CCSP Cisco Secure PIX Firewall Advanced Exam Certification Guide

Greg Bastien
Earl Carter
Christian Degu

Cisco Press

Cisco Press
800 East 96th Street
Indianapolis, IN 46240 USA

CCSP Cisco Secure PIX Firewall Advanced Exam Certification Guide

Greg Bastien
Earl Carter
Christian Degu

Copyright© 2005 Cisco Systems, Inc.

Cisco Press logo is a trademark of Cisco Systems, Inc.

Published by:
Cisco Press
800 East 96th Street
Indianapolis, IN 46240 USA

Printed in the United States of America 1 2 3 4 5 6 7 8 9 0

First Printing October 2004

Library of Congress Cataloging-in-Publication Number: 2003116679

ISBN: 1-58720-123-2

Warning and Disclaimer

This book is designed to provide information about the CCSP Cisco Secure PIX Firewall Advanced Exam Certification. Every effort has been made to make this book as complete and as accurate as possible, but no warranty or fitness is implied.

The information is provided on an "as is" basis. The authors, Cisco Press, and Cisco Systems, Inc. shall have neither liability nor responsibility to any person or entity with respect to any loss or damages arising from the information contained in this book or from the use of the discs or programs that may accompany it.

The opinions expressed in this book belong to the author and are not necessarily those of Cisco Systems, Inc.

Feedback Information

At Cisco Press, our goal is to create in-depth technical books of the highest quality and value. Each book is crafted with care and precision, undergoing rigorous development that involves the unique expertise of members from the professional technical community.

Readers' feedback is a natural continuation of this process. If you have any comments regarding how we could improve the quality of this book, or otherwise alter it to better suit your needs, you can contact us through e-mail at feedback@ciscopress.com. Please make sure to include the book title and ISBN in your message.

We greatly appreciate your assistance.

Corporate and Government Sales

Cisco Press offers excellent discounts on this book when ordered in quantity for bulk purchases or special sales. For more information, please contact: **U.S. Corporate and Government Sales**   1-800-382-3419   corpsales@pearsontechgroup.com

For sales outside of the U.S. please contact: **International Sales**   international@pearsontechgroup.com

Trademark Acknowledgments

All terms mentioned in this book that are known to be trademarks or service marks have been appropriately capitalized. Cisco Press or Cisco Systems, Inc. cannot attest to the accuracy of this information. Use of a term in this book should not be regarded as affecting the validity of any trademark or service mark.

Publisher: John Wait

Editor-in-Chief: John Kane

Executive Editor: Brett Bartow

Acquisitions Editor: Michelle Grandin

Development Editor: Howard A. Jones

Copy Editors: Bill McManus, Christina Palaia

Editorial Assistant: Tammi Barnett

Composition: Argosy

Cisco Representative: Anthony Wolfenden

Cisco Press Program Manager: Nannette M. Noble

Production Manager: Patrick Kanouse

Project Editor: Marc Fowler

Technical Editors: Behzad Behtash, Izak Karmona, Tim Sammut

Book and Cover Designer: Louisa Adair

Indexer: Eric Schroeder

CISCO SYSTEMS

Corporate Headquarters
Cisco Systems, Inc.
170 West Tasman Drive
San Jose, CA 95134-1706
USA
www.cisco.com
Tel: 408 526-4000
    800 553-NETS (6387)
Fax: 408 526-4100

European Headquarters
Cisco Systems International BV
Haarlerbergpark
Haarlerbergweg 13-19
1101 CH Amsterdam
The Netherlands
www-europe.cisco.com
Tel: 31 0 20 357 1000
Fax: 31 0 20 357 1100

Americas Headquarters
Cisco Systems, Inc.
170 West Tasman Drive
San Jose, CA 95134-1706
USA
www.cisco.com
Tel: 408 526-7660
Fax: 408 527-0883

Asia Pacific Headquarters
Cisco Systems, Inc.
Capital Tower
168 Robinson Road
#22-01 to #29-01
Singapore 068912
www.cisco.com
Tel: +65 6317 7777
Fax: +65 6317 7799

Cisco Systems has more than 200 offices in the following countries and regions. Addresses, phone numbers, and fax numbers are listed on the **Cisco.com Web site at www.cisco.com/go/offices.**

Argentina • Australia • Austria • Belgium • Brazil • Bulgaria • Canada • Chile • China PRC • Colombia • Costa Rica • Croatia • Czech Republic Denmark • Dubai, UAE • Finland • France • Germany • Greece • Hong Kong SAR • Hungary • India • Indonesia • Ireland • Israel • Italy Japan • Korea • Luxembourg • Malaysia • Mexico • The Netherlands • New Zealand • Norway • Peru • Philippines • Poland • Portugal Puerto Rico • Romania • Russia • Saudi Arabia • Scotland • Singapore • Slovakia • Slovenia • South Africa • Spain • Sweden Switzerland • Taiwan • Thailand • Turkey • Ukraine • United Kingdom • United States • Venezuela • Vietnam • Zimbabwe

About the Authors

Greg Bastien, CCNP, CCSP, CISSP, is the chief technical officer for Virtue Technologies, Inc. He provides consulting services to various federal agencies and commercial clients and holds a position as adjunct professor at Strayer University, teaching networking and network security classes. He completed his undergraduate and graduate degrees at Embry-Riddle Aeronautical University while on active duty as a helicopter flight instructor in the U.S. Army.

Earl Carter, CCNA, has been working in the field of computer security for eight years. He began learning about computer security while working at the Air Force Information Warfare Center. Earl's primary responsibility was securing Air Force networks against cyber attacks. In 1998 he accepted a job with Cisco Systems to perform intrusion detection system (IDS) research for NetRanger (currently Cisco IDS) and NetSonar (Cisco Secure Scanner). Earl spent approximately one year writing signatures for NetRanger and developing software modules for NetSonar. Currently, he is a member of the Security Technologies Assessment Team (STAT) that is part of Consulting Engineering (CE). His duties involve performing security evaluations on numerous Cisco products as well as consulting with other teams within Cisco to help enhance the security of Cisco products. He has examined various products from the PIX Firewall to the Cisco CallManager. Presently, Earl is working on his CCIE certification with a security emphasis.

Christian Degu, CCNP, CCSP, CISSP, works as a senior network engineer for General Dynamics Network Systems Signal solutions, as consultant to the U.S. Federal Energy Regulatory commission. He holds a master's degree in computer information systems. Christian resides in Alexandria, Virginia.

About the Technical Reviewers

Behzad Behtash is an IT consultant with more than 10 years of internetworking experience, emphasizing wired and wireless network security. Behzad holds a bachelor's degree in chemical engineering from the University of Wisconsin at Madison and currently resides in Oakland, California. He holds the CCNP, CCDP, CCSP, and MSCE certifications and is the author of the Cisco Press title, *CCSP Self-Study: Cisco Secure PIX Firewall Advanced (CSPFA)*, Second Edition.

Izak Karmona, CCSP, CCNA, CSS-1, is a network security consultant in Israel and is currently working toward his CCIE Security certification. Izak has more than 15 years of experience in the networking industry. As part of his job, he provides network design, security, and implementation services to his customers. Izak holds a bachelor's degree in computer sciences from the Technion Institute of Technology at Haifa, Israel.

Tim Sammut, CCIE No. 6642, is a senior network consultant for Northrop Grumman Information Technology. Tim has served in key project roles involving technologies from LAN switching to security to SNA integration and has helped many organizations make the most of their network investment. Tim also holds the CISSP, CCIE Security, and CCIE Service Provider certifications.

Dedications

Greg Bastien: To Ingrid, Joshua, Lukas, and my friends at Virtue Technologies, Inc., especially Todd Schweitzer and Meti Gizaw. Thank you all for your support throughout this project. I would also like to dedicate this work to the men and women of the United States Military for their selflessness and dedication to duty during these difficult times.

Earl Carter: Without my loving family, I would not be where I am today. They always support the projects I undertake. Therefore, I dedicate this book to my wife, Chris, my daughter, Ariel, and my son, Aidan.

Christian Degu: To Meron Tamrat Desta, for your love and the constant support you have given me.

Acknowledgments

Greg Bastien: Network security is no doubt a fast-paced market and keeping up with the changes requires some very short deadlines. We would like to thank the team at Cisco Press for keeping us on track and on time with this project. We would especially like to recognize Michelle Grandin, acquisitions editor, Chris Cleveland, senior development editor, and Howard Jones, development editor, for their efforts with this project.

Earl Carter: First, I want to say that many people helped me during the writing of this book (too many to be list here). Everyone that I have dealt with has been very supportive and cooperative. Thank you very much for all of your support. I would also like to thank Mr. and Mrs. Nowakowski for always encouraging me to do my best in both Taekwondo and in everything that I do. Finally, I want to thank Jesus Christ for gracing me with numerous gifts throughout my life, such as my understanding family who have helped me through the many long hours (and late nights) writing this book.

Contents at a Glance

Contents

Icons Used in This Book

Throughout the book, you will see the following icons used for networking devices:

Router

Bridge

Hub

DSU/CSU

Catalyst
Switch

Multilayer
Switch

ATM
Switch

ISDN/Frame Relay
Switch

Communication
Server

Gateway

Access
Server

Throughout the book, you will see the following icons used for networking devices:

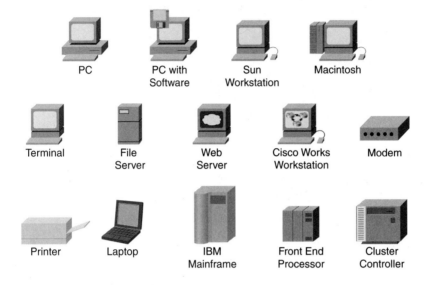

Throughout the book, you will see the following icons used for networking devices:

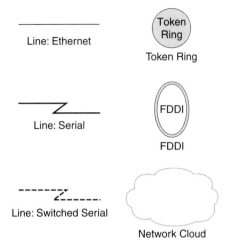

Command Syntax Conventions

The conventions used to present command syntax in this book are the same conventions used in the IOS Command Reference. The Command Reference describes these conventions as follows:

- **Boldface** indicates commands and keywords that are entered literally as shown. In actual configuration examples and output (not general command syntax), boldface indicates commands that are manually input by the user (such as a **show** command).
- *Italics* indicate arguments for which you supply actual values.
- Vertical bars (|) separate alternative, mutually exclusive elements.
- Square brackets [ ] indicate optional elements.
- Braces { } indicate a required choice.
- Braces within brackets [{ }] indicate a required choice within an optional element.

Introduction

This book was created as a tool to assist you in preparing for the Cisco Secure PIX Firewall Advanced Certification Exam (CSPFA 642-521).

Why the "Second Edition"?

Network security is *very* dynamic. New vulnerabilities are identified every day, and new technologies and products are released into the marketplace at nearly the same rate. The first edition of the *CCSP Cisco Secure PIX Firewall Advanced Exam Certification Guide* was on the shelves for approximately four months when Cisco Systems, Inc., completed the production release of PIX Version 6.3(1) and, consequently, updated the certification exam to reflect the additional features available in the new release. This book is written to PIX Version 6.3(3), and we do not anticipate any major revisions to the PIX operating system (OS) in the near future.

Who Should Read This Book?

Network security is a complex business. The PIX Firewall performs some very specific functions as part of the security process. It is very important that you be familiar with many networking and network security concepts before you undertake the CSPFA certification. This book is designed for security professionals or networking professionals who are interested in beginning the security certification process.

How to Use This Book

The book consists of 20 chapters. Each chapter builds upon the chapter that precedes it. The chapters that cover specific commands and configurations include case studies or practice configurations. Chapter 20 includes additional case studies and configuration examples that may or may not work—it is up to you to determine if the configurations fulfill the requirement and why.

This book was written to be a guide to help you prepare for the CSPFA certification exam. It is a tool, not the entire tool box. That is to say, you need to use this book along with other references (specifically Cisco TAC) to help you prepare for the exam. Remember that successfully completing the exam makes a great short-term goal. Being very proficient at what you do should always be your ultimate goal.

The chapters of the book cover the following topics:

- **Chapter 1, Network Security**—Chapter 1 provides an overview of network security, the process and potential threats and discusses how network security has become increasingly more important to business as companies become more intertwined and their network perimeters continue to fade. Chapter 1 discusses the network security policy and two Cisco programs that can assist companies with the design and implementation of sound security policies, processes, and architecture.

- **Chapter 2, Firewall Technologies and the Cisco PIX Firewall**—Chapter 2 covers the different firewall technologies and the Cisco PIX Firewall. It examines the design of the PIX Firewall and discusses some the security advantages of that design.

- **Chapter 3, Cisco PIX Firewall**—Chapter 3 deals with the design of the PIX Firewall in greater detail. This chapter lists the different models of the PIX Firewall and their intended applications. It discusses the various features available with each model and how each model should be implemented.

- **Chapter 4, System Management/Maintenance**—Chapter 4 details the installation and configuration of the PIX Firewall IOS. This chapter covers the different configuration options that allow for remote management of the PIX Firewall.

- **Chapter 5, Understanding Cisco PIX Firewall Translation and Connection**—This chapter covers the different transport protocols and how they are handled by the PIX Firewall. It also discusses network addressing and how the PIX Firewall can alter node or network addresses to secure those elements.

- **Chapter 6, Getting Started with the Cisco PIX Firewall**—This chapter is the meat of the PIX Firewall: basic commands required to get the PIX operational. It discusses the methods for connecting to the PIX Firewall and some of the many configuration options available with the PIX.

- **Chapter 7, Configuring Access**—Chapter 7 introduces the different configurations that enable you to control access to your network(s) using the PIX Firewall. It also covers some of the specific configurations required to allow certain protocols to pass through the firewall.

- **Chapter 8, Syslog and the PIX**—Chapter 8 covers the logging functions of the PIX Firewall and the configuration required to allow the PIX Firewall to log to a syslog server.

- **Chapter 9, Routing and the PIX Firewall**—Chapter 9 discusses routing with the PIX Firewall, the routing protocols supported by the PIX, and how to implement them.

- **Chapter 10, Cisco PIX Firewall Failover**—Chapter 10 details the advantages of a redundant firewall configuration and the steps required to configure two PIX Firewalls in the failover mode.

- **Chapter 11, Virtual Private Networks**—Many businesses have multiple locations that need to be interconnected. Chapter 11 explains the different types of secure connections of virtual private networks (VPNs) that can be configured between the PIX Firewall and other VPN endpoints. It covers the technologies and protocols used for creating and maintaining VPNs across public networks.

- **Chapter 12, Configuring Access VPNs**—Chapter 12 discusses how the PIX Firewall is used for creating remote access virtual private networks.

- **Chapter 13, PIX Device Manager**—The PIX Firewall can now be managed using a variety of different tools. The PIX Device Manager is a web-based graphical user interface (GUI) that can be used to manage the PIX Firewall.

- **Chapter 14, CiscoWorks Management Center for Firewalls (PIX MC)**—CiscoWorks is a product developed for the management of multiple Cisco products in an enterprise environment. Chapter 14 provides an overview of CiscoWorks and discusses a component used for managing the PIX Firewall known as the PIX MC.

- **Chapter 15, Content Filtering on the PIX**—It is a common practice for hackers to embed attacks into the content of a web page. Certain types of program code are especially conducive to this type of attack because of their interactive nature. Chapter 15 discusses these types of code and identifies their dangers.

- **Chapter 16, Overview of AAA and the PIX**—It is extremely important to ensure that only authorized users are accessing your network. Chapter 16 discusses the different methods for configuring the PIX Firewall to interact with authentication, authorization, and accounting (AAA) services. This chapter also introduces the Cisco Secure Access Control Server (Cisco Secure ACS), which is the Cisco AAA server package.

- **Chapter 17, Configuration of AAA on the PIX**—Chapter 17 discusses the specific configuration on the PIX Firewall for communication with the AAA server, including the Cisco Secure ACS. It covers the implementation, functionality, and troubleshooting of AAA on the PIX Firewall.

- **Chapter 18, Attack Guards and Advanced Protocol Handling**—Many different attacks can be launched against a network and its perimeter security devices. Chapter 18 explains some of the most common attacks and how the PIX Firewall can be configured to repel such an attack.

- **Chapter 19, Firewall Services Module**—The PIX Firewall Services Module (FWSM) is a blade designed for the Catalyst 6000 Series switches. The FWSM provides firewall functionality for the core switching infrastructure. Chapter 19 discusses the FWSM in detail.

- **Chapter 20, Case Study and Sample Configuration**—This chapter consists of two case studies that enable you to practice configuring the firewall to perform specific functions. One section includes configurations that may or may not work. You will be asked to determine if the configuration will work correctly and why or why not. The certification exam asks specific questions about configuration of the PIX Firewall. It is very important to become intimately familiar with the different commands and components of the PIX Firewall configuration.

Each chapter follows the same format and incorporates the following tools to assist you by assessing your current knowledge and emphasizing specific areas of interest within the chapter.

- **"Do I Know This Already?" Quiz**—Each chapter begins with a quiz to help you assess your current knowledge of the subject. The quiz is broken down into specific areas of emphasis that allow you to best determine where to focus your efforts when working through the chapter.

- **Foundation Topics**—The foundation topics are the core sections of each chapter. They focus on the specific protocol, concept, or skills that you must master to prepare successfully for the examination.

- **Foundation Summary**—Near the end of each chapter, the foundation topics are summarized into important highlights from the chapter. In many cases the foundation summaries are broken into charts, but in some cases the important portions from each chapter are simply restated to emphasize their importance within the subject matter. Remember that the foundation portions are in the book to assist you with your exam preparation. It is very unlikely that you will be able to complete the certification exam successfully by studying just the foundation topics and foundation summaries, although they are good tools for last-minute preparation just before taking the exam.

- **Q&A**—Each chapter ends with a series of review questions to test your understanding of the material covered. These questions are a great way not only to ensure that you understand the material, but to exercise your ability to recall facts.

- **Case Studies/Scenarios**—The chapters that deal more with configuration of the PIX Firewall have brief scenarios included. These scenarios are there to help you understand the different configuration options and how each component can affect another component within the configuration of the firewall. The final chapter of this book is dedicated to case studies/scenarios.

- **CD-Based Practice Exam**—On the CD included with this book, you will find a practice test with more than 200 questions that cover the information central to the CSPFA exam. With the customizable testing engine, you can take a sample exam that focuses on particular topic areas or randomizes the questions. Each test question includes a link that points to a related section in an electronic Portable Document Format (PDF) copy of the book, also included on the CD.

Figure I-1 depicts the best way to navigate through the book. If you feel that you already have a sufficient understanding of the subject matter in a chapter, you should test yourself with the "Do I Know This Already?" quiz. Based on your score, you should determine whether to complete the entire chapter or move on to the "Foundation Summary" and "Q&A" sections. It is always recommended that you go through the entire book rather than skipping around. It is not possible to know too much about a topic. Only you will know how well you really understand each topic . . . until you take the exam, and then it might be too late.

Figure I-1 *Completing the Chapter Material*

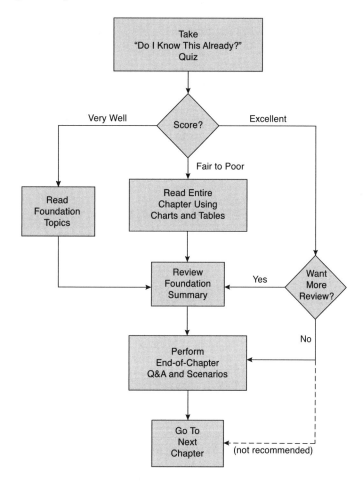

Certification Exam and This Preparation Guide

The questions for each certification exam are a closely guarded secret. The truth is that if you had the questions and could only pass the exam, you would be in for quite an embarrassing situation as soon as you arrived at your first job that required PIX skills. The point is to know the material, not just to pass the exam successfully. We do know what topics you must know to complete this exam. Coincidentally, these are the same topics required for you to be proficient with the PIX Firewall. We have broken down these topics into foundation topics and have covered each topic in the book. Table I-1 lists each foundation topic and provides a brief description of each.

Table I-1 *CSPFA Foundation Topics and Descriptions*

Reference Number	Exam Topic	Description
1	Firewalls	There are three different ways that firewalls process network traffic. Chapter 2 discusses those technologies and the advantages of the technology utilized by the PIX Firewall.
2	PIX Firewall Models	There are currently six different models of the PIX Firewall. Chapter 3 discusses each model, its specifications, and how/when each model would be applied.
3	PIX Services Module	The PIX Firewall Services Module (FWSM) is a blade that provides PIX Firewall functionality to the Catalyst 6000 Series switches. This component is discussed in Chapter 19.
4	PIX Firewall Licensing	Chapter 3 discusses the different licensing options available for the PIX Firewall and how each license applies.
5	User Interface	The command-line interface (CLI) is one of the methods used to configure the PIX Firewall. Chapter 6 covers the CLI and many of the commands used to configure the firewall.
6	Examining the PIX Firewall Status	Verifying the configuration of the PIX Firewall will assist you in troubleshooting connectivity issues. Troubleshooting is discussed as part of each task within the book.
7	ASA Security Levels	The Adaptive Security Algorithm (ASA) is a key component of the PIX Firewall. It is discussed in great detail in Chapters 2, 3, 5, and 6.
8	Basic PIX Firewall Configuration	The basic configuration of the PIX Firewall is discussed in Chapter 6.

Table I-1 *CSPFA Foundation Topics and Descriptions (Continued)*

Reference Number	Exam Topic	Description
9	Syslog Configuration	The logging features of the PIX Firewall are covered in Chapter 8.
10	DHCP Server Configuration	The PIX Firewall can function both as a Dynamic Host Configuration Protocol (DHCP) server and client. These configurations are covered in Chapters 3, 6, and 12.
11	PPPoE and the PIX Firewall	Point-to-Point Protocol over Ethernet (PPPoE) is used to connect multiple hosts using a single dial-up or broadband connection. Some PIX Firewall models support PPPoE. This topic is covered in Chapter 12.
12	Transport Protocols	The transport protocols and how they are handled by the PIX Firewall are discussed in Chapters 5 and 8.
13	Network Address Translation	Network Address Translation (NAT) is used by many different firewalls to secure network segments. This is discussed in Chapters 5 and 6.
14	Configuring DNS Support	As a perimeter device, the PIX Firewall will be required to support the Domain Name Service (DNS). Configuring DNS on the PIX is discussed in Chapter 6.
15	Port Address Translation	Port Address Translation (PAT) is a method used by the PIX Firewall to NAT multiple internal sources to a single external address. This configuration is covered in Chapters 5 and 6.
16	ACLs	Access control lists (ACLs) are used to allow or deny traffic between different network segments that attach by the PIX Firewall. Configuring ACLs is discussed in Chapter 7.
17	Converting Conduits to ACLs	Conduits are from a command set that predated ACLs. They tend to be broader in their function. Conduits and ACLs are covered in Chapter 7.
18	Using ACLs	Configuring and using ACLs are discussed in Chapter 7.
19	Overview of Object Grouping	Service, host, and network objects can be grouped to make processing by the firewall more efficient. Object grouping is discussed in Chapter 7.
20	Getting Started with Object Groups	Object grouping is discussed in Chapter 7.
21	Configuring Object Groups	Object grouping is discussed in Chapter 7.

continues

Table I-1   *CSPFA Foundation Topics and Descriptions (Continued)*

Reference Number	Exam Topic	Description
22	Nested Object Groups	Object groups can be nested into other object groups. Object grouping is discussed in Chapter 7.
23	Advanced Protocols	Many advanced protocols require special handling by the firewall. Some protocols require multiple inbound and outbound connections. The handling of advanced protocols by the PIX Firewall is discussed in Chapters 7 and 18.
24	Multimedia Support	Multimedia protocols are considered advanced protocols. The handling of advanced protocols by the PIX Firewall is discussed in Chapters 7 and 18.
25	Attack Guards	The PIX Firewall can be configured to recognize an attack and react to it. This is covered in Chapter 18.
26	Intrusion Detection	The PIX Firewall can be configured to perform as an intrusion detection system (IDS) as well as a firewall. It also can be configured to work with external IDSs. These issues are covered in Chapter 18.
27	Overview of AAA	AAA is a method of ensuring that you can verify who is accessing your network resources, restrict their access to specific resources, and keep track of what actions they take on the network. Configuring the PIX Firewall to support AAA is discussed in Chapters 16 and 17.
28	Installation of Cisco Secure ACS for Windows NT/2000	Cisco Secure ACS is a Cisco AAA server product. Installing and configuring Cisco Secure ACS is covered in Chapter 17.
29	Authentication Configuration	Configuring Cisco Secure ACS is discussed in Chapters 16 and 17.
30	Downloadable ACLs	Configuring Cisco Secure ACS is discussed in Chapters 16 and 17.
31	Understanding Failover	Mission-critical systems require high-availability solutions to minimize any chance of network outages. Two PIX Firewalls can be configured as a high-availability solution. This configuration is covered in Chapter 10.
32	Serial Failover Configuration	PIX failover configuration is discussed in Chapter 10.
33	LAN-Based Failover Configuration	PIX failover configuration is discussed in Chapter 10.

Table I-1 *CSPFA Foundation Topics and Descriptions (Continued)*

Reference Number	Exam Topic	Description
34	PIX Firewall Enables a Secure VPN	Dedicated circuits between different locations can be cost-prohibitive. It is much less expensive and just as secure to create an encrypted connection between those locations across public network space. Configuring VPNs is discussed in Chapter 11.
35	Prepare to Configure VPN Support	Both ends of a VPN must have a termination point. The PIX Firewall can be configured as a VPN termination point. Configuring VPNs is discussed in Chapter 11.
36	Configure IKE Parameters	Internet Key Exchange (IKE) is a key exchange method used to ensure that the encrypted connection is not easily compromised. Configuring VPNs is discussed in Chapter 11.
37	Configure IPSec Parameters	IP Security (IPSec) is a standard for creating an encrypted VPN connection. Configuring VPNs is discussed in Chapter 11.
38	Test and Verify VPN Configuration	Configuration and troubleshooting of VPNs is discussed in Chapter 11.
39	Cisco VPN Client	Remote users can create a VPN from their computers to the company network using VPN client software. Configuring VPNs and VPN client software is discussed in Chapter 12.
40	Scale PIX Firewall VPNs	Configuring VPNs is discussed in Chapter 11.
41	Remote Access	The PIX Firewall can be managed either locally or remotely. Configuring the PIX to allow remote access is discussed in Chapter 4.
42	Command Authorization	Remote management of the PIX Firewall is discussed in Chapter 4.
43	PDM Overview	The PIX Device Manager (PDM) is a web-enabled tool for remote management of the PIX Firewall. Remote management of the PIX using the PDM is discussed in Chapter 13.
44	Prepare for PDM	The PDM is a web-enabled tool for remote management of the PIX Firewall. Remote management of the PIX using the PDM is discussed in Chapter 13.

continues

Table I-1 *CSPFA Foundation Topics and Descriptions (Continued)*

Reference Number	Exam Topic	Description
45	Using PDM to Configure the PIX Firewall	The PDM is a web-enabled tool for remote management of the PIX Firewall. Remote management of the PIX using the PDM is discussed in Chapter 13.
46	Using PDM to Create a Site-to-Site VPN	The PDM is a web-enabled tool for remote management of the PIX Firewall. Remote management of the PIX using the PDM is discussed in Chapter 13.
47	Using PDM to Create a Remote Access VPN	The PDM is a web-enabled tool for remote management of the PIX Firewall. Remote management of the PIX using the PDM is discussed in Chapter 13.
48	Configuring Access and Translation Rules	The PIX MC is used for management of multiple PIX Firewalls on an enterprise network. Installation, configuration, and use of the PIX MC are addressed in Chapter 14.
49	Reporting, Tools, and Administration	The PIX MC is used for management of multiple PIX Firewalls on an enterprise network. Installation, configuration, and use of the PIX MC are addressed in Chapter 14.
50	Introduction to the Auto Update Server	The auto update server is a component within the PIX MC that can be used to update the PIX Firewall. The auto update server is discussed in Chapter 14.
51	PIX Firewall and AUS Communication Settings	The Auto Update Server (AUS) is a component within the PIX MC that can be used to update the PIX Firewall. The AUS is discussed in Chapter 14.
52	Devices, Images, and Assignments	Use of the PIX MC and the AUS is covered in Chapter 14.
53	Reporting and Administration	Use of the PIX MC and the AUS is covered in Chapter 14.
54	FWSM Overview	The PIX FWSM is a blade that provides PIX Firewall functionality to the Catalyst 6000 Series switches. This component is discussed in Chapter 19.
55	Using PDM with FWSM	The PIX FWSM is a blade that provides PIX Firewall functionality to the Catalyst 6000 Series switches. Management of the FWSM using the PDM is discussed in Chapters 13 and 19.

Overview of the Cisco Certification Process

In the network security market demand for qualified engineers vastly outpaces the supply. For this reason, many engineers consider migrating from routing/networking to network security. Remember that network security is simply security applied to networks. This sounds like an obvious concept, and it is actually a very important one if you are persuing your security certification. You must be very familiar with networking *before* you can begin to apply the security concepts. Although a previous Cisco certification is not required to begin the Cisco Security Certification process, it is a good idea to at least complete the Cisco Certified Networking Associate (CCNA) certification. The skill required to complete the CCNA certification will give you a solid foundation that you can expand into the network security field.

The security certification is called the Cisco Certified Security Professional (CCSP) certification and consists of the following exams:

- **CSPFA**—Cisco Secure Firewall Advanced—642-521
- **SECUR**—Securing Cisco IOS Networks (formerly MCNS)—642-501
- **CSVPN**—Cisco Secure Virtual Private Networks—642-511
- **CSIDS**—Cisco Secure Intrusion Detection System—642-531
- **CSI**—Cisco SAFE Implementation—642-541

Taking the CSPFA Certification Exam

As with any Cisco certification exam, it is best to be thoroughly prepared before taking the exam. There is no way to determine exactly which questions are on the exam, so the best way to prepare is to have a good working knowledge of all subjects covered on the exam. Schedule yourself for the exam and be sure to be rested and ready to focus when taking the exam.

Tracking CCSP Status

You can track your certification progress by checking https://www.certmanager.net/~cisco_s/login.html. You will need to create an account the first time you log on to the site.

How to Prepare for an Exam

The best way to prepare for any certification exam is to use a combination of the preparation resources, labs, and practice tests. This guide has integrated some practice questions and labs to help you better prepare. If possible, try to get some hands-on time with the PIX Firewall. There is no substitute for experience, and it is much easier to understand the commands and concepts when you can actually see the PIX in action. If you do not have access to a PIX

Firewall, a variety of simulation packages are available for a reasonable price. Last, but certainly not least, the Cisco website provides a wealth of information on the PIX Firewall and all of the products it interacts with. No single source can adequately prepare you for the CSPFA exam unless you already have extensive experience with Cisco products and a background in networking or network security. At a minimum, you will want to use this book combined with http://www.cisco.com/public/support/tac/home.shtml to prepare for this exam.

Assessing Exam Readiness

After completing a number of certification exams, I have found that you do not really know if you are adequately prepared for the exam until you have completed about 30 percent of the questions. At this point, if you are not prepared, it is too late. Be sure that you are preparing for the correct exam. This certification exam is CSPFA 3.0 and is a relatively new exam. The best way to determine your readiness is to work through the "Do I Know This Already?" portions of the book, the review questions, and the case studies/scenarios. It is best to work your way through the entire book unless you can complete each subject without having to do any research or look up any answers.

Cisco Security Specialist in the Real World

Cisco is one of the most recognized names on the Internet. You cannot go into a data center or server room without seeing some Cisco equipment. Cisco certified security specialists are able to bring quite a bit of knowledge to the table because of their deep understanding of the relationship between networking and network security. This is why the Cisco certification carries such clout. Cisco certifications demonstrate to potential employers and contract holders a certain professionalism and the dedication required to achieve a goal. Face it, if these certifications were easy to acquire, everyone would have them.

PIX AND Cisco IOS Commands

A firewall or router is not normally something you fiddle with. That is to say, once you have it properly configured, you tend to leave it alone until there is a problem or you need to make some other configuration change. This is the reason that the question mark (?) is probably the most widely used Cisco IOS command. Unless you have constant exposure to this equipment, it can be difficult to remember the numerous commands required to configure devices and troubleshoot problems.

Most engineers remember enough to go in the right direction but use the (?) to help them use the correct syntax. This is life in the real world. Unfortunately, the question mark is not always available in the testing environment. Many questions on this exam require you to select the best command to perform a certain function. It is extremely important that you familiarize yourself with the different commands, the correct command syntax, and functions of each command.

Rules of the Road

We have always found it very confusing when different addresses are used in the examples throughout a technical publication. For this reason we use the address space depicted in Figure I-2 when assigning network segments in this book. Please note that the address space we have selected is all reserved space per RFC 1918. We understand that these addresses are not routable across the Internet and are not normally used on outside interfaces. Even with the millions of IP addresses available on the Internet, there is a slight chance that we could have chosen to use an address that the owner did not want published in this book.

Figure I-2 *Addressing for Examples*

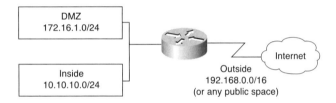

It is our hope that this book will assist you in understanding the examples and the syntax of the many commands required to configure and administer the PIX Firewall.

Good luck!

This chapter covers the following subjects:

- Overview of Network Security

- Vulnerabilities, Threats, and Attacks

- Security Policies

- Network Security as a Process

- Network Security as a "Legal Issue"

- Defense in Depth

- Cisco Architecture for Voice, Video, and Integrated Data (AVVID)

- Cisco Security Architecture for Enterprises (SAFE)

CHAPTER 1

Network Security

Rather than jump directly into what you need to know for the CSPFA 642-521 examination, this chapter presents some background information about network security and its integral role in business today. You need to understand this information because it is the basis for CCSP Certification and is a common theme throughout the five CCSP certification exams.

The term *network security* defines an extremely broad range of very complex subjects. To understand the individual subjects and how they relate to each other, it is important for you first to look at the "big picture" and get an understanding of the importance of the entire concept. Much of an organization's assets consist of data and computer resources that are interconnected and must be protected from unauthorized access. There are many different ways to ensure that network assets are adequately protected. The key is to correctly balance the business need with the requirement for security.

How to Best Use This Chapter

This chapter will give you an understanding of the general principles of network security. It will give you the foundation to understand the specifics of how the PIX Firewall is incorporated into a network architecture.

"Do I Know This Already?" Quiz

The purpose of the "Do I Know This Already?" quiz is to help you decide if you really need to read the entire chapter. If you already intend to read the entire chapter, you do not necessarily need to answer these questions now.

The ten-question quiz, derived from the major sections in the "Foundation and Supplemental Topics" portion of the chapter, helps you determine how to spend your limited study time.

Table 1-1 outlines the major topics discussed in this chapter and the "Do I Know This Already?" quiz questions that correspond to those topics.

Table 1-1 *"Do I Know This Already?" Foundation Topics Section-to-Question Mapping*

Supplemental or Foundation Topics Section	Questions Covered in This Section	Score
Overview of Network Security	1	
Vulnerabilities, Threats, and Attacks	2 to 6	
Security Policies		
Network Security as a Process	7 to 8	
Network Security as a "Legal Issue"		
Defense in Depth		
Cisco AVVID	9	
Cisco SAFE	10	

CAUTION The goal of self assessment is to gauge your mastery of the topics in this chapter. If you do not know the answer to a question or are only partially sure of the answer, you should mark this question wrong for purposes of the self assessment. Giving yourself credit for an answer you correctly guess skews your self-assessment results and might provide you with a false sense of security.

1. Which single method is the best way to secure a network?

    a. Allow dialup access only to the Internet

    b. Install a personal firewall on every workstation

    c. Use very complex passwords

    d. Implement strong perimeter security

    e. None of the above

2. What are the three types of cyber attacks? (Choose three.)

    a. Penetration attack

    b. Access attack

    c. Denial of service attack

    d. Destruction of data attack

    e. Reconnaissance attack

3. What type of threat is directed toward a specific target normally for a specific purpose?

    a. Structured threats

    b. Directed threats

    c. Unstructured threats

    d. Political threats

    e. None of the above

4. What type of threat normally scans networks looking for "targets of opportunity"?

    a. Structured threats

    b. Scanning threats

    c. Unstructured threats

    d. Script kiddies

    e. None of the above

5. What type of scan looks for all services running on a single host?

    a. Ping sweep

    b. Service scan

    c. Horizontal scan

    d. Vertical scan

    e. All of the above

6. What type of attack determines the address space assigned to an organization?

    a. Ping sweep

    b. DNS queries

    c. Vertical scan

    d. Horizontal scan

    e. None of the above

7. What are the steps of the security process?

   a. Secure, test, repair, retest

   b. Test, repair, monitor, evaluate

   c. Lather, rinse, repeat

   d. Evaluate, secure, test

   e. None of the above

8. What constant action sits between the individual steps of the security process?

   a. Test

   b. Retest

   c. Evaluate

   d. Repair

   e. Improve

9. True or false: Cisco AVVID uses only Cisco products.

10. Which of the following is *not* a component of Cisco SAFE?

   a. Perimeter security

   b. Policy implementation

   c. Identity

   d. Security management and monitoring

   e. Application security

The answers to the "Do I Know This Already?" quiz are found in Appendix A, "Answers to the 'Do I Know This Already?' Quizzes and Q&A Sections." The suggested choices for your next step are as follows:

■ **8 or less overall score**—Read the entire chapter. This includes the "Foundation and Supplemental Topics," "Foundation Summary," and "Q&A" sections.

■ **9 or 10 overall score**—If you want more review of these topics, skip to the "Foundation Summary" section and then go to the "Q&A" section. Otherwise, move to the next chapter.

Foundation and Supplemental Topics

This chapter does not contain any foundation topics. However, if you take a look at the foundation topics throughout the book, you will discover that understanding the foundation topics will be difficult if you do not already understand the supplemental topics.

Overview of Network Security

In the past, the term *information security* was used to describe the physical security measures used to keep vital government or business information from being accessed by the public and to protect it against alteration or destruction. These measures included storing valuable documents in locked filing cabinets or safes and restricting physical access to areas where those documents were kept. With the proliferation of computers and electronic media, the old way of accessing data changed. As technology continued to advance, computer systems were interconnected to form computer networks, allowing systems to share resources, including data.

The ultimate computer network, which interconnects almost every publicly accessible computer network, is the Internet. Although the methods of securing data have changed dramatically, the concept of network security remains the same as that of information security.

Because computers can warehouse, retrieve, and process tremendous amounts of data, they are used in nearly every facet of our lives. Computers, networks, and the Internet are integral parts of many businesses. Our dependence on computers continues to increase as businesses and individuals become more comfortable with technology and as technology advances make systems more user-friendly and easier to interconnect.

A single computer system requires automated tools to protect data on that system from users who have local system access. A computer system that is on a network (a *distributed system*) requires that the data on that system be protected not only from local access but also from unauthorized remote access and from interception or alteration of data during transmission between systems. Network security is not a single product, process, or policy but rather a combination of products and processes that support a defined policy. Network security is the implementation of security devices, policies, and processes to prevent unauthorized access to network resources or alteration or destruction of resources or data.

Vulnerabilities, Threats, and Attacks

Attackers who attempt to access a system or network use various methods to find and exploit specific targets. This section discusses the basic concepts of a cyber attack.

Vulnerabilities

To understand cyber attacks, you must remember that computers, no matter how advanced, are still just machines that operate based on predetermined instruction sets. Operating systems and other software packages are simply compiled instruction sets that the computer uses to transform input into output. A computer cannot determine the difference between authorized input and unauthorized input unless this information is written into the instruction sets. Any point in a software package at which a user can alter the software or gain access to a system (that was not specifically designed into the software) is called a *vulnerability*. In most cases, a hacker gains access to a network or computer by exploiting a vulnerability. It is possible to remotely connect to a computer on any of 65,535 ports.

Different applications configure a system to *listen* on specific ports. It is possible to scan a computer to determine which ports are *listening*, and what applications are running on that system. By knowing what vulnerabilities are associated with which applications, you can determine what vulnerabilities exist and how to exploit them. As hardware and software technology continue to advance, the "other side" continues to search for and discover new vulnerabilities. For this reason, most software manufacturers continue to produce *patches* for their products as vulnerabilities are discovered.

Threats

Potential threats are broken into the following two categories:

- **Structured threats**—Threats that are preplanned and focus on a specific target. A structured threat is an organized effort to breach a specific network or organization.

- **Unstructured threats**—Threats that are random and tend to be the result of hackers looking for a target of opportunity. These threats are the most common because an abundance of script files are available on the Internet to users who want to scan unprotected networks for vulnerabilities. Because the scripts are free and run with minimal input from the user, they are widely used across the Internet. Many unstructured threats are not of a malicious nature or for any specific purpose. The people who carry them out are usually just novice hackers looking to see what they can do.

Types of Attacks

The types of cyber attackers and their motivations are too numerous and varied to list. They range from the novice hacker who is attracted by the challenge, to the highly skilled professional who targets an organization for a specific purpose (such as organized crime, industrial espionage, or state-sponsored intelligence gathering). Threats can originate from outside the organization or from inside. *External threats* originate outside an organization and attempt to breach a network either from the Internet or via dialup access. *Internal threats* originate from within an organization and are usually the result of employees or other personnel who have some authorized access to internal network resources. Studies indicate that internal attacks perpetrated by disgruntled employees or former employees are responsible for the majority of network security incidents within most organizations.

There are three major types of network attacks, each with its own specific goal:

- **Reconnaissance attack**—An attack designed not to gain access to a system or network but only to search for and track vulnerabilities that can be exploited later.
- **Access attack**—An attack designed to exploit vulnerability and to gain access to a system on a network. After gaining access, the goal of the user is to
    - Retrieve, alter, or destroy data.
    - Add, remove, or change network resources, including user access.
    - Install other exploits that can be used later to gain access to the network.
- **Denial of service (DoS) attack**—An attack designed solely to cause an interruption on a computer or network.

Reconnaissance Attacks

The goal of this type of attack is to perform reconnaissance on a computer or network. The goal of this reconnaissance is to determine the makeup of the targeted computer or network and to search for and map any vulnerability. A reconnaissance attack can indicate the potential for other, more-invasive attacks. Many reconnaissance attacks are written into scripts that allow novice hackers or script kiddies to launch attacks on networks with a few mouse clicks. Here are some of the more common reconnaissance attacks:

- **Domain Name Service (DNS) query**—Provides the unauthorized user with such information as what address space is assigned to a particular domain and who owns that domain.
- **Ping sweep**—Tells the unauthorized user how many hosts are active on the network. It is possible to drop ICMP packets at the perimeter devices, but this occurs at the expense of network troubleshooting.
- **Vertical scan**—Scans the service ports of a single host and requests different services at each port. This method enables the unauthorized user to determine what type of operating system and services are running on the computer.

■ **Horizontal scan**—Scans an address range for a specific port or service. A very common horizontal scan is the FTP sweep. This is done by scanning a network segment, looking for replies to connection attempts on port 21.

■ **Block scan**—A combination of the vertical scan and the horizontal scan. In other words, it scans a network segment and attempts connections on multiple ports of each host on that segment.

Access Attacks

As the name implies, the goal of an access attack is to gain access to a computer or network. Having gained access, the user may be able to perform many different functions. These functions can be broken into three distinct categories:

■ **Interception**—Gaining unauthorized access to a resource. This could be access to confidential data such as personnel records, payroll records, or research and development projects. As soon as the user gains access, he might be able to read, write to, copy, or move this data. If an intruder gains access, the only way to protect your sensitive data is to save it in an encrypted format (beforehand). This prevents the intruder from being able to read the data.

■ **Modification**—Having gained access, the unauthorized user can alter the resource. This includes not only altering file content but also altering system configurations, changing the level of authorized system access, and escalating authorized privilege levels. Unauthorized system access is achieved by exploiting vulnerability in either the operating system or a software package running on that system. Unauthorized privilege escalation occurs when a user who has a low-level but authorized account attempts to gain higher-level or more-privileged user account information or to increase his or her own privilege level. This gives the user greater control over the target system or network.

■ **Fabrication**—With access to the target system or network, the unauthorized user can create false objects and introduce them into the environment. This can include altering data or inserting packaged exploits such as a virus, worm, or Trojan horse, which can continue attacking the network from within.

— **Virus**—Computer viruses range from annoying to destructive. They consist of computer code that attaches itself to other software running on the computer. This way, each time the attached software opens, the virus reproduces and can continue growing until it wreaks havoc on the infected computer.

— **Worm**—A worm is a virus that exploits vulnerabilities on networked systems to replicate itself. A worm scans a network, looking for a computer with a specific vulnerability. When it finds a host, it copies itself to that system and begins scanning from there as well.

— **Trojan horse**—A Trojan horse is a program that usually claims to perform one function (such as a game) but also does something completely different (such as corrupting data on your hard disk). Many different types of Trojan horses get attached to systems. The effects of these programs range from minor user irritation to total destruction of the computer's file system. Trojan horses are sometimes used to exploit systems by creating user accounts on systems so that an unauthorized user can gain access or upgrade her privilege level. Trojans are also commonly used to enlist computers for a distributed denial of service (DDoS) attack without the knowledge of the system owner.

Denial of Service Attacks

A DoS attack is designed to deny user access to computers or networks. These attacks usually target specific services and attempt to overwhelm them by making numerous requests concurrently. If a system is not protected and cannot react to a DoS attack, that system may be very easy to overwhelm by running scripts that generate multiple requests.

It is possible to greatly increase a DoS attack's magnitude by launching it from multiple systems against a single target. This practice is called a *distributed denial of service (DDoS) attack*. A common practice by hackers is to use a Trojan horse to take control of other systems and enlist them in a DDoS attack.

Security Policies

Security policies are created based upon the security philosophy of the organization. The policy should be a "top-down" policy that is consistent, understandable (nontechnical), widely disseminated within the organization, and fully supported by management. The technical team uses the security policy to design and implement the organization's security structure. The security policy is a formal statement that specifies a set of rules required for gaining access to network assets. The security policy is not a technical document; it is a business document that lays out the permitted and prohibited activities and the tasks and responsibilities regarding security. The network security policy is the core of the network security process. Every organization that maintains networked assets should have a written network security policy. At a minimum, that policy should fulfill the following objectives:

- Analyze the threat based on the type of business performed and type of network exposure

- Determine the organization's security requirements

- Document the network infrastructure and identify potential security breach points

- Identify specific resources that require protection and develop an implementation plan

> **NOTE** An effective network security policy must include physical security to prevent unauthorized users from gaining local access to equipment.

The *security process* is the implementation of the security policy. It is broken into four steps that run continuously, as shown in Figure 1-1. It is important to emphasize that this is a continuous process, that each step leads to the next, and that you should evaluate the results of each step and constantly improve your security posture.

Figure 1-1 *Security Process*

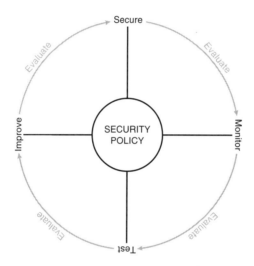

Step 1: Secure

Step 1 is to implement your network security design. This includes hardening your network systems by installing security devices such as firewalls, intrusion detection sensors, and AAA (authentication, authorization, and accounting) servers. Firewalls on the network perimeter prevent unwanted traffic from entering the network. Firewalls within the network verify that only authorized traffic moves from one network segment to another. Restrict access to resources to only authorized users, and implement a strong password convention. Implement data encryption to protect data that is passing from one network to another across an unsecured connection (via the Internet) or to protect sensitive data within your network. Cisco PIX Firewall and Cisco Secure IDS are both industry-leading network security devices that are commonly used for securing the network perimeter and monitoring all traffic that traverses critical points on the network. The purpose of this step is to prevent unauthorized access to the network and to protect network resources.

Step 2: Monitor

After you secure your network, you should monitor the network to ensure that you can detect potential security incidents. By installing Cisco Secure IDS at key points of the network (as part of Step 1), you can monitor both internal and external traffic. It is important to monitor both internal and external traffic because you can check for violations of your network security policy from internal sources and attacks from external sources and determine if any external attacks have breached your network. All your perimeter devices, including firewalls and perimeter routers, provide log data that can be used to verify that your secure configuration is functioning properly and can be filtered to look for specific incidents.

Step 3: Test

Step 3 involves testing the effectiveness of your security design and is the completed by continuing to monitor the solution and generating traffic that should be mitigated by the solution that you implemented. Verify that the security equipment is properly configured and functioning correctly. Several excellent tools are available that you can use to verify the capabilities of your design and determine how effective your security devices will be as they are currently configured.

Step 4: Improve

Step 4 involves using the data from your intrusion detection sensors and your test data to improve the design. An effective security policy is always a work in progress. It continues to improve with every cycle of the process. This does not necessarily mean implementing new hardware with every cycle. The improvement cycle could involve changing certain organizational procedures or documenting new potential threats and vulnerabilities.

The security process is ongoing and constantly changing based on the results of evaluations that occur as part of each step of the process.

Network Security as a "Legal Issue"

Organizations are expected to exercise "reasonable care" to ensure that they protect assets on their networks and to ensure that their network resources are not used against others. Consider the following scenario: An employee of Company X uses his computer (without authorization) to scan the Internet and eventually finds a server that belongs to Company Y that he is able to take control of using a documented exploit. The employee then uses that server to break into the database server at Insurance Company Z and steal the medical records of a celebrity that contain very sensitive and potentially damaging personal information. The stolen information is later distributed to the public. Who is responsible? Of course the employee is ultimately responsible but probably lacks the financial resources that make it worthwhile for the celebrity to seek legal recourse. However, companies X, Y, and Z will all likely become involved in legal action as a result of this theft.

Defense in Depth

Securing a network requires significantly more than implementing a strong network perimeter. The installation of a firewall is a part of the perimeter defense, but it cannot ensure that the entire network is secure. The concept of *defense in depth* refers to the military strategy of having multiple layers of defense. It is an architecture that includes a strong perimeter, intrusion detection/prevention at key points on the network, network monitoring and logging, and a design that allows administrators to dynamically alter the network in response to attacks.

Of course, the concept of defense in depth must always be balanced with the business need of the organization. It simply would not make sense to implement a complex and expensive security architecture for a home office with a couple of computers that do not contain any sensitive data.

Cisco AVVID and Cisco SAFE

Cisco has two programs in place—Cisco AVVID and Cisco SAFE—to help network architects design secure network solutions. Both programs are based on proven solutions that have been tested for full functionality and interoperability and both programs use the strategy of defense in depth.

Cisco AVVID?

AVVID is the Cisco Architecture for Voice, Video, and Integrated Data. Cisco AVVID is an open architecture that is used by Cisco partners to develop various solutions. Every Cisco partner solution is rigorously tested for interoperability with Cisco products. Cisco AVVID is designed for large enterprise networks that require an infrastructure that can support emerging applications such as IP telephone, content delivery, and storage. This *network of networks* concept allows the use of a single network infrastructure to support the concurrent operation of multiple solutions. The Cisco Enterprise Solutions Engineering team creates design guides for use when planning enterprise network infrastructure using Cisco products, software, and features. These solutions provide the following benefits:

■ **Network performance**—This is measured by the following three metrics rather than just throughput:

  — **Application response time**— Measures how quickly an application responds to changes on a network and network congestion by changing its link speed.

  — **Device performance**—Measures the limitations in performance of individual network devices such as switches or routers. A poorly performing device can become a bottleneck to the network, so it is important to ensure that devices are not overtaxed. Device performance measures errors, drops, and CPU usage as well as packet-per-second throughput.

  — **Protocol performance**—Measures the ability of devices to operate dynamically by verifying that devices and the network can handle the use of routing protocols and the Spanning Tree Protocol (STP).

■ **Scalability**— A scalable solution must allow a network to grow into the future. The network must be designed to allow growth in the following areas:

  — **Topology**—A topology must be selected so that changes do not require major reconfiguration of the entire network.

  — **Addressing**—The addressing scheme that you choose should be affected only minimally by changes to the network and should allow for route summarization.

  — **Routing protocols**—The design should be such that changes in the network are easily handled by the routing protocols.

■ **Availability**—Availability is always a major concern to network managers. A network's ability to overcome outages and adapt to changes is paramount. Three availability issues are incorporated into the Cisco AVVID design model:

  — **Equipment and link redundancy**—This includes not only redundant components and high-availability configurations but also redundancy within the equipment, such as dual power supplies and other features designed into the modular products.

  — **Protocol resiliency**—The focus here is to use the most resilient protocol. Multiple redundant protocols do not necessarily provide the best solution.

  — **Network capacity design**—A network design should allow for significant expansion and support the capacity needs and redundancy to reduce the impact of a redundant link failure.

The Cisco AVVID network infrastructure design incorporates many different topologies and technologies to provide optimum efficiency and stability.

Cisco SAFE

Cisco Security Architecture for Enterprises (SAFE) is available for different sizes of networks. The Cisco white papers 'SAFE: A Security Blueprint for Enterprise Networks' and 'SAFE: Extending the Security Blueprint to Small, Midsize, and Remote-User Networks' are guides for network designers and focus on the implementation of secure network designs. Cisco SAFE is based on Cisco AVVID. SAFE uses best practices and the interoperability of various Cisco and Cisco partner products. There are several SAFE white papers available on Cisco.com that focus on the following design fundamentals (from the Cisco Systems white paper "SAFE: A Security Blueprint for Enterprise Networks," copyright 2000):

- Security and attack mitigation based on policy
- Security implementation throughout the infrastructure (not just specialized security devices)
- Secure management and reporting
- Authentication and authorization of users and administrators to critical network resources
- Intrusion detection for critical resources and subnets
- Support for emerging networked applications

The SAFE blueprint is composed of the critical areas of network security:

- **Perimeter security**—Protects access to the network by controlling access on the network's entry and exit points
- **Secure connectivity**—Provides secure communications via virtual private networks (VPNs)
- **Application security**—Ensures that critical servers and applications are protected
- **Identity**—Provides secure authentication and authorization services to ensure that access is restricted to only authorized users.
- **Security management and monitoring**—Allows for centralized management of security resources and the detection of unauthorized activity on the network

NOTE   Cisco SAFE Implementation (exam 642-541) is a requirement for CCSP Certification. For more information, refer to http://www.cisco.com/go/certifications.

Foundation Summary

The "Foundation Summary" is a collection of tables and figures that provide a convenient review of many key concepts in this chapter. If you are already comfortable with the topics in this chapter, this summary can help you recall a few details. If you just read this chapter, this review should help solidify some key facts. If you are doing your final preparation before the exam, these tables and figures are a convenient way to review the day before the exam.

Network Security

There is no single security solution for every network. Network security is a combination of products and processes that support the organization's security policy.

Vulnerabilities, Threats, and Attacks

Vulnerabilities, threats, and attacks are three components that create the environment for a cyber-attack.

Vulnerabilities

Vulnerabilities are unintentional weaknesses in an application, hardware component, or network design that can be exploited to gain entry to a computer system or network. Attackers generally target known vulnerabilities when looking for targets.

Threats

Threats are broken down into two categories based on the intent of the attacker:

- **Structured threats**—Threats that are preplanned and focus on a specific target. A structured threat is an organized effort to breach a specific network or organization.

- **Unstructured threats**—Threats that are random and usually the result of an attacker identifying the vulnerability by scanning the network looking for "targets of opportunity." This type of threat is by far the most common threat because it can be performed using automated tools (scripts) that are readily available on the Internet and can be performed by someone with very limited computer skills.

Attacks

There are three different types of attacks, which are named based on the attacker's intent:

■ **Reconnaissance attack**—Designed to gain information about a specific target network or resource. Typical types of reconnaissance attacks include:

— **DNS query**—Checks the Domain Name Service to see what address space is registered to a specific organization

— **Ping sweep**—Directs ICMP packets at specific host addresses on a network, enabling the attacker to determine what addresses are being used based on the replies received

— **Vertical scan**—Directs a scan against all the service ports of a specific host to determine which services are running on that host

— **Horizontal scan**—Directs a scan for a single service port against a range of network addresses

— **Block scan**—Directs a scan for multiple service ports against a range of network addresses

■ **Access attack**—Designed to gain access to a network or resource. There are three main goals of an access attack:

— **Interception**—Retrieve, alter, or destroy data

— **Modification**—Add, move, or change network resources, including user access

— **Fabrication**—Install exploits that can be used later to gain access to the network or resource

■ **Denial of service attack**—Designed to deny authorized access to the target network or resource

Security Policies

A security policy is the written representation of an organization's security philosophy. The security policy is a guide that defines how the organization does business with respect to its network resources and defines in general terms how the network resources are to be secured. The security policy should fulfill the following objectives:

■ Analyze the threat based on the type of business performed and type of network exposure

■ Determine the organization's security requirements

- Document the network infrastructure and identify potential security breach points
- Identify specific resources that require protection and develop an implementation plan

Network Security as a Process

The security process is driven by the security policy. The *Security Wheel* demonstrates the four ongoing steps used to continuously improve the security of a network:

- **Secure**—Implement the necessary security hardware, management and operational processes, and secure your system configurations to reduce your network exposure.
- **Monitor**—Monitor the network to determine how changes have affected your network and look for additional threats.
- **Test**—Test the current network and system configurations to determine if any vulnerabilities exist.
- **Improve**—Make continuous improvements based on the results of your testing, based on vulnerabilities noted during the network monitoring, or based on normal component upgrades and improvements.

Defense in Depth

- Defense in depth refers to implementing multiple layers of security to mitigate potential threats. Cisco has two specific programs to address defense in depth. Those programs are Cisco AVVID and Cisco SAFE.

Cisco AVVID

- *AVVID* is the Cisco Architecture for Voice, Video, and Integrated Data. Cisco AVVID is an open architecture that is used by Cisco partners to develop various solutions. Cisco AVVID solutions provide the following benefits:
- Network performance
  - Application response time
  - Device performance
  - Protocol performance
- Scalability
  - Topology
  - Addressing
  - Routing protocols

- Availability
    - Equipment and link redundancy
    - Protocol resiliency
    - Network capacity design

Cisco SAFE

- The Cisco white papers 'SAFE: A Security Blueprint for Enterprise Networks' and 'SAFE: Extending the Security Blueprint to Small, Midsize, and Remote-User Networks' are guides for network designers and focus on the implementation of secure network designs. The SAFE blueprints comprise the following components:

- Perimeter security

- Secure connectivity

- Application security

- Identity

- Security management and monitoring

Key Terms

Table 1-2 lists the most important terms used in this chapter.

Table 1-2 *Chapter Key Terms*

Term	Definition
Network security	The implementation of security devices, policies, and processes to prevent the unauthorized access to network resources or the alteration or destruction of resources or data.
Security policy	A formal statement that specifies a set of rules that users must follow while gaining access to corporate network access.
Defense in depth	A network architecture that provides multiple layers of protection.
AVVID	Cisco Architecture for Voice, Video, and Integrated Data.
SAFE	The Cisco Secure Architecture for Enterprises.

Q&A

As mentioned in the Introduction, the questions in this book are more difficult than what you should experience on the exam. The questions are designed to ensure your understanding of the concepts discussed in this chapter and adequately prepare you to complete the exam. You should use the simulated exams on the CD to practice for the exam.

The answers to these questions can be found in Appendix A.

1. What is the difference between the network security policy and the network security process?

2. For unstructured threats, what is the normal anatomy of an attack?

3. What information can you gain from a ping sweep?

4. What is the single most important component when implementing defense in depth?

5. Why could an organization be legally responsible if its systems are compromised during an attack?

This chapter covers the following subjects:

- Firewalls

- PIX Firewall Overview

Firewall Technologies and the Cisco PIX Firewall

The Cisco PIX Firewall is one of many firewalls on the market today. Different manufacturers employ different technologies in their designs. This chapter discusses the different technologies, which technology is employed by the Cisco PIX Firewall, and how.

How to Best Use This Chapter

This chapter is straightforward. It covers a few basic concepts and discusses how they are applied to Cisco PIX Firewall. There are few questions in the "Do I Know This Already?" section, few review questions, and no scenarios.

The fact that this topic is easy does not make it any less important. On the contrary, the concepts in this chapter are the foundation of much of what you need to understand to pass the CSPFA Certification Exam. Unless you do exceptionally well on the "Do I Know This Already?" quiz and are 100 percent confident in your knowledge of this area, you should read through the entire chapter.

"Do I Know This Already?" Quiz

The purpose of the "Do I Know This Already?" quiz is to help you decide if you really need to read the entire chapter. If you already intend to read the entire chapter, you do not necessarily need to answer these questions now.

The ten-question quiz, derived from the major sections in the "Foundation Topics" portion of the chapter, helps you determine how to spend your limited study time.

Table 2-1 outlines the major topics discussed in this chapter and the "Do I Know This Already?" quiz questions that correspond to those topics.

Table 2-1 *"Do I Know This Already?" Foundation Topics Section-to-Question Mapping*

Foundation Topics Section	Questions Covered in This Section	Score
Firewall Technologies	1, 5, 8 to 10	
Cisco PIX Firewall	2 to 4, 6, 7	

CAUTION The goal of self assessment is to gauge your mastery of the topics in this chapter. If you do not know the answer to a question or are only partially sure of the answer, you should mark this question wrong for purposes of the self assessment. Giving yourself credit for an answer you correctly guess skews your self-assessment results and might provide you with a false sense of security.

1. True or false: Packet filtering can be configured on Cisco routers.

2. What design feature enables the Cisco PIX Firewall to outperform conventional application firewalls?

   a. The Packet Selectivity Algorithm

   b. Super-packet filtering

   c. A single embedded operating environment

   d. Hot standby proxy processing

3. True or false: Cut-through proxy technology allows users to do anything they want after authenticating at the firewall.

4. What steps are required to add an ARP entry to a Cisco PIX Firewall?

   a. Edit the /etc/interfaces/outside/arp.conf file.

   b. You do not need to add an ARP entry on a PIX Firewall.

   c. Add the ARP entry using the GUI.

   d. Use the **set arp** command in interface config mode.

5. True or false: There is no limit to the number of connections an application proxy firewall can handle.

6. True or false: The Adaptive Security Algorithm requires a tremendous amount of processing by the firewall. Although the PIX Firewall is not very efficient at processing the ASA, it can handle the task.

7. True or false: Redundancy allows you to configure two or more PIX Firewalls in a cluster to protect critical systems.

8. Of the three firewall technologies, which one generates a separate connection on behalf of the requestor and usually operates at the upper layers of the OSI reference model?

   a. Stateful inspection

   b. Packet filtering

   c. High-speed packet filtering

   d. Application proxy

   e. None of the above

9. Which of the following is *not* one of the three basic firewall technologies?

   a. Stateful inspection

   b. Packet filtering

   c. High-speed packet filtering

   d. Application proxy

   e. None of the above

10. Which firewall technology is commonly implemented on a router?

    a. Stateful inspection

    b. Packet filtering

    c. High-speed packet filtering

    d. Application proxy

    e. None of the above

The answers to the "Do I Know This Already?" quiz are found in Appendix A, "Answers to the 'Do I Know This Already?' Quizzes and Q&A Sections." The suggested choices for your next step are as follows:

- **8 or less overall score**—Read the entire chapter. This includes the "Foundation Topics," "Foundation Summary," and "Q&A" sections.

- **9 or 10 overall score**—If you want more review of these topics, skip to the "Foundation Summary" section and then go to the "Q&A" section. Otherwise, move to the next chapter.

Foundation Topics

Firewall Technologies

To understand the different firewall technologies, you first need to have a good understanding of the Open System Interconnection (OSI) reference model. The seven-layer OSI reference model is the standard for network communication and is the foundation upon which each firewall technology was built. The lower four layers of the OSI reference model are generally considered to be the layers that deal with networking, whereas the upper three layers deal more with application functions.

Firewalls are the primary components required to perform network perimeter security. The function of a firewall is to permit or to deny traffic that attempts to pass through it, based on specific predefined rules. All firewalls perform the function of examining network traffic and directing that traffic based on the rule set; however, the methods that the various firewalls use may differ. The following are the three different types of firewall technologies, each of which is discussed in more detail in the following sections:

- Packet filtering
- Proxy
- Stateful inspection

Packet Filtering

Packet-filtering firewalls are the oldest and most commonly used firewall technologies. A packet-filtering firewall simply inspects incoming traffic for items that occur at the network and transport layers of the OSI reference model. The packet-filtering firewall analyzes IP packets and compares them to a set of established rules called an *access control list* (*ACL*). Packet filtering inspects the packet for only the following elements:

- Source IP address
- Source port
- Destination IP address
- Destination port
- Protocol (listed by name or IP protocol number)

NOTE In addition to the elements just listed, some packet-filtering firewalls check for header information to determine if the packet is from a new connection or an existing connection.

Figure 2-1 depicts how traffic passes through a packet-filtering firewall from the source to the destination as compared to the OSI reference model. Traffic is depicted as passing between the network and transport layers because some network layer items are checked (source and destination addresses) and some transport layer items are checked (the transport protocol, such as TCP or UDP). The items listed in the previous paragraph are verified against the ACL (rule set) to determine if the packets are permitted or denied.

Figure 2-1 *Packet-Filtering Firewall*

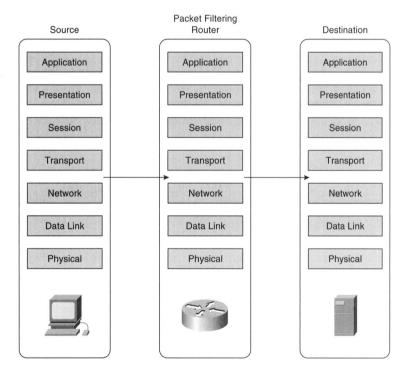

The advantage to using packet filters is that they tend to be very fast because they do not concern themselves with upper-layer data. Some of the disadvantages of packet filtering are as follows:

■   ACLs may be very complex and difficult to manage.

- A packet-filtering firewall may be tricked into permitting access to an unauthorized user who is falsely representing himself (*spoofing*) with an IP address that is authorized by the ACL.

- Many new applications (such as multimedia applications) create multiple connections on random ports with no way to determine which ports will be used until the connection is established. Because access lists are manually configured, it is very difficult to provide support for these applications without reducing the security of the device.

Packet filtering is a feature that is commonly used on routers. Chapter 7, "Configuring Access," discusses ACLs as applied to the Cisco PIX Firewall in greater detail.

Proxy

New Webster's Dictionary of the English Language defines *proxy* as "the agency of a person who acts as a substitute for another person; authority to act for another." Although this definition does not define a proxy firewall, the function is very similar.

A proxy firewall, commonly called a *proxy server,* acts on behalf of hosts on the protected network segments. The protected hosts never actually make any connections with the outside world. Hosts on the protected network send their requests to the proxy server, where they are compared to the rulebase. If the request matches a rule within the rulebase and is allowed, the proxy server sends a request on behalf of the requesting host to the external host and forwards the reply to the requesting host.

Proxies run at the upper layers of the OSI reference model. Once again, the connections are established between the network and transport layers; however, the application proxy then examines the request at the upper layers while verifying the request against the rule set. If the traffic meets the requirements of the upper-layer inspection and is verified against the rule set, the proxy firewall creates a new connection to the destination.

Figure 2-2 depicts, using the OSI reference model, how traffic passes through a proxy firewall from the source to the destination.

Most proxy firewalls are designed to cache commonly used information to expedite the response time to the requesting host. Application proxies tend to be very secure because the packets are inspected at all layers, but performance can suffer for the same reason. The processing workload required to perform proxy services is significant and increases with the number of requesting hosts.

Figure 2-2   *Proxy Firewall*

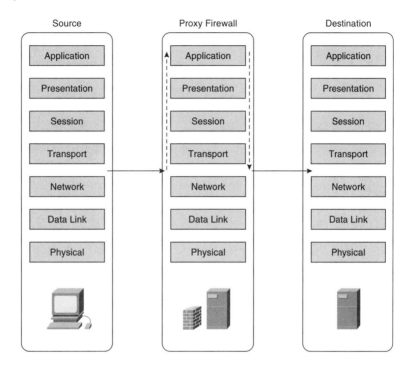

Large networks usually implement several proxy servers, to avoid problems with throughput. The number of applications that a requesting host can access via a proxy is limited. By design, proxy firewalls support only specific applications and protocols. The major disadvantage of proxy servers is that they are applications that run on top of operating systems. A device can be only as secure as the operating system it is running on. If the operating system is compromised, the unauthorized user may be able to take control of the proxy firewall and gain access to the entire protected network.

Stateful Inspection

Stateful inspection, also called *stateful packet filtering,* provides the best combination of security and performance because connections are not only applied to an ACL but also logged in to a small database known as the *state table.* After a connection is established, all session data is compared to the state table. If the session data does not match the state table information for that connection, the connection is dropped.

Figure 2-3 depicts, using the OSI reference model, how traffic passes through a stateful inspection firewall from the source to the destination. Note that the traffic enters between the network and transport layers, and is verified against the state table and the rule set, while basic protocol compliance is checked at the upper layers.

Figure 2-3 *Stateful Inspection Firewall*

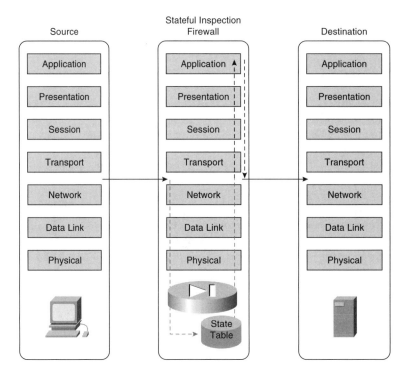

Chapter 3, "Cisco PIX Firewall," covers stateful inspection in further detail.

Stateful packet filtering is the method that is used by the Cisco PIX Firewall.

Cisco PIX Firewall

Four major characteristics of the Cisco Secure PIX Firewall design make it a leading-edge, high-performance security solution:

- Secure real-time embedded system
- Adaptive Security Algorithm
- Cut-through proxy
- Redundancy

Secure Real-Time Embedded System

Unlike most firewalls, the Cisco PIX Firewall runs on a single, proprietary, embedded system. Whereas most firewalls run a firewall application over a general-purpose operating system, the PIX Firewall has a single system that is responsible for operating the device. This single system is beneficial for the following reasons:

- **Better security**—The PIX Firewall operating environment is a single system that was designed with functionality and security in mind. Because there is no separation between the operating system and the firewall application, there are no known vulnerabilities to exploit.

- **Better functionality**—The combined operating environment requires fewer steps when you configure the system. For example, if multiple IP addresses are bound to the external interface of an application firewall that runs over a general operating system, you must configure the networking portions (that is, Address Resolution Protocol [Proxy ARP] entries and routing) on the operating system and then apply the ACLs or rules in the firewall application. On the Cisco PIX Firewall, all these functions are combined into a single system. As soon as an IP address is bound to an interface, the PIX Firewall automatically replies to ARP requests for that address without it having to be specifically configured.

- **Better performance**—Because the operating environment is a single unit, it allows for streamlined processing and much greater performance. The Cisco PIX 535 Firewall can handle 500,000 concurrent connections while maintaining stateful inspection of all connections.

Adaptive Security Algorithm

The *Adaptive Security Algorithm (ASA)* is the key to stateful connection control on the Cisco PIX Firewall. The ASA creates a stateful session flow table (also called the *state table*). Source and destination addresses and other connection information are logged in to the state table. By using the ASA, the Cisco PIX Firewall can perform stateful filtering on the connections in addition to filtering packets. Additionally, the ASA generates random TCP sequence numbers for outbound traffic by making it look like a response to an outbound request is unlikely to succeed.

Cut-Through Proxy

Cut-through proxy is a method of transparently performing authentication and authorization of inbound and outbound connections at the firewall. Cut-through proxy requires very little overhead because it occurs as the session is being established and provides a significant performance advantage over application proxy firewalls. Cut-through proxy is discussed in greater detail in Chapter 3.

Redundancy

The Cisco Secure PIX 515 series and above can be configured in pairs with a primary system and a hot standby. This redundancy and stateful failover make the PIX Firewall a high-availability solution for use in protecting critical network segments. If the primary firewall fails, the secondary automatically assumes the load, dramatically reducing the chances of a network outage. Failover is discussed in greater detail in Chapter 10, "Cisco PIX Firewall Failover."

Foundation Summary

The "Foundation Summary" provides a convenient review of many key concepts in this chapter. If you are already comfortable with the topics in this chapter, this summary can help you recall a few details. If you just read this chapter, this review should help solidify some key facts. If you are doing your final preparation before the exam, this summary provides a convenient way to review the day before the exam.

Firewall Technologies

There are three firewall technologies:

- **Packet filtering**—Inspects the incoming and outgoing packets and allows/denies traffic based on source, destination, protocol, and service.

- **Proxy**—Connections are initiated by the firewall on behalf of the requestor. Traffic does not pass through a proxy-based firewall but rather is re-created by the firewall.

- **Stateful inspection**—Stateful inspection firewalls, also know as *stateful packet filters*, allow/deny traffic based on source, destination, and service while maintaining a state table to keep track of existing connections. This ensures that inbound connections are valid replies to outbound requests.

Cisco PIX Firewall

Four major characteristics of the Cisco Secure PIX Firewall design make it a leading-edge, high-performance security solution:

- **Secure real-time embedded system**—This is a single proprietary embedded system designed for improved security, functionality, and performance.

- **Adaptive Security Algorithm**—The ASA is the key to stateful session control in the PIX Firewall. The ASA maintains state information in the state table and randomly generates TCP sequence numbers to prevent session hijacking.

- **Cut-through proxy**—Cut-through proxy is a method for transparently performing authentication and authorization of inbound and outbound connections at the firewall.

- **Redundancy**—The Cisco Secure PIX 515 series and above can be configured in pairs with a primary system and a hot standby.

Q&A

As mentioned in the Introduction, the questions in this book are more difficult than what you should experience on the exam. The questions are designed to ensure your understanding of the concepts discussed in this chapter and to adequately prepare you to complete the exam. Use the simulated exams on the CD to practice for the exam.

The answers to these questions can be found in Appendix A.

1. What items does a packet filter look at to determine whether to allow the traffic?

2. What are the advantages of the Cisco PIX Firewall over competing firewall products?

3. How many PIX Firewalls can you operate in a high-availability cluster?

4. What is the ASA, and how does the Cisco PIX Firewall use it?

5. Why is cut-through proxy more efficient than traditional proxy?

6. What are the advantages of a real-time embedded system?

This chapter covers the following subjects:

- PIX Firewall Models

- PIX Firewall Licensing

- ASA Security Levels

Cisco PIX Firewall

This chapter discusses the Cisco PIX Firewall in greater detail than Chapter 2, "Firewall Technologies and the Cisco PIX Firewall." It covers the many different models available, including their design and specifications.

How to Best Use This Chapter

Chapter 2 gave you insight into the different firewall technologies and the functionality designed into the Cisco PIX Firewall. This chapter gives you more specific information about this functionality and how this makes the PIX Firewall a truly high-performance solution. This chapter also covers all the PIX Firewall models that are available today and the possible configurations of each model. It is very important for you to understand in great detail the technology that powers the PIX Firewall. Test yourself with the "Do I Know This Already?" quiz, and see how familiar you are with the PIX Firewall in general and with the specifics of each available model.

"Do I Know This Already?" Quiz

The purpose of the "Do I Know This Already?" quiz is to help you decide if you really need to read the entire chapter. If you already intend to read the entire chapter, you do not necessarily need to answer these questions now.

The ten-question quiz, derived from the major sections in the "Foundation Topics" portion of the chapter, helps you determine how to spend your limited study time.

Table 3-1 outlines the major topics discussed in this chapter and the "Do I Know This Already?" quiz questions that correspond to those topics.

Table 3-1 *"Do I Know This Already?" Foundation Topics Section-to-Question Mapping*

Foundation and Supplemental Topics Section	Questions Covered in This Section	Score
PIX Firewall Models	2 to 6	
PIX Firewall Licensing	1, 10	
ASA Security Levels	7 to 9	

CAUTION The goal of self assessment is to gauge your mastery of the topics in this chapter. If you do not know the answer to a question or are only partially sure of the answer, you should mark this question wrong for purposes of the self assessment. Giving yourself credit for an answer you correctly guess skews your self-assessment results and might provide you with a false sense of security.

1. True or false: You do not need a license for any Cisco PIX Firewall. If you own the appliance, you can do anything you want with it.

2. How many physical interfaces does the PIX 525 support?

   a. Eight 10/100 interfaces or three Gigabit interfaces

   b. Eight 10/100 interfaces and three Gigabit interfaces

   c. Six 10/100 interfaces or three Gigabit interfaces

   d. Six 10/100 interfaces and three Gigabit interfaces

   e. None of the above

3. What are the three firewall technologies?

   a. Packet filtering, proxy, connection dropping

   b. Stateful inspection, packet filtering, proxy

   c. Stateful proxy, stateful filtering, packet inspection

   d. Cut-through proxy, ASA, proxy

4. How are optional component cards installed in the PIX Firewall?

   a. ISA slot

   b. USB port

   c. Serial connection

   d. PCI slot

   e. PCMCIA slot

5. What is the maximum clear-text throughput of the PIX 535?

   a. 1.0 Gbps

   b. 1.7 Gbps

   c. 100 Mbps

   d. 565 Mbps

6. How many physical interfaces does a PIX 501 have, and how many network segments does it support?

   a. Six interfaces, two network segments

   b. Six interface, six network segments

   c. Five interfaces, four network segments

   d. Two interfaces, two network segments

   e. None of the above

7. What happens to a reply that does not have the correct TCP sequence number?

   a. It generates an alert.

   b. The connection is dropped.

   c. The connection information is added to the state table.

   d. The session object is modified.

   e. None of the above

8. Which of the following is the best way to remove the ASA from a PIX Firewall?

   a. Use the ASA removal tool, downloaded from Cisco.com.

   b. Use the **asa disable** command in the config mode.

   c. Configure all NATs to a single external address.

   d. Configure all NATs to a single internal address.

   e. You cannot remove the ASA from the PIX Firewall.

9. Which of the following four authentication methods is not supported by the PIX Firewall for performing cut-through proxy?

   a. Local Database

   b. TACACS+

   c. RADIUS

   d. Active Directory

   e. All of the above

10. What encryption algorithms does the PIX Firewall *not* support?

   a. Data Encryption Standard

   b. Triple Data Encryption Standard

   c. Diffie-Hellman

   d. Advanced Encryption Standard 128

   e. Advanced Encryption Standard 256

   f. Answers c, d, and e

The answers to the "Do I Know This Already?" quiz are found in Appendix A, "Answers to the 'Do I Know This Already?' Quizzes and Q&A Sections." The suggested choices for your next step are as follows:

- **8 or less overall score**—Read the entire chapter. This includes the "Foundation Topics," "Foundation Summary," and "Q&A" sections.

- **9 or 10 overall score**—You have a good understanding of the topic. If you want more review of these topics, skip to the "Foundation Summary" section and then go to the "Q&A" section. Otherwise, move to the next chapter.

Foundation Topics

Overview of the Cisco PIX Firewall

As discussed in Chapter 2, the design of the Cisco PIX Firewall provides some significant advantages over application-based firewalls. The Cisco PIX Firewall is designed to be a "performance built, best of breed, all-in-one security appliance." The PIX Firewall appliance provides state-of-the-art stateful firewalling, protocol and application inspection, virtual private networking, inline intrusion prevention, and outstanding multimedia and voice security. Having a single operating environment allows the device to operate more efficiently. Also, because it was designed with security in mind, it is not vulnerable to any known exploits.

Two key components that facilitate the outstanding performance of the PIX Firewall are the Adaptive Security Algorithm (ASA) and cut-through proxy. Both are discussed in detail in the following sections.

Adaptive Security Algorithm

A key part of the Cisco PIX operating environment is the ASA. The ASA is more secure and efficient than packet filtering and provides better performance than application-type proxy firewalls. The ASA segregates the network segments connected to the firewall, maintains secure perimeters, and can control traffic between those segments.

The firewall interfaces are assigned *security levels*. The PIX allows traffic to pass from an interface with a higher security level (inside) to an interface with a lower security level (outside) without an explicit rule for each resource on the higher-level segment. Traffic that is coming from an interface with a lower security level destined for an interface with a higher security level must meet the following two requirements:

- A static translation must exist for the destination.
- An access list or conduit must be in place to allow the traffic.

Access lists and conduits can be used to deny traffic from a higher security level to a lower security level just as they allow traffic from a lower level to a higher level.

NOTE The use of conduits is not supported beyond PIX OS Version 6.3.

The ASA is designed to function as a stateful, connection-oriented process that maintains session information in a *state table*. Applying the security policy and address translation to the state table controls all traffic passing through the firewall. A random TCP sequence number is generated, and the ASA writes the connection information to the state table as an outbound connection is initiated. If the connection is allowed by the security policy, the source address is translated to an external address and the request goes out. Return traffic is compared to the existing state information. If the information does not match, the firewall drops the connection. The security emphasis on the connection rather than on the packets makes it nearly impossible to gain access by hijacking a TCP session.

Figure 3-1 depicts the mechanics of the Adaptive Security Algorithm and how it affects traffic flowing through the PIX Firewall. The following numbered list explains the steps indicated in the figure. Notice that Steps 1 and 5 are performed by the requestor and responder. Steps 2, 3, 4, and 6 are all performed by the PIX Firewall.

1. The internal host initiates an IP connection to an external resource.

2. The PIX writes the following connection information into the state table:

      — Source IP and port

      — Destination IP and port

      — TCP sequencing information

      — Additional TCP/UDP flags

      — A randomly generated TCP sequence number is applied (the state table
        entry is called a "session object")

3. The connection object is compared to the security policy. If the connection is not allowed, the session object is deleted, and the connection is dropped.

4. If the connection is approved by the security policy, the source address is translated and the request is forwarded to the external resource.

5. The external resource replies to the request.

6. The response arrives at the firewall and is compared to the session object. If the response matches the session object, the destination address is translated back to the original address and the traffic passes to the internal host. If it does not match, the connection is dropped.

Figure 3-1 *How ASA Works*

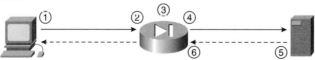

Cut-Through Proxy

The cut-through proxy feature on the Cisco PIX Firewall provides significantly better performance than application proxy firewalls because it completes user authentication at the application layer, verifies authorization against the security policy, and then opens the connection as authorized by the security policy. Subsequent traffic for this connection is no longer handled at the application layer but is statefully inspected, providing significant performance benefits over proxy-based firewalls.

Figure 3-2 depicts the mechanics of cut-through proxy and the four steps that take place prior to the activation of the ASA. The following numbered list explains the steps indicated in the figure:

1. The external user initiates an FTP, HTTP, or Telnet connection to the internal web server.

2. The PIX Firewall replies with a user logon and the user completes the logon.

3. The PIX Firewall uses TACACS+ or RADIUS to communicate the user account information to the AAA server, where it is authenticated.

4. The connection to the web server is opened at the network layer, the session information is written to the connections table, and the ASA process begins.

Figure 3-2 *How Cut-Through Proxy Works*

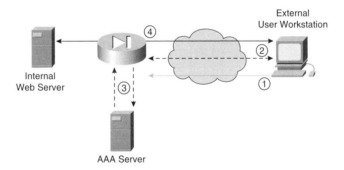

> **NOTE** Users can authenticate to a user database on the PIX Firewall, but it is more efficient to use an external authentication server with RADIUS or TACACS+ because the processing required by the PIX Firewall to maintain and query an internal database increases the firewall's workload.

Cisco PIX Firewall Models and Features

Currently, six models of the Cisco PIX Firewall are available. These models provide services that range from the small office/home office (SOHO) to the enterprise network and Internet service provider (ISP):

- **Cisco Secure PIX 501**—This model is intended for SOHO use and incorporates an integrated 10/100 Ethernet switch.

- **Cisco Secure PIX 506E**—Intended for remote office/branch office (ROBO) use and comes with two 10/100 Ethernet interfaces.

- **Cisco Secure PIX 515E**—Designed for small to medium-size businesses and branch office installations.

- **Cisco Secure PIX 525**—Intended for large enterprise networks and ISPs.

- **Cisco Secure PIX 535**—Intended for very large enterprise networks and ISPs. This model is the most robust of the PIX Firewall series.

- **Cisco Firewall Service Module (FWSM)**—Designed for large enterprise networks and ISPs. The FWSM is a PIX Firewall blade for the Cisco Catalyst 6500 Series Switches and 7600 Series Routers. The FWSM is discussed in great detail in Chapter 19, "Firewall Service Module."

All the PIX firewalls have the functionality described in the following sections incorporated into their design.

Intrusion Protection

PIX firewalls were designed to detect a variety of attacks. They can also be integrated with the Cisco Secure Intrusion Detection Sensor to dynamically react to different threats.

AAA Support

PIX firewalls work with RADIUS or TACACS+ and the Cisco Access Control Server (CSACS) or other AAA products to provide authentication, authorization, and accounting (AAA) functionality. It is also possible to configure a local user database on the PIX rather than integrate with an external authentication server.

X.509 Certificate Support

Digital certificates are your digital identification that verifies you are who you claim to be and validates the integrity of your data. Digital certificates are most commonly combined with encryption to secure data in the following four ways:

- **Authentication**—Digital certificates are used to verify the identity of a user or server.

■ **Integrity**—If data has been digitally signed and it is altered, the digital signature becomes invalid, indicating to the recipient that the data is no longer valid.

■ **Token verification**—Digital tokens are a much more secure product that can be used to replace passwords. Passwords are less secure because several methods are available that can determine a password by using both dictionaries and number/letter/word combination generators to try every conceivable combination of characters until they discover the password. A digital certificate is an encrypted file that resides on your computer and can be decrypted only by your password. To compromise your certificate, a user would have to have *both* the encrypted file and your password.

■ **Encryption**—Digital certificates verify the identity of both ends of an encrypted connection and dynamically negotiate the parameters of that connection. Using digital certificates to negotiate virtual private networks (VPNs) is discussed in detail in Chapter 11, "Virtual Private Networks."

PIX firewalls support the Simple Certificate Enrollment Protocol (SCEP) and can be integrated with the following X.509 digital identification solutions:

■ **Entrust Technologies, Inc.**—Entrust/PKI 4.0

■ **Microsoft Corp.**—Windows 2000 Certificate Server 5.0

■ **VeriSign**—Onsite 4.5

■ **Baltimore Technologies**—UniCERT 3.05

Network Address Translation/Port Address Translation

PIX firewalls can statically or dynamically translate internal private (RFC 1918) addresses or any other address used internally to the assigned public addresses. They can also hide multiple hosts on the internal network behind a single public address. A one-for-one translation of addresses from internal to external, or from external to internal, is referred to as Network Address Translation (NAT). If multiple internal addresses are translated behind a single external address, each outgoing connection uses a different source port. This is called Port Address Translation (PAT).

Firewall Management

PIX firewalls can be managed using one of three methods:

■ **Cisco command-line interface (CLI)**—The CLI uses commands consistent with other Cisco products. The PIX can be configured to allow access to the CLI via console, Telnet, and SSH. All system configurations can be saved as a text file for archive and recovery purposes.

- **PIX Device Manager (PDM)**—The PDM is a graphical user interface (GUI) that can be used to manage the PIX firewall. The GUI connects to the device via a secure connection and provides a simplified method of firewall management. The PDM also provides real-time log data that can be used to track events and do limited troubleshooting.

- **CiscoWorks Management Center for Firewalls (PIX MC)**—The PIX MC is a component of the CiscoWorks Enterprise Management Center. The PIX MC allows you to manage as many as 1000 PIX Firewalls and can be used to manage the entire perimeter of your enterprise network.

Simple Network Management Protocol

PIX firewalls allow limited SNMP support. Because SNMP was designed as a network management protocol and not a security protocol, it can be used to exploit a device. For this reason, the PIX Firewall allows only *read-only* access to remote connections. This enables the manager to remotely connect to the device and monitor SNMP traps but does not allow the manager to change any SNMP settings.

Syslog Support

PIX firewalls log four different types of events onto syslog:

- Security
- Resource
- System
- Accounting

The PIX can be configured to react differently to any of eight severity levels for each event type. Logs are stored in system memory and can be forwarded to a syslog server. It is a recommended practice to select the appropriate log level that generates the syslog details required to track session-specific data.

Virtual Private Networks

All PIX firewalls are designed to function as a termination point, or *VPN gateway,* for VPNs. This functionality allows administrators to create encrypted connections with other networks over the Internet. The VPN performance of each PIX model is listed in its corresponding specifications section later in this chapter.

Optional Firewall Components

Cisco offers five optional components for use with the PIX 515E, 525, or 535 models. These components can increase the performance and functionality of the PIX Firewall. The five optional components include:

- **VPN Accelerator Card (VAC)**—The VAC is a card that fits into a PCI slot of the PIX 515E through 535 firewall appliances and increases VPN performance and security by segregating the processing required for the VPN from all other traffic traversing the firewall. The VAC supports both DES and 3DES encryption.

- **VPN Accelerator Card Plus (VAC+)**—The VAC+ is an improved version of the VAC. It also fits into a PCI slot of the PIX 515E through 535 appliances. The VAC+ supports DES, 3DES, and the Advanced Encryption Standard (AES). The VAC+ requires PIX OS Version 6.3(1) or higher with a DES, 3DES/AES license.

NOTE Only one VAC or VAC+ card can be installed in the PIX appliance.

- **Cisco PIX Firewall FastEthernet Interface Card (PIX-1FE)**—The PIX-1FE is a 10/100 Ethernet interface on a 33-MHz PCI card. This enables you to increase the number of interfaces on the 515E to 535 appliances.

- **Cisco PIX 64-bit/66-MHz Four-Port FastEthernet Interface Card (4FE-66)**—The 4FE-66 interface card is a single PCI card that combines four 10/100 Ethernet interfaces. This interface card works with the 515E, 525, and 535 firewall appliances and allows you to install four 10/100 interfaces per PCI slot up to the maximum number of interfaces per device model.

- **Cisco PIX Firewall 66-MHz Gigabit Ethernet Card (1GE-66)**—The 1GE-66 Gigabit interface fits into the PCI slot of the 525 and 535 firewall appliances. The 1GE-66 allows for full-duplex gigabit (1000BASE-SX) performance, compliant with the IEEE 802.2 and 802.3z Ethernet standards.

NOTE The type and number of interfaces that will function in the PIX Firewall appliance is normally determined by the license installed not the number of available PCI slots.

PIX Firewall Model Capabilities

The following sections describe the characteristics and capabilities of each of the PIX Firewall models. The *throughput* speeds mentioned for each model refer to the speeds at which the firewall can process the data. The actual throughput for the firewall is largely determined by the speed of the firewall interface, the speed of the connected link, or the packet (MTU) size.

Cisco PIX 501

The Cisco PIX 501 Firewall was designed for the SOHO environment. It has a 133-MHz processor, 16 MB of RAM, and 8 MB of Flash memory. It has an outside Ethernet interface and an integrated four-port Ethernet 10/100 switch on the internal side. It has a 9600-baud console port that is used for local device management. The PIX 501 does not support failover.

Connection capabilities for the PIX 501 are as follows:

- Maximum clear-text throughput—60 Mbps
- Maximum throughput (DES)—6 Mbps
- Maximum throughput (AES-128)—4.5 Mbps
- Maximum throughput (3DES)—3 Mbps
- Maximum concurrent connections—7500
- Maximum concurrent VPN peers—10

As shown in Figure 3-3, the front panel of the PIX 501 has a power indicator, a VPN tunnel indicator, and two rows of LEDs for link and network activity. These indicators are divided into two groups:

- The outside Ethernet interface
- The four inside Ethernet interfaces (switch)

Figure 3-3 *PIX 501 Front Panel*

There are several licenses available for the PIX 501 Firewall. Upgrades are available to increase the number of users or to implement VPN support. Table 3-2 describes the available licenses and their function.

Table 3-2 *Cisco PIX 501 Licenses*

License	Function
10 User License	Support for up to ten concurrent connections from different source IP addresses on the internal network to traverse the firewall. Also provides DHCP server support for up to 32 leases.
50 User License	Support for up to 50 concurrent connections from different source IP addresses on the internal network to traverse the firewall. Also provides DHCP server support for up to 128 leases.
Unlimited User License	Support for an unlimited number of concurrent connections from different source IP addresses on the internal network to traverse the firewall. Also provides DHCP server support for up to 256 leases.
DES Encryption License	Support for 56-bit DES encryption.
3DES/AES Encryption License	Support for 168-bit 3DES and up to 256-bit AES encryption.

NOTE DES, 3DES, and AES encryption will be discussed in detail in Chapter 11.

Cisco PIX 506E

The Cisco PIX 506E Firewall was designed for the ROBO environment. It has a 300-MHz Celeron processor, 32 MB of RAM, and 8 MB of Flash memory. It has a fixed outside Ethernet interface and a fixed inside Ethernet interface. It has a 9600-baud console port that is used for local device management. The PIX 506 does not support failover.

Connection capabilities for the PIX 506 are as follows:

- **Maximum clear-text throughput**—100 Mbps
- **Maximum throughput (DES)**—20 Mbps
- **Maximum throughput (3DES)**—17 Mbps
- **Maximum throughput (AES-128)**—30 Mbps
- **Maximum concurrent connections**—25,000
- **Maximum concurrent VPN peers**—25

As shown in Figure 3-4, the PIX 506 has three status LEDs on the front panel that indicate power to the system, that the system is active (the OS is fully loaded), and that there is network activity on any interface.

Figure 3-4   *PIX 506 Front Panel*

As shown in Figure 3-5, the rear of the PIX 506 contains the Ethernet ports and the console port.

Figure 3-5   *PIX 506E Rear Panel*

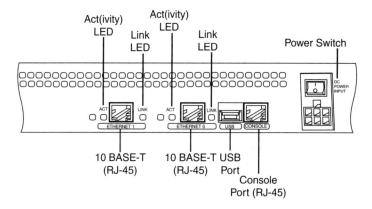

The console can be connected using an RJ-45 to a DB-9 or DB-25 serial adapter, as shown in Figure 3-6.

Figure 3-6 *PIX 506E Console Connection*

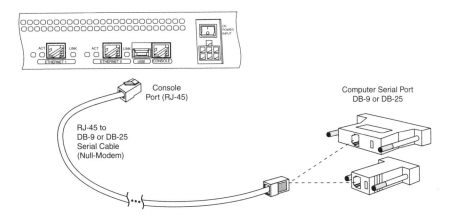

There are three licenses available for the PIX 506E Firewall. The basic license provides unlimited user access and the two upgrades allow for VPN support. Table 3-3 describes the available licenses and their function.

Table 3-3 *Cisco PIX 506E Licenses*

License	Function
Unlimited User License	Support for an unlimited number of concurrent connections from source IP addresses on the internal network to traverse the firewall. Also provides DHCP server support for up to 256 leases. This is the standard license that comes with the PIX 506E.
DES Encryption License	Support for 56-bit DES encryption.
3DES/AES Encryption License	Support for 168-bit 3DES up to 256-bit AES encryption.

Cisco PIX 515E

The Cisco PIX 515E Firewall was designed for small- to medium-size businesses. The PIX 515E is the smallest firewall of the PIX family that is designed to be rack-mountable and is a standard 1U (1.75-inch) configuration. It has a 433-MHz processor, 32 MB or 64 MB of RAM, and 16 MB of Flash memory. It has two fixed 10/100 Ethernet interfaces that have a default configuration of outside (Ethernet 0) and inside (Ethernet 1) and contains two PCI slots for the installation of up to four additional Ethernet interfaces.

The PIX 515E also supports the use of *virtual interfaces* for switched environments using 802.1q VLAN tagging. It has a 9600-baud console port that is used for local device management. The PIX 515E can be configured for failover using a failover cable connected to the 115-kbps serial connection. PIX Firewall OS Version 6.2 provides the functionality for long-distance (LAN-based) failover. This is discussed in greater detail in Chapter 9, "Routing and the PIX Firewall."

Connection capabilities for the PIX 515E are as follows:

- **Maximum clear-text throughput**—188 Mbps
- **Maximum throughput (3DES)**—63 Mbps with VAC
- **Maximum throughput (3DES)**—140 Mbps with VAC+
- **Maximum throughput (AES-128)**—135 Mbps with VAC+
- **Maximum throughput (AES-256)**—140 Mbps with VAC+
- **Maximum concurrent connections**—130,000
- **Maximum concurrent VPN peers**—2000

As shown in Figure 3-7, the PIX 515E has three status LEDs on the front panel that indicate power to the system, that the system is active (the OS is fully loaded and the system is operational), and that there is network activity on any interface. If you have two firewalls running in the failover mode, the active light indicates which firewall is active and which is standby.

Figure 3-7 *PIX 515E Front Panel*

The rear of the PIX 515E contains the Ethernet ports and the console port. The PIX 515E can handle up to four additional Ethernet interfaces. This could be a single four-port Ethernet card (see Figure 3-8) or two single-port cards (see Figure 3-9). The PIX 515E automatically recognizes and numbers any additional interfaces that are installed.

The PIX 515E also can be configured with a VAC or VAC+. The VAC and VAC+ handle much of the VPN traffic processing (encryption and decryption), thus improving the firewall's performance. The VAC and VAC+ are recommended for firewalls that connect multiple high-traffic VPNs.

Figure 3-8 *PIX 515E with Additional Four-Port Interface*

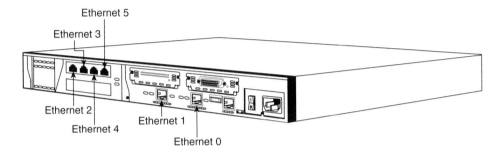

Figure 3-9 *PIX 515E with Two Additional Interfaces*

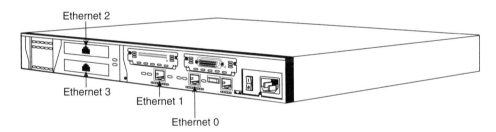

The installation of additional interfaces and failover requires that the software license be upgraded from the basic license (515-R) to the unrestricted license (515-UR). A maximum of three interfaces can be installed using the restricted license.

The console connection for the PIX 515E is the same as for the 506E.

There are three licenses available for the PIX 515E Firewall. Upgrades are available to implement VPN support. Table 3-4 describes the available licenses and their function.

Table 3-4 *Cisco PIX 515E Licenses*

License	Function
Restricted Software License	Support for 32 MB of RAM and up to three 10/100 interfaces. The restricted license supports only limited VPN connectivity and does not support failover.
Unrestricted Software License	Support for 64 MB of RAM, up to six 10/100 interfaces, stateful failover, and integrated VAC or VAC+.
Failover Software License	Support for a "hot standby" system designed to operate in conjunction with an active system running the unrestricted license.

Cisco PIX 525

The Cisco PIX 525 Firewall is an enterprise firewall. It provides perimeter security for large enterprise networks. The PIX 525 is rack-mountable in a 2U (3.5-inch) configuration. It has a 600-MHz processor, up to 256 MB of RAM, and 16 MB of Flash memory. It has two fixed 10/100 Ethernet interfaces. The two fixed interfaces are Ethernet 0, which is the outside interface by default, and Ethernet 1, which is the inside interface by default.

The PIX 525 also includes three PCI slots for the installation of up to six additional Ethernet interfaces. It has a 9600-baud console port that is used for local device management. The PIX 525 can be configured for failover using a failover cable connected to the 115-kbps serial connection or can be configured for LAN-based failover. The PIX 525 also can be configured with a VAC. The VAC handles much of the processing of VPN traffic (encryption and decryption), thus improving the firewall's performance. The VAC is recommended for firewalls that will connect multiple high-traffic VPNs.

Connection capabilities for the PIX 525 are as follows:

- Maximum clear-text throughput—330 Mbps
- Maximum throughput (3DES)—72 Mbps with VAC
- Maximum throughput (3DES)—155 Mbps with VAC+
- Maximum throughput (AES-128)—165 Mbps with VAC+
- Maximum throughput (AES-256)—170 Mbps with VAC+
- Maximum concurrent connections—280,000
- Maximum concurrent VPN peers—2000

As shown in Figure 3-10, the PIX 525 has two LEDs on the front. These LEDs indicate that the firewall has power and that the system is active (the OS is loaded and the system is operational). The active light indicates which firewall is active in a failover pair.

Figure 3-10 *PIX 525 Front Panel*

The rear of the PIX 525, shown in Figure 3-11, is similar in design to the PIX 515E, with fixed interfaces and additional PCI slots. The PIX 525 can support 10/100 Mbps and Gbps Ethernet interface cards.

Figure 3-11 *PIX 525 Rear Panel*

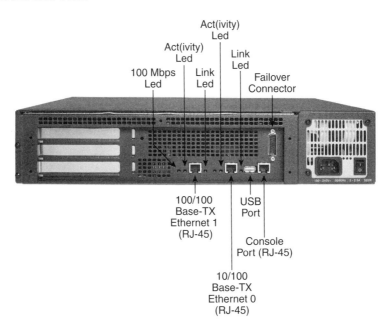

The console connection for the PIX 525 is the same as for the PIX 506E, 515E, and 535.

NOTE The installation of additional physical interfaces and failover requires that the software license be upgraded from the Restricted Bundle.

The three licenses available for the PIX 525 Firewall are similar to those available for the PIX 515E but support a greater amount of RAM and more available physical interfaces. Upgrades are available to increase the number of supported physical interfaces or to implement VPN hardware (VAC/VAC+) support. Table 3-5 describes the available licenses and their function.

Table 3-5 *Cisco PIX 525 Licenses*

License	Function
Restricted Software License	Support for 128 MB of RAM and up to six total 10/100 interfaces or three Gigabit interfaces (plus the two 10/100 onboard interfaces.
Unrestricted Software License	Support for 256 MB of RAM, a total of eight 10/100 interfaces or three Gigabit interfaces (plus the two onboard 10/100 interfaces), stateful failover, and integrated VAC or VAC+.
Failover Software License	Support for a "hot standby" system designed to operate in conjunction with an active system running the unrestricted license.

Cisco PIX 535

The Cisco PIX 535 Firewall is the ultimate enterprise firewall designed for enterprise networks and service providers. The PIX 535 is rack-mountable and fits a 3U configuration. It has a 1-GHz processor, up to 1 GB of RAM, and 16 MB of Flash memory. It has nine PCI slots for the installation of up to ten Ethernet interfaces. It has a 9600-baud console port that is used for local device management, as shown in Figure 3-12.

Figure 3-12 *PIX 535 Rear Panel*

The PIX 535 can be configured for failover using a failover cable connected to the 115-kbps serial connection or configured for LAN-based failover. The PIX 535 is also available with redundant hot-swappable power supplies.

The PIX 535 can also be configured with a VAC or VAC+. The VAC and VAC+ handle much of the VPN traffic processing (encryption and decryption), thus improving the firewall's performance. The VAC and VAC+ are recommended for firewalls that connect multiple high-traffic VPNs.

Connection capabilities for the PIX 535 are as follows:

- **Maximum clear-text throughput**—1.7 GBps
- **Maximum throughput (3DES)**—100 Mbps with VAC
- **Maximum throughput (3DES)**—440 Mbps with VAC+
- **Maximum throughput (128 AES)**—535 Mbps with VAC+
- **Maximum throughput (256 AES)**—440 Mbps with VAC+
- **Maximum concurrent connections**—500,000
- **Maximum concurrent VPN peers**—2000

As shown in Figure 3-13, the PIX 535 has two LEDs on the front. These LEDs indicate that the firewall has power and that the system is active (the OS is loaded and passing traffic). The active light indicates which device of a failover pair is active and which is standby.

Figure 3-13 *PIX 535 Front Panel*

The PCI slots are divided into different bus speeds. The slots are numbered from right to left, and slots 0 through 3 run at 64-bit/66 MHz and can support Gigabit Ethernet interface cards (1GE-66). Slots 4 through 8 run at 32-bit/33 MHz and can support Fast Ethernet interface cards (PIX-1FE and PIX-4FE). Figure 3-14 depicts the rear panel of the PIX 535 Firewall.

Figure 3-14   *PIX 535 Rear Panel*

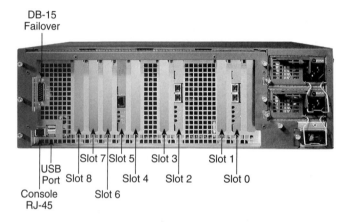

> **NOTE**   Do not mix 33-MHz and 66-MHz cards on the same bus. This causes the overall speed of the 66-MHz bus to be reduced to 33 MHz.

The PIX 535 also supports a VPN accelerator card (VAC and VAC+). It should be installed only on the 32-bit/33-MHz bus.

The console connection for the PIX 535 is the same as for the other PIX models.

The three licenses available for the PIX 535 Firewall are similar to those available for the PIX 515E and 525 but support a greater amount of RAM and more available physical interfaces. Upgrades are available to implement VPN hardware (VAC or VAC+) support. PIX OS Version 6.3 supports logical interfaces and VLANs. Table 3-6 describes the available licenses and their function.

Table 3-6 *Cisco PIX 535 Licenses*

License	Function
Restricted Software License	Support for 512 MB of RAM and up to eight 10/100 interfaces or eight Gigabit interfaces.
Unrestricted Software License	Support for 1 GB of RAM, up to ten 10/100 interfaces or nine Gigabit interfaces, stateful failover, and integrated VAC or VAC+.
Failover Software License	Support for a "hot standby" system designed to operate in conjunction with an active system running the unrestricted license.

NOTE The installation of additional interfaces and failover requires that the software license be upgraded from the Restricted Bundle.

NOTE The PIX 506E through 535 Firewall appliances all have an onboard USB port. At this time the USB port is not used.

Foundation Summary

The "Foundation Summary" provides a convenient review of many key concepts in this chapter. If you are already comfortable with the topics in this chapter, this summary can help you recall a few details. If you just read this chapter, this review should help solidify some key facts. If you are doing your final preparation before the exam, this summary provides a convenient way to review the day before the exam.

Adaptive Security Algorithm

The ASA is an algorithm used by the PIX Firewall to provide better security than packet filters and better performance than application proxies. Each interface of the firewall is assigned a *security level*. Traffic flows through the firewall are managed by the security level combined with ACLs or conduits. TCP sequence numbers for outbound connections are randomly generated by the PIX Firewall to greatly reduce the chances of an inbound TCP session being hijacked.

Cut-Through Proxy

Cut-through proxy is the method used by the PIX Firewall to authorize users and then allow the connection to occur at the network level after completing the ASA process. This greatly improves firewall performance over application proxy firewalls because every packet traversing the firewall is not inspected.

Cisco PIX Firewall Models and Features

The following is a list of the Cisco PIX Firewall models. Table 3-7 lists the capabilities of each model except the FWSM, which is discussed in great detail in Chapter 19.

- **PIX 501**—Designed for SOHO use and has two effective interfaces, a single outside interface and a four-port inside switch.
- **PIX 506E**—Designed for ROBO use and has a single outside interface and a single inside interface.
- **PIX 515E**—Designed for small- to medium-size networks.
- **PIX 525**—Designed for large enterprise networks.
- **PIX 535**—Designed for large enterprise networks and ISPs.
- **FWSM**—A firewall blade designed for the Cisco Catalyst 6500 Series Switch and 7600 Series Router.

Intrusion Protection

PIX firewalls were designed to independently detect and react to a variety of attacks. They can also be integrated with the Cisco Secure Intrusion Detection System to dynamically react to different threats.

AAA Support

The PIX Firewall supports the following AAA technologies:

- **Local database**—It is possible to configure a local AAA database on the PIX Firewall; however, it is not recommended because the additional processing required to utilize the local database can adversely effect the performance of the firewall.

- **RADIUS**—The PIX Firewall supports RADIUS.

- **TACACS+**—The PIX Firewall supports TACACS+.

X.509 Certificate Support

The PIX Firewall supports X.509 certificates for digital identity verification. X.509 certificates are used in conjunction with encryption for the following:

- **Authentication**—Digital certificates are used to authenticate the identity of a user or server.

- **Integrity**—A digital certificate becomes invalid if the digitally signed data has been altered.

- **Token verification**—Digital certificates can be used as a replacement for passwords.

- **Encryption**—Digital certificates simplify the identity authentication process when negotiating a VPN connection.

The Cisco PIX Firewall supports the Simple Certificate Enrollment Protocol (SCEP) and can be integrated with the following X.509 digital identification solutions:

- **Entrust Technologies, Inc.**—Entrust/PKI 4.0

- **Microsoft Corp.**—Windows 2000 Certificate Server 5.0

- **VeriSign**—Onsite 4.5

- **Baltimore Technologies**—UniCERT 3.05

Network Address Translation/Port Address Translation

The PIX Firewall can perform both NAT and PAT.

Firewall Management

PIX firewalls can be managed using one of three methods:

- Cisco command-line interface (CLI)
- PIX Device Manager (PDM)
- CiscoWorks Management Center for Firewalls (PIX MC)

Simple Network Management Protocol

PIX firewalls allow limited SNMP support. Because SNMP was designed as a network management protocol and not a security protocol, it can be used to exploit a device. For this reason, the PIX Firewall allows only read-only access to remote connections. This allows the manager to remotely connect to the device and monitor SNMP traps but does not allow the manager to change any SNMP settings.

Syslog Support

PIX firewalls log four different types of events onto syslog:

- Security
- Resource
- System
- Accounting

Virtual Private Networks

All PIX firewalls are designed to function as a termination point, or *VPN gateway*, for VPNs. This functionality enables administrators to create encrypted connections with other networks over the Internet.

Table 3-7 *PIX Models and Features*

Firewall Model	501	506E	515E	525	535
Intended Business Application	SOHO	ROBO	Small- to medium-size business	Enterprise	Enterprise/ISP
Intrusion Protection	Yes	Yes	Yes	Yes	Yes
AAA Support	Yes	Yes	Yes	Yes	Yes

Table 3-7 *PIX Models and Features (Continued)*

Firewall Model	501	506E	515E	525	535
X.509 Certificate Support	Yes	Yes	Yes	Yes	Yes
AVVID Partner Support	Yes	Yes	Yes	Yes	Yes
Maximum Installed Interfaces	One plus a four-port 10/100 switch	Two 10/100	Six 10/100	Eight 10/100 or three Gigabit and two 10/100	Ten 10/100 or Nine Gigabit
Supports DHCP	Yes	Yes	Yes	Yes	Yes
NAT	Yes	Yes	Yes	Yes	Yes
PAT	Yes	Yes	Yes	Yes	Yes
PPP over Ethernet	Yes	Yes	Yes	Yes	Yes
Cisco PIX Command Line	Yes	Yes	Yes	Yes	Yes
PIX Device Manager	Yes	Yes	Yes	Yes	Yes
Cisco Secure Policy Manager	Yes	Yes	Yes	Yes	Yes
SNMP and Syslog Support	Yes	Yes	Yes	Yes	Yes
Failover Support	No	No	Yes	Yes	Yes
Maximum Throughput	60 Mbps	100 Mbps	188 Mbps	330 Mbps	1.7 GBps
Maximum Throughput (DES)	6 Mbps	20 Mbps	Not listed	Not listed	Not listed
Maximum Throughput (3DES)	3 Mbps	17 Mbps	63-Mbps VAC 140-Mbps VAC+	72-Mbps VAC 155-Mbps VAC+	100-Mbps VAC 440-Mbps VAC+

continues

Table 3-7 *PIX Models and Features (Continued)*

Firewall Model	501	506E	515E	525	535
Maximum Throughput (AES)	4.5 Mbps (128 AES)	30 Mbps (128 AES)	135 Mbps (128 AES) 140 Mbps (256 AES)	165 Mbps (128 AES) 170 Mbps (256 AES)	535 Mbps (128 AES) 440 Mbps (256 AES)
Maximum Concurrent Connections	7500	25,000	130,000	280,000	500,000
Maximum Concurrent VPN Peers	10	25	2000	2000	2000
Processor	133 MHz	300 MHz	433 MHz	600 MHz	1.0 GHz
RAM	16 MB	32 MB	32/64 MB	Up to 256 MB	Up to 1 GB
Flash Memory	8 MB	8 MB	16 MB	16 MB	16 MB

Q&A

As mentioned in the Introduction, the questions in this book are more difficult than what you should experience on the exam. The questions are designed to ensure your understanding of the concepts discussed in this chapter and adequately prepare you to complete the exam. You should take the simulated exams on the CD to practice for the exam.

The answers to these questions can be found in Appendix A.

1. What is the ASA, and how does the Cisco PIX Firewall use it?

2. Why does the ASA generate random TCP sequence numbers?

3. What components of a TCP session does the ASA write to the state table to create a session object?

4. What can cause a session object to be deleted from the state table?

5. What are the three ways to initiate a cut-through proxy session?

6. What X.509 certificates do SCEP and the PIX Firewall support?

7. How many physical interfaces does the PIX 515E support?

8. What is the lowest model number of the PIX Firewall family to support failover?

9. What are three methods of managing a Cisco PIX Firewall?

10. List four advantages of the ASA.

This chapter covers the following topics:

- Accessing the Cisco PIX Firewall

- Command-Level Authorization

- Installing a New Operating System

- Upgrading the Cisco PIX Firewall Operating System

- Creating a Boothelper Disk Using a Windows PC

- Password Recovery

- Overview of Simple Network Management Protocol on the PIX Firewall

- Configuring Simple Network Management Protocol on the PIX Firewall

- Troubleshooting Commands

CHAPTER 4

System Management/ Maintenance

In addition to the nine posted exam topics mentioned in the chapter opener, this chapter also covers the following important system maintenance topics for the Cisco PIX Firewall:

- Activation key upgrade
- Installing a new operating system (OS) on the Cisco PIX Firewall
- Upgrading the Cisco PIX Firewall operating system
- Creating a boot helper disk using a PC running Microsoft Windows
- Password recovery

How to Best Use This Chapter

Chapter 3, "Cisco PIX Firewall," provides insight into the different models of the Cisco PIX Firewall as well as the features and available configurations. This chapter provides information about how to configure access for the Cisco PIX Firewall, how to access the Cisco PIX Firewall, and how to maintain the integrity of the Cisco PIX Firewall through upgrades. In addition, about it discusses password recovery and how to create a boothelper disk. It is very important for you to understand in great detail the technology that powers the Cisco PIX Firewall. Test yourself with the "Do I Know This Already?" quiz and see how familiar you are with these aspects of Cisco PIX Firewall.

"Do I Know This Already?" Quiz

The purpose of the "Do I Know This Already?" quiz is to help you decide if you really need to read the entire chapter. If you already intend to read the entire chapter, you do not necessarily need to answer these questions now.

The ten-question quiz, derived from the major sections in the "Foundation Topics" portion of the chapter, helps you determine how to spend your limited study time.

Table 4-1 outlines the major topics discussed in this chapter and the "Do I Know This Already?" quiz questions that correspond to those topics.

Table 4-1 *"Do I Know This Already?" Foundation Topics Section-to-Question Mapping*

Foundation Topics Section	Questions Covered in This Section	Score
Accessing the Cisco PIX Firewall	7, 8, 10	
Command-Level Authorization	5, 6	
Installing a New Operating System		
Upgrading the Cisco PIX Firewall Operating System	1, 3	
Creating a Boothelper Disk Using a Windows PC		
Password Recovery	2, 4	
Overview of Simple Network Management Protocol on the PIX Firewall		
Configuring Simple Network Management Protocol on the PIX Firewall	9	
Troubleshooting Commands		

CAUTION The goal of self assessment is to gauge your mastery of the topics in this chapter. If you do not know the answer to a question or are only partially sure of the answer, you should mark this question wrong for purposes of the self assessment. Giving yourself credit for an answer you correctly guess skews your self-assessment results and might provide you with a false sense of security.

1. Which command upgrades a PIX Firewall 525 device running a 5.3 OS version to 6.3?

    a. install

    b. setup

    c. copy 6.3

    d. copy tftp flash

2. Which binary file is required to perform a password recovery procedure on a PIX device running OS Version 6.3?

    a. np63.bin

    b. pix52.bin

    c. bh52.bin

    d. pass52.bin

3. What circumstance(s) warrant(s) the use of a boothelper disk in the OS upgrade procedure?

   a. A corrupt binary image

   b. A PIX 520 device

   c. A PIX device running a 6.0 or later PIX OS

   d. No circumstance warrants the use of a boothelper disk.

4. To what is the console password set after a successful password recovery procedure?

   a. password.

   b. cisco.

   c. secret.

   d. It is erased and set to blank.

5. How many privilege levels are there on the PIX Firewall?

   a. 2

   b. 16

   c. 32

   d. 4

6. Which of the following is the highest level of privilege to which a user account can be assigned?

   a. 32

   b. 16

   c. 8

   d. 15

7. Which command changes the SSH password for login?

   a. change ssh password

   b. secret

   c. password

   d. ssh pass

8. What is the default amount of time a Telnet session can be idle?

   a. 2 minutes

   b. 15 minutes

   c. 5 minutes

   d. 12 minutes

9. Which of the following pieces of information are sent to an SNMP management station by the PIX Firewall?

   a. Link up and link down

   b. Running configuration

   c. Show command outputs

   d. Authentication failure

10. Which version of SSH does the PIX Firewall support?

   a. 2.1

   b. 2.2

   c. 3.1

   d. 1

The answers to the "Do I Know This Already?" quiz are found in Appendix A, "Answers to the 'Do I Know This Already?' Quizzes and Q&A Sections." The suggested choices for your next step are as follows:

- **8 or less overall score**—Read the entire chapter. This includes the "Foundation Topics," "Foundation Summary," and "Q&A" sections.

- **9 or 10 overall score**—If you want more review of these topics, skip to the "Foundation Summary" section and then go to the "Q&A" section. Otherwise, move to the next chapter.

Foundation Topics

Accessing the Cisco PIX Firewall

The PIX Firewall can be accessed by using the console port or remotely using the following methods:

- Telnet
- Secure Shell (SSH)
- A browser using PIX Device Manger (PDM)

Console port access allows a single user to configure the Cisco PIX Firewall. A user connects a PC or portable computer to the PIX Firewall through the console access port using a rollover cable.

The following sections describe how to access the PIX Firewall remotely using Telnet and SSH. Chapter 13, "PIX Device Manager," covers using the PDM to access the PIX Firewall and other aspects of the PDM in greater detail.

Accessing the Cisco PIX Firewall with Telnet

You can manage the PIX Firewall by using Telnet from hosts on any internal interface. With Internet Protocol Security (IPSec) configured, you can use Telnet to administer the console of a Cisco PIX Firewall remotely from lower-security interfaces.

To access the PIX Firewall using a Telnet connection, you have to first configure the PIX Firewall for Telnet access:

Step 1   Enter the PIX Firewall **telnet** command:

```
telnet local-ip [mask] [if-name]
```

You can identify a single host or a subnet that can have Telnet access to the PIX Firewall. For example, to let a host on the internal network with an address of 10.1.1.24 access the PIX Firewall, enter the following:

```
telnet 10.1.1.24 255.255.255.255 inside
```

> **NOTE**   If you do not specify the interface name, the **telnet** command adds command statements to the configuration to let the host or network access the Telnet management session from all internal interfaces.

Step 2   Configure the Telnet password using the **password** command:

```
password telnetpassword
```

If you do not set a password, the default Telnet password is **cisco**.

> **NOTE**   The **passwd** command can be used interchangeably with the **password** command.

Step 3   If required, set the duration for how long a Telnet session can be idle before the PIX Firewall disconnects the session. The default duration is 5 minutes. To configure the timeout for 15 minutes, you would enter the following:

```
telnet timeout 15
```

Step 4   (Optional) To protect access to the console with an authentication server, use the **aaa authentication telnet console** command. (Authentication, authorization, and accounting [AAA] authentication is optional.) This requires that you have a username and password on the authentication server or configured locally on the firewall. When you access the console, the PIX Firewall prompts you for these login credentials. If the authentication server is offline, you can still access the console by using the username **pix** and the password set with the **enable password** command.

Step 5   Save the commands in the configuration using the **write memory** command.

As soon as you have Telnet configured on the Cisco PIX Firewall you are ready to access the PIX Firewall using a Telnet session. You can start a Telnet session to the PIX Firewall from the Windows command-line interface (CLI).

Accessing the Cisco PIX Firewall with Secure Shell

Secure Shell (SSH) is an application that runs over Transmission Control Protocol (TCP). SSH provides strong authentication and encryption capabilities. Cisco PIX Firewall supports the SSH remote shell functionality provided in SSH version 1. SSH version 1 also works with Cisco IOS® Software devices. Up to five SSH clients are allowed simultaneous access to the PIX Firewall console.

To gain access to the PIX Firewall console using SSH, at the SSH client, enter the username as **pix** and enter the Telnet password. You can set the Telnet password with the **password** command; the default Telnet password is **cisco**. To authenticate using the AAA server instead, configure the **aaa authenticate ssh console** command. SSH permits up to 100 characters in a username and up to 50 characters in a password.

> **NOTE**   SSH v1.*x* and v2 are entirely different protocols and are incompatible. Make sure that you download a client that supports SSH v1.*x*.

Like Telnet, SSH also first must be configured on the PIX Firewall. To configure SSH, follow these steps:

Step 1   Configure the firewall host name.

   `PIXFW (config)#`*hostname* `FW-PIX`

Step 2   Configure a domain for the PIX Firewall.

   `PIXFW(config)#`*domain-name* `cspa-example.com`

Step 3   Generate the firewall's RSA key pair.

   `PIXFW(config)#`**ca generate rsa key 1024**

Step 4   Save the generated RSA key pair.

   `PIXFW(config)#`**ca save all**

Step 5   Identify a host/network to be used to access the PIX Firewall console using SSH. The syntax for the **ssh** command is as follows:

   `ssh ip_address` [*netmask*] [*interface_name*]

   For example, to let a host on the internal interface with an address of 10.1.1.25 access the PIX Firewall using SSH, enter the following:

   `ssh 10.1.1.25 255.255.255.255 inside`

Step 6   The password used to perform local authentication is the same as the one used for Telnet access. It is set using the **password** command:

   `password eXamP1e`*pass*

Step 7   Specify in the number of minutes a session can be idle before being disconnected. The default duration is 5 minutes, although you can set this duration to be between 1 and 60 minutes. The command to configure this setting is as follows:

   `ssh timeout` *number*

To gain access to the Cisco PIX Firewall console using SSH, you have to install an SSH client. After installing the SSH client, enter the username **pix** (the default), and then enter the password.

When you start an SSH session, a dot (.) appears on the Cisco PIX Firewall console before the SSH user authentication prompt appears:

```
pix(config)# .
```

The display of the dot does not affect the functionality of SSH. The dot appears at the console when you generate a server key or decrypt a message using private keys during SSH key exchange before user authentication occurs. These tasks can take up to 2 minutes or longer. The dot is a progress indicator that verifies that the PIX Firewall is busy and has not hung.

Command-Level Authorization

In some organizations there may be more than one firewall administrator for the PIX Firewall(s). In those instances you can provide those other admins with full rights/privileges to the PIX Firewalls or curtail their ability to accomplish their assigned functions, thereby reducing the chance of unintended (or sometimes malicious) events from occurring on the firewall(s). The PIX operating system provides a mechanism of controlling what type of command a user can execute.

PIX Firewall Version 6.2 and higher supports up to 16 privilege levels. This is similar to what is available with IOS® Software. With this feature, you can assign PIX Firewall commands to one of 16 levels, 0 through 15.

When commands and users have privilege levels set, the two levels are compared to determine if a given user can execute a given command. If the user's privilege level is lower than the privilege level of the command, the user is prevented from executing the command. In the default configuration, each PIX Firewall command is assigned to either privilege level 0 or privilege level 15.

The **privilege** command sets user-defined privilege levels for PIX Firewall commands.

```
[no] privilege [show ¦ clear ¦ configure] level level
    [mode enable ¦ configure] command command
```

Table 4-2 shows the description of the privilege command parameters.

Table 4-2 *Privilege Command Parameter Descriptions*

Parameter	Description
show	Sets the privilege level for the **show** command corresponding to the command specified.
clear	Sets the privilege level for the **clear** command corresponding to the command specified.
configure	Sets the privilege level for the **configure** command corresponding to the command specified.
level	Specifies the privilege level.
level	The privilege level, from 0 to 15. (Lower numbers are lower-privilege levels.)
mode	For commands that are available in multiple modes, use the **mode** parameter to specify the mode in which the privilege level applies.
enable	For commands with both enable and configure modes, this indicates that the level is for the enable mode of the command.
configure	For commands with both enable and configure modes, this indicates that the level is for the configure mode of the command.
command	The command to allow.
command	The command on which to set the privilege level.

For example, the following commands set the privilege of the different command modifiers of the **access-list** command:

```
Privilege show level 9 command access-list
Privilege configure level 11 command access-list
Privilege clear level 10 command access-list
```

The first line sets the privilege of **show access-list** (**show** modifier of **command access-list**) to 9. The second line sets the privilege level of the **configure** modifier to 11, and the last line sets the privilege level of the **clear** modifier to 10.

To set the privilege of all the modifiers of the **access-list** command to a single privilege level of 10, you would enter the following command:

```
Privilege level 10 command access-list
```

Once you have selected the commands for which you want to change the default privileges, you enable the command authorization feature to either LOCAL or TACACS+. The following command enables the command authorization feature to LOCAL:

```
aaa authorization command LOCAL
```

To define a user account in the LOCAL database, enter the following command:

```
Username username {nopassword¦password password [encrypted]} [privilege level]
```

Table 4-3 shows the description of the parameters of the **username** command.

Table 4-3 *Parameters of the* username *Command*

Keyword/Parameter	Description
username	Name of the user (character string from 4 to 15 characters long).
password	Password (a character string from 3 to 16 characters long).
level	The privilege level you want to assign (0–15).
nopassword	Use this keyword to create a user account with no password.
encrypted	Use this keyword to encrypt your keyword.

When users log in to the PIX Firewall, they can enter any command assigned to their privilege level or to lower privilege levels. For example, a user account with a privilege level of 15 can access every command because this is the highest privilege level. A user account with a privilege level of 0 can access only the commands assigned to level 0.

For example, the following command assigns a privilege level of 10 to the user account Fwadmin2.

```
username Fwadmin2 password cspfa2ed privilege 10
```

If no privilege level is specified, the user account is created with a privilege level of 2. You can define as many user accounts as you need. If you are not sure what the privilege level assigned to commands is, use the **show privilege all** command to view the assignments. To view the privilege level assignment of a specific command, enter the following command:

```
Show privilege command command
```

Replace *command* with the command for which you want to display the assigned privilege level. For example, the following command displays the command assignment for the **capture** command:

```
PXFW01# show privilege command capture
privilege show level 15 command capture
privilege clear level 15 command capture
privilege configure level 15 command capture
```

Another useful command to see privilege level is the **show curpriv** command. This displays the current privilege level. The following examples show output from the **show curpriv** command for a user named noc_ops. Username indicates the name the user entered when he or she logged in, P_PRIV indicates that the user has entered the **enable** command, and P_CONF indicates the user has entered the **config terminal** command.

```
PIXFW01(config)# show curpriv
Username : noc_ops
Current privilege level : 15
Current Mode/s : P_PRIV P_CONF
pixfirewall(config)# exit
```

To change between privilege levels, use the **login** command to access another privilege level and the **disable** command to exit that level.

Installing a New Operating System

Installing a new operating system (OS) on a Cisco PIX Firewall is similar in some respects to installing a new OS on your PC. You must consider fundamental questions such as whether you have enough memory and disk space (Flash size for PIX Firewall) when deciding whether to upgrade the operating system. Table 4-4 shows the random-access memory (RAM) and Flash memory requirements for the different versions and releases of the Cisco PIX Firewall OS.

Table 4-4 *PIX Software RAM/Flash Minimum Memory Requirements*

PIX Software Version	Memory
PIX Software Version 4.4(*x*)	2 MB Flash, 16 MB RAM
PIX Software Version 5.0(*x*)	2 MB Flash, 32 MB RAM
PIX Software Version 5.1(*x*)	2 MB Flash, 32 MB RAM
PIX Software Version 5.2(*x*)	16 MB Flash, 32 MB RAM
PIX Software Version 5.3(*x*)	16 MB Flash, 32 MB RAM
PIX Software Version 6.0(*x*)	16 MB Flash, 32 MB RAM
PIX Software Version 6.1(*x*)	16 MB Flash, 32 MB RAM
PIX Software Version 6.2(*x*)	16 MB Flash, 32 MB RAM
[a]PIX Software Version 6.3(*x*)	16 MB Flash, 32 MB RAM

[a] Except the Cisco PIX 501, 506, and 506E Security Appliance models, which require 8 MB of Flash, and Cisco PIX 501 Security Appliance, which requires 16 MB of RAM.

In addition to the memory and Flash requirements, you should consider the model of Cisco PIX Firewall before installing an OS. For example, the OS required for the Cisco PIX Firewall model 506 is 5.1*x* or greater; the Cisco PIX Firewall model 525 needs 5.2*x* or greater; and the Cisco PIX Firewall model 535 needs 5.3*x* or greater.

To determine the RAM memory and Flash memory you have running on your Cisco PIX Firewall, use the **show version** command. The output from this command also tells you which PIX Firewall OS you are currently running, as shown in Example 4-1.

Example 4-1 *Sample Output from the* **show version** *Command*

```
pixfw(config)# show version

Cisco PIX Firewall Version 6.3(1)
Cisco PIX Device Manager Version 3.0(1)

Compiled on Wed 19-Dec-02 14:03 by hyen

pixfw up 1 days 07 hours

Hardware:   PIX-515E, 64 MB RAM, CPU Pentium 433 MHz
Flash i28F640J5 @ 0x300, 16MB
BIOS Flash AT29C257 @ 0xfffd8000, 32KB

0: ethernet0: address is 0001.e300.73fd, irq 10
1: ethernet1: address is 0003.e300.73fc, irq 7
2: ethernet2: address is 00a0.c7c8.133e, irq 9
Licensed Features:
Failover: Disabled
VPN-DES: Enabled
VPN-3DES-AES:        Disabled
Maximum Physical Interfaces: 3
Maximum Interfaces: 10
Cut-through Proxy:  Enabled
Guards:             Enabled
URL-filtering:      Enabled
Inside Hosts:       Unlimited
Throughput:         Unlimited
IKE peers:          Unlimited

This PIX has a Restricted (R) license.

Serial Number: 120430465 (0x1ca2c977)
Running Activation Key: 0xc4e64122 0xc21f5281 0x13652200 0x341f8732
Configuration last modified by enable_15 at 11:22:18.480 UTC Wed Dec 28 2002
<--- More --->
```

As you can see, the OS version is 6.3(1), and the Flash memory size is 16 megabytes (MB).

In Example 4-1, the line that starts with **Running Activation Key** displays the activation key for the PIX Firewall. The activation key is the license key for the PIX Firewall OS. It is important to save your configuration and write down your activation key before upgrading to a newer version of the PIX Firewall OS.

Upgrading Your Activation Key

Three important reasons might prompt you to upgrade or change your activation key:

- Your Cisco PIX Firewall does not have failover activated.

- Your PIX Firewall does not currently have virtual private network Data Encryption Standard (VPN-DES) or virtual private network Triple DES (VPN-3DES) encryption enabled.

- You are upgrading from a connection-based license to a feature-based license.

Before the release of PIX Firewall Version 6.2, the activation keys were changed in monitor mode. Cisco PIX Firewall Version 6.2 introduces a method of upgrading or changing the license for your Cisco PIX Firewall remotely without entering monitor mode and without replacing the software image. With this new feature, you can enter a new activation key for a different PIX Firewall license from the CLI. To enter an activation key, use the following command:

```
activation-key license#
```

You replace *license#* with the key you get with your new license. For example:

```
activation-key 0x14355378 0xabcdef01 0x2645678ab 0xcdef0124
```

After changing the activation key, you must reboot the PIX Firewall to enable the new license. If you are upgrading to a newer version and you are changing the activation key, you must reboot the Cisco PIX Firewall twice—once after the new image is installed, and again after the new activation key has been configured.

If you are downgrading to a lower Cisco PIX Firewall software version, it is important to ensure that the activation key running on your system is not intended for a higher version before you install the lower-version software image. If this is the case, you must first change the activation key to one that is compatible with the lower version before installing and rebooting. Otherwise, your system might refuse to reload after you install the new software image.

The **show activation-key** command output indicates the status of the activation key:

- If the activation key in the PIX Firewall Flash memory is the same as the activation key running on the PIX Firewall, the **show activation-key** output reads as follows:

  ```
  The flash activation key is the SAME as the running key.
  ```

- If the activation key in the PIX Firewall Flash memory is different from the activation key running on the PIX Firewall, the **show activation-key** output reads as follows:

  ```
  The flash activation key is DIFFERENT from the running key.
  The flash activation key takes effect after the next reload.
  ```

- If the PIX Firewall Flash memory software image version is not the same as the running PIX Firewall software image, the **show activation-key** output reads as follows:

  ```
  The flash image is DIFFERENT from the running image.
  The two images must be the same in order to examine the flash activation key.
  ```

Example 4-2 shows sample output from the **show activation-key** command.

Example 4-2   show activation-key *Command Output*

```
pix(config)# show activation-key

Serial Number: 480221353 (0x1c9f98a9)
 Running Activation Key: 0x14355378 0xabcdef01 0x2645678ab 0xcdef0124

Licensed Features:
Failover:          Enabled
VPN-DES:           Enabled
VPN-3DES:          Enabled
Maximum Interfaces: 6
Cut-through Proxy: Enabled
Guards:            Enabled
URL-filtering:     Enabled
Inside Hosts:      Unlimited
Throughput:        Unlimited
IKE peers:         Unlimited

The flash activation key is the SAME as the running key.
pix (config)#
```

Upgrading the Cisco PIX Firewall Operating System

There are three procedures for upgrading a PIX Firewall OS. The use of these procedures is determined by which PIX Firewall OS is currently running on the PIX device and the model of the Cisco PIX Firewall.

- You can use the **copy tftp flash** command with any Cisco PIX Firewall model running PIX Software Version 5.1.1 or later.

- PIX devices that do not have an internal floppy drive (501, 506(E), 515(E), 525, and 535) come with a read-only memory (ROM) boot monitor program that is used to upgrade the image of the Cisco PIX Firewall. For PIX devices that are running Version 5.0 and earlier, a boothelper disk is required to create boothelper mode, similar to ROM monitor mode.

- PIX Firewall Version 6.2 introduces a Hypertext Transfer Protocol (HTTP) client that lets you use the **copy http** command to retrieve PIX Firewall configurations, software images, or Cisco PDM software from any HTTP server.

Upgrading the Operating System Using the copy tftp flash Command

Step 1 Download the binary software image file pix*nnx*.bin, where *nn* is the version number and *x* is the release number (which you can find at Cisco.com in the document "Cisco PIX Firewall Upgrading Feature Licenses and System Software"). Place the image file in the root of your Trivial File Transfer Protocol (TFTP) server.

Step 2 Enter the **copy tftp flash** command.

Step 3 Enter the Internet Protocol (IP) address of the TFTP server.

Step 4 Enter the source filename (the image file you downloaded—*.bin).

Step 5 Enter **Yes** to continue.

Example 4-3 shows a sample upgrade.

Example 4-3 *Upgrading the OS Using the* **copy tftp flash** *Command*

```
PIX# copy tftp flash
Address or name of remote host [127.0.0.1]? 192.168.1.14
Source file name [cdisk]? pix611.bin
copying tftp://192.168.1.14/pix611.bin to flash
[yes¦no¦again]? yes
!!!!!!!!!!!!!!!!!!!!!!!!!!!!!!!!!!!!!!!!!!!!!!!!!!!!!!!!!!!!!!!!!!!!!!!!!!!!!!!!!! !!
Received 2562048 bytes
Erasing current image
Writing 2469944 bytes of image
!!!!!!!!!!!!!!!!!!!!!!!!!!!!!!!!!!!!!!!!!!!!!!!!!!!!!!!!!!!!!!!!!!!!!!!!!!!!!!!!!! !!
Image installed.
PIX#
```

> **NOTE**   Under no circumstances must you ever download a Cisco PIX Firewall image earlier than Version 4.4 with TFTP. Doing so corrupts the Cisco PIX Firewall Flash memory unit and requires special recovery methods that must be obtained from the Cisco Technical Assistance Center (TAC).

Upgrading the Operating System Using Monitor Mode

If you are upgrading your Cisco PIX Firewall from Version 5.0.*x* or earlier to Version 5.1.*x* or later, you will need to use the boothelper or monitor mode method for the upgrade because before Version 5.1, the PIX Firewall software did not provide a way to TFTP an image directly into Flash. Starting with PIX Firewall software Version 5.1, the **copy tftp flash** command was introduced to copy a new image directly into the PIX Firewall's Flash.

The following steps describe how to upgrade the PIX Firewall using monitor mode:

Step 1   Download the binary software image file pix*nnx*.bin, where *nn* is the version number and *x* is the release number (which you can find at Cisco.com in the document "Cisco PIX Firewall Upgrading Feature Licenses and System Software"). Place the image file in the root of your TFTP server.

Step 2   Reload the PIX Firewall, and press the **Esc** key (or enter a BREAK character) to enter monitor mode. For PIX devices running Version 5.0 and earlier, a boothelper disk is required. (See the section "Creating a Boothelper Disk Using a Windows PC" later in this chapter.)

Step 3   Use the **interface** command to specify out of which PIX Firewall interface the TFTP server is connected. The default is **interface 1** (inside). The Cisco PIX Firewall cannot initialize a Gigabit Ethernet interface from monitor or boothelper mode. Use a Fast Ethernet or Token Ring interface instead.

Step 4   Use the **address** command followed by an IP address to specify the PIX Firewall interface IP address.

Step 5   Use the **server** command followed by an IP address to specify the TFTP server's IP address.

Step 6   Use the **file** command followed by the filename of the image on the TFTP server to specify the filename of the Cisco PIX Firewall image.

Step 7   Use the **ping** command followed by the IP address of the TFTP server to verify connectivity. (This is an optional but recommended command to test connectivity.)

Step 8   If needed, enter the **gateway** command to specify the IP address of a
             router gateway through which the server is accessible. (This is also an
             optional command.)

Step 9   Enter **tftp** to start downloading the image from the TFTP server.

Step 10   After the image downloads, you are prompted to install the new image.
             Enter **y** to install the image to Flash.

Step 11   When prompted to enter a new activation key, enter **y** if you want to
             enter a new activation key or **n** to keep your existing activation key.

Upgrading the OS Using an HTTP Client

You can also perform a PIX Firewall OS upgrade by connecting to an HTTP server on which
the image is stored. The **copy http** command enables you to download a software image into
the Flash memory of the firewall from an HTTP server. The syntax for the **copy http**
command is as follows:

```
copy http[s]://[user:password@] location [:port ] / http_pathname flash [: [image
¦ pdm] ]
```

Secure Sockets Layer (SSL) is used when the **copy https** command is specified. The *user* and
password options are used for authentication when logging into the HTTP server. The
location option is the IP address (or a name that resolves to an IP address) of the HTTP
server. The *port* option specifies the port on which to contact the server. The value for port
defaults to port 80 for HTTP and port 443 for HTTP through SSL. The *pathname* option is
the name of the resource that contains the image or PIX Device Manager (PDM) file to copy.

The following example shows how to copy the PIX Firewall software image from an HTTP
server into the Flash memory of your PIX Firewall:

```
copy http://192.168.1.22/software/download flash:image
```

The following example shows how to copy the PIX Firewall software image through HTTP
over SSL (HTTPS), where the SSL authentication is provided by the username dan and the
password example:

```
copy https://dan:example@192.168.1.22/software/download flash:image
```

Creating a Boothelper Disk Using a Windows PC

The boothelper disk, as described earlier in this chapter, provides assistance for Cisco PIX Firewall models 510 and 520 running PIX software Version 5.0(x) or Version 4.x to be upgraded to a newer version:

Step 1   Go to the Cisco website and download the rawrite.exe utility, which you use to write the PIX Firewall binary image to a floppy disk (you must have a Cisco.com account to do this).

Step 2   Download the PIX Firewall binary image (.bin file) that corresponds to the software version to which you are upgrading.

Step 3   Download the corresponding boothelper binary file that matches the version to which you are upgrading.

For example, if you are upgrading from PIX Software Version 5.0 to 6.1(1), you must download three files:

- rawrite.exe

- pix611.bin

- bh61.bin (boothelper file)

Step 4   Run the rawrite.exe program by entering **rawrite** at the DOS prompt. When prompted, enter the name of the boothelper file you want written to the floppy disk, as shown in Example 4-5.

Example 4-4   *Creating a Bootable Disk from Windows*

```
C:\>rawrite
RaWrite 1.2 - Write disk file to raw floppy diskette
Enter source file name: bh61.bin
Enter destination drive: a:
Please insert a formatted diskette into drive A: and press -ENTER- :
Number of sectors per track for this disk is 18.
Writing image to drive A:. Press ^C to abort.
Track: 11 Head: 1 Sector: 16
Done.
C:\>
```

Reboot the PIX Firewall with the disk you created. The PIX Firewall comes up in boothelper mode. Follow the procedure beginning with Step 3 of the earlier section "Upgrading the Operating System Using Monitor Mode" to continue with the upgrade process.

Password Recovery

If you ever find yourself in the unfortunate circumstance of having forgotten or lost the console and Telnet password to your Cisco PIX Firewall, do not panic. Like most Cisco products, PIX devices have a procedure to recover lost passwords. Unlike the Cisco router password recovery process, which entails changing the configuration register number, PIX Firewall uses a different method. PIX Firewall uses a password lockout utility to regain access to the locked-out device. The password lockout utility is based on the PIX Firewall software release you are running. Table 4-5 shows the binary filename (that is included with the utility) and the corresponding PIX Firewall OS on which it is used. These files can be downloaded from the Cisco website.

Table 4-5 *PIX Firewall Password Lockout Utility Filenames*

Filename	PIX Firewall Software Version
nppix.bin	4.3 and earlier releases
np44.bin	4.4 release
np50.bin	5.0 release
np51.bin	5.1 release
np52.bin	5.2 release
np60.bin	6.0 release
np61.bin	6.1 release
np62.bin	6.2 release
np63.bin	6.3 release

When you boot the Cisco PIX Firewall with one of these binary files, the enable password is erased and the Telnet password is reset to **cisco**.

Cisco PIX Firewall Password Recovery: Getting Started

The procedure for password recovery on the Cisco PIX Firewall with a floppy drive is slightly different than with a diskless Cisco PIX Firewall. The difference is in how the Cisco PIX Firewall boots with the binary files listed in Table 4-5. Firewall models that have a floppy drive boot from a disk, and diskless firewall models boot from a TFTP server.

In addition to the binary files, you need the following items:

■ Portable computer or PC
■ Terminal-emulating software

- TFTP software (only for diskless PIX Firewall models)
- The rawrite.exe utility (needed only for firewall models that have floppy drives to create the boot disk)

Password Recovery Procedure for a PIX Firewall with a Floppy Drive (PIX 520)

Step 1   Create the boot disk by running the rawrite.exe file on your portable computer or PC and writing np*xn*.bin to the bootable floppy.

Step 2   Make sure that the terminal-emulating software is running on your PC and that you connected the console cable to the Cisco PIX Firewall.

> **NOTE**   Because you are locked out, you see only a password prompt.

Step 3   Insert the PIX Firewall password lockout utility disk into the PIX Firewall's floppy drive. Push the Reset button on the front of the PIX Firewall.

Step 4   The PIX Firewall boots from the floppy, and you see a message that says "Erasing Flash Password. Please eject diskette and reboot."

Step 5   Eject the disk, and press the Reset button. Now you can log in without a password.

Step 6   When you are prompted for a password, press Enter. The default Telnet password after this process is cisco. The enable password is also erased, and you have to enter a new one.

Password Recovery Procedure for a Diskless PIX Firewall (PIX 501, 506, 506E, 515E, 515, 525, and 535)

Step 1   Start the terminal-emulation software, and connect your portable computer or PC to the console port of the PIX Firewall.

Step 2   After you power on the Cisco PIX Firewall and the startup messages appear, send a BREAK character or press the **Esc** key. The **monitor>** prompt is displayed.

Step 3   At the **monitor>** prompt, use the **interface** command to specify which interface the PIX Firewall traffic should use.

Step 4   Use the **address** command to specify the IP address of the PIX Firewall interface.

Step 5   Use the **server** command to specify the IP address of the remote TFTP server containing the PIX Firewall password recovery file.

Step 6   Use the **gateway** command to specify the IP address of a router gateway through which the server is accessible.

Step 7   Use the **file** command to specify the filename of the PIX Firewall password recovery file, such as np62.bin.

Step 8   Use the **tftp** command to start the download. After the password recovery file loads, the following message is displayed:

```
Do you wish to erase the passwords? [yn] y
Passwords have been erased.
```

Overview of Simple Network Management Protocol on the PIX Firewall

Using Simple Network Management Protocol (SNMP), you can monitor system events on the PIX Firewall. All SNMP values are read only (RO). SNMP events can be read, but information on the PIX Firewall cannot be changed by using SNMP.

The PIX Firewall SNMP traps available to an SNMP management station are as follows:

Generic traps:

■   Link up and link down

■   Cold start

■   Authentication failure

Security-related events sent by the Cisco syslog management information base (MIB):

■   Global access denied

■   Failover syslog messages

■   Syslog messages

PIX Firewall Version 6.2 and later supports monitoring central processing unit (CPU) utilization through SNMP. Overall CPU busy percentage in the last 5-second period, one-minute period, and five-minute period are sent to the SNMP management server.

NOTE   Similar information on CPU utilization can be displayed by typing in **show cpu usage** on the Cisco Pix Firewall.

This feature allows network administrators to monitor PIX Firewall CPU usage using SNMP management software for capacity planning.

Configuring Simple Network Management Protocol on the PIX Firewall

The **snmp-server** command causes the PIX Firewall to send SNMP traps so that the PIX Firewall can be monitored remotely. Use the **snmp-server host** command to specify which systems receive the SNMP traps. Example 4-6 shows a SNMP sample configuration on a PIX Firewall.

Example 4-5   *Sample SNMP Configuration on a PIX Firewall*

```
snmp-server host 10.10.1.22
snmp-server location DC-HQ
snmp-server contact Yung Park
snmp-server community SnMpKey
snmp-server enable traps
```

The **location** and **contact** commands identify where the host is and who administers it. The **community** command specifies the password in use at the PIX Firewall SNMP agent and the SNMP management station for verifying network access between the two systems.

Troubleshooting Commands

The two most important troubleshooting commands on the PIX Firewall are the following:

- debug
- show

The **debug** command provides real-time information that helps you troubleshoot protocols operating with and through the PIX Firewall. There are more than three dozen debug commands that are available on the PIX Firewall.

Like the **debug** command, the **show** command also has many options available on the Cisco PIX Firewall. One helpful **show** command is the **show tech-support** command.

The **debug packet** command sends its output to the Trace Channel. All other **debug** commands do not. Use of Trace Channel changes the way you can view output on your screen during a PIX Firewall console or Telnet session. If a **debug** command does not use Trace Channel, each session operates independently, which means any commands started in the session appear only in the session. By default, a session not using Trace Channel has output disabled by default. The location of the Trace Channel depends on whether you have a simultaneous Telnet console session running at the same time as the console session or you are using only the PIX Firewall serial console:

■ If you are only using the PIX Firewall serial console, all **debug** commands display on the serial console.

■ If you have both a serial console session and a Telnet console session accessing the console, no matter where you enter the **debug** commands, the output displays on the Telnet console session.

■ If you have two or more Telnet console sessions, the first session is the Trace Channel. If that session closes, the serial console session becomes the Trace Channel. The next Telnet console session that accesses the console will then become the Trace Channel.

The **debug** commands, except the **debug crypto** commands, are shared between all Telnet and serial console sessions.

The following is sample output from the **show debug** command output:

```
Pixfw#show debug
debug crypto ipsec 1
debug crypto isakmp 1
debug crypto ca 1
debug icmp trace
```

The **show tech-support** command lists information that technical support analysts need to help you diagnose PIX Firewall problems. Using this command is very similar to running half a dozen **show** commands at once. The syntax for the command is as follows:

```
show tech-support [no-config]
```

The **no-config** option excludes the output of the running configuration. Example 4-7 shows a sample output of the **show tech-support** command with the **no-config** option.

Example 4-6   *Sample Output of the* **show tech-support no config** *Command*

```
Pix_fw# show tech-support no-config

Cisco PIX Firewall Version 6.3(1)
Cisco PIX Device Manager Version 2.1(1)


Compiled on Tue 16-Sept-03 17:49 by morlee


PIXFW01 up 17 days 5 hours


Hardware:   PIX-525, 256 MB RAM, CPU Pentium III 600 MHz
Flash E28F128J3 @ 0x300, 16MB
BIOS Flash AM29F400B @ 0xfffd8000, 32KB
```

continues

Example 4-6   *Sample Output of the* **show tech-support no config** *Command (Continued)*

```
Encryption hardware device : IRE2141 with 2048KB, HW:1.0, CGXROM:1.9, FW:6.5
0: ethernet0: address is 0008.a3db.87ea, irq 10
1: ethernet1: address is 0008.a3db.87eb, irq 11
2: ethernet2: address is 00e0.b605.5817, irq 11
3: ethernet3: address is 00e0.b605.5816, irq 10
4: ethernet4: address is 00e0.b605.5815, irq 9
5: ethernet5: address is 00e0.b605.5814, irq 5
6: ethernet6: address is 0003.47ac.5edd, irq 5
Licensed Features:
Failover:          Enabled
VPN-DES:           Enabled
VPN-3DES:          Enabled

Maximum Interfaces: 8
Cut-through Proxy:  Enabled
Guards:             Enabled
URL-filtering:      Enabled
Inside Hosts:       Unlimited
Throughput:         Unlimited
IKE peers:          Unlimited

Serial Number: 406044528 (0x1833bf0c)
Running Activation Key: 0xb974f13e 0x3253edba 0x0d0365e4 0xbae9e768
Configuration last modified by enable_15 at 13:36:25.580 EST Sat Jan 10 2004

----------------- show clock -----------------
14:26:55.403 EST Sat Jan 10 2004

----------------- show memory -----------------
Free memory:        197058560 bytes
Used memory:        71376896 bytes
------------        ----------------
Total memory:       268435456 bytes

----------------- show conn count -----------------
134 in use, 5168 most used

----------------- show xlate count -----------------
93 in use, 3279 most used

----------------- show blocks -----------------

   SIZE    MAX    LOW    CNT
      4    1600   1581   1600
     80     400    344    400
    256     500      0    500
```

Example 4-6 *Sample Output of the* **show tech-support no config** *Command (Continued)*

```
   1550   2724   1472   1824
   2560      1      0      1
   4096      1      0      1


----------------- show interface -----------------

 interface ethernet0 "outside" is up, line protocol is up
  Hardware is i82559 ethernet, address is 0008.a3db.87ea
  IP address 192.168.100.2, subnet mask 255.255.255.0
  MTU 1500 bytes, BW 100000 Kbit full duplex
    383875955 packets input, 1546242085 bytes, 0 no buffer
    Received 1958243 broadcasts, 0 runts, 0 giants
    22 input errors, 0 CRC, 0 frame, 22 overrun, 0 ignored, 0 abort
    362851238 packets output, 2335666853 bytes, 0 underruns
    0 output errors, 0 collisions, 0 interface resets
    0 babbles, 0 late collisions, 0 deferred
    0 lost carrier, 0 no carrier
    input queue (curr/max blocks): hardware (128/128) software (0/134)
    output queue (curr/max blocks): hardware (0/102) software (0/63)
interface ethernet1 "inside" is up, line protocol is up
  Hardware is i82559 ethernet, address is 0008.a3db.87eb
  IP address 10.20.29.187, subnet mask 255.255.255.0
  MTU 1500 bytes, BW 100000 Kbit full duplex
    328261488 packets input, 1334827221 bytes, 0 no buffer
    Received 16099319 broadcasts, 0 runts, 0 giants
    0 input errors, 0 CRC, 0 frame, 0 overrun, 0 ignored, 0 abort
    428793671 packets output, 3583318676 bytes, 0 underruns
    0 output errors, 0 collisions, 0 interface resets
    0 babbles, 0 late collisions, 0 deferred
    0 lost carrier, 0 no carrier
     input queue (curr/max blocks): hardware (128/128) software (0/128)
    output queue (curr/max blocks): hardware (2/128) software (0/472)
              .
              .
              .
----------------- show cpu usage -----------------

CPU utilization for 5 seconds = 0%; 1 minute: 0%; 5 minutes: 0%

----------------- show process -----------------

    PC       SP       STATE     Runtime    SBASE    Stack Process

Hsi 800b0e09 807d3938 8052ddd8          0 807d29b0 3716/4096 arp_timer
Lsi 800b5271 80846a48 8052ddd8          0 80845ad0 3788/4096 FragDBGC
Cwe 8000a945 80bd5e48 80375d90          0 80bd4ee0 3944/4096 CryptIC PDR poll
```

continues

Example 4-6 *Sample Output of the* **show tech-support no config** *Command (Continued)*

```
Lwe 8000f9fe 80bd6de8 80531508          0 80bd5f70 3704/4096 dbgtrace
Lwe 8020685d 80bd8f48 80507300    4655470 80bd7000 6352/8192 Logger
Hsi 8020a4ed 80bdc010 8052ddd8          0 80bda098 7700/8192 tcp_fast.
                          .
                          .
----------------- show failover -----------------


Failover On

Cable status: Normal
Reconnect timeout 0:00:00
Poll frequency 8 seconds
failover replication http
     This host: Primary - Active
          Active time: 1499048 (sec)
          Interface failover (192.168.10.3): Normal
          Interface intf5 (127.0.0.1): Link Down (Shutdown)
          Interface EXTRA-NET (10.2.0.1): Normal
          Interface Dialindmz (10.2.28.1): Normal
          Interface Serverdmz (10.10.43.2): Normal
          Interface outside (192.168.100.2): Normal
          Interface inside (10.20.29.187): Normal
     Other host: Secondary - Standby
          Active time: 0 (sec)
          Interface failover (192.168.10.2): Normal
          Interface intf5 (0.0.0.0): Link Down (Shutdown)
          Interface EXTRA-NET (10.2.0.2): Normal
          Interface Dialindmz (10.2.28.2): Normal
          Interface Serverdmz (10.10.43.3): Normal
          Interface outside (192.168.100.4): Normal
          Interface inside (10.20.29.24): Normal

Stateful Failover Logical Update Statistics


     Link : failover
     Stateful Obj     xmit      xerr      rcv      rerr
     General        65534709   0       198872    0
     sys cmd        198871     0       198872    0
     up time        2          0       0         0
     xlate          7312548    0       0         0
     tcp conn       58023288   0       0         0
     udp conn       0          0       0         0
     ARP tbl        0          0       0         0
     RIP Tbl        0          0       0         0
```

Example 4-6 *Sample Output of the* show tech-support no config *Command (Continued)*

```
    Logical Update Queue Information
             Cur    Max     Total
    Recv Q:    0     1     198872
    Xmit Q:    0     1     9861326
----------------- show traffic -----------------
outside:
    received (in 1501994.020 secs):
        384156904 packets    1628831642 bytes
        1 pkts/sec    1001 bytes/sec
    transmitted (in 1501994.020 secs):
        363147896 packets    2525315383 bytes
        1 pkts/sec    1000 bytes/sec
inside:
    received (in 1501994.020 secs):
        328515373 packets    1453897436 bytes
        1 pkts/sec    1 bytes/sec
    transmitted (in 1501994.020 secs):
        429046804 packets    3666788039 bytes
        2 pkts/sec    2000 bytes/sec
             .
             .
             .
   ----------------- show perfmon -----------------

PERFMON STATS:    Current      Average
Xlates            0/s          0/s
Connections       4/s          0/s
TCP Conns         1/s          0/s
UDP Conns         3/s          0/s
URL Access        0/s          0/s
URL Server Req    0/s          0/s
TCP Fixup         146/s          0/s
TCPIntercept      0/s          0/s
HTTP Fixup        87/s          0/s
FTP Fixup         0/s          0/s
AAA Authen        0/s          0/s
AAA Author        0/s          0/s
AAA Account       0/s          0/s
```

Foundation Summary

The "Foundation Summary" provides a convenient review of many key concepts in this chapter. If you are already comfortable with the topics in this chapter, this summary can help you recall a few details. If you just read this chapter, this review should help solidify some key facts. If you are doing your final preparation before the exam, this summary provides a convenient way to review the day before the exam.

- The PIX Firewall can be accessed for management purposes in several different ways. It can be accessed through the console port, remotely through Telnet, through SSH, and through the PIX Device Manager (PDM).

- Before upgrading the Cisco PIX Firewall OS, it is important to determine your current hardware settings—namely, the RAM and Flash memory size.

- PIX Firewall Version 6.2 and later supports up to 16 privilege levels. This is similar to what is available with IOS® Software. With this feature, you can assign PIX Firewall commands to one of 16 levels, 0 through 15.

- The **privilege** command sets user-defined privilege levels for PIX Firewall commands.

- The activation key is the license for the PIX Firewall OS. Before the release of PIX Firewall Version 6.2, the activation keys were changed in monitor mode. Cisco PIX Firewall Version 6.2 introduces a method of upgrading or changing the license for your PIX Firewall remotely without entering monitor mode and without replacing the software image using the **activation-key** command.

- There are three ways to perform the PIX Firewall OS upgrade:

  — Using **copy tftp flash**

  — Using monitor mode with a boothelper disk for PIX Firewalls with an OS version earlier than 5.0

  — Using an HTTP client (available only with Version 6.2)

- It is possible to recover from a lockout on a Cisco PIX Firewall caused by forgotten or lost passwords. You can download the corresponding file and boot the PIX Firewall through monitor mode.

- Using SNMP, you can monitor system events on the PIX Firewall. All SNMP values are read only (RO). SNMP events can be read, but information on the PIX Firewall cannot be changed with SNMP.

Q&A

As mentioned in the Introduction, the questions in this book are more difficult than what you should experience on the exam. The questions do not attempt to cover more breadth or depth than the exam; however, they are designed to make sure that you know the answer. Hopefully, these questions will help limit the number of exam questions on which you narrow your choices to two options and then guess. Be sure to use the CD and to take the simulated exams.

The answers to these questions can be found in Appendix A.

1. How many ways can you access the PIX Firewall?

2. What is the command to change the Telnet password?

3. Which command would you use to view the privilege level assigned to the **access-list** command?

4. Which version of SSH does PIX Firewall support?

5. What is the activation key?

6. Give one reason why you would need to change the activation key on your PIX Firewall.

7. How many privilege levels are available on the PIX Firewall?

8. How do you determine which version of the PIX Firewall operating system is installed?

9. Which command would you use to create locally a user called mason with a password of Fr33 on the PIX Firewall?

10. How do you find out what your activation key is?

This chapter covers the following subjects:

- ASA Security Levels

- Transport Protocols

- Network Address Translation

- Port Address Translation

- Configuring DNS Support

CHAPTER 5

Understanding Cisco PIX Firewall Translation and Connection

This chapter presents an overview of the different network transport protocols and how they are processed by the PIX Firewall.

How to Best Use This Chapter

Reconsider the comment in the Introduction about how important it is to *know* the PIX Firewall commands, not just have an idea of what they are and what they do. It is very important to fully understand the concepts discussed in this chapter because they are the basis for the topics discussed in Chapter 6, "Getting Started with the Cisco PIX Firewall." To completely understand how the many different PIX Firewall commands work, you must first have a good understanding of how the Cisco PIX Firewall processes network traffic.

"Do I Know This Already?" Quiz

The purpose of the "Do I Know This Already?" quiz is to help you decide if you really need to read the entire chapter. If you already intend to read the entire chapter, you do not necessarily need to answer these questions now.

The ten-question quiz, derived from the major sections in the "Foundation Topics" portion of the chapter, helps you determine how to spend your limited study time.

Table 5-1 outlines the major topics discussed in this chapter and the "Do I Know This Already?" quiz questions that correspond to those topics.

Table 5-1 *"Do I Know This Already?" Foundation Topics Section-to-Question Mapping*

Foundation Topics Section	Questions Covered in This Section	Score
ASA Security Levels	2, 4	
Transport Protocols	8	
Network Address Translation	1, 3, 5, 6	
Port Address Translation	7, 10	
Configuring DNS Support	9	

CAUTION The goal of self assessment is to gauge your mastery of the topics in this chapter. If you do not know the answer to a question or are only partially sure of the answer, you should mark this question wrong for purposes of the self assessment. Giving yourself credit for an answer you correctly guess skews your self-assessment results and might provide you with a false sense of security.

1. By default, how long will an embryonic connection remain open?

    a. 2 minutes

    b. 3600 seconds

    c. 1800 seconds

    d. Unlimited

    e. 30 minutes

2. You have configured two additional DMZ interfaces on your PIX Firewall. How do you prevent nodes on DMZ1 from accessing nodes on DMZ2 without adding rules to the security policy?

    a. Route all traffic for DMZ2 out the outside interface.

    b. Dynamically NAT all DMZ2 nodes to a multicast address.

    c. Assign a higher security level to DMZ2.

    d. All of the above

3. Which of the following is not a method of address translation supported by the PIX Firewall?

  a. Network Address Translation

  b. Socket Address Translation

  c. Port Address Translation

  d. Static Address Translation

4. What happens if you configure two interfaces with the same security level?

  a. Traffic will pass freely between those connected networks.

  b. Traffic will not pass between those interfaces.

  c. Specific ACLs must allow traffic between those interfaces.

  d. The two interfaces will not apply the **nat** or **global** commands.

5. When should you run the command **clear xlate**?

  a. When updating a conduit on the firewall

  b. When editing the NAT for the inside segment

  c. When adding addresses to the global pool

  d. All of the above

6. How do you define the global addresses used when configuring NAT?

  a. Define a subnet.

  b. Define an address range.

  c. Define individual IP addresses.

  d. You can define only /24 address segments for global addresses.

  e. None of the above

7. How many external IP addresses are required to configure PAT?

  a. A single address

  b. A /24 subnet

  c. A defined address range

  d. Any of the above

  e. None of the above

8. What command shows all active TCP connections on the PIX Firewall?

   a. show conn

   b. show xlate

   c. show connection status

   d. show tcp active

   e. None of the above

9. Why is it difficult to penetrate the PIX Firewall over UDP port 53?

   a. The PIX Firewall allows multiple outbound queries but randomizes the UDP sequence numbers.

   b. The PIX Firewall allows queries to go out to multiple DNS servers but drops all but the first response.

   c. The PIX Firewall allows responses only to outbound DNS queries.

   d. All of the above

10. How many connections can you hide behind a single global address?

   a. 65,536

   b. 255

   c. 17,200

   d. An unlimited number

   e. None of the above

The answers to the "Do I Know This Already?" quiz are found in Appendix A, "Answers to the 'Do I Know This Already?' Quizzes and Q&A Sections." The suggested choices for your next step are as follows:

- **8 or less overall score**—Read the entire chapter. This includes the "Foundation Topics," "Foundation Summary," and "Q&A" sections.

- **9 or 10 overall score**—If you want more review of these topics, skip to the "Foundation Summary" section and then go to the "Q&A" section. Otherwise, move to the next chapter.

Foundation Topics

How the PIX Firewall Handles Traffic

The term *network security* simply refers to the application of security principles to a computer network. To apply security to a network, you must first understand how networks function. It stands to reason that to secure how traffic flows across a network, you must first understand how that traffic flows. This chapter discusses end-to-end traffic flow and how that traffic is handled by the Cisco PIX Firewall.

Interface Security Levels and the Default Security Policy

By default, the Cisco PIX Firewall applies security levels to each interface. The more secure the network segment, the higher the security number. Security levels range from 0 to 100. By default, 0 is applied to Ethernet 0 and is given the default name *outside*; 100 is applied to Ethernet 1 and is given the default name *inside*. Any additional interfaces are configured using the **nameif** command. The security level for these additional interfaces can be from 1 to 99.

The Adaptive Security Algorithm (ASA) allows traffic from a higher security level to pass to a lower security level without a specific rule in the security policy that allows the connection as long as a **nat/global** or **static** command is configured for those interfaces. Any traffic that passes from a lower security level to a higher security level must be allowed by the security policy (that is, access lists or conduits). If two interfaces are assigned the same security level, traffic cannot pass between those interfaces (this configuration is not recommended).

Transport Protocols

Traffic that traverses a network always has a source and destination address. This communication is based on the seven layers of the OSI reference model. Layers 5 through 7 (the upper layers) handle the application data, and Layers 1 through 4 (lower layers) are responsible for moving the data from the source to the destination. The data is created at the application layer (Layer 7) on the source machine. Transport information is added to the upper-layer data, and then network information is added, followed by data-link information. At this point the information is transmitted across the physical medium as electronic signals.

The upper-layer data combined with the transport information is called a *segment*. As soon as the network information is added to the segment, it is called a *packet*. The packet is encapsulated at the data link layer (Layer 2) with the addition of the source and destination

MAC address, at which point it is called a *frame*. Figure 5-1 shows how the data is encapsulated at each layer of the OSI reference model.

Figure 5-1 *Encapsulation of Upper-Layer Data*

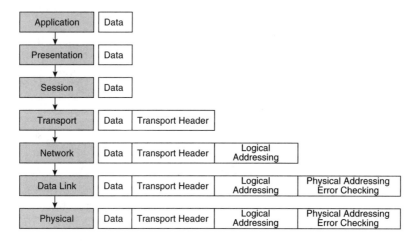

The two transport protocols most commonly used by TCP/IP are Transmission Control Protocol (TCP) and User Datagram Protocol (UDP). These protocols are very different. Each has its strengths and weaknesses. For this reason, they are used in different ways to play on their strengths:

- TCP—A connection-oriented transport protocol that is responsible for reliability and efficiency of communication between nodes. TCP completes these tasks by creating connections as *virtual circuits* that act as two-way communications between the source and destination. TCP is very reliable and guarantees the delivery of data between nodes. TCP also can dynamically modify a connection's transmission variables based on changing network conditions. TCP sequence numbers and TCP acknowledgment numbers are included in the TCP header. These features allow the source and destination to verify the correct, orderly delivery of data. Unfortunately, the overhead required for TCP can make it slow and keeps it from being the optimum transport protocol for some connections.

- UDP—A connectionless transport protocol that is used to get the data to the destination. UDP provides no error checking, no error correction, and no verification of delivery. UDP defers the reliability issues to the upper-layer protocols and simply sends the data without verifying delivery. UDP is a very simple and very fast protocol.

The upper layers determine which of the transport protocols is used when data is encapsulated at the source node.

Figure 5-2 illustrates the TCP communication between nodes that do not have a firewall between them. The TCP "three-way handshake" is a four-step process that requires three different transmissions to negotiate the connection:

1. The source sends a segment to the destination, asking to open a TCP session. A TCP flag is set to SYN, indicating that the source wants to initiate synchronization or a handshake. The source generates a random TCP sequence number. In this example we will use 125.

2. The destination receives the request and sends back a reply with the TCP flags ACK and SYN set, indicating an acknowledgment of the SYN bit (receive flow) and initiation of the transmit flow. It generates and sends its own random TCP sequence number, 388, and replies to the original TCP sequence number by adding 1, sending back a sequence number of 126. The source receives the SYN/ACK and sends back an ACK to indicate the acknowledgment of the SYN for the setup of the receive flow. It adds 1 to the value of the TCP sequence number generated by the destination and sends back the number 389.

3. The acknowledgment is received, the handshake is complete, and the connection is established. Note in Figure 5-2 that the source begins to send data to the destination as soon as the connection is established.

Figure 5-2 *TCP Communication Between Nodes Without a PIX Firewall*

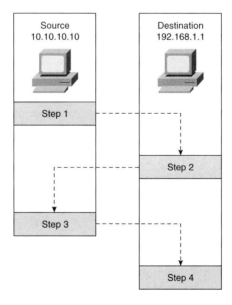

Now look at how this communication is handled by the Cisco PIX Firewall (see Figure 5-3). You first notice that the number of steps required for the same transaction has changed from four to eight and the number of transmissions has increased from three to six, although everything appears to be the same to both the source and destination.

Figure 5-3 *TCP Communication Between Nodes with a PIX Firewall*

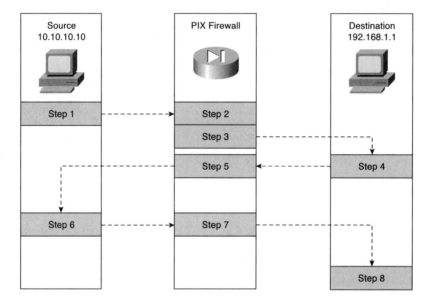

The following is a list of actions taken by the Cisco PIX Firewall when processing a TCP handshake and opening a TCP session (refer to Figure 5-3):

1. The source machine initiates the connection by sending a packet with the SYN flag set. It is received by the Cisco PIX Firewall en route to the destination. The PIX Firewall verifies the connection against the running configuration to determine if translation is to be completed. The running configuration is stored in memory, so this process occurs very quickly. The PIX Firewall checks whether the inside address, 10.10.10.10, is to be translated to an outside address—in this case, 192.168.1.10. If the translation is to be completed, the PIX Firewall creates a *translation slot* if one does not already exist for this connection.

2. All the session information is written to the state table, and the Cisco PIX Firewall randomly generates a new TCP sequence number. This connection slot is marked in the state table as an *embryonic* (half-open) connection.

3. After the connection is verified against the security policy, the PIX Firewall allows the connection outside using the translated source address and the newly generated TCP sequence number.

4. The destination receives the connection request (SYN) and replies with an SYN ACK.

5. The PIX Firewall verifies the SYN ACK from the destination and matches the acknowledgment number against the randomly generated sequence number. It verifies the connection slot and forwards the connection back to the source using the original source address and original sequence number plus 1.

6. Any packets that do not match the session object exactly are dropped and logged.

7. The source completes the connection by responding with an ACK. The acknowledgment number is not randomized as it passes through the PIX Firewall, and the connection slot is marked as *active-established*.

8. The embryonic counter is reset, and data is transmitted between the nodes.

The process used by the PIX Firewall to handle UDP traffic is completely different from the process that it uses for TCP traffic. This is due to UDP's characteristics. UDP is a connectionless protocol that does not negotiate a connection. Without any setup or termination, it is very difficult to determine the state of a UDP session. Because of the inability to determine session state, it is very easy to spoof UDP packets and hijack a UDP session. Some applications use UDP rather than TCP for data transfer. Many of these are real-time applications or applications that either have no reliability requirements or have their reliability requirements handled by the application rather than by the transport protocol. These applications include network video, Common Internet File System (CIFS), NetBIOS, Domain Name System (DNS), and remote-procedure call (RPC) applications.

The default security policy allows UDP packets to pass from a higher security level to a lower security level. For UDP packets to pass in the other direction, they must be allowed by the security policy. It is very important to restrict inbound UDP access as much as possible. Due to UDP's limitations, many applications that operate over UDP are targets for exploitation by hackers.

The Cisco PIX Firewall handles UDP traffic in the following manner:

1. The source machine initiates the UDP connection. It is received by the PIX Firewall en route to the destination. The PIX Firewall applies the default rule and any necessary translation, creates a session object in the state table, and allows the connection to pass to the outside interface.

2. Any return traffic is matched with the session object, and the session timeout is applied. The session timeout is 2 minutes by default. If the response does not match the session object or is not within the timeout, the packet is dropped. If everything matches, the response is allowed through to the requesting source.

3. Any inbound UDP sessions from a lower security level to a higher security level must be allowed by the security policy, or the connection is dropped.

Address Translation

The current Internet Protocol standard being used is version 4 (IPv4). IPv4 addresses consist of 32 bits, which represents approximately 4 billion individual IP addresses. This seems like a tremendous number of addresses, but the Internet continues to grow at an incredible rate, and with the current standard, available addresses will run out. Two solutions are being implemented to help conserve the public address space or increase the number of available public addresses. The first is Internet Protocol version 6 (IPv6), a total redesign of the Internet Protocol that is still in development. The second solution is the use of RFC 1918 addressing combined with Port Address Translation (PAT). RFC 1918 sets aside network space to be used for private networks, and PAT provides a method for hiding literally thousands of private addresses behind a single public address. This private address space is not accessible via the public Internet. Static Network Address Translation (NAT) is used to create a one-to-one relationship between public addresses and RFC 1918 addresses and allows external users to access internal resources.

The Internet Assigned Numbers Authority (IANA) reserved the following address space for private networks:

> 10.0.0.0 through 10.255.255.255: 16,777,214 hosts
> 172.16.0.0 through 172.31.255.255: 1,048,574 hosts
> 192.168.0.0 through 192.168.255.255: 65,534 hosts

RFC 1918 has had a tremendous impact on Internet addressing and the design of public and private networks. The challenge to RFC 1918 addressing is that private addresses cannot be publicly routed. Hence, address translation is implemented. Address translation provides not only a method of conserving public address space, but also an additional level of protection for internal nodes because there is no way to route to a private address from the Internet.

Address translation is the method used by the Cisco PIX Firewall to give internal nodes with private IP addresses access to the Internet. The internal node addresses that are translated are called *local addresses,* and the addresses that are translated as well are called *global addresses.* **nat** and **global** commands are applied to specific interfaces. Most commonly, NAT takes place, translating internal addresses to external addresses, although the PIX Firewall is not limited to this configuration. It is possible to translate any address at one interface to another address at any other interface. Two types of NAT can be implemented on a Cisco PIX Firewall:

- **Dynamic address translation**—Translates multiple local addresses into a limited number of global public addresses or possibly a single global address. This is called *dynamic address translation* because the firewall selects the first available global address and assigns it when creating an outbound connection. The internal source retains the global address for the duration of the connection. Dynamic address translation is broken into two types:

    — **Network Address Translation (NAT)**—Translating multiple local addresses to a pool of global addresses.

    — **Port Address Translation (PAT)**—Translating multiple local addresses to a single global address. This method is called *Port Address Translation* because the firewall uses a single translated source address but changes the source port to allow multiple connections via a single global address. The limitation for PAT is approximately 64,000 hosts because of the limited number of available ports (65,535) and the number of ports already assigned to specific services. Some applications do not work through PAT because they require specific source and destination ports.

- **Static translation**—Allows for a one-to-one translation of local to global addresses. Static translation is commonly used when the internal node must be accessed from the Internet. Web servers and mail servers must have static addresses so that users on the Internet can connect to them via their global address.

Translation Commands

Table 5-2 describes the commands and arguments used to configure NAT, PAT, and static translation on a Cisco PIX Firewall. All the PIX commands are covered in much greater detail in Chapter 6. Table 5-2 helps you understand the syntax of the commands given in the following examples.

Table 5-2 *Translation Commands*

Command	Description
nat	Associates a network with a pool of global addresses.
global	Identifies the global addresses to be used for translation.
static	Maps the one-to-one relationship between local addresses and global addresses.

continues

Table 5-2   *Translation Commands (Continued)*

Command	Description
netmask	A reserved word that is required to identify the network mask.
dns	Specifies that DNS replies that match the **xlate** command should be translated
outside	Allows you to enable or disable address translation for the external addresses.
timeout	Sets the idle timeout for the translation slot.
id	Also called the *nat_id*. The number that matches the **nat** statement with the **global** statement. This is how the PIX Firewall determines which local addresses translate to which global address pool.
internal_if-name	The interface name for the network with the higher security level.
external_if-name	The interface name for the network with the lower security level.
local-ip	The IP addresses or network addresses that are to be translated. This can be a specific network segment (10.10.10.0) or can include all addresses (0.0.0.0).
global_ip	The IP address or range of IP addresses to which the local addresses translate.
network_mask	The network mask for a specific network segment. This applies to both local and global addresses.
max-cons	The maximum number of concurrent connections allowed through a static translation.
em_limit	The maximum number of allowed embryonic connections. The default is 0, which allows unlimited connections. You can limit the number of embryonic connections to reduce an attack's effectiveness by flooding embryonic connections.
norandomseq	Stops the ASA from randomizing the TCP sequence numbers. This normally is used if the firewall is located inside another firewall and data is being scrambled, with both firewalls randomizing the sequence number.

Network Address Translation

NAT allows you to translate a large number of local addresses behind a limited number of global addresses. This lets you keep your internal network addressing scheme hidden from external networks. To configure NAT on a Cisco PIX Firewall, you simply need to define the local and global addresses. In Figure 5-4, all nodes on the internal network are being translated to a pool of addresses on the external network.

Figure 5-4 *Network Address Translation*

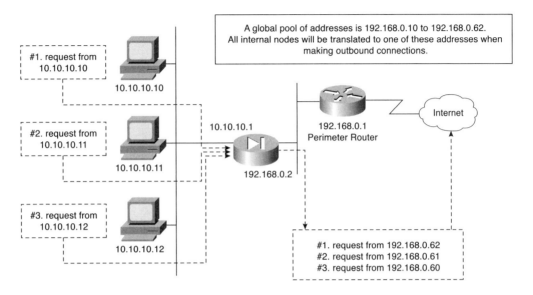

Two commands are required to complete this configuration:

■ **nat**—Defines the addresses to be translated:

```
LabPIX(config)# nat [(internal_if_name)] id local_ip [network_mask]
```

  Here is an example:

```
LabPIX(config)# nat (inside) 1 0.0.0.0 0.0.0.0
```

■ **global**—Defines the pool of addresses to translate to:

```
LabPIX(config)# global [(external_if_name)] id {global_ip[-global_ip] [netmask
network_mask]¦interface}
```

  Here is an example:

```
LabPIX(config)# global (outside) 1 192.168.0.10-192.168.0.62 netmask   255.255.255.192
```

Notice the *id* in both the **nat** and **global** commands. It enables you to assign specific addresses to translate. The addresses in the **nat** command translate to the addresses in the global command that contains the same ID. The only ID that cannot be used here is 0. The command **nat 0** is used on the PIX Firewall to identify addresses that are *not* to be translated. The **nat 0** command is commonly called the "no nat" command.

PIX Firewall OS Version 6.3(2) incorporated the ability to configure a *policy NAT*. This provides the functionality to enable translations to occur on a specific source and destination basis. The policy NAT is configured with the access control lists and will be discussed in greater detail in Chapter 7, "Configuring Access."

Port Address Translation

PAT enables you to translate your local addresses behind a single global address. The commands required to perform PAT are exactly the same as the commands to perform NAT. The only difference in defining PAT is that you define a single global address rather than a range. Figure 5-5 shows all local nodes behind a single global address being translated.

Figure 5-5 *Port Address Translation*

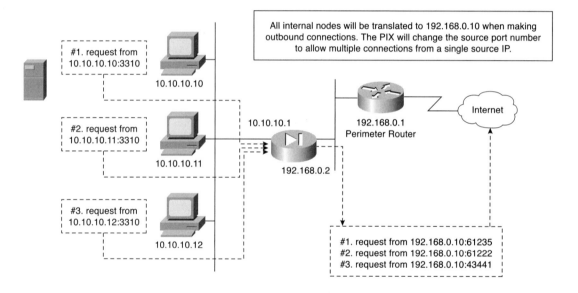

The correct syntax for configuring PAT uses the **nat** and **global** commands and is depicted here:

```
LabPIX(config)# nat [(internal_if_name)] id local_ip network_mask
```

The following is an example of the correct syntax for configuring the **nat** portion of PAT for an internal network consisting of 10.0.0.0 addresses:

```
LabPIX(config)# nat (inside) 4 10.0.0.0 0.0.0.0
```

Here is the **global** command syntax:

```
LabPIX(config)# global [(external_if_name)] id global_ip netmask  network_mask
```

The following is an example of the correct syntax for configuring the **global** portion of PAT for the external address 192.168.0.10:

```
LabPIX(config)# global (outside) 1 192.168.0.10 netmask 255.255.255.255
```

Static Translation

Although static translation is not specifically defined as an exam topic, it is very important for you to know the commands and to understand how static translation works. Static translation maps a single local address to a single global address. It is most commonly used when the local node must be accessed from the public space (Internet).

```
LabPIX(config)# [static] (local_if_name, global_if_name) {global_ip/interface} local_ip
```

In the following command, the local node 10.10.10.9 is configured to have a global address of 192.168.0.9. Remember that the **static** command configures only the address translation. To allow access to the local node from a lower security level interface, you need to configure either a conduit or an access list:

```
LabPIX(config)# static (inside, outside) 192.168.0.9 10.10.10.9
LabPIX(config)# conduit permit tcp host 192.168.0.9 eq www any
```

or

```
LabPIX(config)# access-list 101 permit tcp any host 192.168.0.9 eq www
```

If you are using an access list, you need to create an access group to apply the access list to the correct interface:

```
LabPIX(config)# access-group 101 in interface outside
```

NOTE   Chapter 7 discusses conduits and access lists in greater detail.

This is the configuration used in Figure 5-6. Note that the node is now accessible from the Internet.

Figure 5-6 *Static Translation*

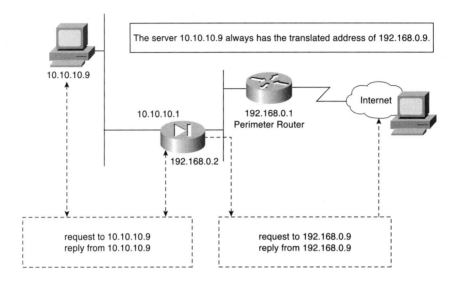

Using the static Command for Port Redirection

One of the improvements of PIX OS Version 6.0 is that the **static** command can be used to redirect services to specific ports and to translate the host's address. This command enables the outside user to connect to a specific address/port and have the PIX Firewall redirect the traffic to the appropriate inside/DMZ server. The syntax for this command is as follows:

```
LabPIX(config)# [static] (local_if_name, global_if_name) {tcp ¦ udp} {global_ip/
interface} local_ip local port netmask mask [norandomseq] [max connections[emb_limit]]
```

For example:

```
LabPIX(config)# static (inside, outside) tcp 192.168.0.9 ftp
   10.10.10.9 2100 netmask 255.255.255.255 0 0
```

The configuration in the preceding example would redirect all traffic that hits the outside interface of the PIX Firewall for IP address 192.168.0.9 on TCP port 21 to 10.10.10.9 on TCP port 2100.

Configuring Multiple Translation Types on the Cisco PIX Firewall

It is a good practice to use a combination of NAT and PAT. If you have more internal hosts than external IP addresses, you can configure both NAT and PAT. Your first group of hosts translates to the global addresses that are listed and the remaining hosts use PAT and translate to the single global address. PAT is configured separately from NAT. If NAT is configured without PAT, once the available global IP address range is depleted, additional translation attempts will be refused. If the location has any servers that need to be accessed from the Internet (web servers, mail servers, and so on), they must be configured for static translation.

In the following examples, the internal network consisting of 254 hosts translates to 52 external addresses (192.168.0.10 to 192.168.0.62). This means that the remaining 202 hosts translate to 192.168.0.63.

```
LabPIX(config)# nat [(local_interface)] id local_ip network_mask
LabPIX(config)# nat (inside) 1 10.10.10.0 255.255.255.0
LabPIX(config)# [global] [(global_interface)] id global_ip [netmask]  network_mask
LabPIX(config)# global (outside) 1 192.168.0.10-192.168.0.62 netmask
  255.255.255.192
LabPIX(config)# [global] [(global_interface)] id global_ip [netmask]  network_mask
LabPIX(config)# global (outside) 1 192.168.0.63 netmask 255.255.255.255
```

NOTE   It is recommended that you segregate from the rest of the internal network any devices that have a static translation and are accessed from the Internet. These devices should be on a separate network segment that connects to an additional interface on the PIX Firewall. This is normally called a *demilitarized zone (DMZ) segment.*

NOTE   The addresses assigned for static translation cannot be part of the global IP pool. This is a one-to-one relationship between the outside address and the address being translated.

Example 5-1 shows the commands for this type of configuration.

Example 5-1   *Configuring Multiple Translation Types*

```
LabPIX(config)# nat (inside) 1 0.0.0.0 0.0.0.0
LabPIX(config)# global (outside) 1 192.168.0.10-192.168.0.61 netmask
  255.255.255.192
LabPIX(config)# global (outside) 1 192.168.0.62 netmask 255.255.255.255
LabPIX(config)# static (DMZ, outside) 192.168.0.2 172.16.1.2
LabPIX(config)# static (DMZ, outside) 192.168.0.3 172.16.1.3
LabPIX(config)# static (DMZ, outside) 192.168.0.4 172.16.1.4
LabPIX(config)# access-list 101 permit tcp [any] host 192.168.0.2 eq
  smtp
LabPIX(config)# access-list 101 permit tcp any host 192.168.0.3 eq www
LabPIX(config)# access-list 101 permit udp [any] host 192.168.0.4 eq
  domain
LabPIX(config)# access-group 101 in interface outside
```

Figure 5-7 depicts the configuration shown in Example 5-1. Note that the traffic that is allowed inbound is routed to the DMZ rather than going to the internal network. Remember that static translation provides the mechanism for external hosts to connect to internal nodes, but because the connection is from a lower security level to a higher security level, there must be a rule in the security policy allowing the connection.

Figure 5-7 *Combined NAT, PAT, and Static Translation*

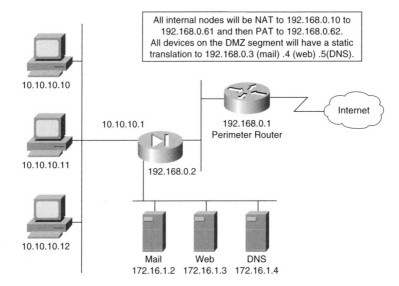

All internal nodes will be NAT to 192.168.0.10 to 192.168.0.61 and then PAT to 192.168.0.62. All devices on the DMZ segment will have a static translation to 192.168.0.3 (mail) .4 (web) .5(DNS).

Bidirectional Network Address Translation

Cisco PIX Firewall software version 6.2 allows NAT of external source IP addresses for packets traveling from the outside interface to an inside interface. All the functionality available with traditional **nat, pat,** and **static** commands is available bidirectionally.

Translation Versus Connection

Consider this scenario: A single user on a workstation located on the internal network is connecting to his web-based e-mail account, making an online stock purchase, researching a new software package that he intends to buy, and backing up a database at a remote branch office. How many connections does he have going from his workstation? It is difficult to tell because many of these tasks require multiple connections between the source and destination. How many translated sessions does he have going? One.

Most configurations create a single translated session, and from that session the user can create multiple connections. It is possible to create multiple translated sessions. This normally occurs when the internal node is accessing resources via different network segments all attached to the firewall (such as outside, DMZ1, DMZ2, and so on).

Translation occurs at the network layer (Layer 3) of the OSI reference model and deals only with packets. Connections, however, deal with the transport layer (Layer 4). Therefore, connections can be considered a subset of a single translation. It is possible to troubleshoot both translation and connection issues. It is recommended that you verify translation before attempting to troubleshoot a connection problem because the connection cannot be established if the translation has not occurred.

The argument or keyword used to troubleshoot translations is **xlate**. You can see the translation table by using the command **show xlate**, or you can clear the table with **clear xlate**. Any time you make a change to the translation table, it is a good idea to use **clear xlate**. This forces the translation slots to drop, and the Cisco PIX Firewall rebuilds the translation table. If you do not run the **clear xlate** command, the system does not drop the translation slots until they time out, which is 3 hours by default. The following commands can make a change to the translation table:

- **nat**—Identifies the internal address that should be translated.
- **global**—Identifies the external address or addresses to which internal addresses translate.
- **static**—Allows external users to connect to specific addresses and have the PIX Firewall redirect that connection specific internal/DMZ address. The **static** command also can be used for port redirection.
- **route**—Provides routing functionality for traffic that is traversing the PIX Firewall.
- **alias**—Was used to translate addresses between overlapping networks but now is used infrequently because of the recent improvements in the functionality of the **nat** and **static** commands.
- **conduit**—Configures the firewall to apply specific rules based on conduits to the traffic. Conduits are not commonly used because of the increased performance and functionality of ACLs.

Table 5-3 documents the options and arguments that are available with the **show xlate** and **clear xlate** commands. Table 5-4 lists the translation flags.

Table 5-3 show/clear xlate *Command Options*

Command Option	Description
detail	If specified, displays the translation type and interface information
[global | local *ip1*[-*ip2*] [netmask *mask*]	Displays active translations by global IP address or local IP address using the network mask to qualify the IP address
interface *if1* [,*if2*] [,*ifn*]	Displays active translations by interface
lport | gport *port* [-*port*]	Displays active translations by local and global ports
state	Displays active translations by state (use the translation flags listed in Table 5-4)

Table 5-4 *Translation Flags*

Flag	Description
s	Static translation slot
d	Dumps the translation slot on the next cleaning cycle
r	Port map translation (PAT)
n	No randomization of TCP sequence number
o	Outside address translations
i	Inside address translations
D	DNS A Resource Record rewrite
I	Identity translation from nat0

If you cannot clear **xlate,** it is possible (but not preferred) to clear the translation table by doing a reload or by rebooting the PIX Firewall.

The command used to troubleshoot connections is **show conn.** This command displays the number and status of all active TCP connections for the specific options selected. Table 5-5 lists the many options for the **show conn** command. Table 5-6 lists the connection flags.

Table 5-5 show conn *Command Options*

Command Option	Description
count	Displays the number of used connections (its accuracy depends on the volume and type of traffic)
detail	Displays the specified translation type and interface information
foreign | **local** *ip* [-*ip2*] **netmask** *mask*	Displays active connections by foreign or local IP address and qualifies connections by network mask
fport | **lport** *port1* [-*port2*]	Displays foreign or local active connections by port
protocol tcp | **udp** | *protocol*	Displays active connections by protocol type
state	Displays active connections by their current state (see Table 5-6)

Table 5-6 *Connection Flags*

Flag	Description
U	Up
f	Inside FIN
F	Outside FIN
r	Inside acknowledged FIN
R	Outside acknowledged FIN
s	Awaiting outside SYN
S	Awaiting inside SYN
M	SMTP data
T	TCP SIP connection
I	Inbound data
O	Outbound data
q	SQL*Net data
d	Dump

continues

Table 5-6 *Connection Flags (Continued)*

Flag	Description
P	Inside back connection
E	Outside back connection
G	Group
a	Awaiting outside ACK to SYN
A	Awaiting inside ACK to SYN
B	Initial SYN from outside
R	RPC
H	H.323
T	UDP SIP connection
m	SIP media connection
t	SIP transient connection
D	DNS

Configuring DNS Support

It is not necessary to configure DNS support on the Cisco PIX Firewall. By default, the PIX Firewall identifies each outbound DNS request and allows only a single response to that request. The internal host can query several DNS servers for a response, and the PIX Firewall allows the outbound queries. However, the PIX Firewall allows only the first response to pass through the firewall. All subsequent responses to the original query are dropped.

PIX Version 6.3(2) includes a DNS fixup protocol that enables you to configure a maximum packet length for connections to UDP port 53. The default value is 512 bytes. If you configure the DNS fixup protocol, the PIX Firewall drops all connections to UDP port 53 that exceed the configured maximum length. The command for this configuration is

```
fixup protocol dns [maximum length <512-65535>]
```

Foundation Summary

The "Foundation Summary" provides a convenient review of many key concepts in this chapter. If you are already comfortable with the topics in this chapter, this summary can help you recall a few details. If you just read this chapter, this review should help solidify some key facts. If you are doing your final preparation before the exam, this summary provides a convenient way to review the day before the exam.

All interfaces on the Cisco PIX Firewall are assigned security levels. The higher the number, the more secure the interface. Traffic is allowed to pass from an interface with a higher security level to an interface with a lower security level without a specific rule in the security policy. By default, the outside interface (Ethernet 0) is assigned a security level of 0, and the inside interface (Ethernet 1) is assigned a security level of 100. All other interfaces must be manually assigned a security level using the **nameif** command. Traffic does not pass through two interfaces if they have the same security level.

The PIX Firewall handles transport protocols completely differently. TCP is a connection-oriented protocol that creates a session and is relatively simple traffic for the PIX Firewall to handle. The TCP sequence number that is generated by the source machine is replaced by a randomly generated number as it passes through the PIX Firewall on its way to the destination. It becomes very difficult to hijack a TCP session because the initial TCP sequence numbers are randomly generated by the firewall and you cannot simply select the next sequence number in a series. Figure 5-8 shows how the PIX Firewall handles a TCP handshake.

Because UDP is a connectionless protocol, determining a connection's state can be very difficult. When outbound UDP traffic is generated, the PIX Firewall completes the necessary address translation and saves the session object in the state. If the response does not arrive within the timeout period (the default is 2 minutes), the connection is closed. If the response arrives within the timeout, the PIX Firewall verifies the connection information. If it matches the session object in the state table, the PIX Firewall allows the traffic. Figure 5-9 shows how the PIX Firewall typically handles UDP traffic.

Figure 5-8 *PIX Firewall Handling TCP Traffic*

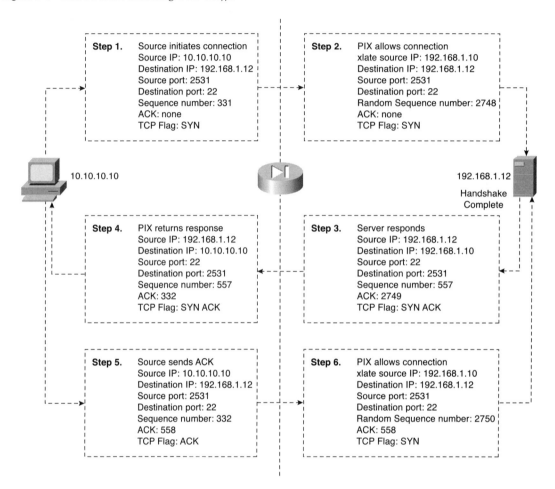

There are two types of address translation:

- **Dynamic address translation**—Is broken into two categories:

  — **Network Address Translation (NAT)**—Multiple local hosts translate to a pool of global addresses.

  — **Port Address Translation (PAT)**—Multiple local hosts translate to a single global address.

Figure 5-9 *PIX Firewall Handling UDP Traffic*

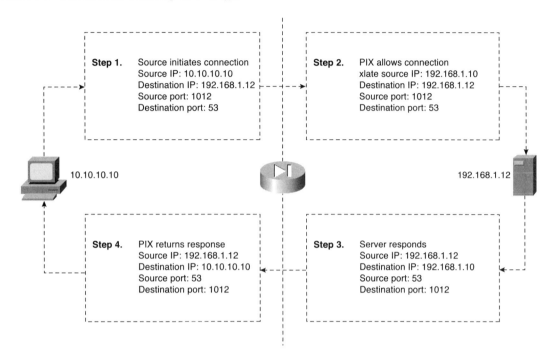

- **Static translation**—A single local address translates to a single global address. Static rules provide the translation to allow connection from a lower security level to a higher security level, but this connection must be allowed in the security policy. This connection can be allowed using either the **conduit** or **access-list** command. Access lists must be part of an access group and must be configured to a specific interface.

Multiple connections can take place through a single translation. Translations take place at the network layer, and connections occur at the transport layer. Therefore, connections are a subset of translations. Two specific commands are used to troubleshoot translation:

- **show xlate**—Displays translation slot information. Many options are available to display specific information about the address translations.

- **clear xlate**—Clears the translation table. Again, many options enable you to clear specific portions of the translation table.

A single command with numerous options is used to troubleshoot connections:

- **show conn**—Displays the number of and information about the active connections for the options specified.

Q&A

As mentioned in the Introduction, the questions in this book are more difficult than what you should experience on the exam. The questions are designed to ensure your understanding of the concepts discussed in this chapter and adequately prepare you to complete the exam. You should use the simulated exams on the CD to practice for the exam.

The answers to these questions can be found in Appendix A.

1. What is the difference between TCP and UDP?

2. What is the default security for traffic origination on the inside network segment going to the outside network?

3. True or false: You can have multiple translations in a single connection.

4. What commands are required to configure NAT on a Cisco PIX Firewall?

5. How many nodes can you hide behind a single IP address when configuring PAT?

6. What is an embryonic connection?

7. What is the best type of translation to use to allow connections to web servers from the Internet?

8. How does the Cisco PIX Firewall handle outbound DNS requests?

9. True or false: The quickest way to clear the translation table is to reboot the PIX Firewall.

10. True or false: If you configure a static translation for your web server, everyone can connect to it.

11. What does the PIX Firewall normally change when allowing a TCP handshake between nodes on different interfaces and performing NAT?

12. What does the PIX Firewall normally change when allowing a TCP handshake between nodes on different interfaces and performing PAT?

13. True or false: TCP is a much better protocol than UDP because it does handshakes and randomly generates TCP sequence numbers.

14. What are the two commands (syntax) to perform Network Address Translation of all internal addresses?

15. When would you want to configure NAT and PAT for the same inside segment?

16. What is RFC 1918?

17. Why is there an *id* field in the **nat** command?

This chapter covers the following subjects:

- User interface

- Configuring the PIX Firewall

- Time settings and NTP support

- DHCP server configuration

CHAPTER 6

Getting Started with the Cisco PIX Firewall

This chapter describes the basic preparation and configuration required to use the network firewall features of the Cisco PIX Firewall. It focuses on how to establish basic connectivity from the internal network to the public Internet.

How to Best Use This Chapter

This chapter provides an overview of the initial configuration steps required to get a PIX Firewall operational. Besides explaining the basic configuration steps it also explains the operation of the PIX Firewall user interface. If you are at all familiar with the PIX Firewall, you will probably find the topics in this chapter very easy to understand. Test yourself with the "Do I Know This Already?" quiz

"Do I Know This Already?" Quiz

The purpose of the "Do I Know This Already?" quiz is to help you decide if you really need to read the entire chapter. If you already intend to read the entire chapter, you do not necessarily need to answer these questions now.

The nine-question quiz, derived from the major sections in the "Foundation Topics" portion of the chapter, helps you determine how to spend your limited study time.

Table 6-1 outlines the major topics discussed in this chapter and the "Do I Know This Already?" quiz questions that correspond to those topics.

Table 6-1 *"Do I Know This Already?" Foundation Topics Section-to-Question Mapping*

Foundations Topics Section	Questions Covered in This Section	Score
User Interface	5, 7	
Configuring the PIX Firewall	1 to 4, 8	
Time Settings and NTP Support	6	
DHCP Server Configuration	9	

> **CAUTION**   The goal of self assessment is to gauge your mastery of the topics in this
> chapter. If you do not know the answer to a question or are only partially sure of the
> answer, you should mark this question wrong for purposes of the self assessment. Giving
> yourself credit for an answer you correctly guess skews your self-assessment results and
> might provide you with a false sense of security.

1. Which command tests connectivity?

   a. ping

   b. nameif

   c. ip address

   d. write terminal

2. Which command saves the configuration you made on the Cisco PIX Firewall?

   a. write terminal

   b. show start-running config

   c. write memory

   d. save config

3. Which command assigns security levels to interfaces on the PIX Firewall?

   a. ip address

   b. route

   c. nameif

   d. secureif

4. Which command flushes the ARP cache of the PIX Firewall?

   a. flush arp cache

   b. no arp cache

   c. clear arp

   d. You cannot flush the ARP cache.

5. Which of following configures a message when a firewall administrator enters the **enable** command?

    a. banner motd enter the enable password

    b. banner enable enter the enable password

    c. banner exec enter the enable password

    d. banner login enter the enable password

6. Why would you want authentication enabled between the PIX and the NTP server?

    a. To ensure that the PIX does synchronize with an unauthorized NTP server

    b. To maintain the integrity of the communication

    c. To increase the speed of communication

    d. To reduce latency

7. How do you access the enable mode?

    a. Enter the **enable** command and the enable password.

    b. Enter the **privilege** command and the privilege password.

    c. Enter the super-secret password.

    d. Enter only the command **privilege**.

8. How do you view the current configuration on your PIX Firewall?

    a. show running-config

    b. show current

    c. write memory

    d. save config

9. In a DHCP client configuration, what is the command to release and renew the IP address on the outside interface?

    a. ipconfig release

    b. ip address dhcp outside

    c. outside ip renew

    d. ip address renew outside

The answers to the "Do I Know This Already?" quiz are found in Appendix A, "Answers to the 'Do I Know This Already?' Quizzes and Q&A Sections." The suggested choices for your next step are as follows:

- **7 or less overall score**—Read the entire chapter. This includes the "Foundation Topics," "Foundation Summary," and "Q&A" sections.

- **8 or 9 overall score**—If you want more review on these topics, skip to the "Foundation Summary" section and then go to the "Q&A" section. Otherwise, move to the next chapter.

Foundation Topics

Access Modes

The Cisco PIX Firewall contains a command set based on Cisco IOS® Software technologies that provides three administrative access modes:

■ Unprivileged mode is available when you first access the PIX Firewall through console or Telnet. It displays the > prompt. This mode lets you view only restricted settings.

■ You access privileged mode by entering the **enable** command and the enable password. The prompt then changes from > to #. In this mode you can change a few of the current settings and view the existing Cisco PIX Firewall configuration. Any unprivileged command also works in privileged mode. To exit privileged mode, enter the **disable** or **exit** command.

■ You access configuration mode by entering the **configure terminal** command. This changes the prompt from # to (config)#. In this mode you can change system configurations. All privileged, unprivileged, and configuration commands work in this mode. Use the **exit** or **^z** command to exit configuration mode.

> **NOTE**   PIX Version 6.2 supports 16 privilege levels. This new feature enables you to assign Cisco PIX Firewall commands to one of the 16 levels. These privilege levels can also be assigned to users. This is discussed in detail in Chapter 4, "System Management/ Maintenance."

Configuring the PIX Firewall

Six important commands are used to produce a basic working configuration for the PIX Firewall:

> interface
> nameif
> ip address
> nat
> global
> route

Before you use these commands, it can prove very useful to draw a diagram of your Cisco PIX Firewall with the different security levels, interfaces, and Internet Protocol (IP) addresses. Figure 6-1 shows one such diagram that is used for the discussion in this chapter.

Figure 6-1 *Documenting Cisco PIX Firewall Security Levels, Interfaces, and IP Addresses*

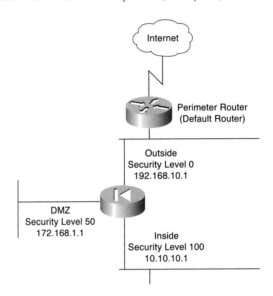

interface Command

The **interface** command identifies the interface hardware card, sets the speed of the interface, and enables the interface all-in-one command. All interfaces on a Cisco PIX Firewall are shut down by default and are explicitly enabled by the **interface** command. The basic syntax of the **interface** command is as follows:

```
interface hardware-id hardware-speed [shutdown]
```

Table 6-2 describes the command parameters for the **interface** command.

Table 6-2 interface *Command Parameters*

Command Parameter	Description
hardware-id	Indicates the interface's physical location on the Cisco PIX Firewall.
hardware-speed	Sets the connection speed, depending on which medium is being used. **auto** sets Ethernet speeds automatically. However, it is recommended that you configure the speed manually. **1000sxfull**—Sets full-duplex Gigabit Ethernet. **1000basesx**—Sets half-duplex Gigabit Ethernet.

Table 6-2 interface *Command Parameters (Continued)*

Command Parameter	Description
hardware-speed (continued)	**1000auto**—Automatically detects and negotiates full-/half-duplex Gigabit Ethernet. **10baset**—Sets 10 Mbps half-duplex Ethernet (very rare these days). **10full**—Sets 10 Mbps full-duplex Ethernet. **100full**—Sets 100 Mbps full-duplex Ethernet. **100basetx**—Sets 100 Mbps half-duplex Ethernet. Make sure that the *hardware-speed* setting matches the port speed on the switch to which the interface is connected. **aui**—Set 10 for Mbps Ethernet half-duplex communication with an attachment unit interface (AUI) cable interface. **auto**—Sets Ethernet speed automatically. The **auto** keyword can be used only with the Intel 10/100 automatic speed-sensing network interface card. You should not use this option to maintain compatibility with switches and other devices in your network. **bnc**—Set for 10-Mbps Ethernet half-duplex communication with a Bayonet-Neill-Concelman (BNC) cable interface.
shutdown	Administratively shuts down the interface. This parameter performs a very similar function in Cisco IOS Software. However, unlike with Cisco IOS, the command **no shutdown** cannot be used here. To place an interface in an administratively up mode, you reenter the **interface** command without the **shutdown** parameter.

Example 6-1 shows some examples of the **interface** command:

Example 6-1 *Sample Configuration for the* **interface** *Command*

```
Pix(config)# interface ethernet0 auto
Pix(config)# interface ethernet1 100full
Pix(config)# interface ethernet2 100basetx shut
```

nameif Command

As the name intuitively indicates, the **nameif** command is used to name an interface and assign a security value from 1 to 99. The outside and inside interfaces are named by default and have default security values of 0 and 100, respectively. By default, the interfaces have their hardware ID. Ethernet 0 is the outside interface, and Ethernet 1 is the inside interface. The names that are configured by the **nameif** command are user-friendly and are easier to use for advanced configuration later.

> **NOTE**   The **nameif** command can also be used to assign security values of 0 and 100. The names "inside" and "outside" are merely reserved for security levels 100 and 0, respectively, and are assigned by default, but they can be changed.

The syntax of the **nameif** command is as follows:

```
nameif hardware-id if-name security-level
```

Table 6-3 describes the command parameters for the **nameif** command.

Table 6-3   nameif *Command Parameters*

Command Parameter	Description
hardware-id	Indicates the interface's physical location on the Cisco PIX Firewall.
if-name	Specifies the name by which you refer to this interface. The name cannot have any spaces and must not exceed 48 characters.
security-level	Specifies a numerical value from 1 to 99 indicating the security level.

Example 6-2 shows some examples of the **nameif** command:

Example 6-2   *Sample Configuration for the* nameif *Command*

```
nameif ethernet0 outside security0
nameif ethernet1 inside security100
nameif ethernet2 dmz security20
```

The *security-level* value controls how hosts/devices on the different interfaces interact with each other. By default, hosts/devices connected to interfaces with higher security levels can access hosts/devices connected to interfaces with lower-security interfaces. Hosts/devices connected to interfaces with lower-security interfaces cannot access hosts/devices connected to interfaces with higher-security interfaces without the assistance of access lists.

You can verify your configuration by using the **show nameif** command.

ip address Command

All the interfaces on the Cisco PIX Firewall that will be used must be configured with an IP address. The IP address can be configured manually or through Dynamic Host Configuration Protocol (DHCP). The DHCP feature is usually used on Cisco PIX Firewall small office/home office (SOHO) models. DHCP is discussed later in this chapter.

The **ip address** command is used to configure IP addresses on the PIX interfaces. The **ip address** command binds a logical address (IP address) to the hardware ID. Table 6-4 describes the parameters for the **ip address** command, the syntax of which is as follows:

    ip address *if-name ip-address [netmask]*

Table 6-4   **ip address** *Command Parameters*

Command Parameter	Description
if-name	Specifies the interface name that was configured using the **nameif** command.
ip-address	Specifies the IP address of the interface.
netmask	Specifies the appropriate network mask. If the mask value is not entered, the PIX assigns a classful network mask.

Example 6-3 shows configuration of the inside interface with an IP address of 10.10.10.14/24:

Example 6-3   *Sample Configuration for the* **ip address** *Command*

```
ip address inside 10.10.10.14 255.255.255.0
```

Use the **show ip** command to view the configured IP address on the PIX interface.

nat Command

The **nat** (which stands for Network Address Translation) command lets you dynamically translate a set of IP addresses (usually on the inside) to a global set of IP addresses.

> **NOTE**   PIX Version 6.2 and later support bidirectional translation of inside network IP addresses to global IP addresses and translation of outside IP addresses to inside network IP addresses.

The **nat** command is always paired with a **global** command, with the exception of the **nat 0** command. Table 6-5 describes the command parameters for the **nat** command, the syntax of which is as follows:

```
nat (if-name) nat-id local-ip [netmask]
```

Table 6-5 nat *Command Parameters*

Command Parameter	Description
(if-name)	Specifies the internal network interface name.
nat-id	Specifies the ID number to match with the global address pool.
local-ip	Specifies the IP address that is translated. This is usually the inside network IP address. It is possible to assign all of the inside network for the *local-ip* through **nat (inside) 1 0 0**.
netmask	Specifies the network mask for the local IP address.

Example 6-4 shows an example of the **nat** command.

Example 6-4 *Sample Configuration for the* nat *Command*

```
nat (inside) 1 10.10.10.0 255.255.255.0
nat (inside) 2 172.16.1.0 255.255.255.0
```

Chapter 5, "Understanding Cisco PIX Firewall Translation and Connection," discusses NAT in greater detail.

Configuring Port Address Translation

Port Address Translation (PAT) can be configured using the same command as Network Address Translation (NAT). PAT maps a single global IP address to many local addresses. PAT extends the range of available outside addresses at your site by dynamically assigning unique port numbers to the outside address as a connection is requested. A single IP address has up to 65,535 ports available for making connections. For PAT, the port number uniquely identifies each connection.

PAT translates a group of local addresses to a single global IP address with a unique source port (above 1024). When a local host accesses the destination network, the Firewall services module assigns it the global IP address and then a unique port number. Each host receives the same IP address, but because the source port numbers are unique, the responding traffic, which includes the IP address and port number as the destination, can be assigned to the correct host. It is highly unlikely that you would run out of addresses in PAT configuration because there are more than 64,000 ports available.

PAT enables you to use a single global address, thus conserving routable addresses. You can even use the destination actual interface IP address as the PAT IP address (this type of configuration is used, but not limited to, the outside interface). PAT does not work with multimedia applications that have an inbound data stream different from the outgoing control path.

In large enterprise environments, to use NAT you must have a large number of routable addresses in the global pool. If the destination network requires registered addresses, such as the Internet, you might encounter a shortage of usable addresses. This can be a disadvantage.

PAT does not work with applications that have an inbound data stream on one port and the outgoing control path on another, such as multimedia applications. For those situations, it is more advantageous to use NAT. Example 6-5 shows a sample configuration for PAT.

Example 6-5 *Sample Configuration for Configuring PAT on the Inside Interface*

```
nat (inside) 1 10.10.30.0 255.255.255.0
global (outside) 1 interface
```

global Command

The **global** command is used to define the address or range of addresses into which the addresses defined by the **nat** command are translated. It is important that the *nat-id* be identical to the *nat-id* used in the **nat** command. The *nat-id* pairs the IP address defined by the **global** and **nat** commands so that network translation can take place. The syntax of the **global** command is as follows:

```
global (if-name) nat-id global-ip | global-ip-global-ip [netmask netmask]
```

Table 6-6 describes the parameters and options for the **global** command.

Table 6-6 **global** *Command Parameters*

Command Parameter	Description
(if-name)	Specifies the external network where you use these global addresses.
nat-id	Identifies the global address and matches it with the **nat** command with which it is pairing.
global-ip	Specifies a single IP address. When a single IP address is specified, the PIX automatically performs PAT. A warning message indicating that the PIX will use PAT for all addresses is displayed on the console.
global-ip-global-ip	Defines a range of global IP addresses to be used by the PIX to NAT.
netmask	Specifies the network mask for the global IP address(es).

There should be enough global IP addresses to match the local IP addresses specified by the **nat** command. If there are not, you can leverage the shortage of global addresses by PAT entry, which permits more than 64,000 hosts to use a single IP address. PAT divides the available ports per global IP address into three ranges:

- 0 to 511
- 512 to 1023
- 1024 to 65535

PAT assigns a unique source port for each User Datagram Protocol (UDP) or Transmission Control Protocol (TCP) session. It attempts to assign the same port value of the original request, but if the original source port has already been used, PAT starts scanning from the beginning of the particular port range to find the first available port and then assigns it to the conversation. PAT has some restrictions in its use. For example, it cannot support H.323. Example 6-6 shows a configuration using a range of global IP addresses and a single IP address for PAT.

Example 6-6   *Sample Configuration for NAT and PAT*

```
nat (inside) 1 10.0.0.0 255.0.0.0
global (outside) 1 192.168.100.20-192.168.100.50 netmask 255.255.255.0
global (outside) 1 192.168.100.55 netmask 255.255.255.0
```

When a host or device tries to start a connection, the PIX Firewall checks the translation table to see whether there is an entry for that particular IP address. If there is no existing translation, a new *translation slot* is created. The default time that a translated IP address is kept in the translation table is 3 hours. You can change this with the **timeout xlate** *hh:mm:ss* command. To view the translated addresses, use the **show xlate** command.

route Command

The **route** command tells the Cisco PIX Firewall where to send information that is forwarded on a specific interface and that is destined for a particular network address. You add static routes to the PIX using the **route** command.

Table 6-7 describes the **route** command parameters, the syntax of which is as follows:

```
route if-name ip-address netmask gateway-ip [metric]
```

Table 6-7   route *Command Parameters*

Command Parameter	Description
if-name	Specifies the name of the interface from which the data leaves.
ip-address	Specifies the IP address to be routed.
netmask	Specifies the network mask of the IP address to be routed.
gateway-ip	Specifies the IP address of the next-hop address. Usually this is the IP address of the perimeter router.
metric	Specifies the number of hops to *gateway-ip*.

Example 6-7 shows a default route configuration on a Cisco PIX Firewall:

Example 6-7   *Default Route of 192.168.1.3*

```
route outside 0.0.0.0 0.0.0.0 192.168.1.3 1
```

> **NOTE**   On the PIX Firewall, only one default route is permitted.

The **1** at the end of the route indicates that the gateway router is only one hop away. If a metric is not specified in the **route** command, the default is 1. You can configure only one default route on the PIX Firewall. It is good practice to use the **clear arp** command to clear the ARP cache of the PIX Firewall before testing your new route configuration.

Routing Information Protocol

The Routing Information Protocol (RIP) can be enabled to build the Cisco PIX Firewall routing table. RIP configuration specifies whether the PIX updates its routing tables by passively listening to RIP traffic and whether the interface broadcasts itself as a default route for network traffic on that interface. When using RIP version 2 with PIX software versions earlier than 5.3, it is important to configure the router providing the RIP updates with the network address of the PIX interface. The default version is 1 if not explicitly specified. The syntax to enable RIP is as follows:

```
rip if-name default ¦ passive [version [1 ¦ 2]] [authentication [text ¦ md5
   key (key-id)]]
```

Table 6-8 describes the **rip** command parameters.

Table 6-8 *rip Command Parameters*

Command Parameter	Description
if-name	Specifies the interface name.
default	Broadcasts a default route on the interface.
passive	Enables passive RIP on the interface. The Cisco PIX Firewall listens for RIP routing broadcasts and uses that information to populate its routing tables.
version	Specifies the RIP version number. Use version 2 for RIP update encryption. Use version 1 to provide backward compatibility with the earlier versions.
authentication	Enables authentication for RIP version 2.
text	Sends RIP updates in clear text.
md5	Encrypts RIP updates using MD5 encryption.
key	Specifies the key to encrypt RIP updates. This value must be the same on the routers and on any other device that provides RIP version 2 updates. The *key* is a text string up to 16 characters in length.
key-id	Specifies the key identification value. The *key-id* can be a number from 1 to 255. Use the same *key-id* that is used on the routers and any other device that provides RIP version 2 updates.

Testing Your Configuration

Making sure that the configuration you entered works is an important part of the configuration process. At this point you test basic connectivity from the inside interface out to the other interfaces. Use the **ping** and **debug** commands to test your connectivity.

The **ping** command sends an Internet Control Message Protocol (ICMP) echo request message to the target IP address and expects an ICMP echo reply. By default, the PIX denies all inbound traffic through the outside interface. Based on your network security policy, you should consider configuring the PIX to deny all ICMP traffic to the outside interface, or any other interface you deem necessary, by entering the **icmp** command. The **icmp** command controls ICMP traffic that terminates on the PIX. If no ICMP control list is configured, the PIX accepts all ICMP traffic that terminates at any interface (including the outside interface). For example, when you first configure the PIX, it is a good idea to be able to ping an interface and get a response. The following makes that possible for the outside interface:

```
icmp permit any any outside
```

The **icmp permit any any outside** command is used during the testing/debugging phase of your configuration process. Make sure that you change it so it does not respond to ping requests after you complete testing. It is a security risk to leave it set to accept and respond to ICMP packets.

After the **icmp permit** command has been configured, you can ping the outside interface on your Cisco PIX Firewall and ping from hosts on each firewall interface. For example:

```
ping outside 192.168.1.1
```

You also can monitor ping results by starting **debug icmp trace**.

Saving Your Configuration

Configuration changes that you have made stay in the random access memory (RAM) of the PIX Firewall unless you save them to Flash memory. If for any reason the PIX must be rebooted, the configuration changes you made are lost. So, when you finish entering commands in the configuration, save the changes to Flash memory by using the **write memory** command, as follows:

```
Pix# write memory
```

NOTE   There is one obvious advantage of not having configuration changes committed to Flash memory immediately. For example, if you make a configuration change that you cannot back out from, you simply reboot and return to the settings you had before you made the changes.

You are now finished configuring the Cisco PIX Firewall. This basic configuration lets protected network users start connections and prevents users on unprotected networks from accessing (or attacking) protected hosts.

Use the **write terminal** or **show running-config** command to view your current configuration.

Support for Domain Name System Messages

PIX Firewall fully supports NAT and PAT Domain Name System (DNS) messages originating from either a more secure interface or less secure interfaces. This means that if a client on an inside network requests DNS resolution of an inside address from a DNS server on an outside interface, the DNS A record is translated correctly. To illustrate this point, Figure 6-2 shows a user from inside obtaining DNS resolution from the outside (maybe from an Internet service provider) for a web server on the inside.

Figure 6-2 *User Obtaining DNS Resolution from the Outside*

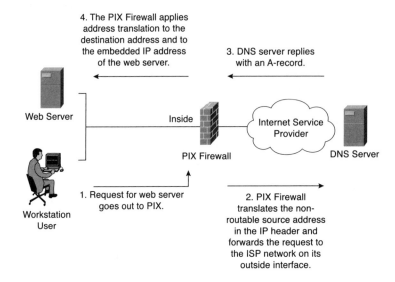

Configuring Dynamic Host Configuration Protocol on the Cisco PIX Firewall

The Cisco PIX Firewall can be configured as either of the following:

- DHCP server
- DHCP client

Using the PIX Firewall Dynamic Host Configuration Protocol Server

The DHCP server is usually used in, but not limited to, SOHO environments. The address pool of a PIX Firewall DHCP server must be within the same subnet of the PIX Firewall interface that is enabled, and you must specify the associated PIX Firewall interface with *if-name*. In other words, the client must be physically connected to the subnet of a PIX Firewall interface. The size of the pool is limited to 32 addresses with a 10-user license and 128 addresses with a 50-user license on the PIX 501. The unlimited user license on the PIX 501 and all other PIX Firewall platforms supports 256 addresses. To configure DHCP on the PIX, use the **dhcpd** command. The following is the syntax for the **dhcpd** command:

```
dhcpd address ip1[-ip2] if-name
dhcpd auto-config [outside]
dhcpd dns dns1 [dns2]
dhcpd wins wins1 [wins2]
```

```
 dhcpd lease lease-length
 dhcpd domain domain-name
 dhcpd enable if-name
 dhcpd option 66 ascii {server-name ¦ server-ip-str}
 dhcpd option 150 ip server-ip1 [ server-ip2]
dhcpd ping-timeout timeout
 debug dhcpd event
debug dhcpd packet
```

Table 6-9 describes the different **dhcpd** command parameters.

Table 6-9   dhcpd *Command Parameters*

Parameter	Description
address *ip1*- [*ip2*]	Specifies the IP pool address range.
auto-config	Enables the PIX to configure DNS, Windows Internet Naming Service (WINS), and domain name values automatically from the DHCP client to the DHCP server. If the user also specifies DNS, WINS, and domain parameters, the command line interface (CLI) parameters overwrite the **auto-config** parameters.
binding	Specifies the binding information for a given server IP address and its associated client hardware address and lease length.
code	Specifies the DHCP option code, either 66 or 150.
dns *dns1* [*dns2*]	Specifies the IP addresses of the DNS servers for the DHCP client.
domain *domain-name*	Specifies the DNS domain name; for example, cspfa2.com.
if-name	Specifies the interface on which to enable the DHCP server.
lease *lease-length*	Specifies the length of the lease, in seconds, granted to the DHCP client from the DHCP server. The lease indicates how long the client can use the assigned IP address. The default is 3600 seconds. The minimum lease length is 300 seconds, and the maximum lease length is 2,147,483,647 seconds.
option 150	Specifies thc Trivial File Transfer Protocol (TFTP) server IP address(es) designated for Cisco IP Phones in dotted-decimal format. DHCP **option 150** is site-specific; it gives the IP addresses of a list of TFTP servers.
option 66	Specifies the TFTP server IP address designated for Cisco IP Phones and gives the IP address or the host name of a single TFTP server.
outside	Specifies the outside interface of the firewall.
ping-timeout	Specifies the timeout value of a ping, in milliseconds, before an IP address is assigned to a DHCP client.
server-ip(1,2)	Specifies the IP address(es) of a TFTP server.
server-ip-str	Specifies the TFTP server in dotted-decimal format, such as 1.1.1.1, which is treated as a character string by the PIX Firewall DHCP server.

continues

Table 6-9   dhcpd *Command Parameters (Continued)*

Parameter	Description
server-name	Specifies an American Standard Code for Information Interchange (ASCII) character string representing the TFTP server.
statistics	Provides statistical information, such as address pool, number of bindings, malformed messages, sent messages, and received messages.
wins *wins1 [wins2]*	Specifies the IP addresses of the Microsoft NetBIOS name servers (Windows Internet Naming Service servers). The second server address is optional.

In addition to supporting a DHCP client and DHCP server configuration, the PIX also supports a DHCP relay configuration. The DHCP relay configuration enables the PIX to assist in dynamic configuration of IP device hosts on any Ethernet interface. When the PIX Firewall receives a request from a host on an interface, it forwards the request to a user-configured DHCP server on another interface. The DHCP relay agent is a feature that is provided by PIX Version 6.3.

PIX Firewall Version 6.3 allows any number of integrated DHCP servers to be configured, and on any interface. The DHCP client can be configured only on the outside interface, and the DHCP relay agent can be configured on any interface. The DHCP server and DHCP relay agent cannot be configured concurrently on the same PIX Firewall, but the DHCP client and DHCP relay agent can be configured concurrently.

As with all other DHCP servers, DNS, Windows Internet Naming Service (WINS), IP address lease time, and domain information on the PIX can be configured. The following six steps are required to enable the DHCP server feature on the PIX:

Step 1   Enable the DHCP daemon on the Cisco PIX Firewall to listen to DHCP requests from clients:

```
pix(config)#dhcpd enable inside
```

Step 2   Specify the IP address range that the PIX DHCP server assigns:

```
pix(config)#dhcpd address 10.10.10.15-10.10.10.100 inside
```

Step 3   Specify the lease length to grant to the client (the default is 3600 seconds):

```
pix(config)#dhcpd lease 2700
```

Step 4   Specify a DNS server (optional):

```
pix(config)#dhcpd dns 192.168.10.68 192.168.10.73
```

Step 5   Specify a WINS server (optional):

```
pix(config)#dhcpd wins 192.168.10.66
```

Step 6   Configure the domain name the client will use (optional):

```
pix(config)#dhcpd domain axum.com
```

Configuring the PIX Firewall Dynamic Host Configuration Protocol Client

DHCP client support on the Cisco PIX Firewall is designed for use in SOHO environments in which Digital Subscriber Line (DSL) and cable modems are used. The DHCP client can be enabled only on the outside interface of the PIX Firewall. When the DHCP client is enabled, DHCP servers on the outside provide the outside interface with an IP address.

> **NOTE**   The DHCP client does not support failover configuration.

The DHCP client feature on the PIX Firewall is enabled by the **ip address dhcp** command:

```
ip address outside dhcp [setroute] [retry retry-cnt]
```

The **setroute** option tells the Cisco PIX Firewall to set its default route using the default gateway parameter that the DHCP server returns. Do not configure a default route when using the **setroute** option.

> **NOTE**   **ip address dhcp** is used to release and renew the outside interface's IP address.

To view current information about the DHCP lease, enter the following command:

```
show ip address outside dhcp
```

The partial configuration in Example 6-8 demonstrates how to use three new features that are associated with each other: DHCP server, DHCP client, and PAT using the interface IP address to configure a PIX Firewall in a SOHO environment with the inside interface as the DHCP server:

Example 6-8   *Sample Configuration for the* **dhcpd** *Command*

```
Ip address outside dhcp setroute
Ip address inside 10.100.1.1 255.255.255.0
dhcpd address 10.100.1.50-10.100.1.60 inside
dhcpd dns 192.168.1.106 192.168.1.107
dhcpd wins 192.168.1.106
dhcpd lease 1200
```

continues

Example 6-8   *Sample Configuration for the* **dhcpd** *Command (Continued)*

```
dhcpd domain cspfa.com
dhcpd enable inside
nat (inside) 1 0 0
global (outside) 1 interface
```

Configuring Time Settings on the Cisco PIX Firewall

The PIX obtains its time setting information in two ways:

- By Network Time Protocol (NTP) server
- By system clock

Network Time Protocol

The Network Time Protocol (NTP) is used to implement a hierarchical system of servers that provide a source for a precise synchronized time among network systems. It is important to maintain a consistent time throughout all network devices, such as servers, routers, and switches. When analyzing network events, logs are an important source of information. Analyzing and troubleshooting network events can be difficult if there is a time inconsistency between network devices on the network. Furthermore, some time-sensitive operations, such as validating certificates and certificate revocation lists (CRLs), require precise time stamps.

Cisco PIX Firewall Version 6.2 and later enable you obtain the system time from NTP version 3 servers.

The syntax to enable an NTP client on the PIX Firewall is as follows:

```
ntp server ip-address [key number] source if-name [prefer]
```

Table 6-10 describes the parameters of the **ntp** command.

Table 6-10   **ntp** *Command Parameters*

Command Parameter	Description
ip-address	Specifies the IP address of the time server with which the PIX synchronizes.
key	This keyword indicates that you are configuring the NTP client to use the specified authentication key (identified by *number*) when sending packets to the NTP server.
number	Specifies the authentication key. This value is useful when you use multiple keys and multiple servers for identification purposes.
source	Specifies the interface. If the **source** keyword is not specified, the routing table is used to determine the interface.

Table 6-10 ntp *Command Parameters (Continued)*

Command Parameter	Description
if-name	Specifies the interface name used to send packets to the NTP server.
prefer	Specifies the preferred time server. This option reduces switching back and forth between servers by making the specified server the preferred time server.

Communication of messages between the PIX and the NTP servers can be authenticated to prevent the PIX from synchronizing time with rogue NTP servers. The three commands used to enable NTP authentication are as follows:

```
ntp authenticate
ntp authentication-key number md5 value
ntp trusted-key number
```

NOTE   NTP uses port 123 for communication.

The **ntp authenticate** command enables NTP authentication and refuses synchronization with an NTP server unless the server is configured with one of the authentication keys specified using the **ntp trusted-key** command.

The **ntp authentication-key** command is used to define authentication keys for use with other NTP commands to provide a higher degree of security. The *number* parameter is the key number (1 to 4294967295). The **md5** option is the encryption algorithm. The *value* parameter is the key value (an arbitrary string of up to 32 characters).

The **ntp trusted-key** command is used to define one or more key numbers that the NTP server is required to provide in its NTP packets for the PIX Firewall to accept synchronization with that NTP server. The Cisco PIX Firewall requires the NTP server to provide this key number in its NTP packets, which provides protection against synchronizing the PIX system clock with an NTP server that is not trusted.

NTP configuration on the PIX can be verified and viewed by using the following **show** commands:

- The **show ntp** command displays the current NTP configuration.
- The **show ntp associations** [**detail**] command displays the configured network time server associations.
- The **show ntp status** command displays the NTP clock information.

To remove the NTP configuration, use the **clear ntp** command.

PIX Firewall System Clock

The second method of configuring the time setting on the PIX Firewall is by using the system clock. The system clock is usually set when you answer the initial setup interview question when you are configuring a new Cisco PIX Firewall. You can change it later using the **clock set** command:

```
clock set hh:mm:ss month day year
```

Three characters are used for the *month* parameter. The *year* is a four-digit number. For example, to set the time and date to 17:51 and 20 seconds on April 9, 2003, you would enter the following:

```
clock set 17:51:20 apr 9 2003
```

NOTE   The system clock, unlike NTP, is not synchronized with other network devices.

Cisco PIX Firewall Version 6.2 includes improvements to the **clock** command. The **clock** command now supports daylight saving (summer) time and time zones. To configure daylight saving time, enter the following command:

```
clock summer-time zone recurring [week weekday month hh:mm week weekday
    month hh:mm [offset]]
```

Table 6-11 describes the parameters for the **clock** command.

Table 6-11   clock *Command Parameters*

Command Parameter	Description
summer-time	Automatically switches to summer time (for display purposes only).
zone	Specifies the name of the time zone.
recurring	Indicates that summer time should start and end on the days specified by the values that follow this keyword. The summer time rule defaults to the United States rule.
week	Specifies the week of the month. The week is 1 through 4.
week day	Sets the day of the week (Sunday, Monday).
month	Specifies the full name of the month, such as April.
hh:mm	Specifies the time in 24-hour clock format.
offset	Specifies the number of minutes to add during summer. The default is 60 minutes.

Time zones are set only for display. Setting a time zone does not change the internal PIX time, which is kept according to Coordinated Universal Time (UTC). To set the time zone, use the **clock timezone** command. The syntax for the command is as follows:

```
clock timezone zone hours [minutes]
```

The following **clock summer-time** command specifies that summer time starts on the first Sunday in April at 2 A.M. and ends on the last Sunday in October at 2 A.M.:

```
pix(config)# clock summer-time PDT recurring 1 Sunday April 2:00 last Sunday
   October 2:00
```

You can check your clock configuration by simply entering the show clock command as shown in Example 6-9 below:

Example 6-9   show clock *Sample Output*

```
PIXFW# show clock
10:04:06.334 PDT Thu Feb 13 2004
```

Configuring Login Banners on the PIX Firewall

PIX Firewall Version 6.3 introduces support for message-of-the-day (MOTD), EXEC, and login banners, similar to the feature included in Cisco IOS Software. Banner size is limited only by available system memory or Flash memory.

You can create a message as a warning for unauthorized use of the firewall. In some jurisdictions, civil and/or criminal prosecution of crackers who break into your system are made easier if you have incorporated a warning banner that informs unauthorized users that their attempts to access the system are in fact unauthorized. In other jurisdictions, you may be forbidden to monitor the activities of even unauthorized users unless you have taken steps to notify them of your intent to do so. One way of providing this notification is to put the information into a banner message configured with the PIX **banner** command.

Legal notification requirements are complex and vary in each jurisdiction and situation. Even within jurisdictions, legal opinions vary, and this issue should be discussed with your own legal counsel. In cooperation with counsel, you should consider which of the following information should be put into your banner:

- A notice that the system can be logged in to or used only by specifically authorized personnel, and perhaps information about who may authorize use

- A notice that any unauthorized use of the system is unlawful and may be subject to civil and/or criminal penalties

- A notice that any use of the system may be logged or monitored without further notice and that the resulting logs may be used as evidence in court

- Specific notices required by specific local laws

From a security, rather than a legal, point of view, your login banner usually should not contain any specific information about your router, its name, its model, what software it is running, or who owns it; such information may be abused by crackers.

The banner messages can be displayed when a user enters privileged EXEC mode, upon line activation, on an incoming connection to a virtual terminal, or as a message of the day. To create a banner message, use the following command:

```
Banner {exec¦login¦motd} text
```

Table 6-12 describes the parameters of the **banner** command.

Table 6-12 banner *Command Parameters*

Parameter	Description
exec	Configures the system to display a banner before displaying the enable prompt.
login	Configures the system to display a banner before the password login prompt when accessing the firewall using Telnet.
motd	Configures the system to display a message-of-the-day banner.
text	Specifies the line of message text to be displayed in the firewall command-line interface. Subsequent *text* entries are added to the end of an existing banner unless the banner is cleared first. The tokens $(domain) and $(hostname) are replaced with the host name and domain name of the firewall.

Spaces are allowed, but tabs cannot be entered using the command-line interface (CLI). You can dynamically add the host name or domain name of the PIX Firewall by including $(hostname) and $(domain) in the string. Example 6-10 shows a sample configuration using the **banner** command.

Example 6-10 *A Sample Configuration of the* **banner** *Command*

```
pixfw(config)# banner login Warning Notice
This is a U.S. Government computer system, which may be accessed and used only
 for authorized Government business by authorized personnel. Unauthorized access
 or use of this computer system may subject violators to criminal, civil, and/or
administrative action.
All information on this computer system may be intercepted, recorded, read, copied,
 and disclosed by and to authorized personnel for official purposes, including criminal
 investigations. Such information includes sensitive data encrypted to comply with
confidentiality and privacy requirements. Access or use of this computer system
by any person, whether authorized or unauthorized, constitutes consent to these
 terms. There is no right of privacy in this system.  ^d
```

To replace a banner, use the **no banner** command before adding the new lines. The **no banner** {**exec** | **login** | **motd**} command removes all the lines for the banner option specified. The **no banner** command removes all the lines for the banner option specified and does not selectively delete text strings. The **clear banner** command removes all the banners.

Sample PIX Configuration

Example 6-11 shows sample output for a PIX configuration. Included are some of the commands discussed in this chapter.

Example 6-11 *Sample PIX Configuration*

```
pix# show config
: Saved
: Written by deguc at 11:29:39.859 EDT Fri Aug 8 2002
PIX Version 6.2(2)
nameif ethernet0 outside security0
nameif ethernet1 inside security100
nameif ethernet2 dmz security20
enable password GgtfiV2tiX5zk297 encrypted
passwd kP3Eex5gnkza7.w9 encrypted
hostname pix
domain-name axum.com
clock timezone EST -5
clock summer-time EDT recurring
fixup protocol ftp 21
fixup protocol http 80
fixup protocol h323 h225 1720
fixup protocol h323 ras 1718-1719
fixup protocol ils 389
fixup protocol rsh 514
fixup protocol rtsp 554
fixup protocol smtp 25
fixup protocol sqlnet 1521
fixup protocol sip 5060
fixup protocol skinny 2000
names
pager lines 24
no logging on
interface ethernet0 100full
interface ethernet1 100full
interface ethernet2 100full
mtu outside 1500
mtu inside 1500
mtu dmz 1500
```

continues

Example 6-11 *Sample PIX Configuration (Continued)*

```
ip address outside 192.168.1.1 255.255.255.224
ip address inside 10.10.10.1 255.255.0.0
ip address dmz 172.16.1.1 255.255.255.0
ip audit info action alarm
ip audit attack action alarm
no failover
pdm location 10.10.10.14 255.255.255.255 inside
arp timeout 14400
global (outside) 1 192.168.1.20-192.168.1.110 netmask 255.255.255.224
global (outside) 1 192.168.1.111
global (dmz) 1 172.16.1.10-172.16.1.20 netmask 255.255.255.224

nat (inside) 1 0.0.0.0 0.0.0.0 0 0
nat (dmz) 1 0.0.0.0 0.0.0.0 0 0
route outside 0.0.0.0 0.0.0.0 192.168.1.3 1
timeout xlate 3:00:00
timeout conn 1:00:00 half-closed 0:10:00 udp 0:02:00 rpc 0:10:00 h323 0:05:00
  sip 0:30:00 sip-media 0:02:00
timeout uauth 0:05:00 absolute
aaa-server TACACS+ protocol tacacs+
aaa-server RADIUS protocol radius
aaa-server LOCAL protocol local
 http server enable
http 10.10.10.14 255.255.255.255 inside
no snmp-server location
no snmp-server contact
snmp-server community public
no snmp-server enable traps
floodguard enable
no sysopt route dnat
telnet 10.10.10.14  255.255.255.255 inside
telnet timeout 5
 terminal width 80
Cryptochecksum:62a73076955b1060644fdba1da64b15f
```

Foundation Summary

The "Foundation Summary" provides a convenient review of many key concepts in this chapter. If you are already comfortable with the topics in this chapter, this summary can help you recall a few details. If you just read this chapter, this review should help solidify some key facts. If you are doing your final preparation before the exam, this summary provides a convenient way to review the day before the exam.

Table 6-13 provides a quick reference to the commands needed to configure the Cisco PIX Firewall, time server support, and the DHCP server.

Table 6-13 *Command Reference*

Command	Description
enable	Specifies to activate a process, mode, or privilege level.
interface	Identifies the speed and duplex settings of the network interface boards.
nameif	Enables you to name interfaces and assign security levels.
ip address	Identifies addresses for network interfaces and enables you to set how many times the PIX Firewall polls for DHCP information.
nat	Enables you to associate a network with a pool of global IP addresses.
global	Defines a pool of global addresses. The global addresses in the pool provide an IP address for each outbound connection and for inbound connections resulting from outbound connections. Ensure that associated **nat** and **global** command statements have the same *nat-id*.
route	Specifies a default or static route for an interface.
write terminal	Displays the current configuration on the terminal.
rip	Enables IP routing table updates from received RIP broadcasts.
dhcpd	Controls the DHCP server feature.
ntp server	Synchronizes the PIX Firewall with the network time server that is specified and authenticates according to the authentication options that are set.
clock	Lets you specify the time, month, day, and year for use with time-stamped syslog messages.

Q&A

As mentioned in the Introduction, the questions in this book are more difficult than what you should experience on the exam. The questions are designed to ensure your understanding of the concepts discussed in this chapter and adequately prepare you to complete the exam. You should use the simulated exams on the CD to practice for the exam.

The answers to these questions can be found in Appendix A.

1. How do you access privileged mode?

2. What is the function of the **nameif** command?

3. Which six commands produce a basic working configuration for a Cisco PIX Firewall?

4. Why is the **route** command important?

5. What is the command to flush out the Address Resolution Protocol (ARP) cache on a Cisco PIX Firewall?

6. What is the syntax to configure a message-of-the-day (MOTD) banner that says, "System shall not be available on 18:00 Monday January 19th for 2 hours due to system maintenance"?

7. What is the command used to configure PAT on the PIX Firewall?

8. Which command releases and renews an IP address on the PIX?

9. Give at least one reason why it is beneficial to use NTP on the Cisco PIX Firewall.

10. Why would you want to secure the NTP messages between the Cisco PIX Firewall and the NTP server?

This chapter covers the following subjects:

- ACLs

- Using ACLs

- Overview of object grouping

- Getting started with group objects

- Configuring group objects

- Nested object groups

- Advanced protocols

- Multimedia support

CHAPTER 7

Configuring Access

Managing controlled access to network resources from an untrusted (Internet) network is a very important function of the Cisco PIX Firewall. Access lists, network address translations, authentication, and authorization are ways to provide access through the PIX Firewall in a controlled fashion. In addition, PIX software Version 6.2 and later has new features such as object grouping and TurboACL, which make managing and implementing a complex security policy much easier and more scalable.

How Best to Use This Chapter

Limiting access to systems and services on your network is one of the primary responsibilities of the PIX Firewalls that you deploy on a network. This chapter provides the information on how to restrict network traffic using access lists, hide internal addresses using Network Address Translation (both static and dynamic), as well as configuring fixup protocols that monitor common protocols to dynamically open up access through the PIX Firewall. Understanding these concepts is vital to successfully securing your network using a PIX Firewall. Test yourself with the "Do I Know This Already?" quiz and see how familiar you are configuring access restrictios on PIX Firewalls.

"Do I Know This Already?" Quiz

The purpose of the "Do I Know This Already?" quiz is to help you decide if you really need to read the entire chapter. If you already intend to read the entire chapter, you do not necessarily need to answer these questions now.

The ten-question quiz, derived from the major sections in the "Foundation Topics" portion of the chapter, helps you determine how to spend your limited study time.

Table 7-1 outlines the major topics discussed in this chapter and the "Do I Know This Already?" quiz questions that correspond to those topics.

Table 7-1 *"Do I Know This Already?" Foundation Topics Section-to-Question Mapping*

Foundation Topics Section	Questions Covered in This Section	Score
ACLs	1 to 3, 7, 8	
Using ACLs	6, 10	
Getting Started With Object Groups	4	
Configuring Object Groups	5	
Advanced Protocols	8, 9	

CAUTION   The goal of self assessment is to gauge your mastery of the topics in this chapter. If you do not know the answer to a question or are only partially sure of the answer, you should mark this question wrong for purposes of the self assessment. Giving yourself credit for an answer you correctly guess skews your self-assessment results and might provide you with a false sense of security.

1. Which of the following are constraints when configuring policy NAT?

   a. A global address *can* be used concurrently for NAT and PAT.

   b. An access list must be used *only twice* with the **nat** command.

   c. Access lists for policy NAT *cannot* contain deny statements.

   d. An access list must be used only once with the **nat** command.

2. What is the maximum number of access list entries in one access list that TurboACL supports?

   a. 19

   b. 2000

   c. 16,000

   d. 10

3. What is the minimum number of access list entries needed in an access list for TurboACL to compile?

   a. 4

   b. 19

   c. 16,000

   d. No minimum is required.

4. Which of the following is *not* one of four options for object types when you create an object group?

   a. Network

   b. Protocol

   c. Application

   d. Services

5. Which command lets you create a network object group?

   a. **object-group network** *group-id*

   b. **enable object-group network** *group-id*

   c. **create network object-group**

   d. **network object-group enable**

6. Which command enables TurboACL globally on the PIX Firewall?

   a. **turboacl global**

   b. **access-list compiled**

   c. **access-list turboacl**

   d. You cannot enable TurboACL globally.

7. What is the minimum memory requirement for TurboACL to work?

   a. 8 MB

   b. 100 KB

   c. 2.1 MB

   d. 4 MB

8. How many SMTP commands are made by the PIX application inspection function?

   a. 3

   b. 2

   c. 7

   d. 5

9. What will be the results if you disable FTP fixups?

    a. Nothing

    b. All inbound FTP is disabled.

    c. All outbound FTP is disabled.

    d. FTP traffic will be disabled in both directions.

10. Which of the following is the correct syntax for mapping an internal web server with an IP address of 10.10.10.15 to an outside IP address of 192.168.100.15 for HTTP traffic?

    a. static (inside, outside) 192.168.100.15 80 10.10.10.15 netmask 255.255.255.255 eq www

    b. static (inside, outside) 192.168.100.15 80 10.10.10.15 netmask 255.255.255.255

    c. static (inside, outside) tcp 192.168.100.15 80 10.10.10.15 www netmask 255.255.255.255

    d. static (inside, outside) 192.168.100.15 80 10.10.10.15 netmask 255.255.255.255

The answers to the "Do I Know This Already?" quiz are found in Appendix A, "Answers to the 'Do I Know This Already?' Quizzes and Q&A Sections." The suggested choices for your next step are as follows:

■ **8 or less overall score**—Read the entire chapter. This includes the "Foundation Topics," "Foundation Summary," and "Q&A" sections.

■ **9 or 10 overall score**—If you want more review on these topics, skip to the "Foundation Summary" section and then go to the "Q&A" section. Otherwise, move to the next chapter.

Foundation Topics

Configuring Inbound Access Through the PIX Firewall

A two-step approach lets connections initiated from lower-security interfaces access higher-security interfaces:

Step 1   Network Address Translation

Step 2   Access lists

Static Network Address Translation

Static Network Address Translation (NAT) creates a permanent, one-to-one mapping between an address on an internal network (a higher-security-level interface) and an external network (a lower-security-level interface) in all PIX versions. For an external host to initiate traffic to an inside host, a static translation rule needs to exist for the inside host. Without the persistent translation rule, the translation cannot occur.

> **NOTE**   Access from a lower security level to a higher security level can also be configured using a **nat 0 access-list** address rule.

> **NOTE**   Unlike NAT and Port Address Translation (PAT), static NAT requires a dedicated address on the outside network for each host, so it does not save registered Internet Protocol (IP) addresses.

The syntax for the **static** command is as follows:

```
static [(prenat-interface, postnat-interface)] {mapped-address ¦ interface}
   real-address [dns] [netmask mask] [max-conns [emb-limit]] [norandomseq]
```

Table 7-2 describes the **static** command parameters.

Table 7-2 static *Command Parameters*

Command Parameter	Description
prenat-interface	Usually the inside interface, in which case the translation is applied to the inside address.
postnat-interface	The outside interface when *prenat-interface* is the inside interface. However, if the outside interface is used for *prenat-interface*, the translation is applied to the outside address, and the *postnat-interface* is the inside interface.
mapped-address	The address into which *real-address* is translated.
interface	Specifies to overload the global address from **interface**.
real-address	The address to be mapped.
dns	Specifies that DNS replies that match the xlate are translated.
netmask	A reserved word that is required before you specify the network mask.
mask or *network-mask*	Pertains to both *global-ip* and *local-ip*. For host addresses, always use 255.255.255.255. For network addresses, use the appropriate class mask or subnet mask. For example, for Class A networks, use 255.0.0.0. A sample subnet mask is 255.255.255.224.
norandomseq	Does not randomize the TCP/IP packet's sequence number. Use this option only if another inline firewall is also randomizing sequence numbers and the result is scrambling the data. Using this option opens a security hole in the PIX Firewall.
max-conns	The maximum number of connections permitted through the static IP address at the same time.
emb-limit	The embryonic connection limit. An embryonic connection is one that has started but has not yet completed. Set this limit to prevent an attack by a flood of embryonic connections. The default is 0, which means unlimited connections.

The following example maps a server with an internal Internet Protocol (IP) address of 10.1.100.10 to the IP address 192.168.100.10:

```
PIXFIREWALL(conf)#static (inside, outside) 192.168.100.10 10.1.100.10 netmask
   255.255.255.255
```

The **static** command can also be used to translate an IP subnet:

```
PIXFIREWALL(conf)#static (inside, outside) 192.168.100.0 10.1.100.0 netmask
   255.255.255.0
```

The following syntax shows a server with an internal IP address of 10.1.100.10 translated to IP address 192.168.100.10.

```
PIXFIREWALL(conf)#static (inside, outside) 192.168.100.10 10.1.100.10 255.255.255.255
```

Static Port Address Translation

In PIX Version 6.0, the port redirection feature was added to allow outside users to connect to a particular IP address/port and have the PIX Firewall redirect the traffic to the appropriate inside server; the **static** command was modified. The shared address can be a unique address or a shared outbound PAT address, or it can be shared with the external interface. For example, static PAT lets you redirect inbound Transmission Control Protocol (TCP) and User Datagram Protocol (UDP) services. Using the **interface** option of the **static** command, you can use static PAT to permit external hosts to access TCP or UDP services residing on an internal host. (As always, though, an access list should also be in place to control access to the internal host.) The command to configure static PAT is as follows:

```
static [(internal-if-name, external-if-name)] {tcp ¦ udp}{global-ip ¦ interface}
    global-port local-ip local-port [netmask mask][max-conns [emb-limit
    [norandomseq]]]
```

Static PAT supports all applications that are supported by (regular) PAT, including the same application constraints. Like PAT, static PAT does not support H.323 or multimedia application traffic. The following example enables static port address translation (static PAT) for File Transfer Protocol (FTP) traffic:

```
static (inside, outside) tcp 192.168.1.14 ftp 10.1.2.8 ftp
```

The next example shows the following:

- The PIX redirects external users' Telnet requests to 192.168.1.24 to IP address 10.1.2.19.

- The PIX redirects external users' Hypertext Transfer Protocol (HTTP) port 8080 requests to 192.168.1.24 to PAT address 10.1.2.20 port 80.

```
static (inside,outside) tcp 192.168.1.24 telnet 10.1.2.19 telnet netmask
    255.255.255.255
static (inside,outside) tcp 192.168.1.24 8080 10.1.2.20 www netmask
    255.255.255.255
access-list 101 permit tcp any host 192.168.1.24 eq 8080
access-list 101 permit tcp any host 192.168.1.24 eq telnet
```

Notice that the outside IP address 192.168.1.24 is the same for both mappings, but the internal IP address is different. Also notice that external users directed to 192.168.1.24:8080 are sent as HTTP requests to 10.1.2.20, which is listening on port 80.

Transmission Control Protocol Intercept Feature

Before Version 5.3, the Cisco PIX Firewall offered no mechanism to protect systems that could be reached using a static and TCP conduit from TCP SYN attacks. When the embryonic connection limit was configured in a **static** command statement, the earlier PIX versions simply dropped new connection attempts as soon as the embryonic threshold was reached. A mild TCP SYN attack could potentially create service disruption to the server in question. For **static** command statements without an embryonic connection limit, PIX

Firewall passes all traffic. If the affected system does not have TCP SYN attack protection (most operating systems do not offer sufficient protection), the affected system's embryonic connection table overloads, and all traffic stops.

With the TCP intercept feature, as soon as the optional embryonic connection limit is reached, and until the embryonic connection count falls below this threshold, every SYN bound for the affected server is intercepted. For each SYN, the PIX Firewall responds on behalf of the server with an empty SYN/ACK segment. The PIX Firewall retains pertinent state information, drops the packet, and waits for the client's acknowledgment. If the ACK is received, a copy of the client's SYN segment is sent to the server, and a TCP three-way handshake is performed between the PIX Firewall and the server. If this three-way handshake completes, the connection resumes as normal. If the client does not respond during any part of the connection phase, PIX Firewall retransmits the necessary segment.

This feature requires no change to the Cisco PIX Firewall command set but demonstrates that the embryonic connection limit on the **static** command now has a new behavior.

nat 0 Command

As mentioned earlier in the text, one can configure access to higher-security subnets by using the **nat** 0 command. For instance, if you have a host with a public address on the inside network and the outside network needs access to this host, you can use **nat** 0, which disables address translation so that inside IP addresses are visible to the outside. The following short example demonstrates the use of the **nat** 0 command:

```
nat (inside) 0 192.168.1.10 255.255.255.255
```

This can also be configured as follows:

```
access-list 121 permit 192.168.1.10 255.255.255.255 any
nat (inside) 0 access-list 121
```

Policy Network Address Translation

Policy NAT provides additional capabilities in configuring address translation. The Policy NAT feature lets you identify local traffic for address translation by specifying the source and destination addresses (or ports), whereas regular NAT uses only ports/source addresses. In other words, the same local traffic for address translation can have multiple "global" translations depending on the destination IP address or port. This is aptly demonstrated in Figure 7-1.

Figure 7-1 *Identifying Multiple External Addresses Using Policy NAT*

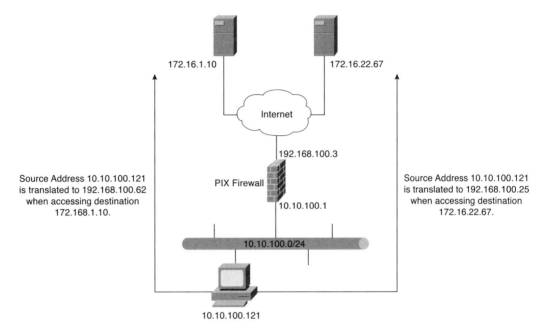

The translation configuration for Figure 7-1 is as follows:

```
pixfw(config)#access-list 120 permit ip 10.10.100.0
    255.255.255.0 172.16.1.10 255.255.255.255

pixfw(config)#access-list 130 permit ip 10.10.100.0
    255.255.255.0 172.16.22.67 255.255.255.255
pixfw(config)#nat (inside) 1 access-list 120
pixfw(config)#global (outside) 1 192.168.100.62 255.255.255.255
pixfw(config)#nat (inside) 2 access-list 130
pixfw(config)#global (outside) 2 192.168.100.25 255.255.255.255
```

There are constraints of which you have to be aware when configuring Policy NAT:

■ A global address cannot be used concurrently for NAT and PAT.

■ Access lists for policy NAT cannot contain deny statements. Access lists must contain only permit statements.

■ Use an access list between the **nat** and **static** commands.

■ **static** commands are matched and executed before **nat** commands.

NOTE   Policy NAT does not support SQL*Net, which is supported by regular NAT.

Access Lists

An access list typically consists of multiple access control entries (ACEs) organized internally by PIX Firewall as a linked list. When a packet is subjected to access list control, the Cisco PIX Firewall searches this linked list linearly to find a matching element. The matching element is then examined to determine if the packet is to be transmitted or dropped. By default, all **access-list** commands have an implicit deny unless you explicitly specify permit. In other words, by default, all access in an access list is denied unless you explicitly grant access using a permit statement.

The general syntax of the **access-list** command is as follows:

```
access-list id [line line-num] deny¦permit {protocol ¦
object-group prot-obj-grp-id} {source-addr source-mask} ¦
object-group netw-grp-grp-id [operator port [port] ¦ interface if-name
¦ object-group service-obj-grp-id ]
{destination-addr destination-mask} ¦ object-group new-obj-grp-id ¦
[operator port [port] ¦ object-group service-obj-grp-id]}
[log [disable¦default] ¦ [level]]
```

Table 7-3 describes the parameters for the **access-list** command.

Table 7-3   access-list *Command Parameters*

Parameter	Description
id	Name of an access list. You can use either a name or number.
line-num	The line number at which to insert a remark or an ACE.
deny	The **deny** option does not allow a packet to traverse the PIX Firewall.
permit	The **permit** option selects a packet to traverse the PIX Firewall.
protocol	Name or number of an IP protocol. It can be one of the keywords **icmp, ip, tcp,** or **udp,** or an integer in the range of 1 to 254 representing an IP protocol number. To match any Internet protocol, including ICMP, TCP, and UDP, use the keyword **ip.**
object-group	Specifies an object group.
source-addr	Address of the network or host from which the packet is being sent.
source-mask	Netmask bits (mask) to be applied to *source-addr*, if the source address is for a network mask.
port	Specifies services to which you permit or deny access. Specify services by the port that handles it, such as **smtp** for port 25, **www** for port 80, and so on. You can specify ports by either a literal name or a number in the range of 0 to 65,535.

Table 7-3   access-list *Command Parameters (Continued)*

Parameter	Description
interface *if-name*	The name of the firewall interface.
obj-grp-id	An existing object group.
destination-addr	IP address of the network or host to which the packet is being sent.
destination-mask	Netmask bits (mask) to be applied to *destination-addr* , if the destination address is a network mask.
**log disable	default |** *level*	When the **log** option is specified, it generates syslog message 106100 for the ACE to which it is applied. An optional syslog *level* (0–7) may be specified for the generated syslog messages (106100). If no *level* is specified, the default level is 6 (informational) for a new ACE. If the **log disable** option is specified, access list logging is completely disabled. No syslog message, including message 106023, will be generated.
interval *secs*	The time interval in seconds, from 1 to 600, at which to generate an 106100 syslog message. The default interval is 300 seconds for a new ACE.

The **access-list** command creates the rule you want. The created rule is applied by using the **access-group** command to the desired PIX interface. It is also important to note that unlike Cisco IOS software access lists, which use wildcards (that is, 0.0.0.255 for a Class C address) to identify their network masks, PIX software uses a regular subnet mask (that is, 255.255.255.0 for a Class C address) when defining the network mask.

> **NOTE**   Specify only one **access-group** command for each interface. PIX Firewall allows you to configure only one access group per interface.

The syntax for the **access-group** command is as follows:

```
access-group id in interface interface-name
```

The *id* is the same identifier that was specified in the **access-list** command. The *interface-name* parameter is the name of the interface.

Example 7-1 illustrates the use of the **static** and **access-list** commands to permit connections from lower-security interfaces to higher-security interfaces on the PIX Firewall.

Example 7-1 *Permitting Connections from Lower-Security Interfaces to Higher-Security Interfaces on the PIX Firewall*

```
pixfirewall(config)# static (inside, outside) 192.168.1.10 10.1.100.10
  netmask 255.255.255.255
pixfirewall(config)# access-list acl-out permit tcp any host 192.168.1.10 eq www
pixfirewall(config)# access-group acl-out in interface outside
```

The **static** command statically translates 10.1.100.10 to 192.168.1.10. The **access-list** command permits HTTP access only to host 10.1.100.10 (translated into 192.168.1.10). The **access-group** command applies the access list acl-out to the outside interface.

To view the created access list, use the **show access-list** *id* command, where *id* is the access list name or number.

Access lists also can be used to control outbound access on the PIX Firewall. An outbound access list restricts users from starting connections from a trusted network to a less trusted network; for example, users from an inside interface accessing hosts or networks on the outside interface. By default, outbound access is permitted, so you use the **deny** action to restrict access when using an outbound access list.

For example, if you want to restrict users on the inside interface from accessing a website at address 172.16.68.20 on the outside interface, you would use the commands shown in Example 7-2.

Example 7-2 *Restricting Inside Users' Access to an External Web Server on Port 80*

```
pixfirewall(config)# access-list acl-in deny tcp any host 172.16.68.20 eq www
pixfirewall(config)# access-list acl-in permit ip any any
pixfirewall(config)# access-group acl-in in interface inside
```

This access list configuration lets any user start World Wide Web (WWW) connections to any destination, with the exception of 172.16.68.20.

> **NOTE** Access lists are implemented by using the **access-list** and **access-group** commands. These commands are used instead of the **conduit** and **outbound** commands, which were used in earlier versions of PIX Firewall software. Pix Firewall software Version 6.3 does support the **conduit** and **outbound** commands. To convert PIX the configuration file that contains **conduit** and **outbound** commands to a supported configuration file that contains the equivalent **access-list** commands, Cisco Systems has created a tool. This tool can be found at http://www.cisco.com/cgi-bin/tablebuild.pl/pix (the link requires a cisco.com account).

Organizing and Managing Access Control Entries

It is quite common to have several access lists with several access-list elements in them on a PIX Firewall. To deal with this sometimes becomes arduous, especially in the following situations:

- When attempting to identify the reason for each ACE in the access list because no descriptions or comments are included for software releases earlier than Version 6.3

- When removing a single ACE from an access list at the command line on software earlier than Version 6.3, which becomes a several-step process

Configuring a remark or comment allows you and other administrators to understand and identify access-list entries. PIX Firewall Version 6.3 and later lets you include comments about entries in any access control list (ACL). A remark can be up to 100 characters and can precede or follow an **access-list** command. The following is the syntax for configuring an access-list remark:

access-list *acl-id* **remark** *text*

The ACL remark can be placed before or after an **access-list** command statement, but it should be placed in a consistent position so that it is clear which remark describes which **access-list** command. For example, it would be confusing to have some remarks before the associated **access-list** commands and some remarks after the associated **access-list** commands. Example 7-3 shows a sample configuration on how to create comments for ACEs.

Example 7-3 *Configuring Comments for ACEs*

```
Pixfw(config)#access-list 115 remark Allow network engineering group to telnet
PixfW(config)#access-list 115 permit tcp 192.168.1.0 255.255.255.224 host
   10.10.100.20 telnet
PixfW(config)#access-list 115 remark Allowsales group to login
PixfW(config)#access-list 115 permit tcp 192.168.3.0 255.255.255.224 host
   10.10.100.12
```

In addition to adding remarks to access lists, Version 6.3 and later add numbering to access-list elements. Each ACE and remark has an associated line number. Line numbers can then be used to insert or delete elements at any position in an access list. These numbers are maintained internally in increasing order starting from 1. The line numbers are always maintained in increasing order, with an individual line number for each ACE.

> **NOTE** All ACEs resulting from a single object group **access-list** command statement have a single line number. Consequently, you cannot insert an ACE in the middle of object-group ACEs.

The **show access-list** command displays the line numbers. The line numbers, however, are not shown in the configuration. Example 7-4 shows a sample output from a **show access-list** command.

Example 7-4 *Sample Output from the* **show access-list** *Command*

```
pixfw(config)#show access-list 115
access-list 115 ; 4 elements
access-list 115 line 1 remark-Allow network engineering group
    to telnet (hitcnt=0)
access-list 115 line 2 permit tcp 192.168.1.0 255.255.255.224 host 10.10.100.20
   telnet (hitcnt=0)
access-list 115 line 3 remark-Allow sales group to login (hitcnt=0)
access-list 115 line 4 permit tcp 192.168.3.0 255.255.255.224 host
    10.10.100.12 (hitcnt=0)
```

To remove remarks from an access list, simply use the following command:

> `no access-list` *id* `line` *line-num* `remark` *text*

or

> `no access-list` *id* `line` *line-num*

Both remove the remark at the specified line number.

TurboACL

TurboACL is a feature introduced with Cisco PIX Firewall Version 6.2 that improves the average search time for ACLs containing a large number of entries. The search time for long ACLs is improved because this feature causes the PIX Firewall to compile tables for ACLs.

The TurboACL feature can be enabled globally on the entire PIX Firewall and then disabled for specific ACLs. It also can be enabled only for specific ACLs. Search performance improvement is realized in ACLs that have more than 19 ACEs. For ACLs that contain few ACEs, TurboACL does not improve performance. The TurboACL feature is applied only to ACLs with 19 or more entries. The implementation of TurboACL in PIX Firewall Version 6.2 supports access lists with up to 16,000 ACEs.

The minimum memory required for TurboACL is 2.1 megabytes (MB). Approximately 1 MB of memory is required for every 2000 ACE elements. High-end PIX Firewall models, such as the PIX 525 and PIX 535, are the most appropriate for memory-demanding TurboACL.

> **NOTE** Because some models of Cisco PIX Firewall, such as the PIX 501, have limited memory, implementing the TurboACL feature might cause problems, such as not being able to load Cisco PIX Device Manager (PDM).

Configuring Individual TurboACL

The individual TurboACL command can be used to enable Turbo configuration for individual ACLs when TurboACL is not globally enabled. The syntax of this command is as follows:

```
[no] access-list acl-name compiled
```

This command is used to enable or disable TurboACL on a specific ACL individually. The *acl-name* parameter in the command must specify an existing ACL. This command causes the TurboACL process to mark the ACL specified by *acl-name* as Turbo-configured and Turbo-compiles the ACL if the ACL has 19 or more ACEs and has not yet been Turbo-compiled.

If you enter the **no** form of this command, the TurboACL process deletes the TurboACL structures associated with the ACL and marks the ACL as non-Turbo.

Globally Configuring TurboACL

The syntax for enabling TurboACL for the entire PIX Firewall is as follows:

```
[no] access-list compiled
```

This configures TurboACL on all ACLs having 19 or more entries. This command causes the TurboACL process to scan all existing ACLs. During the scan, TurboACL marks and Turbo-compiles any ACL that has 19 or more ACEs and that has not yet been Turbo-compiled.

The command **no access-list compiled**, which is the default, causes the TurboACL process to scan all compiled ACLs and mark every one as non-Turbo. It also deletes all existing TurboACL structures.

Object Grouping

Another feature that is incorporated into the PIX Firewall Version 6.2 software is object grouping, which allows you to group objects such as hosts (servers and clients), services, and networks and apply security policies and rules to the group. Object grouping lets you apply access rules to logical groups of objects. When you apply an access list to an object group, the command affects all objects defined in the group. Object grouping provides a way to reduce the number of access rules required to describe complex security policies. This in turn reduces the time spent configuring and troubleshooting access rules in large or complex networks.

The syntax for creating object groups is as follows:

```
[no] object-group object-type grp-id
```

Use the first parameter, *object-type,* to identify the type of object group you want to configure. There are four options:

- network
- protocol
- service
- icmp-type

Replace *grp-id* with a descriptive name for the group.

network Object Type

The **network** object type is used to group hosts and subnets. Server and client hosts can be grouped by functions. For example, mail servers, web servers, or a group of client hosts that have special privileges on the network can be grouped accordingly.

Example 7-5 shows a web servers object group.

Example 7-5   *Configuring an Object Group*

```
pixfirewall(config)#object-group network web-servers
pixfirewall(config-network)#description Public web servers
pixfirewall(config-network)#network-object host 192.168.1.12
pixfirewall(config-network)#network-object host 192.168.1.14
pixfirewall(config-network)# exit
pixfirewall(config)#access-list 102 permit tcp any object-group web-servers eq www
pixfirewall(config)#access-group 102 in interface outside
```

Notice that when you enter the **object-group** command, the system enters the appropriate subcommand mode for the type of object you are configuring. In this case, you see the config-network subcommand prompt. The **network-object host** subcommand adds the host to the network object group. The description is optional, but it is helpful to include it.

> **NOTE** It is also possible to use a name instead of an IP address when defining the network host. For example:
>
> ```
> pixfw(config)# object-group network mis-ftp-servers
> pixfw(config-network)#network-object host 10.10.100.154
> pixfw(config-network)#network-object host 10.10.100.155
> pixfw(config-network)#network-object host 10.10.100.156
> pixfw(config-network)#exit
> ```

To display the configured object group, use the **show object-group** command, as shown in Example 7-6.

Example 7-6 *Displaying Configured Object Groups*

```
pix(config)# show object-group
object-group network web-servers
  description: Public web servers
  network-object host 192.168.1.12
  network-object host 192.168.1.14
```

protocol Object Type

The **protocol** object type identifies a group of IP protocols using keywords such as **icmp, tcp, udp,** or an integer in the range of 1 to 254 representing an IP protocol number. The syntax for the command is **object-group protocol** *grp-id*. To add a single protocol to the current protocol object group, use the **protocol-object** *protocol* command. Example 7-7 shows how to use object-group protocol subcommand mode to create a new protocol object group.

Example 7-7 *Creating a New Protocol Object Group*

```
pixfw(config)#object-group protocol grp-citrix
pixfw(config-protocol)#protocol-object tcp
pixfw(config-protocol)#protocol-object 1494
pixfw(config-protocol)#exit
```

service Object Type

The **service** object type identifies port numbers that can be grouped. This is particularly useful when you are managing an application. The syntax for **service** *object-type* is

      [no] **object-group** *service obj-grp-id* **tcp ¦ udp ¦ tcp-udp**

As soon as you are in the **service** subcommand, the command **port-object eq service** adds a single TCP or UDP port number to the service object group. The **port-object range** *begin-service end-service* command adds a range of TCP or UDP port numbers to the service object group. Example 7-8 shows how to use object-group service subcommand mode to create a new port (service) object group.

Example 7-8   *Creating a New Port (Service) Object Group*

```
pixfw(config)#object-group service mis-service tcp
pixfw(config-service)#port-object eq ftp
pixfw(config-service)#port-object range 5200 6000
pixfw(config-service)#exit
```

icmp-type Object Type

Internet Control Message Protocol (ICMP) object groups can be created to group certain types of ICMP messages. For example, ICMP messages of ECHO-REQUEST, ECHO-REPLY, and DESTINATION-UNREACHABLE with numerical type values of 8, 0, and 3, respectively, can be grouped as shown in Example 7-9.

Example 7-9   *Grouping ICMP Messages*

```
pix(config)# object-group icmp-type icmp-test
pix(config-icmp-type)# icmp-object 0
pix(config-icmp-type)# icmp-object 3
pix(config-icmp-type)# icmp-object 8
```

Nesting Object Groups

You can add an object group within an object group. The **object-group** command allows logical grouping of the same type of objects and construction of hierarchical object groups for structured configuration. To nest an object group within another object group, use the **group-object** command. Example 7-10 illustrates the use of nested object groups.

Example 7-10   *Configuring Nested Object Groups*

```
pixfirewall(config)# object-group network web-servers
pixfirewall(config-network)# description web servers
pixfirewall(config-network)# network-object host 192.168.1.12
pixfirewall(config-network)# network-object host 192.168.1.14
pixfirewall(config-network)# exit

pixfirewall(config)# object-group network Public-servers
pixfirewall(config-network)# description Public servers
pixfirewall(config-network)# network-object host 192.168.1.18
pixfirewall(config-network)# group-object web-servers
pixfirewall(config-network)# exit
```

Access Control List Logging

The ACL logging feature is part of PIX Firewall Version 6.3 that lets you log the number of permits or denies of a flow during a specific period of time. A flow is defined by protocol, source IP address, source port, destination IP address, and destination port. When a flow is permitted or denied, the system checks to see if the flow already exists in the system. If not, an initial syslog message with a hit count of 1 for the flow is generated. The flow entry is then created and the hit count for the flow is incremented every time the flow is permitted or denied. The command syntax to enable logging of the number of permits or denies of a flow by an ACL entry is as follows:

```
access-list acl-id [log [disable¦default] ¦ [level] [interval seconds]]
```

For an existing flow, a syslog message is generated at the end of each configurable interval to report the nonzero hit count for the flow in the current interval. After the syslog message is generated, the hit count for the flow is reset to 0 for the next interval. If there is no hit recorded during the interval, the flow is deleted and no syslog message is generated. Large numbers of flows may concurrently exist at any point in time. To prevent unlimited consumption of memory and central processing unit (CPU) resources, a limit is placed on the number of concurrent deny flows. When the limit is reached, no new deny flow will be created until the existing deny flows expire. To specify the maximum number of concurrent deny flows that can be created, enter the following command:

```
access-list deny-flow-max num-of-flows
```

The deny-flow-max keyword specifies the maximum number of concurrent deny flows that can be created. New values for this option go into effect immediately. The default is set for the maximum number of flows allowed, which depends on the amount of memory available on the PIX Firewall, as follows:

64 MB or greater—Maximum value/default value is 4096.

16 MB or greater—Maximum value/default value is 1024.

Less than 16 MB—Maximum value/default value is 256.

When the maximum number of flows has been reached, a syslog message (106101) is generated. By default, this message is repeated once every 300 seconds.

The syslog message generated for the ACL entry has the following format:

```
106101: access-list <acl-id> <grant> <prot> <intf/src-ip(src-port)> ->
    <intf/dst-ip(dest-port)> hit-cnt <nnn> (first hit¦n-second interval)
```

Table 7-4   *syslog Format Description*

Field	Description
<grant>	Displays whether the flow is permitted or denied.
<prot>	Displays the protocol type: tcp, udp, icmp, or an IP protocol number.

continues

Table 7-4 *syslog Format Description (Continued)*

Field	Description
<intf>	Displays the interface name (as configured by the **nameif** command) for the source or destination of the logged flow. This can include logical (virtual LAN) interfaces.
<src-ip>	Displays the source IP address of the logged flow.
<dst-ip>	Displays the destination IP address of the logged flow.
<src-port>	Displays the source port of the logged flow (TCP or UDP). For ICMP, this field is 0.
<dst-port>	Displays the destination port of the logged flow (TCP or UDP). For ICMP, this field is icmp-type.
<nnn>	Displays the number of times this flow was permitted or denied by the ACL entry in the configured time interval. The value is 1 when the first syslog message is generated for the flow.
first hit	Displays the first message generated for this flow.
n-second interval	Displays the interval over which the hit count is accumulated.

Using the fixup Command

The ports that are specified by the **fixup** command are the services that the PIX Firewall listens for. The **fixup** command can be used to change the default port assignments or to enable or disable application inspection for the following protocols and applications:

- FTP
- H.323
- HTTP
- Internet Locator Service (ILS)
- Remote Shell (RSH)
- Real-Time Streaming Protocol (RTSP)
- Session Initiation Protocol (SIP)
- Skinny (or Simple) Client Control Protocol (SCCP)
- Simple Mail Transfer Protocol (SMTP)
- SQL*Net
- Domain Name System (DNS)
- Trivial File Transfer Protocol (TFTP)
- Computer Telephony Integration Quick Buffer Encoding (CTIQBE)

The basic syntax for the **fixup** command is as follows:

```
[no] fixup protocol [protocol] [port]
```

To change the default port assignment, identify the protocol and the new port number to assign. Use the **no fixup protocol** command to reset the application inspection entries to the default configuration. The **clear fixup** command removes **fixup** commands from the configuration you added. However, it does not remove the default **fixup protocol** commands.

The following example shows how to define multiple ports for HTTP by entering separate commands:

```
fixup protocol http 8080
fixup protocol http 8888
```

These commands do not change the standard HTTP port assignment (80). After you enter these commands, the PIX Firewall listens for HTTP traffic on ports 80, 8080, and 8888. You can view the explicit (configurable) **fixup protocol** settings by using the **show fixup** command, as shown in Example 7-11.

Example 7-11 *Displaying Configurable* fixup protocol *Settings*

```
Pixfirewall# show fixup
fixup protocol dns maximum-length 512
fixup protocol ftp 21
fixup protocol h323 h225 1720
fixup protocol h323 ras 1718-1719
fixup protocol http 80
fixup protocol ils 389
fixup protocol rsh 514
fixup protocol rtsp 554
fixup protocol sip 5060
fixup protocol sip udp 5060
fixup protocol skinny 2000
fixup protocol smtp 25
fixup protocol sqlnet 1521
```

Advanced Protocol Handling

Some applications require special handling by the Cisco PIX Firewall application inspection function. These types of applications typically embed IP addressing information in the user data packet or open secondary channels on dynamically assigned ports. The application inspection function works with NAT to help identify the location of embedded addressing information.

In addition to identifying embedded addressing information, the application inspection function monitors sessions to determine the port numbers for secondary channels. Many protocols open secondary TCP or UDP ports to improve performance. The initial session on a well-known port is used to negotiate dynamically assigned port numbers. The application inspection function monitors these sessions, identifies the dynamic port assignments, and permits data exchange on these ports for the duration of the specific session. Multimedia applications and FTP applications exhibit this kind of behavior.

File Transfer Protocol

The FTP application inspection inspects FTP sessions and performs four tasks:

- Prepares a dynamic secondary data connection
- Tracks the **ftp** command-response sequence
- Generates an audit trail
- Translates the embedded IP address using NAT

FTP application inspection prepares secondary channels for FTP data transfer. The channels are allocated in response to a file upload, a file download, or a directory listing event, and they must be prenegotiated. The port is negotiated through the PORT or PASV (227) commands.

You can use the **fixup** command to change the default port assignment for FTP. The command syntax is as follows:

```
[no] fixup protocol ftp [strict] [port]
```

The **port** option lets you configure the port at which the PIX Firewall listens for FTP traffic.

The **strict** option prevents web browsers from sending embedded commands in FTP requests. Each **ftp** command must be acknowledged before a new command is allowed. Connections sending embedded commands are dropped. The **strict** option lets only the server generate the PASV reply command (227) and lets only the client generate the PORT command. The PASV reply and PORT commands are checked to ensure that they do not appear in an error string.

If you disable FTP fixups with the **no fixup protocol ftp** command, outbound users can start connections only in passive mode, and all inbound FTP is disabled.

Domain Name System

DNS uses a UDP connection. This makes DNS queries subject to generic UDP handling based on activity timeouts. DNS, therefore, requires application inspection. As soon as the first response is received for a DNS query, the UDP connection is terminated. This is known as DNS guard and is discussed further in Chapter 18, "Attack Guards and Advanced Protocol Handling." The DNS inspection task includes the following:

- Compares the ID of the DNS reply to the ID of the DNS query.

- Translates the DNS A record.

- Confirms the length of the DNS packet is less than the maximum length specified by the user. Otherwise, the packet is dropped.

Simple Mail Transfer Protocol

SMTP packets are closely monitored. An SMTP server responds to client requests with numeric reply codes and optional human-readable strings. SMTP application inspection controls and restricts the commands that the user can use as well as the messages that the server returns. SMTP inspection performs three primary tasks:

- Monitors the SMTP command-response sequence.

- Permits only 7 of the 14 SMTP commands (HELO, MAIL, RCPT, DATA, RSET, NOOP, and QUIT).

- Generates an audit trail. Audit record 108002 is generated when an invalid character embedded in the mail address is replaced.

Multimedia Support

PIX Firewall supports several popular multimedia applications. Its application inspection function dynamically opens and closes UDP ports for secure multimedia connections. Supported multimedia applications include the following:

- Microsoft Netshow

- Microsoft Netmeeting

- Intel Internet Video Phone

- VDOnet VDOLive

- RealNetworks RealAudio and RealVideo

- VocalTech

- White Pine Meeting Point

- White Pine CuSeeMe

- Xing StreamWorks

- VXtreme WebTheatre

Foundation Summary

The "Foundation Summary" provides a convenient review of many key concepts in this chapter. If you are already comfortable with the topics in this chapter, this summary can help you recall a few details. If you just read this chapter, this review should help solidify some key facts. If you are doing your final preparation before the exam, this summary provides a convenient way to review the day before the exam.

Rules or translations have to be put in place to allow data traffic to and from hosts in a network. Rules are usually made up of a static **nat** command and access list. The static **nat** command identifies the subnet or host to which connections will be permitted to go. Access lists are then configured to identify and permit the type of traffic to the subnet or host identified by the **static** command.

TurboACL is a feature introduced with Cisco PIX Firewall Version 6.2 that improves the average search time for ACLs containing a large number of entries. TurboACL feature is applied only to access lists with a minimum of 19 ACEs to a maximum of 16,000 ACEs.

The object grouping feature enables you to group objects such as hosts (servers and clients), services, and networks and apply security policies and rules to the group. The four types of object groups are these:

- network
- protocol
- service
- icmp-type

PIX Firewall supports several popular multimedia applications. Its application inspection function dynamically opens and closes UDP ports for secure multimedia connections. Popular multimedia applications such as RealPlayer and Microsoft NetMeeting are supported by Cisco PIX Firewall.

Q&A

As mentioned in the Introduction, the questions in this book are more difficult than what you should experience on the exam. The questions are designed to ensure your understanding of the concepts discussed in this chapter and adequately prepare you to complete the exam. You should use the simulated exams on the CD to practice for the exam.

The answers to these questions can be found in Appendix A.

1. What do static NAT settings do?

2. What is the difference between regular network address translation and policy-based network translation?

3. Which command would you use to create the description/remark "Linda's group extranet server access" for access list 112?

4. About how many ACEs in one access list does TurboACL support?

5. How would you change the default port assignment for FTP?

6. What is the minimum memory required to run TurboACL?

7. What is the command to enable TurboACL globally on the PIX Firewall?

8. What is the minimum number of ACEs needed for TurboACL to compile?

9. What is the function of object groups?

10. What are the four object type options available when you are creating object groups?

This chapter covers the following subjects:

- Understanding How Syslog Works

- Configuring Syslog on the Cisco PIX Firewall

- Configuring the PIX Device Manager to View Logging

CHAPTER 8

Syslog and the PIX

System logging, otherwise known as *syslog*, on the Cisco PIX Firewall makes it possible for you as an administrator to gather information about the PIX unit's traffic and performance. You can use syslog messages generated by the PIX to troubleshoot and analyze suspicious activity on the network.

This chapter describes how to configure syslog on the Cisco PIX Firewall and interpret the messages it generates.

How to Best Use This Chapter

Monitoring and logging the traffic on your network is an important step in monitoring the health of your network and identifying attacks against your network. Syslog messages provide valuable information concerning the health of your PIX Firewall. These messages can also indicate attacks that are being launched against your network. Understanding the meaning and severity of various Syslog messages is the first step toward using these messages to actively monitor the operation of your network. Test yourself with the "Do I Know This Already?" quiz and see how familiar you are with the Syslog functionality available on PIX Firewalls.

"Do I Know This Already?" Quiz

The purpose of the "Do I Know This Already?" quiz is to help you decide if you really need to read the entire chapter. If you already intend to read the entire chapter, you do not necessarily need to answer these questions now.

The nine-question quiz, derived from the major sections in the "Foundation Topics" portion of the chapter, helps you determine how to spend your limited study time.

Table 8-1 outlines the major topics discussed in this chapter and the "Do I Know This Already?" quiz questions that correspond to those topics.

Table 8-1 *"Do I Know This Already?" Foundation Topics Section-to-Question Mapping*

Foundation Topics Section	Questions Covered in This Section	Score
How Syslog Works	2 to 5, 7, 8	
Configuring Syslog on the Cisco PIX Firewall	6	
Configuring the PIX Device Manager to View Logging	1, 9	

> **CAUTION** The goal of self assessment is to gauge your mastery of the topics in this chapter. If you do not know the answer to a question or are only partially sure of the answer, you should mark this question wrong for purposes of the self assessment. Giving yourself credit for an answer you correctly guess skews your self-assessment results and might provide you with a false sense of security.

1. What is the command for sending syslog messages to the Telnet session?

   a. logging console

   b. logging monitor

   c. telnet logging

   d. send log telnet

2. Which of the following is the correct command syntax to set the logging level to 5 for syslog message 403503?

   a. logging message 403503 level 5

   b. logging 403503 5

   c. logging message 403503 5

   d. logging 403503 level 5

3. The PIX Firewall can be configured to send syslog messages to all of the following except which one?

   a. Console

   b. Telnet session

   c. Serial port

   d. Syslog server

4. Which of the following is *not* an example of a severity level for syslog configuration?

    a. Emergency

    b. Alert

    c. Prepare

    d. Warning

5. What is syslogd?

    a. A message type that forms the syslog services

    b. A service that runs on UNIX machines

    c. A hardware subcomponent that is required for syslog configuration on the PIX

    d. Cisco application software

6. Which port does syslogd use by default?

    a. UDP 512

    b. TCP 514

    c. TCP 512

    d. UDP 514

7. Which of the following logging severity levels are matched up correctly?

    a. Error → 4

    b. Alert → 2

    c. Warning → 4

    d. Notification → 1

8. Which of the following is the highest-importance logging level?

    a. 9

    b. 7

    c. 0

    d. 3

9. By using which command could you view the logging setting from the command line?

    a. show log setting

    b. show logging

    c. show syslog

    d. view log

The answers to the "Do I Know This Already?" quiz are found in Appendix A, "Answers to the 'Do I Know This Already?' Quizzes and Q&A Sections." The suggested choices for your next step are as follows:

- **7 or less overall score**—Read the entire chapter. This includes the "Foundation Topics," "Foundation Summary," and "Q&A" sections.

- **8 or 9 overall score**—If you want more review of these topics, skip to the "Foundation Summary" section and then go to the "Q&A" section. Otherwise, move to the next chapter.

Foundation Topics

How Syslog Works

The syslog message facility in the Cisco PIX Firewall is a useful means to view troubleshooting messages and to watch for network events such as attacks and denials of service. The Cisco PIX Firewall reports on events and activities using syslog messages, which report on the following:

- **System status**—When the Cisco PIX Firewall reboots or a connection by Telnet or the console is made or disconnected
- **Accounting**—The number of bytes transferred per connection
- **Security**—Dropped User Datagram Protocol (UDP) packets and denied Transmission Control Protocol (TCP) connections
- **Resources**—Notification of connection and translation slot depletion

It is important to become familiar with the logging process and logging command parameters on the PIX before you dive in and start configuring the PIX for logging. Syslog messages can be sent to several different output destinations on or off the PIX unit:

- **PDM logging**—Logging messages can be sent to the PIX Device Manager (PDM).
- **Console**—Syslog messages can be configured to be sent to the console interface, where the PIX administrator (you) can view the messages in real time as they happen when you are connected to the console interface.
- **Internal memory buffer**—Syslog messages can be sent to the buffer.
- **Telnet console**—Syslog messages also can be configured to be sent to Telnet sessions. This configuration helps you remotely administer and troubleshoot PIX units without being physically present at the location of the firewall.
- **Syslog servers**—This type of configuration is particularly useful for storing syslog messages for analysis on performance, trends, and packet activities on the PIX unit. Syslog messages are sent to UNIX servers/workstations running a syslog daemon or to Windows servers running PIX Firewall Syslog Server (PFSS).
- **SNMP management station**—Syslog traps can be configured to be sent to an SNMP management station.

After you decide where to send the syslog messages, you have to decide what type of messages you want to see at the output destination.

All syslog messages have a severity level; however, not all syslog messages are required to have a facility.

Logging Facilities

When syslog messages are sent to a server, it is important to indicate through which *pipe* the PIX will send the messages. The single syslog service, syslogd, can be thought of as having multiple pipes. It uses the pipes to decide where to send incoming information based on the pipe through which the information arrives. Syslogd is a daemon/service that runs on UNIX machines. In this analogy, the *logging facilities* are the pipes by which syslogd decides *where* to send information it receives—that is, to which file to write.

Eight logging facilities (16 through 23) are commonly used for syslog on the PIX. On the syslog server, the facility numbers have a corresponding identification—local0 to local7. The following are the facility numbers and their corresponding syslog identification:

- local0 (16)
- local1 (17)
- local2 (18)
- local3 (19)
- local4 (20)
- local5 (21)
- local6 (22)
- local7 (23)

The default facility is local4 (20). To change the default logging facility on the PIX you use the **logging facility** *facility* command. The following command shows the logging facility changed to 21:

```
Pix(config)# logging facility 21
```

Logging Levels

Different *severity levels* are attached to incoming messages. You can think of these levels as indicating the type of message. The PIX can be configured to send messages at different levels. Table 8-2 lists these levels from highest to lowest importance.

Table 8-2 *Logging Severity Levels*

Level/Keyword	Numeric Code	System Condition
Emergency	0	System unusable message
Alert	1	Take immediate action
Critical	2	Critical condition
Error	3	Error message
Warning	4	Warning message
Notification	5	Normal but significant condition
Informational	6	Information message
Debug	7	Debug message, log FTP commands, and WWW URLs

Many of the **logging** commands require that you specify a severity level threshold to indicate which syslog messages can be sent to the output locations. The lower the level number, the more severe the syslog message. The default severity level is 3 (error). During configuration, you can specify the severity level as either a number or a keyword, as described in Table 8-2. The level you specify causes the Cisco PIX Firewall to send the messages of that level and below to the output location. For example, if you specify severity level 3 (error), the PIX sends severity level 0 (emergency), 1 (alert), 2 (critical), and 3 (error) messages to the output location.

Changing Syslog Message Levels

PIX Firewall Version 6.3 gives you the option to modify the level at which a specific syslog message is issued and to disable specific syslog messages. Previous versions of PIX Firewall let you specify only the message level or disable all messages to a specific syslog server. This new feature provides you with more flexibility because you can specify which message you are logging and at what level. To change the logging level for all syslog servers, enter the following command syntax:

```
logging message syslog_id [level levelid]
```

To change the level of a specific syslog message, enter the following command syntax:

```
logging message syslog_id level levelid
```

The variables *syslogid* and *levelid* represent the numeric identifier and severity level assigned to the syslog message, respectively, as shown in Table 8-2.

Example 8-1 shows how you can view the level of a syslog message and display its current and default levels:

Example 8-1   *Changing the Level of a Syslog Message*

```
pixfirewall(config)#n
syslog 403503: default-level errors (enabled)


pixfirewall(config)#logging message 403503 level 6
pixfirewall(config)#show logging message 403503
syslog 403503: default-level errors, current-level informational (enabled)
```

To disable a particular syslog message, enter the following command:

```
no logging message messageid
```

How Log Messages Are Organized

Syslog messages are listed numerically by message code. Each message is followed by a brief explanation and a recommended action. If several messages share the same explanation and recommended action, the messages are presented together, followed by the common explanation and recommended action.

The explanation of each message indicates what kind of event generated the message. Possible events include the following:

- Authentication, authorization, and accounting (AAA) events
- Connection events (for example, connections denied by the PIX configuration or address translation errors)
- Failover events reported by one or both units of a failover pair
- File Transfer Protocol (FTP)/Uniform Resource Locator (URL) events (for example, successful file transfers or blocked Java applets)
- Mail Guard/SNMP events
- PIX management events (for example, configuration events or Telnet connections to the PIX console port)
- Routing errors

How to Read System Log Messages

System log messages received at a syslog server begin with a percent sign (%) and are structured as follows:

```
%PIX-level-message-number: message-text
```

- **PIX** identifies the message facility code for messages generated by the PIX Firewall.

- *level* reflects the severity of the condition described by the message. The lower the number, the more serious the condition.

- *message-number* is the numeric code that uniquely identifies the message.

- *message-text* is a text string describing the condition. This portion of the message sometimes includes IP addresses, port numbers, or usernames.

You can find more information on syslog messages at http://www.cisco.com/en/US/products/sw/secursw/ps2120/products_system_message_guide_book09186a00801582a9.html.

Configuring Syslog on the Cisco PIX Firewall

The **logging** command is used to configure logging on the PIX Firewall. Logging is disabled by default. Table 8-3 describes the parameters of the **logging** command.

Table 8-3   logging *Command Parameters*

Command	Description
logging on	Enables the transmission of syslog messages to all output locations. You can disable sending syslog messages with the **no logging on** command.
no logging message *n*	Allows you to disable specific syslog messages. Use the **logging message** *message_number* command to resume logging of specific disabled messages.
logging buffered *n*	Stores syslog messages in the PIX Firewall so that you can view them with the **show logging** command. Cisco Systems recommends that you use this command to view syslog messages when the PIX Firewall is in use on a network.
clear logging	Clears the message buffer created with the **logging buffered** command.
clear logging message	Reenables all disabled syslog messages.

continues

Table 8-3 logging *Command Parameters (Continued)*

Command	Description
logging console *n*	Displays syslog messages on the PIX Firewall console as they occur. Use this command when you are debugging problems or when there is minimal load on the network. Do not use this command when the network is busy because it can reduce the PIX Firewall performance.
logging monitor *n*	Displays syslog messages when you access the PIX Firewall console with Telnet.
logging host [*interface*] *ip_address* [*protocol/ port*]	Specifies the host that receives the syslog messages. The PIX Firewall can send messages across UDP or TCP (which you specify by setting the *protocol* variable). The default UDP port is 514. The default TCP port is 1470.
logging history *severity_level*	Sets the logging level for SNMP traps.
logging queue *msg_count*	Specifies how many syslog messages can appear in the message queue while waiting for processing. The default is 512 messages. Use the **show logging queue** command to view queue statistics.
logging timestamp	Specifies that each message sent to the syslog server should include a timestamp to indicate when the event occurred.
logging trap *n*	Sets the logging level for syslog messages.
show logging disabled	Displays a complete list of disabled syslog messages.
show logging	Lists the current syslog messages and which **logging** command options are enabled.
logging standby	Lets the failover standby unit send syslog messages.

Configuring the PIX Device Manager to View Logging

The PDM Log panel, shown in Figure 8-1, allows you to view syslog messages that are captured in the PDM Log buffer in the PIX Firewall memory. You may select the level of syslog messages you want to view. When you view the PDM Log, all the buffered syslog messages at and below the logging level you choose are displayed.

Figure 8-1 *PDM Log Viewer Screen*

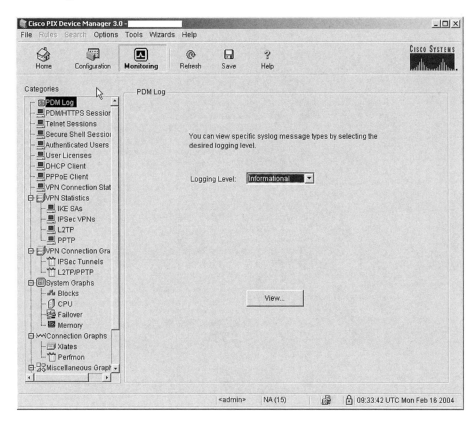

The PDM logging panel has the following fields:

■ **Logging Level**—Enables you to choose the level of syslog messages to view.

To view the logs using the PDM interface, click the View button shown in Figure 8-1. Figure 8-2 shows a sample output of logs viewed from the PDM logging panel.

Figure 8-2 *Sample PDM Logging Output*

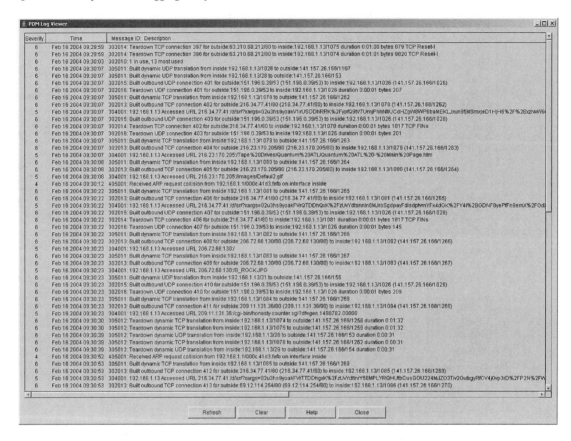

PDM is discussed in further detail in Chapter 13, "PIX Device Manager."

Configuring Syslog Messages at the Console

Configuring logging on the console interface is useful when you are troubleshooting or observing traffic patterns directly from the PIX Firewall. This gives you real-time information about what is happening on the PIX Firewall. To configure logging at the PIX console interface, use the **logging console** command as follows. After logging into configuration mode, enter the following:

```
Pixfw(config)#logging on
Pixfw(config)#logging console 5
```

The 5 indicates the logging level. In this case, it is logging notification. From the console you can see the logs in real time.

Sending Syslog Messages to a Telnet Session

Remotely troubleshooting or viewing real-time PIX traffic patterns can be done by configuring the PIX to send logging information to a Telnet session. The **logging monitor** command configures the PIX to send syslog messages to Telnet sessions. For example, after logging into configuration mode, enter the following:

```
Pixfirewall (config)#logging monitor 6
Pixfirewall(config)#terminal monitor
```

In this example, syslog messages 0 to 6, or emergency to informational, are sent to a Telnet session. To disable logging to Telnet, you use the **no logging monitor** command.

The *terminal monitor* displays messages directly to the Telnet session. You can disable the direct display of messages by entering the **terminal no monitor** command. A Telnet session sometimes is lost in busy networks when the **logging monitor** command is used.

Configuring the Cisco PIX Firewall to Send Syslog Messages to a Log Server

Configuring the PIX to send logging information to a server helps you collect and maintain data that can later be used for forensic and data traffic analysis. PIX syslog messages are usually sent to a syslog server or servers. PIX uses UDP port 514 by default to send syslog messages to a syslog server. The syntax for configuring the PIX Firewall to send syslog messages to a syslog server is as follows:

```
Pixfirewall(config)#Logging host [interface] ip_address [tcp[/port] |udp[/port]]
   [format emblem]
```

The variables *[interface]* and *ip-address* are replaced with the name of the interface on which the syslog resides and the Internet Protocol (IP) address of the syslog server, respectively. PIX Firewall Version 6.3 introduces support for EMBLEM format. EMBLEM syslog format is designed to be consistent with the Cisco IOS® Software format and is more compatible with CiscoWorks management applications such as Resource Manager Essentials (RME) syslog analyzer. Use the option **format emblem** to send messages to the specified server in EMBLEM format.

> **NOTE**   This option is available only for UDP syslog messages, used by the RME syslog analyzer.

The following steps show you how to configure the PIX to send syslog messages:

Step 1   Designate a host to receive the messages with the **logging host** command:

```
Pixfirewall(config)#logging host inside  10.1.1.10
```

You can specify additional servers so that if one goes offline, another is available to receive messages.

Step 2   Set the logging level with the **logging trap** command:

```
Pixfirewall(config)#logging trap informational
```

If needed, set the **logging facility** command to a value other than its default of 20. Most UNIX systems expect the messages to arrive at facility 20.

> **NOTE**   In the event that all syslog servers are offline, the Cisco PIX Firewall stores up to 100 messages in its memory. Subsequent messages that arrive overwrite the buffer starting from the first line. PIX buffer logging is enabled by the command **logging buffered** *level*.

Step 3   Start sending messages with the **logging on** command. To disable sending messages, use the **no logging** command.

Step 4   To view your logging setting enter **show logging**.

Centrally managing several PIX Firewalls can be challenging if you cannot identify the origin of a particular message that is sent to the central log server. PIX Firewall Version 6.2(3) and later support defining a unique device ID for log messages sent to a syslog server. If several PIX Firewalls are configured to send their syslog messages to a single syslog server, a unique identification can be configured so the message source can be identified. To enable this option, use the following command:

```
logging device-id {hostname | ipaddress if_name | string text}
```

Table 8-4 gives a description of the parameters of the **logging device-id** command.

Table 8-4   logging device-id *Command Parameters*

Parameter	Description
hostname	The name of the PIX Firewall
ipaddress	Specifies to use the IP address of the specified PIX Firewall interface to uniquely identify the syslog messages from the PIX Firewall
if-name	The name of the interface with the IP address that is used to uniquely identify the syslog messages from the PIX Firewall
string text	Specifies the text string to uniquely identify the syslog messages from the PIX Firewall

When this feature is enabled, the message will include the specified device ID (either the hostname or IP address of the specified interface—even if the message comes from another interface—or a string) in messages sent to a syslog server. The PIX Firewall will insert the specified device ID into all non-EMBLEM-format syslog messages.

> **NOTE**   The device ID does not appear in EMBLEM-formatted messages, Simple Network Management Protocol (SNMP) traps, or on the firewall console, management session, or buffer. This command does not affect the syslog message text in EMBLEM format or its display on the PIX Firewall console or in the log file.

To disable this feature, use the following command:

```
no logging device-id
```

Configuring SNMP Traps and SNMP Requests

SNMP requests can be used to query the PIX on its system status information. If you want to send only the cold start, link up, and link down generic traps, no further configuration is required. SNMP traps send information about a particular event only when the configured threshold is reached.

To configure the PIX to receive SNMP requests from a management station, you must do the following:

- Configure the IP address of the SNMP management station with the **snmp-server host** command.
- Set the **snmp-server** options for **location, contact,** and the **community** password as required.

To configure SNMP traps on the PIX, you must do the following:

- Configure the IP address of the SNMP management station with the **snmp-server host** command.
- Set the **snmp-server** options for **location, contact,** and the **community** password as required.
- Set the trap with the **snmp-server enable traps** command.
- Set the logging level with the **logging history** command.

Configuring a Syslogd Server

Because syslogd was originally a UNIX concept, the features available in the syslogd products on non-UNIX systems depend on the vendor implementation. Features might include dividing incoming messages by facility or debug level or both, resolving the names of the sending devices, and reporting facilities. For information on configuring the non-UNIX syslog server, refer to the vendor's documentation.

> **NOTE** Configuring the syslog server is not covered on the PIX CSPFA 642-521 exam.

To configure syslog on UNIX, follow these steps:

Step 1 On SunOS, AIX, HPUX, or Solaris, as root, make a backup of the /etc/ syslog.conf file before modifying it.

Step 2 Modify /etc/syslog.conf to tell the UNIX system how to sort out the syslog messages coming in from the sending devices—that is, which *logging-facility.level* goes in which file. Make sure there is a tab between the *logging-facility.level* and *file-name*.

Step 3 Make sure the destination file exists and is writable.

Step 4 The **#Comment** section at the beginning of syslog.conf usually explains the syntax for the UNIX system.

Step 5 Do not put file information in the **ifdef** section.

Step 6 As root, restart syslogd to pick up changes.

For example, if /etc/syslog.conf is set for

```
local7.warn      /var/log/local7.warn
```

warning, error, critical, alert, and emergency messages coming in on the local7 logging facility are logged in the local7.warn file. Notification, informational, and debug messages coming in on the local7 facility are not logged anywhere.

If /etc/syslog.conf is set for

```
*.debug          /var/log/all.debug
```

all message levels from all logging facilities go to this file.

PIX Firewall Syslog Server

PFSS lets you view PIX Firewall event information from a Windows NT system. It includes special features not found on other syslog servers:

■ The ability to receive syslog messages by TCP or UDP

■ Full reliability, because messages can be sent using TCP

PFSS can receive syslog messages from up to ten PIX units. You can install this product for use with any model of Cisco PIX Firewall. If you have specified that the PIX send syslog messages using TCP, the Windows NT disk might become full and the PIX unit stops its traffic. If the Windows NT file system is full, the Windows system beeps, and the PFSS disables all TCP connections from the PIX unit(s) by closing its TCP listen socket. The PIX tries to reconnect to the PFSS five times, and during the retry it stops all new connections through the PIX.

Foundation Summary

The "Foundation Summary" provides a convenient review of many key concepts in this chapter. If you are already comfortable with the topics in this chapter, this summary can help you recall a few details. If you just read this chapter, this review should help solidify some key facts. If you are doing your final preparation before the exam, this summary provides a convenient way to review the day before the exam.

The syslog message facility in the Cisco PIX Firewall is a useful means to view troubleshooting messages and to watch for network events such as attacks and service denials. Syslog messages can be configured to be sent to the following:

- PDM Log
- Console
- Telnet console
- Internal memory/buffer
- Syslog server
- SNMP management station

Common to all ways of viewing syslog messages is the message level, or severity. The level specifies the types of messages sent to the syslog host, as shown in Table 8-6.

Table 8-5 *Logging Severity Levels*

Level	Numeric Code	System Condition
Emergency	0	System unusable message
Alert	1	Take immediate action
Critical	2	Critical condition
Error	3	Error message
Warning	4	Warning message
Notification	5	Normal but significant condition
Informational	6	Information message
Debug	7	Debug message, log FTP commands, and WWW URLs

System log messages received at a syslog server begin with a percent sign (%) and are structured as follows:

```
%PIX-level-message_number: message_text
```

You can set the *level* with the **logging** command so that you can view syslog messages on the PIX Firewall console, from a syslog server, or with SNMP.

Q&A

As mentioned in the Introduction, the questions in this book are more difficult than what you should experience on the exam. The questions are designed to ensure your understanding of the concepts discussed in this chapter and adequately prepare you to complete the exam. You should use the simulated exams on the CD to practice for the exam.

The answers to these questions can be found in Appendix A.

1. What command would you use to view logs that are in memory?

2. On which port does syslogd listen by default?

3. What is the total number of logging facilities available for PIX Firewall syslog configuration?

4. What is the command for sending syslog messages to Telnet sessions?

5. For what is the **logging trap** command used?

6. What is the command used to enable logging on the failover PIX unit?

7. Why would you use the *timestamp* command parameter?

8. What is PFSS?

This chapter covers the following subjects:

- Overview of General Routing Principles

- Overview of PIX Firewall Routing Functionality

- Configuring Static Routes

- Configuring Dynamic Routes

- Configuring VLANs and VLAN Tagging

- Permitting Multicast Traffic

CHAPTER 9

Routing and the PIX Firewall

Configuring your PIX Firewall to forward traffic to other networks is crucial for the correct operation of your PIX Firewall. Forwarding traffic to the next hop on its path toward its final destination is known as *routing*. Although the PIX Firewall is not a router, it does provide sufficient routing features to effectively pass traffic through its interfaces. This functionality covers Ethernet VLAN tagging, static routes, dynamic routes, and even multicast traffic.

How to Best Use This Chapter

Protecting your network with a PIX Firewall provides a strong perimeter defense, but for valid traffic to reach your protected network, you must understand how to configure routing on your PIX Firewall. This can be as simple as defining a single static default route or as complex as configuring your PIX Firewall to use the Open Shortest Path First (OSPF) routing protocol. The concepts in this chapter explain how to configure your PIX Firewall to forward network traffic across your network. Test yourself with the "Do I Know This Already?" quiz, and see how familiar you are with the routing functionality available on PIX Firewalls.

"Do I Know This Already?" Quiz

The purpose of the "Do I Know This Already?" quiz is to help you decide if you really need to read the entire chapter. If you already intend to read the entire chapter, you do not necessarily need to answer these questions now.

The ten-question quiz, derived from the major sections in the "Foundation and Supplemental Topics" portion of the chapter, helps you determine how to spend your limited study time.

Table 9-1 outlines the major topics discussed in this chapter and the "Do I Know This Already?" quiz questions that correspond to those topics.

Table 9-1 *"Do I Know This Already?" Foundation Topics Section-to-Question Mapping*

Foundation Topics Section	Questions Covered in This Section	Score
Overview of PIX Firewall Routing Functionality	1	
Configuring Static Routes	2	
Configuring Dynamic Routes	6, 9, 10	
Configuring VLANs and VLAN Tagging	4, 7, 8	
Permitting Multicast Traffic	3, 5	

CAUTION The goal of self assessment is to gauge your mastery of the topics in this chapter. If you do not know the answer to a question or are only partially sure of the answer, you should mark this question wrong for purposes of the self assessment. Giving yourself credit for an answer you correctly guess skews your self-assessment results and might provide you with a false sense of security.

1. Which dynamic routing protocol(s) are supported by PIX Firewall Version 6.3?

    a. RIP

    b. OSPF

    c. BGP

    d. EIGRP

    e. Answers a and b

2. Which command do you use to configure static routes?

    a. interface

    b. mroute

    c. route

    d. static

    e. None of the above

3. Which command do you use to configure the PIX Firewall to statically receive a multicast session?

   a. igmp forward

   b. igmp static

   c. multicast static

   d. igmp join-group

   e. None of the above

4. What type of Ethernet VLAN tagging does the PIX Firewall support?

   a. ISL

   b. 802.1x

   c. 802.1q

   d. 802.3

   e. None of the above

5. IP multicasting is a technique that

   a. consumes more network bandwidth by sending IP traffic to multiple hosts on the network.

   b. enables the PIX Firewall to communicate with multiple hosts on the network.

   c. sends traffic to specific Class C IP addresses.

   d. sends traffic to specific Class D IP addresses, thus enabling multiple recipients to receive the same traffic stream.

   e. None of the above

6. Which of the following is true with respect to PIX Firewall RIP support?

   a. RIP routing updates cannot be propagated by the PIX Firewall.

   b. The PIX Firewall can advertise a default route.

   c. Authentication is supported only for RIP version 2.

   d. Answers a, b, and c

   e. None of the above

7. Which PIX Firewall command do you use to create logical interfaces?

   a. interface

   b. nameif

   c. logical

   d. static

   e. None of the above

8. Which PIX command enables you to configure the security level for logical interfaces?

   a. static

   b. interface

   c. nameif

   d. logical

   e. None of the above

9. Which OSPF subcommand defines which Type 3 LSA traffic to filter?

   a. network

   b. area

   c. router ospf

   d. prefix-list

   e. access-list

10. The PIX Firewall can propagate which types of routes?

    a. BGP

    b. OSPF

    c. RIP

    d. Static

    e. None of the above

The answers to the "Do I Know This Already?" quiz are found in Appendix A, "Answers to the 'Do I Know This Already?' Quizzes and Q&A Sections." The suggested choices for your next step are as follows:

- **8 or less overall score**—Read the entire chapter. This includes the "Foundation and Supplemental Topics," "Foundation Summary," and "Q&A" sections.

- **9 or 10 overall score**—If you want more review on these topics, skip to the "Foundation Summary" section and then go to the "Q&A" section. Otherwise, move to the next chapter.

Foundation and Supplemental Topics

General Routing Principles

Although your PIX Firewall is not a router, it does need to provide certain routing and switching functionality. Whenever your PIX Firewall processes valid traffic, it must determine which interface provides the correct path for the destination network. It may also have to tag the traffic for the appropriate VLAN. Not only can your PIX Firewall route valid traffic, you can also configure it to forward multicast traffic. Sending multicast traffic to a multicast broadcast address enables multiple systems to receive a data stream that otherwise would have to be sent to each individual system.

This chapter focuses on the following three features that enable your PIX Firewall to effectively route and switch traffic:

■ Ethernet VLAN tagging

■ IP routing

■ Multicast routing

Ethernet VLAN Tagging

To pass traffic between the different virtual LANs (VLANs) on your switched network, Ethernet packets can be tagged with a VLAN identifier that indicates the VLAN to which the traffic belongs. Ethernet tagging enables you to pass traffic for different VLANs across the same Layer 2 interface. The following sections explain how to use Ethernet VLAN tagging with your PIX Firewall.

Understanding VLANs

At the Ethernet layer, you can partition your network using VLANs. These VLANs limit the scope of broadcast traffic on your network because each VLAN represents an individual broadcast domain. By dividing your switched network using VLANs, you improve the security of your network by limiting the scope of broadcast traffic that is vital for the operation of your network, such as Address Resolution Protocol (ARP) traffic and Dynamic Host Configuration Protocol (DHCP) traffic.

Understanding Trunk Ports

Usually, you configure a switch as a member of a specific VLAN. This automatically associates all of the regular Ethernet traffic received on that port with that VLAN. Sometimes, however, you may want a single port to receive traffic from multiple VLANs. A switch port that accepts traffic from multiple VLANs is known as a *trunk port*.

To differentiate between the different VLANs, each packet is tagged with a specific VLAN identifier. This identifier informs the switch to which VLAN the traffic needs to be forwarded. By using trunk lines on your switch, your PIX Firewall can send and receive traffic from multiple VLANs using only a single physical interface.

Understanding Logical Interfaces

Your PIX Firewall has a limited number of physical interfaces. This limits the number of Layer 3 networks to which the PIX Firewall can be directly connected. If you use VLANs to segment your network into smaller broadcast domains, each of these VLANs represents a different Layer 3 network. By using logical interfaces, you can accommodate multiple VLANs by using trunk lines on your switch ports and configuring multiple logical interfaces on a single physical interface on your PIX Firewall. Logical interfaces overcome the physical interface limitation by enabling a single physical interface to handle multiple logical interfaces.

Table 9-2 shows the maximum number of interfaces allowed using a restricted license, while Table 9-3 shows the maximum number of interfaces allowed for an unrestricted license.

Table 9-2 *Maximum Interfaces for Restricted License*

Cisco Secure PIX Model	Total Interfaces	Physical Interfaces	Logical Interfaces
515E	5	3	5
525	8	6	6
535	10	8	8

NOTE VLANs are not supported on the PIX 501 and PIX 506/506E.

Table 9-3 *Maximum Interfaces for Unrestricted License*

Cisco Secure PIX Model	Total Interfaces	Physical Interfaces	Logical Interfaces
501	2	2	Not supported
506E	2	2	Not supported
515E	10	6	8
525	12	8	10
535	24	10	22

NOTE The maximum number of logical interfaces that you can use is equal to the total number of interfaces available minus the total number of physical interfaces that you currently have configured on your PIX Firewall.

Unique VLAN tags differentiate the traffic to each logical interface. Currently, the PIX Firewall supports configuring multiple 802.1Q VLANs on a physical port and the ability to send and receive 802.1Q tagged packets. The PIX Firewall does not perform any trunk negotiations or participate in bridging protocols.

To create a logical interface on the PIX Firewall, you use the **interface** command, the syntax for which is as follows:

```
interface hardware-id vlan-id [physical¦logical] [shutdown]
```

The parameters for the **interface** command are shown in Table 9-4.

Table 9-4 **interface** *Command Parameters*

Parameter	Description
hardware-id	Specifies the network interface on which the command will be applied (such as Ethernet0)
vlan-id	The VLAN identifier to be associated with either the logical or physical interface
physical	Keyword indicating that the command applies to the physical actual interface
logical	Keyword indicating that the command applies to a logical interface instead of the physical interface
shutdown	Keyword indicating that the interface should be administratively shut down

Suppose that interface Ethernet0 on your PIX Firewall is connected to VLAN 30 and that you want to configure three logical interfaces on that same physical interface for VLAN 40 through VLAN 42. The commands to accomplish this are as follows:

```
pix515a(config)# interface Ethernet0 vlan30 physical
pix515a(config)# interface Ethernet0 vlan40 logical
pix515a(config)# interface Ethernet0 vlan41 logical
pix515a(config)# interface Ethernet0 vlan42 logical
```

NOTE   The VLAN assigned to the physical interface represents the native VLAN. You do not need to assign a VLAN to the physical interface to assign logical interfaces to an interface.

Managing VLANs

After you create your logical interfaces, you also need to assign the following parameters to each logical interface:

- Interface name
- Security level
- IP address

Using the **nameif** interface command, you can assign an interface name and a security level to a logical interface. The syntax for the **nameif** command is as follows:

```
nameif {hardware-id¦vlan-id} interface-name security-level
```

Table 9-5 shows the parameters for the **nameif** command.

Table 9-5   nameif *Command Parameters*

Parameter	Description
hardware-id	Specifies the network interface on which the command will be applied (such as Ethernet0)
vlan-id	The VLAN identifier associated with the logical interface
interface-name	The name to be assigned to the specified interface
security-level	The security level for the specified interface in the range from 0–100, with 0 being the outside interface and 100 being the inside interface

Finally, you need to complete your logical interface configuration by assigning an IP address to the logical interface. To assign an IP address to an interface, you use the **ip address** command. The syntax for this command is as follows:

```
ip address interface-name ip-address
```

> **NOTE** The *interface-name* corresponds to the name that you assigned with the **nameif** command.

IP Routing

At the IP layer, your PIX Firewall routes traffic based on the IP addresses in the network traffic. It does not provide all the functionality of a router, but it does enable you to define the following two types of routes:

■ Static routes

■ Dynamic routes

Static Routes

Static routes are manually configured routes that do not frequently change. They essentially direct your PIX Firewall to send traffic destined for a specific network to a specific router that has connectivity to the destination network. Static routes are perhaps best explained by using a network example. Figure 9-1 illustrates a simple network configuration with hosts on both the 10.10.10.0 and 10.10.20.0 networks.

Figure 9-1 *Static Routes*

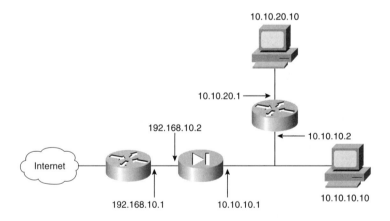

When you configure the inside interface on the PIX Firewall with a Class C address of 10.10.10.1, the PIX Firewall automatically creates a route that enables it to send traffic for the 10.10.10.0 network to the inside interface (identified by the keyword CONNECT when viewing the routes). The PIX Firewall may also receive traffic for the host whose IP address is 10.10.20.10. By default, if the PIX Firewall receives traffic for 10.10.20.10, it will not know where to send it. To enable the PIX Firewall to know where to send traffic for

10.10.20.10, you can configure a static route using the **route** command. The syntax for the **route** command is as follows:

```
route interface-name destination-ip netmask gateway [metric]
```

The parameters for the **route** command are explained in Table 9-6. Using the network in Figure 9-1, you can define a static route for the 10.10.20.0 network using the following command:

```
pix515a(config)# route inside 10.10.20.0 255.255.255.0 10.10.10.2 1
```

Table 9-6   route *Command Parameters*

Parameter	Description
interface-name	The name of the interface on the PIX Firewall through which the traffic will travel to reach the destination network (the name assigned in the **nameif** command).
destination-ip	The destination IP address(es) of the traffic to which the route pertains.
netmask	The network mask of the route, which indicates the number of addresses covered by the route (for example, a Class C network pertains to 256 different addresses and is specified as 255.255.255.0).
gateway	The IP address of the gateway to which the routed traffic will be sent.
metric	The cost of the route. Normally, this indicates the number of hops to the destination network. When routing, this value is used to choose the best route when multiple routes exist.

Default Route

Configuring multiple routes can be a time-consuming task, especially for the traffic bound for the Internet. Therefore, you can create a special route known as a default route. This route is automatically used for any traffic that does not match any other routes on the system. When configuring the default route, you use a destination IP address of 0.0.0.0 and a netmask of 0.0.0.0.

Instead of using the address of a gateway router when you are configuring a static route, you can specify the IP address of one of the PIX Firewall's own interfaces. When you create a route in this manner, the PIX Firewall does not have a destination IP address to which to send the traffic. Therefore, the PIX Firewall broadcasts an ARP request on the specified interface to determine the address to which to send the traffic. Any router that has a route to the destination address can generate a proxy ARP (using its own interface's Ethernet address), enabling the PIX Firewall to update its ARP cache with an entry for the IP address of the traffic. The PIX Firewall uses this proxy ARP to then send the traffic to the router that has a route to the destination IP address.

> **NOTE** Although you can configure the PIX Firewall to generate an ARP request to determine the destination address to which to send traffic, this configuration is not recommended. ARP is an unauthenticated protocol and this configuration can pose a security risk.

Static routes are stored in your PIX Firewall configuration and restored when your PIX Firewall is reloaded. To view the routes on your PIX Firewall, you use the **show route** command. This command displays all the routes in the PIX Firewall's routing table, such as shown in Example 9-1.

Example 9-1 *Output of the* show route *Command*

```
pix515a# show route
    intf5 0.0.0.0 0.0.0.0 10.89.141.1 1 OTHER static
    inside 10.10.10.0 255.255.255.0 10.10.10.1 1 CONNECT static
    inside 10.10.20.0 255.255.255.0 10.10.10.2 2 OTHER static
    intf5 10.89.141.0 255.255.255.0 10.89.141.80 1 CONNECT static
    intf4 172.16.1.0 255.255.255.0 172.16.1.1 1 CONNECT static
    outside 192.168.10.0 255.255.255.0 192.168.10.80 1 CONNECT static
pix515a#
```

The static routes with the keyword CONNECT indicate routes that are automatically created when you define the IP address for an interface. The routes with the OTHER keyword indicate static routes that have been manually entered.

Sometimes you may want to remove the static routes that you have already configured. You can do this using the **clear route** command.

> **NOTE** You can also remove individual routes by placing the **no** keyword in front of the original command used to create the static route.

Dynamic Routes

Besides creating static routes manually, the PIX Firewall also supports some dynamic routing functionality. Dynamic routes are created based on routing protocols that automatically add entries into the PIX Firewall's routing table. The PIX Firewall supports the following two different routing protocols, but only one can be active on a single PIX Firewall:

■ Routing Information Protocol (RIP)

■ Open Shortest Path First (OSPF)

The PIX Firewall can learn new routes based on the RIP routing broadcasts, but the PIX Firewall does not have the functionality to propagate these learned routes to other devices. With OSPF, the PIX Firewall learns new routes, and it can also propagate that information to other devices.

> **NOTE** Authentication should be used with all routing protocols whenever possible. Route redistribution between OSPF and other protocols (such as RIP) is a prime target for attackers. By subverting the routing information, an attacker can potentially bypass your defined security configuration.

Configuring RIP

To enable the PIX Firewall to learn new routes based on RIP routing updates, you use the **rip** command. The syntax for the **rip** command is as follows:

```
rip if-name default¦passive [version {1¦2}] [authentication {text¦md5} key key id]
```

Table 9-7 describes the various parameters for the **rip** command.

Table 9-7 rip *Command Parameters*

Parameter	Description
if-name	The name of the interface to which the rip configuration will apply (the name assigned in the **nameif** command).
default	Keyword indicating that you want to broadcast the address of the specified interface as a default route.
passive	Enables passive RIP on the interface. The PIX Firewall listens for RIP routing updates and uses the information received to populate its routing table.
version	Keyword used to specify the version of RIP to use. This keyword must be followed by either **1** or **2**, to indicate the RIP version to use.
authentication	Keyword to enable RIP version 2 authentication.
text	Keyword indicating that RIP updates should be sent in the clear.
md5	Keyword indicating that RIP updates should use MD5 authentication.
key	The key to encrypt routing updates. This key is a text string of up to 16 characters.
key_id	The key identification value in the range between 1 and 255. The same key_ID must be used on all of your RIP-enabled devices that communicate with one another.

By configuring RIP on a specific PIX Firewall interface, your firewall watches for RIP routing updates. It then uses this information to update its routing table. The information cannot be distributed by the PIX Firewall to other devices. The PIX Firewall can, however, broadcast the address of one of its interfaces as a default route.

To turn off RIP on a specific interface, you use the **no** keyword in front of the original RIP configuration command. You can also remove all the RIP configuration commands from your configuration by using the **clear rip** command.

Suppose that you want to enable RIP on the outside interface by using MD5 authentication, using MYKEY as the key and a key_id of 2. The command to accomplish this is as follows:

```
Pix515a(config)# rip outside passive version 2 authentication md5 MYKEY 2
```

NOTE   Because authentication is supported only with RIP version 2, you must specify version 2 in the command. The default is RIP version 1.

OSPF Overview

Route propagation and greatly reduced route convergence times are two of the many benefits that occur by using OSPF. OSPF is widely deployed in large internetworks because of its efficient use of network bandwidth and its rapid convergence after changes in topology. The PIX Firewall implementation supports intra-area, interarea, and external routes. The distribution of static routes to OSPF processes and route redistribution between OSPF processes are also included.

NOTE   The PIX 501 does not support OSPF functionality.

An OSPF router that has interfaces in multiple areas is called an Area Border Router (ABR). A router that redistributes traffic or imports external routes (Type 1 or Type 2) between routing domains is called an Autonomous System Boundary Router (ASBR). An ABR uses link-state advertisements (LSAs) to send information about available routes to other OSPF routers. Using ABR Type 3 LSA filtering, you can have separate private and public areas, with the PIX Firewall acting as an ABR. Type 3 LSAs (interarea routes) can be filtered from one area to another. This lets you use NAT and OSPF together without advertising private networks.

The PIX Firewall OSPF supported features are as follows:

■   Support for intra-area, interarea, and external routes

- Support for virtual links
- Authentication for OSPF packets
- The capability to configure the PIX Firewall as a designated router, ABR, and limited ASBR
- ABR Type 3 LSA filtering
- Route redistribution

NOTE   Your PIX Firewall can filter only Type 3 LSAs. If you configure your PIX Firewall to function as an ASBR in a private network, then information about your private networks will be sent to the public interfaces, because Type 5 LSAs describing private networks will be flooded to the entire autonomous system (including the public areas) unless you configure two separate OSPF processes.

OSPF Commands

To configure OSPF on your PIX Firewall, you use various commands. To enable OSPF on your PIX Firewall, you use the **router ospf** command. The syntax is as follows:

```
router ospf pid
```

The *pid* represents a unique identification for the OSPF routing process in the range from 1 to 65535. Each OSPF routing process on a single PIX Firewall must be unique, and PIX Firewall Version 6.3 supports a maximum of two different OSPF routing processes.

After you issue the **router ospf** command, the PIX command prompt enters a subcommand mode indicated by a command prompt similar to the following:

```
pix515a(config-router)#
```

In subcommand mode, you can configure various OSPF parameters (see Table 9-8).

Table 9-8   router ospf *Subcommand Options*

Parameter	Description
area	Configures OSPF areas
compatible	Runs OSPF in RFC 1583 compatible mode
default-information	Distributes a default route
distance	Configures administrative distances for OSPF process
ignore	Suppresses syslog for receipt of Type 6 (MOSPF) LSAs
log-adj-changes	Logs OSPF adjacency changes

Table 9-8 router ospf *Subcommand Options (Continued)*

Parameter	Description
network	Adds/removes interfaces to/from OSPF routing process
redistribute	Configures route redistribution between OSPF processes
router-id	Configures router ID for an OSPF process
summary-address	Configures summary address for OSPF redistribution
timers	Configures timers for an OSPF process

Using the **network** command, you can define which interfaces will be running OSPF. Using the **network** command also enables you to add networks to or remove networks from the OSPF routing process and define OSPF area information for each network. The syntax for the **network** command is as follows:

```
network prefix-ip-address netmask area area-id
```

The parameters for the **network** command are shown in Table 9-9.

Table 9-9 network *Command Parameters*

Parameter	Description
prefix-ip-address	IP address of the network being configured.
netmask	The network mask, which indicates the number of addresses covered by the area (for example, a Class C network pertains to 256 different addresses and is specified as 255.255.255.0).
area	Keyword indicating that the area information will follow.
area-id	The ID of the area to be associated with this OSPF address range.

OSPF advertises routes to networks. To prevent information about your private network from being advertised, you need to filter LSAs. The **prefix-list** and **area** commands enable you to filter Type 3 LSA advertisements. This filtering is based on the prefix list defined by the **prefix-list** command. Once configured, only the specified prefixes are sent from one area to another, and all other prefixes are restricted to their OSPF area. The syntax for the **prefix-list** command is as follows:

```
prefix-list list-name [seq seq-number] {permit¦deny prefix/len}
```

> **NOTE** Unlike the other OSPF configuration commands, the **prefix-list** command is executed from normal configuration mode instead of the OSPF subcommand mode.

Table 9-10 shows the parameters for the **prefix-list** command.

Table 9-10   **prefix-list** *Command Parameters*

Parameter	Description
list-name	The name of the prefix list.
seq	Keyword indicating that you want to provide a sequence number.
seq-number	Specifies the sequence number for the prefix list entry in the range from 1 to 4294967295.
permit	Keyword indicating that the specified prefix list should be allowed.
deny	Keyword indicating that the specified prefix list should be disallowed.
prefix	Prefix address that is being identified.
len	A network mask indicator that identifies the number of valid bits in the prefix (for instance to specify a Class C address, the *len* value is 24).

After configuring a prefix list, you apply that prefix list to an area by using the **area** command. Filtering can be applied to traffic going into or coming out of an OSPF area or to both the incoming and outgoing traffic for an area. The syntax for the **area** command is as follows:

```
area area-id filter-list prefix {prefix-list-name in|out}
```

The parameters for the **area** command are shown in Table 9-11.

Table 9-11   **area** *Command Parameters*

Parameter	Description
area-id	The identifier of the area on which filtering is being configured
filter-list	Keyword indicating that you are configuring LSA filtering
prefix	Keyword indicating that you are specifying a configured prefix list to use for filtering
prefix-list-name	The name of the prefix list that you created using the **prefix-list** command
in	Keyword that applies the configured prefix to prefixes advertised inbound to the specified area
out	Keyword that applies the configured prefix to prefixes advertised outbound from the specified area

Running two separate OSPF processes on your PIX Firewall enables you to perform address filtering when your PIX Firewall is configured as an ASBR. LSA Type 5 advertisements pass between areas on the same OSPF process (and cannot be filtered like LSA Type 3 advertisements), but they do not pass between separate OSPF processes. Using two OSPF processes can be advantageous in various situations, such as the following:

- NAT is being used
- OSPF is operating on the public and private interfaces
- LSA Type 5 advertisement filtering is required

Autonomous System Boundary Router

An ASBR is located on the edge of your OSPF autonomous system and is responsible for advertising external routes for the entire OSPF autonomous system.

When using two OSPF processes, one process is usually configured for the external interface while the other process handles the private interfaces. Each OSPF process is configured by using a separate **router ospf** command with a different process identification (PID) number for each process.

In some situations, it may be advantageous to distribute route advertisements between separate OSPF processes, such as to enable routes received on the public interface to pass to the OSPF process running on the private interfaces. To redistribute routes between different OSPF processes or domains, you use the **redistribute ospf** subcommand, the syntax for which is as follows:

```
redistribute ospf pid
```

Because the **redistribute ospf** command is executed from the OSPF subcommand mode, *pid* identifies the OSPF process identification (PID) whose LSA Type 3 advertisements you want forwarded to the current OSPF process.

Configuring OSPF

Figure 9-2 shows a typical OSPF deployment configuration. In this configuration the PIX Firewall is operating as an ABR. Because you do not want the information about private networks sent out on the public interface, LSA filtering is applied to the Internet interface. NAT is applied only to the inside interface (for the private networks).

Figure 9-2 *PIX OSPF Network*

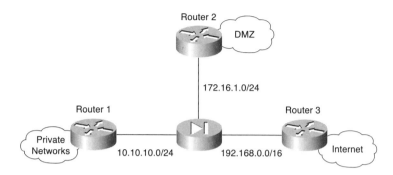

In this configuration, the inside interface learns routes from both the DMZ and the outside interface, but you do not want private routes to be propagated to either the DMZ or the public interfaces.

Configuring OSPF on your PIX Firewall requires you to perform the following steps:

Step 1 Enable OSPF.

Step 2 Define the PIX Firewall interfaces that need to run OSPF.

Step 3 Define OSPF areas.

Step 4 Configure LSA filtering to protect private addresses.

Using the configuration shown in Figure 9-2, the following commands configure OSPF based on the scenario described:

```
pix515a(config)# router ospf 1
pix515a(config-router)# area 0 filter-list prefix ten in
pix515a(config-router)# network 192.168.0.0 255.255.0.0 area 0
pix515a(config-router)# network 172.16.1.0 255.255.255.0 area 172.16.1.0
pix515a(config-router)# network 10.10.10.0 255.255.255.0 area 10.10.10.0
pix515a(config-router)# prefix-list ten deny 10.10.10.0/24
pix515a(config)#
pix515a(config)# router ospf 1
pix515a(config-router)# prefix-list ten permit 172.16.1.0/24
pix515a(config)#
```

NOTE If you configure your PIX Firewall as an ASBR, then you need to configure multiple OSPF processes on the firewall if you want to perform address filtering.

When configuring OSPF, you should also enable one of the following authentication mechanisms:

- Password
- MD5 (message digest algorithm 5)

You enable authentication for each area individually by using the following command:

```
area area-id authentication [message-digest]
```

Next, you need to define the authentication to be used for communication with the specific routers with which each area will be communicating. You do so by defining a *virtual-link* using the **area** command. Continuing with the example shown in Figure 9-2, to enable MD5 authentication with a key ID of 4 and a key of Ab1&05K! for **area 172.16.1.0** when communicating with router 172.16.1.250, you would use the following commands:

```
pix515a(config)# router ospf 1
pix515a(config-router)# area 172.16.1.0 authentication message-digest
pix515a(config-router)# area 172.16.1.0 virtual-link
     172.16.1.250 authentication message-digest
     message-digest-key 4 md5 Ab1&05K!
```

NOTE To enable password authentication (using a password of R5!s4&Px*) for the same router (instead of using MD5), you would use the following commands:

```
pix515a(config)# router ospf 1
pix515a(config-router)# area 172.16.1.0 authentication
pix515a(config-router)# area 172.16.1.0 virtual-link
     172.16.1.250 authentication authentication-key
     R5!s4&Px*
```

Viewing the OSPF Configuration

After setting up OSPF on your PIX Firewall, it is helpful to be able to view the configuration. Using the **show ospf** command, you can view your entire OSPF configuration. When you enter this command, you see output similar to Example 9-2, depending on the OSPF features that you have configured.

Example 9-2 *Output from the* show ospf *Command*

```
pix515a# show ospf

 Routing Process "ospf 1" with ID 192.168.10.80 and Domain ID 0.0.0.1
 Supports only single TOS(TOS0) routes
 Supports opaque LSA
 It is an area border router
 SPF schedule delay 5 secs, Hold time between two SPFs 10 secs
 Minimum LSA interval 5 secs. Minimum LSA arrival 1 secs
```

Example 9-2 *Output from the* **show ospf** *Command (Continued)*

```
Number of external LSA 0. Checksum Sum 0x      0
Number of opaque AS LSA 0. Checksum Sum 0x      0
Number of DCbitless external and opaque AS LSA 0
Number of DoNotAge external and opaque AS LSA 0
Number of areas in this router is 3. 3 normal 0 stub 0 nssa
External flood list length 0
   Area BACKBONE(0) (Inactive)
       Number of interfaces in this area is 1
       Area has message digest authentication
       SPF algorithm executed 4 times
       Area ranges are
       Area-filter ten in
       Number of LSA 2. Checksum Sum 0x  35a8
       Number of opaque link LSA 0. Checksum Sum 0x      0
       Number of DCbitless LSA 0
       Number of indication LSA 0
       Number of DoNotAge LSA 0
       Flood list length 0
   Area 10.10.10.0
       Number of interfaces in this area is 1
       Area has no authentication
       SPF algorithm executed 4 times
       Area ranges are
       Number of LSA 3. Checksum Sum 0x  ec7b
       Number of opaque link LSA 0. Checksum Sum 0x      0
       Number of DCbitless LSA 0
       Number of indication LSA 0
       Number of DoNotAge LSA 0
       Flood list length 0
   Area 172.16.1.0
       Number of interfaces in this area is 1
       Area has message digest authentication
       SPF algorithm executed 6 times
       Area ranges are
       Number of LSA 2. Checksum Sum 0x 104d9
       Number of opaque link LSA 0. Checksum Sum 0x      0
       Number of DCbitless LSA 0
       Number of indication LSA 0
       Number of DoNotAge LSA 0
       Flood list length 0

pix515a(config)#
```

Multicast Routing

IP multicasting is a mechanism that conserves network bandwidth by delivering a stream of information simultaneously to multiple recipients. Some common applications that take advantage of IP multicasting include the following:

- Video conferencing
- Distance learning
- News feeds

IP multicasting actually involves sending an IP packet to a single multicast IP address. Routers send Internet Group Management Protocol (IGMP) query messages to locate hosts that belong to any multicast groups (wishing to receive specific multicast traffic). Any host that wishes to receive multicast traffic must join the multicast group by using an IGMP report message that indicates all the multicast groups to which it belongs. When a host no longer wishes to receive a multicast data stream, it sends an IGMP Leave message to the multicast router.

You can configure your PIX Firewall to act as a Stub Multicast Router (SMR) because it forwards requests only between end hosts and multicast routers. Instead of supporting the functionality of a fully operational multicast router, the PIX Firewall functions only as an IGMP proxy agent. To illustrate the configuration tasks associated with configuring your PIX Firewall as an SMR, you need to understand the following topics:

- Multicast commands
- Inbound multicast traffic
- Outbound multicast traffic
- Debugging multicast

Multicast Commands

Configuring multicast functionality on your PIX Firewall requires you to understand various multicast configuration commands. The major multicast configuration commands are as follows:

- **multicast interface**
- **mroute command**
- **igmp forward**
- **igmp join-group**
- **igmp access-group**

- igmp version
- igmp query-interval
- igmp query-max-response-time

multicast interface Command

The **multicast interface** command identifies the interface that will pass multicast traffic. It also enables the multicast subcommand mode in which the other multicast commands must be entered. The syntax for this command is

```
multicast interface interface-name [max-groups number]
```

The parameters for this command are shown in Table 9-12.

Table 9-12 multicast interface *Command Parameters*

Parameter	Description
interface-name	The name of the interface that will be configured for passing multicast traffic and to which other multicast commands will be applied
max-groups	Keyword indicating that you want to limit the number of multicast groups allowed on the interface
number	A numeric value (1–2000) indicating the maximum number of groups allowed on the interface (default value is 500)

mroute Command

To configure your PIX Firewall to forward multicast traffic when the multicast router is on the inside interface, you need to use the **mroute** command. The syntax for this command is as follows:

```
mroute source source-mask in-interface dest dest-mask out-interface
```

The parameters for the **mroute** command are shown in Table 9-13.

Table 9-13 mroute forward *Command Parameters*

Parameter	Description
source	The source address of the multicast transmission device
source-mask	The network mask associated with the multicast source address
in-interface	The interface on which the multicast traffic enters the PIX Firewall
dest	The Class D address of the multicast group

continues

Table 9-13 mroute forward *Command Parameters (Continued)*

Parameter	Description
dest-mask	The network mask associated with the destination multicast address
out-interface	The interface on which the multicast traffic leaves the PIX Firewall

> **NOTE** To clear static multicast routes created with the **mroute** command, you use the **clear mroute** command. To actually stop the PIX Firewall from forwarding multicast traffic, you use the **no** keyword in front of your original **mroute** command.

igmp forward Command

To join a multicast group, the host IGMP message must reach the multicast router. The **igmp forward** command enables you to cause one PIX Firewall interface to pass IGMP messages to another interface. The syntax for this command is as follows:

```
igmp forward interface interface-name
```

The parameters for the **igmp forward** command are shown in Table 9-14.

Table 9-14 igmp forward *Command Parameters*

Parameter	Description
interface	Keyword indicating that the next parameter will be an interface name
interface-name	The name of the interface to forward the IGMP messages that are received on the current interface being configured

igmp join-group Command

To statically configure the PIX Firewall to join a multicast group, you can use the **igmp join-group** command. This command is useful if you have clients who are unable to send the IGMP messages on their own. The syntax for this command is as follows:

```
igmp join-group group
```

The only parameter for the **igmp join-group** command is the multicast group (multicast address) that is statically being joined. Multicast addresses use the entire range of 224.0.0.0 through 239.255.255.255 (Class D addresses); however, you can configure a value only in the range of 224.0.0.2 through 239.255.255.255 for the **igmp join-group** command.

> **NOTE** The multicast address 224.0.0.0 is the base address for IP multicasting, and 224.0.0.1 is permanently assigned to a group that includes all IP hosts.

igmp access-group Command

To limit which multicast groups (addresses) are allowed on a specific interface, you use the **igmp access-group** command. To use this command, you must first create an access list (using the **access-list** command) that defines the allowed multicast addresses. The syntax for this command is as follows:

```
igmp access-group access-list-id
```

igmp version Command

To define the IGMP version, you use the **igmp version** command. The syntax for this command is as follows:

```
igmp version 1|2
```

> **NOTE**   The default version for IP multicasting is 2.

igmp query-interval Command

To configure the frequency, in seconds, at which IGMP query messages are sent by an interface, you use the **igmp query-interval** command. The default value is 60, but you can specify a value from 1 to 65535. The syntax for this command is as follows:

```
igmp query-interval seconds
```

> **NOTE**   To set the query interval back to the default value, you use the **no igmp query-interval** command.

igmp query-max-response-time Command

When using IGMP version 2, you can specify the maximum query response time, in seconds, using the **igmp query-max-response-time.** The default value is 10, but you can configure a value in the range from 1 to 65535.

> **NOTE**   To set the query interval back to the default value, you use the **no igmp query-max-response-time** command.

Inbound Multicast Traffic

Allowing inbound multicast traffic involves the configuration shown in Figure 9-3. In this configuration, the multicast router is located outside the PIX Firewall and the hosts that want to receive multicast traffic are being protected by the PIX Firewall.

Figure 9-3 *Inbound Multicast Configuration*

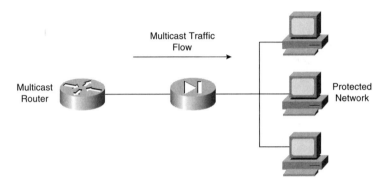

Because the hosts that need to receive the multicast traffic are separated from the multicast router by your PIX Firewall, you need to configure the PIX Firewall to forward IGMP reports from the hosts protected by the firewall to the multicast router. You also need to forward multicast transmissions from the multicast router. The following configuration steps enable this multicast configuration:

Step 1 Use the **multicast interface** command to enable multicast processing on a specific interface and place the interface in multicast promiscuous mode. This also places the command line in multicast subcommand mode, designated by the *(config-multicast)#* prompt.

Step 2 Use the **igmp forward** command to enable IGMP forwarding on the interfaces connected to hosts that will receive multicast transmissions. This also enables the interface to forward all IGMP Host Report and Leave messages.

Step 3 (Optional) If your network contains clients that cannot respond to IGMP messages but still require the reception of multicast traffic, you use the **igmp join-group** command to statically join the PIX Firewall to the specific multicast group.

Step 4   (Optional) Define an access list to define which Class D addresses (multicast addresses) are allowed to traverse the PIX Firewall. Then, use the **igmp access-group** command to apply the access list to a specific interface.

Assume that you want to allow protected hosts to join the multicast group 224.0.1.100 from a multicast router that is located outside the protected network. To accomplish this, you would use the following commands:

```
pix515a(config)# access-list 120 permit udp any host 224.0.1.100
pix515a(config)# multicast interface outside
pix515a(config-multicast)# igmp access-group 120
pix515a(config-multicast)# exit
pix515a(config)# multicast interface inside
pix515a(config-multicast)# igmp forward interface outside
pix515a(config-multicast)# exit
```

Outbound Multicast Traffic

Allowing outbound multicast traffic involves the configuration shown in Figure 9-4. In this configuration, the multicast transmission source is located inside the PIX Firewall and the hosts that want to receive multicast traffic are not protected by the PIX Firewall.

Figure 9-4   *Outbound Multicast Configuration*

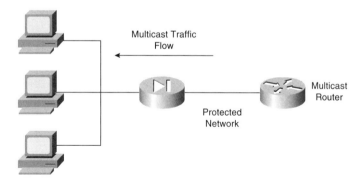

When the multicast transmission source is on the protected or secure interface of the PIX Firewall, you must specifically configure the PIX Firewall to forward the multicast transmissions. The following configuration steps enable this multicast configuration:

Step 1   Use the **multicast interface** command to enable multicast forwarding on each PIX Firewall interface.

Step 2   Use the **mroute** command to create a static route from the multicast transmission source to the next-hop router interface.

Suppose that your multicast router is located at 10.10.10.100 and broadcasting to the multicast group 230.0.1.100. To get the PIX Firewall to forward multicast transmissions from this multicast router to the outside interface, you would use the following commands:

```
pix515a(config)# multicast interface outside
pix515a(config-multicast) exit
pix515a(config)# multicast interface inside
pix515a(config-multicast)# mroute 10.10.10.100 255.255.255.255
     inside 230.0.1.100 255.255.255.255 outside
pix515a(config-multicast)# exit
pix515a(config)#
```

Debugging Multicast

Not only can you configure IP multicasting, you can also debug the operation of your IP multicasting configuration. The commands that you use to do so fall into the following two categories:

■ Commands to view the multicast configuration

■ Commands to debug multicast traffic

Commands to View the Multicast Configuration

You can use the following commands to view your multicast configuration:

■ **show multicast**

■ **show igmp**

■ **show mroute**

The **show multicast** command displays the multicast settings for either a specific interface or all the interfaces. The syntax for this command is as follows:

```
show multicast [interface interface-name]
```

If you do not specify an interface, then the information for all the PIX Firewall interfaces is displayed.

The **show igmp** command displays information about either a specific IGMP group or all the IGMP groups for a specific interface. The syntax for this command is as follows:

```
show igmp [group¦interface interface-name] [detail]
```

The final command that you can use to view your multicast configuration is **show mroute**, which displays the current multicast routes. Its syntax is as follows:

```
show mroute [destination [source]]
```

Commands to Debug Multicast Traffic

After you configure IP multicasting on your PIX Firewall, you may need to debug multicast traffic to identify configuration problems. Two commands that are useful for debugging multicast traffic are as follows:

- **debug igmp**—Enables debugging for IGMP events
- **debug mfwd**—Enables debugging for multicast forwarding events

> **NOTE**   To disable either of these debugging commands, simply place a **no** in front of the command (for instance, **no debug igmp**).

Foundation Summary

The "Foundation Summary" provides a convenient review of many key concepts in this chapter. If you are already comfortable with the topics in this chapter, this summary can help you recall a few details. If you just read this chapter, this review should help solidify some key facts. If you are doing your final preparation before the exam, this summary provides a convenient way to review the day before the exam.

The PIX Firewall needs to support some basic routing and switching functionality. This functionality falls into the following three areas:

- Ethernet VLAN tagging
- IP routing
- Multicast routing

To support traffic from multiple VLANs, the PIX Firewall supports 802.1Q tagging and the configuration of multiple logical interfaces on a single physical interface. For each logical interface that you establish, you must configure the following parameters:

- Interface name
- Security level
- IP address

For IP routing, the PIX Firewall supports both static and dynamic routes. Using the **route** command, you can configure static routing information on the PIX Firewall. The PIX Firewall also supports dynamic updates from the following two routing protocols:

- RIP
- OSPF

With RIP, the PIX Firewall can only *receive* RIP routing updates. It does not support the capability to propagate those updates to other devices. It can, however, advertise one of its interfaces as a default route.

Using OSPF, the PIX Firewall can actually propagate route information and actively participate in the OSPF routing protocol. Some of the OSPF functionality supported by the PIX Firewall includes the following:

- Support for intra-area, interarea, and external routes
- Support for virtual links

- Authentication for OSPF packets
- The capability to configure the PIX Firewall as a designated router, ABR, and limited ASBR
- ABR Type 3 LSA filtering
- Route redistribution

Configuring OSPF on your PIX Firewall requires you to perform the following steps:

Step 1   Enable OSPF.

Step 2   Define the PIX Firewall interfaces that need to run OSPF.

Step 3   Define OSPF areas.

Step 4   Configure LSA filtering to protect private addresses.

You enable OSPF using the **router ospf** command. The **network** command enables you to define which IP addresses fall into which areas, and which interfaces use OSPF. The **prefix-list** and **area** commands enable you to filter Type 3 LSAs to prevent the PIX Firewall from advertising information about private networks. If you configure your PIX Firewall as an ASBR OSPF router, then using multiple OSPF processes enables you to perform address filtering.

Finally, you can configure the PIX Firewall to operate as a Stub Multicast Router (SMR). This enables you to support various applications such as remote learning and video conferencing. The multicast transmission source can be either inside or outside the PIX Firewall. Some of the important multicast configuration commands include the following:

- **multicast interface**
- **igmp forward**
- **igmp join-group**
- **igmp access-group**
- **igmp version**
- **igmp query-interval**
- **igmp query-max-response-time**

Q&A

As mentioned in the Introduction, the questions in this book are more difficult than what you should experience on the exam. The questions are designed to ensure your understanding of the concepts discussed in this chapter and adequately prepare you to complete the exam. You should use the simulated exams on the CD to practice for the exam.

The answers to these questions can be found in Appendix A.

1. What type of Ethernet tagging does the PIX Firewall support?

2. Which command do you use to configure logical interfaces?

3. What three basic configuration parameters do you need to define for each logical interface?

4. What command do you use to define static routes on the PIX Firewall?

5. What is the default route and what values do you use for the IP address and netmask when creating the default route?

6. The PIX Firewall provides functionality for which two routing protocols?

7. Can the PIX Firewall propagate RIP routes?

8. Which LSAs can the PIX Firewall filter, and why is this important?

9. Which two commands enable you to configure LSA filtering?

10. What are the steps involved in setting up OSPF on your PIX Firewall?

11. Can the PIX Firewall operate as a fully functional multicast router?

12. If you have clients that cannot send IGMP messages, which command do you use to statically configure the PIX Firewall to receive messages from a multicast group?

13. What is the range of addresses for multicast traffic?

14. If the multicast transmission source is protected by the PIX Firewall, which command do you use to configure the PIX Firewall to allow clients to access it?

15. Which two commands can you use to view the multicast configuration on the PIX Firewall?

16. Which command enables you to view the routes currently in use on the PIX Firewall?

17. Which command enables you to pass OSPF routing information between multiple OSPF domains or processes?

18. Why would you run multiple OSPF processes on your PIX Firewall?

This chapter covers the following subjects:

- Understanding Failover

- Failover Configuration

- LAN-Based Failover Configuration

CHAPTER 10

Cisco PIX Firewall Failover

Today, most businesses rely heavily on critical application servers that support the business process. The interruption of these servers due to network device failures or other causes has a great financial cost, not to mention the irritation such an interruption causes in the user community. With this in mind, Cisco has designed most of its devices, including the PIX Firewall products (models 515 and up), such that they can be configured in a redundant or highly available configuration.

The failover feature makes the Cisco PIX Firewall a highly available firewall solution. The purpose of this feature is to ensure continuity of service in case of a failure on the primary unit.

The failover process requires two PIX Firewalls—one primary (active mode) and one secondary (standby mode). The idea is to have the primary PIX Firewall handle all traffic from the network and to have the secondary PIX Firewall wait in standby mode in case the primary fails, at which point it takes over the process of handling all network traffic. If a primary (active) unit fails, the secondary PIX Firewall changes its state from standby mode to active, assumes the IP address and MAC address of the previously active unit and begins accepting traffic for it. The new standby unit assumes the IP address and MAC address of the unit that was previously the standby unit, thus completing the failover process.

How to Best Use This Chapter

Computer networks are a vital component to the operation of most businesses. Protecting these networks from attacks using firewalls is also vital. Many businesses deploy some type of power backup (on critical systems) to insure that these important components continue to operate in the case of a temporary power failure. Similarly, depending on a single device to protect important networks is not acceptable in many environments. Using multiple PIX Firewalls operating in a failover configuration enables your network to remain operational (and protected from attack) even if a single PIX Firewall fails. Test yourself with the "Do I Know This Already?" quiz and see how familiar you are with the failover functionality available on PIX Firewalls.

"Do I Know This Already?" Quiz

The purpose of the "Do I Know This Already?" quiz is to help you decide if you really need to read the entire chapter. If you already intend to read the entire chapter, you do not necessarily need to answer these questions now.

The eleven-question quiz, derived from the major sections in the "Foundation Topics" portion of the chapter, helps you determine how to spend your limited study time.

Table 10-1 outlines the major topics discussed in this chapter and the "Do I Know This Already?" quiz questions that correspond to those topics.

Table 10-1 *"Do I Know This Already?" Foundation Topics Section-to-Question Mapping*

Foundation Topics Section	Questions Covered in This Section	Score
Understanding Failover	1 to 3, 5, 6, 8 to 10	
LAN-Based Failover Configuration	4, 7	
Serial Failover Configuration	11	

> **CAUTION** The goal of self assessment is to gauge your mastery of the topics in this chapter. If you do not know the answer to a question or are only partially sure of the answer, you should mark this question wrong for purposes of the self assessment. Giving yourself credit for an answer you correctly guess skews your self assessment results and might provide you with a false sense of security.

1. Which of the following causes a failover event?

   a. A reboot or power interruption on the active PIX Firewall

   b. Low HTTP traffic on the outside interface

   c. Issuance of the **failover active** command on the standby PIX Firewall

   d. Low memory utilization for several consecutive seconds

2. What is the command to view failover configuration?

   a. **show failover**

   b. **failover**

   c. **view failover**

   d. **show me failover**

3. Which of the following is/are replicated in stateful failover operation?

    a. Configuration

    b. TCP connection table, including timeout information for each connection

    c. Translation (xlate) table

    d. Negotiated H.323 UDP protocols

    e. All of the above

4. Which of the following is *not* replicated in stateful failover operation?

    a. User authentication (uauth) table

    b. ISAKMP and IPSec SA table

    c. ARP table

    d. Routing information

    e. All of the above

5. What is the command to force configuration replication to the standby unit?

    a. **write standby**

    b. **copy to secondary**

    c. **force secondary**

    d. **force conf**

6. Which of the following is a stateful failover hardware restriction?

    a. The stateful failover configuration is supported only by PIX Firewall 535 models.

    b. Only fiber connections can be used in a stateful failover hardware configuration.

    c. A PIX Firewall with two FDDI cards cannot use stateful failover, because an additional FDDI interface is not supported.

    d. There is no hardware restriction for stateful failover configuration.

7. What command assigns an IP address to the standby Cisco PIX Firewall?

    a. **secondary ip address** *ip address*

    b. **failover ip address** *if-name ip-address*

    c. **ip address** *ip address* **secondary**

    d. **ip address** *ip address* **failover**

8. What is the command to configure a LAN-based failover?

    a. conf lan failover

    b. failover ip LAN

    c. failover lan interface *if-name*

    d. lan interface failover

9. What is an advantage of a LAN-based failover?

    a. It quickly fails over to a peer when a power failure on the active unit takes place.

    b. It does not have the 6-foot-cable distance limitation for failover communication.

    c. It is preconfigured on the PIX Firewall.

    d. All of the above

10. What is the default failover poll, in seconds?

    a. 10 seconds

    b. 15 seconds

    c. 30 seconds

    d. 25 seconds

11. Which of the following is true about the serial link cable connection in a PIX Firewall failover configuration?

    a. Serial link cable can transfer data at 100 Mbps.

    b. The two units maintain the heartbeat network over the cable.

    c. Network link status is not communicated over the serial link.

    d. Keepalive packets and configuration replication are communicated over the serial link.

The answers to the "Do I Know This Already?" quiz are found in Appendix A, "Answers to the 'Do I Know This Already?' Quizzes and Q&A Sections." The suggested choices for your next step are as follows:

- **8 or less overall score**—Read the entire chapter. This includes the "Foundation Topics," "Foundation Summary," and "Q&A" sections.

- **9 to 11 overall score**—If you want more review on these topics, skip to the "Foundation Summary" section and then go to the "Q&A" section. Otherwise, move to the next chapter.

Foundation Topics

What Causes a Failover Event?

In a PIX Firewall failover configuration, one of the PIX Firewalls is considered the *active* unit, and the other is the *standby* unit. As their names imply, the active unit performs normal network functions and the standby unit monitors and is ready to take control should the active unit fail to perform its functionality. A failover event occurs after a series of tests determines that the primary (active) unit can no longer continue providing its services, at which time the standby PIX Firewall assumes the role of the primary. The main causes of failover are shown in Table 10-2.

Table 10-2 *Possible Failover Event Situations*

Failure Condition	Reasons that Standby becomes Active
No Failure	**Failover active**—An administrator can force the standby unit to change state by using the **failover active** command, which causes failover to occur. This is the only situation in which failover occurs without the primary (active) unit having any problems.
Power loss or reload	**Cable errors**—The cable is wired so that each unit can distinguish between a power failure in the other unit and an unplugged cable. If the standby unit detects that the active unit is turned off (or resets), it takes active control.
	Loss of power—When the primary (active) unit loses power or is turned off, the standby unit assumes the active role.
PIX Firewall hardware failure	**Memory exhaustion**—If block memory exhaustion occurs for 15 straight seconds on the active unit the standby unit becomes the active unit.
Network failure	**Failover communication loss**—If the standby unit does not hear from the active unit for more than twice the configured poll time (or a maximum of 30 seconds), and the cable status is OK, a series of tests is conducted before the standby unit takes over as active.

What Is Required for a Failover Configuration?

The hardware and software for the primary and standby PIX Firewalls must match in the following respects for failover configuration to work properly:

- Firewall model

- Software version (which should be the version with unrestricted [UR] licensing)

- Flash memory size

- RAM size

- Activation key

- Number and type of interfaces

> **NOTE**   Failover for 501 and 506E models is not supported.

The only additional hardware that is needed to support failover is the failover cable. Both units in a failover pair communicate through the failover cable. The failover cable is a modified RS-232 serial link cable that transfers data at 115 kbps. It is through this cable that the two units maintain the heartbeat network. This cable is not required for LAN-based failover. Some of the messages that are communicated over the failover cable are the following:

- Hello (keepalive packets)

- Configuration replication

- Network link status

- State of the unit (active/standby)

- MAC address exchange

It is also important to examine the labels on each end of the failover cable. One end of the cable is labeled "primary," and the other end is labeled "secondary." To have a successful failover configuration, the end labeled "primary" should be connected to the primary unit, and the end labeled "secondary" should be connected to the secondary unit. Changes made to the standby unit are never replicated to the active unit.

In addition to the hardware and software requirements, it is also important to correctly configure the switches where the PIX Firewalls directly connect. *Port Fast* should be enabled on all the ports where the PIX Firewall interface directly connects, and trunking and channeling should be turned off. This way, if the PIX Firewall's interface goes down during failover, the switch does not have to wait 30 seconds while the port is transitioned from a listening state to a learning state to a forwarding state.

Port Fast

Many Cisco switches provide a Port Fast option for switch ports. Configuring this option on a switch port enables a simplified version of the Spanning-Tree Protocol that eliminates several of the normal spanning-tree states. The pre-forwarding states are bypassed to more quickly transition ports into the forwarding states. Port Fast is an option that you can enable on a per-port basis. It is recommended only for end-station attachments.

Failover Monitoring

The failover feature in the Cisco PIX Firewall monitors failover communication, the power status of the other unit, and hello packets received at each interface. If two consecutive hello packets are not received within an amount of time determined by the failover feature, failover starts testing the interfaces to determine which unit has failed and transfers active control to the standby unit. At this point, the "active" LED on the front of the standby PIX Firewall lights up and the "active" LED on the failed PIX Firewall unit dims.

> **NOTE**   The **failover poll** *seconds* command enables you to determine how long failover waits before sending special failover hello packets between the primary and standby units over all network interfaces and the failover cable. The default is 15 seconds. The minimum value is 3 seconds, and the maximum is 15 seconds.

Failover uses the following tests to check the status of the units for failure:

- **Link up/down test**—If an interface card has a bad network cable or a bad port, is administratively shut down, or is connected to a failed switch, it is considered failed.

- **Network activity test**—The unit counts all received packets for up to 5 seconds. If any packets are received at any time during this interval, the interface is considered operational and testing stops. If no traffic is received, the ARP test begins.

- **Address Resolution Protocol test**—The unit's ARP cache is evaluated for the ten most recently acquired entries. One at a time, the PIX Firewall sends ARP requests to these machines, attempting to stimulate network traffic. After each request, the unit counts all received traffic for up to 5 seconds. If traffic is received, the interface is considered operational. If no traffic is received, an ARP request is sent to the next machine. If at the end of the list no traffic has been received, the ping test begins.

- **Ping test**—A broadcast ping request is sent out. The unit then counts all received packets for up to 5 seconds. If any packets are received at any time during this interval, the interface is considered operational and testing stops. If no traffic is received, failover takes place.

Configuration Replication

Configuration changes, including initial failover configurations to the Cisco PIX Firewall, are done on the primary unit. The standby unit keeps the current configuration through the process of configuration replication. For configuration replication to occur, the two PIX Firewall units should be running the same software release. Configuration replication usually occurs when:

■ The standby unit completes its initial bootup and the active unit replicates its entire configuration to the standby unit.

■ Configurations are made (commands) on the active unit and the commands/changes are sent across the failover cable to the standby unit.

■ Issuing the **write standby** command on the active unit forces the entire configuration in memory to be sent to the standby unit.

When the replication starts, the PIX Firewall console displays the message Sync Started. When the replication is complete, the PIX Firewall console displays the message Sync Completed. During the replication, information cannot be entered on the PIX Firewall console.

The **write memory** command is important, especially when failover is being configured for the first time. During the configuration replication process, the configuration is replicated from the active unit's running configuration to the running configuration of the standby unit. Because the running configuration is saved in RAM (which is unstable), you should issue the **write memory** command on the primary unit to save the configuration to Flash memory.

Stateful Failover

In stateful failover mode, more information is shared about the connections that have been established with the standby unit by the active unit. The active unit shares per-connection state information with the standby unit. If and when an active unit fails over to the standby unit, an application does not reinitiate its connection because stateful information from the active unit updates the standby unit.

> **NOTE** Some applications are latency-sensitive. In some cases, the application times out before the failover sequence is completed. In these cases, the application must reestablish the session.

Replicated state information includes the following:

■ TCP connection table, including timeout information for each connection

- Translation (xlate) table and status
- Negotiated H.323 UDP ports, SIP, and MGCP UDP media connections
- Port allocation table bitmap for PAT
- HTTP replication

Because failover cannot be prescheduled, the state update for the connection is packet-based. This means that every packet passes through the PIX Firewall and changes a connection's state, and triggers a state update.

However, some state information does not get updated to the standby unit in a stateful failover:

- User authentication (uauth) table
- ISAKMP and the IPSec SA table
- ARP table
- Routing information

Most UDP state tables are not transferred, with the exception of dynamically opened ports that correspond to multichannel protocols such as H.323.

In addition to the failover cable, stateful failover setup requires a 100-Mbps or Gigabit Ethernet interface to be used exclusively for passing state information between the active and standby units. IP 105 is used to pass data over this interface.

The stateful failover interface can be connected to any of the following:

- Category 5 crossover cable directly connecting the primary unit to the secondary unit
- 100BASE-TX full duplex on a dedicated switch or a switch's dedicated VLAN
- 1000BASE-SX full duplex on a switch's dedicated VLAN

A Cisco PIX Firewall with two FDDI cards cannot use stateful failover because an additional Ethernet interface with FDDI is not supported in stateful failover.

LAN-Based Failover

The distance restriction of 6 feet of serial cable between two PIX Firewall devices in a failover configuration is no longer a limitation starting with PIX Firewall Version 6.2. LAN-based failover is a new feature (available only on PIX Firewall 6.2 or higher) that extends PIX Firewall failover functionality to operate through a dedicated LAN interface without the serial failover cable. This feature provides a choice of failover configuration on the PIX Firewall.

The obvious benefit of LAN-based failover is that it removes the 6-foot distance limitation from the PIX Firewall devices in a failover configuration. If the LAN-based failover command interface link goes down, the PIX Firewall notifies the peer through "other" interfaces, and then the standby unit takes over. If all connectivity between the two PIX Firewall units is lost, both PIX Firewalls could become active. Therefore, it is best to use a separate switch for the LAN-based failover command interface, so that a failed switch will not cause all connectivity to be lost between the two PIX Firewall units.

The weakness of LAN-based failover is the delayed detection of its peer power loss, consequently causing a relatively longer period for failover to occur.

NOTE   Crossover Ethernet cables cannot be used to connect the LAN-based failover interface. Additionally, it is recommended that you dedicate a LAN interface for LAN-based failover, but the interface can be shared with stateful failover under lightly loaded configurations.

Cisco PIX Firewall Version 6.2 enhances failover functionality so that the standby unit in a PIX Firewall failover pair can be configured to use a virtual MAC address. This eliminates potential "stale" ARP entry issues for devices connected to the PIX Firewall failover pair in the unlikely event that both firewalls in a failover pair fail at the same time.

Configuring Failover

To configure failover, you need to become familiar with a few key commands. Table 10-3 shows the commands used to configure and verify failover.

Table 10-3 *PIX Firewall Failover Commands*

Command	Description
failover lan enable	Enables LAN-based failover.
failover	Enables the failover function on the PIX Firewall. Use this command after you connect the failover cable between the primary and secondary unit. Use the **no failover** command to disable the failover feature.
failover lan key *key-secret*	Specifies the shared secret key.
failover active	Makes the PIX Firewall unit it is issued on the active unit. This command is usually used to make the primary unit active again after repairs have been made to it.

Table 10-3 *PIX Firewall Failover Commands (Continued)*

Command	Description
failover ip address *if-name ip-address*	Issued on the primary unit to configure the standby unit's IP address. This is the IP address that the standby interface uses to communicate with the active unit. Therefore, it has the same subnet as the system address.[a] The *if-name* argument is the interface name, such as **outside**. The *ip-address* is the interface name's IP address.
failover link *stateful-if-name*	Enables stateful failover on the specified interface.
show failover	This popular command displays the status of the failover configuration.
failover poll *seconds*	Specifies how long failover waits before sending special hello packets between the primary and secondary units. The default is 15 seconds. The minimum is 3 seconds, and the maximum is 15 seconds.
failover reset	Can be entered from either unit (active or standby), preferably the active unit. This forces the units back to an unfailed state and is used after repairs have been made.
write standby	Enter the **write standby** command from the active unit to synchronize the current configuration from RAM-to-RAM memory to the standby unit.
failover lan interface *interface-name*	Configures LAN-based failover.
failover lan unit primary | **secondary**	Specifies the primary or secondary PIX Firewall to use for LAN-based failover.
failover replicate http	Allows the stateful replication of HTTP sessions in a stateful failover environment.

[a] The system address is the same address as the active unit IP address. When the active unit fails, the standby assumes the system address so that there is no need for the network devices to be reconfigured for a different firewall address.

Figure 10-1 shows two PIX Firewall units in a failover configuration. Example 10-1 shows a sample configuration for a PIX Firewall Failover configuration.

Figure 10-1 *Network Diagram of Failover Configuration*

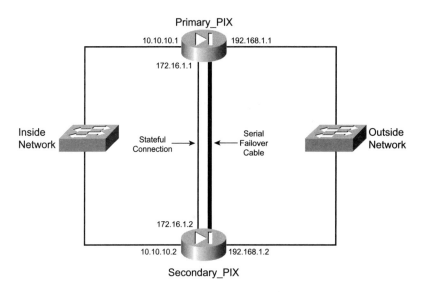

Example 10-1 *Sample Configuration for primary-PIX*

```
hostname primary-PIX
nameif ethernet0 outside security0
nameif ethernet1 inside security100
nameif ethernet2 failover security10
interface ethernet0 100full
interface ethernet1 100full
interface ethernet2 100full
ip address outside 192.168.1.1 255.255.255.0
ip address inside 10.10.10.1 255.255.255.0
ip address failover 172.16.10.1 255.255.255.224
failover ip address outside 192.168.1.2
failover ip address inside 10.10.10.2
failover ip address failover 172.16.10.2
global (outside) 1 192.168.1.15-192.168.1.40 netmask 255.255.255.224
nat (inside) 1 0.0.0.0 0.0.0.0 0 0
```

Configuring failover involves defining your configuration on the primary PIX Firewall. This
configuration is then replicated to the standby PIX Firewall. The following steps illustrate the
tasks needed to define a basic PIX Firewall configuration utilizing a serial failover
deployment.

> **NOTE**   Before you begin the failover configuration, be sure that you connect the failover cable to the units correctly. Also be sure that the standby unit is not powered on.

Step 1   Enable failover:

```
Primary-pix (config)# failover
```

Step 2   Assign interface ethernet2 a name for stateful failover:

```
Primary-pix (config)# nameif ethernet2 failover securitry10
```

Step 3   Set the interface speed:

```
Primary-pix (config)# interface ethernet2 100full
```

Step 4   Assign an IP address to the interface:

```
Primary-pix (config)# ip address failover 172.16.10.1 255.255.255.240
```

Step 5   Verify your failover configuration:

```
Primary-pix (config)# show failover
```

Step 6   Configure the secondary unit IP address from the primary unit by using the **failover ip address** command. Add the **failover ip address** command for *all* interfaces, including the one for the dedicated failover interface and any unused interfaces:

```
Primary-pix (config)# failover ip address outside 192.168.1.2
Primary-pix (config)# failover ip address inside 10.10.10.2
Primary-pix (config)# failover ip address failover 172.16.10.2
```

Step 7   Save your configuration:

```
Primary-pix (config)# write memory
```

Step 8   Use the **show ip address** command to view the addresses you specified:

```
Primary-pix (config)# show ip address
System IP Addresses:
     ip address outside 192.168.1.1 255.255.255.0
     ip address inside 10.10.10.1 255.255.255.0
     ip address failover 172.16.10.1 255.255.255.240
Current IP Addresses:
     ip address outside 192.168.1.1 255.255.255.0
     ip address inside 10.10.10.1 255.255.255.0
     ip address failover 172.16.10.1 255.255.255.244
```

The current IP addresses are the same as the system IP addresses on the failover active unit. When the primary unit fails, the current IP addresses become those of the standby unit.

Step 9   Enable stateful failover:

```
Primary-pix (config)# failover link failover
```

Step 10   Power up the secondary unit. At this point, the primary unit starts replicating the configuration to the secondary.

Step 11   Verify your failover configuration:

```
Primary-pix (config)# show failover
Failover On
Serial Failover Cable status: My side not connected
Reconnect timeout 0:00:00
Poll frequency 15 seconds
Last Failover at: 22:19:11 UTC Mon Jan 19 2004
        This host: Primary - Active
                Active time: 345 (sec)
                Interface failover (172.16.10.1): Normal
                Interface outside (192.168.1.1): Normal
                Interface inside (10.10.10.1): Normal
        Other host: Secondary - Standby
                Active time: 0 (sec)
                Interface failover (172.16.10.1): Normal
                Interface outside (192.168.1.1): Normal
                Interface inside (10.10.10.1): Normal
Stateful Failover Logical Update Statistics
        Link : failover
        Stateful Obj    xmit        xerr        rcv         rerr
        General         0           0           0           0
        sys cmd         0           0           0           0
        up time         0           0           0           0
        xlate           0           0           0           0
        tcp conn        0           0           0           0
        udp conn        0           0           0           0
        ARP tbl         0           0           0           0
        RIP Tbl         0           0           0           0

        Logical Update Queue Information
                        Cur         Max         Total
        Recv Q:         0           0           0
        Xmit Q:         0           0           0
```

The **show failover** command displays the last occurrence of a failover. The first part of the **show failover** command output describes the cable status. Each interface on the PIX Firewall unit has one of the following values:

- **Normal**—The active unit is working, and the standby unit is ready.

- **Waiting**—Monitoring of the other unit's network interfaces has not yet started.

- **Failed**—The PIX Firewall has failed.

- **Shutdown**—The interface is turned off.

The second part of the **show failover** command describes the status of the stateful failover configuration. Each row is for a particular static object count:

- **General**—The sum of all stateful objects.

- **Sys cmd**—Refers to logical update system commands, such as **login** and **stay alive**.

- **Up time**—The value for PIX up time that the active PIX Firewall unit passes on to the standby unit.

- **Xlate**—The PIX Firewall translation information.

- **Tcp conn**—The PIX Firewall dynamic TCP connection information.

- **Udp conn**—The PIX Firewall dynamic UDP connection information.

- **ARP tbl**—The PIX Firewall dynamic ARP table information.

- **RIF tbl**—The dynamic router table information.

The **Stateful Obj** has these values:

- **Xmit**—Indicates the number of packets transmitted.

- **Xerr**—Indicates the number of transmit errors.

- **Rcv**—Indicates the number of packets received.

- **rerr**—Indicates the number of receive errors.

Step 12   Enter the **write memory** command from the active unit to synchronize the current configuration to the Flash memory on the standby unit.

Foundation Summary

The "Foundation Summary" provides a convenient review of many key concepts in this chapter. If you are already comfortable with the topics in this chapter, this summary can help you recall a few details. If you just read this chapter, this review should help solidify some key facts. If you are doing your final preparation before the exam, this summary provides a convenient way to review the day before the exam.

Failover enables you to connect a second PIX Firewall unit to your network to protect your network should the first unit go offline. If you use stateful failover, you can maintain operating state for TCP connections during the failover from the primary unit to the standby unit.

Failover is triggered by some of the following events:

- Loss of power
- The standby unit is forced by an administrator to be active
- Cable errors
- Memory exhaustion
- Failover communication loss

Failover requires you to purchase a second PIX Firewall unit, sold as a failover unit, that works only as a failover unit. You need to ensure that both units have the same software version (which should be the version with unrestricted licensing), activation key type, Flash memory, and the same RAM. After you configure the primary unit and attach the necessary cabling, the primary unit automatically copies the configuration over to the standby unit.

If a failure is due to a condition other than a loss of power on the other unit, failover begins a series of tests to determine which unit failed. This series of tests begins when hello messages are not heard for two consecutive 15-second intervals (the interval length depends on how you set the **failover poll** command). Hello messages are sent over both network interfaces and the failover cable. Failover uses the following tests to determine the other unit's availability:

- Link up/down
- Network activity
- Address Resolution Protocol
- Ping

The stateful failover feature passes per-connection stateful information to the standby unit. After a failover occurs, the same connection information is available at the new active unit. Most end-user applications do not have to reconnect to maintain the communication session.

Q&A

As mentioned in the Introduction, the questions in this book are more difficult than what you should experience on the exam. The questions are designed to ensure your understanding of the concepts discussed in this chapter and adequately prepare you to complete the exam. You should use the simulated exams on the CD to practice for the exam.

The answers to these questions can be found in Appendix A.

1. What are some things that trigger a failover event?

2. What command assigns an IP address to the standby PIX Firewall?

3. How many PIX Firewall devices can be configured in a failover configuration?

4. What are the disadvantages of LAN-based failover?

5. What is some of the information that is updated to the standby unit in a stateful failover configuration?

6. What command forces replication to the standby unit?

7. What command configures a LAN-based failover?

8. What is the default failover poll, in seconds?

9. Does configuration replication save the running configuration to Flash memory on the standby unit during normal operations?

10. How long does it take to detect a failure?

This chapter covers the following subjects:

- Examining the PIX Firewall status

- PIX Firewall enables a secure VPN

- Prepare to configure VPN support

- Configure IKE parameters

- Configure IPSec parameters

- Test and verify VPN configuration

- Scale PIX Firewall VPNs

CHAPTER 11

Virtual Private Networks

Virtual private networks (VPNs) have become crucial components of nearly all enterprise networks. The ability of VPN technologies to create a secure link interconnecting offices over the Internet saves companies the expense of dedicated connections. Additionally, VPN connections enable remote users to connect to their headquarters securely.

How to Best Use This Chapter

This chapter provides an overview of the different VPN technologies available and discusses where the Cisco PIX Firewall can be used as an endpoint for VPNs. You must become very familiar with the methodology used to implement VPNs and how that methodology is applied to the PIX. As you read through this chapter, consider how encryption technology is applied in general, and then focus on the configuration steps required to configure the PIX. If you are at all familiar with configuring VPNs on any Cisco Systems product, you will probably find this chapter very easy.

"Do I Know This Already?" Quiz

The purpose of the "Do I Know This Already?" quiz is to help you decide if you really need to read the entire chapter. If you already intend to read the entire chapter, you do not necessarily need to answer these questions now.

The ten-question quiz, derived from the major sections in the "Foundation Topics" portion of the chapter, helps you determine how to spend your limited study time.

Table 11-1 outlines the major topics discussed in this chapter and the "Do I Know This Already?" quiz questions that correspond to those topics.

Table 11-1 *"Do I Know This Already?" Foundation Topics Section-to-Question Mapping*

Foundations Topics Section	Questions Covered in This Section	Score
Examining the PIX Firewall status	10	
PIX Firewall enables a secure VPN	9	
Prepare to configure VPN support	6, 7	
Configure IKE parameters	2, 3	
Configure IPSec parameters	1, 4	
Test and verify VPN configuration	10	
Scale PIX Firewall VPNs	5, 8	

CAUTION The goal of self assessment is to gauge your mastery of the topics in this chapter. If you do not know the answer to a question or are only partially sure of the answer, you should mark this question wrong for purposes of the self assessment. Giving yourself credit for an answer you correctly guess skews your self-assessment results and might provide you with a false sense of security.

1. Which type of encryption is stronger?

    a. Group 2 Diffie-Hellman

    b. AES-128

    c. 3DES

    d. AES-192

    e. DES

2. Which service uses UDP port 500?

    a. IPSec

    b. OAKLEY

    c. IKE

    d. None of the above

3. Which service uses TCP port 50?

   a. IKE

   b. AH

   c. OAKLEY

   d. ESP

   e. None of the above

4. What is the size of the output for a MD5 hash?

   a. There is no fixed size.

   b. 256 bits

   c. 255 bits

   d. 128 bits

   e. None of the above

5. What is the most scalable VPN solution?

   a. Manual-ipsec with CAs

   b. IKE using OAKLEY

   c. IKE using CAs

   d. CAs using preshared keys

   e. None of the above

6. What is the function of the access list with regard to VPNs?

   a. It tells the PIX what traffic should be allowed.

   b. It tells the PIX what traffic should be encrypted.

   c. It tells the PIX what traffic should be denied.

   d. None of the above

7. What is the configuration value for the unlimited ISAKMP phase 1 lifetime?

   a. Unlim

   b. 99999

   c. 86400

   d. 19200

   e. 0

8. The X509v3 standard applies to which standard or protocol?

   a. Authentication Header format

   b. ESP header format

   c. Digital certificates

   d. Diffie-Hellman negotiation

   e. AES encryption

9. What are three types of VPNs?

   a. Hardware, software, and concentrator

   b. Manual, dynamic, and very secure

   c. Dialup, cable, and LAN

   d. Access, intranet, and extranet

   e. Internet, extranet, and dialup

10. What command will allow you to watch the IKE negotiations?

    a. **debug isakmp sa**

    b. **debug crypto isakmp**

    c. **view isakmp neg**

    d. **view crypto isakmp**

    e. **debug isakmp crypto**

The answers to the "Do I Know This Already?" quiz are found in Appendix A, "Answers to the 'Do I Know This Already?' Quizzes and Q&A Sections." The suggested choices for your next step are as follows:

- **8 or less overall score**—Read the entire chapter. This includes the "Foundation Topics," "Foundation Summary," and "Q&A" sections.

- **9 or 10 overall score**—If you want more review of these topics, skip to the "Foundation Summary" section and then go to the "Q&A" section. Otherwise, move to the next chapter.

Foundation Topics

Overview of Virtual Private Network Technologies

Before the creation of VPN technologies, the only way for companies to secure network communications between different locations was to purchase or lease costly dedicated connections. VPNs allow companies to create secure encrypted tunnels between locations over a shared network infrastructure such as the Internet. A VPN is a service that offers secure, reliable connectivity over a shared public network infrastructure. VPNs are broken into three types based on the business component accessing the VPN and the assets available by using the VPN:

- **Access VPNs**—An access VPN, as shown in Figure 11-1, provides secure communications with remote users. Access VPNs are used by users who connect using dialup or other mobile connections. A user working from home would most likely use an access VPN to connect to the company network. Access VPNs usually require some type of client software running on the user's computer. This type of VPN is commonly called a *remote-access VPN*.

Figure 11-1 *Access VPN*

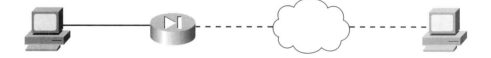

- **Intranet VPNs**—An intranet VPN is used to interconnect a company's different locations securely. This allows all locations to have access to the resources available on the enterprise network. Intranet VPNs link headquarters, offices, and branch offices over a shared infrastructure using connections that are always encrypted. This type of VPN is normally configured as a *site-to-site VPN*.

- **Extranet VPNs**—Extranet VPNs provide a secure tunnel between customers, suppliers, and partners over a shared infrastructure using connections that are always encrypted. This type of VPN is also normally configured as a site-to-site VPN. The difference between an intranet VPN and an extranet VPN is the network access that is granted at either end of the VPN. Figure 11-2 shows a site-to-site VPN, the configuration commonly used for both intranet and extranet VPNs.

Figure 11-2 *Site-to-Site VPN*

Internet Protocol Security

Internet Protocol Security (IPSec) is not a protocol. It is a framework of open-standard protocol suites designed to provide data authentication, data integrity, and data confidentiality. IPSec runs at the Internet Protocol (IP) layer and uses Internet Key Exchange (IKE) to negotiate the security association (SA) between the peers. There are actually two *phases* of negotiation that must take place. The *phase 1* negotiation establishes the IKE SA. The IKE SA must be established to begin the *phase 2* negotiations to establish the IPSec SA. The following items must be negotiated as phase 1 of IKE SA negotiation:

- Encryption algorithm
- Hash algorithm
- Authentication method
- Diffie-Hellman group

As soon as the IKE SA negotiation is complete, the established SA is bidirectional.

The phase 2 negotiations establish unidirectional SAs between two IPSec peers. The SAs determine the keying, protocols, and algorithms to be used between the peers. Two primary security protocols are included as part of the IPSec standard supported by the PIX:

- **Encapsulating Security Payload (ESP)**—ESP provides data authentication, encryption, and antireplay services. ESP is protocol number 50 assigned by the Internet Assigned Numbers Authority (IANA). ESP is primarily responsible for getting the data from the source to the destination in a secure manner, verifying that the data has not been altered, and ensuring that the session cannot be hijacked. ESP also can be used to authenticate the sender, either by itself or in conjunction with Authentication Header (AH). ESP can be configured to encrypt the entire data packet or only the packet's payload. Figure 11-3 shows how ESP encapsulates the Internet Protocol version 4 (IPv4) packet, which portions are encrypted, and which are authenticated.

Figure 11-3 *ESP Encapsulation*

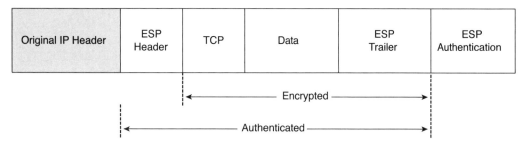

IPv4 Packet without ESP Encapsulation

IPv4 Packet with ESP Encapsulation

- **Authentication Header (AH)**—AH provides data authentication and antireplay services. AH is protocol number 51 assigned by the IANA. The primary function of AH is origin authentication. AH does not provide any data encryption. It provides only origin authentication or verifies that the data is from the sender. This functionality also prevents session hijacking. AH does not work with Network Address Translation (NAT) because the address translation occurs prior to the IPSec SA being established. NAT will change the IP address of the original IP header, creating a mismatch with the AH and causing the hash to fail. Figure 11-4 shows how AH is inserted into the IPv4 packet.

It is important to note that ESP authenticates only the payload, and AH authenticates the entire packet including the IP header.

Figure 11-4 *AH Insertion into the IPv4 Packet*

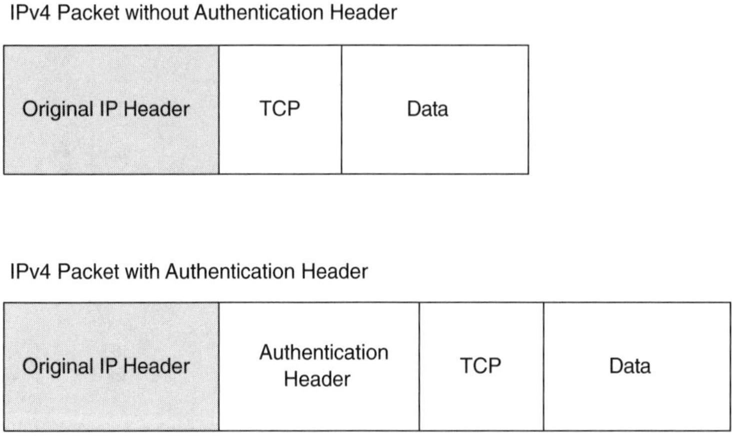

IPv4 Packet without Authentication Header

Original IP Header	TCP	Data

IPv4 Packet with Authentication Header

Original IP Header	Authentication Header	TCP	Data

Support for Network Address Translation and Port Address Translation

PIX Version 6.3 supports ESP with NAT using a new *fixup* protocol that allows for application inspection of ESP. PIX OS Version 6.3 also supports ESP with Port Address Translation (PAT) by restricting ESP to a single port (port 0) but with only a single ESP tunnel. Application inspection of ESP is disabled by default and can be enabled with the **fixup protocol esp-ike** command. This fixup protocol performs ESP tunnel serialization and the matching and recording of Security Parameter Indexes (SPIs) for each ESP connection. The SPI is a number that combines with the destination IP address and security protocol to uniquely identify the SA. AH does not support either a NAT or PAT device between the two AH peers.

Another feature supported by PIX Version 6.3 is NAT Traversal. NAT Traversal allows ESP packets to pass through one or more NAT devices. The command for NAT Traversal is **isakmp nat-traversal** [*natkeepalives*]. The values for *natkeepalives* is between 10 and 3600 seconds.

Supported Encryption Algorithms

Both ESP and AH can be configured to use a specific encryption algorithm and hash algorithms. An encryption algorithm is the mathematical algorithm used to encrypt and decrypt the data. The hash algorithm is used to ensure data integrity.

> **NOTE**   The Cisco PIX Firewall requires an activation key (license) to implement the IPSec features. Refer to Chapter 3, "Cisco PIX Firewall," for the specific licenses available for each firewall model.

The PIX supports the following encryption algorithms:

- **Data Encryption Standard (DES)**—DES is a 56-bit symmetric encryption algorithm. Although it is still widely used, DES is somewhat outdated and should not be used if your data is highly sensitive. It is commonly used for VPN connections to locations outside the United States that cannot purchase higher levels of encryption because of U.S. technology export policies.

- **Triple Data Encryption Standard (3DES)**—3DES is a 168-bit symmetric key cipher derived by encrypting the data three consecutive times using DES. The data is encrypted using a 56-bit key, decrypted using a second 56-bit key, and then reencrypted using a third 56-bit key.

- **Advanced Encryption Standard (AES)**—AES is a symmetric block cipher based on the Rijndael algorithm that encrypts and decrypts data using cryptographic keys of 128, 192, or 256 bit lengths. The encrypted data is placed into 128-bit blocks that are combined into *cipher block chains*.

A hash algorithm takes a message as input and creates a fixed-length output called the *message digest*. The message digest is put into the digital signature algorithm, which generates or verifies the signature for the message. Signing the message digest rather than the actual message usually improves the processing of the message, because the message digest is smaller than the message. The same hash algorithm must be used by the originator and verifier of the message. The Cisco PIX Firewall supports the Keyed-Hash Message Authentication Code (HMAC) variant of the following hash algorithms:

- **Secure Hash Algorithm 1 (SHA-1)**— The output of SHA-1 is 160 bit. Because the output is larger than Message Digest 5 (MD5), SHA-1 is considered more secure.

- **Message Digest 5 (MD5)**—The output of MD5 is 128 bit. MD5 is slightly faster to process because of its smaller message digest.

Internet Key Exchange

Internet Key Exchange is the protocol that is responsible for negotiation. IKE is the short name for ISAKMP/Oakley, which stands for Internet Security Association and Key Management Protocol (with Oakley distribution). The terms *IKE* and *ISAKMP* are used interchangeably throughout this chapter. IKE operates over User Datagram Protocol (UDP) port 500 and negotiates the key exchange between the ISAKMP peers to establish a bidirectional SA. This process requires that the IPSec systems first authenticate themselves to each other and establish ISAKMP (IKE) shared keys. This negotiation is called *phase 1* negotiation, and it is during this phase that the Diffie-Hellman key agreement is performed. During phase 1, IKE creates the IKE SA, which is a secure channel between the two IKE peers. IKE authenticates the peer and the IKE messages between the peers during IKE phase 1. Phase 1 consists of *main mode* or *aggressive mode*.

A main mode negotiation consists of six message exchanges:

- The first two messages simply negotiate the exchange policy.
- The second two messages exchange Diffie-Hellman public-key values and an 8- to 256-bit *nonce* (a random number generated by a peer).
- The last two messages authenticate the key exchange.

Figure 11-5 shows main mode key exchanges.

NOTE There are three message exchanges in an aggressive mode exchange:

Figure 11-5 *Main Mode Key Exchanges*

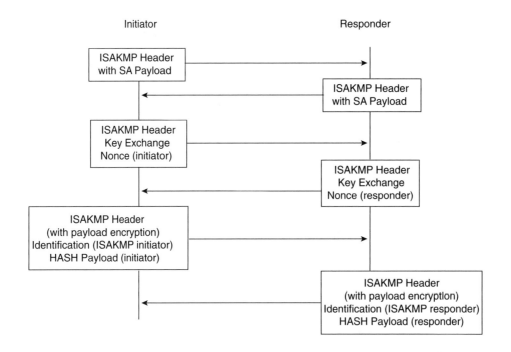

- The first two messages negotiate policy, exchange public-key values, and authenticate the responder.

- The third message authenticates the initiator and is normally postponed until the negotiation is complete and is not sent as clear text.

Figure 11-6 shows aggressive mode key exchanges.

> **NOTE**   Diffie-Hellman is a public-key cryptography protocol that is used between two IPSec peers to derive a shared secret over an unsecured channel without transmitting it to each peer. The PIX Firewall supports three Diffie-Hellman groups: Group 1 is 768-bit, group 2 is 1024-bit, and group 5 is 1536-bit.

Figure 11-6 *Aggressive Mode Key Exchanges*

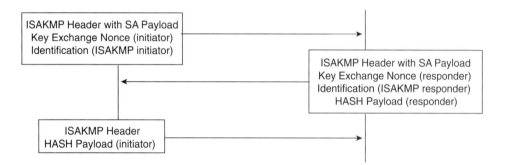

Peers that want to participate in the IPSec session *must* authenticate themselves to each other before IKE can proceed. Peer authentication occurs during the main mode/aggressive mode exchange during IKE phase 1. The IKE protocol is very flexible and supports multiple authentication methods as part of the phase 1 exchange. The two entities must agree on a common authentication protocol through a negotiation process. IKE phase 1 has three methods to authenticate IPSec peers in Cisco products:

- **Preshared keys**—Case-sensitive key values entered into each peer manually and used to authenticate the peer.

- **RSA signatures**—A public-key cryptographic system that uses a digital certificate authenticated by an RSA signature.

- **RSA encrypted nonces**—Use Rivest-Shamir-Adleman (RSA) encryption to encrypt a nonce value (a random number generated by the peer) and other values. The PIX Firewall does not support this authentication type.

Having completed the phase 1 negotiation, IKE provides a secure channel for the completion of phase 2. The phase 2 exchange occurs only after the IKE SA negotiation is complete. It is used to derive keying material and negotiate policies for non-ISAKMP SAs (such as the IPSec SA). IKE performs the following functions and provides the following benefits:

- It automatically negotiates the security parameters for SAs between peers, removing the requirement of manually configuring each peer.
- It provides the capability to configure an SA's lifetime.
- It allows the encryption key to change dynamically while the IPSec session is open.
- It provides antireplay (hijacking) protection to IPSec services.
- It provides dynamic authentication of SA peers.
- It provides support for certification authorities.
- It allows for the scalable implementation of IPSec.

Perfect Forward Secrecy

Perfect Forward Secrecy (PFS) is the function of two parties agreeing on a temporary session key that is different for each message. This provides confidence that the compromise of the long-term private key does not compromise previous session keys. PFS prevents an eavesdropper from being able to decrypt traffic even if the eavesdropper has the private keys from both parties because the parties negotiate the temporary session key.

Certification Authorities

IKE interoperates with X.509v3 certificates for authentication that requires public keys. Certification authorities (CAs) manage certificate requests, issue digital certificates, and publish certificate revocation lists (CRLs) to list certificates that are no longer valid. A digital certificate contains information about the user or device and includes a copy of its public key. This technology enables IPSec-protected networks to scale, because the peers simply exchange digital certificates that have been authenticated by a CA, removing the requirement to configure the preshared key manually for each IPSec peer. The PIX interoperates with CA server products from the following vendors:

- Baltimore Technologies
- Entrust Corporation
- Microsoft Corporation
- VeriSign

After ensuring that you have correctly configured the firewall host name, domain name, and the system date/time, you can initiate enrollment with a CA server. It is important that your date and time are correctly configured so that you can verify the validity of the certificate when received. The process that a PIX uses to enroll with a CA server is as follows:

Step 1   The firewall generates an RSA key pair.

Step 2   The firewall contacts the CA server and obtains the CA server's certificate, which contains the public key.

Step 3   The firewall requests a signed certificate from the CA server using the generated key and the public key from the CA.

Step 4   The CA administrator verifies the request and returns the signed certificate.

Configuring the PIX Firewall as a Virtual Private Network Gateway

Configuring the Cisco PIX Firewall as a VPN gateway or VPN termination point is a process that requires four specific tasks:

- Selecting the configuration
- Configuring IKE
- Configuring IPSec
- Testing and troubleshooting the connection

Selecting the Configuration

Selecting a standardized configuration is perhaps the most important step in creating a VPN. You need to follow these steps when selecting your configuration:

Step 1   Determine which hosts will participate in this connection and which devices to use as VPN gateways. The Cisco PIX Firewall can create a VPN connection to another PIX, VPN appliances, routers, other third-party firewalls that support IPSEC, and so on.

Step 2   Gather information about the peers and all hosts and networks that will participate in this VPN.

Step 3   Select which phase 1 and phase 2 IKE policies to use based on the number and location of the peers.

Step 4   Verify the current configuration of your Cisco PIX Firewall to ensure
that you do not select any policies (such as access control lists [ACLs],
ISAKMP policies, or crypto maps) that conflict with the current
configuration:

- Ensure that you have connectivity with your peers. If you are unable
to connect with a peer in the clear, you will be unable to create an
encrypted connection.

- Ensure that perimeter devices such as routers are allowing the traffic
required to create and maintain the VPN connection. Most notable
are UDP port 500 (used for IKE negotiation), protocol 50 (ESP), and
protocol 51 (AH).

It is extremely important to ensure that VPN peers have configurations with matching
elements. If both peers are not configured to have compatible VPN components, they will be
unable to create the encrypted connection.

Configuring IKE

Remember that IKE is the method used by the peers to negotiate and establish the SA.
Determining which IKE configuration to use is not difficult. Most companies have a standard
configuration that they employ when creating any VPN connection. If you do not have a
preestablished policy, you should select a policy that allows your minimum amount of
security to be not less than that required for the most sensitive data to travel across the
connection. The following steps are required to configure IKE on a Cisco PIX Firewall:

Step 1   Enable IKE—This is a simple command on the PIX. You turn on IKE
by enabling it on a specific interface. The syntax for the command is
isakmp enable *if_name*. For example:

```
tgpix(config)# isakmp enable outside
```

Step 2   Create your IKE policies (phase 1)—To create the IKE policies, you
select certain options and configure them as policies. Again, it is
extremely important that both peers are configured in the same manner.
Any undefined policies use the current default values. You must make
the following choices when creating the policy:

- **Authentication method**—Preshared secret or RSA signature

NOTE   You need to configure your SA peer's preshared secret for each IP address.

- **Message encryption algorithm**—DES, 3DES, AES, AES-192, or AES-256

- **Message integrity algorithm**—SHA-1 or MD5

- **Key exchange parameters**—Diffie-Hellman group 1, group 2, or group 5

- **IKE established SA lifetime**—The default is 86,400 seconds. PIX Version 6.3(2) now supports an unlimited ISAKMP SA (phase 1) lifetime by using a value of 0. This allows for VPN connectivity with third-party VPN products that do not support rekeying the ISAKMP SA. An unlimited ISAKMP SA lifetime will be much less secure than a constantly rekeyed SA and should be used only if required to support connections to third-party gateways.

The **isakmp policy** command is a simple command with several options. In the event that you do not select a specific option, the PIX Firewall will automatically choose a default value. Table 11-1 describes the **isakmp policy** command parameters.

Table 11-2   **isakmp policy** *Command Parameters*

Parameter	Description
priority	Allows you to prioritize your ISAKMP policies. Policy priorities range from 1 to 65,534, with 1 being the highest priority.
authentication pre-share	Specifies that the peer authentication method is the preshared key. This requires that the preshared key be manually configured on both peers.
authentication rsa-sig	Specifies that the peer authentication method is RSA signatures. This method allows peer authentication to be completed automatically and is a more scalable solution. This is the default setting.
encryption des	Specifies that the encryption algorithm is DES. This is the default setting.
encryption 3des	Specifies that the encryption algorithm is 3DES.
encryption aes	Specifies that the encryption algorithm is AES-128.
encryption aes-192	Specifies that the encryption algorithm is AES-192.
encryption aes-256	Specifies that the encryption algorithm is AES-256.
group 1	Specifies that Diffie-Hellman group 1 (768-bit) is used. This is the default setting.

continues

Table 11-2   isakmp policy *Command Parameters (Continued)*

Parameter	Description
group 2	Specifies that Diffie-Hellman group 2 (1024-bit) is used.
group 5	Specifies the Diffie-Hellman group 5 (1536-bit) is used.
hash md5	Specifies that the MD5 hash algorithm is used.
hash sha	Specifies that the SHA-1 hash algorithm is used. This is the default setting.
lifetime	Specifies the SA's lifetime. The range is from 60 seconds to unlimited. The default setting is 86,400 seconds.

For example, to configure ISAKMP policies configured for VPN peers, you would have a configuration similar to this:

```
LOCAL PIX FIREWALL>>>>>>>>>>>
tgpix(config)# isakmp policy 10 authentication pre-share
tgpix(config)# isakmp policy 10 encryption 3des
tgpix(config)# isakmp policy 10 group 2
tgpix(config)# isakmp policy 10 hash md5
tgpix(config)# isakmp policy 10 lifetime 86400
tgpix(config)# isakmp enable outside

REMOTE PIX FIREWALL>>>>>>>>>>
gonderpix (config)# isakmp policy 10 authentication pre-share
gonderpix (config)# isakmp policy 10 encryption 3des
gonderpix (config)# isakmp policy 10 group 2
gonderpix (config)# isakmp policy 10 hash md5
gonderpix (config)# isakmp policy 10 lifetime 86400
gonderpix (config)# isakmp enable outside
```

Note that the policies are the same on both peers; however, it is not a requirement for the policy number to match on each peer.

Step 3   Configure the preshared key—You can configure the same preshared key for all your SAs. This method is not recommended, however, because it is more secure to specify a different key for each SA. To configure the preshared key, you need to determine how the peers identify themselves. SA peers can identify themselves by IP address or host name. It is recommended that you use the same method of identification for all SAs. If you choose to identify the peers by host name, the negotiations could fail if a Domain Name System (DNS) issue prevents the host name from resolving correctly. Here is the command for configuring identification:

```
isakmp identity (address ¦ hostname)
```

Here is the command for configuring the preshared key:

```
isakmp key string address ¦ peer-address [netmask mask]
```

NOTE You can configure your preshared key with a wildcard IP address and netmask, but this is not recommended and could be considered a security risk.

To configure ISAKMP policies for both Cisco PIX Firewalls with the ISAKMP identities and **isakmp key** commands added, use a configuration similar to this:

```
LOCAL PIX FIREWALL>>>>>>>>>>
tgpix(config)# isakmp policy 10 authentication pre-share
tgpix(config)# isakmp policy 10 encryption 3des
tgpix(config)# isakmp policy 10 group 2
tgpix(config)# isakmp policy 10 hash md5
tgpix(config)# isakmp policy 10 lifetime 86400
tgpix(config)# isakmp enable outside
tgpix(config)# isakmp identity address
tgpix(config)# isakmp key abc123 address 192.168.2.1 netmask 255.255.255.255

REMOTE PIX FIREWALL>>>>>>>>>>
gonderpix (config)# isakmp policy 10 authentication pre-share
gonderpix (config)# isakmp policy 10 encryption 3des
gonderpix (config)# isakmp policy 10 group 2
gonderpix (config)# isakmp policy 10 hash md5
gonderpix (config)# isakmp policy 10 lifetime 86400
gonderpix (config)# isakmp enable outside
gonderpix (config)# isakmp identity address
gonderpix (config)# isakmp key abc123 address 192.168.1.1 netmask
  255.255.255.255
```

Step 4   Verify your configuration—Because of the complexity of the configurations, it is a good idea to verify your configuration. Remember that both peers must have an exactly matched phase 1 policy for the key exchange to occur, which is the first step in establishing the VPN connection. As always, the **show** command is a very effective tool for checking your configuration. You can get extended output with

show isakmp policy, or you can see the commands that were input
with **show isakmp.** You get the same output with **write terminal** as with
show isakmp. Here is some sample output from **show isakmp:**

```
tgpix# show isakmp
isakmp policy 10 authentication pre-share
isakmp policy 10 encryption 3des
isakmp policy 10 group 2
isakmp policy 10 hash md5
isakmp policy 10 lifetime 86400
isakmp enable outside

isakmp key ***** 192.168.2.1 netmask 255.255.255.255
```

You can see that policy 10 uses preshared secrets for authentication,
3DES encryption, the group 2 (1024-bit) Diffie-Hellman key exchange,
MD5 hash, and a connection lifetime of 86,400 seconds (24 hours), and
it is enabled on the outside interface.

Here is some sample output from **show isakmp policy:**

```
tgpix# show isakmp policy
Protection suite or priority  10
    encryption algorithm:    Three key triple DES
    hash algorithm:          Message Digest 5
    authentication method:   Pre-Shared Key
    Diffie-Hellman group:    #2 (1024 bit)
    lifetime:         86400 seconds, no volume limit
Default protection suite
    encryption algorithm:    DES - Data Encryption Standard (56-bit keys)
hash algorithm:          Secure Hash Standard
    authentication method:   Rivest-Shamir-Adleman Signature
    Diffie-Hellman group:    #1 (768 bit)
    lifetime:         86400 seconds, no volume limit
```

In this output, you can see the two ISAKMP policies that are configured
on the firewall (policy 10 and default). If you do not configure a specific
ISAKMP policy, the default values are used.

Configuring IPSec

Now that you have successfully configured IKE on your firewall, you are ready to configure
IPSec. Follow these steps:

Step 1   Create a crypto access list to define the traffic to protect.

Step 2   Configure a transform set that defines how the traffic is protected.

Step 3   Create a crypto map entry.

Step 4   Apply the crypto map set to an interface.

Step 1: Creating a Crypto Access List

Crypto access lists are used to identify which IP traffic is to be protected by encryption and which traffic is not. After the access list is defined, the crypto maps reference it to identify the type of traffic that IPSec protects. The **permit** keyword in the access list causes IPSec to protect all IP traffic that matches the access list criteria. If the **deny** keyword is used in the access list, the traffic is not encrypted. The crypto access lists specified at the remote peer should be mirror images of the access lists specified at the local peer. This ensures that traffic that has IPSec protection applied locally can be processed correctly at the remote peer. The crypto map entries should also support common transforms and should refer to the other system as a peer.

It is not recommended that you use the **permit ip any any** command, because it causes all outbound traffic to be encrypted (and all encrypted traffic to be sent to the peer specified in the corresponding crypto map entry), and it requires encryption of all inbound traffic. With this type of access list, the firewall drops all inbound packets that are not encrypted.

The syntax for the **access-list** command is as follows:

```
access-list acl_name permit ¦ deny protocol src_addr src_mask
    [operator port[port]] dest_addr dest_mask [operator port[port]]
```

Table 11-3 lists and describes the command arguments and options for the **access-list** command.

Table 11-3 access-list *Command Parameters*

Parameter	Description
acl-name	Specifies the access list name or number.
permit	Encrypts the packet.
deny	Does not encrypt the packet.
protocol	Specifies the protocol by name or IP protocol number. Protocols include **icmp**, **tcp**, **udp**, and **ip**. (**ip** is the keyword for any.)
src_addr, dest-addr	Specifies the IP address of the network or host for the source and destination. The term **any** is the wildcard for 0.0.0.0 0.0.0.0. It is also possible to use the word **host** to indicate a 32-bit mask.
src_mask, dest-mask	Specifies the subnet masks of the source or destination network.

continues

Table 11-3 access-list *Command Parameters (Continued)*

Parameter	Description
operator	An optional field. It includes the following options: **lt** = less than **gt** = greater than **eq** = equal to **neq** = not equal to **range** = inclusive range
port	Specifies the TCP or UDP port used for the IP service.

> **NOTE** The configuration examples in this chapter build on each other (they include the previous portion). The specific items that are being addressed as part of the current configuration are highlighted.

Example 11-1 shows the current ISAKMP policy configuration with the access list added:

Example 11-1 *Crypto Access List*

```
tgpix(config)# isakmp policy 10 authentication pre-share
tgpix(config)# isakmp policy 10 encryption 3des
tgpix(config)# isakmp policy 10 group 2
tgpix(config)# isakmp policy 10 hash md5
tgpix(config)# isakmp policy 10 lifetime 86400
tgpix(config)# isakmp enable outside
tgpix(config)# isakmp identity address
tgpix(config)# isakmp key abc123 address 192.168.2.1 netmask 255.255.255.255
tgpix(config)# access-list 90 permit ip 10.10.10.0 255.255.255.0 10.10.20.0  255.255.255.0
```

Step 2: Configuring a Transform Set

A transform set defines the combination of encryption algorithms and message integrity algorithms to be used for the IPSec tunnel. Transforms are combined to make *transform sets*. Both peers agree on the transform set during the IPSec negotiation. You can define multiple transform sets because both peers search for a common transform set during the IKE negotiation. If a common transform set is found, it is selected and applied to the protected traffic. Table 11-4 shows the transform sets supported on the Cisco PIX Firewall.

Table 11-4 *PIX-Supported IPSec Transforms*

Transform	Description
ah-md5-hmac	AH-MD5-HMAC transform used for authentication
ah-sha-hmac	AH-SHA-HMAC transform used for authentication
esp-null	ESP transform that does not provide any encryption
esp-des	ESP transform using DES encryption (56-bit)
esp-3des	ESP transform using 3DES encryption (168-bit)
esp-aes	ESP transform using AES encryption (128-bit)
esp-aes-192	ESP transform using AES-192 encryption (192-bit)
esp-aes-256	ESP transform using AES-256 encryption (256-bit)
esp-md5-hmac	ESP transform with HMAC-MD5 authentication, used with either ESP-DES or ESP-3DES to provide additional integrity of ESP packets
esp-sha-hmac	ESP transform with HMAC-SHA authentication, used with either ESP-DES or ESP-3DES to provide additional integrity of ESP packets

NOTE *hmac* represents *Keyed-Hashing for Message Authentication* and is outlined in RFC 2104.

The syntax for the **transform-set** command is as follows:

```
crypto ipsec transform-set transform-set-name transform1 [transform2 [transform3]]
```

Example 11-2 shows the current ISAKMP policy configuration with the access list and transform set defined:

Example 11-2 *Crypto Transform Set*

```
tgpix(config)# isakmp policy 10 authentication pre-share
tgpix(config)# isakmp policy 10 encryption 3des
tgpix(config)# isakmp policy 10 group 2
tgpix(config)# isakmp policy 10 hash md5
tgpix(config)# isakmp policy 10 lifetime 86400
tgpix(config)# isakmp enable outside
tgpix(config)# isakmp identity address
tgpix(config)# isakmp key abc123 address 192.168.2.1 netmask 255.255.255.255
tgpix(config)# access-list 90 permit ip 10.10.10.0 255.255.255.0 10.10.20.0
  255.255.255.0
tgpix(config)# crypto ipsec transform-set strong esp-3des esp-md5-hmac
```

Step 3: Configuring IPSec Security Association Lifetimes

To preclude any opportunity to gather sufficient network traffic using a single encryption key, it is important to limit the key lifetime. This forces a key exchange, changing the encryption scheme and greatly reducing the possibility of cracking the key. Technology continues to advance, producing computers that can break code at faster rates. However, these systems require a certain amount of traffic encrypted under a single key. The idea is to change encryption keys before any system can feasibly crack your encryption. The PIX enables you to configure your SA lifetimes, forcing a key exchange. It is possible to limit the SA lifetime either by the amount of traffic passing through the connection or by how long the encrypted connection remains open. The command for configuring SA lifetimes is as follows:

```
crypto ipsec security-association lifetime [kilobytes | seconds]
```

Example 11-3 shows the current configuration, including an SA lifetime of 15 minutes (900 seconds):

Example 11-3 *Crypto IPSec SA Lifetime*

```
tgpix(config)# isakmp policy 10 authentication pre-share
tgpix(config)# isakmp policy 10 encryption 3des
tgpix(config)# isakmp policy 10 group 2
tgpix(config)# isakmp policy 10 hash md5
tgpix(config)# isakmp policy 10 lifetime 86400
tgpix(config)# isakmp enable outside
tgpix(config)# isakmp identity address
tgpix(config)# isakmp key abc123 address 192.168.2.1 netmask 255.255.255.255
tgpix(config)# access-list 90 permit ip 10.10.10.0 255.255.255.0 10.10.20.0
  255.255.255.0
tgpix(config)# crypto ipsec transform-set strong esp-3des esp-md5-hmac
tgpix(config)# crypto ipsec security-association lifetime seconds 900
```

Step 4: Configuring Crypto Maps

Just as the **isakmp policy** command configures the parameters for the IKE negotiations, crypto map tells the PIX Firewall how to negotiate the IPSec SA. The **crypto map** command is the final piece of the puzzle that is used on both peers to establish the SA. Again, it is extremely important that the settings are compatible on both ends. If both peers do not have a compatible configuration, they cannot establish the VPN connection. This does not mean that the configuration must be an exact match (like the **isakmp** configurations), but the peers must have matching elements within the crypto map. Many different components are covered by the **crypto map** command. The following parameters are set using this command:

- **What traffic is to be encrypted and what traffic is not**—Earlier in this chapter, the **access-list** command was said to designate which traffic the PIX should encrypt. This is correct; however, the access list is applied by the **crypto map**.

- **What type of IPSec to apply to the connection**—The **crypto map** tells the firewall which transform set to use.

- **How the SA is to be initially established**—This tells the firewall if the SA is manually established or established using IKE.

- **Who the peer is for this SA**—This can be one or more peers. You can configure a primary peer and backup peers. In the event that the firewall cannot establish the connection with the primary peer, it will attempt to connect to the secondary, and so on. These additional peers are called *backup gateways*.

- **What the SA's local address is**—The crypto map is applied to a specific interface on the PIX.

- **Any additional options that should be configured for this SA**—This can include setting a specific timeout in kilobytes or adding an authentication, authorization, and accounting (AAA) server.

Three steps are required for configuring crypto maps:

Step 1   Creating a crypto map entry

Step 2   Applying the crypto map set to an interface

Step 3   Specifying that IPSec traffic be permitted

It is important that you ensure that all three steps are completed. Although each line of the crypto map is considered "creating the crypto map," specific lines apply the crypto map and specify the IPSec traffic. These lines are discussed next.

Normally, you have at least five **crypto map** entries with the same name. These entries combine to list your IPSec SA configuration. Each line of the configuration has its own purpose. The following text shows and explains the syntax of each line.

```
crypto map map-name seq-num ipsec-isakmp
```

This line establishes the crypto map by name and sequence number and specifies that IKE negotiates the SA.

```
crypto map map-name seq-num match address acl_name
```

This line binds the access list to the crypto map. It establishes which traffic is encrypted and which is not. This line specifies which IPSec traffic is permitted. It defines the traffic as "interesting."

```
crypto map map-name seq-num set transform-set transform-set-name
```

This line identifies which transform set is to be used. The *transform-set-name* is assigned to the transform set using the **crypto ipsec transform-set** command.

```
crypto map map-name seq-num set peer ip-address
```
This line identifies the SA peer by IP address.

```
crypto map map-name interface if_name
```
This line applies the crypto map to a specific interface. In much the same way that the **access-group** command is used to bind the access lists to an interface for standard ACLs, this command binds the entire crypto map process (including the crypto access list) to the interface. This line applies the crypto map set to a specific interface on the firewall.

Additional **crypto map** entries can include **set pfs**, **set security-association lifetime**, and **client authentication** settings.

Example 11-4 shows the current configuration, including the crypto map entries. Note that the access list is numbered 90 and the **match address** command references **90**. The **ipsec transform-set** is named **strong**, and the **set transform-set** references the name **strong**.

Example 11-4 *Crypto Map Entries*

```
tgpix(config)# isakmp policy 10 authentication pre-share
tgpix(config)# isakmp policy 10 encryption 3des
tgpix(config)# isakmp policy 10 group 2
tgpix(config)# isakmp policy 10 hash md5
tgpix(config)# isakmp policy 10 lifetime 86400
tgpix(config)# isakmp enable outside
tgpix(config)# isakmp identity address
tgpix(config)# isakmp key abc123 address 192.168.2.1 netmask 255.255.255.255
tgpix(config)# access-list 90 permit ip 10.10.10.0 255.255.255.0 10.10.20.0
  255.255.255.0
tgpix(config)# crypto ipsec transform-set strong esp-3des esp-md5-hmac
tgpix(config)# crypto ipsec security-association lifetime seconds 900
tgpix(config)# crypto map gonder 10 ipsec-isakmp
tgpix(config)# crypto map gonder 10 match address 90
tgpix(config)# crypto map gonder 10 set transform-set strong
tgpix(config)# crypto map gonder 10 set peer 192.168.2.1
tgpix(config)# crypto map gonder interface outside
```

Table 11-5 describes the different **crypto map** command arguments and options that are available when you are configuring crypto maps.

Table 11-5 crypto map *Arguments and Options*

Argument/Option	Description
map-name	You can apply multiple crypto maps on a single PIX Firewall. It is a good idea to assign a name that allows you to keep track of which crypto map goes with which access list. The easiest way to do this is to use the same name or number for both components.
seq-num	Because you can add multiple crypto maps to the PIX, you must give each a sequence number so that the system can process each in the correct order. The lower the number, the higher the priority.
ipsec-isakmp	Indicates that the PIX uses IKE to negotiate the SA. This is the recommended configuration.
ipsec-manual	Indicates that the SA is configured manually and that IKE is not used to negotiate it. This is not the recommended configuration because it is difficult to ensure that both peers are configured correctly and because a manual session does not expire (no renegotiation of the keys).
set session-key	Manually specifies the session keys within the crypto map entry.
inbound	Manual IPSec requires that session keys be configured directionally. You must specify both inbound and outbound session keys.
outbound	Manual IPSec requires that session keys be configured directionally. You must specify both inbound and outbound session keys.
match address	Identifies the access list for the IPSec SA.
acl-name	The name of the access list that indicates that the traffic should be encrypted.
set peer	Specifies the SA peer using either of the following two arguments.
hostname	Identifies the SA peer's host name and any backup gateways.
ip-address	Identifies the SA peer's IP address(es) and any backup gateways.
interface	Identifies the interface that is to be used for the local SA peer address.
If-name	The interface name.

continues

Table 11-5   crypto map *Arguments and Options (Continued)*

Argument/Option	Description
set pfs	Initiates PFS, which provides an additional layer of security to the SA negotiation and renegotiation. It requires that a new Diffie-Hellman exchange occur every time a key negotiation takes place. This causes the key exchange to use a new key for every negotiation rather than renegotiating based on a key that is currently being used. This process increases the processor load on both peers.
group 1	Indicates that the Diffie-Hellman group 1 (768-bit) modulus should be used when the key exchange for the **esp-des** and **esp-3des** transforms is performed.
group 2	Indicates that the Diffie-Hellman group 2 (1024-bit) modulus should be used when the key exchange for the **esp-des** and **esp-3des** transforms is performed.
group 5	Indicates that the Diffie-Hellman group 5 (1536-bit) modulus should be used. This group should always be used with **aes**, **aes-192**, and **aes-256** due to the large key sizes used by AES.
set transform-set	Specifies the transform to be used for the crypto map entry. You can list up to six transform sets by priority. The PIX automatically selects the most secure transform that is listed on both peers.
transform-set-name	Specifies the transform set by name.
set security-association lifetime	A second location for configuring the SA lifetime. This setting will override the global SA lifetime for a specific crypto map.
seconds *seconds*	The SA lifetime in seconds.
kilobytes *kilobytes*	The SA lifetime in kilobytes.
dynamic	Specifies that the crypto map entry must reference a preexisting dynamic crypto map.
dynamic-map-name	Specifies the dynamic crypto map.
aaa-server-name	Specifies the AAA server that authenticates the user during IKE authentication. The PIX Firewall supports Terminal Access Controller Access Control System (TACACS+) and Remote Authentication Dial-In User Service (RADIUS) for this function.

sysopt connection permit-ipsec Command

The **sysopt** command reconfigures the system options. The command **sysopt connection permit-ipsec** implicitly permits all packets that arrive from the IPSec tunnel to bypass any checking of access lists, conduits, or **access-group** command statements for IPSec connections. If the **sysopt connection permit-ipsec** command is not specified, an explicit rule (conduit or ACL) must be coded to allow the traffic arriving from the IPSec tunnel through the firewall.

Example 11-5 shows the current configuration with this command included:

Example 11-5   sysopt connection permit-ipsec

```
tgpix(config)# isakmp policy 10 authentication pre-share
tgpix(config)# isakmp policy 10 encryption 3des
tgpix(config)# isakmp policy 10 group 2
tgpix(config)# isakmp policy 10 hash md5
tgpix(config)# isakmp policy 10 lifetime 86400
tgpix(config)# isakmp enable outside
tgpix(config)# isakmp identity address
tgpix(config)# isakmp key abc123 address 192.168.2.1 netmask 255.255.255.255
tgpix(config)# nat (inside) 0 access list 90
tgpix(config)# access-list 90 permit ip 10.10.10.0 255.255.255.0 10.10.20.0
  255.255.255.0
tgpix(config)# crypto ipsec transform-set strong esp-3des esp-md5-hmac
tgpix(config)# crypto ipsec security-association lifetime seconds 900
tgpix(config)# crypto map gonder 10 ipsec-isakmp
tgpix(config)# crypto map gonder 10 match address 90
tgpix(config)# crypto map gonder 10 set transform-set strong
tgpix(config)# crypto map gonder 10 set peer 192.168.2.1
tgpix(config)# crypto map gonder interface outside
tgpix(config)# sysopt connection permit-ipsec
```

Troubleshooting the Virtual Private Network Connection

Configuring an SA peer can be extremely complicated and must be exact. If both peers are not configured correctly, they cannot successfully establish the VPN connection. The most common VPN issue is an incorrect configuration of either of the SA peers. The first step of troubleshooting a VPN should always be to compare the configurations of both peers and verify that they match. Three commands and a variety of command options are available to help you troubleshoot VPN issues:

- show
- clear
- debug

show Command

The **show** command lets you view different portions of the configuration and see the condition of ISAKMP and IPSec SAs. Table 11-6 explains the different **show** commands.

Table 11-6 show *Commands*

Command	Description
show isakmp	Displays all ISAKMP configurations.
show isakmp policy	Displays only configured ISAKMP policies.
show access-list	Displays configured access lists.
show crypto map	Displays all configured crypto map entries.
show crypto ipsec transform-set	Displays all configured IPSec transform sets.
show crypto ipsec security-association lifetime	Displays the global SA lifetime. If not defined specifically by a **crypto ipsec security-association lifetime** command, it displays the default lifetime values.
show crypto isakmp sa	Displays the status of current IKE SAs.
show crypto ipsec sa	Displays the status of current IPSec SAs.

Example 11-6 displays the output from the **show crypto isakmp sa** command on the PIX Firewall in 192.168.1.2 that is configured for a VPN connection to 192.168.2.1.

Example 11-6 show crypto isakmp sa *Command Output*

```
tgpix# show crypto isakmp sa
dst          src          state     conn-id    slot
192.168.2.1  192.168.1.1  QM_IDLE   1          0
```

Example 11-7 displays the output from **show crypto ipsec sa** for the same firewall.

Example 11-7 show crypto ipsec sa *Command Output*

```
tgpix# show crypto ipsec sa
interface: outside
    Crypto map tag: 10, local addr. 192.168.1.1
   local  ident (addr/mask/port/port): (10.10.10.0/255.255.255.0/0/0)
   remote ident (addr/mask/prot/port): (192.168.2.1/255.255.255.255/0/0)
   current_peer: 192.128.1.1
   dynamic allocated peer ip: 192.168.2.1
     PERMIT, flags={}
```

Example 11-7 show crypto ipsec sa *Command Output (Continued)*

```
#pkts encaps: 345, #pkts encrypt: 345, #pkts digest 0
#pkts decaps: 366, #pkts decrypt: 366, #pkts verify 0
#pkts compressed: 0, #pkts decompressed: 0
#pkts not compressed: 0, #pkts compr. failed: 0, #pkts decompress failed: 0
#send errors 0, #recv errors 0
 local crypto endpt.: 192.168.1.1, remote crypto endpt.: 192.168.2.1
 path mtu 1500, ipsec overhead 56, media mtu 1500
 current outbound spi: 9a46ecae
 inbound esp sas:
  spi: 0x50b98b5(84646069)
    transform: esp-3des esp-md5-hmac ,
    in use settings ={Tunnel, }
    slot: 0, conn id: 1, crypto map: Chapter11
    sa timing: remaining key lifetime (k/sec): (460800/21)
    IV size: 8 bytes
    replay detection support: Y
 inbound ah sas:
 inbound pcp sas:
 outbound esp sas:
  spi: 0x9a46ecae(2588339374)
    transform: esp-3des esp-md5-hmac ,
    in use settings ={Tunnel, }
    slot: 0, conn id: 2, crypto map: Chapter11
    sa timing: remaining key lifetime (k/sec): (460800/21)
    IV size: 8 bytes
    replay detection support: Y
 outbound ah sas:
```

clear Command

The **clear** command allows you to remove current settings. You must be very careful when using the **clear** command to ensure that you do not remove portions of your configuration that are needed. The most common use of the **clear** command for troubleshooting VPN connectivity is to clear current sessions and force them to regenerate. Table 11-7 explains the two **clear** commands used to troubleshoot VPN connectivity.

Table 11-7 clear *Commands*

Command	Description
clear isakmp sa	Removes all ISAKMP statements from the configuration
clear [crypto] isakmp sa	Clears all active ISAKMP SAs
clear [crypto] ipsec sa	Clears all active IPSec SAs

debug Command

The **debug** command lets you watch the VPN negotiation take place. This command is available only from configuration mode on the PIX and will not display any output in a Telnet session. Table 11-8 explains the two **debug** commands most commonly used to troubleshoot VPN connectivity.

Table 11-8 debug *Commands*

Command	Description
debug crypto isakmp	Displays IKE communication between the PIX and its IPSec peers
debug crypto ipsec	Displays IPSec communication between the PIX and its IPSec peers

Example 11-8 displays the output from the **debug crypto isakmp** command on the PIX Firewall in 192.168.1.1 that is configured for a VPN connection to 192.168.2.1. Note the highlighted comments "atts are not acceptable" and "atts are acceptable" that are generated during the negotiation as address transforms attempt to find a match.

Example 11-8 debug **crypto isakmp** *Command Output*

```
crypto_isakmp_process_block: src 192.168.1.1, dest 192.168.2.1
OAK_AG exchange
ISAKMP (0): processing SA payload. message ID = 0
ISAKMP (0): Checking ISAKMP transform 1 against priority 1 policy
ISAKMP:        encryption DES-CBC
ISAKMP:        hash MD5
ISAKMP:        default group 1
ISAKMP:        auth pre-share
ISAKMP (0): atts are not acceptable. Next payload is 3
ISAKMP (0): Checking ISAKMP transform 3 against priority 1 policy
ISAKMP:        encryption ESP_3DES
ISAKMP:        hash HMAC-MD5
ISAKMP:        default group 2
ISAKMP:        auth pre-share
ISAKMP (0): atts are acceptable. Next payload is 3
ISAKMP (0): processing KE payload. message ID = 0
ISAKMP: Created a peer node for 192.168.2.1
OAK_QM exchange
ISAKMP (0:0): Need config/address
ISAKMP (0:0): initiating peer config to 192.168.2.1. ID = 2607270170 (0x9b67c91a)
return status is IKMP_NO_ERROR
crypto_isakmp_process_block: src 192.168.2.1, dest 192.168.1.1
ISAKMP_TRANSACTION exchange
ISAKMP (0:0): processing transaction payload from 192.168.2.1. message ID =
  2156506360
ISAKMP: Config payload CFG_ACK
ISAKMP (0:0): peer accepted the address!
```

Example 11-8   debug crypto isakmp *Command Output (Continued)*

```
ISAKMP (0:0): processing saved QM.
oakley_process_quick_mode:
OAK_QM_IDLE
ISAKMP (0): processing SA payload. message ID = 448324052
ISAKMP : Checking IPSec proposal 1
ISAKMP: transform 1, ESP_DES
ISAKMP:    attributes in transform:
ISAKMP:        authenticator is HMAC-MD5
ISAKMP:        encaps is 1
IPSec(validate_proposal): transform proposal (prot 3, trans 2, hmac_alg 1) not
  supported
ISAKMP (0): atts not acceptable. Next payload is 0
ISAKMP : Checking IPSec proposal 2
ISAKMP: transform 1, ESP_3DES
ISAKMP:    attributes in transform:
ISAKMP:        authenticator is HMAC-MD5
ISAKMP:        encaps is 1
ISAKMP (0): atts are acceptable.
ISAKMP (0): processing NONCE payload. message ID = 448324052
ISAKMP (0): processing ID payload. message ID = 44
ISAKMP (0): processing ID payload. message ID = 44
INITIAL_CONTACTIPSec(key_engine): got a queue event...
```

Example 11-9 displays the output from **debug crypto ipsec** for the same firewall. Notice that this **debug** command actually depicts the real address of the node behind the firewall that is initiating the VPN connection.

Example 11-9   debug crypto ipsec *Command Output*

```
IPSec(key_engine): got a queue event...
IPSec(spi_response): getting spi 0xd532efbd(3576885181) for SA
        from  192.168.2.1  to  192.168.1.1  for prot 3
return status is IKMP_NO_ERROR
crypto_isakmp_process_block: src 192.168.2.1, dest 192.168.1.1
OAK_QM exchange
oakley_process_quick_mode:
OAK_QM_AUTH_AWAIT
ISAKMP (0): Creating IPSec SAs
        inbound SA from  192.168.2.1  to  192.168.1.1  (proxy 10.10.10.3 to
  192.168.1.1.)
        has spi 3576885181 and conn_id 2 and flags 4
        outbound SA from  192.168.1.1  to  192.168.2.1  (proxy 192.168.1.1 to
  10.10.10.3)
        has spi 2749108168 and conn_id 1 and flags 4IPSec(key_engine): got a queue
  event...
IPSec(initialize_sas): ,
```

continues

Example 11-9 debug crypto ipsec *Command Output (Continued)*

```
  (key eng. msg.) dest= 192.168.1.1, src= 192.168.2.1,
    dest_proxy= 192.168.1.1/0.0.0.0/0/0 (type=1),
    src_proxy= 10.10.10.3/0.0.0.0/0/0 (type=1),
    protocol= ESP, transform= esp-3des esp-md5-hmac ,
    lifedur= 0s and 0kb,
    spi= 0xd532efbd(3576885181), conn_id= 2,        keysize= 0, flags= 0x4
IPSec(initialize_sas): ,
  (key eng. msg.) src= 192.168.1.1, dest= 192.168.2.1,
    src_proxy= 192.168.1.1/0.0.0.0/0/0 (type=1),
    dest_proxy= 10.10.10.3/0.0.0.0/0/0 (type=1),
    protocol= ESP, transform= esp-3des esp-md5-hmac ,
    lifedur= 0s and 0kb,
    spi= 0xa3dc0fc8(2749108168), conn_id= 1, keysize= 0, flags= 0x4
return status is IKMP_NO_ERROR
```

Configuring PIX Firewalls for Scalable Virtual Private Networks

Earlier in this chapter, you learned about the different methods of negotiating an IPSec connection:

- Manual IPSec, which requires you to configure each peer manually. This method is not recommended by Cisco because it does not allow for key exchanges and, therefore, would be rather easy to decrypt, given enough time and traffic. Obviously, manual IPSec is not a scalable solution.

- IKE, which dynamically negotiates your SA using preshared keys or digital certificates. Preshared keys still require you to enter a preshared key manually into each IPSec peer.

- IKE with digital certificates, which is the most dynamic solution that lets IKE negotiate your IPSec SA and a CA server authenticating each peer. This system is completely dynamic, very secure, and very scalable.

Foundation Summary

The "Foundation Summary" provides a convenient review of many key concepts in this chapter. If you are already comfortable with the topics in this chapter, this summary can help you recall a few details. If you just read this chapter, this review should help solidify some key facts. If you are doing your final preparation before the exam, this summary provides a convenient way to review the day before the exam.

There are three different VPN types: access, intranet, and extranet. Access VPNs are used for remote users and normally require client software. Intranet and extranet VPNs are configured as site-to-site VPNs.

VPN peers need to authenticate each other and negotiate the IPSec SA. The negotiation is completed automatically using IKE. The authentication is completed using preshared keys, RSA signatures (certificates), or RSA nonces. The PIX Firewall does not support RSA nonces. To configure IKE on the PIX, you use the following commands:

- **isakmp policy**

  — Configures the authentication type

  — Configures the message encryption algorithm

  — Configures the message integrity algorithm

  — Configures the key exchange parameters

  — Defines the SA lifetime (reinitiates the Diffie-Hellman key exchange)

- **isakmp enable**—Applies the ISAKMP policy to an interface, allowing that interface to receive UDP 500 traffic

- **isakmp identity**—Identifies the local peer by IP address or host name

- **isakmp key**—If you are using a preshared key, defines the key and the peer (by IP address)

After you configure IKE, you are ready to configure IPSec. Follow these steps:

Step 1   Use the **access-list** command to configure the access list so that the PIX knows which traffic should be encrypted.

Step 2   Use the **transform-set** command to create transform sets to define the encryption and integrity to be used for the session.

Step 3   Use the **ipsec security-association lifetime** command (optional) to define the SA lifetime to reduce the opportunity of others to crack your encryption.

Step 4   Configure the crypto map:

- Define the SA negotiation (manual or IKE)

- Apply the access list to the crypto map

- Apply the transform set to the crypto map

- Identify the SA peer by IP address or host name

- Apply the crypto map to an interface

Three commands (and many options for each) are available to troubleshoot VPN connectivity:

- **show**—Displays the current configuration or current SA status

- **clear**—Removes the current configuration or setting (usually used to regenerate the connection)

- **debug**—Allows you to see ongoing sessions and key negotiations

Cisco VPN Client is used to connect remote users to internal resources by an encrypted tunnel. The package handles all the negotiation and encryption and can operate using any connection to the Internet.

To develop a scalable VPN solution, you must implement a dynamic means of authentication. The most effective and scalable method today is the use of IKE and certification authorities.

Q&A

As mentioned in the Introduction, the questions in this book are more difficult than what you should experience on the exam. The questions are designed to ensure your understanding of the concepts discussed in this chapter and adequately prepare you to complete the exam. You should take the simulated exams on the CD to practice for the exam.

The answers to these questions can be found in Appendix A.

1. Why is **manual-ipsec** not recommended by Cisco?

2. What is the difference between an access VPN and an intranet VPN?

3. Which hash algorithm is configured by default for phase 1?

4. What are the two methods of identifying SA peers?

5. What happens if you have different ISAKMP policies configured on your potential SA peers, and none of them match?

6. Where do you define your authentication method?

7. What is the default lifetime if not defined in **isakmp policy**?

8. Do your transform sets have to match exactly on each peer?

9. What is the difference between the **isakmp** lifetime and the **crypto map** lifetime?

10. What command do you use to delete any active SAs?

11. What is the command for defining a preshared key?

12. What is the first thing you should check if you are unable to establish a VPN?

13. What is the command to apply an access list to a crypto map?

14. What is the difference between ESP and AH?

Scenario

This scenario gives you the opportunity to configure three locations (New York, Los Angeles, and Atlanta) for a site-to-site fully meshed VPN. The configurations for the three locations are listed with specific items missing. By reviewing the network layout and each firewall configuration you will find the items that are missing from the individual firewall configurations.

VPN Configurations

Clearly, the most detail-oriented and time-consuming portion of configuring VPNs is ensuring that both peers have matching configurations. This task usually becomes more complicated because you might have access to only one peer and are relying on someone else to configure the other end. A single discrepancy between the configurations can prevent the key exchange from completing or prevent encryption from occurring. It is best to compare the configurations on both peers before attempting the connection rather than trying to troubleshoot the VPN after an unsuccessful connection.

In this scenario, you are working as a consultant and have been assigned the task of configuring a full-mesh VPN between corporate headquarters and two branch offices. Figure 11-7 shows the layout of each network and how the VPNs are to connect.

Figure 11-7 *VPN Network Layout*

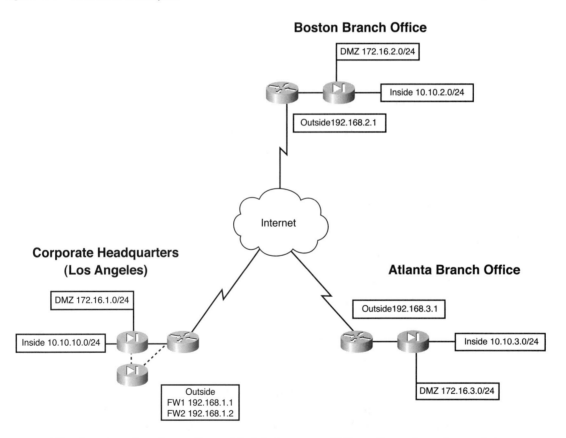

The three locations have all provided their current PIX configurations, but each has a significant amount of information missing. It is your responsibility to complete each of the configurations and ensure that they are correct. Example 11-10 shows the configuration for the corporate headquarters in Los Angeles:

Example 11-10 *PIX Configuration for Los Angeles*

```
1.    : Saved
2.    :
3.    PIX Version 6.3(3)
4.    nameif ethernet0 outside security0
5.    nameif ethernet1 inside security100
6.    nameif ethernet2 DMZ security70
7.    enable password HtmvK15kjhtlyfvcl encrypted
8.    passwd Kkjhlkf1568Hke encrypted
9.    hostname LosAngeles
10.   domain-name www.Chapter11.com
11.   fixup protocol ftp 21
12.   fixup protocol http 80
13.   fixup protocol h323 1720
14.   fixup protocol rsh 514
15.   fixup protocol smtp 25
16.   fixup protocol sqlnet 1521
17.   fixup protocol sip 5060
18.   fixup protocol skinny 2000
19.   names
20.   access-list inbound permit icmp any host 192.168.1.10
21.   access-list inbound permit tcp any host 192.168.1.10  eq www
22.   access-list inbound permit tcp any host 192.168.1.10 eq 443
23.   access-list inbound permit tcp any host 192.168.1.11  eq www
24.   access-list inbound permit tcp any host 192.168.1.11 eq 443
25.   access-list inbound permit tcp any host 192.168.1.12  eq www
26.   access-list inbound permit tcp any host 192.168.1.12 eq 443
27.   access-list inbound permit tcp any host 192.168.1.13  eq ftp
28.   access-list inbound permit tcp any host 192.168.1.13 eq 443
29.   access-list DMZ permit udp 172.16.1.0 255.255.255.0 host 10.10.10.240 eq ntp
30.   access-list VPN permit ip 10.10.10.0 255.255.255.0 10.10.2.0 255.255.255.0
31.   _____
32.   _____
33.   _____
34.   pager lines 24
35.   logging on
36.   logging timestamp
37.   interface ethernet0 auto
38.   interface ethernet1 auto
39.   interface ethernet2 auto
40.   mtu outside 1500
41.   mtu inside 1500
42.   ip address outside 192.168.1.1 255.255.255.0
```

continues

Example 11-10 *PIX Configuration for Los Angeles (Continued)*

```
43.  ip address inside 10.10.10.1 255.255.255.0
44.  ip address DMZ 172.16.1.1 255.255.255.0
45.  failover
46.  failover timeout 0:00:00
47.  failover poll 15
48.  failover ip address outside 192.168.1.2
49.  failover ip address inside 10.10.10.2
50.  failover ip address DMZ 172.16.1.2
51.  arp timeout 14400
52.  global (outside) 1 192.168.1.20-250
53.  nat (inside) 1 0.0.0.0 0.0.0.0
54.  nat (inside) 0 access-list VPN
55.  static (inside,DMZ) 10.10.10.240 10.10.10.240 netmask 255.255.255.255 0 0
56.  static (DMZ,outside) 192.168.1.10 172.16.1.10 netmask 255.255.255.255 0 0
57.  static (DMZ,outside) 192.168.1.11 172.16.1.11 netmask 255.255.255.255 0 0
58.  static (DMZ,outside) 192.168.1.12 172.16.1.12 netmask 255.255.255.255 0 0
59.  static (DMZ,outside) 192.168.1.13 172.16.1.13 netmask 255.255.255.255 0 0
60.  access-group inbound in interface outside
61.  access-group DMZ in interface DMZ
62.  route outside 0.0.0.0 0.0.0.0 192.168.1.254 1
63.  timeout xlate 3:00:00
64.  timeout conn 1:00:00 half-closed 0:10:00 udp 0:02:00 rpc 0:10:00 h323 0:05:00
     sip 0:30:00 sip_media 0:02:00
65.  timeout uauth 0:05:00 absolute
66.  aaa-server TACACS+ protocol tacacs+
67.  aaa-server RADIUS protocol radius
68.  no snmp-server location
69.  no snmp-server contact
70.  snmp-server community public
71.  no snmp-server enable traps
72.  floodguard enable
73.  sysopt connection permit-ipsec
74.  no sysopt route dnat
75.  crypto ipsec transform-set
76.  crypto ipsec transform-set NothingNew esp-3des esp-sha-hmac
77.  _____
78.  _____
79.  _____
80.  crypto map Chapter11 10 set transform-set Chapter11
81.  crypto map Chapter11 20 ipsec-isakmp
82.  _____
83.  _____
84.  _____
85.  crypto map Chapter11 interface outside
86.  _____
87.  _____
88.  _____
```

Example 11-10 *PIX Configuration for Los Angeles (Continued)*

```
89. _____
90. _____
91. _____
92. _____
93. _____
94. _____
95. terminal width 80
96. Cryptochecksum:e0clmj3546549637cbsFds54132d5
```

Example 11-11 shows the configuration for the Boston branch office.

Example 11-11 *PIX Configuration for Boston*

```
1.  : Saved
2.  :
3.  PIX Version 6.3(3)
4.  nameif ethernet0 outside security0
5.  nameif ethernet1 inside security100
6.  nameif ethernet2 DMZ security70
7.  enable password ksjfglkasglc encrypted
8.  passwd kjngczftglkacytiur encrypted
9.  hostname Boston
10. domain-name www.Chapter11.com
11. fixup protocol ftp 21
12. fixup protocol http 80
13. fixup protocol smtp 25
14. fixup protocol skinny 2000
15. names
16. access-list inbound permit icmp any host 192.168.2.10
17. access-list inbound permit tcp any host 192.168.2.10   eq www
18. access-list inbound permit tcp any host 192.168.2.10 eq 443
19. access-list DMZ permit udp 172.16.2.0 255.255.255.0 host 10.10.2.240 eq ntp
20. access-list_____
21. access-list_____
22. access-list_____
23. access-list_____
24. pager lines 24
25. logging on
26. logging timestamp
27. interface ethernet0 auto
28. interface ethernet1 auto
29. interface ethernet2 auto
30. mtu outside 1500
31. mtu inside 1500
32. ip address outside 192.168.2.1 255.255.255.0
```

continues

Example 11-11 *PIX Configuration for Boston (Continued)*

```
33.  ip address inside 10.10.2.1 255.255.255.0
34.  ip address DMZ 172.16.2.1 255.255.255.0
35.  arp timeout 14400
36.  global (outside) 1 192.168.2.20-200
37.  nat (inside) 1 0.0.0.0 0.0.0.0 0 0
38.  nat (inside) 0 access-list VPN
39.  static (inside,DMZ) 10.10.2.240 10.10.2.240 netmask 255.255.255.255 0 0
40.  static (DMZ,outside) 192.168.2.10 172.16.2.10 netmask 255.255.255.255 0 0
41.  access-group inbound in interface outside
42.  access-group DMZ in interface DMZ
43.  route outside 0.0.0.0 0.0.0.0 192.168.2.254 1
44.  timeout xlate 3:00:00
45.  timeout conn 1:00:00 half-closed 0:10:00 udp 0:02:00
46.  timeout uauth 0:05:00 absolute
47.  aaa-server TACACS+ protocol tacacs+
48.  aaa-server RADIUS protocol radius
49.  no snmp-server location
50.  no snmp-server contact
51.  snmp-server community public
52.  no snmp-server enable traps
53.  floodguard enable
54.  _____
55.  _____
56.  _____
57.  crypto map Chapter11 10 ipsec-isakmp
58.  crypto map Chapter11 10 match address LosAngeles
59.  _____
60.  crypto map Chapter11 10 set transform-set Chapter11
61.  crypto map Chapter11 20 ipsec-isakmp
62.  crypto map Chapter11 20 match address Atlanta
63.  crypto map Chapter11 20 set peer 192.168.3.1
64.  _____
65.  _____
66.  isakmp enable outside
67.  isakmp key ******** address 192.168.1.1 netmask 255.255.255.255
68.  isakmp key ******** address 192.168.3.1 netmask 255.255.255.255
69.  isakmp identity address
70.  isakmp policy 20 authentication pre-share
71.  _____
72.  _____
73.  _____
74.  _____
75.  terminal width 80
76.  Cryptochecksum:e0c04954fcabd239ae291d58fc618dd5
```

Example 11-12 shows the configuration for the Atlanta branch office.

Example 11-12 *PIX Configuration for Atlanta*

```
1.   : Saved
2.   :
3.   PIX Version 6.3(3)
4.   nameif ethernet0 outside security0
5.   nameif ethernet1 inside security100
6.   nameif ethernet2 DMZ security70
7.   enable password ksjfglkasglc encrypted
8.   passwd kjngczftglkacytiur encrypted
9.   hostname Atlanta
10.  domain-name www.Chapter11.com
11.  fixup protocol ftp 21
12.  fixup protocol http 80
13.  fixup protocol smtp 25
14.  fixup protocol skinny 2000
15.  names
16.  access-list inbound permit icmp any host 192.168.3.10
17.  access-list inbound permit tcp any host 192.168.3.10  eq www
18.  access-list inbound permit tcp any host 192.168.3.10 eq 443
19.  access-list DMZ permit udp 172.16.3.0 255.255.255.0 host 10.10.3.240 eq ntp
20.  access-list_____
21.  access-list_____
22.  access-list_____
23.  access-list_____
24.  pager lines 24
25.  logging on
26.  logging timestamp
27.  interface ethernet0 auto
28.  interface ethernet1 auto
29.  interface ethernet2 auto
30.  mtu outside 1500
31.  mtu inside 1500
32.  ip address outside 192.168.3.1 255.255.255.0
33.  ip address inside 10.10.3.1 255.255.255.0
34.  ip address DMZ 172.16.3.1 255.255.255.0
35.  arp timeout 14400
36.  global (outside) 1 192.168.3.20-200
37.  nat (inside) 1 0.0.0.0 0.0.0.0 0 0
38.  nat (inside) 0 access-list VPN
39.  static (inside,DMZ) 10.10.3.240 10.10.3.240 netmask 255.255.255.255 0 0
40.  static (DMZ,outside) 192.168.3.10 172.16.3.10 netmask 255.255.255.255 0 0
41.  access-group inbound in interface outside
42.  access-group DMZ in interface DMZ
43.  route outside 0.0.0.0 0.0.0.0 192.168.3.254 1
```

continues

Example 11-12 *PIX Configuration for Atlanta (Continued)*

```
44.  timeout xlate 3:00:00
45.  timeout conn 1:00:00 half-closed 0:10:00 udp 0:02:00
46.  timeout uauth 0:05:00 absolute
47.  aaa-server TACACS+ protocol tacacs+
48.  aaa-server RADIUS protocol radius
49.  no snmp-server location
50.  no snmp-server contact
51.  snmp-server community public
52.  no snmp-server enable traps
53.  floodguard enable
54.  sysopt connection permit-ipsec
55.  crypto ipsec transform-set_____
56.  crypto ipsec transform-set NothingNew esp-3des esp-sha-hmac
57.  crypto map Chapter11 10 ipsec-isakmp
58.  crypto map_____
59.  crypto map_____
60.  crypto map Chapter11 10 set transform-set Chapter11_____
61.  crypto map_____
62.  crypto map_____
63.  crypto map_____
64.  crypto map Chapter11 20 set transform-set Chapter11_____
65.  crypto map_____
66.  isakmp_____
67.  isakmp key ********_____
68.  isakmp key_____
69.  isakmp identity address_____
70.  isakmp policy 20_____
71.  isakmp policy 20 encryption 3des
72.  isakmp policy 20 hash md5
73.  isakmp policy 20 group 2
74.  isakmp policy 20 lifetime 86400
75.  terminal width 80
76.  Cryptochecksum:e0c04954fcabd239ae291d58fc618dd5
```

Each line of the configuration is numbered, and certain lines have not been completed. Your job is to complete the lines and verify each configuration against the configuration of the VPN peer. The following sections give the blank lines for each configuration. The completed configurations are listed at the end of the chapter, along with a full description of each element from the configuration in Los Angeles. You will not find all the information needed to complete the configuration on a single firewall. Remember that the configurations must match on each end of the VPN.

Los Angeles Configuration

Fill in the missing lines in Example 11-10:

Line 31: _____

Line 32: _____

Line 33: _____

Line 77: _____

Line 78: _____

Line 79: _____

Line 82: _____

Line 83: _____

Line 84: _____

Line 86: _____

Line 87: _____

Line 88: _____

Line 89: _____

Line 90: _____

Line 91: _____

Line 92: _____

Line 93: _____

Line 94: _____

Boston Configuration

Fill in the missing lines in Example 11-11:

Line 20: _____

Line 21: _____

Line 22: _____

Line 23: _____

Line 54: _____

Line 55: _____

Line 56: _____

Line 59: _____

Line 64: _____

Line 65: _____

Line 71: _____

Line 72: _____

Line 73: _____

Line 74: _____

Atlanta Configuration

Fill in the missing lines in Example 11-12:

Line 20: _____

Line 21: _____

Line 22: _____

Line 23: _____

Line 55: _____

Line 58: _____

Line 59: _____

Line 61: _____

Line 62: _____

Line 63: _____

Line 65: _____

Line 66: _____

Line 67: _____

Line 68: _____

Line 70: _____

Completed PIX Configurations

To reduce confusion, it is a good idea to use a common naming convention when creating access lists, transforms, and crypto maps. Example 11-13 shows the completed configuration for the Los Angeles headquarters.

Example 11-13 *Completed Configuration for Los Angeles*

```
1.    : Saved
2.    :
3.    PIX Version 6.3(3)
4.    nameif ethernet0 outside security0
5.    nameif ethernet1 inside security100
6.    nameif ethernet2 DMZ security70
7.    enable password HtmvK15kjhtlyfvcl encrypted
8.    passwd Kkjhlkf1568Hke encrypted
9.    hostname LosAngeles
10.   domain-name www.Chapter11.com
11.   fixup protocol ftp 21
12.   fixup protocol http 80
13.   fixup protocol h323 1720
```

continues

Example 11-13 *Completed Configuration for Los Angeles (Continued)*

```
14.  fixup protocol rsh 514
15.  fixup protocol smtp 25
16.  fixup protocol sqlnet 1521
17.  fixup protocol sip 5060
18.  fixup protocol skinny 2000
19.  names
20.  access-list inbound permit icmp any host 192.168.1.10
21.  access-list inbound permit tcp any host 192.168.1.10  eq www
22.  access-list inbound permit tcp any host 192.168.1.10 eq 443
23.  access-list inbound permit tcp any host 192.168.1.11  eq www
24.  access-list inbound permit tcp any host 192.168.1.11 eq 443
25.  access-list inbound permit tcp any host 192.168.1.12  eq www
26.  access-list inbound permit tcp any host 192.168.1.12 eq 443
27.  access-list inbound permit tcp any host 192.168.1.13  eq ftp
28.  access-list inbound permit tcp any host 192.168.1.10 eq 443
29.  access-list DMZ permit udp 172.16.1.0 255.255.255.0 host 10.10.10.240 eq ntp
30.  access-list VPN permit ip 10.10.10.0 255.255.255.0 10.10.2.0 255.255.255.0
31.  access-list VPN permit ip 10.10.10.0 255.255.255.0 10.10.3.0 255.255.255.0
32.  access-list Boston permit ip 10.10.10.0 255.255.255.0 10.10.2.0 255.255.255.0
33.  access-list Atlanta permit ip 10.10.10.0 255.255.255.0 10.10.3.0 255.255.255.0
34.  pager lines 24
35.  logging on
36.  logging timestamp
37.  interface ethernet0 auto
38.  interface ethernet1 auto
39.  interface ethernet2 auto
40.  mtu outside 1500
41.  mtu inside 1500
42.  ip address outside 192.168.1.1 255.255.255.0
43.  ip address inside 10.10.10.1 255.255.255.0
44.  ip address DMZ 172.16.1.1 255.255.255.0
45.  failover
46.  failover timeout 0:00:00
47.  failover poll 15
48.  failover ip address outside 192.168.1.2
49.  failover ip address inside 10.10.10.2
50.  failover ip address DMZ 172.16.1.2
51.  arp timeout 14400
52.  global (outside) 1 192.168.1.20-192.168.1.250
53.  nat (inside) 1 0.0.0.0 0.0.0.0 0 0
54.  nat (inside) 0 access-list VPN
55.  static (inside,DMZ) 10.10.10.240 10.10.10.240 netmask 255.255.255.255 0 0
56.  static (DMZ,outside) 192.168.1.10 172.16.1.10 netmask 255.255.255.255 0 0
57.  static (DMZ,outside) 192.168.1.11 172.16.1.11 netmask 255.255.255.255 0 0
```

Example 11-13 *Completed Configuration for Los Angeles (Continued)*

```
58.  static (DMZ,outside) 192.168.1.12 172.16.1.12 netmask 255.255.255.255 0 0
59.  static (DMZ,outside) 192.168.1.13 172.16.1.13 netmask 255.255.255.255 0 0
60.  access-group inbound in interface outside
61.  access-group DMZ in interface DMZ
62.  route outside 0.0.0.0 0.0.0.0 192.168.1.254 1
63.  timeout xlate 3:00:00
64.  timeout conn 1:00:00 half-closed 0:10:00 udp 0:02:00 rpc 0:10:00 h323 0:05:00
     sip 0:30:00 sip_media 0:02:00
65.  timeout uauth 0:05:00 absolute
66.  aaa-server TACACS+ protocol tacacs+
67.  aaa-server RADIUS protocol radius
68.  no snmp-server location
69.  no snmp-server contact
70.  snmp-server community public
71.  no snmp-server enable traps
72.  floodguard enable
73.  sysopt connection permit-ipsec
74.  no sysopt route dnat
75.  crypto ipsec transform-set Chapter11 esp-3des esp-md5-hmac
76.  crypto ipsec transform-set NothingNew esp-3des esp-sha-hmac
77.  crypto map Chapter11 10 ipsec-isakmp
78.  crypto map Chapter11 10 match address Boston
79.  crypto map Chapter11 10 set peer 192.168.2.1
80.  crypto map Chapter11 10 set transform-set Chapter11
81.  crypto map Chapter11 20 ipsec-isakmp
82.  crypto map Chapter11 20 match address Atlanta
83.  crypto map Chapter11 20 set peer 192.168.3.1
84.  crypto map Chapter11 20 set transform-set Chapter11
85.  crypto map Chapter11 interface outside
86.  isakmp enable outside
87.  isakmp key ******** address 192.168.2.1 netmask 255.255.255.255
88.  isakmp key ******** address 192.168.3.1 netmask 255.255.255.255
89.  isakmp identity address
90.  isakmp policy 20 authentication pre-share
91.  isakmp policy 20 encryption 3des
92.  isakmp policy 20 hash md5
93.  isakmp policy 20 group 2
94.  isakmp policy 20 lifetime 86400
95.  terminal width 80
96.  Cryptochecksum:e0clmj3546549637cbsFds54132d5
```

Example 11-14 shows the completed configuration for the Boston branch office.

Example 11-14 *Completed Configuration for Boston*

```
1.   : Saved
2.   :
3.   PIX Version 6.3(3)
4.   nameif ethernet0 outside security0
5.   nameif ethernet1 inside security100
6.   nameif ethernet2 DMZ security70
7.   enable password ksjfglkasglc encrypted
8.   passwd kjngczftglkacytiur encrypted
9.   hostname Boston
10.  domain-name www.Chapter11.com
11.  fixup protocol ftp 21
12.  fixup protocol http 80
13.  fixup protocol smtp 25
14.  fixup protocol skinny 2000
15.  names
16.  access-list inbound permit icmp any host 192.168.2.10
17.  access-list inbound permit tcp any host 192.168.2.10   eq www
18.  access-list inbound permit tcp any host 192.168.2.10 eq 443
19.  access-list DMZ permit udp 172.16.2.0 255.255.255.0 host 10.10.2.240 eq ntp
20.  access-list VPN permit ip 10.10.2.0 255.255.255.0 10.10.10.0 255.255.255.0
21.  access-list VPN permit ip 10.10.2.0 255.255.255.0 10.10.3.0 255.255.255.0
22.  access-list LosAngeles permit ip 10.10.2.0 255.255.255.0 10.10.10.0
     255.255.255.0
23.  access-list Atlanta permit ip 10.10.2.0 255.255.255.0 10.10.3.0 255.255.255.0
24.  pager lines 24
25.  logging on
26.  logging timestamp
27.  interface ethernet0 auto
28.  interface ethernet1 auto
29.  interface ethernet2 auto
30.  mtu outside 1500
31.  mtu inside 1500
32   ip address outside 192.168.2.1 255.255.255.0
33.  ip address inside 10.10.2.1 255.255.255.0
34.  ip address DMZ 172.16.2.1 255.255.255.0
35.  arp timeout 14400
36.  global (outside) 1 192.168.2.20-192.168.2.200
37.  nat (inside) 1 0.0.0.0 0.0.0.0 0 0
38.  nat (inside) 0 access-list VPN
39.  static (inside,DMZ) 10.10.2.240 10.10.2.240 netmask 255.255.255.255 0 0
40.  static (DMZ,outside) 192.168.2.10 172.16.2.10 netmask 255.255.255.255 0 0
```

Example 11-14 *Completed Configuration for Boston (Continued)*

```
41.  access-group inbound in interface outside
42.  access-group DMZ in interface DMZ
43.  route outside 0.0.0.0 0.0.0.0 192.168.2.254 1
44.  timeout xlate 3:00:00
45.  timeout conn 1:00:00 half-closed 0:10:00 udp 0:02:00
46.  timeout uauth 0:05:00 absolute
47.  aaa-server TACACS+ protocol tacacs+
48.  aaa-server RADIUS protocol radius
49.  no snmp-server location
50.  no snmp-server contact
51.  snmp-server community public
52.  no snmp-server enable traps
53.  floodguard enable
54.  sysopt connection permit-ipsec
55.  crypto ipsec transform-set Chapter11 esp-3des esp-md5-hmac
56.  crypto ipsec transform-set NothingNew esp-3des esp-sha-hmac
57.  crypto map Chapter11 10 ipsec-isakmp
58.  crypto map Chapter11 10 match address LosAngeles
59.  crypto map Chapter11 10 set peer 192.168.1.1
60.  crypto map Chapter11 10 set transform-set Chapter11
61.  crypto map Chapter11 20 ipsec-isakmp
62.  crypto map Chapter11 20 match address Atlanta
63.  crypto map Chapter11 20 set peer 192.168.3.1
64.  crypto map Chapter11 20 set transform-set Chapter11
65.  crypto map Chapter11 interface outside
66.  isakmp enable outside
67.  isakmp key ******** address 192.168.1.1 netmask 255.255.255.255
68.  isakmp key ******** address 192.168.3.1 netmask 255.255.255.255
69.  isakmp identity address
70.  isakmp policy 20 authentication pre-share
71.  isakmp policy 20 encryption 3des
72.  isakmp policy 20 hash md5
73.  isakmp policy 20 group 2
74.  isakmp policy 20 lifetime 86400
75.  terminal width 80
76.  Cryptochecksum:e0c04954fcabd239ae291d58fc618dd5
```

Example 11-15 shows the completed configuration for the Atlanta branch office.

Example 11-15 *Completed Configuration for Atlanta*

```
1.   : Saved
2.   :
3.   PIX Version 6.3(3)
4.   nameif ethernet0 outside security0
5.   nameif ethernet1 inside security100
6.   nameif ethernet2 DMZ security70
7.   enable password ksjfglkasglc encrypted
8.   passwd kjngczftglkacytiur encrypted
9.   hostname Atlanta
10.  domain-name www.Chapter11.com
11.  fixup protocol ftp 21
12.  fixup protocol http 80
13.  fixup protocol smtp 25
14.  fixup protocol skinny 2000
15.  names
16.  access-list inbound permit icmp any host 192.168.3.10
17.  access-list inbound permit tcp any host 192.168.3.10   eq www
18.  access-list inbound permit tcp any host 192.168.3.10 eq 443
19.  access-list DMZ permit udp 172.16.3.0 255.255.255.0 host 10.10.3.240 eq ntp
20.  access-list VPN permit ip 10.10.3.0 255.255.255.0 10.10.2.0 255.255.255.0
21.  access-list VPN permit ip 10.10.3.0 255.255.255.0 10.10.10.0 255.255.255.0
22.  access-list LosAngeles permit ip 10.10.3.0 255.255.255.0 10.10.10.0
     255.255.255.0
23.  access-list Boston permit ip 10.10.3.0 255.255.255.0 10.10.2.0 255.255.255.0
24.  pager lines 24
25.  logging on
26.  logging timestamp
27.  interface ethernet0 auto
28.  interface ethernet1 auto
29.  interface ethernet2 auto
30.  mtu outside 1500
31.  mtu inside 1500
32.  ip address outside 192.168.3.1 255.255.255.0
33.  ip address inside 10.10.3.1 255.255.255.0
34.  ip address DMZ 172.16.3.1 255.255.255.0
35.  arp timeout 14400
36.  global (outside) 1 192.168.3.20-192.168.3.200
37.  nat (inside) 1 0.0.0.0 0.0.0.0 0 0
38.  nat (inside) 0 access-list VPN
39.  static (inside,DMZ) 10.10.3.240 10.10.3.240 netmask 255.255.255.255 0 0
40.  static (DMZ,outside) 192.168.3.10 172.16.3.10 netmask 255.255.255.255 0 0
41.  access-group inbound in interface outside
42.  access-group DMZ in interface DMZ
43.  route outside 0.0.0.0 0.0.0.0 192.168.3.254 1
44.  timeout xlate 3:00:00
```

Example 11-15 *Completed Configuration for Atlanta (Continued)*

```
45.   timeout conn 1:00:00 half-closed 0:10:00 udp 0:02:00
46.   timeout uauth 0:05:00 absolute
47.   aaa-server TACACS+ protocol tacacs+
48.   aaa-server RADIUS protocol radius
49.   no snmp-server location
50.   no snmp-server contact
51.   snmp-server community public
52.   no snmp-server enable traps
53.   floodguard enable
54.   sysopt connection permit-ipsec
55.   crypto ipsec transform-set Chapter11 esp-3des esp-md5-hmac
56.   crypto ipsec transform-set NothingNew esp-3des esp-sha-hmac
57.   crypto map Chapter11 10 ipsec-isakmp
58.   crypto map Chapter11 10 match address LosAngeles
59.   crypto map Chapter11 10 set peer 192.168.1.1
60.   crypto map Chapter11 10 set transform-set Chapter11
61.   crypto map Chapter11 20 ipsec-isakmp
62.   crypto map Chapter11 20 match address Boston
63.   crypto map Chapter11 20 set peer 192.168.2.1
64.   crypto map Chapter11 20 set transform-set Chapter11
65.   crypto map Chapter11 interface outside
66.   isakmp enable outside
67.   isakmp key ******** address 192.168.1.1 netmask 255.255.255.255
68.   isakmp key ******** address 192.168.2.1 netmask 255.255.255.255
69.   isakmp identity address
70.   isakmp policy 20 authentication pre-share
71.   isakmp policy 20 encryption 3des
72.   isakmp policy 20 hash md5
73.   isakmp policy 20 group 2
74.   isakmp policy 20 lifetime 86400
75.   terminal width 80
76.   Cryptochecksum:e0c04954fcabd239ae291d58fc618dd5
```

How the Configuration Lines Interact

Figure 11-8 shows the completed configuration for Los Angeles, with a brief explanation for each entry. Note that each entry is connected to one or more other entries on the right. This diagram depicts how the lines of the configuration are dependent on each other. Keep this in mind when trying to troubleshoot a VPN configuration. It might help you to find which line is missing or incorrectly configured.

Figure 11-8 *LA Configuration with Comments*

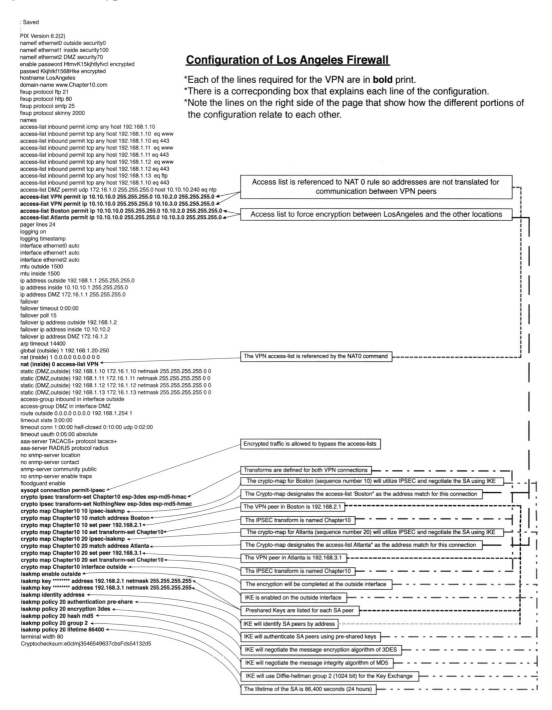

```
: Saved
:
:
PIX Version 6.2(2)
nameif ethernet0 outside security0
nameif ethernet1 inside security100
nameif ethernet2 DMZ security70
enable password HtmvK15kjhtlyfvcl encrypted
passwd Kkjhlkf1568Hke encrypted
hostname LosAngeles
domain-name www.Chapter10.com
fixup protocol ftp 21
fixup protocol http 80
fixup protocol smtp 25
fixup protocol skinny 2000
names
access-list inbound permit icmp any host 192.168.1.10
access-list inbound permit tcp any host 192.168.1.10  eq www
access-list inbound permit tcp any host 192.168.1.10 eq 443
access-list inbound permit tcp any host 192.168.1.11  eq www
access-list inbound permit tcp any host 192.168.1.11 eq 443
access-list inbound permit tcp any host 192.168.1.12  eq www
access-list inbound permit tcp any host 192.168.1.12 eq 443
access-list inbound permit tcp any host 192.168.1.13  eq ftp
access-list inbound permit tcp any host 192.168.1.10 eq 443
access-list DMZ permit udp 172.16.1.0 255.255.255.0 host 10.10.10.240 eq ntp
access-list VPN permit ip 10.10.10.0 255.255.255.0 10.10.2.0 255.255.255.0
access-list VPN permit ip 10.10.10.0 255.255.255.0 10.10.3.0 255.255.255.0
access-list Boston permit ip 10.10.10.0 255.255.255.0 10.10.2.0 255.255.255.0
access-list Atlanta permit ip 10.10.10.0 255.255.255.0 10.10.3.0 255.255.255.0
pager lines 24
logging on
logging timestamp
interface ethernet0 auto
interface ethernet1 auto
interface ethernet2 auto
mtu outside 1500
mtu inside 1500
ip address outside 192.168.1.1 255.255.255.0
ip address inside 10.10.10.1 255.255.255.0
ip address DMZ 172.16.1.1 255.255.255.0
failover
failover timeout 0:00:00
failover poll 15
failover ip address outside 192.168.1.2
failover ip address inside 10.10.10.2
failover ip address DMZ 172.16.1.2
arp timeout 14400
global (outside) 1 192.168.1.20-250
nat (inside) 1 0.0.0.0 0.0.0.0 0 0
nat (inside) 0 access-list VPN
static (DMZ,outside) 192.168.1.10 172.16.1.10 netmask 255.255.255.255 0 0
static (DMZ,outside) 192.168.1.11 172.16.1.11 netmask 255.255.255.255 0 0
static (DMZ,outside) 192.168.1.12 172.16.1.12 netmask 255.255.255.255 0 0
static (DMZ,outside) 192.168.1.13 172.16.1.13 netmask 255.255.255.255 0 0
access-group inbound in interface outside
access-group DMZ in interface DMZ
route outside 0.0.0.0 0.0.0.0 192.168.1.254 1
timeout xlate 3:00:00
timeout conn 1:00:00 half-closed 0:10:00 udp 0:02:00
timeout uauth 0:05:00 absolute
aaa-server TACACS+ protocol tacacs+
aaa-server RADIUS protocol radius
no snmp-server location
no snmp-server contact
snmp-server community public
no snmp-server enable traps
floodguard enable
sysopt connection permit-ipsec
crypto ipsec transform-set Chapter10 esp-3des esp-md5-hmac
crypto ipsec transform-set NothingNew esp-3des esp-md5-hmac
crypto map Chapter10 10 ipsec-isakmp
crypto map Chapter10 10 match address Boston
crypto map Chapter10 10 set peer 192.168.2.1
crypto map Chapter10 10 set transform-set Chapter10
crypto map Chapter10 20 ipsec-isakmp
crypto map Chapter10 20 match address Atlanta
crypto map Chapter10 20 set peer 192.168.3.1
crypto map Chapter10 20 set transform-set Chapter10
crypto map Chapter10 interface outside
isakmp enable outside
isakmp key ******** address 192.168.2.1 netmask 255.255.255.255
isakmp key ******** address 192.168.3.1 netmask 255.255.255.255
isakmp identity address
isakmp policy 20 authentication pre-share
isakmp policy 20 encryption 3des
isakmp policy 20 hash md5
isakmp policy 20 group 2
isakmp policy 20 lifetime 86400
terminal width 80
Cryptochecksum:e0clmj3546549637cbsFds54132d5
```

Configuration of Los Angeles Firewall

*Each of the lines required for the VPN are in **bold** print.
*There is a correcponding box that explains each line of the configuration.
*Note the lines on the right side of the page that show how the different portions of the configuration relate to each other.

Access list is referenced to NAT 0 rule so addresses are not translated for communication between VPN peers

Access list to force encryption between LosAngeles and the other locations

The VPN access-list is referenced by the NAT0 command

Encrypted traffic is allowed to bypass the access-lists

Transforms are defined for both VPN connections

The crypto-map for Boston (sequence number 10) will utilize IPSEC and negotiate the SA using IKE

The Crypto-map designates the access-list 'Boston' as the address match for this connection

The VPN peer in Boston is 192.168.2.1

Ths IPSEC transform is named Chapter10

The crypto-map for Atlanta (sequence number 20) will utilize IPSEC and negotiate the SA using IKE

The Crypto-map designates the access-list Atlanta" as the address match for this connection

The VPN peer in Atlanta is 192.168.3.1

Ths IPSEC transform is named Chapter10

The encryption will be completed at the outside interface

IKE is enabled on the outside interface

Preshared Keys are listed for each SA peer

IKE will identify SA peers by address

IKE will authenticate SA peers using pre-shared keys

IKE will negotiate the message encryption algorithm of 3DES

IKE will negotiate the message integrity algorithm of MD5

IKE will use Diffie-hellman group 2 (1024 bit) for the Key Exchange

The lifetime of the SA is 86,400 seconds (24 hours)

This chapter covers the following subjects:

- DHCP server configuration

- PPPoE and the PIX Firewall

- PIX Firewall enables a secure VPN

- Prepare to configure VPN support

- Cisco VPN Client

- Scale PIX Firewall VPNs

Configuring Access VPNs

The Cisco Easy VPN, a software enhancement for Cisco PIX Firewalls and security appliances, greatly simplifies virtual private network (VPN) deployment for remote offices and telecommuters. By centralizing VPN management across all Cisco VPN devices, Cisco Easy VPN reduces the complexity of VPN deployments. Cisco Easy VPN enables you to integrate various remote VPN solutions (Cisco IOS® routers, Cisco PIX Firewalls, Cisco VPN 3002 Hardware Clients, and Cisco VPN Software Clients) within a single deployment using a consistent VPN policy and key management method that greatly simplifies administration of the remote clients.

How to Best Use This Chapter

Using VPNs to protect traffic from remote locations is a vital portion of your overall network security solution. Understanding how the Cisco Easy VPN simplifies VPN deployment and management is crucial to securing access from all of your remote locations. Chapter 11, "Virtual Private Networks," explains the technologies and protocols used for creating and maintaining VPNs across public networks. This chapter explains how you can apply those VPNs to secure various remote configurations using the Cisco Easy VPN solution. Test yourself with the "Do I Know This Already?" quiz and see how familiar you are with the Cisco Easy VPN functionality available on PIX Firewalls.

"Do I Know This Already?" Quiz

The purpose of the "Do I Know This Already?" quiz is to help you decide if you really need to read the entire chapter. If you already intend to read the entire chapter, you do not necessarily need to answer these questions now.

The ten-question quiz, derived from the major sections in the "Foundation and Supplemental Topics" portion of the chapter, helps you determine how to spend your limited study time.

Table 12-1 outlines the major topics discussed in this chapter and the "Do I Know This Already?" quiz questions that correspond to those topics.

Table 12-1 *"Do I Know This Already?" Foundation Topics Section-to-Question Mapping*

Supplemental or Foundation Topics Section	Questions Covered in This Section	Score
Introduction to Cisco Easy VPN		
Overview of the Easy VPN Server	1	
Overview of Easy VPN Remote Feature	2, 3	
Easy VPN Remote Modes of Operation	4, 5	
Overview of Cisco VPN Software Client	6	
PIX Easy VPN Remote Configuration	7	
Point-to-Point Protocol over Ethernet and the PIX Firewall	8, 10	
Dynamic Host Configuration Protocol Server Configuration	9	

CAUTION The goal of self assessment is to gauge your mastery of the topics in this chapter. If you do not know the answer to a question or are only partially sure of the answer, you should mark this question wrong for purposes of the self assessment. Giving yourself credit for an answer you correctly guess skews your self-assessment results and might provide you with a false sense of security.

1. What is the Easy VPN Server functionality known as *Initial Contact*?

    a. Ability to cause the Easy VPN Server to delete any existing connections, thus preventing SA synchronization problems

    b. The first connection between an Easy VPN Client and Easy VPN Server

    c. The initial message sent from the Easy VPN Server to the Easy VPN Client

    d. The initial message sent from the Easy VPN Client to the Easy VPN Server

    e. None of the above

2. Which of the following platforms does not support the Easy VPN Remote feature functionality?

    a. 800 Series routers

    b. 900 Series routers

    c. 7200 Series routers

    d. 1700 Series routers

    e. None of the above

3. Which two IKE authentication mechanisms do the Easy VPN Remote Clients support? (Choose two.)

    a. Username/password

    b. Preshared keys

    c. Diffie-Hellman

    d. Digital certificates

    e. XAUTH

4. How many different operation modes does the Easy VPN Remote feature support?

    a. 1

    b. 4

    c. 2

    d. 3

    e. None of the above

5. In which Easy VPN Remote mode are the IP addresses of the remote systems visible on the Easy VPN Server network?

    a. Client mode

    b. Network extension mode

    c. Server mode

    d. No Easy VPN Remote modes support this functionality.

    e. All Easy VPN Remote modes

6. The Cisco VPN Software Client supports which key management techniques?

    a. IKE main mode

    b. IKE aggressive mode

    c. Diffie-Hellman groups 1, 2, 5, and 7

    d. Answers a and b

    e. Answers a, b, and c

7. What is Secure Unit Authentication (SUA)?

   a. The ability to require the hosts on the remote protected network to be authenticated individually based on the IP address of the inside host

   b. The ability to require one-time passwords, two-factor authentication, and similar authentication schemes before the establishment of a VPN tunnel to the Easy VPN Server

   c. An authentication mechanism between the remote systems and the Easy VPN Remote Client

   d. An authentication mechanism that the Cisco VPN Software Client uses to connect with the Easy VPN Remote feature

   e. None of the above

8. Which authentication mechanisms are supported with PPPoE?

   a. PAP

   b. CHAP

   c. MS-CHAP

   d. Answers a and b

   e. Answers a, b, and c

9. Which command enables the PIX Firewall to pass configuration parameters learned from a DHCP server to its DHCP clients?

   a. dhcpd auto_config

   b. dhcpd option 150

   c. dhcpd address

   d. dhcpd bind

   e. None of the above

10. Which of the following is false with regard to the PIX Firewall?

    a. You can pass configuration parameters learned from the DHCP client to the PIX's DHCP clients.

    b. You can pass configuration parameters learned from the PPPoE client to the PIX's DHCP clients.

    c. You can enable the DHCP client and the DHCP server simultaneously.

    d. You can enable the PPPoE client and the DHCP client on the same interface simultaneously.

    e. All of the statements are true.

The answers to the "Do I Know This Already?" quiz are found in Appendix A, "Answers to the 'Do I Know This Already?' Quizzes and Q&A Sections." The suggested choices for your next step are as follows:

- **8 or less overall score**—Read the entire chapter. This includes the "Foundation and Supplemental Topics," "Foundation Summary," and "Q&A" sections.

- **9 or 10 overall score**—If you want more review of these topics, skip to the "Foundation Summary" section and then go to the "Q&A" section. Otherwise, move to the next chapter.

Foundation and Supplemental Topics

Introduction to Cisco Easy VPN

Cisco Easy VPN greatly simplifies VPN deployment for remote offices and telecommuters. Based on a Cisco Unified Client Framework, Cisco Easy VPN centralizes management across all Cisco VPN devices, thus greatly reducing the complexity in configuring and deploying VPN configurations. The Cisco Easy VPN consists of the following two components (see Figure 12-1):

- Easy VPN Server
- Easy VPN Remote feature

Easy VPN Server

The Easy VPN Server enables Cisco IOS® routers, PIX Firewalls, and Cisco VPN 3000 Series concentrators to serve as VPN headend devices when remote offices are running the Easy VPN Remote feature. The configuration works for both site-to-site and remote access configurations. With Cisco Easy VPN, security policies defined at the headend are pushed to the remote VPN device, ensuring that the connection has up-to-date policies in place before the connection is established.

Mobile workers running the VPN Client software on their PCs can initiate Internet Protocol Security (IPSec) tunnels that are terminated on the Easy VPN Server. This flexibility enables telecommuters and traveling employees to access critical data and applications easily that reside at the headquarter facilities.

Easy VPN Remote Feature

The Easy VPN Remote feature enables PIX Firewalls, Cisco VPN 3002 Hardware Clients, Cisco VPN Software Clients, and certain Cisco IOS® routers to act as remote VPN clients. The Easy VPN Server can push security policies to these clients, thus minimizing VPN configuration requirements at remote locations. This cost-effective solution is ideal for remote offices with little information technology (IT) support as well as large deployments where it is impractical to configure individual remote devices.

Figure 12-1   *Cisco Easy VPN*

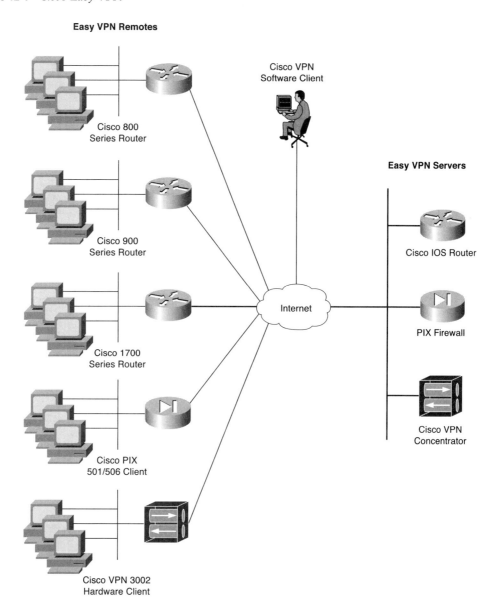

Overview of the Easy VPN Server

The Easy VPN Server serves as the headend for your VPN configuration. To utilize Cisco Easy VPN effectively, you need to understand the following characteristics of the PIX Firewall Easy VPN Server:

■ Major features

■ Server functions

■ Supported servers

Major Features

The PIX Firewall Version 6.3 VPN Server includes the following major features:

■ Support for Easy VPN Remote clients

■ Ability for remote users to communicate using IPSec with supported PIX Firewall gateways

■ Central management of IPSec policies that are pushed to the clients by the server

Server Functions

The PIX Firewall Version 6.3 VPN Server supports the following functionality:

■ Mode Configuration version 6

■ Extended Authentication (XAUTH) version 6

■ Internet Key Exchange (IKE) dead peer detection (DPD)

■ Split tunneling control

■ Initial Contact

■ Group-based policy control

Dead Peer Detection

Dead peer detection (DPD) enables two IPSec peers to determine if each other is still "alive" during the lifetime of the VPN connection. This functionality is useful to clean up valuable VPN resources that are allocated to a peer that no longer exists.

A Cisco VPN device can be configured to send and reply to DPD messages. DPD messages are sent when no other traffic is traversing the IPSec tunnel. If a configured amount of time passes without a DPD message, a dead peer can be detected. DPD messages are unidirectional and automatically sent by Cisco VPN Clients. DPD is configured on the server only if the server wishes to send DPD messages to VPN Clients to assess their health.

> **Initial Contact**
>
> If a Cisco VPN Client is suddenly disconnected, the gateway might not immediately detect this, so the current connection information (IKE and IPSec security associations [SAs]) will still be valid. Then, if the VPN Client attempts to reestablish a connection, the new connection will be refused because the gateway still has the previous connection marked as valid. To avoid this scenario, *Initial Contact* has been implemented in all Cisco VPN products. Initial Contact enables the VPN Client to send an initial message that instructs the gateway to ignore and delete any existing connections from that client, thus preventing connection problems caused by SA synchronization issues.

The Cisco Easy VPN supports the IPSec options and attributes shown in Table 12-2.

Table 12-2 *IPSec Options and Attributes*

IPSec Option	Attributes
Authentication Algorithms	• Keyed-Hash Message Authentication Code (HMAC) • Message Digest 5 (MD5) • HMAC Secure Hash Algorithm (SHA-1)
Authentication Types	• Preshared keys • Rivest-Shamir-Adleman (RSA) digital signatures (not supported by Cisco Easy VPN Remote phase II)
Diffie-Hellman (DH) Groups	• Group 1 • Group 2 • Group 5
IKE Encryption Algorithms	• Data Encryption Standard (DES) • Triple Data Encryption Standard (3DES) • Advanced Encryption Standard (AES)
IPSec Encryption Algorithms	• DES • 3DES • AES • NULL
IPSec Protocol Identifiers	• Encapsulating Security Payload (ESP) • IP Payload Compression Protocol (IPComp) • STAC-Lempel-Ziv Compression (LZS)
IPSec Protocol Mode	• Tunnel Mode

Supported Servers

The Easy VPN Remote feature requires that the destination peer be a VPN gateway or concentrator that supports the Easy VPN Server. Some of the currently supported Easy VPN Server platforms include the following:

- Cisco 806, 826, 827, and 828 routers (Cisco IOS Software Release 12.2[8]T or later)
- Cisco 1700 Series routers (Cisco IOS Software Release 12.2[8]T or later)
- Cisco 2600 Series routers (Cisco IOS Software Release 12.2[8]T or later)
- Cisco 3620, 3640, and 3660 routers (Cisco IOS Software Release 12.2[8]T or later)
- Cisco 7100 Series VPN routers (Cisco IOS Software Release 12.2[8]T or later)
- Cisco 7200 Series routers (Cisco IOS Software Release 12.2[8]T or later)
- Cisco 7500 Series routers (Cisco IOS Software Release 12.2[8]T or later)
- Cisco uBR905 and uBR925 cable access routers (Cisco IOS Software Release 12.2[8]T or later)
- Cisco VPN 3000 Series (Software Release 3.11 or later)
- Cisco PIX 500 Series (Software Release 6.2 or later)

Overview of Easy VPN Remote Feature

The Cisco Easy VPN Remote feature enables Cisco PIX Firewalls, Cisco VPN 3002 Hardware Clients, Cisco VPN Software Clients, and certain IOS routers to act as remote Cisco VPN Clients. The Cisco Easy VPN Remote feature provides for automatic management of the following items:

- Negotiating tunnel parameters
- Establishing tunnels according to parameters
- Automatically creating the Network Address Translation (NAT)/Port Address Translation (PAT) and associated access list if necessary
- Authenticating users
- Managing security keys for encryption and decryption
- Authenticating, encrypting, and decrypting data through the VPN tunnel

This section explains the following characteristics of the Easy VPM Remote feature:

- Supported clients
- Easy VPN remote connection process
- XAUTH configuration

Supported Clients

The Easy VPN Remote feature supports the following client platforms:

■ Cisco VPN Software Client

■ Cisco VPN 3002 Hardware Client

■ Cisco PIX 501 and 506/506E VPN Clients

■ Cisco Easy VPN Remote router clients

Cisco VPN Software Client

The Cisco Easy VPN Remote feature supports the Cisco VPN Client software (software version 3.*x* and later). Simple to deploy and operate, this client software enables customers to establish secure, end-to-end encrypted tunnels to any Easy VPN Server. The Cisco VPN Software Client is available from the Cisco.com website for any central-site remote access VPN product and is included free of charge with the Cisco VPN 3000 Concentrator.

VPN access policies and configurations are downloaded to the Cisco VPN Software Client from the Easy VPN Server when the client establishes a connection. This configuration simplifies deployment, management, and scalability. By preconfiguring the client software, the initial user login requires little user intervention even in mass deployment scenarios.

The Cisco VPN Software Client operates with the following operating systems:

■ Microsoft Windows 95, 98, Me, NT 4.0, 2000, and XP

■ Linux

■ Solaris (UltraSPARC 32- and 64-bit)

■ MAC OS X 10.1

Cisco VPN 3002 Hardware Client

The Cisco VPN Hardware Client has the Cisco VPN Software Client software built into it, enabling it to emulate the Cisco 3000 Series VPN Concentrator Software Client. You simply can connect the remote PCs into the Hardware Client instead of loading the Cisco VPN Software Client software on the remote PCs.

The Hardware Client comes in the following two versions:

■ Hardware Client

■ Hardware Client 8E

> **NOTE** Both Hardware Client models have one public Ethernet interface. The difference between the two Hardware Clients is that the 8E has eight private 10/100BaseT ports instead of only one. These eight ports utilize auto Medium Dependent Interface Crossover (MDIX) technology that eliminates the need for crossover cables when connecting a device to a port.

The Hardware Client operates in one of the following two modes:

■ Client mode

■ Network extension mode

You can select the modes locally using the command-line interface (CLI) or the graphical user interface (GUI) or remotely using an IPSec tunnel or Secure Shell (SSH).

The Hardware Client is powered by an external power supply and can auto sense either 110V or 220V.

Cisco PIX 501 and 506 VPN Clients

The following two PIX Firewall models are commonly used as VPN clients:

■ PIX 501

■ PIX 506/506E

The PIX 501 delivers enterprise-class security for small offices and telecommuters. For small offices with always-on broadband connections, the PIX 501 provides security functionality, numerous networking features, and powerful remote management capabilities in a compact single-box solution.

Up to four individual systems can share a single broadband connection, using the integrated four-port auto-sensing, auto MDIX switch for the inside interface. Like the Hardware Client, this switch eliminates the need for crossover cables when connecting a device to a port. The Ethernet ports support 10/100BASE-T (100BASE-T with the 6.3 software release). The PIX 501 also provides a RS-232 console port interface (RJ-45 connector and 9600 baud).

The PIX 506/506E enables companies to utilize the power of the Internet to enable users to work remotely from home securely. It delivers full firewall protection in conjunction with IPSec and VPN functionality. Connecting simultaneously with up to 25 VPN peers, the PIX 506/506E provides a complete implementation of IPSec standards. It comes with two integrated 10/100BASE-T (100BASE-T with the 6.3 software release) ports in a compact platform (8 inches by 12 inches by 1.7 inches). Updates to image files are downloaded using the Trivial File Transfer Protocol (TFTP).

> **NOTE**   Before software release 6.3, the Ethernet ports on the PIX 501 and 506/506E were 10BASE-T. After upgrading to the 6.3 software release on either the PIX 501 or 506/506E, these ports become 10/100BASE-T ports. This speed enhancement is accomplished strictly by a software update (no hardware upgrades are necessary).

Cisco Easy VPN Remote Router Clients

To provide a comprehensive solution, Cisco Easy VPN also supports several router-based clients. You can use the following router platforms as Cisco Easy VPN remote clients:

- Cisco 800 Series routers (806, 826, 827,828)
- Cisco 900 Series routers (uBR905, uBR925)
- Cisco 1700 Series routers (1710, 1720, 1721, 1750, 1751, 1760)

Cable modems, xDSL routers, and other forms of broadband access provide Internet access, but many situations require VPN connections to secure data that traverses the Internet. Establishing a VPN connection between two VPN endpoints, however, can be complicated because it usually requires coordination between administrators to perform the tedious tasks necessary to define the connection parameters.

Cisco Easy VPN Remote eliminates most of the tedious work by implementing the Cisco VPN Client protocol. This protocol allows many of the VPN parameters to be configured on the access server. Once the access server is configured, the additional configuration on the VPN Client is minimal. When the IPSec client initiates the VPN connection, the VPN remote access server pushes the required IPSec policies to the IPSec client and creates the corresponding IPSec tunnel.

Easy VPN Remote Connection Process

When the Easy VPN Remote Client initiates a connection with the Easy VPN Server gateway, the interaction between the peers involves the following major steps:

Step 1   VPN Client initiates the IKE phase 1 process.

Step 2   VPN Client negotiates an IKE SA.

Step 3   Easy VPN Server accepts the SA proposal.

Step 4   Easy VPN Server initiates a username/password challenge.

Step 5   Mode configuration process is initiated.

Step 6   IKE quick mode completes the connection.

Step 1: VPN Client Initiates Internet Key Exchange Phase 1 Process

When initiating the VPN connection, the client can use one of the following two IKE authentication mechanisms:

■ Preshared keys

■ Digital certificates

When using preshared keys, the client initiates IKE aggressive mode negotiation. The group name entered in the configuration GUI (ID-KEY-ID) is used to identify the group profile associated with the VPN Client.

Using digital certificates requires the client to initiate IKE main mode negotiation. The Organizational Unit (OU) field of the distinguished name (DN) is used to identify the group profile associated with the VPN Client.

Step 2: VPN Client Negotiates an Internet Key Exchange Security Association

The client attempts to establish a SA between the tythbzclient and server peer Internet Protocol (IP) addresses by sending multiple IKE proposals to the Easy VPN Server. To reduce manual configuration on the VPN Client, these IKE proposals include several combinations of the following parameters:

■ Encryption and hash algorithms

■ Authentication methods

■ Diffie-Hellman (DH) group sizes

Proposing multiple IKE proposals with various parameters means that one combination is likely to match one of the options configured on the server.

Step 3: Easy VPN Server Accepts the Security Association Proposal

After receiving the various proposals from the VPN Client, the Easy VPN Server searches for a valid match in its configuration. The first proposal to match is accepted. To ensure that the most secure proposal is always accepted, you should store the valid proposals on the server in order from the most secure option to the least secure option.

Step 4: Easy VPN Server Initiates a Username/Password Challenge

If the Easy VPN Server is configured for XAUTH, the VPN Client waits for a username/password challenge once the proposal is accepted. The username and password entered by the user are checked against the data stored in an authentication, authorization, and accounting (AAA) server.

> **NOTE** VPN devices that handle remote Cisco VPN Clients should always be configured to enforce user authentication.

Step 5: Mode Configuration Process Is Initiated

After successfully authenticating with the Easy VPN Server, the VPN Client requests the remaining configuration parameters from the Easy VPN Server such as the following:

- IP address
- Domain Name System (DNS) information
- Split tunneling configuration

> **NOTE** The IP address is the only required parameter in the group profile. All other parameters are optional.

Step 6: Internet Key Exchange Quick Mode Completes the Connection

After the VPN Client receives the various configuration parameters from the Easy VPN Server, IKE quick mode is initiated to negotiate the IPSec SA establishment.

Extended Authentication Configuration

XAUTH enables the Easy VPN Server to require username/password authentication in order to establish the VPN connection. This authentication is performed by an AAA server. To configure the Easy VPN Server to use XAUTH for remote VPN clients, you must set up the Easy VPN Server and configure it to perform XAUTH. The complete configuration process involves performing the following tasks:

- Create an Internet Security Association and Key Management Protocol (ISAKMP) policy for remote Cisco VPN Client access
- Create an IP address pool
- Define a group policy for mode configuration push
- Create a transform set
- Create a dynamic crypto map
- Assign the dynamic crypto map to a static crypto map
- Apply the static crypto map to an interface
- Configure XAUTH
- Configure NAT and NAT 0
- Enable IKE DPD

Create an Internet Security Association and Key Management Protocol Policy

To create the ISAKMP policy you must use the standard ISAKMP configuration commands to define the following parameters:

- Authentication type

- Encryption algorithm

- Hash algorithm

- Diffie-Hellman group ID

- SA lifetime

The syntax for these commands is as follows:

```
isakmp policy priority authentication {pre-share/rsa-sig}
isakmp policy priority encryption {aes¦aes-192¦aes-256¦des¦3des}
isakmp policy priority group {1¦2¦5}
isakmp policy priority hash {md5¦sha}
isakmp policy priority lifetime seconds
```

Table 12-3 outlines the parameters for the **isakmp policy** command.

Table 12-3 isakmp policy *Parameters*

Parameter	Description
aes	Specifies AES with a 128-bit key to be the encryption algorithm used by the IKE policy.
aes-192	Specifies AES with a 192-bit key to be the encryption algorithm used by the IKE policy.
aes-256	Specifies AES with a 256-bit key to be the encryption algorithm used by the IKE policy.
des	Specifies DES with a 56-bit key to be the encryption algorithm used by the IKE policy.
3des	Specifies triple DES to be the encryption algorithm used by the IKE policy.
encryption	Keyword indicating that the next parameter specifies the encryption algorithm for the IKE policy
group	Keyword indicating that the next parameter is a Diffie-Hellman group. You can specify 1, 2, or 5 (1 is the default).
hash	Keyword indicating that the next parameter specifies the hash algorithm to be used by the IKE policy.

Table 12-3 isakmp policy *Parameters (Continued)*

Parameter	Description
lifetime	Keyword indicating that the next parameter specifies the lifetime for the IKE policy.
md5	Specifies that the MD5 hash algorithm will be used by the IKE policy.
pre-share	Specifies that the IKE policy will use preshared keys for initial authentication.
priority	An integer (1 to 65,534) uniquely identifying the IKE policy and assigning it a priority (1 is the highest priority, and 65,534 is the lowest priority).
rsa-sig	Specifies that the IKE policy will use RSA signatures for initial authentication.
sha	Specifies that the SHA-1 hash algorithm will be used by the IKE policy. This is the default hash algorithm.

For instance, suppose that you want to configure an ISAKMP policy based on the following criteria:

- Preshare key initial authentication
- AES encryption algorithm (128-bit)
- SHA hash algorithm
- Diffie-Hellman group 5

The commands to define this ISAKMP policy are as follows:

```
Pix(config)# isakmp enable outside
Pix(config)# isakmp policy 30 authentication pre-share
Pix(config)# isakmp policy 30 encryption aes
Pix(config)# isakmp policy 30 hash sha
Pix(config)# isakmp policy 30 group 5
```

Create an Internet Protocol Address Pool

If the remote client is using the Easy VPN Server to obtain its IP address, you must define a local address pool using the **ip local pool** command. The syntax for this command is as follows:

```
ip local pool {pool_name low_ip_address [-high_ip_address]}
```

For instance, suppose that you want to assign the remote clients addresses in the range from 10.20.100.1 through 10.20.100.254. Using a pool name of *vpn-pool*, then the command line would be as follows:

```
Pix(config)# ip local pool vpn_pool 10.20.100.1-10.20.100.254
```

Define Group Policy for Mode Configuration Push

Several parameters are pushed to the VPN Client from the Easy VPN Server. These parameters are specified by the group policy assigned to a set of remote VPN Clients. The major group policy parameters are as follows:

- IKE preshared key
- DNS servers
- Windows Internet Naming Service (WINS) servers
- DNS domain
- Local IP address pool
- Idle timeout

> **NOTE** Each remote VPN user belongs to a specific VPN group. As users establish VPN tunnels to the Easy VPN Server, they identify to which group they belong.

You configure these parameters using the **vpngroup** command. The syntax for these commands is as follows:

```
vpngroup group_name password preshared_key
vpngroup group_name dns-server primary-server [secondary-server]
vpngroup group_name wins-server primary-server [secondary-server]
vpngroup group_name default-domain domain_name
vpngroup group_name address-pool pool_name
vpngroup group_name idle-time seconds
```

Create Transform Set

A transform identifies an encryption algorithm and hash algorithm pair. A group of transforms defines a transform set. For each group policy, you can define one or more transforms to indicate which pairs of algorithms are acceptable for new IPSec connections. You specify the transform information for your group policy using the **crypto ipsec transform-set** command. The syntax for this command is as follows:

```
crypto ipsec transform-set transform-set-name transform1 [transform2 [transform3]]
```

You can assign up to three different transforms to a specific transform set name. The order in which the transforms are listed indicates the order in which the transforms will be checked. Therefore, you must place the highest-priority (most secure) transforms first so that they will be matched before less-secure transforms. A remote client, however, can end up using any of the transforms that you specify in the list.

> **NOTE** For an IPSec-manual crypto map, you can specify only a single transform. When using IPSec-ISAKMP or dynamic crypto map entries, however, you can specify up to six transform sets.

The transform sets that you can use are as follows:

- ah-md5-hmac
- ah-sha-hmac
- esp-aes
- esp-aes-192
- esp-aes-256
- esp-des
- esp-3des
- esp-null
- esp-md5-hmac
- esp-sha-hmac

Each transform defines either **ah** or **esp** (indicating either Authentication Header [AH] or Encapsulating Security Payload [ESP]). The keyword used in the transform is an algorithm abbreviation (see Table 12-4).

Table 12-4 *Encryption and Hash Algorithms*

Keyword	Algorithm
aes	Advanced Encryption Standard
des	Data Encryption Standard
3des	Triple Data Encryption Standard
md5	MD5 message digest algorithm
sha	SHA message digest algorithm

Create a Dynamic Crypto Map

When your VPN Clients connect to the Easy VPN Server, they will negotiate the parameters of the IPSec session. Creating a dynamic crypto map enables you to define a crypto map that does not have all of the parameters configured. It acts as a sort of policy template in which the missing parameters get configured to match the remote peer's requirements (as part of the IPSec negotiation). By using dynamic crypto maps, your Easy VPN Servers do not have to be preconfigured for all of the requirements of your remote peers, thus making the configuration process more flexible.

> **NOTE** Dynamic crypto maps are not used to initiate IPSec SAs with remote peers. They are used only when remote peers initiate IPSec SAs and during the evaluation of traffic coming to the server.

You create dynamic crypto maps using the **crypto dynamic-map** command. The syntax for this command is as follows:

```
crypto dynamic-map dynamic-map-name dynamic-map-seqnum
```

Assign a Dynamic Crypto Map to a Static Crypto Map

After creating a dynamic crypto map, you need to assign the dynamic crypto map to a static crypto map using the **crypto map** command. The syntax for this command is as follows:

```
crypto map map-name seq-num {ipsec-isakmp¦ipsec-manual} [dynamic dynamic-map-name]
```

Apply the Static Crypto Map to an Interface

Once the static crypto map has been created, you need to identify to which interface the map needs to be applied by using another variation of the **crypto map** command. The syntax for this command is as follows:

```
crypto map map-name interface interface-name
```

Configure Extended Authentication

Configuring XAUTH on the Easy VPN Server for your remote VPN Clients involves the following three steps:

Step 1   Enable AAA login authentication.

Step 2   Define AAA server IP address and encryption key.

Step 3   Enable IKE XAUTH for the crypto map.

To enable AAA login authentication, you use the **aaa-server** command. The syntax for this command is as follows:

```
aaa-server server-tag protocol {tacacs+¦radius}
```

Besides enabling AAA login authentication, you need to configure the location of the AAA server by specifying its IP address. The syntax for this variation of the **aaa-server** command is as follows:

```
aaa-server server-tag [(if_name)] host server-ip [key][timeout seconds]
```

Finally, you need to enable IKE XAUTH for the crypto map that you defined using another variation of the **crypto map** command. This syntax for this command is as follows:

```
crypto map map-name client [token] authentication aaa-server-name
```

> **NOTE**   The optional keyword **token** when specified informs the PIX Firewall that the AAA server uses a token-card system and to thus prompt the user for a username and password during the IKE authentication.

An example configuration for XAUTH that utilizes Terminal Access Controller Access Control System Plus (TACACS+) is as follows:

```
pix515a(config)# aaa-server MYSERVER protocol tacacs+
pix515a(config)# aaa-server MYSERVER (inside) host 192.168.1.15 S3cr3TK3y!
pix515a(config)# crypto map MYMAP client authentication MYSERVER
```

Configure Network Address Translation and NAT 0

The traffic traversing the IPSec tunnel is encrypted. Some traffic originating from the Easy VPN Server network, however, simply must be translated using NAT and then sent without being encrypted. Figure 12-2 shows a situation in which a remote VPN Client is connecting across the Internet to the PIX VPN Server.

Figure 12-2   *Configuring NAT and NAT 0*

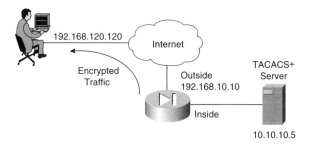

Traffic from the TACACS+ server destined for 192.168.120.120 needs to be encrypted and sent through the IPSec tunnel without translation. Traffic to the Internet (from the TACACS+

server), however, needs to be translated (by NAT) but not encrypted. The commands to perform this configuration are as follows:

```
pix515a(config)# access-list 101 permit ip 10.10.10.0 255.255.255.0 192.168.120.120
   255.255.255.255
pix515a(config)# nat (inside) 0 access-list 101
pix515a(config)# nat (inside) 1 0.0.0.0 0.0.0.0
pix515a(config)# global (outside) 1 interface
```

Traffic that matches **access-list 101** is encrypted and sent through the IPSec tunnel to the remote system. Other traffic is translated (by NAT) and transmitted without encryption out the same interface.

Enable Internet Key Exchange Dead Peer Detection

Dead peer detection (DPD) allows two IPSec peers to determine that the other is still "alive" during the lifetime of the VPN connection. In many situations, the one peer may reboot or the link may be unexpectedly disconnected for some other reason. The other peer may not quickly detect that the connection has been terminated. DPD enables an IPSec peer to send notification of the disconnection to the user, attempt to switch to another IPSec host, or clean up valuable resources that were allocated to a peer that is no longer connected.

A Cisco VPN device can be configured to send and reply to DPD messages. DPD messages are sent when no other traffic is traversing the IPSec tunnel. If a configured amount of time passes without a reply to a DPD message, a dead peer can be detected. DPD messages are unidirectional and are automatically sent by Cisco VPN Clients. DPD is configured on the server only if the server wishes to send DPD messages to VPN Clients to assess their health.

You use the **isakmp keepalive** command to enable the PIX Firewall gateway to send IKE DPD messages. You need to specify the number of seconds between DPD messages and the number of seconds between retries (if a DPD message does not receive a response). The syntax for this command is as follows:

```
isakmp keepalive seconds [retry_seconds]
```

Easy VPN Remote Modes of Operation

The Easy VPN Remote supports the following two modes of operation:

- Client mode
- Network extension mode

In client mode, the Easy VPN Server automatically creates NAT/PAT associations that allow the PCs and other hosts on the client side of the VPN connection to form a private network that does not use any IP addresses in the address space of the Easy VPN Server.

> **NOTE**   The NAT/PAT translations and access control list (ACL) configurations created by the Easy VPN Remote feature are not written to either the startup configuration or the running configuration. You can view these configurations, however, using the **show ip nat statistics** and **show access-list** commands (or the **show vpnclient detail** on the PIX Firewall) when the configuration is active.

In network extension mode, the PCs and other hosts at the client end of the IPSec tunnel are assigned fully routable IP addresses that are reachable from the server network (by the IPSec tunnel session), forming one logical network. In this mode, PAT is not used so that client systems have direct access to the PCs and hosts on the destination network.

Client Mode

Client mode enables you to deploy a VPN quickly and easily in a small office/home office (SOHO) environment. In situations where there is no need to access the devices behind the VPN client directly and ease of use and quick installation are important, the client mode is the ideal solution.

In client mode, the Easy VPN Remote device uses PAT to isolate the private network from the public network. PAT causes all of the traffic from the SOHO network to appear on the private network as a single source IP address. Figure 12-3 illustrates the Easy VPN Remote client mode of operation. The remote clients are on the 192.168.10.0 network. Traffic from these clients is converted (by PAT) to a single address (10.20.10.2).

Figure 12-3   *Easy VPN Remote Client Mode*

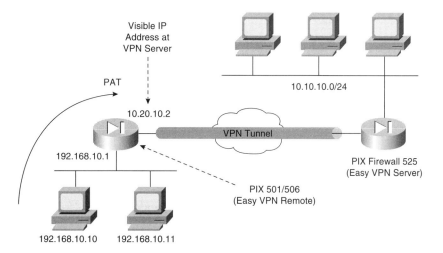

Network Extension Mode

In network extension mode, all SOHO PCs connected to the Easy VPN Remote device are uniquely addressable by the VPN tunnel. This allows devices to connect directly to PCs behind the Easy VPN Remote device. Figure 12-4 illustrates the Easy VPN Remote network extension mode. The remote client hosts are assigned IP addresses that are fully routable by the destination network through the tunnel.

Figure 12-4 *Easy VPN Remote Network Extension Mode*

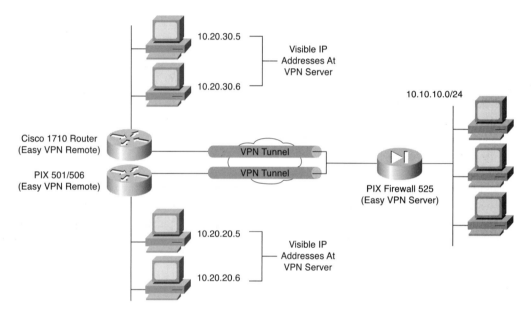

Overview of Cisco VPN Software Client

The Cisco VPN Software Client is software that enables you to establish secure end-to-end encrypted tunnels to any Easy VPN Server. The Cisco VPN Software Client is IPSec compliant and available from Cisco.com for customers with SMARTnet support and is included free of charge with the concentrator.

The Cisco VPN Software Client can easily be preconfigured for mass deployment situations. Initial logins require very little user intervention because VPN access policies and configurations are downloaded from the Easy VPN Server and pushed to the Cisco VPN Client when a connection is established, enabling simple deployment and management.

The Cisco VPN Software Client provides support for the following operating systems:

■ Windows 95, 98, Me, NT 4.0, 2000, and XP

■ Linux

■ Solaris (UltraSPARC 32- and 64-bit)

■ MAC OS X 10.1

Features

The Cisco VPN Software Client provides numerous features and benefits. Some of the major benefits of the Cisco VPN Software Client include the following:

■ Intelligent peer availability detection

■ Simple Certificate Enrollment Protocol (SCEP)

■ Data compression (LZS)

■ Command-line options for connecting, disconnecting, and monitoring connection status

■ Configuration file with option locking

■ Support for Microsoft network login (all Windows platforms)

■ DNS, WINS, and IP address assignment

■ Load balancing and backup server support

■ Centrally controlled policies

■ Integrated personal firewall (stateful firewall): Zone Labs technology (Windows only)

■ Personal firewall enforcement: Zone Alarm, BlackICE (Windows only)

> **NOTE** The Cisco VPN Software Client supports more features than the Easy VPN Server platforms. You should always compare the Cisco VPN Software Client specifications against the Easy VPN Server supported and unsupported feature list. For instance, although the Cisco VPN Client supports Zone Labs and BlackICE firewall features, the Easy VPN Server does not. The features supported on the Easy VPN Server determine which policies and configurations can be pushed from the Easy VPN Server to the VPN Client.

Specifications

Effectively utilizing the Cisco VPN Software Client on your network requires an understanding of its major functional specifications. The specifications for the Cisco VPN Software Client fall into the following major categories:

■ Tunneling protocols

■ Encryption and authentication

■ Key management techniques

- Data compression
- Digital certificates
- Authentication methodologies
- Policy and profile management

Tunneling Protocols

The Cisco VPN Software Client supports the following tunneling options:

- IPSec Encapsulating Security Payload (ESP)
- IPSec over Transmission Control Protocol (TCP): NAT or PAT
- IPSec over User Datagram Protocol (UDP): NAT, PAT, or firewall

NOTE   IPSec over TCP and IPSec over UDP refer to the VPN Client encapsulating the IPSec traffic inside of either TCP or UDP packets. By encapsulating the complete IPSec packets inside of another transport protocol (such as UDP), the integrity checks on the IPSec packets remain valid even when a NAT device changes the IP addresses on the outer transport protocol.

Encryption and Authentication

The Cisco VPN Software Client supports the following encryption algorithms:

- DES
- 3DES
- AES (128- and 256-bit)

It also supports the following cryptographic hash algorithms:

- MD5
- SHA-1

Key Management Techniques

The Cisco VPN Client supports the following key management techniques:

- IKE main mode
- IKE aggressive mode
- Diffie-Hellman (DH) groups 1, 2, 5, and 7

Data Compression

The only supported data compression technique is LZS. LZS provides an algorithm for compressing Point-to-Point Protocol (PPP)–encapsulated packets (see RFC 1974).

Digital Certificates

Digital certificates help to verify the identity of the peers in an IPSec session. The digital certificate functionality provided by the Cisco VPN Software Client falls into the following categories:

- Enrollment mechanisms
- Certificate authorities
- Smart cards

Enrollment mechanisms define the means by which digital certificates are securely issued. *Certificate authorities* (CAs) actually issue the certificates by signing them with their own private key. The Cisco VPN Software Client supports the following CAs:

- Entrust
- GTE Cybertrust
- Netscape
- Baltimore
- RSA Keon
- VeriSign
- Microsoft

Using smart cards also can help secure the login process by verifying the identification of the user. The Cisco VPN Software Client supports various smart cards by using the Microsoft crypto application programming interface (API) CRYPT-NOHASHOID, including the following:

- ActivCard (Schlumberger cards)
- eToken from Aladdin
- Gemplus
- Datakey

Authentication Methodologies

Authentication is crucial for providing secure remote access through VPN tunnels. The Cisco VPN Software Client supports XAUTH and Remote Authentication Dial-In User Service (RADIUS) with support for the following:

- State (token cards)
- Security Dynamics (RSA SecurID ready)
- Microsoft Windows NT domain authentication
- Microsoft Challenge Handshake Authentication Protocol version 2 (MS-CHAPv2)— Windows NT password authentication
- X.509 version 3 digital certificates

Policy and Profile Management

You can easily distribute Cisco VPN Software Clients with preconfigured Profile Configuration Files (PCFs) that regulate the operation of the client software. You can also centrally control policies such as the following:

- DNS information
- WINS information
- IP address
- Default domain name

Cisco VPN Client Manual Configuration Tasks

When using the Cisco VPN Software Client, the Easy VPN Server can push the VPN policy to help facilitate the management of the client systems. Initially, however, you still need to install the Cisco VPN Software Client on the remote system. This manual process involves the following tasks:

- Installing the Cisco VPN Software Client
- Creating a new connection entry
- Modifying VPN Client options (optional)

Installing the Cisco VPN Software Client

Installation of the Cisco VPN Software Client varies slightly between the different supported operating systems. The best source of detailed installation information is the release notes that accompany the Cisco VPN Software Client that you are installing. Installing the Cisco VPN Software Client on a Windows-based system follows the usual software installation process. The on-screen instructions ensure the installation is quick and not very complicated.

After the software is installed, the following new options are added to your Programs menu (see Figure 12-5):

- **Help**—Accesses the Cisco VPN Client Help text
- **Set MTU**—Enables you to set the maximum transmission unit (MTU) for a specific interface
- **VPN Client**—Launches the Cisco VPN Client so that you can choose a connection and establish a VPN session

Figure 12-5 *Cisco VPN Software Client Program Menu*

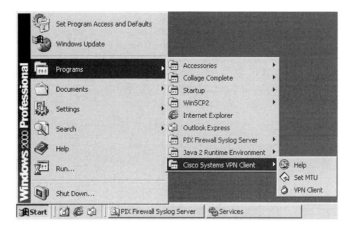

If you try to launch the Cisco VPN Client when you already have a session established, it displays the same window you see when you launch the Cisco VPN Client Software (see Figure 12-6).

Figure 12-6 *VPN Client Window*

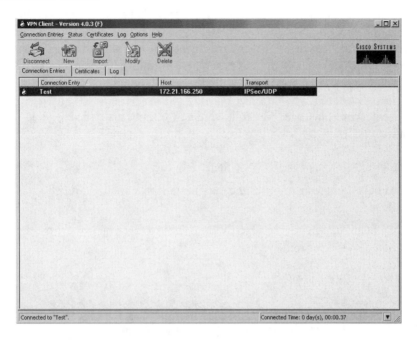

Either typing **Ctrl-S** or selecting **Statistics** from the **Status** drop-down menu displays the following information about your connection (see Figure 12-7):

- **Client IP address**—The IP address assigned to the Cisco VPN Client for the current session.

- **Server IP address**—The IP address of the Easy VPN Server to which the client is currently connected.

- **Bytes Received**—The total number of bytes received by the client software.

- **Bytes Sent**—The total number of bytes sent by the client software.

- **Packets Encrypted**—The total number of data packets transmitted.

- **Packets Decrypted**—The total number of data packets received.

- **Packets Discarded**—The total number of packets rejected because they did not come from the Easy VPN Server.

- **Packets Bypassed**— The total number of packets that were not processed (such as Address Resolution Protocol [ARP] and Dynamic Host Configuration Protocol [DHCP] packets).

- **Encryption**—The data encryption method in use for traffic in the tunnel.

- **Authentication**—The data or packet authentication method used for traffic through the tunnel.

- **Transparent Tunneling**—The status of transparent tunneling (either active or inactive).

- **Local LAN Access**—Indicates whether local local area network (LAN) access is enabled or disabled.

- **Compression**—Indicates whether data compression is in effect and identifies the compression being used (currently, only LZS compression is supported).

Transparent Tunneling

Transparent tunneling enables a secure transmission between the VPN Client and a secure VPN Server when the traffic passes through an intermediary device that is performing NAT (such as a firewall). Transparent tunneling encapsulates Internet Protocol 50 (ESP) traffic within either UDP or TCP packets to prevent the IPSec traffic from being changed by the NAT/PAT device. Transparent tunneling is commonly used with VPN Client deployments that are behind a home router that is performing NAT/PAT.

Figure 12-7 *VPN Client Statistics Window*

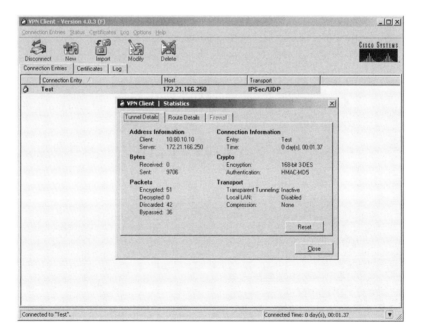

Creating a New Connection Entry

After installing the Cisco VPN Software Client on your system, you need to create a connection entry that will define the properties of your VPN connection, such as the following:

- IP address of Easy VPN Remote server
- Group name
- Group password

Creating a new connection entry involves the following steps on a Windows 2000 system:

Step 1 Choose **Start > Programs > Cisco Systems VPN Client > VPN Client**. The Cisco VPN Client window is displayed.

Step 2 Click **New** to launch the new connection wizard.

Step 3 Enter a name for the new connection in the Name of the new connection entry field. Optionally, you can also provide a description for this connection in the Description of the new connection entry.

Step 4 After entering the name, click **Next**.

Step 5 Enter the IP address or DNS name for the public interface on the Easy VPN Server in the Remote Server field.

Step 6 Click **Next**.

Step 7 Select the **Group Access Information** radio button, and enter the following information:

- Group name that matches a group on the Easy VPN Server
- Group password
- Group password confirmation

Step 8 Click **Next**.

Step 9 Click **Finish**.

Modifying VPN Client Options

Besides creating a new connection entry, you can also optionally define various characteristics of the connection entry. These options are accessible by using the **Options** drop-down menu on the main Cisco VPN Software Client screen (see Figure 12-8).

Figure 12-8   *Cisco VPN Software Client Options*

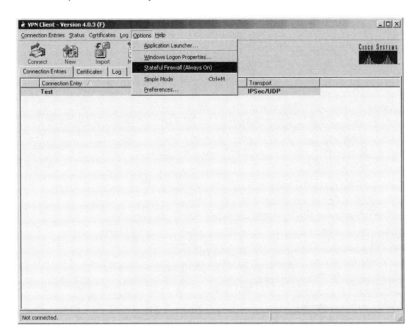

From the **Options** drop-down menu, you can configure the characteristics of the current connection entry as listed in Table 12-5.

Table 12-5   *Cisco VPN Software Client Options*

Option	Description
Application Launcher	Defines an application that you want to launch before establishing the VPN connection. This is used in conjunction with the Windows Login Properties option.
Windows Login Properties	Enables the Cisco VPN Client to make a connection to the concentrator before the user logs in.
Stateful Firewall (Always On)	Blocks all inbound traffic to the Cisco VPN Client that is not related to the outbound session when set to Always On.
Simple Mode	Changes the VPN Client window to a smaller compressed version. You then use the Advanced Mode option to return to the original window.
Preferences	Enables you to configure basic VPN Client preferences such as whether the VPN Client window automatically hides itself upon establishing a successful VPN connection.

> **NOTE** If you want to know the version of the Cisco VPN Software Client installed on your PC, you can right-click the **Cisco VPN Dialer** icon in the system tray. This will also indicate if the stateful firewall functionality is always on because Stateful Firewall (Always On) will have a check mark next to it if enabled.

Clicking the **Modify** icon enables you to configure the following characteristics of the Cisco VPN Client:

- VPN Client authentication properties
- VPN Client transport properties
- VPN Client backup servers
- VPN Client dialup properties

Although these properties vary slightly between the supported operating systems, the major general properties that you can configure are as follows:

- Enabling transparent tunneling
- Allowing IPSec over UDP
- Allowing IPSec over TCP
- Allowing local LAN access
- Configuring peer response timeout

> **NOTE** Allowing IPSec over TCP (or UDP) enables you to use the VPN Client in an environment where your traffic must go though a firewall or router that is using NAT or PAT. This option must also be configured on the Easy VPN Server for it to operate correctly.

The Authentication tab of the VPN Client Properties window enables you to configure the VPN Client to use either a group name and password or digital certificates for authentication (see Figure 12-9).

Figure 12-9 *Authentication Tab of the VPN Client Properties Window*

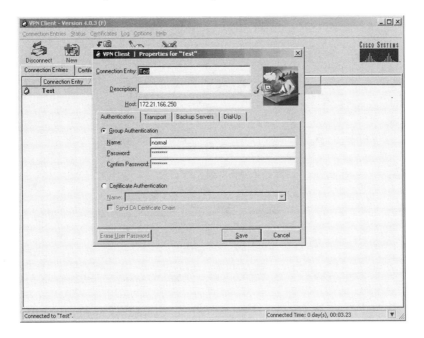

The Transport tab in the VPN Client Properties window enables you to configure the transparent tunneling properties for the VPN connection (see Figure 12-10). Transparent tunneling enables your VPN connection to travel across devices that are performing NAT or PAT on the traffic. Without transparent tunneling, the traffic would be considered invalid because the integrity checks on the packets would fail.

The Backup Servers tab of the VPN Client Properties window defines backup Easy VPN Servers (see Figure 12-11), and the Dial-Up tab of the VPN Client Properties window defines whether the connection to the Internet using dialup networking is enabled (see Figure 12-12).

An enterprise network may have multiple Easy VPN Servers. Backup servers for the connections enable your Cisco VPN Clients to utilize these alternate Easy VPN Servers if the primary Easy VPN Server is unavailable. When establishing a VPN connection, clients attempt to connect to the primary Easy VPN Server first. If that device is unavailable, one of the backup servers will be used.

NOTE You also can configure the backup servers on the Easy VPN Server and have them pushed to the VPN Client after a successful connection. Then, on subsequent connections, the VPN Client can use these backup servers if the primary server is unavailable.

Figure 12-10 *Transport Tab of the VPN Client Properties Window*

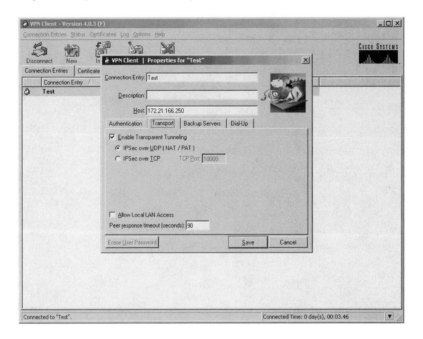

Figure 12-11 *Backup Servers Tab of the VPN Client Properties Windows*

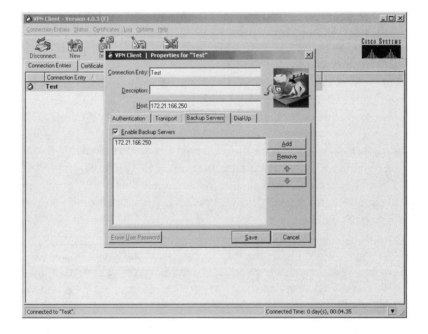

Figure 12-12 *Dial-Up Tab of the VPN Client Properties Window*

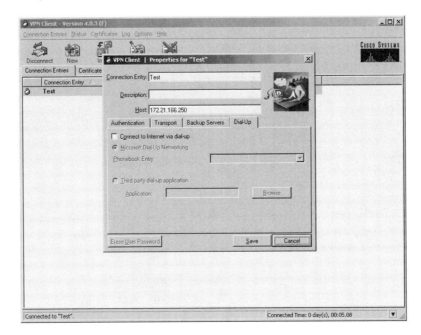

PIX Easy VPN Remote Configuration

The Easy VPN Server controls the policy enforced on the PIX Firewall Easy VPN Remote device. To establish the initial connection to the Easy VPN Server, you must complete some configuration locally on the remote client device. You can perform this configuration using the Cisco PIX Device Manager (PDM) or by using the command-line interface. These configuration tasks fall into the following categories:

- Basic configuration
- Client device mode
- SUA
- Individual User Authentication (IUA)

Basic Configuration

To enable the PIX Easy VPN Remote client to communicate with the Easy VPN Server, you need to identify the location of the Easy VPN Server using the **vpnclient server** command. The syntax for this command is as follows:

```
vpnclient server {Primary_IP} [Secondary_IPs]
```

You need to specify the IP address of the primary Easy VPN Server. In addition to the primary Easy VPN Server, you also can specify up to ten additional secondary Easy VPN Servers. If the primary server is not accessible, the client will use one of the secondary servers.

To enable the VPN Client you need to use the **vpnclient enable** command. The syntax for this command is as follows:

```
vpnclient enable
```

If you use preshared keys, you also must specify this key value using the **vpnclient vpngroup** command. The syntax for this command is as follows:

```
vpnclient vpngroup {groupname} password {preshared_key}
```

The client needs to use the preshared key to encrypt the information being transmitted to the server.

One other basic configuration task involves XAUTH. If you use XAUTH, you need to specify the username and password for the VPN Client using AAA or the **vpnclient username** command. The syntax for this command is as follows:

```
vpnclient username {xuath_username} password {xauth_password}
```

Client Device Mode

The Cisco VPN Client operates in the following two modes (see the "Easy VPN Remote Modes of Operation" section earlier in the chapter for more information):

- Client mode
- Network extension mode

To configure the client device mode, you use the **vpnclient mode** command. The syntax for this command is as follows:

```
vpnclient mode {client-mode|network-extension-mode}
```

Client mode applies NAT/PAT to all IP addresses of the clients connected to the higher-security (inside) interface. Network extension mode, on the other hand, does not apply NAT/PAT to any IP addresses of clients on the higher-security interface.

Secure Unit Authentication

Secure Unit Authentication (SUA) is a feature introduced in PIX Firewall Software Version 6.3 to improve security when using a PIX Firewall as an Easy VPN Remote device. With SUA, the Easy VPN Remote Server can require one-time passwords, two-factor authentication, and similar authentication schemes before the establishment of a VPN tunnel to the Easy VPN Server.

SUA is configured as part of the VPN policy on the Easy VPN Server and cannot be configured directly on the VPN Remote device. The Easy VPN Remote device downloads the VPN policy (after connecting to the Easy VPN Server), which enables or disables SUA.

Client Operation with Secure Unit Authentication Disabled

When SUA is disabled and the Easy VPN Remote device is operating in network extension mode, a connection is automatically initiated by the PIX VPN Remote device for the remote protected hosts. In client mode, the connection is initiated whenever traffic from the remote protected network is sent through the PIX Firewall to the network protected by the Easy VPN Server.

Client Operation with Secure Unit Authentication Enabled

When SUA is enabled, static credentials included in the local configuration of the Easy VPN Remote device are ignored. A connection request is initiated as soon as any Hypertext Transfer Protocol (HTTP) request is sent from the remote network to the network protected by the Easy VPN Remote Server. All other traffic to the network protected by the Easy VPN Server is dropped until a VPN tunnel is established.

NOTE   You also can initiate a connection request from the command-line interface (CLI) of the Easy VPN Remote device.

Before a VPN tunnel is established, any HTTP request to the network protected by the Easy VPN Server is redirected to a Uniform Resource Locator (URL) in the following format:

```
https://<inside-ip-address>/vpnclient/connstatus.html
```

inside-ip-address is the inside (protected) interface of the Easy VPN Remote device. For instance, if the inside interface of the Easy VPN Remote device is 10.10.10.1, the requests will be redirected to the following URL:

```
https://10.10.10.1/vpnclient/connstatus.html
```

You can check the status of the VPN tunnel by manually entering this URL into your browser (from one of the remote protected hosts). This URL displays a page containing a *Connect* link that displays an authentication page. If authentication is successful, the VPN tunnel has been established.

> **NOTE** You can also activate the connection by manually entering this URL into your browser (on a remote protected host).

To enable SUA, you use the following command on the Easy VPN Server:

```
vpngroup groupname secure-unit-authentication
```

groupname is the alphanumeric identifier for the VPN group for which you want to enable SUA.

After the tunnel is established, other users on the remote network (protected by the Easy VPN Remote device) can access the network protected by the Easy VPN Server without further authentication. If you want to control access by individual users, you need to implement Individual User Authentication (IUA). IUA is explained in the next section.

Individual User Authentication

IUA causes the hosts on the remote protected network (behind the Easy VPN Remote device) to be authenticated individually based on the IP address of the inside host. IUA supports authentication based on both static and dynamic password mechanisms.

Similar to SUA, IUA is enabled by the VPN policy downloaded from the Easy VPN Server and cannot be configured locally. When IUA is enabled, each user on the remote protected network is prompted for a username and password when trying to initiate a connection to the network protected by the Easy VPN Server. Unlike SUA, which requires an HTTP connection to initiate the authentication request, when IUA is enabled the user will automatically be prompted for authentication (to establish the tunnel) whenever any traffic is sent across the tunnel.

A PIX Firewall (serving as an Easy VPN Server) downloads the contact information for the AAA server to the Easy VPN Remote device. The Easy VPN Remote device then sends authentication requests directly to the AAA server.

> **NOTE** A Cisco 3000 Series VPN Concentrator used as an Easy VPN Server performs proxy authentication to the AAA server. The Easy VPN Remote device sends each authentication request to the Cisco 3000 Series VPN Concentrator instead of directly to the AAA server.

To enable IUA, you use the following command on the Easy VPN Server:

> **vpngroup** *groupname* **user-authentication**

groupname is the alphanumeric identifier for the VPN group for which you want to enable IUA.

You also must use the following command on the Easy VPN Server to specify the AAA server to use for authentication:

> **vpngroup** *groupname* **authentication-server** *server-tag*

The *server-tag* identifies the AAA server to use for the specified VPN group.

To specify the length of time that the VPN tunnel will remain open without any user activity, you use the following command on the Easy VPN Server:

> **vpngroup** *groupname* **user-idle-timeout** *seconds*

You specify the idle time for the specified VPN group in seconds.

Point-to-Point Protocol over Ethernet and the PIX Firewall

Beginning with software version 6.2, you can configure the PIX Firewall as a Point-to-Point Protocol over Ethernet (PPPoE) client. Many Internet service providers (ISPs) deploy PPPoE because it provides high-speed broadband access using their existing remote access infrastructure. PPPoE is also easy for customers to use.

Figure 12-13 depicts a typical PPPoE network configuration that uses a PIX Firewall to secure a low-cost always-on Internet connection. The PIX Firewall can secure various broadband connections including the following:

- Digital Subscriber Line (DSL)
- Cable modem
- Fixed wireless

Figure 12-13 *PIX Firewall PPPoE Client Configuration*

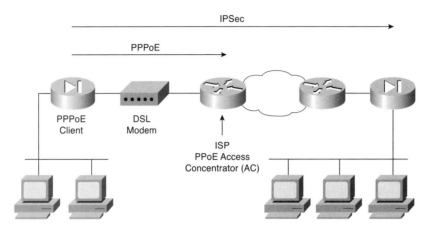

PPPoE (see RFC 2516) provides an authenticated method for assigning IP addresses to client systems by combining the following two widely accepted standards:

■ Point-to-Point Protocol (PPP)

■ Ethernet

PPP

Point-to-Point Protocol (PPP) provides a secure and reliable mechanism to transport multiprotocol datagrams over point-to-point links. It has been reliably used for many years to transmit data from dialup clients across modem-based connections.

PPPoE is composed of the following two main phases:

■ Active discovery phase

■ PPP session phase

PPPoE connects a network of systems over a simple bridging access device to a remote Access Concentrator (AC). In the active discovery phase, the PPPoE client locates the AC (or PPPoE server). After locating an AC, the PPPoE client establishes a PPP session.

When establishing a session, PPP options are negotiated and authentication is performed. Once the session is completely established, the information from the client is sent across the Ethernet network by encapsulating the PPP messages in unicast Ethernet packets. The session ID enables the AC to determine to which client the PPP messages belong.

After configuration, the PIX Firewall automatically connects to a service provider's AC without user intervention. By setting the MTU to 1492 bytes, the PIX Firewall can encapsulate PPPoE messages inside regular Ethernet frames by attaching PPPoE/PPP headers.

The PIX Firewall PPPoE Client can operate in environments that are using other firewall features such as the following:

- NAT to or from the outside interface (or over a VPN)
- URL content filtering before transmission (to or from outside interface)
- Firewall rules on traffic before transmission to or from the outside interface (or over a VPN)

If your ISP distributes certain configuration parameters, such as DNS and WINS, the PIX Firewall's PPPoE Client can retrieve these parameters and automatically pass these parameters to its Dynamic Host Configuration Protocol (DHCP) clients. You need to use the **dhcpd auto-config** command on the PIX Firewall to enable your DHCP clients to receive the configuration parameters automatically from the PPPoE client.

> **NOTE**   Although the PIX Firewall DHCP server operates with the PPPoE client, the PPPoE client and the DHCP clients are mutually exclusive. Therefore, if you configure the PPPoE client on the outside interface, the DHCP client functionality is automatically disabled on that interface. Similarly, if you enable the DHCP client on the outside interface, the PPPoE client is automatically disabled on the outside interface.

> **NOTE**   The PIX Firewall's PPPoE Client is not interoperable with failover, Layer Two Tunneling Protocol (L2TP), or Point-to-Point Tunneling Protocol (PPTP).

Configuring the PPPoE client on the PIX Firewall involves the following tasks:

- Configuring the Virtual Private Dial-Up Networking (VPDN) group
- Configuring VPDN group authentication
- Assigning the VPDN group username
- Configuring the VPDN username and password
- Enabling the PPPoE client

Configuring the Virtual Private Dial-Up Networking Group

The first task in configuring the PIX Firewall PPPoE Client is to define the VPDN group using the following command:

```
vpdn group group-name request dialout pppoe
```

Configuring Virtual Private Dial-Up Networking Group Authentication

Your ISP may require you to use authentication with PPPoE. The PIX Firewall PPPoE Client supports the following authentication protocols:

- Password Authentication Protocol (PAP)
- Challenge Handshake Authentication Protocol (CHAP)
- Microsoft Challenge Handshake Authentication Protocol (MS-CHAP)

To define the authentication protocol for the PPPoE client, you use the following command:

```
vpdn group group-name ppp authentication pap¦chap¦mschap
```

> **NOTE** ISPs that use CHAP or MS-CHAP may refer to the username as the remote system name and the password as the CHAP secret.

Assigning the Virtual Private Dial-Up Networking Group Username

To assign the username provided by your ISP to the VPDN group you use the following command:

```
vpdn group group-name localname username
```

Configuring the Virtual Private Dial-Up Networking Username and Password

The PIX Firewall uses a username and password pair to authenticate to the AC. To assign a username and password pair for PPPoE authentication, you use the following command:

```
vpdn username username password password
```

> **NOTE** The username specified must be the username that has already been associated with the VPDN group specified for PPPoE (using the **vpdn group** command).

Enabling the Point-to-Point over Ethernet Client

By default the PPPoE client on the PIX Firewall is disabled. Use the following command to enable the PPPoE client:

```
ip address interface-name pppoe [setroute]
```

You also can enable PPPoE by manually entering the IP address using the following command:

```
ip address interface-name ip-address netmask pppoe [setroute]
```

This command causes the PIX Firewall to use the specified IP address instead of negotiating with the PPPoE server to assign an address dynamically.

The parameters for the **ip address** command are shown in Table 12-6.

Table 12-6 ip address *Command Parameters*

Parameter	Description
interface-name	The name of the outside interface on the PIX Firewall
ip-address	The IP address assigned to the PIX Firewall's outside interface
netmask	The subnet mask assigned to the PIX Firewall's outside interface
setroute	Configures the PIX Firewall to use the default gateway parameter that the DHCP or PPPoE server returns as the default route

The **setroute** keyword causes a default route to be created based on the default gateway parameter returned by either the DHCP or PPPoE server. This keyword, however, cannot override an existing default route. If you use the **setroute** keyword when a default route already exists, the PIX Firewall will be unable to override the existing default route with the information learned from PPPoE. Therefore, if you already have an existing default route configured on the PIX Firewall, you must delete the default route before using the **setroute** keyword.

Monitoring the Point-to-Point over Ethernet Client

The **show vpdn** command displays information about the PPPoE traffic on the PIX Firewall. Without any other keywords, this command displays information about the PPPoE tunnels and sessions, such as in the following:

```
pix515a# show vpdn
```

```
%No active L2TP tunnels


PPPoE Tunnel and Session Information (Total tunnels=1 sessions=1)


Tunnel id 0, 1 active sessions
  time since change 4294967 secs
  Remote MAC Address 00:02:3B:02:32:2E
  9005625 packets sent, 11376588 received, 1755681415 bytes sent, -407696198 received
Remote MAC is 00:02:3B:02:32:2E
  Session state is SESSION_UP
    Time since event change 4294967 secs, interface outside
    PPP interface id is 1
    9005625 packets sent, 1265856 received, 1755681415 bytes sent, 865125131 received
pix515a#
```

To view the information only on your VPDN sessions, you can add the **session** keyword to the **show vpdn** command, as in the following:

```
pix515a# show vpdn session


%No active L2TP tunnels


PPPoE Tunnel and Session Information (Total tunnels=1 sessions=1)


Remote MAC is 00:02:3B:02:32:2E
  Session state is SESSION_UP
    Time since event change 4294967 secs, interface outside
    PPP interface id is 1
    9005664 packets sent, 1265894 received, 1755684373 bytes sent, 865127247 received
pix515a#
```

To view the information only on your VPDN tunnels, you can add the **tunnel** keyword to the **show vpdn** command, as in the following:

```
pix515a# show vpdn tunnel


%No active L2TP tunnels


PPPoE Tunnel and Session Information (Total tunnels=1 sessions=1)


Tunnel id 0, 1 active sessions
  time since change 4294967 secs
  Remote MAC Address 00:02:3B:02:32:2E
  9005704 packets sent, 11376666 received, 1755687225 bytes sent, -407691806 received
pix515a#
```

You can use the **show vpdn pppinterface** command when a PPPoE connection is established to view the address of the AC. If the PIX Firewall cannot locate the AC, the address displayed is 0.0.0.0. The syntax for this command is as follows:

```
show vpdn pppinterface [id interface_name]
```

The output of the **show vpdn pppinterface** command is similar to the following:

```
pix515a# show vpdn pppinterface

PPP virtual interface id = 1
PPP authentication protocol is PAP
Server ip address is 214.8.252.151
Our ip address is 88.235.123.14
Transmitted Pkts: 1002469, Received Pkts: 1265984, Error Pkts: 0
MPPE key strength is None
  MPPE_Encrypt_Pkts: 0,   MPPE_Encrypt_Bytes: 0
  MPPE_Decrypt_Pkts: 0,   MPPE_Decrypt_Bytes: 0
  Rcvd_Out_Of_Seq_MPPE_Pkts: 0

pix515a#
```

To view the local usernames, you use the **show vpdn username** command, and the **show vpdn group** command displays the configured VPDN groups. The syntax for these commands is as follows:

```
show vpdn username [specific-name]
show vpdn group [specific-group-name]
```

To view the IP address assigned by the PPPoE server on an established PPPoE session, you use the **show ip address** command using the interface on which PPPoE is enabled. The syntax for this command is as follows:

```
show ip address interface-name pppoe
```

Finally, you can debug the PPPoE packets processed by the PIX Firewall with the **debug pppoe** command. The syntax for this command is as follows:

```
debug pppoe {event¦error¦packet}
```

Dynamic Host Configuration Protocol Server Configuration

DHCP provides automatic allocation of reusable network addresses on a Transmission Control Protocol/Internet Protocol (TCP/IP) network. Without DHCP, IP addresses must be manually entered on each computer or device that is connected to the network. Automatic allocation dramatically reduces administration and user error.

DHCP can also distribute other configuration parameters such as DNS and WINS server addresses and domain names. The system requesting an IP address and configuration parameters is known as the *DHCP client*. The system that automatically allocates the IP addresses is known as the *DHCP server*.

> **NOTE** Because the DHCP client does not know the IP address of the DHCP server, the initial DHCP requests are broadcast to every host on the network segment. Instead of deploying a DHCP server on every network segment, you can configure your IOS® router to forward the DHCP requests to a single DHCP server by using the **ip helper-address** command.

Any PIX Firewall (Version 5.2 or later) provides both DHCP server and DHCP client functionality. As a DHCP server, the PIX Firewall provides hosts protected by the firewall with the network parameters necessary for them to access the enterprise or corporate network. As a DHCP client, the PIX Firewall can obtain its own IP address and network mask and optionally a default route from the DHCP server.

DHCP Overview

DHCP communications consist of several messages sent between the DHCP client and DHCP server by broadcast messages. This exchange of messages consists of the following events:

Step 1   The client broadcasts a DHCPDISCOVER message on its local subnet to locate available DHCP servers that can provide it an IP address.

Step 2   Any DHCP servers that receive the DHCPDISCOVER message can respond with a DHCPOFFER message that includes an available IP address and other configuration parameters.

Step 3   Based on the DHCPOFFER messages received, the client chooses one of the offers. It then broadcasts a DHCPREQUEST message requesting the offered parameters from the chosen DHCP server and implicitly declining all of the other offers received.

Step 4   The DHCP server selected in the DHCPREQUEST message responds with a DHCPACK message containing the configuration parameters for the requesting client.

> **NOTE** If the selected DHCP server cannot satisfy the DHCPREQUEST (for instance, the requested address has already been assigned to another system), it sends a DHCPNAK message to the DHCP client.

Configuring the PIX Firewall Dynamic Host Configuration Protocol Server

Configuring the PIX Firewall to operate as a DHCP server involves the following tasks:

- Configuring the address pool
- Specifying WINS, DNS, and the domain name
- Configuring the DHCP options
- Configuring the DHCP lease length
- Enabling the DHCP server

NOTE   Configuring the PIX Firewall to serve as a DHCP server also requires you to assign a static IP address to the inside interface. This is one of the basic configuration tasks when setting up your PIX Firewall.

Configuring the Address Pool

A DHCP server needs to know which addresses it can assign to DHCP clients. It must also keep track of the IP addresses that it has already given out. The **dhcpd address** command specifies the range of IP addresses for the PIX DHCP server to distribute. The syntax for this command is as follows:

```
dhcpd address ipaddress1 [-ipaddress2] [interface]
```

NOTE   To remove an existing DHCP address pool, use the **no dhcpd address** command.

Table 12-7 shows the parameters for the **dhcpd address** command.

Table 12-7   dhcpd address *Command Parameters*

Parameter	Description
ipaddress1	The low IP address of the IP address pool.
ipaddress2	The high IP address of the IP address pool.
interface	Name of the PIX Firewall interface (the default is the inside interface).

NOTE   The DHCP address pool is limited to 32 addresses for the PIX Firewall 501 with a 10-user license. With the 50-user license, 128 addresses are supported. The maximum size of the address pool is 256 addresses for the Unlimited license and for all other PIX models.

Specifying WINS, DNS, and the Domain Name

Besides providing IP addresses to DHCP clients, a DHCP server can also provide other configuration parameters, such as the following:

- WINS servers
- DNS servers
- Domain name

To configure the DNS servers that the PIX DHCP server provides in its DHCPOFFER messages, you use the **dhcpd dns** command. The syntax for this command is as follows:

```
dhcpd dns dns-server1 [dns-server2]
```

To configure the WINS servers that the PIX DHCP server provides in its DHCPOFFER messages, you use the **dhcpd wins** command. The syntax for this command is as follows:

```
dhcpd wins wins-server1 [wins-server2]
```

Finally, you also can specify the domain name that will be provided to the DHCP clients using the **dhcpd domain** command. The syntax for this command is as follows:

```
dhcpd domain domain_name
```

Configuring Dynamic Host Configuration Protocol Options

Because Cisco IP Phones use TFTP to load phone images, the PIX Firewall supports the **dhcpd option** command to define the TFTP servers that will be identified to the client by DHCP. The syntax for this command is as follows:

```
dhcpd option 66 ascii {server-name¦server-ip-str}
dhcpd option 150 ip server-ip1 [server-ip2]
```

> **NOTE**   The difference between these two commands is that the **option 150** enables you to specify a list of TFTP servers to be used by the DHCP client.

Configuring Dynamic Host Configuration Protocol Lease Length

The **dhcpd lease** command specifies the amount of time (in seconds) that the DHCP clients can use the assigned IP address received from the DHCP server. The syntax for this command is as follows:

```
dhcpd lease lease_length
```

> **NOTE**   The default lease length is 3600 seconds. The minimum lease length that you can specify is 300 seconds, and the maximum lease length that you can specify is 2,147,483,647 seconds.

Enabling the Dynamic Host Configuration Protocol Server

You enable DHCP on the PIX Firewall on a per-interface basis. The command to enable the DHCP daemon on an interface is **dhcpd enable**. The syntax for this command is as follows:

```
dhcpd enable [interface-name]
```

For instance, to enable DHCP on the inside interface you would use the following command:

```
dhcpd enable inside
```

Dynamic Host Configuration Protocol Server Auto Configuration

The PIX Firewall can serve as a DHCP server, DHCP client, or a DHCP server and DHCP client simultaneously. When the PIX Firewall is operating as a DHCP client, it can pass the configuration parameters learned (such as DNS, WINS, and the domain name) automatically to the clients that its DHCP server services. To enable the PIX Firewall to pass the learned DHCP configuration parameters to its DHCP clients automatically, you use the **dhcpd auto-config** command. The syntax for this command is as follows:

```
dhcpd auto-config [client_interface_name]
```

> **NOTE** The **dhcpd auto-config** command also enables the PIX Firewall to pass information learned from its PPPoE interface to its DHCP clients.

The *client_interface_name* represents the interface on which you have enabled the PIX Firewall to operate as a DHCP client using the **ip address** *interface* **dhcp** command.

Dynamic Host Configuration Protocol Debugging Commands

To help debug the operation of your PIX DHCP server and PIX DHCP client, you can use the following two commands:

```
debug dhcpd {event|packet}
debug dhcpc {detail|error|packet}
```

The **debug dhcpd** command displays information associated with the DHCP server running on the PIX Firewall. The **event** keyword displays information about the events related to the DHCP server, and the **packet** keyword displays information about the packets received for the DHCP server.

The **debug dhcpc** command displays information about the PIX DHCP client running on the PIX Firewall. The **packet** keyword specifies information about the packets received for the DHCP client. The **detail** keyword provides detailed information on the packets received by the DHCP client. The **error** keyword enables you to view information on the error messages associated with the DHCP client running on the PIX Firewall.

To show or clear the IP address bindings that the PIX DHCP server has issued, you use the following two commands:

```
show dhcpd [binding¦statistics]
clear dhcpd [binding¦statistics]
```

Both of these commands accept the same two keywords. The **binding** keyword causes the command to operate only on the DHCP leases (binding of an IP address to a specific Layer 2 Ethernet address). The **statistics** keyword operates on the statistics that are tracked on the DHCP server. The following information illustrates the output from the **show dhcpd** commands:

```
pix515a# show dhcpd
dhcpd address 10.10.10.129-10.10.10.254 inside
dhcpd lease 84400
dhcpd ping timeout 750
dhcpd dns 10.200.10.32 10.100.20.40
dhcpd enable inside
pix515a# show dhcpd statistics

Address pools        1
Automatic bindings   1
Expired bindings     1
Malformed messages   0

Message              Received
BOOTREQUEST          0
DHCPDISCOVER         1
DHCPREQUEST          2
DHCPDECLINE          0
DHCPRELEASE          0
DHCPINFORM           0

Message              Sent
BOOTREPLY            0
DHCPOFFER            1
DHCPACK              1
DHCPNAK              0

pix515a(config)# show dhcpd bindings

IP address      Hardware address      Lease expiration      Type
10.10.10.129    00A0.CC5C.8163        46500 seconds         automatic
10.10.10.130    00E0.B605.43B2        32503 seconds         automatic
pix515a#
```

Foundation Summary

The "Foundation Summary" provides a convenient review of many key concepts in this chapter. If you are already comfortable with the topics in this chapter, this summary can help you recall a few details. If you just read this chapter, this review should help solidify some key facts. If you are doing your final preparation before the exam, this summary provides a convenient way to review the day before the exam.

Cisco Easy VPN greatly simplifies VPN deployment for remote offices and telecommuters. The Cisco Easy VPN centralizes management across all Cisco VPN devices, thus greatly reducing the complexity in configuring and deploying VPN configurations. It comprises the following two components:

■ Easy VPN Server

■ Easy VPN Remote feature

The PIX Firewall Version 6.3 VPN Server supports the following major features:

■ Support for Easy VPN Remote Clients

■ Ability for remote users to communicate using IPSec with supported PIX Firewall gateways

■ Central management of IPSec policies that are pushed to the clients by the server

The PIX Firewall Version 6.3 VPN Server supports the following functionality:

■ Mode configuration version 6

■ XAUTH version 6

■ IKE DPD

■ Split tunneling control

■ Initial Contact

■ Group-based policy control

The Cisco Easy VPN Remote feature enables certain IOS® routers, Cisco PIX Firewalls, Cisco VPN 3002 Hardware Clients, and Cisco VPN Software Clients to act as remote Cisco VPN Clients. The Cisco Easy VPN Remote feature provides for automatic management of the following items:

■ Negotiating tunnel parameters

■ Establishing tunnels according to parameters

- Automatically creating the NAT/PAT and associated access list if necessary
- Authenticating users
- Managing security keys for encryption and decryption
- Authenticating, encrypting, and decrypting data through the tunnel

The Easy VPN Remote feature supports the following client platforms:

- Cisco VPN Software Client
- Cisco VPN 3002 Hardware Client
- Cisco PIX 501 and 506/506E VPN Clients
- Cisco Easy VPN Remote router clients

When the Easy VPN Remote Client initiates a connection with the Easy VPN Server gateway, the interaction between the peers involves the following major steps:

Step 1   VPN Client initiates the IKE phase 1 process.

Step 2   VPN Client negotiates an IKE SA.

Step 3   Easy VPN Server accepts the SA proposal.

Step 4   The Easy VPN Server initiates a username/password challenge.

Step 5   Mode configuration process is initiated.

Step 6   IKE quick mode completes the connection.

XAUTH enables the Easy VPN Server to require username/password authentication to establish the VPN connection. This authentication is performed by a AAA server. To configure the Easy VPN Server to use XAUTH for remote VPN Clients, you need to perform the following tasks:

- Create an ISAKMP policy for remote Cisco VPN Client access
- Create an IP address pool
- Define a group policy for mode configuration push
- Create a transform set
- Create a dynamic crypto map
- Assign the dynamic crypto map to a static crypto map
- Apply the static crypto map to an interface
- Configure XAUTH
- Configure NAT and NAT 0
- Enable IKE DPD

The Easy VPN Remote feature supports the following two modes of operation:

- Client mode
- Network extension mode

The Cisco VPN Software Client is software that enables you to establish secure end-to-end encrypted tunnels to any Easy VPN Server. Some of the major benefits of the Cisco VPN Software Client are the following:

- Intelligent peer availability detection
- SCEP
- Data compression (LZS)
- Command-line options for connecting, disconnecting, and monitoring connection status
- Configuration file with option locking
- Support for Microsoft network login (all platforms)
- DNS, WINS, and IP address assignment
- Load balancing and backup server support
- Centrally controlled policies
- Integrated personal firewall (stateful firewall): Zone Labs technology (Windows only)
- Personal firewall enforcement: Zone Alarm, BlackICE (Windows only)

The Easy VPN Server controls the policy enforced on the PIX Firewall Easy VPN Remote device. To establish the initial connection to the Easy VPN Server, you must complete some configuration locally on the client end such as configuring the client device mode. You also can enable the following two features on the Easy VPN Server:

- SUA
- IUA

Beginning with software version 6.2, you can configure the PIX Firewall as a PPPoE client. Using PPPoE, the PIX Firewall can secure various broadband connections including the following:

- DSL
- Cable modem
- Fixed wireless

PPPoE is composed of the following two main phases:

- Active discovery phase
- PPP session phase

The PIX Firewall PPPoE Client can operate in environments that are using other firewall features such as the following:

- NAT to or from the outside interface (or over a VPN)
- URL content before transmission (to or from outside interface)
- Firewall rules on traffic before transmission to or from the outside interface (or over a VPN)

Configuring the PPPoE client on the PIX Firewall involves the following tasks:

- Configuring the VPDN group
- Configuring VPDN group authentication
- Assigning the VPDN group username
- Configuring the VPDN username and password
- Enabling the PPPoE client

Any PIX Firewall (Version 5.2 or later) provides both DHCP server and DHCP client functionality. As a DHCP server, the PIX Firewall provides hosts protected by the firewall with the network parameters necessary for them to access the enterprise or corporate network. As a DHCP client, the PIX Firewall can obtain its own IP address and network mask and optionally a default route from the DHCP server.

Configuring the PIX Firewall to operate as a DHCP server involves the following tasks:

- Configuring the address pool
- Specifying WINS, DNS, and the domain name
- Configuring DHCP options
- Configuring the DHCP lease length
- Enabling the DHCP server

Q&A

As mentioned in the Introduction, the questions in this book are more difficult than what you should experience on the exam. The questions are designed to ensure your understanding of the concepts discussed in this chapter and adequately prepare you to complete the exam. You should use the simulated exams on the CD to practice for the exam.

The answers to these questions can be found in Appendix A.

1. Which two major components comprise the Easy VPN solution?

2. Which three types of devices can serve as Easy VPN Servers?

3. What is DPD?

4. What is Initial Contact?

5. Which client platforms support the Easy VPN Remote feature?

6. Which router platforms can be used as Cisco Easy VPN Clients?

7. What are the six major steps that occur when the Easy VPN Remote client initiates a connection with the Easy VPN Server gateway?

8. When initiating the VPN connection, the client can use which two IKE authentication mechanisms?

9. What is XAUTH?

10. Which two modes of operation does the Easy VPN Remote support?

11. In which Easy VPN Remote mode are the addresses of the remote system visible on the Easy VPN Server network?

12. What feature enables the Cisco VPN Software Client to be simple to deploy and manage?

13. Which encryption algorithms are supported by the Cisco VPN Software Client?

14. What is SUA?

15. What is IUA?

16. What is PPPoE?

17. What type of DHCP functionality does the PIX Firewall (Version 5.2 or later) provide?

18. Which command enables you to configure the PIX Firewall to pass configuration parameters learned by using either PPPoE or DHCP to its DHCP clients?

This chapter covers the following subjects:

- PDM Overview

- PDM Operating Requirements

- Preparing for PDM

- Using PDM to Configure the PIX Firewall

- Using PDM to Create a Site-to-Site VPN

- Using PDM to Create a Remote-Access VPN

CHAPTER 13

PIX Device Manager

Cisco PIX Device Manager (PDM) is a browser-based configuration tool that is designed to help you configure and monitor your Cisco PIX Firewall graphically, without requiring you to have extensive knowledge of the Cisco PIX Firewall command-line interface (CLI).

This chapter begins with an overview of PDM and the workstation requirements needed to run PDM, followed by PDM installation instructions. All of these tasks are necessary to get PDM operational on your PIX Firewall. Besides initially setting up PDM, this chapter also outlines how you can use PDM to perform various PIX Firewall configuration tasks such as the following:

- Defining system properties
- Defining hosts and networks
- Configuring translation rules
- Configuring access rules
- Creating a Site-to-Site VPN
- Creating a Remote-Access VPN

How to Best Use This Chapter

Effectively managing the configuration on your PIX Firewall is a very important step in protecting you network from attack. The Cisco PIX Device Manager (PDM) provides a graphical interface that enables you to easily perform common configuration tasks on your PIX Firewall. Using PDM also reduces configuration errors compared to manually entering commands on the command line. Test yourself with the "Do I Know This Already?" quiz and see how familiar you are with the functionality provided by PDM.

"Do I Know This Already?" Quiz

The purpose of the "Do I Know This Already?" quiz is to help you decide if you really need to read the entire chapter. If you already intend to read the entire chapter, you do not necessarily need to answer these questions now.

The ten-question quiz, derived from the major sections in the "Foundation Topics" portion of the chapter, helps you determine how to spend your limited study time.

Table 13-1 outlines the major topics discussed in this chapter and the "Do I Know This Already?" quiz questions that correspond to those topics.

Table 13-1 *"Do I Know This Already?" Foundation Topics Section-to-Question Mapping*

Foundations Topics Section	Questions Covered in This Section	Score
PDM Overview	1, 3 to 5, 10	
Prepare PDM	2	
Using PDM to Configure the PIX Firewall	6 to 8	

CAUTION The goal of self assessment is to gauge your mastery of the topics in this chapter. If you do not know the answer to a question or are only partially sure of the answer, you should mark this question wrong for purposes of the self assessment. Giving yourself credit for an answer you correctly guess skews your self-assessment results and might provide you with a false sense of security.

1. How many tabs does PDM have under its Configuration button?

    a. Three

    b. Five

    c. Eight

    d. Six

2. How do you connect to PDM?

    a. By accessing the PIX Firewall through Telnet and entering PDM

    b. By entering http://inside_interface_ip in your browser

    c. By entering https://inside_interface_ip in your browser

    d. By entering https://PIX_PDM in your browser

3. What version of PIX Firewall software is required for PDM 3.0 to run?

    a. 6.1

    b. 5.2

    c. 6.3

    d. 6.0

4. Which model of the PIX Firewall does PDM support?

    a. 515

    b. 525

    c. 535

    d. All of the above

5. Where does PDM reside?

    a. On a Windows NT/2000 server

    b. On a Red Hat Linux 7.0 server

    c. On a Solaris server

    d. In the PIX Flash memory

6. What default security mechanism does PDM employ for browsers to connect to it?

    a. RSA

    b. Biometrics

    c. MD5

    d. SSL

7. Which of the following is a prerequisite for access rules to be created?

    a. Hosts or networks must be defined before access rule creation.

    b. Dynamic or static translation must be defined before access rule creation.

    c. There are no prerequisites.

    d. Answers a and b

8. What is a translation exemption rule?

    a. A rule that exempts addresses from being encrypted or translated

    b. A rule that denies access to addresses

    c. A rule that increases security on selected addresses

    d. None of the above

9. What is the optimum configuration file size to use with PDM?

    a. 100 KB

    b. 1500 KB

    c. 110 MB

    d. 25 KB

10. Which of the following is required to access PDM?

    a. Cisco Secure access control server

    b. Transport Layer Security (TLS) enabled

    c. JavaScript and Java enabled on the browser

    d. A VPN connection to the PIX Firewall

The answers to the "Do I Know This Already?" quiz are found in Appendix A, "Answers to the 'Do I Know This Already?' Quizzes and Q&A Sections." The suggested choices for your next step are as follows:

- **8 or less overall score**—Read the entire chapter. This includes the "Foundation Topics," "Foundation Summary," and "Q&A" sections.

- **9 or 10 overall score**—If you want more review on these topics, skip to the "Foundation Summary" section and then go to the "Q&A" section. Otherwise, move to the next chapter.

Foundation Topics

PDM Overview

PDM is a browser-based configuration tool that is designed to help you set up, configure, and monitor your Cisco PIX Firewall graphically. It is installed as a separate software image on the PIX Firewall and resides in the Flash memory of all PIX units running PIX Firewall Version 6.0 and higher. PDM uses tables, drop-down menus, and task-oriented selection menus to assist you in administering your PIX Firewall. Additionally, PDM maintains compatibility with the PIX Firewall CLI and includes a tool for using the standard CLI commands within the PDM application. PDM also lets you print or export graphs of traffic through the PIX Firewall and system activity.

> **NOTE**   PDM is a signed Java applet that downloads from the PIX Firewall to your web browser.

Figure 13-1 shows the PDM GUI with the three main buttons: Home, Configuration, and Monitoring.

Figure 13-1 *PIX Device Manager GUI*

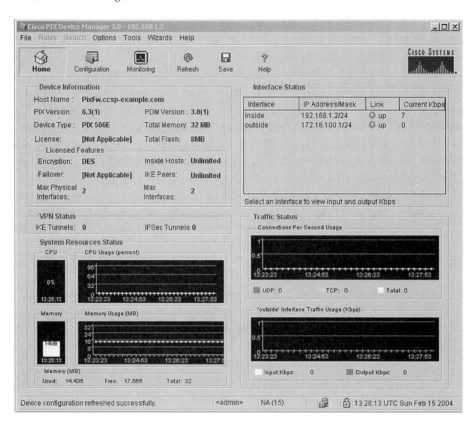

If your Cisco PIX Firewall unit is new and came with PIX Firewall Version 6.3, the software is already loaded in Flash memory. If you are upgrading from a previous version of Cisco PIX Firewall, you need to use Trivial File Transfer Protocol (TFTP) from the PIX Firewall unit's inside interface to copy the PDM image to your PIX Firewall. PDM works with PIX Firewall Version 6.0 and later, and it can operate on the PIX 501, 506E, 515E, 520, 525, and 535 units as soon as they are upgraded to Version 6.0 or later.

PDM is designed to assist you in managing your network security by

■ Letting you visually monitor your Cisco PIX Firewall system, connections, IDS, and traffic on the interfaces.

■ Creating new PIX Firewall configurations or modifying existing configurations that were originally implemented using the PIX Firewall CLI or Cisco Secure Policy Manager.

■ Using visual tools such as task-oriented selections and drop-down menus to configure your Cisco PIX Firewall.

- Using Secure Sockets Layer (SSL) to secure communication between PDM and the PIX Firewall.

- Monitoring and configuring PIX Firewall units individually.

Multiple Cisco PIX Firewalls can be monitored and configured from a single workstation via the web browser. It is also possible to have up to five administrators accessing a given PIX Firewall via PDM at the same time.

Three versions of PDM are available:

- **PDM Version 1.1**—Requires PIX Firewall software Version 6.0 or later

- **PDM Version 2.1**—Requires PIX Firewall software Version 6.2 or later

- **PDM Version 3.0**—Requires PIX Firewall software Version 6.3

For the CSPFA exam, this chapter focuses on PDM Version 3.0 running on PIX Firewall Version 6.3.

PIX Firewall Requirements to Run PDM

Like all software, PDM 3.0 has minimum hardware and software requirements for it to work. PDM 3.0 is available on all PIX 501, PIX 506/506E, PIX 515/515E, PIX 520, PIX 525, and PIX 535 platforms running PIX Firewall Version 6.3. Depending on the type of model PDM will be running on, it must have at least 16 MB of RAM and the Flash memory sizes listed in Table 13-2.

Table 13-2 *Flash Memory Requirements for each PIX Model to Support PDM 3.0*

PIX Firewall Model	Flash Memory Required
PIX 501	8 MB
PIX 506/506E	8 MB
PIX 515/515E	16 MB
PIX 520	16 MB
PIX 525	16 MB
PIX 535	16 MB

To use PDM version 3.0 to manage your PIX Firewall, you must meet the following minimum requirements:

- You must have an activation (license) key that enables Data Encryption Standard (DES) or the more secure 3DES, which PDM requires for support of the SSL protocol.

- PIX Firewall software Version 6.0 or higher.

- Minimum of 8 MB of Flash memory on the PIX unit.

The optimal configuration file size to use with PDM is less than 100 KB (which is approximately 1500 lines). Cisco PIX Firewall configuration files larger than 100 KB might interfere with PDM's performance on your workstation. You can determine the size of your configuration file by entering the command **show flashfs** at a PIX CLI prompt. Then, look for a line in the output that begins with file 1. The length number on the same line is the configuration file size in bytes. Example 13-1 provides sample output from **show flashfs**.

Example 13-1 show flashfs *Command Output*

```
pix# show flashfs
flash file system:  version:2  magic:0x12345679
  file 0: origin:       0 length:1540152
  file 1: origin: 1572864 length:6458
  file 2: origin:       0 length:0
  file 3: origin: 2752512 length:4539600
  file 4: origin:16646144 length:280
pix#
```

PDM Workstation Requirement

PDM, as mentioned earlier, is accessed via a browser interface. The following sections provide an overview of PDM requirements for:

- Browser

- Windows-based workstation

- Sun Solaris–based workstation

- Linux-based workstation

PDM 3.0 does not support Windows 3.1 or Windows 95 operating systems.

Browser Requirements

The following are the requirements to access PDM from a browser:

- JavaScript and Java must be enabled. If you are using Microsoft Internet Explorer, your JDK version should be 1.1.4 or higher. To check which version you have, launch PDM. When the PDM information window comes up, the field JDK Version indicates your JDK version. If you have an older JDK version, you can get the latest JVM from Microsoft by downloading the product called Virtual Machine.

- Browser support for SSL must be enabled. The supported versions of Internet Explorer and Netscape Navigator support SSL without requiring additional configuration.

Windows Requirements

The following are required to access PDM from a Windows NT/2000 operating system:

■ Windows 2000 (Service Pack 3), Windows NT 4.0 (Service Pack 4 and higher), Windows 98, Windows ME, or Windows XP.

■ Supported browsers: Internet Explorer 5.0 (Service Pack 1) or higher (5.5 recommended), Netscape Communicator 4.51 or higher (4.76 recommended). Internet Explorer is recommended because of its faster load times.

■ Any Pentium III or equivalent processor running at 450 MHz or higher.

■ At least 256 MB of RAM.

■ A 1024×768-pixel display and at least 256 colors are recommended.

SUN Solaris Requirements

The following requirements apply to the use of PDM with Sun SPARC:

■ Sun Solaris 2.8 or later running CDE or OpenWindows window manager.

■ SPARC microprocessor.

■ Supported browser: Netscape 4.78.

■ At least 128 MB of RAM.

■ A 1024×768-pixel display and 256 colors are recommended.

NOTE   PDM does not support Solaris on IBM PCs.

Linux Requirements

The following requirements apply to the use of PDM with Linux:

■ Pentium III or equivalent running at 450 MHz or higher.

■ Red Hat Linux 7.0 running the GNOME or KDE 2.0 desktop environment.

■ Supported browser: Netscape Communicator 4.7x on Red Hat 7.x and Mozilla 1.0.1 on Red Hat 8.x.

■ At least 128 MB of RAM.

■ A 1024×768-pixel display and 256 colors.

PDM Installation

Before installing PDM, follow these steps:

Step 1   Save or print your PIX Firewall configuration and write down your activation key.

Step 2   If you are upgrading from a previous version of PIX Firewall software, you need to obtain the PDM software from Cisco in the same way you download the PIX Firewall software. Then, use TFTP to download the image to your PIX unit.

Step 3   If you upgrade your Cisco PIX Firewall software to Version 6.3 and you plan to use PDM, both the PIX image and the PDM image must be installed on your failover units.

The install procedure is very similar to that of the Cisco PIX Firewall image upgrade. Example 13-2 shows the installation procedures for PDM installation.

Example 13-2   *PDM Installation Procedures*

```
PIXFIREWALL(config)# copy tftp flash:pdm
Address or name of remote host [127.0.0.1] 192.168.1.2
Source file name [cdisk] pdm-301.bin
copying tftp://192.168.1.2/ pdm-301.bin to flash:pdm
[yes ¦ no ¦ again]y
```

After you successfully install your PDM, you are ready to access it using your web browser. On a browser running on a workstation that has a network connection to the PIX unit, enter the following:

```
https://PIX_Inside_Interface_IP_Address
```

This launches the PDM applet, as shown in Figure 13-2. Use your enable password and leave the username blank to access the PDM interface when prompted to provide a username and password.

> **NOTE**   When you access PDM, the PIX Firewall prompts you for login credentials. You can restrict access via the enable password, which is encrypted and stored locally on the PIX Firewall. You can also use an external authentication server to store username and password information, which you will be asked by PDM to provide when you request access.

Figure 13-2   *Launching the PDM Applet*

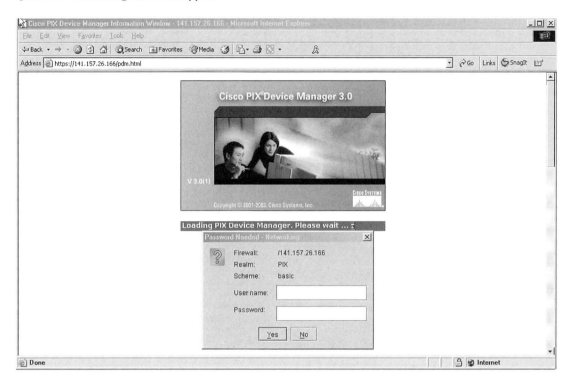

> **NOTE**   Remember that you have to use HTTPS, not HTTP, when accessing PDM.
> Otherwise, the browser cannot connect.

Using PDM to Configure the Cisco PIX Firewall

The Cisco PIX Firewall Device Manager Startup Wizard, shown in Figure 13-3, walks you
through the initial configuration of your Cisco PIX Firewall. You are prompted to enter
information about your PIX Firewall. The Startup Wizard applies these settings, so you
should be able to start using your PIX Firewall right away.

Figure 13-3   *Cisco PIX Firewall Device Manager Startup Wizard*

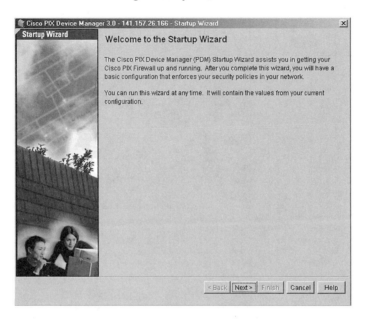

The Startup Wizard configures the following attributes on your Cisco PIX Firewall:

■ A host name for your PIX Firewall.

■ A domain name for your PIX Firewall.

■ A default gateway for your PIX Firewall.

■ An enable password that is required to access PDM or the PIX Firewall's CLI.

■ The speed and IP address information of the outside interface on the PIX Firewall.

■ Your PIX Firewall's other interfaces, such as the inside or DMZ interfaces, can be configured from the Startup Wizard.

■ Network Address Translation (NAT) or Port Address Translation (PAT) rules for your PIX.

■ Dynamic Host Configuration Protocol (DHCP) settings for the inside interface, as a DHCP server.

■ If you are using a PIX 501 or 506E, the Startup Wizard lets you configure Cisco Easy VPN Remote device settings, which let the PIX Firewall act as a VPN client and establish a VPN tunnel to the VPN server.

The Startup Wizard helps you set up a *shell configuration*—a basic configuration for your Cisco PIX Firewall, as the initial "setup" program does for the CLI. To customize and modify your PIX Firewall configuration, PDM provides the Configuration button. After you click the Configuration button on PDM, you see five main tabs for configuring and modifying the PIX Firewall configuration:

- System Properties
- Hosts/Networks
- Translation Rules
- Access Rules
- VPN

The sections that follow examine in more detail the System Properties, Hosts/Networks, Translation Rules, and Access Rules tabs. The section "Using PDM to Create a Site-to-Site VPN," later in the chapter, describes all actions associated with the VPN tab.

System Properties

The System Properties tab, shown in Figure 13-4, lets you view and configure all the parameters that can be configured using the Startup Wizard. Basic configurations such as interface definition, password, clock, and Telnet configuration are all done on this tab. In addition to the basic configuration, the System Properties tab lets you perform advanced configuration that is typically done at the CLI. You can configure logging; authentication, authorization, and accounting (AAA); DHCP services; routing; failover; multicast; intrusion detection; and more through the user-friendly interface of the System Properties tab.

Figure 13-4 *System Properties Tab on PDM*

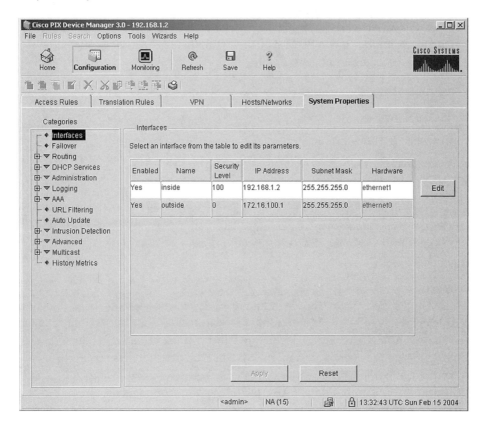

Complicated configurations such as AAA have been made significantly more intuitive and easier with the system properties under AAA. The AAA Server Groups pane, shown in Figure 13-5, allows you to specify up to 14 AAA server groups for your network.

Figure 13-5 *AAA Server Groups Pane Under the System Properties Tab*

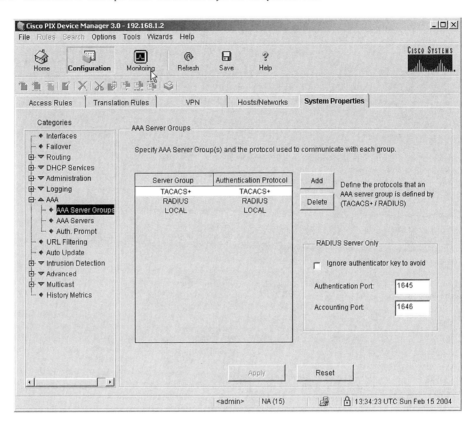

Each AAA server group directs different types of traffic to the authentication servers in its group. If the first authentication server listed in the group fails, the PIX Firewall seeks authentication from the next server in the group. You can have up to 14 groups, and each group can have up to 14 AAA servers, for a total of up to 196 AAA servers.

The Authentication Prompt pane lets you change the AAA challenge text for HTTP, FTP, and Telnet access. Figure 13-6 shows prompt messages that can be configured when users authenticate by an AAA server.

Figure 13-6 *Configurable Prompt Messages*

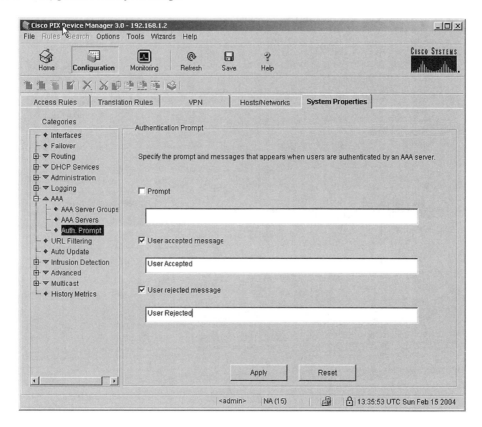

If configured, the prompt text appears above the username and password prompts that users view when logging in. If you do not use this feature, FTP users view FTP authentication, HTTP users view HTTP authentication, and challenge text does not appear for Telnet access. If the user authentication occurs from Telnet, you can use the User Accepted Message and User Rejected Message options to display different authentication prompts if the authentication server accepts or rejects the authentication attempt.

Another example of a command-line task that has been streamlined by the System Properties tab is URL filtering. The URL Filtering pane lets you prevent internal users from accessing external URLs that you designate using the Websense filtering server. After you have defined your URL filtering server(s) and related parameters on this pane, use the Filter Rules pane (located on the Access Rules panel) to define the rules that will be used to enforce URL filtering.

NOTE A total of 16 URL servers can be configured.

The PIX Firewall can be configured to use either N2H2 or Websense, but not both. For example, if the PIX Firewall unit is configured to use two Websense servers, when N2H2 is selected, a warning appears after you add the first N2H2 server and click Apply To PIX. All the previously configured Websense servers are dropped, and the new N2H2 server is added. This also takes place when you switch from N2H2 to Websense. Content filtering is discussed further in Chapter 15, "Content Filtering on the PIX Firewall."

Hosts/Networks

The Hosts/Networks tab, shown in Figure 13-7, lets you view, edit, add to, and delete from the list of hosts and networks defined for the selected interface defined previously on the System Properties tab.

Figure 13-7 *Hosts/Networks Tab on PDM*

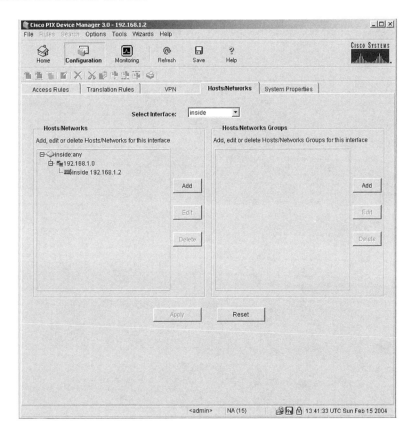

PDM requires that you define any host or network that you intend to use in access rules and translations. These hosts or networks are organized below the interface from which they can be reached.

Access rules reference these hosts or networks in a rule's source and destination conditions, whereas translation rules reference them in a rule's original address condition. When defining either type of rule, you can reference a host or a network by clicking Browse in the appropriate Add or Edit Rule dialog box. Additionally, you can reference the host or network by name if a name is defined for it.

In addition to defining the basic information for these hosts or networks, you can define route settings and NAT rules for any host or network. You also can configure route settings on the System Properties tab and configure translation rules on the Translation Rules tab. These different configuration options accomplish the same results. The Hosts/Networks tab provides another way to modify these settings on a per-host or per-network basis.

Translation Rules

The Translation Rules tab, shown in Figure 13-8, lets you view all the address translation rules or NAT exemption rules applied to your network.

Figure 13-8 *Translation Rules Tab on PDM*

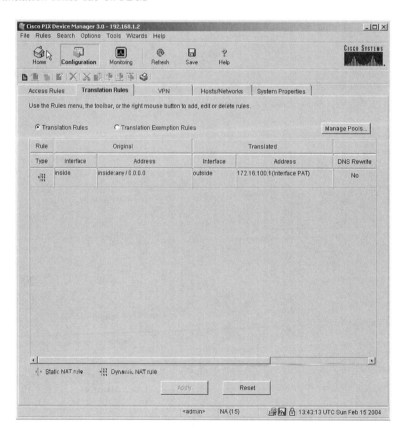

The Cisco PIX Firewall supports both NAT, which provides a globally unique address for each outbound host session, and PAT, which provides a single, unique global address for more than 64,000 simultaneous outbound or inbound host sessions. The global addresses used for NAT come from a pool of addresses to be used specifically for address translation. The unique global address that is used for PAT can be either one global address or the IP address of a given interface.

From the Translation Rules tab, you also can create a translation exemption rule, which lets you specify traffic that is exempt from being translated. The exemption rules are grouped by interface in the table, and then by direction. If you have a group of IP addresses that will be translated, you can exempt certain addresses from being translated by using the exemption rules. If you have a previously configured access list, you can use that to define your exemption rule. PDM writes a **nat 0** command to the CLI. You can re-sort your exemption's view by clicking the column heading.

It is important to note that the order in which you apply translation rules can affect how the rules operate. PDM lists the static translations first and then the dynamic translations. When processing NAT, the Cisco PIX Firewall first translates the static translations in the order they are configured. You can select **Rules > Insert Before** or **Rules > Insert After** to determine the order in which static translations are processed. Because dynamically translated rules are processed on a best-match basis, the option to insert a rule before or after a dynamic translation is disabled.

Access Rules

The Access Rules tab, shown in Figure 13-9, shows your entire network security policy expressed in rules. This tab combines the concepts of access lists, outbound lists, and conduits to describe how a specific host or network interacts with another host or network to permit or deny a specific service and/or protocol. This tab also lets you define AAA rules and filter rules for ActiveX and Java.

> **NOTE**   PDM does not support conduits and ACLs simultaneously on the same configuration.

Figure 13-9 *Access Rules Tab on PDM*

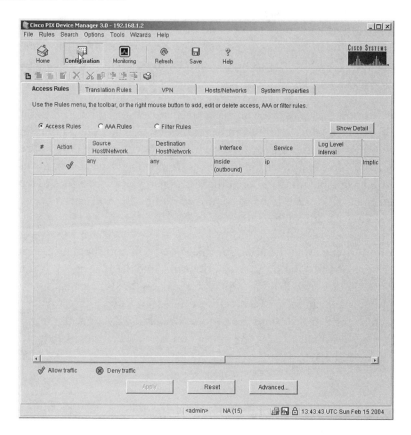

Keep in mind the following points when creating access rules with PDM:

■ It is important to remember that you cannot define any access rules until static or dynamic NAT has been configured for the hosts or networks on which you want to permit or deny traffic.

■ You cannot use unavailable commands until your rule meets certain conditions, such as defining hosts or networks. Unavailable commands appear dimmed on the Rules menu. For example, Insert Before and Insert After are available only after a rule is highlighted. Paste is available only when a rule has been copied or cut.

■ Access rules are listed in sequential order and are applied in the order in which they appear on the Access Rules tab. This is the order in which the PIX Firewall evaluates them. An implicit, unwritten rule denies all traffic that is not permitted. If traffic is not explicitly permitted by an access rule, it is denied.

Null Rules

A null rule indicates that an access rule was configured for a host that is not visible on another interface. This rule is null because no traffic can flow between these two hosts even though the access rule would permit it. Table 13-3 shows an example of how a null rule is displayed on the Access Rules tab.

Table 13-3 *Null Rule Example*

#	Action	Source Host/ Network	Destination Host/ Network	Interface	Service	Description
1	✔	(null rule)	(null rule)	[inbound]	tcp	

A rule can become null when PDM reads in an existing configuration where any of the following exists:

■ Rules for inbound traffic without a static translation

■ Rules for outbound traffic that is not NATed

■ Rules that have no hosts or networks are defined for either source or destination

Monitoring

The Monitoring button, shown in Figure 13-10, is one of the most useful tools to help you make sense of the different statistics that the Cisco PIX Firewall can generate. The different panes on the Monitoring tab help you to analyze your PIX Firewall's performance using colorful graphs.

Figure 13-10 *Monitoring Button on the PDM Menu Bar*

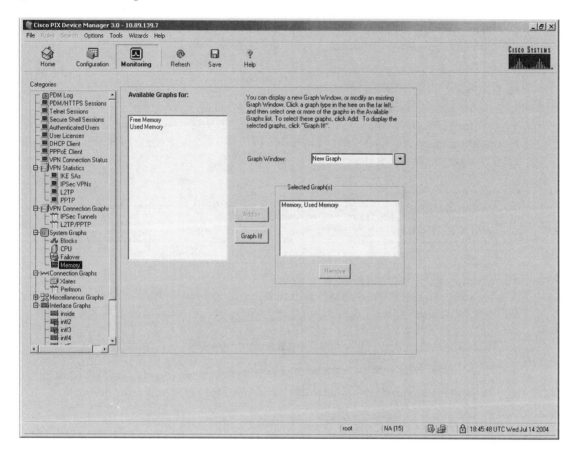

- The Monitoring tab enables you to examine the operation of the PIX Firewall. When monitoring the operation of the PIX Firewall, you can directly view the settings or statistics for many features and parameters. For other features, you have the option of displaying a graph that represents the features usage over time. The left hand column in Figure 13-10 shows the different categories of information that you can monitor on your PIX Firewall.

NOTE After specifying the information to be graphed, the graphical information is displayed in a separate window (New Graph window) when you click the **Graph It!** button (see Figure 13-10).The graphical information displayed in the New Graph window can be printed or bookmarked in your browser for later recall. The data may also be exported for use by other applications.

Selecting any of the following options in the Categories list (left column in Figure 13-10) provides a corresponding pane of monitoring statistics for the Cisco PIX Firewall:

- **PDM Log**—Displays the syslog messages currently in the PDM Log buffer on the PIX Firewall. A snapshot of the PDM Log buffer contents on the PIX Firewall can be displayed.

- **PDM/HTTPS**—Enables you to monitor connections made to the PIX Firewall using PDM. A snapshot of the current PDM user sessions to the PIX Firewall is displayed.

- **Telnet Sessions**—Enables you to monitor connections made to the PIX Firewall using Telnet. A snapshot of current Telnet sessions to the PIX Firewall is displayed.

- **Secure Shell Sessions**—Enables you to monitor connections made to the PIX Firewall using Secure Shell (SSH). When the Secure Shell pane is displayed, a snapshot of the current SSH sessions to the PIX Firewall is available.

- **User Licenses**—Displays the number of current users, which is subtracted from the maximum number of users for your PIX Firewall licensing agreement.

- **DHCP Client**—Displays DHCP-assigned interface parameters when DHCP addressing is configured on the outside interface of the PIX Firewall. A snapshot of the current DHCP lease information is displayed.

- **PPPoE Client**—Enables you to configure the PIX Firewall to automatically connect users on the inside interface to ISPs via the outside interface. The PPPoE Client pane displays information about current PPPOE client connections.

- **VPN Statistics**—Lets you graphically monitor the following functions:

  — Number of active IPSec tunnels

  — Layer 2 Tunneling Protocol (L2TP) active tunnels

  — L2TP active sessions

  — Point-to-Point Tunneling Protocol (PPTP) active tunnels

  — PPTP active sessions

  — Detailed IPSec information (similar to the CLI command **show ipsec sa detail**)

- **System Graphs**—Enables you to build the New Graph window, which monitors the PIX Firewall's system resources, including block utilization, CPU utilization, failover statistics, and memory utilization.

- **Connection Graphs**—Enables you to monitor a wide variety of performance statistics for PIX Firewall features, including statistics for xlates, connections, AAA, fixups, URL filtering, and TCP intercept.

- **IDS (located under Miscellaneous Graphs)**—Enables you to monitor intrusion detection statistics, including packet counts for each Intrusion Detection System (IDS) signature supported by the PIX Firewall.

- **Interface Graphs**—Enables you to monitor per-interface statistics, such as packet counts and bit rates, for each enabled interface on the PIX Firewall.

> **NOTE**   If an interface is not enabled using the System Properties tab, no graphs are available for that interface.

Using PDM for VPN Configuration

Chapter 11, "Virtual Private Networks," explained how to configure VPN on the Cisco PIX Firewall via the CLI. One of the difficult configuration and troubleshooting issues occurs with VPNs. Quite often, typos occur when you create a VPN configuration via the CLI. For novice administrators of the Cisco PIX Firewall, remembering the commands and their sequence can sometimes be difficult. PDM presents a user-friendly VPN Wizard that creates both site-to-site and remote-access VPNs for the Cisco PIX Firewall (accessible via the Wizards menu on PDM). Administrators are prompted for unique parameters such as IP addresses, and they use drop-down menus to configure their VPN. The following sections discuss the steps involved in creating a site-to-site VPN and a remote-access VPN using the VPN Wizard on PDM.

Using PDM to Create a Site-to-Site VPN

The following steps and corresponding figures show a sample site-to-site VPN configuration using the VPN Wizard on PDM:

Step 1   Select the Site to Site VPN radio button, as shown in Figure 13-11, to create a site-to-site VPN configuration. This configuration is used between two IPSec security gateways, which can include Cisco PIX Firewalls, VPN concentrators, or other devices that support site-to-site IPSec connectivity. Use this window to also select the type of VPN tunnel you are defining and to identify the interface on which the tunnel will be enabled. In Figure 13-11, the outside interface is selected as the VPN termination point.

Figure 13-11   *VPN Wizard with Site to Site VPN Selected*

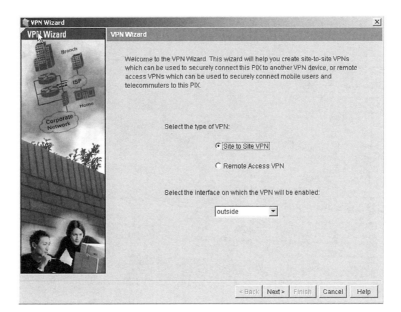

Step 2   In the Remote Site Peer window, shown in Figure 13-12, you specify the IP address of the remote IPSec peer that will terminate the VPN tunnel you are configuring. Also, you use this window to identify which of the following methods of authentication you want to use:

   • Preshared keys

   • Certificates

Figure 13-12 shows the Remote Site Peer window configured with the remote IPSec peer and the preshared authentication keys.

Figure 13-12 *Remote Site Peer Window*

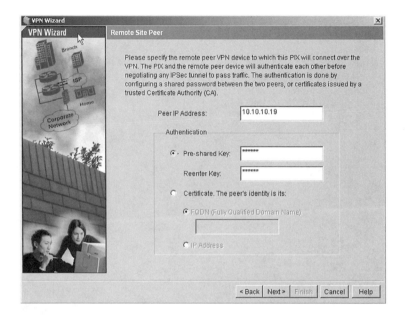

Step 3 Configure the encryption and authentication algorithms for IKE Phase I in the IKE Policy window, as shown in Figure 13-13.

Figure 13-13 *IKE Policy Window*

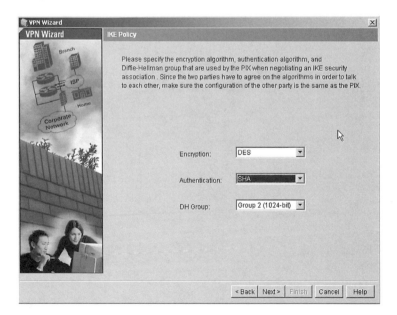

Step 4   Configure the transform set to specify the encryption and authentication algorithms used by IPSec, as shown in Figure 13-14. IPSec provides secure communication over an insecure network, such as the public Internet, by encrypting traffic between two IPSec peers, such as your local PIX and a remote PIX or VPN concentrator.

Figure 13-14 *Transform Set Window*

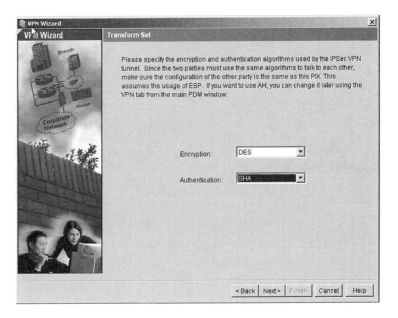

Step 5   Identify the traffic you want to protect using the current IPSec tunnel, as shown in Figure 13-15. The current IPSec tunnel protects packets that are sent to or received from the hosts or networks you select in this window. Use this window to identify the hosts and networks protected by your local Cisco PIX Firewall. In Figure 13-15, packets that are sent to and received from the 192.168.1.0/16 network are protected.

Figure 13-15 *IPSec Traffic Selector Window: On Local Site*

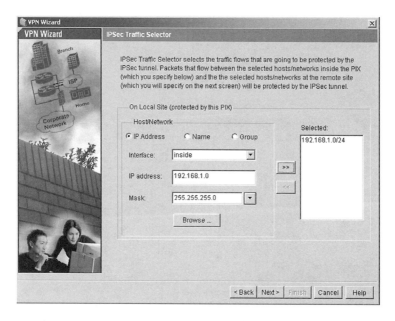

Step 6   Identify the hosts and networks protected by the remote IPSec peer, as shown in Figure 13-16.

Figure 13-16 *IPSec Traffic Selector Window: On Remote Site*

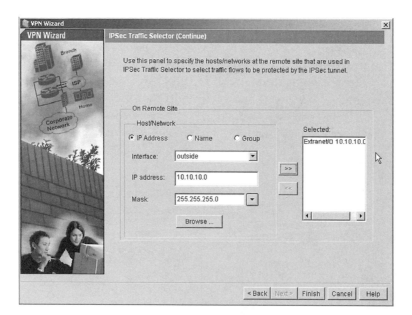

Step 7   At this point, the site-to-site VPN configuration has been completed.

Using PDM to Create a Remote-Access VPN

With a remote-access VPN, your local Cisco PIX Firewall provides secure connectivity between individual remote users and the LAN resources protected by your local PIX Firewall. To start the VPN Wizard, go to the Wizards menu on PDM and select the VPN Wizard option.

Step 1   From the opening window of the PDM VPN Wizard, shown in Figure 13-17, select the Remote Access VPN radio button to create a remote-access VPN configuration. This configuration enables secure remote access for VPN clients, such as mobile users. A remote-access VPN allows remote users to securely access centralized network resources. When you select this option, the system displays a series of panels that let you enter the configuration required for this type of VPN. In Figure 13-17, the outside interface is selected as the interface on which the current VPN tunnel will be enabled.

Figure 13-17   *VPN Wizard with Remote Access VPN Selected*

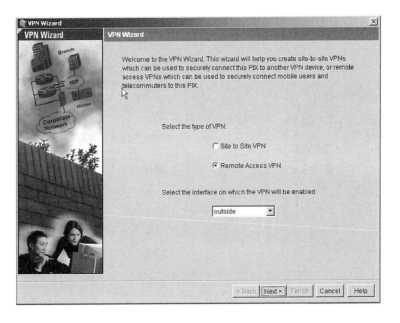

Step 2 In the Remote Access Client window, shown in Figure 13-18, identify the type of remote-access client that will use the current VPN tunnel to connect to your local Cisco PIX Firewall. The options are as follows:

- **Cisco VPN Client**—Select to support remote-access clients using Cisco VPN Client v3.*x* or higher (Cisco Unified VPN Client Framework)

- **Cisco VPN 3000 Client**—Select to support remote-access clients using Cisco VPN 3000 Client, Release 2.5/2.6

- **Microsoft Windows client using PPTP**—Select to support remote-access clients using Microsoft Windows client using PPTP

- **Microsoft Windows client using L2TP**—Select to support remote-access clients using Microsoft Windows client using L2TP

Figure 13-18 *Remote Access Client Window*

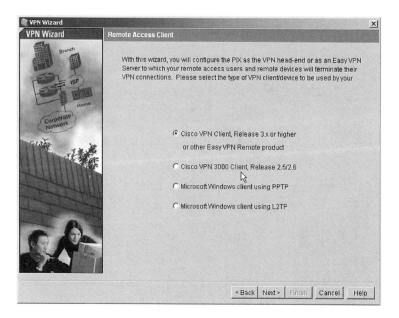

Step 3 Create a VPN client group to group remote-access users who are using the Cisco VPN client. The attributes associated with a group are applied and downloaded to the clients that are part of a given group. The Group Password is a preshared key to be used for IKE authentication. Figure 13-19 shows the VPN Client Group window with Sales as a group name and the Pre-shared Key radio button selected for IKE authentication.

Figure 13-19 *VPN Client Group Window*

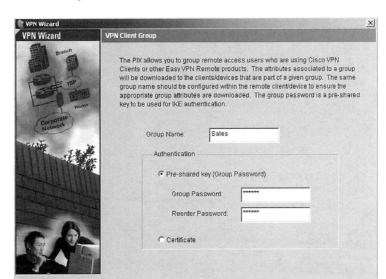

A preshared key is a quick and easy way to set up communications with a limited number of remote peers. To use this method of authentication, exchange the preshared key with the remote-access user through a secure and convenient method, such as an encrypted e-mail message.

NOTE Preshared keys must be exchanged between each pair of IPSec peers that needs to establish secure tunnels. This authentication method is appropriate for a stable network with a limited number of IPSec peers. It might cause scalability problems in a network with a large or increasing number of IPSec peers.

Step 4 Use the Extended Client Authentication window, shown in Figure 13-20, to require VPN client users to authenticate from a AAA server for access to the private network on your PIX Firewall. Extended client authentication is optional and is not required for VPN client access to the private network.

Figure 13-20 *Extended Client Authentication Window*

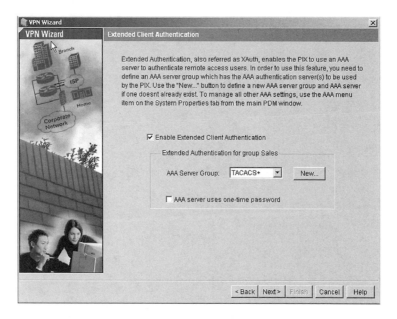

Extended Authentication (XAuth) is a feature within the IKE protocol. XAuth lets you deploy IPSec VPNs using TACACS+ or RADIUS as your user authentication method. This feature, which is designed for VPN clients, provides user authentication by prompting the user for a username and password and verifies them with the information stored in your TACACS+ or RADIUS database. XAuth is negotiated between IKE Phase 1 (the IKE device authentication phase) and IKE Phase 2 (the IPSec SA negotiation phase). If XAuth fails, the IPSec security association is not established, and the IKE security association is deleted.

The AAA server must be defined before XAuth will work on the Cisco PIX Firewall. You can define the AAA server using the New button. This opens the AAA Server Group pane, where you can define the location of the AAA server, the group name, and the protocol used for AAA.

Step 5 Define the location of the AAA server, the group name, and the protocol used for AAA, as shown in Figure 13-21.

Figure 13-21 *AAA Server Group Window*

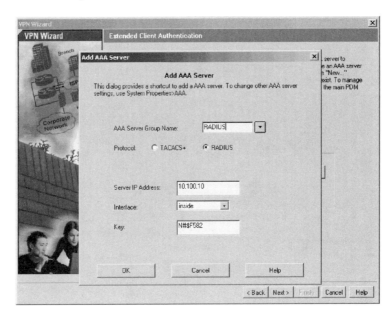

Step 6   Create a pool of local addresses that can be used to assign dynamic addresses to remote-access VPN clients. Enter a descriptive identifier for the address pool. Figure 13-22 shows a sample configuration for the remote sales group in the Address Pool window.

Figure 13-22 *Address Pool Window*

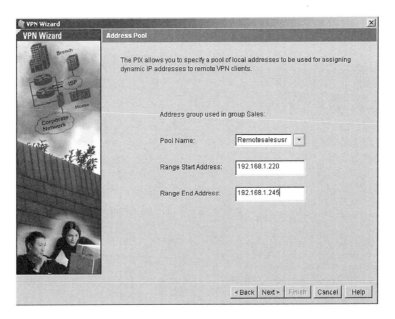

Step 7 (Optional) Configure the DNS and WINS addresses that can be pushed down to the remote client, as shown in Figure 13-23.

Figure 13-23 *Attributes Pushed to Client Window*

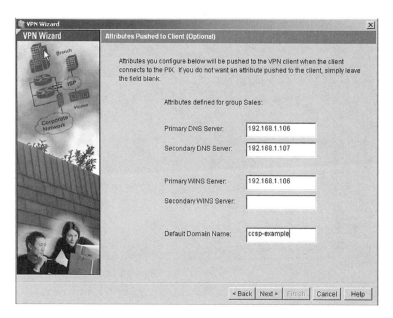

Step 8 Specify the encryption and authentication algorithms used by IKE (Phase 1), as shown in Figure 13-24.

Figure 13-24   *IKE Policy Window*

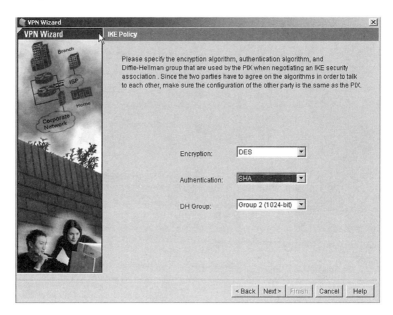

Step 9   Specify the encryption and authentication algorithms used by the IPSec VPN tunnel, as shown in Figure 13-25.

Figure 13-25 *Transform Set Window*

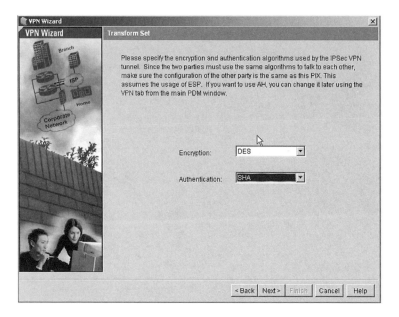

Step 10   (Optional) The Address Translation Exemption window, shown in Figure 13-26, identifies local hosts/networks that are to be exempted from address translation. By default, the PIX Firewall hides the real IP address of internal networks from outside hosts through dynamic or static NAT. The security provided by NAT is essential to minimize the risk of being attacked by untrusted outside hosts, but it might be inappropriate for those who have been authenticated and protected by VPN.

As shown at the bottom of Figure 13-26, a check box option is available to enable split tunneling. A split tunnel allows the VPN client to access the networks protected by the VPN headend via the VPN tunnel and the Internet in clear data (outside the VPN tunnel) simultaneously.

NOTE   Split tunneling is scalable and reduces the drain on institutional computing and network resources. A potential drawback is that this VPN client could be a relay agent if someone on the clear-data side compromised the client's workstation and used that workstation to get information from the VPN-protected networks.

Step 11   At this point the remote-access VPN configuration is complete.

Figure 13-26   *Address Translation Exemption Window*

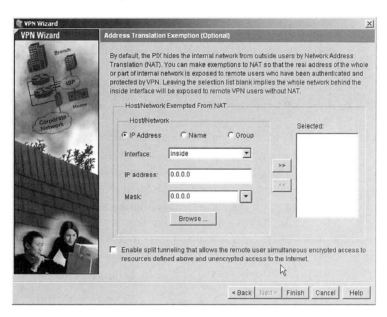

Foundation Summary

The "Foundation Summary" provides a convenient review of many key concepts in this chapter. If you are already comfortable with the topics in this chapter, this summary can help you recall a few details. If you just read this chapter, this review should help solidify some key facts. If you are doing your final preparation before the exam, this summary provides a convenient way to review the day before the exam.

PDM is a browser-based configuration tool designed to help you set up, configure, and monitor your Cisco PIX Firewall graphically. It is installed as a separate software image on the Cisco PIX Firewall and resides in the Flash memory of all PIX Firewall units running PIX Firewall Version 6.0 and higher. Multiple PIX Firewall units can be monitored and configured using PDM from a single workstation via the web browser.

PDM uses tables, drop-down menus, and task-oriented selection menus to assist you in administering your Cisco PIX Firewall. To provide secure management access to your PIX Firewall, PDM allows access only via HTTPS. Five main tabs are available on PDM to configure the Cisco PIX Firewall:

- System Properties
- Hosts/Networks
- Translation Rules
- Access Rules
- VPN

The optimal configuration file size to use with PDM is less than 100 KB (which is approximately 1500 lines). Cisco PIX Firewall configuration files larger than 100 KB might interfere with PDM's performance on your workstation.

Q&A

The questions in this book are more difficult than what you should experience on the exam. The questions are designed to ensure your understanding of the concepts discussed in this chapter and to adequately prepare you to complete the exam. Use the simulated exams on the CD to practice for the exam.

The answers to these questions can be found in Appendix A.

1. When reading an existing configuration using PDM, what three situations can cause access rules to become null?

2. What is a translation exemption rule?

3. What are the three main buttons on the PIX PDM?

4. How do you access PDM?

5. What version of PIX Firewall software is required to run PDM Version 3.0?

6. Which models of Cisco PIX Firewall are supported by PDM?

7. What versions of Windows does PDM support?

8. Where does PDM reside?

9. What is the quickest method to configure site-to-site VPN using PDM?

10. What is the command to install or upgrade PDM on the PIX Firewall?

This chapter covers the following subjects:

- Configuring access and translation rules using CiscoWorks Management Center for Firewalls (Firewall MC)

- Reporting, tool use, and administration using Firewall MC

- Introduction to the Auto Update Server (AUS)

- Cisco PIX Firewall and AUS communication settings using AUS

- Devices, images, and assignments in AUS

- Reporting and administration through AUS

It also covers the following supplemental topics:

- Firewall MC installation

- Key features and concepts of Firewall MC

- Importing devices into Firewall MC

- Device management and groups in Firewall MC

- Multiple firewall management in Firewall MC

CHAPTER 14

CiscoWorks Management Center for Firewalls (PIX MC)

Configuring your Cisco PIX Firewalls with a graphical interface enables you to manage their operation efficiently. Chapter 13, "PIX Device Manager," explains how to use the PIX Device Manager (PDM) to configure a single PIX system. This graphical interface is very effective to administer just a few PIX systems, but if you manage a larger number of PIX devices, you need a different application. The CiscoWorks Management Center for Firewalls (Firewall MC) enables you to manage multiple PIX devices easily from a single graphical interface. This chapter explains in detail the major features of Firewall MC and how you can use that functionality to manage multiple PIX devices across your network.

To manage the configuration of multiple firewalls effectively, you must also maintain current software images. The Auto Update Server (AUS) enables you to maintain and deploy up-to-date software images on your managed firewalls. This chapter explains how you can use the AUS to manage the images on your managed firewalls.

How to Best Use This Chapter

This chapter provides an overview of both the Firewall MC and the AUS. Unlike the PDM, the Firewall MC provides a graphical user environment suited to managing large numbers of firewalls, and the AUS enables you to maintain current images and configurations efficiently on a large number of firewalls. Understanding these applications is vital if you manage a large number of firewalls. If you are at all familiar with these applications, you will probably find this chapter very easy. Test yourself with the "Do I Know This Already?" quiz.

"Do I Know This Already?" Quiz

The purpose of the "Do I Know This Already?" quiz is to help you decide if you really need to read the entire chapter. If you already intend to read the entire chapter, you do not necessarily need to answer these questions now.

The ten-question quiz, derived from the major sections in the "Foundation and Supplemental Topics" portion of the chapter, helps you determine how to spend your limited study time.

Table 14-1 outlines the major topics discussed in this chapter and the "Do I Know This Already?" quiz questions that correspond to those topics.

Table 14-1 *"Do I Know This Already?" Foundation Topics Section-to-Question Mapping*

Supplemental or Foundations Topics Section	Questions Covered in This Section	Score
CiscoWorks Management Center for Firewalls Overview	6	
CiscoWorks	5	
Firewall MC Interface	4	
Basic User Task Flow		
Device Management	8	
Configuration Tasks	1, 2, 10	
Reports	3	
Administration Tasks	7	
CiscoWorks Auto Update Server (AUS)	9	

CAUTION The goal of self assessment is to gauge your mastery of the topics in this chapter. If you do not know the answer to a question or are only partially sure of the answer, you should mark this question wrong for purposes of the self assessment. Giving yourself credit for an answer you correctly guess skews your self-assessment results and might provide you with a false sense of security.

1. Which of the following are types of building blocks? (Choose two.)

   a. Network objects

   b. Address translation pools

   c. Access rules

   d. Static translation rules

   e. Dynamic translation rules

2. What are the three types of access rules?

   a. Firewall rules

   b. Static translation rules

   c. AAA rules

   d. Dynamic translation rules

   e. Filter rules

3. What are the three reports supported by Firewall MC?

   a. Device Report

   b. Activity Report

   c. Configuration Differences report

   d. Device Setting Report

   e. Deployment reports

4. When making changes to device configurations in Firewall MC, the changes can apply to which firewalls?

   a. A single firewall

   b. The firewalls in a group

   c. All of the managed firewalls

   d. Firewalls belonging to multiple groups

   e. Answers a, b, and c

5. Which software manages login access to the Firewall MC?

   a. CiscoWorks

   b. Firewall MC

   c. Windows OS

   d. Auto Update Server

   e. None of the above

6. Firewall MC groups comprise which items? (Choose two.)

    a. Configuration lists

    b. Devices

    c. Subgroups

    d. Software images

    e. Access lists

7. What are the three steps involved in updating device configurations when workflow is enabled?

    a. Define, deploy, review

    b. Define, test, evaluate

    c. Create, test, review

    d. Define, approve, deploy

    e. None of the above

8. Which of the following is not an option when importing devices into Firewall MC?

    a. Import configuration file for a device

    b. Import configuration file for multiple devices

    c. Import configuration from PDM

    d. Create firewall device

    e. Import configuration from device

9. Which of the following is not a configuration tab in AUS?

    a. Devices

    b. Deployment

    c. Images

    d. Assignments

    e. Admin

10. Which translation rules define a permanent mapping between an internal IP address and a public IP address?

    a. Dynamic translation rules

    b. AAA rules

    c. Web filter rules

    d. Static translation rules

    e. None of the above

The answers to the "Do I Know This Already?" quiz are found in Appendix A, "Answers to the 'Do I Know This Already?' Quizzes and Q&A Sections." The suggested choices for your next step are as follows:

■ **8 or less overall score**—Read the entire chapter. This includes the "Foundation and Supplemental Topics," "Foundation Summary," and "Q&A" sections.

■ **9 or 10 overall score**—If you want more review of these topics, skip to the "Foundation Summary" section and then go to the "Q&A" section. Otherwise, move to the next chapter.

Foundation and Supplemental Topics

CiscoWorks Management Center for Firewalls Overview

The CiscoWorks Management Center for Firewalls (Firewall MC) enables you to manage the configuration of multiple PIX Firewall devices deployed throughout your network. Firewall MC is a Web-based application that provides centralized management for devices on your network and accelerates the deployment of firewalls to protect your network. Some features of Firewall MC are as follows:

- Web-based interface for configuring and managing multiple firewalls
- Configuration hierarchy and user interface to facilitate configuration of firewall settings
- Support for PIX Firewall Version 6.0 and later
- Ability to import configurations from existing firewalls
- Ability to support dynamically addressed PIX Firewalls
- Support for up to 1000 PIX Firewalls
- Secure Sockets Layer (SSL) protocol support for client communications to CiscoWorks
- Support for Workflow and audit trails

To obtain maximum functionality from Firewall MC, you need to understand the following items:

- Key concepts
- Supported devices
- Installation

Key Concepts

To use Firewall MC effectively to manage and configure the PIX Firewalls on your network, you need to understand certain key concepts. These concepts fall into the following three categories:

- Configuration hierarchy
- Configuration elements
- Workflow process

Configuration Hierarchy

All devices managed by Firewall MC are grouped in a hierarchical structure beneath a global group. By placing managed devices in different groups and subgroups, you can simplify your configuration and management tasks because each group can include devices with similar attributes, such as similar access rules and configuration settings.

Each device managed by Firewall MC can be a member of only one specific group. A group is composed of one or more of the following items:

■ Subgroups

■ Devices

Devices inherit properties either from a specific group or individually from a specific device. Inheritance of properties allows your configuration changes to apply to multiple managed devices using less administrative effort.

Configuration Elements

Through Firewall MC, you can configure various characteristics of the managed firewalls deployed throughout your network. These characteristics fall into the following four major categories:

■ Device settings

■ Access rules

■ Translation rules

■ Building blocks

Device settings control specific configuration parameters on your PIX Firewalls, such as interface and routing properties. Access rules regulate network traffic and fall into the two categories shown in Table 14-2. Translation rules define the address translations that your firewalls will perform on network traffic. Building blocks associate names with specific objects, such as subnets, that you can then use when defining rules. All of the configuration elements are explained in detail later in this chapter.

Table 14-2 *Access Rule Types*

Access Rule Type	Description
Mandatory	Rules that apply to an enclosed group and that are ordered down to the devices in the group. These rules cannot be overwritten.
Default	Rules that apply to all of the devices in a group. These rules can be overwritten.

Workflow Process

The workflow process divides configuration changes made using Firewall MC into the following three steps:

Step 1   Define configuration.

Step 2   Implement configuration (approve).

Step 3   Deploy configuration.

A collection of configuration changes made for a specific purpose is called an *activity*. After you submit an activity to be deployed, it is converted into a set of configuration files known as a *job*. Finally, the job is scheduled for deployment on the network. A different person can approve each of these steps. Activities and job management are explained in detail later in the chapter.

Supported Devices

Firewall MC Version 1.2.1 supports PIX Firewall Versions 6.0, 6.1, 6.2, and 6.3.*x* along with the Firewall Service Module (FWSM) Version 1.1.*x*.

> **NOTE**   Not all PIX command-line interface (CLI) commands are configurable by using Firewall MC. For a complete list of Firewall MC[en]supported commands and devices refer to http://www.cisco.com/en/US/products/sw/cscowork/ps3992/products-device-support-tables-list.html.

The following PIX hardware models are supported by Firewall MC Version 1.2.1:

- PIX 501
- PIX 506/506E
- PIX 515/515E
- PIX 525
- PIX 535
- FWSM

Installation

Firewall MC requires CiscoWorks Common Services to run. Therefore, before you can install Firewall MC, you must install CiscoWorks Common Services (Version 2.2). Common Services provides services for the following:

- Interacting with the CiscoWorks desktop

- Setting up the CiscoWorks server
- Administering the CiscoWorks server
- Adding external connections to the CiscoWorks server
- Database administration for Firewall MC applications
- System administration
- Logging
- Diagnosing problems with the CiscoWorks server

For CiscoWorks to operate efficiently, your CiscoWorks server and client computers must meet certain hardware requirements.

Server Requirements

When installing Firewall MC, you need to understand the hardware and software requirements for the different components. To support all of the functionality provided by Firewall MC and the underlying CiscoWorks foundation, your CiscoWorks server must meet the following minimum requirements:

- IBM PC-compatible computer
- 1-gigahertz (GHz) or faster processor
- Color monitor with video card capable of viewing 256 colors
- CD-ROM drive
- 10Base-T or faster network connection
- Minimum of 1 gigabyte (GB) of random-access memory (RAM)
- 2 GB of virtual memory
- Minimum of 9 GB of free hard drive space (NTFS)
- Open Database Connectivity (ODBC) Driver Manager 3.510 or later
- Windows 2000 Professional and Windows 2000 Server (with Service Pack 3 or 4)

> **NOTE**   Requirements for the CiscoWorks server are frequently updated. For the latest server requirements, refer to the documentation on the Cisco website.

Client Requirements

Although the Firewall MC runs on a server, access to Firewall MC is by a browser running on a client system. Client systems also must meet certain minimum requirements to ensure successful system operation. Your client systems should meet the following minimum requirements:

- IBM PC-compatible
- 300-megahertz (MHz) or faster processor
- Minimum 256 MB of RAM
- 400 MB of virtual memory (free space on hard drive)

Along with these requirements, your clients must be running one of the following operating systems:

- Windows 2000 Professional or Server (with Service Pack 3 or later)
- Windows XP Professional (with Service Pack 1) with Microsoft Virtual Machine
- Windows 98

One final requirement is that your client systems must use one of the following web browsers:

- Internet Explorer 6.0 (Service Pack 1) with Microsoft Virtual Machine
- Netscape Navigator 4.78
- Java Virtual Machine (JVM) version 5.1

NOTE   Requirements for the CiscoWorks clients are frequently updated. For the latest client requirements, refer to the documentation on the Cisco website.

PIX Bootstrap Commands

When you initially configure your PIX Firewall, you run the **setup** command to configure many of the basic components of the operational configuration. The **setup** command prompts you for the following items:

- Enable password
- Clock Universal Time Coordinate (UTC)
- Date
- Time
- Inside Internet Protocol (IP) address
- Inside network mask
- Host name
- Domain name
- IP address of host running PDM

Besides this information, you must also configure the firewall to allow modification from a browser connection and specify which hosts or network is allowed to initiate these Hypertext

Transfer Protocol (HTTP) connections. Complete the following steps to enable the Firewall MC server to update the configuration on your firewall:

Step 1 Enable the firewall configuration to be modified from a browser by using the following command:

```
http server enable
```

Step 2 Specify the host or network authorized to initiate HTTP connections to the firewall by using the following command:

```
http ip-address [netmask] [interface-name]
```

Step 3 Store the current configuration in Flash memory using the following command:

```
write memory
```

CiscoWorks

CiscoWorks is the heart of the Cisco family of comprehensive network management tools that allow you to access and manage the advanced capabilities of the Cisco AVVID (Architecture for Voice, Video and Integrated Data) easily. It provides the foundation upon which Firewall MC (and other management center applications such as the AUS) is built. Therefore, before you can access the Firewall MC application, you must first log in to CiscoWorks. To use Firewall MC, you need to understand the following CiscoWorks functionality:

■ Login process

■ User authorization roles

■ Adding users

Login Process

To access the applications supported by CiscoWorks, such as Firewall MC and AUS, you must first log in to the CiscoWorks server desktop. The CiscoWorks server desktop is the interface used for CiscoWorks network management applications, such as Firewall MC.

To log in to CiscoWorks, you connect to the CiscoWorks desktop using a web browser. By default, the CiscoWorks web server listens on port 1741. So, if your CiscoWorks desktop is on a machine named *CW.cisco.com* through your Domain Name System (DNS) with an IP address of 10.10.20.10, you could connect to it by entering either of the following Universal Resource Locators (URLs):

■ http://CW.cisco.com:1741/

■ http://10.10.20.10:1741/

> **NOTE** You can also enable CiscoWorks to use HTTP over SSL (HTTPS) instead of HTTP. When you install some management centers (such as the Management Center for Cisco Security Agents), they enable HTTPS on CiscoWorks automatically. When HTTPS is enabled, you need to connect to port 1742.

At the initial CiscoWorks window, log in to CiscoWorks by entering a valid username and password (see Figure 14-1).

> **NOTE** Initially, you can log in using the administration account created during installation. The default value is *admin* for both the username and password (unless you changed these values during the installation process). For security reasons, you should change these values.

Figure 14-1 *CiscoWorks Login Window*

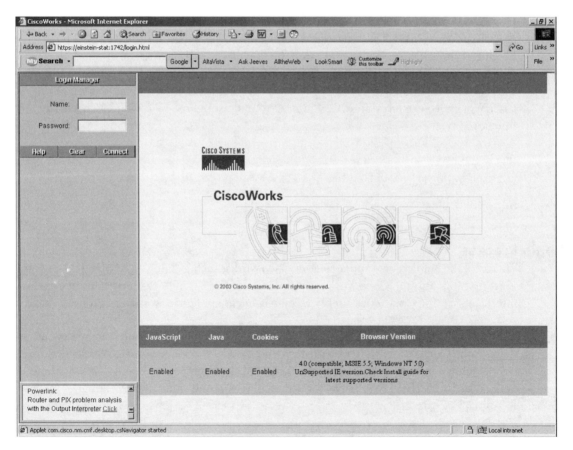

User Authorization Roles

CiscoWorks enables you to define different roles for different users. A role can enable a user to perform specific operations when using CiscoWorks and any of the applications that are built upon CiscoWorks (such as Firewall MC). CiscoWorks supports five different user roles that are relevant to Firewall MC operations (see Table 14-3).

Table 14-3   *CiscoWorks User Roles*

User Role	Description
Help Desk	Provides read-only access for the entire system
Approver	Can review policy changes and accept or reject changes
Network Operator	Can create and submit jobs
Network Administrator	Can perform administrative tasks on Firewall MC
System Administrator	Performs all operations

NOTE   You can assign each user multiple authorization roles (depending on the user's responsibilities). CiscoWorks also supports two other roles: *Export Data* and *Developer*. These roles are not relevant to the Firewall MC operations.

Adding Users

As part of your Firewall MC configuration, you must configure accounts for the various users that need to access Firewall MC. The CiscoWorks Add User window enables you to create new accounts that have access to the CiscoWorks applications. To create a new account in CiscoWorks, perform the following steps:

Step 1   Log in to the CiscoWorks desktop.

Step 2   Choose **Server Configuration > Setup > Security > Add Users**. The Add User window appears (see Figure 14-2).

Figure 14-2 *CiscoWorks Add User Window*

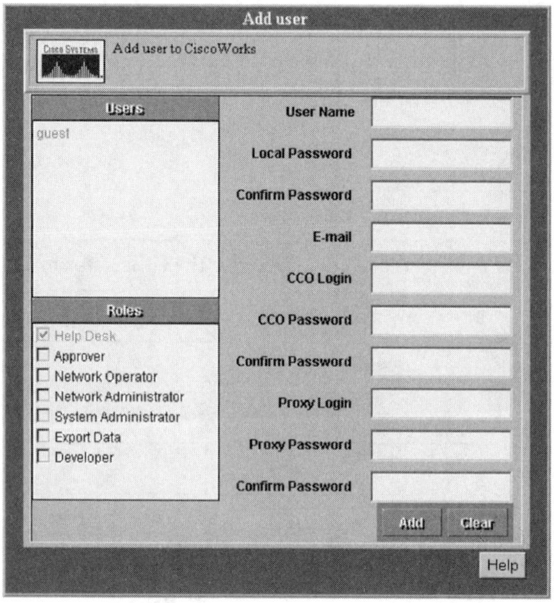

Step 3   Enter values for the new user (Table 14-4 describes the various fields).

Table 14-4 *CiscoWorks Add User Fields*

Field	Description
User Name	Username of the account being added
Local Password	Password for the new user
Confirm Password	Confirmation of the user's password
E-Mail	(Optional) User's e-mail address
CCO Login	(Optional) User's Cisco Connection Online (CCO) login name
CCO Password	User's CCO password (required only if CCO login is specified)

continues

Table 14-4 *CiscoWorks Add User Fields (Continued)*

Field	Description
Confirm Password	Confirmation of user's CCO password (required only if CCO password is entered)
Proxy Login	(Optional) User's proxy login (required only if your network requires use of a proxy server)
Proxy Password	User's proxy password (required only if Proxy Login is specified)
Confirm Password	Confirmation of user's proxy login (required only if Proxy Login is specified)

Step 4   Using the **Roles** section of the **Add User** window, select the roles associated with the user's responsibilities. You can assign multiple roles to a single user, giving that user a combination of user rights.

Step 5   Click **Add** to complete the addition of the user to the CiscoWorks database.

Firewall MC Interface

Although the Firewall MC user interface is graphical and easy to use, it is helpful to understand how the interface is structured. The Firewall MC user interface is composed of the following major sections (see Figure 14-3):

- Configuration tabs
- Options bar
- Table of contents (TOC)
- Path bar
- Instruction box
- Content area
- Scope bar
- Object Selector handle
- Tools bar
- Activity bar

Figure 14-3 *Firewall MC User Interface*

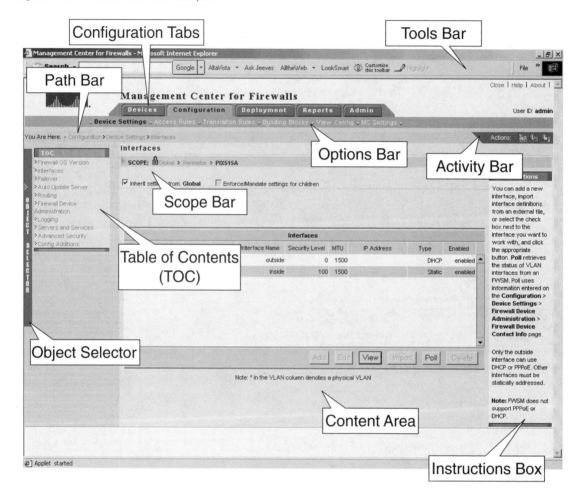

Configuration Tabs

The configuration tasks are broken down into the following five major categories:

- **Devices**—Enables you to import device configurations and define device groups to be managed by the system

- **Configuration**—Enables you to change the operational configuration of the devices managed by the system

- **Deployment**—Enables you to generate configuration files, manage firewall configuration files, and submit or manage new jobs

- **Reports**—Enables you to generate reports, view scheduled reports, and view reports
- **Admin**—Enables you to configure system settings

> **NOTE**   When you enable workflow, the Deployment tab changes to Workflow.

To access any of the categories, click the tab labeled with the appropriate name. The tabs are located across the top of the Firewall MC display.

Options Bar

After clicking one of the major configuration tabs, the options for that selection are displayed in a list located in the window just below the configuration tabs. Figure 14-3 shows a window in which the Configuration tab has been selected. The options associated with the Configuration tab are as follows:

- Device Settings
- Access Rules
- Translation Rules
- Building Blocks
- View Config
- MC Settings

Click an option to display the information in the content area or a menu of available choices (known as the TOC) on the left side of the Firewall MC interface.

Table of Contents

The *table of contents* (*TOC*) is a menu of choices that is displayed on the left side of the Firewall MC interface. It presents a list of suboptions you can select based on the option chosen. As shown in Figure 14-3, for instance, the Configuration > Device Settings option has the following selections:

- Firewall OS Version
- Interfaces
- Failover
- Auto Update Server
- Routing
- Firewall Device Administration
- Logging

- Servers and Services
- Advanced Security
- Config Additions

Path Bar

The *path bar* provides a visual road map indicating where you are with respect to the Firewall MC interface. It is located above the TOC and below the options bar, and it begins with the text "You Are Here."

Figure 14-3 shows a situation in which the value of the path bar is Configuration > Device Settings > Interfaces. This indicates that you performed the following steps to reach the current window:

Step 1   You clicked the **Configuration** tab.

Step 2   You clicked the **Device Settings** option.

Step 3   You clicked the **Interfaces** TOC option.

Instructions Box

Some pages provide you with an *Instructions box* on the right side of the Firewall MC display. When displayed, this box provides you with a brief overview of the page that you have selected. The Instructions box provides less information than the Help option on the tools bar.

Content Area

The *content area* displays the information associated with the option that you selected (when no TOC selections are available) or the selection in the TOC that you click.

Scope Bar

The *Scope bar* displays the object or objects that you have selected using the Object Selector. Figure 14-3 shows a situation in which you have selected the firewall named PIX515A from the Perimeter firewall group, which is part of the Global group. When you perform configuration changes, the Scope bar indicates which devices will receive updated configuration information.

Object Selector

When making configuration changes using Firewall MC, you need to specify to which device or devices you want to apply changes. By clicking the *Object Selector*, you can select individual firewalls or firewall groups (see Figure 14-4). Any changes that you specify are then applied to that firewall or firewall group. The Scope bar indicates the device or group that you currently have selected.

Figure 14-4   *Object Selector*

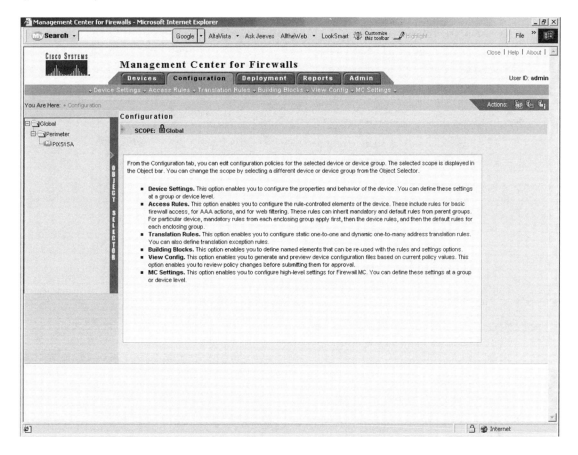

Tools Bar

Located in the upper-right portion of the Firewall MC interface is the *Tools bar*. The Tools bar has the following options:

■   Close

- Help
- About

Click **Close** to log out of the current Firewall MC user session. Select **Help** to open another browser window that displays detailed context-sensitive help information on using Firewall MC. Finally, click **About** to display information about the version of Firewall MC that you are using.

Activity Bar

The activity bar displays activities and Actions icons that vary depending on the information that you are changing. The activity bar is shown only when you are operating in either the Devices or Configuration tabs of the Firewall MC. The Actions icons that can be shown are as follows:

- **Add**—Add a new activity
- **Open**—Open a new or existing activity (selected from a popup window)
- **Close**—Close the activity shown by the activity bar
- **Save and Deploy**—Save and generate a device configuration file
- **Submit**—Submit an activity
- **Reject**—Reject an activity
- **Approve**—Approve an activity
- **Undo**—Discard the activity shown by the activity bar
- **View Details**—show the details of the current changes

> **NOTE** Some of the activity options are not available unless you enable workflow. Workflow is explained later in the chapter.

Basic User Task Flow

Firewall MC provides you with a flexible graphical user environment in which to manage and configure the firewall devices deployed throughout the network. When you first begin to use Firewall MC, however, you might become confused as to where to start. Therefore, it is helpful to understand the basic user task flow involved in using Firewall MC. The following steps illustrate the basic task flow:

Step 1   Create device groups.

Step 2   Import/create devices.

Step 3   Configure building blocks.

Step 4   Configure device settings.

Step 5   Configure access and translation rules.

Step 6   Generate and view the configuration.

Step 7   Deploy the configuration.

> **NOTE**   The approval process for configuration changes is disabled by default. If you enable this process (see the "Workflow Setup" section later in the chapter), before you can deploy your changes you will have to follow the approval process for those changes.

Each step is explained in detail in the following sections. Each section is broken down based on the five configuration tabs available in the Firewall MC interface:

■   Device management

■   Configuration tasks

■   Deployment tasks

■   Reports

■   Administration tasks

Device Management

When using the Firewall MC, all managed devices are members of a group named Global. You also can group your firewalls into subgroups that share similar properties (such as configuration settings or geographic location). Grouping similar devices facilitates management of those devices. You can also import existing configurations into Firewall MC. These activities are accessed through the Devices configuration tab. The tasks in this section include the following:

■   Managing groups

■   Importing devices

■   Managing devices

Managing Groups

Select **Devices > Managing Groups** to add new groups to the system, modify existing groups, and delete existing groups (see Figure 14-5). When defining group names, it is helpful to use descriptive names that clearly identify the different groups. For example, you may identify your groups based on geographic region or department within the company.

> **NOTE** Subgroup names must be unique within an enclosing group.

Figure 14-5 *Managing Groups*

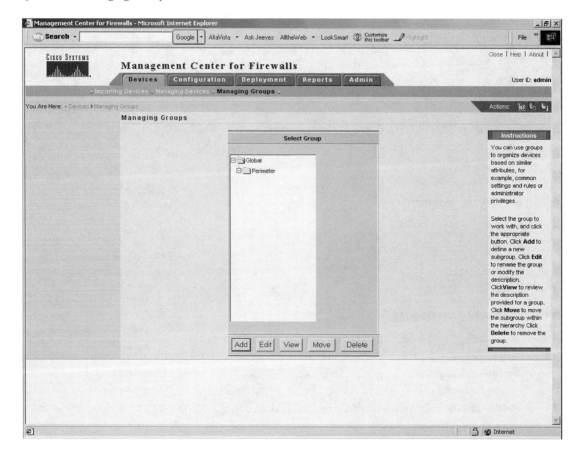

When managing groups, you can perform the following operations:

- **Add**—Add new groups
- **Edit**—Rename existing groups
- **View**—View the description for a group
- **Move**—Move the group to a new location in the hierarchy
- **Delete**—Remove an existing group

Importing Devices

After defining your device groups, you can then import devices into those groups using the Devices > Import Devices option. When importing devices, you perform the following four basic steps:

Step 1   Select the target group.

Step 2   Select the import type.

Step 3   Define firewall device basic information.

Step 4   Review summary details.

You have several options when importing devices into Firewall MC (see Figure 14-6). Table 14-5 explains the various import options that are available.

Table 14-5   *Device Import Options*

Import Option	Description
Create Firewall Device	Allows you to add a single device manually.
Import configuration from device	Allows you to provide device credentials manually that enable the Firewall MC server to communicate directly with the device to retrieve the configuration.
Import configuration file for a device	Allows you to import configuration information for a single device from a configuration file.
Import multiple firewall configurations from a CSV file	Allows the Firewall MC server to communicate directly with multiple firewalls (specified in a comma-separated value [CSV] file) to retrieve configuration information.
Import configuration files for multiple devices	Allows you to import multiple configuration files from a single directory. Each file contains configuration information for a single device.

NOTE   You can import from a device only once. To reimport a device's configuration, you must first delete the device and then import it again.

Figure 14-6 *Select Import Type*

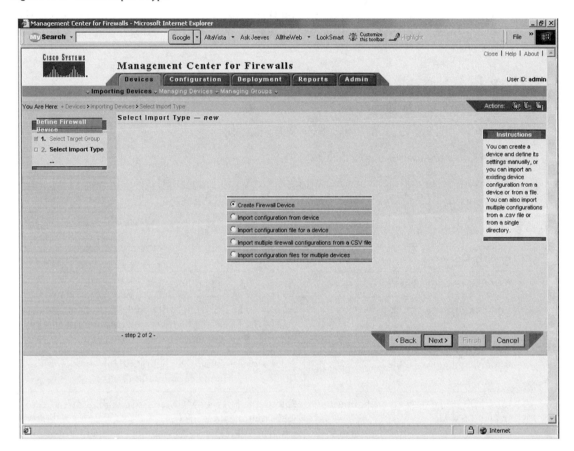

If you select the Import configuration from device option as the import type, you must provide the following parameters that Firewall MC needs to communicate with the device being imported (see Figure 14-7):

- **Contact User Name**—(Optional) The username used when connecting to the firewall
- **Contact IP Address**—The IP address used to connect to the firewall
- **Password**—The firewall enable password

Figure 14-7 *Firewall Contact Information*

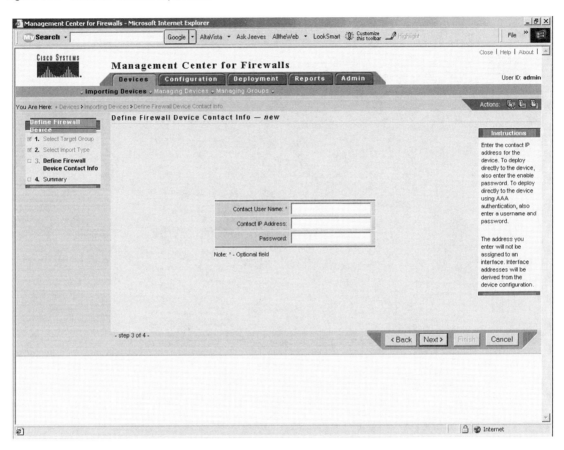

After specifying all of the characteristics for the device being imported, you will see an Import Status window (see Figure 14-8). This window displays the progress of the actual import process, and it automatically updates itself every 60 seconds. You can also force the window to update by clicking the **Refresh** button.

Figure 14-8 *Import Status Window*

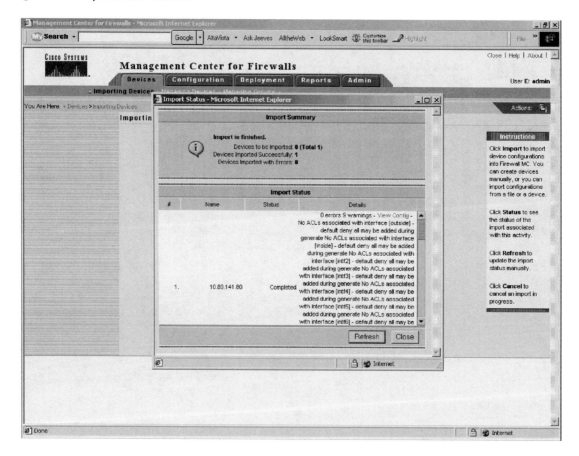

When the import is complete, you can view the configuration of the device by clicking the **View Config** link located in the Details section of the Import Status window (see Figure 14-8).

Managing Devices

Sometimes you need to remove devices or move them from one group to another. To perform these types of device operations, select **Devices > Managing Devices**. The Managing Devices window enables you to move a device from one group to another and remove existing devices (see Figure 14-9).

Figure 14-9 *Managing Devices*

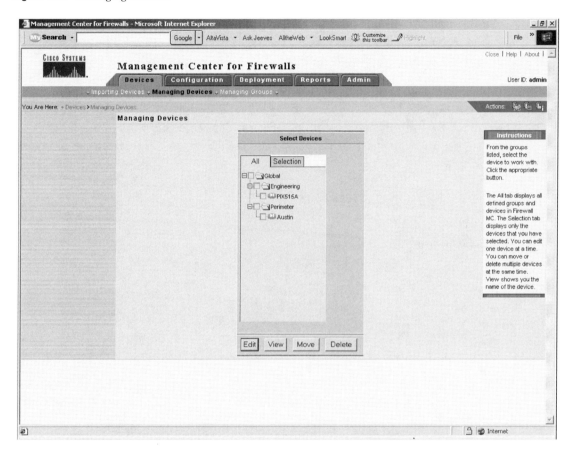

Configuration Tasks

The majority of the tasks that you perform in Firewall MC involves configuration tasks. Configuration settings control individual features of a firewall device. When defining these settings, you can apply them either to a specific firewall or to all of the firewalls in a group by selecting a group instead of an individual firewall. The scope of the changes that you make depends on the object that you select using the Object Selector before making the configuration changes (see the section entitled "Object Selector" earlier in this chapter). These tasks can be broken down into the following categories, each of which is discussed in detail in this section:

- Configuring device settings

- Defining access rules
- Defining translation rules
- Creating building blocks
- Generating and viewing configuration information

Configuring Device Settings

Through the Firewall MC, you can configure many device-specific properties on your managed firewalls. Following are the majority of the device settings that you can configure through Firewall MC:

- PIX operating system version
- Interfaces
- Failover
- Routing
- PIX Firewall administration
- Logging
- Servers and services
- Advanced security
- Firewall MC controls

One common task is changing the properties of the interfaces on the firewalls managed by the Firewall MC software. If you configure a firewall using Setup, it configures only the inside interface. Before you can define the access or translation rules, you must configure the rest of the interfaces on the firewall.

Defining Access Rules

Access rules, which control the traffic that flows through your firewall, are used to define your network security policy. Each access rule is a member of an order list of rules that Firewall MC stores in a table. Rules are processed from first to last. A firewall uses the first matching rule to determine whether the traffic is permitted or denied.

You can configure the following three types of access rules (see Figure 14-10):

- Firewall rules
- Authentication, authorization, and accounting (AAA) rules
- Web filter rules

Figure 14-10 *Access Rules*

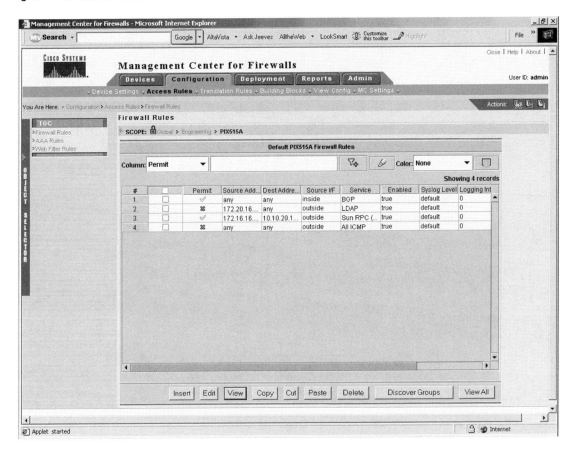

In Firewall MC, you can view a list of access rules that spans all of the different interfaces (see Figure 14-10). Each access rule shown is converted into a single entry in an access control list (ACL) on a specific interface for the managed firewall.

Defining Translation Rules

Translation rules enable you to configure and view the address translations that you are using on the network. You can configure the following types of translation rules using Firewall MC:

- Static translation rules
- Dynamic translation rules
- Translation exception rules (NAT 0 ACL)

> **NOTE** Firewall MC supports both Network Address Translation (NAT) and Port
> Address Translation (PAT).

Static translation rules permanently map an internal IP address to a publicly accessible global
IP address. These rules assign a host on a higher-security-level interface to a global IP address
on a lower-security interface. This enables the hosts from the lower-security zone to
communicate with the host from the higher-security zone. Figure 14-11 shows a static
translation rule that assigns the local address of a protected host (10.10.10.20/32 on the
inside interface) to a global address (192.168.10.20/32 on the outside) that is accessible by
external systems.

Figure 14-11 *Static Translation Rules*

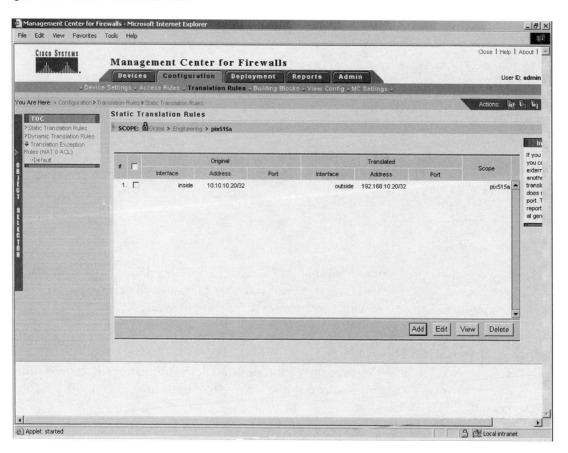

Unlike static translation rules, dynamic translation rules do not permanently map an internal IP address to a global IP address. These rules dynamically map an internal IP address to a global IP address from a pool of IP addresses when using NAT or to a single IP address when using PAT. Figure 14-12 shows a dynamic translation rule that translates traffic from any address on the inside interface to a global address using the address translation pool named *public* for outbound traffic.

Figure 14-12 *Dynamic Translation Rules*

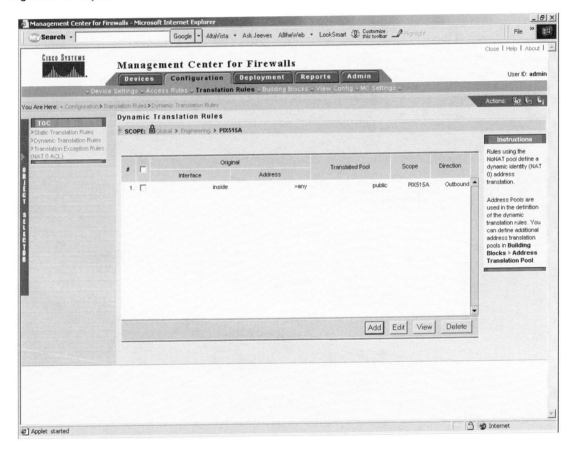

Before you can configure a dynamic translation rule, however, you need to define the appropriate address translation pool. This pool identifies which addresses can be temporarily associated with outbound traffic from a specific internal host. For more information on address translation pools, refer to the following section, "Creating Building Blocks."

Creating Building Blocks

Building blocks enable you to optimize your configuration. Building blocks define groups of objects such as hosts, protocols, or services. You can then issue a command that affects every item in the group by specifying the name of the group. Basically, you can use the names of the building blocks in place of corresponding data values when configuring device settings or defining rules. You can configure the following types of building blocks, each of which is described within this section:

- Network objects
- Service definitions
- Service groups
- AAA server groups
- Address translation pools

Network Objects

Network objects enable you to group a range of network addresses specified by an IP address and a network mask. These network objects can then be used in access rules and translation rules. In Figure 14-13, the network object named DMZ is associated with the Class C network 172.16.10.0/24.

Figure 14-13 *Network Objects*

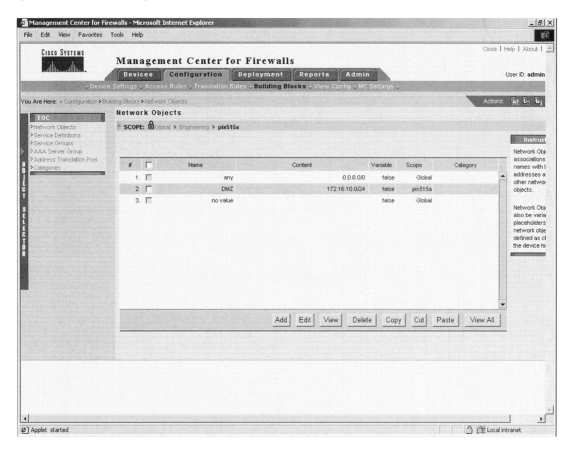

You can use DMZ in access and translation rules by clicking the **Select** button whenever you normally specify an IP address (see Figure 14-14). The Selecting Network Objects window is displayed (see Figure 14-15). To use one of the list objects, click the object name, and then click **Select=>** to move the name to the Selected Objects column.

Figure 14-14 *Creating a Static Translation Rule*

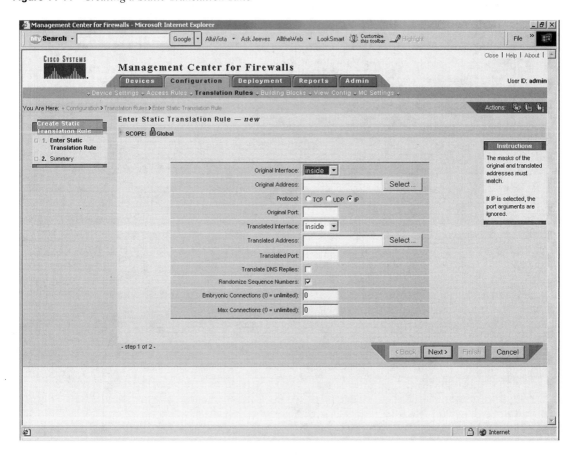

Figure 14-15 *Selecting Network Objects*

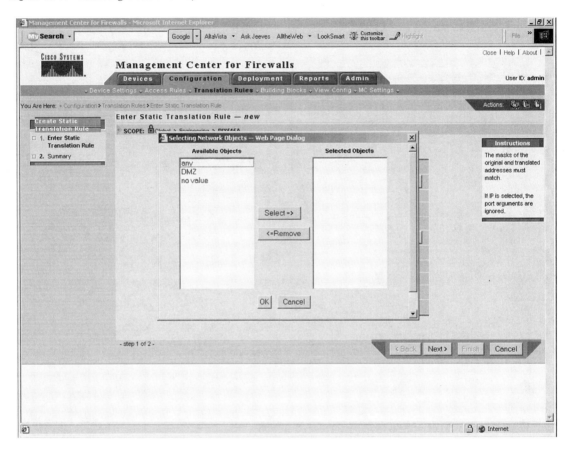

Service Definitions

Service definitions enable you to define objects that associate IP protocols, Transmission Control Protocol (TCP) and User Datagram Protocol (UDP) source and destination ports, and Internet Control Message Protocol (ICMP) message types with a specific name (see Figure 14-16). These service definitions are then used in firewall device protocol groups, service groups, and ICMP-type groups, respectively.

Figure 14-16 *Service Definitions*

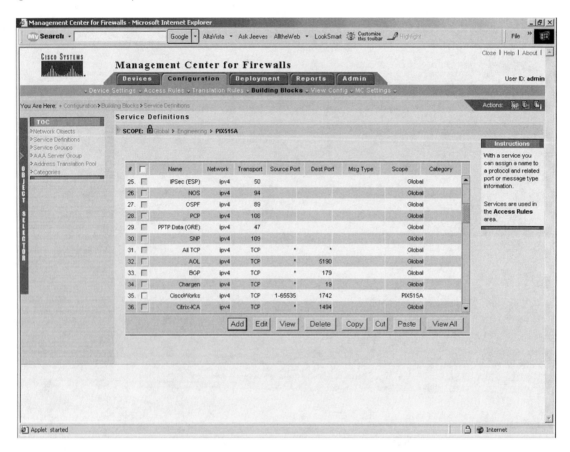

Similar to other building blocks, you can use service definitions whenever you would normally specify a service (such as defining firewall rules) by clicking the **Add** button. This opens the Selecting Services window (see Figure 14-17), enabling you to select the appropriate service definition.

Figure 14-17 *Selecting Services*

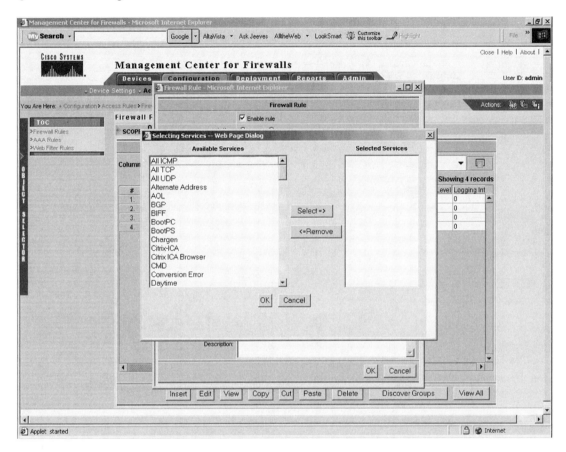

Service Groups

Service groups enable you to define objects that associate a name with a group of service definitions (see Figure 14-18). For instance, you can create a service group that permits both HTTPS and Secure Shell (SSH) traffic.

Figure 14-18 *Service Groups*

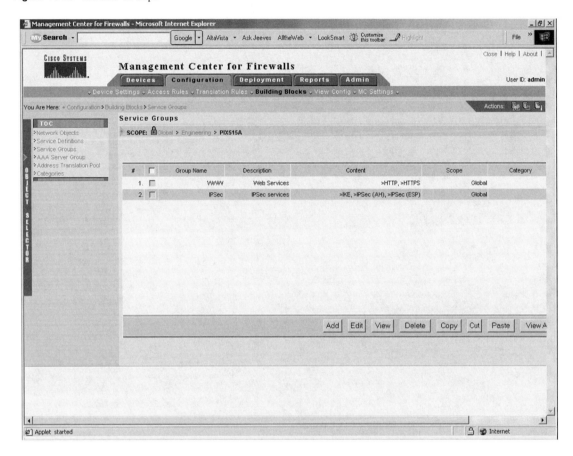

AAA Server Groups

AAA server groups enable you to define separate groups of Terminal Access Controller Access Control System Plus (TACACS+) and Remote Authentication Dial-In User Service (RADIUS) servers that are used for different types of traffic. Traffic will attempt to authenticate with the fist server in the AAA server group. If this server is inaccessible, the next server in the group is tried.

NOTE You can define 14 AAA server groups, each containing 14 distinct AAA servers, supporting a total of 196 AAA servers.

Address Translation Pools

Address translation pools enable you to associate a name with a group of addresses that will be used to create dynamic address translations for outbound traffic. When defining an address translation pool, you need to specify the parameters shown in Table 14-6.

Table 14-6 *Address Translation Pool Parameters*

Parameter	Description
Pool Name	Name used when applying the pool to a dynamic translation rule.
Interface	Logical name of the interface where the pool will be used.
PAT: Use interface address for closing PAT Check Box	Select this check box to indicate that the IP address of the interface will be used as the PAT address when all of the other addresses in the pool have been used.
Address Range(s)/Mask (optional)	Set of addresses (in addition to the interface address) that will be used for dynamic translations.

For address translation pools, PAT is used when you have more internal addresses than external addresses. The firewall automatically uses the last available address to perform PAT. If you select the **PAT** check box (see Figure 14-19) when defining the address translation pool, after all of the addresses in the pool are used, the interface address is used for PAT.

Figure 14-19 *Defining an Address Translation Pool*

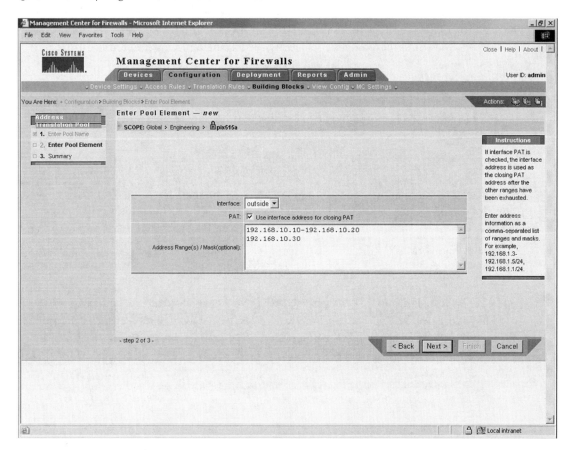

Generating and Viewing Configuration Information

Selecting **Configuration > View Config > Generate Config** allows you to generate the configuration for a specific device. The Scope bar indicates for which device the configuration will be generated. Once the configuration is generated, you can then view the information in the content area (see Figure 14-20).

Figure 14-20 *Viewing Generated Configuration*

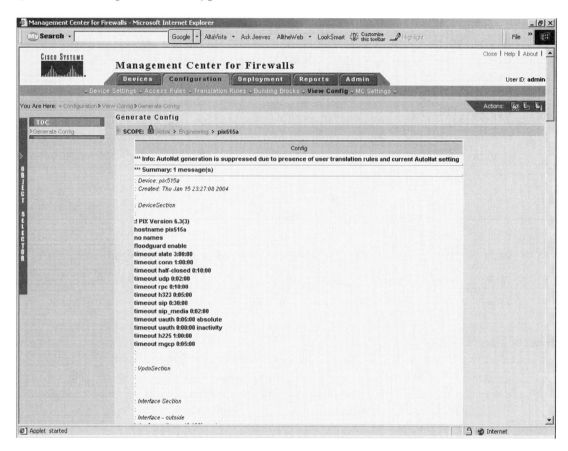

MC Settings

Selecting **Configuration > MC Settings** allows you to control how Firewall MC operates when it discovers commands configured outside of Firewall MC or unsupported and error commands imported into Firewall MC. It also identifies the directories in which imported and deployed configurations will be placed.

When configuring the MC settings, you have the following options:

- Management
- Deployment
- Import

- Feature Tracking
- Object Grouping

> **NOTE**   When configuring the AUS, you use the Deployment option to redirect configuration updates to the AUS instead of sending them directly to the managed device.

Deployment Tasks

After you make changes to the configuration for a managed device, you must deploy those changes on the actual firewalls on your network. You have the following two options when you select the Deployment configuration tab:

- Deploy Saved Changes
- Summary Report

> **NOTE**   These are the options available when workflow is not enabled. If workflow is enabled, refer to the "Workflow Setup" section later in the chapter for the options that are available.

Deploy Saved Changes

Select **Deployment > Deploy Saved Changes** to cause the Firewall MC to generate the updated configuration files for the device or devices specified by the Scope bar. The Generate Summary window initially shows the deployment options as unavailable until the generation process is complete. Once the generation process is finished, you can deploy the changes to your managed firewalls (see Figure 14-21) using the following options:

- Deploy Now
- Deploy Later

> **NOTE**   Click the **Save & Deploy** icon on the activity bar to select the **Deploy Saved Changes** functionality without accessing it through the Deployment configuration tab.

Figure 14-21 *Generate Summary Window*

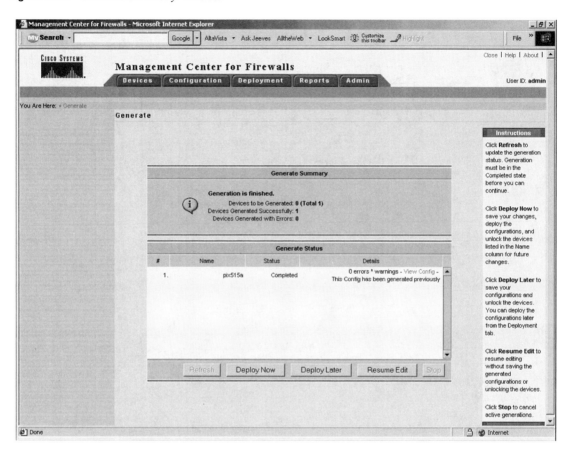

Click the **Deploy Now** button to deploy the new configurations to your managed devices immediately, or click the **Deploy Later** button to delay deploying the new configurations.

After you deploy new configurations, a deployment summary window appears (see Figure 14-22). This window summarizes the results of the deployment process and lets you know the status of the deployment process. It also indicates whether the deployment generated any errors or warnings on the managed firewalls when the configuration commands were executed.

Figure 14-22 *Deployment Status Summary Window*

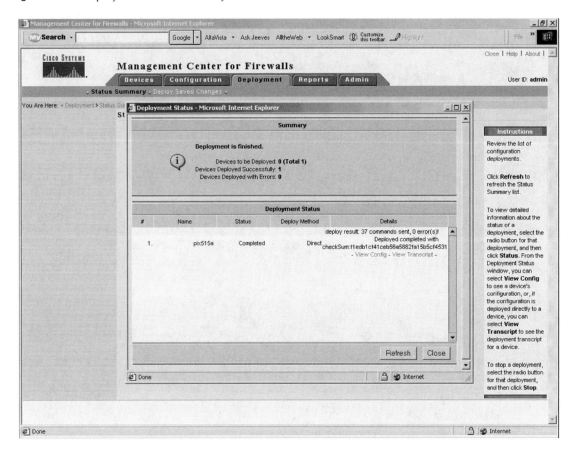

The Deployment Status Summary window (in Figure 14-22) contains the following two links that you can use to view information about your deployed changes:

- View Config
- View Transcript

Click the **View Config** link to display the deployed configuration for the managed firewall (see Figure 14-23), or click the **View Transcript** link to display a window that shows a transcript of all configuration commands that were executed and their success status (see Figure 14-24).

Figure 14-23 *Viewing the Config Window*

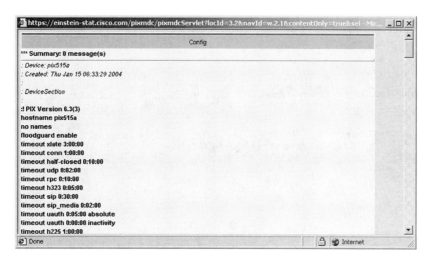

Figure 14-24 *Viewing the Deploy Transcript Window*

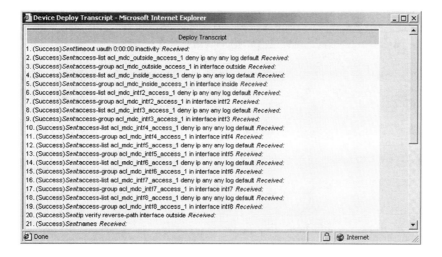

Summary Report

Select **Deployment > Status Summary** to display the history of the deployment changes that you have made to your managed firewalls (see Figure 14-25).

Figure 14-25 *Status Summary Window*

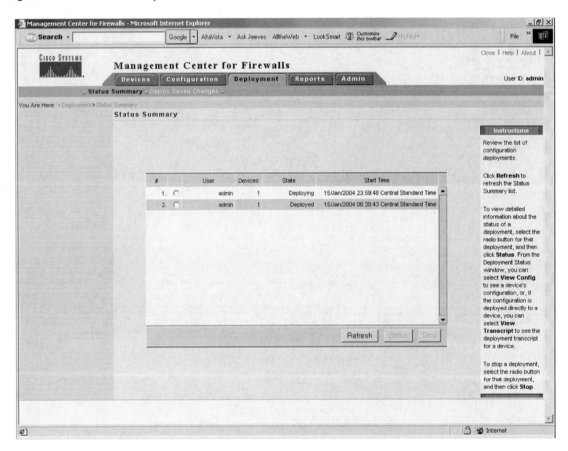

Reports

In the Reports tab, you can view the following three reports:

- Activity Report
- Configuration Differences report
- Device Setting Report

Activity Report

The Activity Report, as the name implies, displays information about the activities or configuration changes that have occurred on the Firewall MC (see Figure 14-26). For each activity, the report provides the following two pieces of information:

- User that performed the activity and when the change happened
- The actual configuration changes that were made

NOTE   If you do not have workflow enabled, the Activity Report shows only the changes that were made. It does not identify the user that performed the changes.

Figure 14-26 *Activity Report*

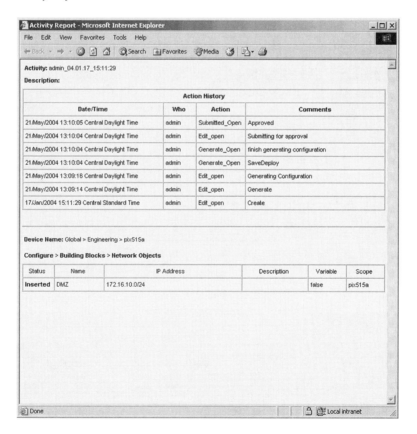

Configuration Differences Report

The Configuration Differences report enables you to determine if the running configuration on a managed firewall matches the latest configuration that you deployed to it. You can also use this report to determine which managed firewalls have an updated configuration waiting to be deployed. You can generate reports based on the following two options:

- The approved configuration does not match the deployed configuration.
- The deployed configuration does not match the running configuration.

Initially, you select the device or group on which you want to check for configuration differences. This displays a window indicating the firewalls that have configuration differences. To view the actual differences, click the **View Configuration Differences** link next to a specific device. This displays a window outlining the actual configuration differences (see Figure 14-27).

Figure 14-27 *Configuration Differences Report*

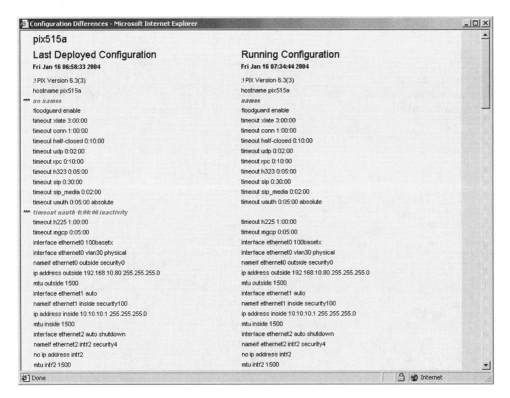

Device Setting Report

The Device Setting Report enables you to view the device settings for a device or device group. Each setting also indicates how the setting was derived. Each setting is determined based on one of the following categories:

- Inherited
- Mandatory
- Overridden

You have the following two options when generating this report:

- Show inheritance only
- Show inheritance and values

The Show inheritance only option displays a list of all of the device settings, indicating how the setting was derived (see Figure 14-28). The Show inheritance and values option includes the actual values for the settings in addition to how the settings were derived (see Figure 14-29).

Figure 14-28 *Show Inheritance Only Device Setting Report*

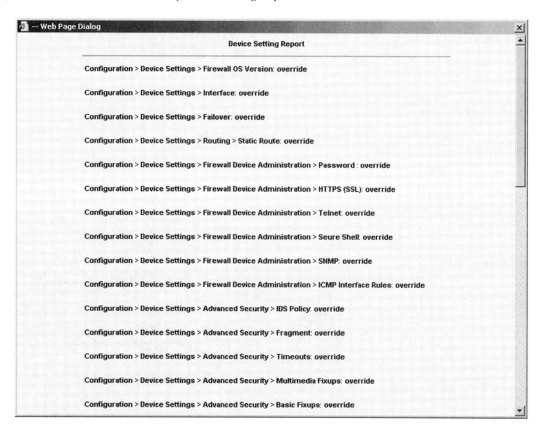

Figure 14-29 *Show Inheritance and Values Device Setting Report*

Device Setting Report

Configuration > Device Settings > Firewall OS Version: override

Supported Version: PIX6.3(3)

Configuration > Device Settings > Interface: override

Hardware ID	VLAN ID	Speed	Interface Name	Security Level	MTU	IP Addess	Address Type	Enabled
ethernet0	vlan30	basetx100	outside	0	1500	192.168.10.80 / 24	staticip	enabled
ethernet1		aut	inside	100	1500	10.10.10.1 / 24	staticip	enabled
ethernet2		aut	intf2	4	1500	127.0.0.1 / 32	staticip	disabled
ethernet3		aut	intf3	6	1500	127.0.0.1 / 32	staticip	disabled
ethernet4		aut	intf4	8	1500	172.16.1.1 / 24	staticip	enabled
ethernet5		aut	intf5	10	1500	10.89.141.80 / 24	staticip	enabled
ethernet0	vlan40		intf6	12		127.0.0.1 / 32	staticip	enabled
ethernet0	vlan41		intf7	14		127.0.0.1 / 32	staticip	enabled
ethernet0	vlan42		intf8	16		127.0.0.1 / 32	staticip	enabled

Configuration > Device Settings > Failover: override

Failover Poll Time (seconds): 15

Configuration > Device Settings > Routing > Static Route: override

Interface	IP Address	Gateway IP	Metric
inside	10.10.20.0 / 24	10.10.10.2	2
intf5	0.0.0.0 / 0	10.89.141.1	1

Administration Tasks

The administration tasks fall into the following categories:

■ Workflow Setup

■ Maintenance

■ Support

Workflow Setup

The Firewall MC software enables you to configure firewalls as well as groups of firewalls. By default, when you make changes, they are propagated to your firewalls as soon as you save and deploy the changes. If you enable workflow (by selecting **Admin > Workflow Setup**), however, there is a distinct process that you must follow to deploy your changes to the appropriate firewalls. This process allows you to track changes down to the individual user that performed the changes. The workflow process establishes the following three distinct steps in the configuration process:

Step 1   Define configuration changes.

Step 2   Approve configuration changes.

Step 3   Deploy configuration changes.

A separate person can be in charge of each step, thus dividing the responsibility for updating the configuration on the managed firewalls.

When using workflow, policy changes (known as *activities* and *jobs*) regulate the deployment of configuration files. You can require formal approval for activities, jobs, or both. The Firewall MC interface also changes. The Deployment configuration tab is replaced with a Workflow configuration tab (see Figure 14-30).

Figure 14-30   *Firewall MC Interface with Workflow Enabled*

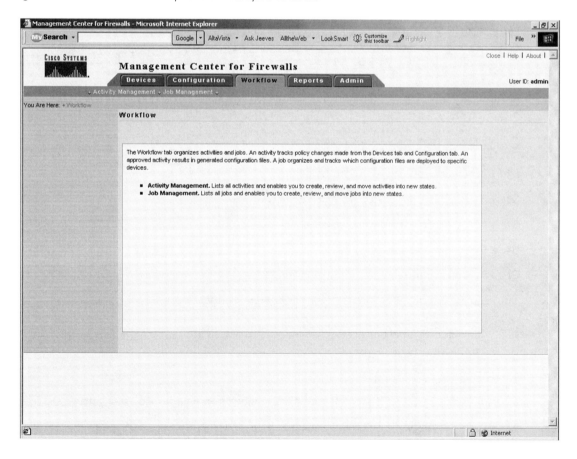

Through workflow, you regulate activities (configuration changes) by using the following options:

- **Add**—Creates a new activity
- **Open**—Opens an existing activity to add more configuration changes
- **Close**—Changes the state of the activity so that it can be submitted
- **Status**—Displays the status of an activity
- **Info**—Displays the changes that make up the activity
- **Submit**—Submits an activity for approval
- **Undo**—Rolls back activity changes
- **Approve**—Approves the changes in an activity
- **Reject**—Rejects the changes in an activity
- **Cancel**—Cancels an active import or any generate actions currently in operation for the activity

> **NOTE** The various activity options are unavailable unless they are valid for the activity selected. For instance, you cannot approve an activity that has not been submitted.

Creating a job to deploy configuration changes (from specified activities) involves the following steps:

Step 1 Specify a job name.

Step 2 Select the activities to be deployed.

Step 3 Select the devices to receive the changes.

Step 4 Review the devices selected.

Step 5 Change the job state.

Step 6 Examine summary information.

You regulate and manage jobs using the following options:

- **Add**—Creates a new job
- **Status**—Displays detailed status of a job
- **Submit**—Submits a job for approval
- **Rollback**—Enables you to roll back the configuration on a firewall to a previous version
- **Approve**—Approves the job for deployment

- **Reject**—Rejects the job
- **Deploy**—Deploys the changes in an approved job
- **Cancel**—Cancels the deployment or rollback operation that is currently in process

NOTE The various job options are unavailable unless they are valid for the activity selected. For instance, you cannot approve a job that has not been submitted.

Maintenance

Depending on how frequently you perform configuration updates, you may want to remove old activity and job records periodically. Select **Admin > Maintenance** to configure how often activity and job records are automatically purged from the database (see Figure 14-31). For both activities and jobs, you can specify how old an entry must be before it is automatically removed from the database (the default is 30 days).

Figure 14-31 *Maintenance Window*

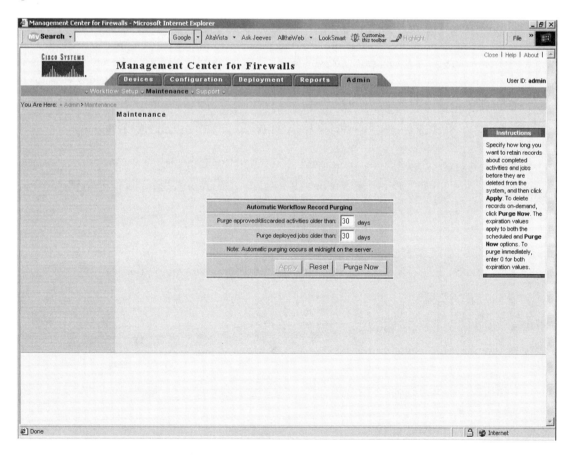

Support

When debugging your system, you may need to obtain some important operational information about your system. Select **Admin > Support** to run a program specifically designed to collect information to assist in troubleshooting the operation of your Firewall MC system.

CiscoWorks Auto Update Server

Maintaining current images on your managed devices can be a time-consuming task. The AUS is a tool that you can use to upgrade device configuration files and maintain current software images on your managed firewalls. The main advantage of AUS is that it can manage devices that obtain their addresses through Dynamic Host Configuration Protocol (DHCP). Remotely managed PIX Firewalls are often dynamically addressed, which means they cannot be managed by traditional network management servers.

The managed devices use an auto update feature to initiate a management connection periodically to the AUS. The device provides AUS with its current state and device information. The AUS then responds to the device by providing a list of versions of the software images and configuration files that the device should be running. The device compares the file versions with the versions it is running. If there are differences, the device downloads the new versions from the URLs provided by the AUS. Once the device is up-to-date with the new file versions, it sends AUS its state and device information again.

Some of the major features provided by AUS (Version 1.0) include the following:

- Web-based interface for maintaining multiple PIX Firewalls
- Support for PIX Firewall Version 6.0 and later (Version 6.2 and later for AUS Version 1.1)
- Support for dynamically addressed PIX Firewalls
- Support for up to 1000 PIX Firewalls

AUS Version 1.1 adds new functionality, including the following major features:

- Installation on Solaris
- Additional report formats
- Support for configuration files

Supported Devices

AUS supports PIX Firewalls running Versions 6.0 and later. In addition, AUS supports the following PIX hardware platforms:

- PIX 501
- PIX 506/506E
- PIX 515/515E
- PIX 525
- PIX 535

Installation

CiscoWorks Common Services (Version 2.2) is required for AUS. The requirements for the CiscoWorks server are described in the "CiscoWorks Management Center for Firewalls Overview" section earlier in this chapter. Once you have the CiscoWorks server built, the installation of AUS is easy and involves the following steps:

Step 1   Insert the AUS CD into the CD drive on the CiscoWorks server. If autorun is enabled, the installation process starts automatically. If not, you must locate the setup.exe file and run it. Once the installation process starts, the Welcome window is displayed.

Step 2   Click **Next.** The software license window is displayed.

Step 3   If you agree to the software license agreement, click **Yes.** (If you click **No,** the installation process will stop.) The system requirements window is displayed.

Step 4   Click **Next.** The Verification window is displayed.

Step 5   Click **Next.** A popup window is displayed that asks if you want to change the AUS database password. Click **Yes** to change the password.

Step 6   Click **Finish.** The AUS installation is now complete.

> **NOTE**   AUS operates in unison with the Firewall MC to update the configuration files on firewalls running in auto update mode. AUS and the Firewall MC, however, do not have to be collocated on the same machine. Because of their different roles and responsibilities, these systems are typically installed on separate machines with Firewall MC located in your network operations center (NOC) and the AUS deployed on a demilitarized zone (DMZ) network.

Communication Settings

To configure and use AUS effectively, you need to understand the AUS communication architecture. The following steps describe the interaction between the PIX Firewall, Firewall MC, and AUS (see Figure 14-32).

Step 1   The Firewall MC deploys a configuration file to the AUS.

Step 2   At a configured polling interval, the managed PIX Firewall contacts the AUS to determine if there are any pending updates.

Step 3   The AUS sends a list of image files and/or configuration files that the PIX Firewall should be running.

Step 4   The PIX Firewall checks its configuration and image against the information provided by the AUS. If the PIX Firewall is not using the most current files, it requests the updated files from the AUS.

Step 5   The needed files are downloaded to the PIX Firewall.

Figure 14-32   *AUS Communication Flow*

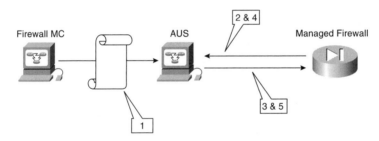

AUS Activation

To enable your managed firewalls to communicate with the AUS, you need to perform certain configuration changes using Firewall MC. The sequence of the changes is as follows:

Step 1   From the PIX console, enable the firewall to accept HTTP connections from the AUS.

Step 2   From Firewall MC, configure the following items:

- AUS and PIX Firewall communications
- PIX Firewall unique identification parameters
- AUS contact information

Step 3   Deploy the updated configuration to the managed firewall.

Step 4   From Firewall MC, modify the PIX Firewall Configuration Deployment options so that configuration updates are sent to the AUS server instead of the device.

Auto Update Server and PIX Firewall Communications

After you configure the PIX Firewall to accept HTTP connections from the AUS, you need to configure the AUS communications parameters on the PIX Firewall by completing the following steps:

Step 1   Log in to CiscoWorks, and launch Firewall MC.

Step 2   Choose **Configuration > Device Settings** to access the device configuration settings.

Step 3   If workflow is enabled, you need to select an existing activity or create a new activity from the activity bar.

Step 4   Use the Object Selector to select a specific group or device.

Step 5   Select **Auto Update Server > Device AUS Settings** from the TOC. The Device AUS Settings window is displayed (see Figure 14-33).

Figure 14-33 *Device AUS Settings Window*

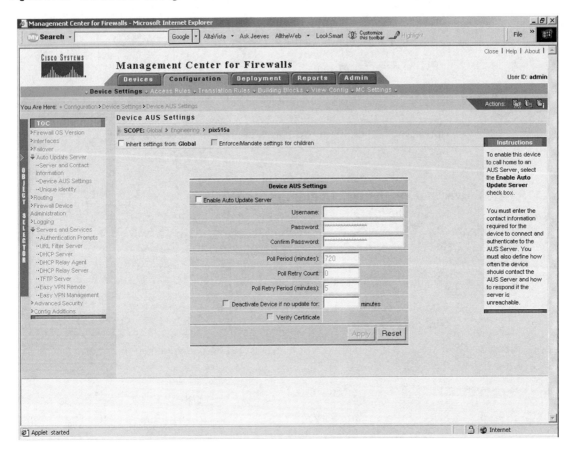

Step 6   Check the **Enable Auto Update Server** check box.

Step 7   Enter the unique ID (username) the PIX Firewall will use to contact the AUS in the **Username** field.

Step 8   Enter the password for the username specified.

Step 9   Confirm the password by entering it in the **Confirm Password** field.

Step 10   Enter the number of minutes in the **Poll Period** field (the default is 720 minutes). This parameter specifies the time that the PIX Firewall will wait between connections to the AUS to check for updates.

Step 11   Enter the number of times that the PIX Firewall will try to contact the AUS (if the initial attempt fails) in the **Poll Retry Count** field (the default is 0).

Step 12   Enter the number of minutes between poll retries in the **Poll Retry Period** field (the default is 5 minutes).

Step 13   If you want the PIX Firewall to deactivate itself if an update is not received in a specified number of minutes, check the **Deactivate Device if no update for** check box and specify the number of minutes.

Step 14   Click **Apply.**

PIX Firewall Unique Identification Parameters

When the PIX Firewall communicates with the AUS, the PIX Firewall must uniquely identify itself to the AUS. This unique identification enables the AUS to search its database of current assignments to locate entries that pertain to the specific PIX Firewall that is communicating with it. To configure the PIX Firewall unique identity parameters, complete the following steps:

Step 1   Log in to CiscoWorks, and launch Firewall MC.

Step 2   Choose **Configuration > Device Settings** to access the device configuration settings.

Step 3   If workflow is enabled, you need to select an existing activity or create a new activity from the activity bar.

Step 4   Use the Object Selector to select a specific group or device.

Step 5   Select **Auto Update Server > Unique Identity** from the TOC. The Device Unique Identity window is displayed (see Figure 14-34).

Figure 14-34 *Device Unique Identity Window*

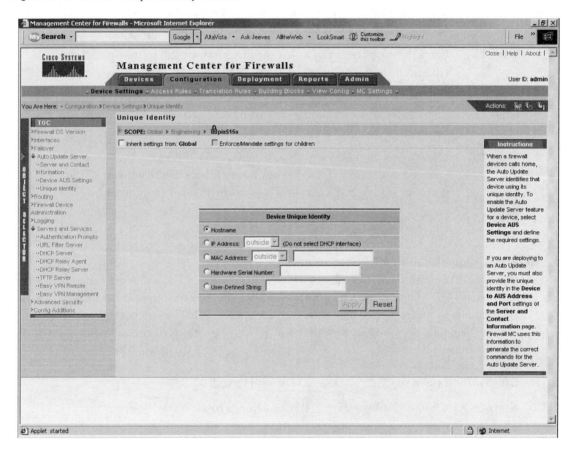

Step 6 Choose the unique identifier by selecting the radio button next to one of the following items:

- Hostname
- IP Address
- MAC Address
- Hardware Serial Number
- User-Defined String

Step 7 Click **Apply.**

Auto Update Server Contact information

Next you need to specify the contact information for the AUS. The Firewall MC will use this information to communicate with the AUS. To configure the AUS contact information, complete the following steps:

Step 1   Log in to CiscoWorks, and launch Firewall MC.

Step 2   Choose **Configuration > Device Settings** to access the device configuration settings.

Step 3   If workflow is enabled, you need to select an existing activity or create a new activity from the activity bar.

Step 4   Use the Object Selector to select a specific group or device.

Step 5   Select **Auto Update Server > Server and Contact Information** from the TOC. The Server and Contact Information window is displayed (see Figure 14-35).

Figure 14-35   *AUS Server and Contact Information Window*

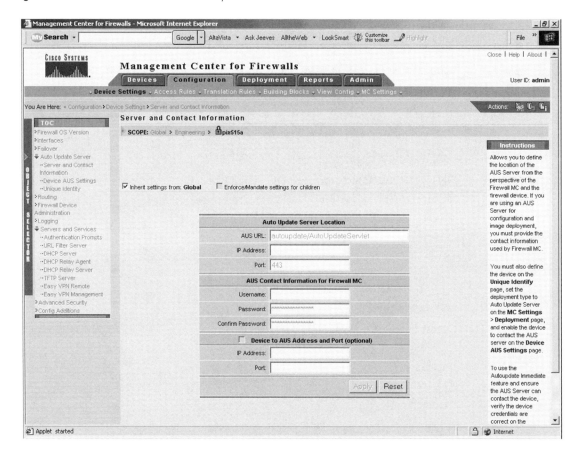

Step 6   Enter the directory path where the updates are stored on the AUS (the default path is Autoupdate/AutoUpdateServlet).

Step 7   Enter the IP address of the AUS server.

Step 8   Enter the port (default 443).

Step 9   In the **Username** field, enter the CiscoWorks username that Firewall MC will use to communicate with the AUS.

Step 10 In the **Password** field, enter the password for the username specified.

Step 11 In the **Confirm Password** field, confirm the password by entering it again.

Step 12 Click **Apply.**

PIX Firewall Configuration Deployment

Finally, you need to configure the Firewall MC to send configuration updates to the AUS instead of the actual device. To specify this configuration change, complete the following steps:

Step 1   Log in to CiscoWorks, and launch Firewall MC.

Step 2   Choose **Configuration > MC Settings** to access the Firewall MC configuration settings.

Step 3   If workflow is enabled, you need to select an existing activity or create a new activity from the activity bar.

Step 4   Use the Object Selector to select a specific group or device.

Step 5   Select **Deployment** from the TOC. The Deployment window is displayed (see Figure 14-36).

Figure 14-36 *Deployment Window*

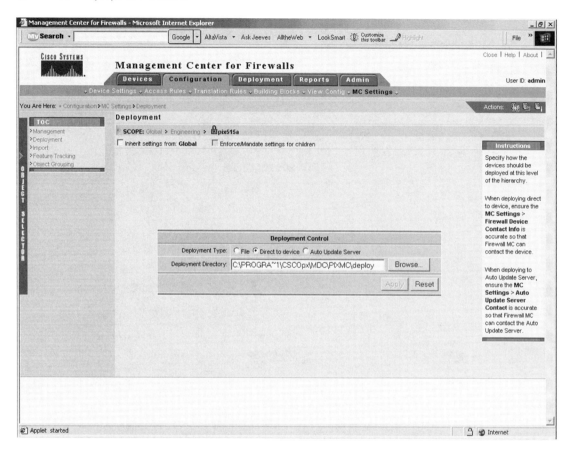

Step 6   Select the **Auto Update Server** radio button.

Step 7   Click **Apply.**

NOTE   Before changing the deployment parameters, you need to verify that you have deployed the initial AUS configuration information to the managed firewall. Once you change the deployment options, the device will not receive any more updates from the Firewall MC (because the updates are then sent to the AUS). If the managed firewall does not have the AUS settings, it will be unable to obtain any configuration updates.

Auto Update Server Interface

Besides configuring the communication between the AUS, Firewall MC, and your managed firewalls, you also need to understand the AUS interface to use it efficiently. The interface is divided into the following sections (see Figure 14-37):

- Path bar
- Options bar
- Configuration tabs
- Tools bar
- Instructions box
- Content area

NOTE You access the AUS by first logging in to CiscoWorks (refer to the "CiscoWorks" section earlier in the chapter). After logging in to CiscoWorks, you launch the AUS by clicking the AUS option VPN/Security Management Solution drawer.

Figure 14-37 *AUS User Interface*

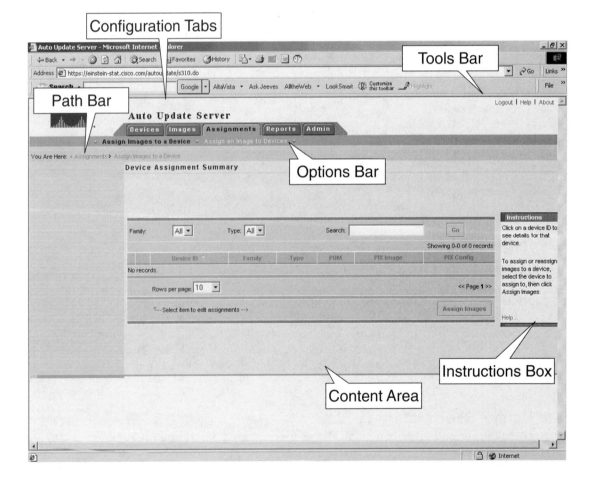

Path Bar

The path bar provides a visual road map indicating where you are with respect to the AUS interface. It is located below the options bar and begins with the text "You Are Here."

Figure 14-37 shows a situation in which the value of the path bar is Assignments > Assign Images to a Device. This indicates that you performed the following steps to reach the current window:

Step 1   You clicked the **Assignments** tab.

Step 2   You clicked the **Assign Images to a Device** option.

Options Bar

After clicking one of the major configuration tabs, the options for that selection are displayed in a list that is located on the screen just below the configuration tabs. Figure 14-37 shows a window in which the user clicked the Assignments tab. The options associated with the Assignments tab are as follows:

- Assign Images to a Device
- Assign an Image to Devices

Configuration Tabs

The configuration tasks are broken down into the following five major categories:

- **Devices**—Displays summary information about devices
- **Images**—Provides information about PIX Firewall software images, PDM images, and configuration files and allows you to add and delete PIX Firewall software images and PDM images
- **Assignments**—Allows you to view and change device-to-image assignments and image-to-device assignments
- **Reports**—Displays reports
- **Admin**—Enables you to perform administrative tasks, such as configuring NAT settings and changing your database password

To access one of the categories, click the tab labeled with the appropriate name. The tabs are located across the top of the AUS display.

Tools Bar

Located at the upper-right portion of the AUS interface is the tools bar. From the tools bar, you can access the following items:

- Logout
- Help
- About

Click **Logout** to log out of the current AUS user session. Click **Help** to open another browser window that displays detailed context-sensitive help information for using AUS. Finally, click the **About** option to display information about the version of AUS that you are using.

Instructions Box

Some pages provide you with an Instructions box on the right side of the AUS display. When displayed, this box provides you with a brief overview of the page that you have selected. The Instructions box provides less information than that provided through the **Help** option on the tools bar.

Content Area

The content area is the portion of the window in which you perform application tasks.

Configuring Devices

Click the **Devices** tab to display the Device Summary table (see Figure 14-38). The table shows all of PIX Firewalls being managed by the AUS. The table provides information such as the device ID, platform family, and the last time that the PIX Firewall contacted the AUS (see Table 14-7). To sort the table by a specific column, click the name of a column. You can also filter the information displayed by using the drop-down menus for Family, Type, or Device Status. Another option for limiting the number of entries displayed is to search for specific devices by entering a textual search string.

Table 14-7 *Device Summary Table Parameters*

Parameter	Description
Device ID	Displays the name the firewall uses to identify itself to the AUS.
Family	Series to which the firewall belongs (such as PIX)
Type	The type of device within the device family (such as PIX 515)
Up to Date	Indicates whether the devices is running the latest files
Last Contact	Indicates the last time that the firewall contacted the AUS

Figure 14-38 *Device Summary Table*

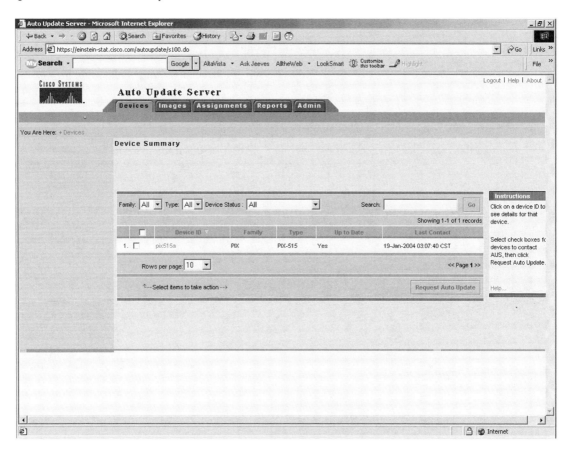

Configuring Images

The AUS enables you to manage the following items for your managed firewalls:

- PIX Firewall images
- PDM images
- PIX Firewall configuration files

In the Images configuration tab, you can add or delete both PIX Firewall software images and PDM images (see Figure 14-39). PIX Firewall configuration files can be added to AUS only by deploying them from Firewall MC. Table 14-8 describes the fields in the Software Images table.

Table 14-8 *Software Images Table Parameters*

Parameter	Description
Image Name	Name of the image that is stored in AUS
Type	Type of image (either PIX image, PDM image, or configuration file)
Version	Version of the image
Create Timestamp	Time the image was added to AUS
No. of References	Number of devices that have been assigned to the image

Figure 14-39 *Software Images Table*

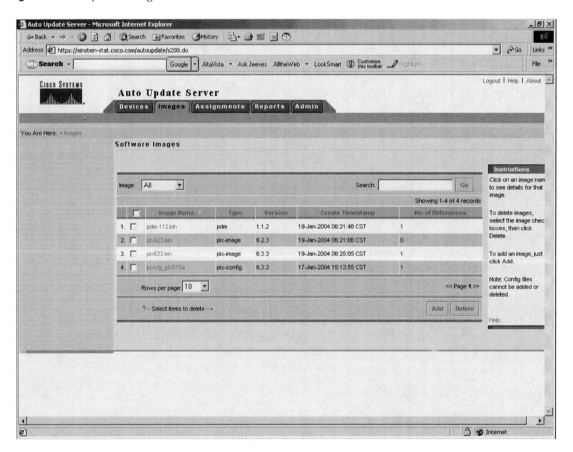

Configuring Assignments

When a new image becomes available, you can perform the following steps:

Step 1   Download the image file.

Step 2   Add the image to AUS.

Step 3   Assign the image to one or more devices.

Click the **Assignments** tab to assign image files to specific managed firewalls. You have the following two options when assigning images to your managed firewalls:

- Assign Images to a Device
- Assign an Image to Devices

Assign Images to a Device

The Assign Images to a Device option enables you to view the images assigned to your managed devices based on a table that is sorted by the device ID (see Figure 14-40). Besides viewing the currently assigned images, you can also assign a different image for a specific device based on its device ID.

Figure 14-40 *Device Assignment Summary Table*

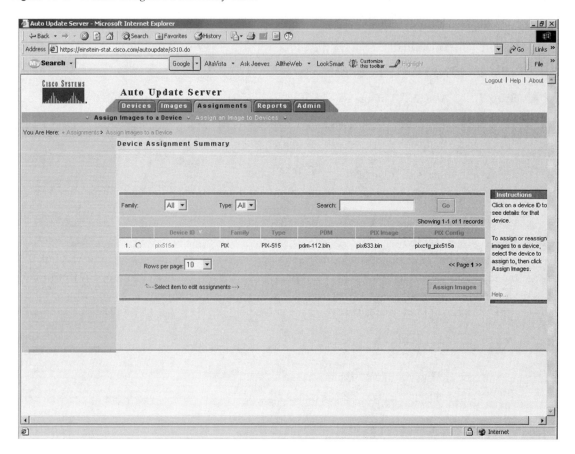

Assign an Image to Devices

The Assign an Image to Devices option enables you to view the images assigned to your managed devices based on a table that is sorted by the image name (see Figure 14-41). You also can assign a specific image listed in the table to one or more managed devices.

Figure 14-41 *Image Assignment Summary Table*

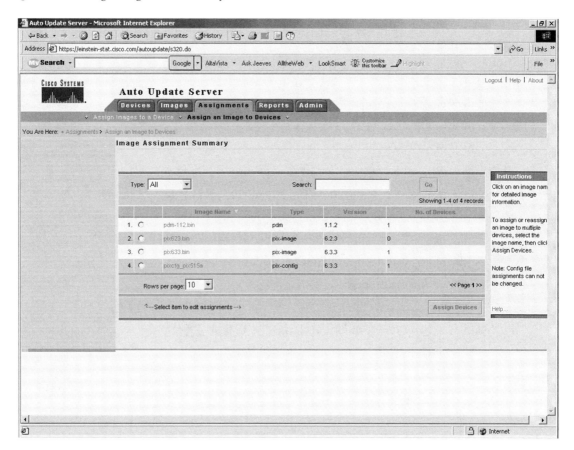

Reports

The Reports tab enables you to view the different reports supported by AUS. The AUS supports the following two types of reports:

■ System Info Report
■ Event Report

System Info Report

The System Info Report displays general system information about the AUS along with the statistics for the last 24 hours (see Figure 14-42). The information provided by the System Info Report includes the following:

- AUS URL
- Number of devices managed
- Number of files that the AUS contains
- Number of assignments
- Most downloaded configuration file (in the last 24 hours)
- Number of unique configuration files downloaded (in the last 24 hours)
- Number of successful configuration file downloads (in the last 24 hours)
- Number of failed configuration file downloads (in the last 24 hours)
- Number of successful auto updates (in the last 24 hours)
- Number of failed auto updates (in the last 24 hours)
- Device that contacted the server most (in the last 24 hours)
- Number of bytes downloaded (in the last 24 hours)
- Number of new assignments (in the last 24 hours)

Figure 14-42 *System Info Report*

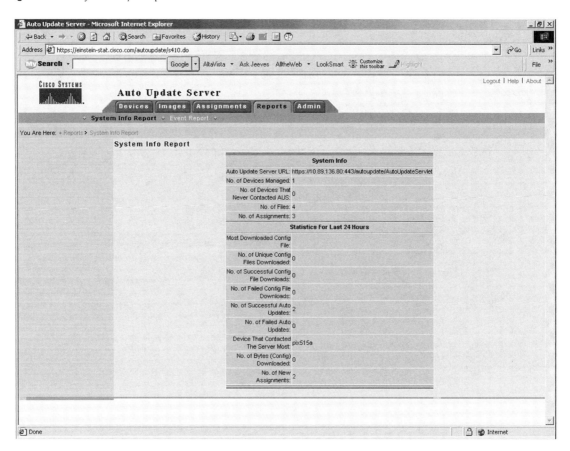

Event Report

The Event Report displays information about the devices that have contacted the AUS (see Figure 14-43). Each entry in the report represents an event and the result of the event. These events can also be notifications from the managed firewalls indicating errors (such as problems with a downloaded configuration file). Some of the events that you may observe are shown in Table 14-9.

Figure 14-43 *Event Report*

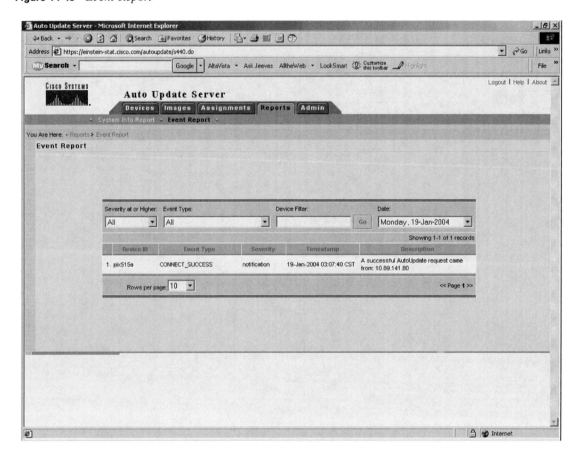

Table 14-9 *Event Types*

Event	Description
CONNECT-SUCCESS	A managed firewall contacted the AUS successfully.
CONNECT-FAILURE	A problem occurred during an auto update attempt. Some possible causes include the following: • Error while parsing XML information • Invalid login credentials • Connectivity problems
DEVICE-CONFIG-ERROR	The managed firewall reported to the AUS that errors occurred while loading the downloaded configuration file.

Table 14-9 *Event Types (Continued)*

Event	Description
GENERAL-DEVICE-ERROR	The managed firewall reported a nonconfiguration file error to AUS. Some possible causes include the following: • Problems connecting to AUS servlet • Invalid checksum for downloaded image
DOWNLAOD-SUCCESS	The file was successfully sent to the managed firewall (does not necessarily indicate that image file is successfully installed).
DOWNLOAD-FAILURE	An error occurred while the image or configuration was being downloaded. Possible causes included the following: • Connectivity problems • Invalid credentials
AUS-IMMEDIATE-SUCCESS	The AUS successfully contacted and updated the managed device.
AUS-IMMEDIATE-FAILURE	An error occurred while updating a managed device. Possible causes include the following: • The server does not have connectivity to device (NAT problems) • The login credentials are incorrect
SYSTEM-ERROR	An internal error occurred.

Administrative Tasks

The Administrative tab enables you to change the following characteristics of the AUS:

■ NAT settings
■ Database password change

The NAT Settings option enables you to configure the actual address of the AUS server along with a NAT address. This option is used when the AUS server is separated from the managed devices by a NAT device.

The Database Password Change option lets you change the password that is used to authenticate access to the AUS database.

Foundation Summary

The "Foundation Summary" provides a convenient review of many key concepts in this chapter. If you are already comfortable with the topics in this chapter, this summary can help you recall a few details. If you just read this chapter, this review should help solidify some key facts. If you are doing your final preparation before the exam, this summary provides a convenient way to review the day before the exam.

CiscoWorks Management Center for Firewalls (Firewall MC) enables you to manage multiple firewalls across your network. The Firewall MC software operates on top of CiscoWorks Common Services (Version 2.2) that provide basic functionality such as user authentication. Some of the features of Firewall MC include the following:

- Web-based interface for configuring and managing multiple firewalls
- Configuration hierarchy and user interface to facilitate configuration of firewall settings
- Support for PIX Firewall Version 6.0 and later
- Ability to import configurations from existing firewalls
- Ability to support dynamically addressed PIX Firewalls
- Support for up to 1000 PIX Firewalls
- SSL protocol support for client communications to CiscoWorks
- Support for workflow and audit trails

Firewall MC supports the following firewall platforms:

- PIX 501
- PIX 506/506E
- PIX 515/515E
- PIX 525
- PIX 535
- FWSM

To manage firewalls using Firewall MC, you must configure the firewall to allow HTTP access from the Firewall MC. The Firewall MC interface is divided into the following major configuration tabs:

- **Devices**—Enables you to import device configurations and define device groups to be managed by the system

- **Configuration**—Enables you to change the operational configuration of the devices managed by the system

- **Deployment**—Enables you to generate configuration files, manage firewall configuration files, and submit or manage new jobs

- **Reports**—Enables you to generate reports, view scheduled reports, and view reports

- **Admin**—Enables you to configure system settings

The basic user task flow for using Firewall MC involves the following steps:

Step 1   Create device groups.

Step 2   Import/create devices.

Step 3   Configure building blocks.

Step 4   Configure device settings.

Step 5   Configure access and translation rules.

Step 6   Generate and view the configuration.

Step 7   Deploy the configuration.

You must define the firewalls that Firewall MC will manage. Device management falls into the following categories:

- Managing groups
- Importing devices
- Managing devices

After importing the device to be managed, you must perform various configuration tasks. Configuration tasks using the Firewall MC fall into the following topics:

- Configuring device settings
- Defining access rules
- Defining translation rules
- Creating building blocks
- Generating and viewing configuration information

Some of the device settings that you can configure through Firewall MC include the following:

- PIX operating system version
- Interfaces

- Fail over
- Routing
- PIX Firewall administration
- Logging
- Servers and services
- Advanced security
- Firewall MC controls
- Configuring access and translation rules

Access rules define your network security policy by controlling the flow of network traffic through your firewalls. The three types of access rules are as follows:

- Firewall rules
- AAA rules
- Web filter rules

Translation rules define the translation of private IP addresses to public IP address and fall into the following three categories:

- Static translation rules
- Dynamic translation rules
- Translation exception rules (NAT 0 ACL)

To optimize your configuration, you can define building blocks that can then be used when defining other items (such as access and translation rules). You can configure the following types of building blocks:

- Network objects
- Service definitions
- Service groups
- AAA server groups
- Address translation pools

Firewall MC supports the following types of reports:

- Activity Report
- Configuration Differences report
- Device Setting Report

After making configuration changes, you need to deploy those changes to your managed firewalls. By default these changes are deployed to your managed firewalls as soon as you save your configuration changes. If you enable workflow, however, then updating configurations involves the following three steps:

Step 1   Define configuration changes.

Step 2   Approve configuration changes.

Step 3   Deploy configuration changes.

Using workflow, configuration changes become activities, and deploying those activities become jobs. You can require approval for activities, jobs, or both.

The AUS enables you to maintain current images efficiently on your managed firewalls. Like Firewall MC, the AUS runs on top of CiscoWorks Common Services. AUS supports the following types of images:

- PIX Firewall software images
- PDM software images
- PIX configuration files

Some of the major features provided by AUS (Version 1.0) include the following:

- Web-based interface for maintaining multiple PIX Firewalls
- Support for PIX Firewall operating system 6.0 and later
- Support for dynamically addressed PIX Firewalls
- Support for up to 1000 PIX Firewalls

AUS Version 1.1 added new functionality including the following major features:

- Installation on Solaris
- Additional report formats
- Support for configuration files

PIX Firewall software images and PDM software images can be directly added to the AUS. PIX configuration files must be deployed from Firewall MC to be added to the AUS.

The configuration tasks in the AUS (Version 1.0) are broken down into the following five major categories:

- **Devices**—Displays summary information about devices

- **Images**—Provides information about PIX Firewall software images, PDM images, and configuration files and allows you to add and delete PIX Firewall software images and PDM images

- **Assignments**—Allows you to view and change device-to-image assignments and image-to-device assignments

- **Reports**—Displays reports

- **Admin**—Enables you to perform administrative tasks, such as configuring NAT settings and changing your database password

Q&A

As mentioned in the Introduction, the questions in this book are more difficult than what you should experience on the exam. The questions are designed to ensure your understanding of the concepts discussed in this chapter and adequately prepare you to complete the exam. You should use the simulated exams on the CD to practice for the exam.

The answers to these questions can be found in Appendix A.

1. Which software performs user authentication for Firewall MC and AUS?

2. Which type of building block enables you to associate multiple protocols with a single name?

3. What types of translation rules can you configure in Firewall MC?

4. What types of access rules does Firewall MC enable you to configure?

5. What types of images does AUS support?

6. Which images can you not add directly through the AUS interface?

7. Which type of translation rule defines a permanent mapping between private IP addresses and public IP addresses?

8. What is an address translation pool?

9. What is a network object?

10. What are three of the device settings that you can configure through Firewall MC?

11. What type of building block do you need to define to create a dynamic translation rule?

12. What is workflow?

13. Can AUS be used to manage firewalls that use dynamic addresses assigned by DHCP?

14. What building blocks can you configure with Firewall MC, and how are they used?

15. What three reports does Firewall MC support?

16. Name the three possible methods from which each device setting in a managed configuration can be derived.

17. What are the four steps used to import a device into Firewall MC?

18. What are the steps required to add images to AUS?

This chapter covers the following subject:

- URL Filtering

- ActiveX Object Filtering

- Java Applet Filtering

CHAPTER 15

Content Filtering on the PIX

Up to now, you have focused on how to configure the PIX Firewall and how to protect against unwanted traffic from outside in. This chapter focuses specifically on outbound traffic and content filtering—traffic moving from inside out.

More and more companies today have some form of network policy in place. Websites that are not related to their business or that are otherwise considered inappropriate are prohibited for use by their employees. This chapter discusses how the Cisco PIX Firewall mitigates some of the threats posed by Java applets and ActiveX objects and how the Cisco PIX Firewall enforces URL filtering.

How to Best Use This Chapter

Users on your network frequently surf the Internet looking for information. Some websites contain content that is not appropriate for a business environment. Besides inappropriate content, many attacks also originate from traffic brought into your network by internal users surfing the Internet via ActiveX objects and Java applets. Filtering ActiveX objects and Java applets along with restricting access to specific URLs is an important aspect in your overall network security policy. Test yourself with the "Do I Know This Already?" quiz and see how familiar you are with the content filtering functionality available on PIX Firewalls.

"Do I Know This Already?" Quiz

The purpose of the "Do I Know This Already?" quiz is to help you decide if you really need to read the entire chapter. If you already intend to read the entire chapter, you do not necessarily need to answer these questions now.

The ten-question quiz, derived from the major sections in the "Foundation Topics" portion of the chapter, helps you determine how to spend your limited study time.

Table 15-1 outlines the major topics discussed in this chapter and the "Do I Know This Already?" quiz questions that correspond to those topics.

Table 15-1 *"Do I Know This Already?" Foundation Topics Section-to-Question Mapping*

Foundations Topics Section	Questions Covered in This Section	Score
URL Filtering	2 to 10	
Configuring Java and ActiveX Filtering	1	

> **CAUTION** The goal of self assessment is to gauge your mastery of the topics in this chapter. If you do not know the answer to a question or are only partially sure of the answer, you should mark this question wrong for purposes of the self assessment. Giving yourself credit for an answer you correctly guess skews your self-assessment results and might provide you with a false sense of security.

1. How does the PIX Firewall filter Java applets and ActiveX objects?

    a. By commenting out the <OBJECT> </OBJECT> tags or the <APPLET> </APPLET> tags in the HTML page.

    b. By deleting the <OBJECT CLASSID> </OBJECT> tags or the <APPLET> </APPLET> tags in the HTML page.

    c. It notifies the content-filtering server, which in turn disables the ActiveX objects and Java applets.

    d. The PIX Firewall does not filter ActiveX objects or Java applets.

2. What is the command to designate or identify the URL-filtering server?

    a. filter url-server

    b. url-server

    c. filtering server

    d. server url

3. What is the longest URL length supported by Cisco PIX Firewall Version 6.2 with Websense Enterprise URL-filtering software?

    a. 12 KB

    b. 15 KB

    c. 4 KB

    d. 6 KB

4. What is the command to filter URLs?

    a. **filter url**

    b. **url-filter**

    c. **url-server**

    d. **filter web page**

5. What happens when the only URL-filtering server is unavailable?

    a. If the **allow** option is set, the PIX Firewall forwards HTTP traffic without filtering.

    b. SMTP traffic is dropped because the URL-filtering server is unavailable.

    c. HTTP requests are queued until the URL-filtering server is available.

    d. The PIX Firewall reverts to the onboard URL-filtering engine to filter HTTP traffic.

6. What is the default port used by the N2H2 server to communicate with the Cisco PIX Firewall?

    a. TCP/UDP 1272

    b. TCP 5004 only

    c. TCP/UDP 4005

    d. UDP 5004 only

7. What command identifies N2H2 servers on a Cisco PIX Firewall?

    a. **websense url filter** *server-ip*

    b. **filter url** *server-ip* **vendor n2h2**

    c. **url-server** (*if-name*) **vendor n2h2 host** *local-ip*

    d. All of the above

8.   How many URL servers can be configured on a single Cisco PIX Firewall?

  a. 5

  b. 12

  c. 3

  d. 16

9.   What command disables URL caching on the Cisco PIX Firewall?

  a. no url-cache

  b. caching-url

  c. disable url-cache

  d. None of the above

10.   Which of the following URL-filtering servers supports FTP and HTTPS filtering?

  a. N2H2

  b. Cisco Works

  c. Websense

  d. CSACS

The answers to the "Do I Know This Already?" quiz are found in Appendix A, "Answers to the 'Do I Know This Already?' Quizzes and Q&A Sections." The suggested choices for your next step are as follows:

■ **8 or less overall score**—Read the entire chapter. This includes the "Foundation Topics," "Foundation Summary," and "Q&A" sections.

■ **9 or 10 overall score**—If you want more review on these topics, skip to the "Foundation Summary" section and then go to the "Q&A" section. Otherwise, move to the next chapter.

Foundation Topics

Filtering ActiveX Objects and Java Applets

ActiveX objects and Java applets are designed to make the browsing experience more interactive. Based on the Component Object Model (COM), ActiveX objects are written for a specific platform of Microsoft Windows. When the user displays a page containing ActiveX or Java, the browser downloads the control dynamically. ActiveX objects are native programs, so they can do all the things that local programs can do. For example, they can read and write to the hard drive, execute programs, perform network administration tasks, and determine which system configuration they are running on. While ActiveX objects and Java applets can perform powerful tasks, they can also be used maliciously to damage systems.

One way to prevent the threats posed by ActiveX objects and Java applets is to disallow ActiveX objects and Java applets at the browser or user level. Users can configure their web browsers not to run ActiveX objects or Java applets. Although you can disable ActiveX objects and Java applets within the browser, this requires a great deal of effort for a large enterprise network. In these cases, it is easier to prevent the ActiveX objects and Java applets from reaching the browser.

When configured for filtering, the Cisco PIX Firewall filters ActiveX objects and Java applets from HTML web pages before those pages reach the browser. Java applet and ActiveX object filtering of HTML files is performed by selectively replacing the <APPLET> and </APPLET> tags and the <OBJECT> and </OBJECT> tags with comments.

Filtering Java Applets

The **filter java** command filters out Java applets that return to the Cisco PIX Firewall from an outbound connection. The user still receives the HTML page, but the web page source for the applet is commented out so that the applet cannot execute. The syntax for **filter java** is

```
filter java port[-port] local-ip mask foreign-ip-mask
```

The following example specifies that Java applet blocking applies to web traffic on port 80 from local subnet 10.10.10.0 and for connections to any foreign host:

```
filter java http 10.10.10.0 255.255.255.0 0 0
```

Table 15-2 describes the different parameters for the **filter** command.

Table 15-2 **filter** *Command Parameters*

Parameter	Description
activex	Blocks inbound ActiveX objects, Java applets, and other HTML <OBJECT> tags from outbound packets.
allow	Filters URL only. When the server is unavailable, lets outbound connections pass through the Cisco PIX Firewall without filtering. If you omit this option, and if the N2H2 or Websense server goes offline, Cisco PIX Firewall stops outbound port 80 (web) traffic until the N2H2 or Websense server is back online.
cgi-truncate	Sends a CGI script as an URL.
except	Filters URL only. Creates an exception to a previous filter condition.
foreign-ip	The IP address of the lowest security level interface to which access is sought. You can use 0.0.0.0 (or, in shortened form, 0) to specify all hosts.
java	Filters out Java applets returning from an outbound connection.
local-ip	The IP address of the highest security level interface from which access is sought. You can set this address to 0.0.0.0 (or, in shortened form, 0) to specify all hosts.
local-mask	Network mask of *local-ip*. You can use 0.0.0.0 (or, in shortened form, 0) to specify all hosts.
longurl-deny	Denies the URL request if the URL is over the URL buffer size limit or if the URL buffer is unavailable.
longurl-truncate	Sends only the originating host name or IP address to the Websense server if the URL is over the URL buffer limit.
mask	Subnet mask.
port	The port that receives Internet traffic on the Cisco PIX Firewall. Typically, this is port 80, but other values are accepted. The **http** or **www** literal can be used for port 80.
proxy-block	Prevents users from connecting to an HTTP proxy server.
url	Filters URLs from data moving through the Cisco PIX Firewall.
interact-block	Prevents users from connecting to the FTP server through an interactive program.

NOTE Table 15-2 lists the parameters for the **filter** command that appear in this chapter.

Filtering ActiveX Objects

The **filter activex** command filters out ActiveX objects and other HTML <OBJECT> usages from inbound packets. These controls include custom forms, calendars, and extensive third-party forms for gathering or displaying information. The syntax for filtering ActiveX objects is as follows:

```
filter activex port local-ip local-mask foreign-ip foreign-mask
```

Note that if the <OBJECT> and </OBJECT> HTML tags split across network packets or if the code in the tags is longer than the number of bytes in the maximum transmission unit (MTU), Cisco PIX Firewall cannot block the tag.

Filtering URLs

Most organizations today have human resources policies that specify indecent materials cannot be brought into the workplace. Similarly, most organizations have network security policies that prohibit users from visiting websites that are categorized as indecent or inappropriate to the business mission of the organization.

Using other content-filtering vendor products, the Cisco PIX Firewall enforces network security policy as it relates to URL filtering. When a user issues an HTTP request to a website, the Cisco PIX Firewall sends the request to the web server and to the URL-filtering server at the same time. If the policy on the URL-filtering server permits the connection, the Cisco PIX Firewall allows the reply from the website to reach the user who issued the original request. If the policy on the URL-filtering server denies the connection, the Cisco PIX Firewall redirects the user to a block page, indicating that access was denied.

The PIX Firewall works in conjunction with two types of URL-filtering application servers:

- **Websense Enterprise**—Supported by Cisco PIX Firewall Version 5.3 and later
- **N2H2 Sentian**—Supported by Cisco PIX Firewall Version 6.2

Identifying the URL-Filtering Server

The **url-server** command designates the server that is running the N2H2 or Websense URL-filtering application. The PIX Firewall allows you to configure a maximum of 16 URL servers (with the first one entered being the primary URL server), and you can use only one URL-filtering server at a time, either N2H2 or Websense. Configuration is performed both on the PIX Firewall and the URL-filtering server. You can identify more than one URL-filtering server by entering the **url-server** command multiple times. The primary URL-filtering server is the first server that you identify. The syntax for identifying an N2H2 URL-filtering server is as follows:

> url-server [(*if-name*)] vendor n2h2 host *local-ip* [port *number*]
> [timeout *seconds*] [protocol {TCP ¦ UDP}]

The default protocol is TCP. The **timeout** parameter in the **url-server** command is the maximum idle time permitted before the PIX Firewall switches to the next URL-filtering server you specified. The default time is 5 seconds.

The following example identifies an N2H2 URL-filtering server with an IP address of 10.10.10.13:

> pixfw(config)#url-server (inside) vendor n2h2 host **10.10.10.13**

The default port used by the N2H2 server to communicate with the Cisco PIX Firewall via TCP or UDP is 4005.

The syntax for identifying a Websense URL-filtering server is as follows:

> url-server [(*if-name*)] vendor websense host *local-ip* [timeout *seconds*]
> [protocol {TCP ¦ UDP} version{1¦4}]

The following example identifies a Websense URL-filtering server with an IP address of 10.10.10.14:

> pixfw(config)# url-server (inside) vendor websense host **10.10.10.14**

To view the URL-filtering server, use the **show url-server** command, as shown in Example 15-1.

Example 15-1 *Displaying the URL-Filtering Server Information*

```
pixfw# show url-server
url-server (inside) vendor n2h2 host 10.10.10.13 port 4005 timeout 5 protocol TCP
```

Configuring URL-Filtering Policy

You must identify and enable the URL-filtering server before you use the following filtering commands. If all URL-filtering servers are removed, any associated filtering commands are also removed. The **filter url** command enables you to prevent outbound users from accessing URLs that you designate as inadmissible. The syntax for filtering URLs is as follows:

> filter url *port* [except] *local-ip local-mask foreign-ip foreign-mask* [allow]
> [proxy-block] [longurl-truncate ¦ longurl-deny] [cgi-truncate]

With URL filtering enabled, the Cisco PIX Firewall stops outbound HTTP, HTTPS, and FTP traffic until a URL-filtering server permits the connection. If the primary URL-filtering server and the secondary server do not respond, then outbound web traffic (port 80) stops until the URL-filtering server comes back online. However, the **allow** option causes the Cisco PIX Firewall to forward HTTP traffic without filtering when the URL-filtering server(s) is unavailable.

> **NOTE**   PIX Firewall Version 6.3 supports filtering of HTTPS and FTP sites for Websense servers. HTTPS and FTP filtering are not supported for the N2H2 URL-filtering server.

The following example filters all HTTP traffic:

```
filter url http 0 0
```

You can make an exception to URL-filtering policies by using the **except** parameter in the **filter url** command. For example:

```
pixfw(config)#filter url http 0 0 0 0
pixfw(config)#filter url except 10.10.10.20 255.255.255.255 0 0
```

This policy filters all HTTP traffic with the exception of HTTP traffic that originates from host 10.10.10.20.

Websense database version 4 contains the following enhancements:

- URL filtering allows the Cisco PIX Firewall to check outgoing URL requests against the policy defined on the Websense server.

- Username logging tracks the username, group, and domain name on the Websense server.

- Username lookup lets the Cisco PIX Firewall use the user authentication table to map the host's IP address to the username.

There are instances in which the web server replies to a user HTTP request faster than the URL-filtering servers. In these instances, the **url-cache** command provides a configuration option to buffer the response from a web server if its response is faster than that from the N2H2 or Websense URL-filtering server. This prevents the web server's response from being loaded twice, improving throughput. The syntax of the **url-cache** command is as follows:

```
url-cache {dst ¦ src-dst} size kbytes
```

Table 15-3 describes the parameters for the **url-cache** command.

Table 15-3 url-cache *Command Parameters*

Parameter	Description
dst	Caches entries based on the URL destination address. Select this mode if all users share the same URL-filtering policy on the N2H2 or Websense server.
src-dst	Caches entries based on the source address initiating the URL request and the URL destination address. Select this mode if users do not share the same URL-filtering policy on the N2H2 or Websense server.
size *kbytes*	Specifies a value for the cache size within the range 1 to 128 KB.

Use the **url-cache** command to enable URL caching, set the size of the cache, and display cache statistics.

Caching also stores URL access privileges in memory on the Cisco PIX Firewall. When a host requests a connection, the Cisco PIX Firewall first looks in the URL cache for matching access privileges before it forwards the request to the N2H2 or Websense server.

The **clear url-cache** command removes **url-cache** command statements from the configuration, and the **no url-cache** command disables caching.

Filtering HTTPS and FTP

As mentioned in the previous section, HTTPS and FTP filtering can be configured on the PIX Firewall using Websense servers. These new features provide a convenient mechanism of enforcing access policy in your environment. Just as it does with HTTP filtering, the PIX Firewall sends FTP requests to both the destination and the Websense server when a user makes an FTP request. If the Websense server denies the connection, the PIX Firewall alters the FTP return code to show that the connection was denied. If the Websense server permits the connection, the PIX Firewall allows the successful FTP return code to reach the user unchanged.

HTTPS filtering, on the other hand, works by preventing the completion of SSL connection negotiation if the site is not allowed. The browser displays an error message such as "The Page or the content cannot be displayed." The command syntax to enable FTP and HTTPS filtering is as follows:

```
filter ftp dest-port localIP local-mask foreign-IP foreign-mask
    [allow] [interact-block]
filter https dest-port localIP local-mask foreign-IP foreign-mask [allow]
```

Filtering Long URLs

Cisco PIX Firewall Version 6.1 and earlier versions do not support filtering URLs longer than 1159 bytes. Cisco PIX Firewall Version 6.2 supports filtering URLs up to 6000 bytes for the Websense URL-filtering server. The default is 2000 bytes. In addition, Cisco PIX Firewall Version 6.2 introduces the **longurl-truncate** and **cgi-truncate** parameters to allow handling of URL requests longer than the maximum permitted size. The format for these options is as follows:

```
filter url [http ¦ port[-port]] local-ip local-mask foreign-ip foreign-mask] [allow]
    [proxy-block] [longurl-truncate ¦ longurl-deny ¦ cgi-truncate]
```

Table 15-4 identifies the major parameters for the **filter url** command.

Table 15-4 **filter url** *Command Parameters*

Parameter	Description
http	Specifies that the filtering be applied to port 80
port	Specifies that the filtering be applied to whatever port (or port range) is specified by either *port* or *port-port*
local-ip	Specifies the source IP addresses for which filtering will be applied
local-mask	Specifies the network mask for *local-ip* (note: using **0.0.0.0** specifies all hosts)
foreign-ip	Specifies the destination IP addresses for which filtering will be applied
foreign-mask	Specifies the network mask for *foreign-ip* (note: using **0.0.0.0** specifies all hosts)
allow	Allows the connection to pass through the firewall without filtering if the filtering server is unavailable
proxy-block	Prevents users from connecting to an HTTP proxy server
longurl-truncate	Causes the Cisco PIX Firewall to send only the host name or IP address portion of the URL for evaluation to the URL-filtering server, when the URL is longer than the maximum length permitted
longurl-deny	Denies outbound traffic if the URL is longer than the maximum permitted
cgi-truncate	Sends a CGI script as the URL

Cisco PIX Firewall Version 6.2 supports a maximum URL length of 1159 bytes for the N2H2 URL-filtering server. To increase the maximum length of a single URL (for Websense only), enter the following command:

```
url-block url-size size
```

The value of the *size* variable is 2 to 6 KB.

Viewing Filtering Statistics and Configuration

The **show url-cache** command with the **stat** option displays the URL caching statistics. Example 15-2 demonstrates sample output from this command.

Example 15-2 show url-cache *Command Output*

```
PIX# show url-cache stat
URL Filter Cache Stats
----------------------
    Size:        128KB
 Entries:        1415
  In Use:           1
 Lookups:           0
    Hits:           0
```

The significant fields in this output are as follows:

- **Size**—The size of the cache in kilobytes, set with the **url-cache** *size* option
- **Entries**—The maximum number of cache entries based on the cache size
- **In Use**—The current number of entries in the cache
- **Lookups**—The number of times the Cisco PIX Firewall has looked for a cache entry
- **Hits**—The number of times the Cisco PIX Firewall has found an entry in the cache

You can view more statistics about URL filtering and performance with the **show url-server stats** and **show perfmon** commands. Example 15-3 shows output from **show url-server stats**.

Example 15-3 show url-server stats *Command Output*

```
PIX(config)# show url-server stats
URL Server Statistics:
----------------------
Vendor                    Websense
URLs total/allowed/denied    2370/1958/412
URL Server Status:
------------------
10.10.10.13      UP
```

Example 15-4 shows output from the **show perfmon** command.

Example 15-4   show perfmon *Command Output*

```
PIX# show perfmon
PERFMON STATS:    Current      Average
Xlates              0/s          0/s
Connections         0/s          2/s
TCP Conns           0/s          2/s
UDP Conns           0/s          0/s
URL Access          0/s          2/s
URL Server Req      0/s          3/s
TCP Fixup           0/s          0/s
TCPIntercept        0/s          0/s
HTTP Fixup          0/s          3/s
FTP Fixup           0/s          0/s
AAA Authen          0/s          0/s
AAA Author          0/s          0/s
AAA Account         0/s          0/s
```

Foundation Summary

The "Foundation Summary" provides a convenient review of many key concepts in this chapter. If you are already comfortable with the topics in this chapter, this summary can help you recall a few details. If you just read this chapter, this review should help solidify some key facts. If you are doing your final preparation before the exam, this summary provides a convenient way to review the day before the exam.

The **filter java** command lets you filter Java applets out of HTTP traffic before it reaches a user's web browser. The Java applets are commented out in the HTML information that the user's web browser receives so that it will not attempt to process them. Similarly, the **filter activex** command enables you to filter ActiveX objects and other HTML <OBJECT> usages from inbound HTTP packets.

The **filter url** command lets you prevent outbound users from accessing World Wide Web URLs that you designate using one of the following URL-filtering server applications:

- **Websense Enterprise**—Supported by PIX Firewall Version 5.3 or later
- **N2H2 Sentian**—Supported by PIX Firewall Version 6.2

When a user issues an HTTP request to a website, the PIX Firewall sends the request to the web server and to the URL-filtering server at the same time. If the URL-filtering server permits the connection, the PIX Firewall allows the reply from the website to reach the user who issued the original request. If the URL-filtering server denies the connection, the PIX Firewall redirects the user to a block page, indicating that access was denied.

Q&A

As mentioned in the Introduction, the questions in this book are more difficult than what you should experience on the exam. The questions are designed to ensure your understanding of the concepts discussed in this chapter and adequately prepare you to complete the exam. You should use the simulated exams on the CD to practice for the exam.

The answers to these questions can be found in Appendix A.

1. With what two URL-filtering servers does the PIX Firewall work?

2. What command filters out Java applets from HTML pages?

3. Why are Java applets and ActiveX objects considered a threat?

4. How does the Cisco PIX Firewall filter Java applets and ActiveX objects?

5. What is the command to designate or identify the URL-filtering server?

6. Which PIX Firewall version supports the Websense URL-filtering server?

7. What is the longest URL filter, in bytes, that is possible with Cisco PIX Firewall Version 6.1 and earlier?

8. What is the longest URL filter that is supported by Cisco PIX Firewall 6.2?

9. What is the command to filter URLs?

10. How would you configure the PIX Firewall to buffer the response from a web server if its response is faster than that from the N2H2 or Websense URL-filtering server on the PIX Firewall?

This chapter covers the following subjects:

- Overview of AAA
- Installation of Cisco Secure ACS for Windows NT/2000
- Authentication Configuration

CHAPTER 16

Overview of AAA and the PIX

This chapter presents authentication, authorization, and accounting, more commonly known as AAA. It discusses how the Cisco PIX Firewall is incorporated with AAA servers and the relationship between the Cisco PIX Firewall and the AAA servers. This chapter also introduces Cisco Secure Access Control Server (ACS), an AAA server product offered by Cisco.

How to Best Use This Chapter

If you are very familiar with AAA but are not very familiar with Cisco Secure ACS, you should skim the first half of this chapter to reinforce your knowledge of AAA and to focus on the installation of Cisco Secure ACS. The AAA process is relatively simple to understand, although there are quite a few different configuration options. This chapter explains the AAA process, discusses how the Cisco PIX Firewall fits into this process, and covers the installation of Cisco Secure ACS.

"Do I Know This Already?" Quiz

The purpose of the "Do I Know This Already?" quiz is to help you decide if you really need to read the entire chapter. If you already intend to read the entire chapter, you do not necessarily need to answer these questions now.

The nine-question quiz, derived from the major sections in the "Foundation Topics" portion of the chapter, helps you determine how to spend your limited study time.

Table 16-1 outlines the major topics discussed in this chapter and the "Do I Know This Already?" quiz questions that correspond to those topics.

Table 16-1   *"Do I Know This Already?" Foundation Topics Section-to-Question Mapping*

Foundations Topics Section	Questions Covered in This Section	Score
Overview of AAA	1, 4	
Installation of Cisco Secure ACS for Windows NT/2000	2, 3, 5, 8, 9	
Authentication Configuration	6, 7	

> **CAUTION**   The goal of self assessment is to gauge your mastery of the topics in this chapter. If you do not know the answer to a question or are only partially sure of the answer, you should mark this question wrong for purposes of the self assessment. Giving yourself credit for an answer you correctly guess skews your self-assessment results and might provide you with a false sense of security.

1. Which platform does Cisco Secure ACS for Windows Version 3.2 currently support?

    a. Windows XP Professional

    b. Windows 2000 Server

    c. Windows NT Workstation

    d. Windows 2000 Professional

2. What is a new feature of Cisco Secure ACS for Windows Version 3.2?

    a. A password generator

    b. A password database

    c. Additional configuration steps for your Cisco IOS Network Access Server

    d. New graphics and tables

3. If you are installing Cisco Secure ACS 3.2 for Windows and do not understand a configuration option, what should you do?

    a. Check the explanation page.

    b. Push F7 for help.

    c. Select the About Cisco Secure ACS drop-down option.

    d. Open a case with Cisco TAC.

4. Which of the following are *not* connection types for authenticating to a PIX Firewall? (Select all that apply.)

   a. Telnet

   b. SSH

   c. FTP

   d. HTTPS

5. When installing Cisco Secure ACS Version 3.2 for Windows, you have the option to authenticate users against an existing user database. Which database can you check?

   a. A currently configured Cisco Secure ACS

   b. Any RADIUS server on the network

   c. The primary domain controller (PDC)

   d. The Windows user database

6. What access does cut-through proxy allow a user after they have successfully authenticated?

   a. Access to anything on the network

   b. Access only to web servers

   c. Access based on the user profile (authorization)

   d. Access only to the Cisco Secure ACS

7. What options are available to authenticate users on a PIX Firewall?

   a. Local user database

   b. Remote RADIUS server

   c. Remote TACACS+ server

   d. All of the above

   e. None of the above

8. What technologies does the Cisco Secure ACS use to communicate with the NAS? (Choose two.)

   a. TACACS

   b. RADIUS

   c. TACACS+

   d. RADIUS+

   e. Virtual Telnet

9. What does the Cisco Secure ACS consider the PIX Firewall to be (i.e., what is it referred to as, during configuration of the Cisco Secure ACS)?

   a. A perimeter security device

   b. A Network Access Server

   c. Cisco Secure ACS does not work with the PIX Firewall.

   d. None of the above

The answers to the "Do I Know This Already?" quiz are found in Appendix A, "Answers to the 'Do I Know This Already?' Quizzes and Q&A Sections." The suggested choices for your next step are as follows:

■ **7 or less overall score**—Read the entire chapter. This includes the "Foundation Topics," "Foundation Summary," and "Q&A" sections.

■ **8 overall score**—If you want more review of these topics, skip to the "Foundation Summary" section and then go to the "Q&A" section. Otherwise, move to the next chapter.

Foundation Topics

Overview of AAA and the Cisco PIX Firewall

Authentication, authorization, and accounting (AAA) has become an extremely important component in any network infrastructure. AAA is used in our everyday lives not only for network security but also for physical security, or any other function that requires access control. This chapter discusses the AAA process, its components, the responsibilities of each component, and how the Cisco PIX Firewall fits into the equation.

Definition of AAA

The best way to understand AAA is to look at the three components individually. Each is distinct and has its own responsibility. AAA is now integrated into nearly every situation that requires access control. Access control can be applied to users, hosts on a network (such as servers and workstations), networking components (such as routers, switches, VPN appliances, and firewalls), and other automated devices that require access and that perform a function. This chapter discusses AAA as it pertains to a user, but you will see how the principles can apply to many automated functions. The three components of AAA are as follows:

- **Authentication**—The process of validating an identity. The identity that is being validated could be a user, a computer, a networking component, and so on. Authentication is by far the most important step. No access is granted until the requestor has been authenticated. There are three layers of user authentication:

    — **What the user knows**—This normally is a user password or passphrase.

    — **What a user has**—This normally is a user token or badge issued to the user by whomever has authority over what the user is attempting to access.

    — **What a user is**—This area includes biometrics, such as checking the user's fingerprint or retinal scan against a stored image in the database.

    Many organizations do not incorporate all three layers of authentication; however, it is very common to use a minimum of two layers at one time.

- **Authorization**—After the user has been authenticated, he or she is granted access rights to perform specific functions.

■   **Accounting**—After the user is granted access, the accounting function tracks what tasks the user performs and saves that information in a log that can be reviewed later. Accountability of users and their actions is an issue that is becoming increasingly important in the security of enterprise networks.

The three functions of AAA can be performed by a single server or can be divided among several servers. Most large enterprise networks create a hierarchy of AAA servers, with the lower-level servers tending to user functions and the upper-level servers working as a central point for updating and distributing user information.

AAA and the Cisco PIX Firewall

So how does the PIX Firewall factor into the AAA equation? Any user who requests access or a service that is configured for authentication and who goes through the PIX Firewall is prompted by the firewall for a username and password. If the PIX Firewall has a local database configured for user authentication, it matches this user information against that database and permits or denies access.

In PIX Firewall Version 6.2, the local database can be used only for console authorization and command authorization. If the PIX Firewall is configured to use a separate AAA server, it forwards the user information to that server for authentication and authorization. In this case, the PIX Firewall and the AAA server act in a client/server mode, with the PIX Firewall being the client. The PIX Firewall acts as a network access server (NAS) but operates as a client to the AAA server. It is a common practice to configure redundant AAA servers. It is also possible to configure a local database on the PIX Firewall for use when no other AAA servers can be contacted.

> **NOTE**   The local user database on a Cisco PIX Firewall can be processor-intensive and should be used only for small organizations with a limited number of users.

Remember that the AAA server not only authenticates the user but also tells the firewall what the user is authorized to do. If a user is authorized to access websites via HTTP and attempts to connect to the same servers over FTP, that connection is dropped at the firewall even though that user has been authenticated. Additionally, the AAA server should log the fact that the user attempted to make a connection that was outside the user's authority. The use of specific authorization and accounting functions is not a prerequisite for the use of authentication. It is possible to configure only authentication, which by default authorizes access to authenticated users.

Cut-Through Proxy

Cut-through proxy is a feature on the Cisco PIX Firewall that allows transparent AAA services and a seamless connection through the firewall to the destination. It provides significantly better performance than application-proxy firewalls because it completes user authentication at the application layer, verifies authorization against the security policy, and then opens the connection as authorized by the security policy. In other words, the connection request needs to go up to the application layer only once to be authorized. After that, all authorized traffic is passed at the lower layers, dramatically increasing the rate at which it can pass through the firewall.

There are three ways to connect to the Cisco PIX Firewall and activate the cut-through proxy:

- HTTP
- FTP
- Telnet

The firewall responds to each of these connections with a username and password prompt. Figure 16-1 shows the Telnet user authentication prompt. The user information is either authenticated against a local database on the PIX Firewall or forwarded to an AAA server for authentication. After the user is authenticated, the firewall completes the connection that is requested (if authorized).

Figure 16-1 *Telnet Logon Prompt*

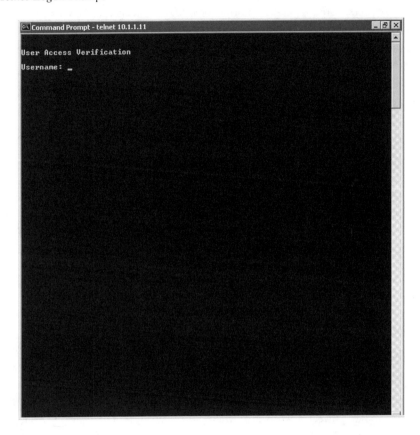

Figure 16-2 shows the steps for cut-through proxy on a Cisco PIX Firewall.

Figure 16-2 *Cut-Through Proxy Steps*

Step 7: Communication is established between source and destination and ASA process begins.

Step 6: Connection completed with web server.

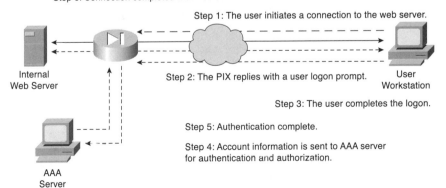

Step 1: The user initiates a connection to the web server.

Step 2: The PIX replies with a user logon prompt.

Step 3: The user completes the logon.

Step 5: Authentication complete.

Step 4: Account information is sent to AAA server for authentication and authorization.

Supported AAA Server Technologies

The Cisco PIX Firewall supports two AAA server authentication protocols:

- **Remote Authentication Dial-In User Service (RADIUS)**—RADIUS was developed by Livingston Enterprises as an AAA server. It uses a UDP connection between the client (NAS) and the server (AAA). RADIUS combines the authentication and authorization into a single response to a query from the NAS. By default, RADIUS authentication is performed on TCP port 1645.

- **Terminal Access Controller Access Control System Plus (TACACS+)**—TACACS+ was developed by Cisco Systems as an alternative to RADIUS. TACACS+ uses a TCP connection between the client and server and divides the authentication and authorization into separate transmissions. The default port for TACACS+ is TCP port 49.

Cisco Secure Access Control Server

Cisco Secure ACS is an AAA server product developed by Cisco that can run on Windows NT/2000 Server and UNIX, although Cisco has discontinued support for the Windows NT and UNIX platforms. It supports a number of NASs, including the Cisco PIX Firewall. Cisco Secure ACS supports both RADIUS and TACACS+.

Minimum Hardware and Operating System Requirements for Cisco Secure ACS

Table 16-2 documents the minimum requirements needed by a system to run Cisco Secure ACS Version 3.2.

Table 16-2 *Cisco Secure ACS Version 3.2 System Requirements*

System Requirement Type	Requirements
Hardware	Pentium III Processor, 550 MHz or greater.
	256 MB of RAM.
	250 MB of available drive space. Additional space is required if you intend to run the Cisco Secure ACS database on this system.
	Screen resolution of 800×600 pixels and 256-color display.
Operating system	Microsoft Windows NT Server with Service Pack 6a (no longer supported).
	Microsoft Windows 2000 Server with Service Pack 3 or 4.

continues

Table 16-2 *Cisco Secure ACS Version 3.2 System Requirements (Continued)*

System Requirement Type	Requirements
Operating system *(continued)*	Microsoft Windows 2000 Advanced Server with Service Pack 3 or 4, without Microsoft Clustering Services installed and without any other Windows 2000 Advanced Server features enabled. Microsoft Windows Server 2003, Enterprise Edition for Cisco Secure ACS Version 3.2.3.
Browser	Microsoft Internet Explorer 6.0 Service Pack 1. Netscape Communicator 7.0 for Windows or Solaris.

Installing Cisco Secure ACS Version 3.2 on Windows Server

You can download a 90-day trial version of Cisco Secure ACS from the Cisco Software Center at Cisco.com. You must register as a user to receive your *CCO login*. You must have the CCO login to download software from the software center. The installation of Cisco Secure ACS is an easy, step-by-step process. It is a good idea to verify that your Windows 2000 Server is up to the current patch level. When you are ready to begin the installation, just run setup.exe. Figure 16-3 shows the initial Cisco Secure ACS installation window.

Figure 16-3 *Cisco Secure ACS Setup Welcome Window*

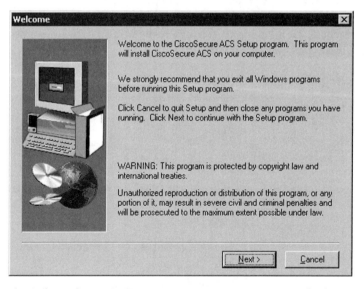

The second window, shown in Figure 16-4, prompts you to verify that your system is ready for this installation. Before this installation, you should verify that your Windows 2000

server is up to date, including Internet Explorer, and that you have connectivity with the NAS. In this case, the PIX Firewall functions as the NAS.

Figure 16-4 *Preinstallation Window*

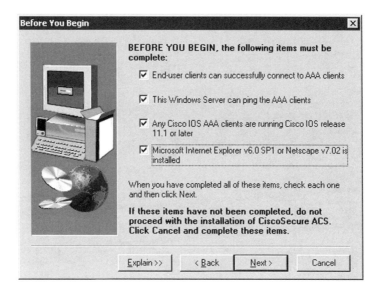

You are prompted to specify the installation directory, as shown in Figure 16-5. You can use the default directory, C:\Program Files\CiscoSecure ACS v3.2, or select another directory for the installation.

Figure 16-5 *Installation Directory (Default)*

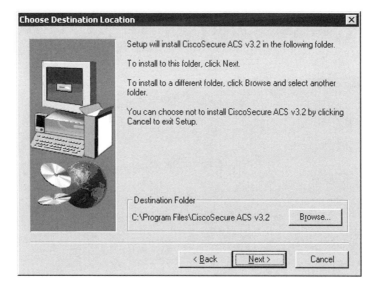

In the next window, shown in Figure 16-6, you select whether to authenticate against only the Cisco Secure ACS user database or the combination of the Cisco Secure ACS database and the Windows user database. The latter selection lets you use Windows username/password management and integrate Windows performance monitoring, which provides you with real-time login statistics.

For the purpose of this installation, the Cisco Secure ACS database only is used.

Figure 16-6 *User Database Window*

In the next window, shown in Figure 16-7, you are prompted to select any of ten possible choices for the connection type to the NAS. Remember that the Cisco PIX Firewall is acting as the NAS. For this configuration, TACACS+ (Cisco IOS) is selected.

Figure 16-7 *NAS Technology (TACACS+ Selected)*

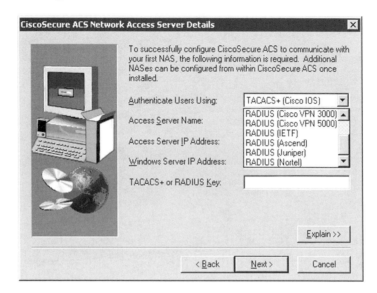

You next need to finish the NAS information to complete the connection between the AAA server and the NAS. Figure 16-8 shows the NAS Details window. Note the Explain button in the lower-right corner. Click this button to get an explanation of each of the settings, as shown in Figure 16-9.

Figure 16-8 *NAS Information (RADIUS Selected)*

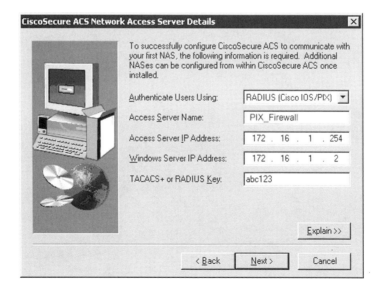

Figure 16-9 *Explanation of Settings*

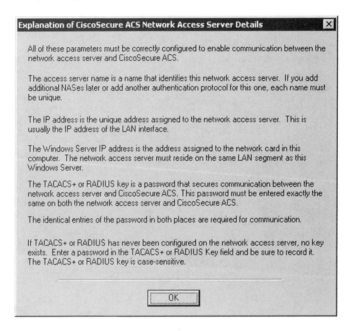

After you click Next in the NAS Details window, you are prompted to select the advanced features that you want to appear in the user interface, as shown in Figure 16-10. This allows you to determine how much (or how little) detail you want to see when working in the user interface. If you click the Explain button, you see the explanation window shown in Figure 16-11, which describes each of the available options. These settings can be configured during the initial configuration (installation), or you can skip this step and change the settings after Cisco Secure ACS is installed.

Figure 16-10   *Available Options in the User Interface*

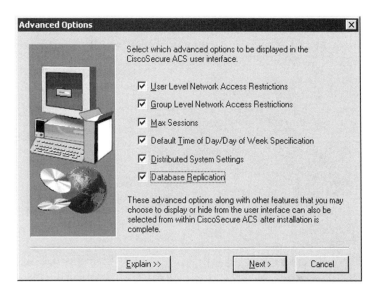

Figure 16-11   *Explanation of Advanced Options*

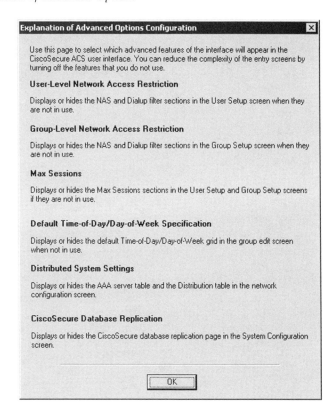

Next you select from three actions (Restart All, Restart RADIUS/TACACS+, Reboot) for the AAA server to initiate if a communications failure occurs between the Cisco Secure ACS and the NAS. These settings also include SMTP settings and the user account for the Cisco Secure ACS to send an alert to if a failure occurs. Figures 16-12 and 16-13 show the settings window and the settings explanation window, respectively.

Figure 16-12 *Alert Action and Notification Settings*

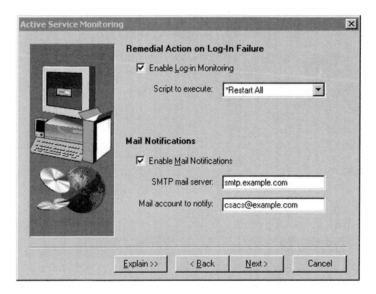

Figure 16-13 *Explanations for Alert Action and Notification Settings*

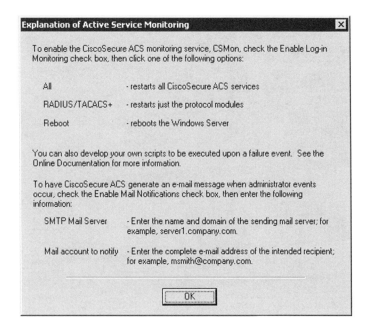

Cisco Secure ACS Version 3.2 includes an optional NAS Configuration window, shown in Figure 16-14, to assist you with the initial configuration of the Cisco IOS software. If you need further explanation, click the Explain button to review the window shown in Figure 16-15. This option works only when you are using a Cisco IOS Router as your NAS. This option should not be selected when using the PIX Firewall as the NAS.

Figure 16-14 *Cisco IOS Configuration Options*

Figure 16-15 *Cisco IOS Configuration Explanation*

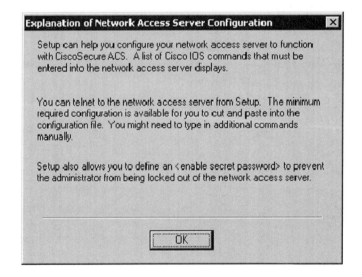

The installation/configuration of Cisco Secure ACS skips several steps if you do not elect to configure the Cisco IOS components. Figure 16-16 depicts the window that appears when the Cisco Secure ACS configuration is nearly complete. This window includes options for starting the Cisco Secure ACS Service, launching the Cisco Secure ACS Administrator from your browser, and viewing the Cisco Secure ACS Readme file.

Figure 16-16   *Cisco Secure ACS Startup Options*

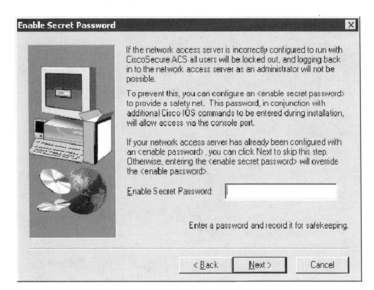

Cisco Secure ACS displays an activity bar as the Cisco Secure ACS Service is started (see Figure 16-17). Figure 16-18 shows the final configuration window that appears when the installation is complete.

Figure 16-17 *Service Start Flash Window*

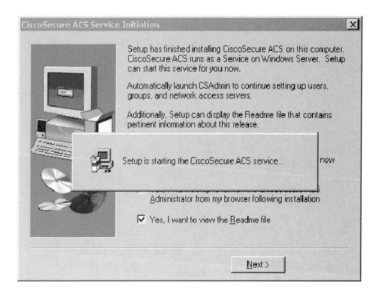

Figure 16-18 *Cisco Secure ACS Installation Complete*

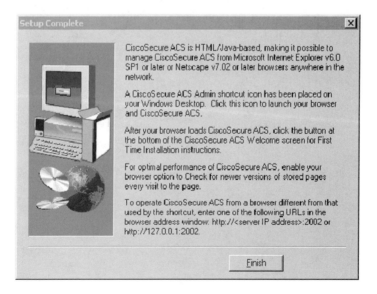

If you selected the option to launch the Cisco Secure ACS administration browser window, the system launches a window that is similar to Figure 16-19.

Figure 16-19 *Cisco Secure ACS Administration Window*

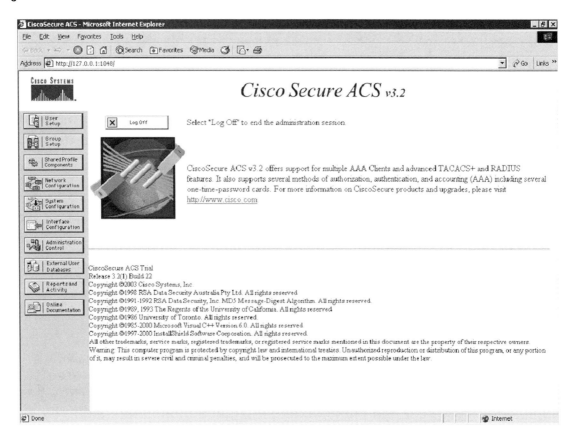

Congratulations! You have completed the installation of Cisco Secure ACS on a Windows server. Chapter 17, "Configuration of AAA on the PIX," shows you how to configure Cisco Secure ACS.

Foundation Summary

The "Foundation Summary" provides a convenient review of many key concepts in this chapter. If you are already comfortable with the topics in this chapter, this summary can help you recall a few details. If you just read this chapter, this review should help solidify some key facts. If you are doing your final preparation before the exam, this summary provides a convenient way to review the day before the exam.

Authentication, authorization, and accounting are three separate functions performed by AAA servers to allow access to resources. Each of these functions has a specific goal. If you are using AAA, then authenticating the user is key. No access is granted if the requestor is not authenticated. The use of authorization and accounting are dependant on authentication, but it is not necessary to configure either authorization or accounting to make authentication function properly. The list below defines each of the components of AAA.

- **Authentication**—Identifies the entity (user)
- **Authorization**—Gives the user access based on his or her profile
- **Accounting**—Maintains a record of user access

Cisco PIX Firewall Version 6.2 can maintain an internal user database for console authentication and command authorization or connect to an external AAA server. The PIX Firewall supports both RADIUS and TACACS+ technologies. Figure 16-20 shows the steps that the AAA server takes during the entire AAA process.

Figure 16-20 *AAA Server Steps*

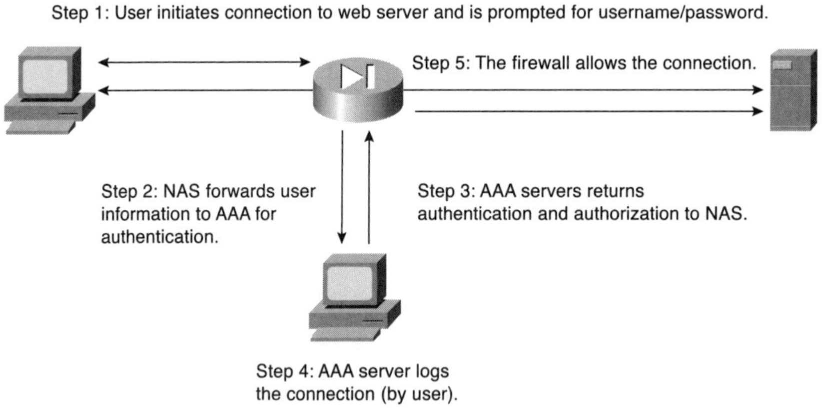

Step 1: User initiates connection to web server and is prompted for username/password.

Step 5: The firewall allows the connection.

Step 2: NAS forwards user information to AAA for authentication.

Step 3: AAA servers returns authentication and authorization to NAS.

Step 4: AAA server logs the connection (by user).

Cisco Secure ACS is available for Windows Server and can be configured for TACACS+ and RADIUS. The Cisco Secure ACS installation on Windows is an easy, step-by-step wizard installation.

Q&A

As mentioned in the Introduction, the questions in this book are more difficult than what you should experience on the exam. The questions are designed to ensure your understanding of the concepts discussed in this chapter and adequately prepare you to complete the exam. You should use the simulated exams on the CD to practice for the exam.

The answers to these questions can be found in Appendix A.

1. What is the relationship between the Cisco PIX Firewall and the AAA server?

2. What three methods are used to authenticate to the Cisco PIX Firewall?

3. How does the Cisco PIX Firewall process cut-through proxy?

4. What are the main differences between RADIUS and TACACS+?

5. What patch level must you have Windows 2000 Professional configured to before you install Cisco Secure ACS?

6. Why is it important to authenticate a user before you complete authorization?

7. What are the three layers of authentication?

8. What is the purpose of the Explain button during the Cisco Secure ACS installation?

9. What do you need to verify before installing Cisco Secure ACS?

10. Why is it important to have Internet Explorer up to date on your Cisco Secure ACS?

11. True or false: With authorization configured, cut-through proxy authenticates users and then allows them to connect to anything.

12. True or false: The Cisco Secure ACS installation on Windows Server is a relatively simple, wizard-based installation.

This chapter covers the following subjects:

- Examining the Cisco PIX Firewall Status

- Overview of AAA

- Installation of Cisco Secure ACS for Windows NT/2000

- Authentication Configuration

- Downloadable ACLs

CHAPTER 17

Configuration of AAA on the PIX

This chapter addresses the commands necessary to configure authentication, authorization, and accounting (AAA) on the Cisco PIX Firewall. As mentioned in the Introduction, remembering the PIX commands is important. In the real world, it is possible to navigate your way around the PIX Firewall and figure out the correct syntax for a command. This is not possible in the testing environment. You will be asked to select a command that performs a certain function from a list of very similar commands. It is *very* important that you understand the correct syntax for each PIX command.

How to Best Use This Chapter

This chapter covers the communications between the Cisco PIX Firewall and the Cisco Secure Access Control Server (ACS). You will learn how to configure the PIX Firewall to work with an AAA server and how to configure the Cisco Secure ACS to work with the PIX Firewall. The configurations for authentication, authorization, and accounting are very similar and should be relatively simple to remember. Quite a few commands and options are available for configuring each AAA component, but each command and option is used for nearly every component. Cisco Secure ACS is a simple GUI package that includes online help. You need to become familiar with the tabs on the navigation bar and how the different configurations interact.

"Do I Know This Already?" Quiz

The purpose of the "Do I Know This Already?" quiz is to help you decide if you really need to read the entire chapter. If you already intend to read the entire chapter, you do not necessarily need to answer these questions now.

The 11-question quiz, derived from the major sections in the "Foundation Topics" portion of the chapter, helps you determine how to spend your limited study time.

Table 17-1 outlines the major topics discussed in this chapter and the "Do I Know This Already?" quiz questions that correspond to those topics.

Table 17-1 *"Do I Know This Already?" Foundation Topics Section-to-Question Mapping*

Foundations Topics Section	Questions Covered in This Section	Score
Examining the PIX Firewall Status	1	
Overview of AAA	2	
Installation of Cisco Secure ACS for Windows NT/2000	4, 5, 7, 8	
Authentication Configuration	3, 9, 11	
Downloadable ACLs	6	

CAUTION The goal of self assessment is to gauge your mastery of the topics in this chapter. If you do not know the answer to a question or are only partially sure of the answer, you should mark this question wrong for purposes of the self assessment. Giving yourself credit for an answer you correctly guess skews your self-assessment results and might provide you with a false sense of security.

1. What is the best way to authenticate an H.323 connection?

   a. Authenticate to the H.323 server

   b. Telnet to the H.323 server

   c. Virtual Telnet to the PIX Firewall for authentication

   d. Virtual HTTP to the Cisco Secure ACS for authentication

2. What three services are used to authenticate by default in the PIX Firewall?

   a. FTP, HTTP, HTTPS

   b. FTP, Telnet, SSH

   c. Auth-proxy, Local-auth, console

   d. FTP, HTTPS, Telnet

   e. None of the above

3. Which options are mandatory in every **aaa authentication** command on the PIX Firewall? (Select all that apply.)

   a. include/exclude

   b. inbound/outbound

   c. local-ip/mask

   d. group-tag

   e. acl-name

4. How do you configure client IP address assignment on the Cisco Secure ACS when using the PIX Firewall as the AAA client?

   a. Edit the AAA-client IP address in the System Configuration window.

   b. Edit the AAA-client information in the Network Configuration window.

   c. Edit the AAA Server information in the Interface Configuration window.

   d. Edit the PIX Firewall information in the Network Configuration window.

   e. None of the above

5. Why is it a good idea to rename your groups in Cisco Secure ACS?

   a. To get the groups into a hierarchical format

   b. To increase the performance of the Cisco Secure ACS

   c. To simplify administration of users and groups

   d. You cannot rename groups after they have been created.

   e. None of the above

6. You are trying to create downloadable IP ACLs in Cisco Secure ACS, but the option is not available. What are two possible reasons?

   a. You are running an older version of Cisco Secure ACS that does not support downloadable ACLs.

   b. The PIX Firewall cannot connect to the Cisco Secure ACS.

   c. Your authentication protocol is not RADIUS.

   d. You do not have User-Level or Group-Level Downloadable ACLs selected in the Interface Configuration window, Advanced Options pane.

7. Where do you see the logs on the Cisco Secure ACS?

   a. Interface Configuration window

   b. Reports and Activity window

   c. Network Configuration window

   d. System Configuration window

8. You are installing Cisco Secure ACS on your new Windows 2000 Professional, but you cannot get it to load correctly. What is most likely the problem?

   a. Cisco Secure ACS requires server software.

   b. Your patch level is not up to date.

   c. You are running a personal firewall or host-based IDS that is blocking the installation.

   d. You do not have administrative privileges on that system.

   e. All of the above

9. True or false: Cisco Secure ACS comes with its own online documentation.

10. True or false: The **show aaa** command shows you everything that has to do with your AAA server in its configuration.

11. What happens to virtual HTTP if you disable **timeout uauth absolute**?

   a. The user cannot authenticate.

   b. The user authenticates and never has to reauthenticate because the connection stays open.

   c. The user can authenticate but cannot connect to the server.

   d. None of the above

The answers to the "Do I Know This Already?" quiz are found in Appendix A, "Answers to the 'Do I Know This Already?' Quizzes and Q&A Sections." The suggested choices for your next step are as follows:

- **9 or less overall score**—Read the entire chapter. This includes the "Foundation Topics," "Foundation Summary," and "Q&A" sections.

- **10 or 11 overall score**—If you want more review of these topics, skip to the "Foundation Summary" section and then go to the "Q&A" section. Otherwise, move to the next chapter.

Foundation Topics

Chapter 16, "Overview of AAA and the PIX," provided a good overview of the AAA process and the Cisco Secure ACS for Windows 2000. This chapter addresses the configuration of the Cisco PIX Firewall and the Cisco Secure ACS required to build an operational AAA solution. The PIX Firewall must be configured to communicate with the Cisco Secure ACS, and the Cisco Secure ACS must be configured to control the PIX Firewall. Although the PIX Firewall configuration is completed using the command-line interface, the commands required are rather simple and fairly intuitive. The Cisco Secure ACS is completely web-based, with instructions on every page, and it is very simple to configure. After completing this chapter, you should be intimately familiar with the configurations of both the PIX Firewall and the Cisco Secure ACS combined as a functional AAA solution.

Specifying Your AAA Servers

Only two components are required to build an AAA solution:

- AAA server

- Network access server (NAS)

It is possible to divide the AAA functions among multiple devices to reduce the processing required by any single server. It is also possible for a single AAA server to support multiple NASs. The point is that there is no single solution. The number of AAA servers and NASs should be tailored to support the size and scope of the network being accessed. Configuring the PIX Firewall to connect to an AAA server requires only a few commands. Of course, quite a few options are available with each command. In this exercise, the PIX Firewall is configured to connect to a Cisco Secure ACS located on the DMZ segment. Figure 17-1 depicts the network configuration used for the examples in this chapter. Note that the Cisco Secure ACS is located on a DMZ segment rather than on the inside or outside segments. This allows you to restrict access to the Cisco Secure ACS from either segment, making the system more secure.

Figure 17-1 *Cisco PIX Firewall and Cisco Secure ACS Topology for Chapter*

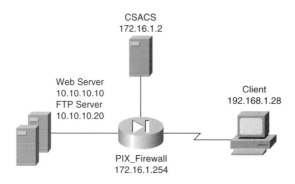

Configuring AAA on the Cisco PIX Firewall

Four steps are required to configure AAA on the PIX Firewall:

Step 1   Identify the AAA server and the NAS.

Step 2   Configure authentication.

Step 3   Configure authorization.

Step 4   Configure accounting.

Each of these steps can be completed for the PIX Firewall to communicate with the AAA servers; however, it is possible to configure authentication without authorization or accounting. Each step is discussed in detail in the following sections.

Step 1: Identifying the AAA Server and NAS

You must be sure to have the correct information about your AAA server before you attempt to configure your PIX Firewall. You use the **aaa-server** command (from configuration mode on the PIX Firewall) to specify the AAA server. Remember that you are dealing with at least two devices: the PIX Firewall and the Cisco Secure ACS.

You must configure the PIX Firewall to recognize the Cisco Secure ACS as its AAA server for authentication. You also must configure the Cisco Secure ACS to communicate with the PIX Firewall with the necessary account information so that the Cisco Secure ACS can validate authentication requests from the PIX Firewall. To accomplish both tasks, you need to use the following commands:

```
aaa-server group-tag protocol auth-protocol
aaa-server group-tag [if-name] host server-ip key [timeout seconds]
```

You must define the following command options and parameters for the configuration to be successful:

- **aaa-server**—Designates the AAA server or server group. A group can have as many as 14 servers, and the PIX Firewall can handle up to 14 groups of AAA servers, for a total of 196 AAA servers. This enables you to tailor which AAA servers handle certain services and lets you configure your AAA servers for redundancy. When a user logs in, the NAS contacts the first server in the group (see the *group-tag* description). If it does not receive a response within the designated timeout period, it moves to the next server in the group.

- *group-tag*—The name used for the AAA server group. The *group-tag* is also used in the **aaa authentication, aaa authorization**, and **aaa accounting** commands.

- **protocol** *auth-protocol*—The type of AAA server used (TACACS+ or RADIUS).

- *if-name*—The interface name for the interface on which the AAA server resides. This designates how the firewall connects to the AAA server.

- **host** *server-ip*—The AAA server's IP address.

- *key*—A shared secret between the Cisco Secure ACS (server) and the PIX Firewall (client). It is an alphanumeric password that can be as many as 127 characters.

- **timeout** *seconds*—How long the PIX Firewall waits between transmission attempts to the AAA server. The PIX Firewall makes four attempts to connect with the AAA server before trying to connect to the next AAA server in the group. The default timeout is 5 seconds; the maximum timeout is 30 seconds. Using the default timeout of 5 seconds, the PIX Firewall attempts four transmissions, waiting 5 seconds between each attempt, for a total of 20 seconds.

For the network example in this chapter, you would enter the syntax shown in Example 17-1.

Example 17-1 *Identifying AAA Servers on the PIX Firewall*

```
PIXFirewall(config)# aaa-server TACACS+ protocol tacacs+
PIXFirewall(config)# aaa-server TACACS+ (DMZ) host 172.16.1.2 abc123 timeout 20
```

For smaller networks with a limited number of users, you can authenticate to a database configured locally on the PIX Firewall. This is not a recommended configuration for medium-size to large networks because the processing required to maintain and authenticate against a local database reduces the firewall's performance. As of PIX Firewall Version 6.2 the AAA server group "local" is predefined for console authentication and command authorization. The command to configure authentication to a local database is **aaa-server local**.

> **NOTE** To remove the **AAA server** from the configuration, enter **no aaa-server.** This disables the AAA server function, but the configuration for that server remains on the PIX Firewall.

You finish configuring the Cisco Secure ACS to connect to the PIX Firewall by selecting the PIX Firewall during the Cisco Secure ACS installation, as shown in Figure 17-2.

Figure 17-2 *Selecting the Network Access Server*

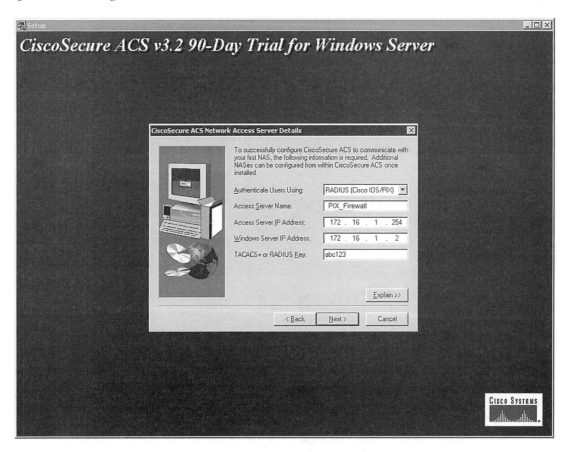

You also can create additional NASs or edit the current NAS settings in Cisco Secure ACS by clicking the Network Configuration button in the Cisco Secure ACS main window. Remember that the Cisco Secure ACS calls the NAS the "AAA client." Figure 17-3 shows the settings for the PIX Firewall in the Cisco Secure ACS. Notice that the authentication protocol has been changed from RADIUS to TACACS+.

Figure 17-3   *Configuring NAS in Cisco Secure ACS*

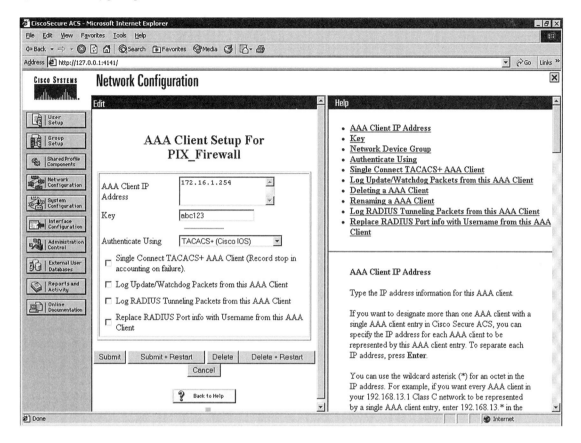

> **NOTE**   The TACACS+ or RADIUS key specified on Cisco Secure ACS must exactly match the key specified in the **aaa-server** command for communication between the Cisco Secure ACS server and the NAS to be established.

Step 2: Configuring Authentication

Now that you have the AAA server and the NAS configured to communicate with each other, you need to configure both for user authentication. First you need to configure the authentication parameters on the PIX Firewall, and then you need to create the user accounts on the Cisco Secure ACS. Three types of authentication are supported on the PIX Firewall:

- TACACS+
- RADIUS
- LOCAL

Both TACACS+ and RADIUS support numerous vendor-specific attributes (VSAs) or attribute value (AV) pairs. For a list of the specific VSAs or AV pairs and their definitions, see the *User Guide for Cisco Secure ACS for Windows Version 3.2*.

The **aaa authentication** command has three different types. The following list describes the options and variables you find collectively within all three:

- **include**—Creates a rule with a specified service.

- **exclude**—Creates an exception to a previously defined rule.

- *authen-service*—The service that is included or excluded. It is the application with which the user accesses the network. The PIX Firewall can authenticate only via FTP, HTTP, and Telnet. You can configure the *authen-service* as "any" to allow the PIX Firewall to authenticate any of the three, but this does not allow your users to authenticate using any protocol other than FTP, HTTP, or Telnet.

- **inbound**—Specifies that the PIX Firewall is to authenticate inbound traffic (originates on the outside interface and is directed to the inside interface).

- **outbound**—Specifies that the PIX Firewall is to authenticate outbound traffic (originates on the inside interface and is directed to the outside interface).

- *if-name*—The interface name from which the users should be authenticated. This is optional. By default, the user must authenticate before being allowed through the PIX Firewall. Therefore, outbound traffic authenticates at the inside interface, and inbound traffic authenticates at the outside interface.

- *local-ip*—The host address or network segment with the highest security level. As with the other address definitions on the PIX Firewall, 0 is used to define "any."

- *local-mask*—The subnet mask that applies to the *local-ip*; 0 is used to define "any."

- *foreign-ip*—Defines the address space with the lowest security level. The use of 0 defines "any."

- *foreign-mask*—The subnet mask that applies to the *foreign-ip*; 0 is used to define "any."

- *group-tag*—The name used for the AAA server group. The *group-tag* is also used in the **aaa-server**, **aaa authorization**, and **aaa accounting** commands.

The following sections describe the three different formats and functions of the **aaa authentication** command in greater detail.

Manually Designating AAA Authentication Parameters

The first command enables you to manually designate the authentication parameters using the items in the preceding list. The syntax for this command is as follows:

```
aaa authentication include ¦ exclude authen-service inbound ¦ outbound if-name local-ip
    local-mask foreign-ip foreign-mask group-tag
```

Example 17-2 shows the syntax for requiring all inbound traffic to authenticate except for traffic connecting from host 192.168.1.28 based on the network shown in Figure 17-1.

Example 17-2   *Configuring AAA Authentication on the PIX Firewall*

```
PIXFirewall(config)# aaa authentication include any outside 0 0 0 0 TACACS+
PIXFirewall(config)# aaa authentication exclude http outside 0 0 192.168.1.28
  255.255.255.255 TACACS+
```

The *local-ip* must be the actual IP address configured on a system without Network Address Translation. To configure this authentication, you must ensure that you have a static address translation or NAT configured for your *local-ip* but you must list the original IP address as the *local-ip*.

Designating AAA Authentication Parameters Via Access Lists

It is also possible to configure your AAA authentication to reference access lists using the **match** command. This configuration removes the requirement of manually defining the local and foreign addresses. The syntax for AAA authentication using access lists is as follows:

```
aaa authentication match acl-name if-name server-tag
```

Example 17-3 is an example of the **aaa authentication** command, including the referenced access list.

Example 17-3   *Configuring aaa authentication match*

```
PIXFirewall(config)# static (inside,outside) 192.168.200.1 10.10.10.10 netmask
  255.255.255.255
PIXFirewall(config)# access-list PIXTEST permit tcp any host  192.168.200.1 eq 80
PIXFirewall(config)# access-group PIXTEST in interface outside
PIXFirewall(config)# aaa authentication match PIXTEST outside TACACS+
```

The static translation and access group are also included in this example because each is required to have the correct public address and to apply the access list.

> **NOTE**   Chapter 7, "Configuring Access," discusses access lists in greater detail.

One additional command you should use when configuring authentication is **sysopt uauth allow-http-cache**. This command allows the system to cache user authentication for HTTP requests, which relieves the user from having to reauthenticate when navigating the Internet when HTTP authentication is required. This could be a security concern in certain situations and, thus, you should carefully consider it before you add it to the PIX Firewall configuration.

Console Access Authentication

The final type of AAA authentication is for direct connections to the Cisco PIX Firewall. It is very important to restrict access to the firewall as much as possible. One way to increase your firewall's security is to require all access to the firewall to be authenticated by an AAA server. Console access is traditionally password protected; however, the **aaa authentication console** command prompts the user to authenticate differently, depending on the method used to access the PIX Firewall:

- **serial**—Causes the user to be prompted before the first command of the command-line prompt when connecting directly to the firewall via a serial cable. Users are continually prompted until they successfully log in.

- **telnet**—Causes the user to be prompted before the first command-line prompt when attempting a Telnet session to the CLI. Users are continually prompted until they successfully log in.

- **ssh**—Causes the user to be prompted before the first command-line prompt when attempting a Secure Shell (SSH) session to the CLI. If users are unable to successfully authenticate within three attempts, they are disconnected and receive the message "Rejected by Server."

- **http**—This option is selected when you use the PIX Device Manager (PDM) to manage your PIX Firewall. PDM users see a pop-up window in their browser (PIX Device Manager). Users are continually prompted until they successfully log in.

- **enable**—With this option, the PIX Firewall requires AAA server authentication to enter privileged mode. The **enable** option prompts the user for a username and password before entering privileged mode for serial, Telnet, and SSH connections. If users are unable to successfully authenticate after three attempts, they see the "Access Denied" message.

> **NOTE** By default, the PDM can access the PIX Firewall with no username and the enable password unless the **aaa authentication http console** *group-tag* command is set.

The PIX Firewall supports usernames that are up to 127 characters and passwords that are up to 63 characters. Usernames and passwords cannot contain the @ character. The PDM is limited to a maximum of 30 characters for the username and 15 characters for the password.

> **NOTE**   To remove the **aaa authentication** from the configuration, enter **no aaa authentication**.

Authentication of Services

The Cisco PIX Firewall is designed to authenticate users via FTP, HTTP, and Telnet. Many other services that pass through the PIX Firewall require authentication. To fulfill this requirement, the PIX Firewall supports *virtual services*. The PIX Firewall can perform functions for servers that do not exist and configures the PIX Firewall to authenticate users who want to connect to services other than FTP, HTTP, and Telnet. After a user has been authenticated, that user can access whatever authorized services they are requesting.

If your company uses Microsoft NetMeeting to communicate among its many different branch offices. NetMeeting runs on the H.323 protocol, which uses a number of different ports. To allow this access, users must authenticate via FTP, HTTP, or Telnet. If you do not have a server available to accept the FTP, HTTP, or Telnet connections, you can configure the PIX Firewall to accept the connections via a virtual service.

Virtual Telnet

Virtual Telnet enables the user to authenticate using Telnet and use a service that does not support authentication. The PIX Firewall accepts the user's connection and challenges the user for a username and password. The username and password are verified by the TACACS+ or RADIUS server. If the user successfully authenticates, the connection to the user's requested service is completed. An additional server is not required to accept the connection, because the PIX Firewall creates a virtual server to handle the authentication requests. Virtual Telnet sessions can be inbound or outbound on the PIX Firewall.

To configure virtual Telnet on the PIX Firewall, you must first create the virtual server on a segment that can be reached via the PIX Firewall. Normally this is an address on the firewall's outside interface. In Figure 17-4, the virtual IP address is 192.168.1.4. This public IP address can be accessed from both inside networks and public networks (such as the Internet). The syntax of the **virtual telnet** command is as follows:

```
virtual telnet ip-address
```

Figure 17-4 *Assigning the IP Address for Virtual Services for Outbound Traffic*

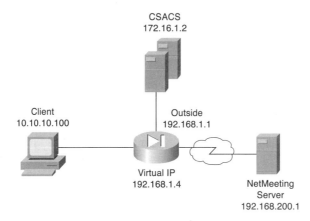

Example 17-4 shows the virtual Telnet configuration that authenticates host 10.10.10.100 when you make an outbound connection to a NetMeeting server located on the Internet.

Example 17-4 *Configuring Virtual Telnet Outbound Connections*

```
PIXFirewall(config)# ip address outside 192.168.1.1 255.255.255.0
PIXFirewall(config)# ip address inside 10.10.10.1 255.255.255.0
PIXFirewall(config)# global (outside) 1 192.168.1.20-192.168.1.40 netmask
  255.255.255.0
PIXFirewall(config)# nat (inside) 1 0 0 0 0
PIXFirewall(config)# aaa-server TACACS+ protocol tacacs+
PIXFirewall(config)# aaa-server TACACS+ (DMZ) host 172.16.1.2 abc123 timeout 20
PIXFirewall(config)# aaa authentication include any inside 0 0 0 0 TACACS+
PIXFirewall(config)# virtual telnet 192.168.1.4
```

Now let us change the positions of the client and server. This time the NetMeeting server is behind the PIX Firewall, and the client is on the Internet. Figure 17-5 depicts the configuration with the NetMeeting server on the internal network and the client on the Internet.

Figure 17-5   *Assigning the IP address for Virtual Services for Inbound Traffic*

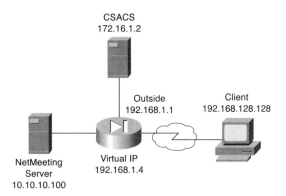

The PIX Firewall configuration must change to allow the inbound traffic to connect to the NetMeeting server. First, the NetMeeting server needs to have a public IP address, which means that you need to perform static translation. Second, you need to configure the access lists to allow the inbound traffic. Example 17-5 shows the configuration required to allow inbound connections to a destination on the protected network.

Example 17-5   *Configuring Virtual Telnet Inbound Connections*

```
PIXFirewall(config)# ip address outside 192.168.1.1 255.255.255.0
PIXFirewall(config)# ip address inside 10.10.10.1 255.255.255.0
PIXFirewall(config)# global (outside) 1 192.168.1.20-192.168.1.40 netmask 255.255.255.0
PIXFirewall(config)# nat (inside) 1 0 0 0 0
PIXFirewall(config)# aaa-server TACACS+ protocol tacacs+
PIXFirewall(config)# aaa-server TACACS+ (DMZ) host 172.16.1.2 abc123 timeout 20
PIXFirewall(config)# aaa authentication include any outside 0 0 0 0 TACACS+
PIXFirewall(config)# virtual telnet 192.168.1.4
PIXFirewall(config)# static (inside, outside) 192.168.1.4 10.10.10.100 netmask
  255.255.255.255 0 0
PIXFirewall(config)# access-list NetMeeting permit tcp any host 192.168.1.4 eq 23
PIXFirewall(config)# access-list NetMeeting permit tcp 192.168.128.128
  255.255.255.255 192.168.1.4 255.255.255.255 eq H323
PIXFirewall(config)# access-group NetMeeting in interface outside
```

NOTE   To remove the virtual Telnet from the configuration, enter **no virtual telnet**.

Virtual HTTP

Virtual HTTP functions similarly to virtual Telnet in that the PIX Firewall acts as the HTTP server via an additional IP address assigned to the firewall. Users might believe that they are accessing the web server, but they are actually accessing the virtual server for the authentication prompt, being authenticated by an AAA server, and being redirected to their destination after successful authentication. The syntax for **virtual http** is

```
virtual http ip-address [warn]
```

The *warn* option is used for text-based browsers that cannot automatically be redirected. The option adds a link that would be used to redirect to the virtual HTTP server.

Normally the *ip-address* should be an address that the inside network routes to the PIX Firewall. This way, the internal users access it directly, and the external users connect to it via static address translation at the firewall. Of course, the inbound users require authentication and also must be permitted by an access list or conduit. Example 17-6 depicts the configuration for virtual HTTP on the PIX Firewall. This is the configuration shown in Figure 17-5.

Example 17-6 *Configuring Virtual HTTP Inbound Connections*

```
PIXFirewall(config)# ip address outside 192.168.1.1 255.255.255.0
PIXFirewall(config)# ip address inside 10.10.10.1 255.255.255.0
PIXFirewall(config)# global (outside) 1 192.168.1.20-192.168.1.40 netmask 255.255.255.0
PIXFirewall(config)# nat (inside) 1 0 0 0 0
PIXFirewall(config)# aaa-server TACACS+ protocol tacacs+
PIXFirewall(config)# aaa-server TACACS+ (DMZ) host 172.16.1.2 abc123 timeout 20
PIXFirewall(config)# static (inside, outside) 192.168.1.5 10.10.10.5 netmask
  255.255.255.255 0 0
PIXFirewall(config)# aaa authentication include any outside 192.168.1.5 255.255.255.255
  0 0 TACACS+
PIXFirewall(config)# access-list WebTest permit tcp any host 192.168.1.5 eq www
PIXFirewall(config)# access-group WebTest in interface outside
PIXFirewall(config)# virtual http 192.168.1.5
```

NOTE   To remove the virtual HTTP from the configuration, enter **no virtual http**.

Authentication Prompts

The **auth-prompt** command is used to configure the exact text used when the user is challenged to authenticate, successfully authenticates, or does not authenticate. This command sets the text for FTP, HTTP, and Telnet session authentication. The syntax of this command is

```
auth-prompt [prompt | accept | reject] string
```

The *string* is the text that is displayed. It can be up to 235 characters in length for FTP and Telnet connections. It is limited to 120 characters for HTTP connections using Netscape Navigator, and it is limited to 37 characters for HTTP connections using Microsoft Internet Explorer. The *string* should not include any special characters. It ends either by typing a question mark (?) or by pressing the Enter key.

The **auth-prompt** command has three options:

- **prompt**—Configures the text that is displayed when the user is prompted to authenticate: "Access to this location is restricted, please provide username and password."

- **accept**—Configures the text that is displayed if the user successfully authenticates using a Telnet session: "User Authentication complete, please continue." No text is displayed for authentication using FTP or HTTP.

- **reject**—Configures the text that is displayed if the user is unable to successfully authenticate using a Telnet session: "Authentication unsuccessful; if you feel that you have received this message in error please contact your systems administrator." The text for FTP and HTTP authentication sessions cannot be configured on the PIX Firewall.

Authentication Timeout

After a user is successfully authenticated, their user information is saved in cache for a predetermined amount of time. You set this time by configuring the **timeout uauth** command. It is specified in hours, minutes, and seconds. If the user session idle time exceeds the timeout, the session is terminated and the user is prompted to authenticate during the next connection. To disable caching of users, use the **timeout uauth** 0 command. Be sure not to use **timeout uauth** 0 when using **virtual http**. This setting prevents any connections to the real web server after successful authentication at the PIX Firewall.

> **NOTE**   If the firewall is performing NAT, the **timeout uauth** value must be less than the **timeout xlate** value to ensure that the user authentication times out before the address translation.

Two command options or settings are associated with the **timeout uauth** command:

- **absolute**—The default setting for the **uauth** timer. This setting sets the timer to prompt the user to reauthenticate after the timer elapses only when the user starts a new connection. If the user leaves the session open and the timer elapses, and the user closes the browser without clicking another link, the user is not prompted to reauthenticate. Setting the **uauth** timer to 0 disables caching of user authentication and therefore disables the **absolute** option.

- **inactivity**—The inactivity timer starts after the connection becomes idle. If the user establishes a new connection before the duration of the inactivity timer, the user is not required to reauthenticate. If a user establishes a new connection after the inactivity timer expires, the user must reauthenticate.

Example 17-7 depicts the **timeout** command with the **absolute** and **inactivity** settings. The first command sets the timer to 4 hours and tells the system not to prompt the user after the session times out unless the user initiates another session. The second command defines a 30-minute period of inactivity as an idle session and tells the system to start the timer at that point.

Example 17-7 *Configuring Timeout on the PIX Firewall*

```
PIXFirewall(config)# timeout uauth 4:00:00 absolute
PIXFirewall(config)# timeout uauth 0:30:00 inactivity
```

The final command associated with timeouts is **clear uauth.** This command forces the system to delete the authorization cache for all users. This makes the system reauthenticate every user when they initiate their next connection.

Step 3: Configuring Authorization

When discussing authorization, you should first understand the difference between authentication and authorization:

- Authentication identifies who the user is.

- Authorization determines what the user can do.

- Authentication can be implemented without authorization.

- Authorization cannot be used unless the user has successfully authenticated.

Authorization is not a requirement but rather a method of allowing you to become more granular in what access you give specific users. After users have successfully authenticated, they can be given the access they have requested. This access is configured using the **aaa authorization** command, the syntax for which is very similar to the **aaa authentication** command, except for the service. The PIX Firewall does not permit or deny any traffic based solely on the **aaa authorization** commands. This configuration merely tells the firewall which services it needs to reference the AAA server for authorization before allowing or denying the connection. A TACACS+ server performs AAA authorization. The server is configured using the following syntax:

```
aaa authorization include | exclude svc if-name local-ip
        local-mask foreign-ip foreign-mask
```

tacacs-server-tag specifies the TACACS+ server to be used for authorization.

author-service is the service defined for **aaa authorization**. The *author-service* parameter defines any service that requires authorization by listing them as **include** or **exclude** and the interface that the traffic is passing through. Services not listed are implicitly authorized. *author-service* can be **any, ftp, http, telnet,** or *protocol/port*. Authorization of services is configured using the following syntax:

```
aaa authorization include ¦ exclude service if-name local-ip
    local-mask foreign-ip foreign-mask
```

Example 17-8 shows the commands used to authorize outbound DNS requests and all inbound services except HTTP requests from 192.168.1.28 to any destination.

Example 17-8 *Configuring Authorization on the PIX Firewall*

```
PIXFirewall(config)# aaa authorization include any outside 0 0 0 0 TACACS+
PIXFirewall(config)# aaa authorization exclude http outside 0 0 192.168.1.28
  255.255.255.255 TACACS+
PIXFirewall(config)# aaa authorization include udp/53 inside 0 0 0 0 TACACS+
```

> **NOTE** To remove the AAA authorization from the configuration, enter **no aaa authorization.**

Cisco Secure ACS and Authorization

After the Cisco PIX Firewall is configured correctly, you must configure authorization on your Cisco Secure ACS. If your Cisco Secure ACS is already configured with the PIX Firewall as the NAS, a few steps remain to configure authorization:

Step 1   Configure user accounts within the Cisco Secure ACS.

Step 2   Assign users to a group.

Step 3   Apply authorization rules to the group.

Steps 1 and 2: Configuring User Accounts Within the Cisco Secure ACS and Assigning Users to a Group

To configure new users in Cisco Secure ACS, click the User Setup button on the left navigation bar. When the User Setup window appears, shown in Figure 17-6, enter the username in the User box and then click Add/Edit.

In the Edit pane of the User Setup window, shown in Figure 17-7, you can configure many options pertaining to the user account:

■ **Account Disabled**—Checking this box lets you create accounts for users who are not yet ready to begin using the system. For example, suppose you are told that the company has hired a new employee who is scheduled to begin working in three weeks. You can configure the user account and then turn it on by deselecting the check box when the new employee starts work.

■ **Supplementary User Info**—An optional field for entering user information. It is a very good idea to complete these fields because they help you keep track of your user accounts as your user base grows:

— **Real Name**—The user's name, not the user account name.

— **Description**—A description of the user. Normally this field describes the user's position within the company.

Figure 17-6 *Creating User Accounts on the Cisco Secure ACS*

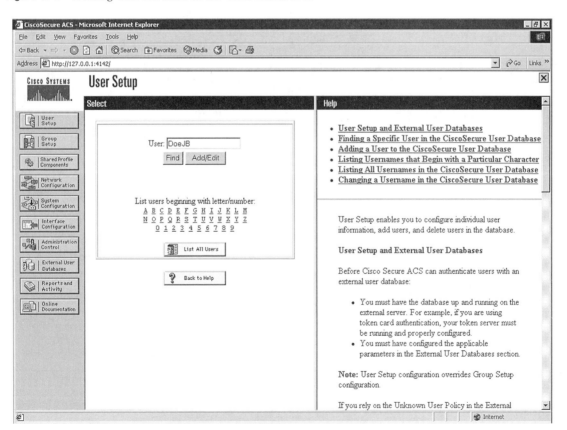

■ **User Setup**—Select the type of authentication database, and enter the user password:

— **Password Authentication**—Two types of password authentication are available on the Cisco Secure ACS by default. You can add a number of additional authentication types by clicking the External User Databases button on the left navigation bar. Select the authentication type from the drop-down menu:

CiscoSecure Database—Authenticates the user from a database installed locally on the Cisco Secure ACS.

Windows NT/2000—Authenticates the user against a Windows NT/2000 Server that is located on the same system that is running the Cisco Secure ACS or any Windows NT/2000 system that has a trust relationship with the domain that the Cisco Secure ACS is part of.

External User Database—You can add multiple configurations for each of the following authentication services: Vasco Token Server, RSA SecurID Token Server, RADIUS Token Server, External ODBC Database, Windows NT/2000, Novell NDS, Leap Proxy RADIUS Server, Generis LDAP, SafeWord Token Server, CryptoCard Token Server, AXENT Token Server, and ActivCard Token Server.

Figure 17-7 *Configuring User Accounts on the Cisco Secure ACS*

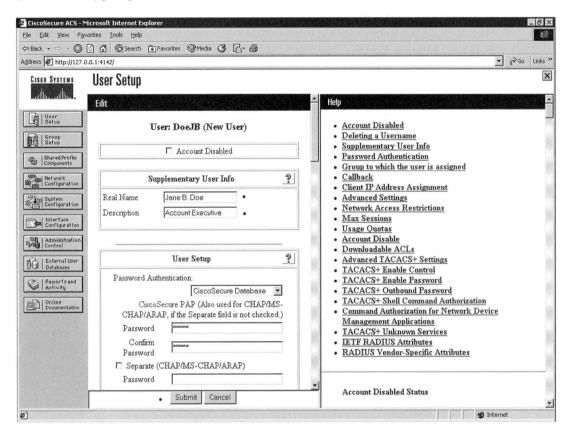

— **Password and Confirm Password**—Enter and confirm the user's password.

— **Separate (CHAP/MS-CHAP/ARAP) Password**—This feature is not used on the PIX Firewall.

— **Group**—Select a user group from the drop-down box. All users are assigned to the Default Group unless they are specifically assigned to another group. Grouping the users and applying rules to groups enables you to efficiently administer the authentication services.

— **Callback**—This feature is not used on the PIX Firewall.

— **Client IP Address Assignment**—This feature is not used on the PIX Firewall.

■ **Network Access Restrictions**—Defines per-user network access restrictions.

- **Max Sessions**—Contains three radio buttons that define the maximum number of concurrent sessions the user can have:

  — **Unlimited**—The user can maintain an unlimited number of concurrent sessions through the firewall.

  — **Fill in the Box**—Defines the maximum number of concurrent sessions.

  — **Use Group Settings**—The default setting. The maximum number is defined at the group level.

- **Account Disable**—Configures the parameters for disabling a user account based on the date or a number of failed logon attempts. Do not confuse this option with the Account Disabled option at the top of the User Setup window.

  — **Never**—The default setting. It allows the user unlimited attempts to log on.

  — **Disable Account If:**

  Date Exceeds—Select the date from the drop-down boxes. The default setting is 30 days after the account is created.

  Failed Attempts Exceed—Add the number of allowed failed attempts to the box.

  An indicator shows the number of failed attempts since the last successful logon.

  There is a check box for you to reset the failed attempts count. If this box is checked the reset will occur when you click the submit button.

Step 3: Applying Authorization Rules to the Group

Now that you have created the user account and assigned the user to a group, it is time to apply authorization rules to the group. Click the Group Setup button on the navigation bar on the left.

Figure 17-8 shows the available selections in the initial Group Setup window.

Figure 17-8 *Configuring a Group Setup on the Cisco Secure ACS*

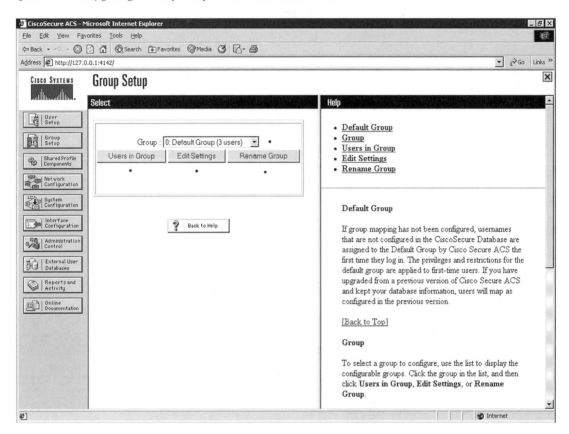

You can select the group from the drop-down box and select any of the following three options for that group:

- **Users in Group**—Replaces the Help pane on the right side of the window with a list of the users assigned to the selected group, as shown in Figure 17-9. Each username is a link to that user's configuration in the User Setup window.

- **Edit Settings**—Allows you to edit the specific settings for the selected group. This is where the authorization rules are applied to the group.

- **Rename Group**—Enables you to rename groups to simplify administration. You can add users to groups based on like positions or job functions (such as marketing, sales, infrastructure, and security).

Figure 17-9 *Users in Group*

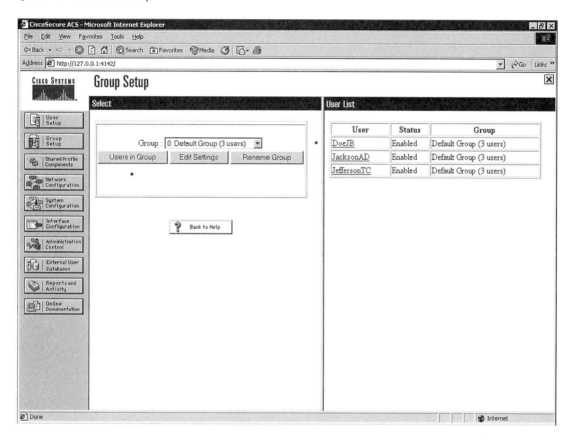

You configure commands by editing the settings for a specific group. Select Group Setup from the navigation bar, click Edit Settings, and scroll down to the Shell Command Authorization Set. You see radio buttons and a Command box that is a subset of the Command Authorization Set, as shown in Figure 17-10.

To configure shell command authorization for AAA clients using TACACS+, set the options in this section as applicable:

■ **None**—If you do not want to apply TACACS+ shell command authorization for users who belong to this group, select this option (selected in Figure 17-10).

■ **Assign a Shell Command Authorization Set for Any Network Device**—To apply a shell command authorization set to all TACACS+ AAA clients, select this option and then select the set you want from the corresponding list.

Figure 17-10 *Command Authorization Sets*

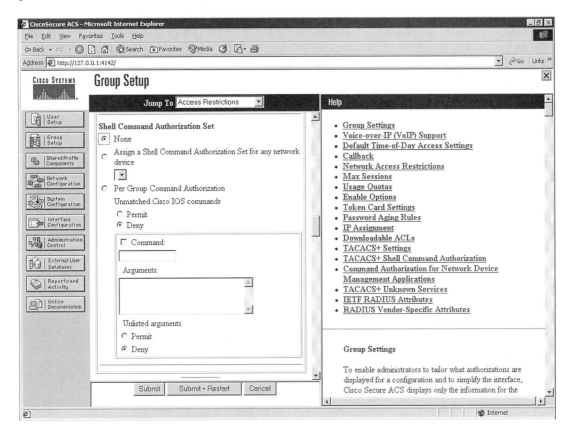

- **Assign a Shell Command Authorization Set on a Per Network Device Group Basis**—In ACS Version 3.1 and later, to apply a shell command authorization set to the TACACS+ AAA clients who belong to a particular Network Device Group (NDG), select this option, and then use the following options:

  — **Device Group**—From the list, select the NDG to which you want to assign a shell command authorization set.

  — **Command Set**—From the list, select the shell command authorization set you want to apply to the NDG.

  — **Add Association**—Click to add the NDG and command set selected to the Device Group/Command Set list.

  — **Remove Association**—To remove an NDG/command set association, select the NDG/command set association you want to remove from the Device Group/Privilege list, and then click Remove Association.

Shell command authorization sets are created and configured in the Shared Profile Components window.

- **Per Group Command Authorization**—To set TACACS+ shell command authorization on a command-by-command basis, select this option, and then use the following options:

  — **Unmatched Cisco IOS Commands**—To determine how Cisco Secure ACS handles commands that you do not specify in this section, select either Permit or Deny as applicable.

  — **Command**—Select this check box, and then enter the command in the corresponding box. The command can be listed by name for well-known commands such as **telnet**, **ftp**, or **http**; otherwise the command should be listed by protocol/port number (i.e., tcp/23).

  — **Arguments**—In this case the term "argument" refers to the target address. This box lists to which target host you should allow (or deny) access via the previously listed command. These should be entered in the format **permit** *argument* or **deny** *argument*. This allows you to specify which commands are permitted or denied.

  — **Unlisted Arguments**—To permit only the arguments listed, select Deny. To allow users to issue all arguments not specifically listed, select Permit. This setting allows you to permit or deny all commands and arguments not listed previously.

Figure 17-11 shows the configuration that would allow Telnet access to hosts at 172.16.1.5 and 172.16.1.7.

Figure 17-11 *Configuring Per User Command Authorization*

User Setup

Shell Command Authorization Set

○ None

○ As Group

○ Assign a Shell Command Authorization Set for any network device

　[∨]

◉ Per User Command Authorization

Unmatched Cisco IOS commands

　○ Permit

　◉ Deny

　☑ Command:

　telnet

　Arguments:

　permit 172.16.1.5
　permit 172.16.1.7

　Unlisted arguments

　○ Permit

　◉ Deny

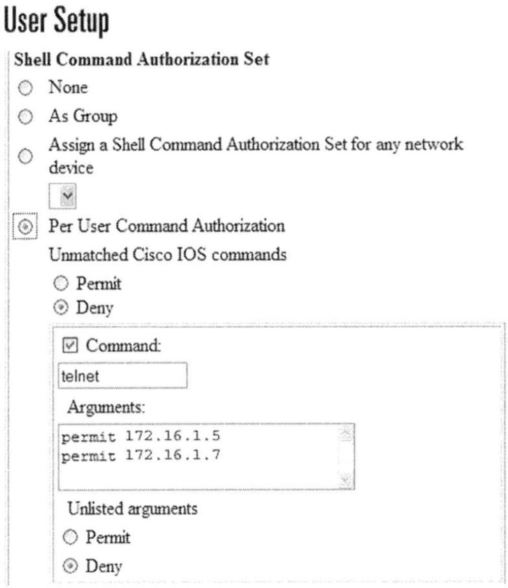

The excerpt of a PIX Firewall configuration below corresponds the Figure 17-11:

```
nameif ethernet0 outside security0
nameif ethernet1 inside security100
nameif ethernet2 dmz1 security50

ip address inside 192.168.1.231 255.255.255.0
ip address dmz1 10.10.1.1 255.255.255.0

access-list from-inside-to-dmz permit tcp 192.168.1.0 255.255.255.0 host 10.10.1.3 eq
5631
access-list from-inside-to-dmz permit udp 192.168.1.0 255.255.255.0 host 10.10.1.3 eq
5632
access-list from-inside-to-dmz permit tcp 192.168.1.0 255.255.255.0 host 10.10.1.5 eq
telnet
access-list from-inside-to-dmz deny ip any host 10.10.1.3

access-list 121 permit tcp any host 10.10.1.3
access-list 121 permit udp any host 10.10.1.3
access-list 121 permit tcp any host 10.10.1.5 eq telnet

access-list 101 permit ip 192.168.1.0 255.255.255.0 host 10.10.1.3

nat (inside) 0 access-list 101

static (inside,dmz1) 192.168.1.1 192.168.1.1 netmask 255.255.255.255 0 0

access-group from-inside-to-dmz in interface inside
```

```
aaa-server AuthOutbound protocol tacacs+
aaa-server AuthOutbound (inside) host 192.168.1.4 xxxxxxxx timeout 10

aaa authentication match 121 inside AuthOutbound
aaa authorization match 121 inside AuthOutbound

virtual telnet 10.10.1.5
```

This PIX Firewall will not allow any connections from its inside hosts (192.168.1.0) to host 10.10.1.3 on DMZ1 except PCAnywhere (TCP/5631 and UDP/5632) application. But to allow this connection it asks authentication as well as authorization using a Cisco Secure ACS. A user on the 192.168.1.1 host would telnet to virtual telnet address at 10.10.1.5, authenticate and afterwards will run his PCAnywhere application with the target host as 10.10.1.3. The Cisco Secure ACS will authorize this user if in its database for this user has the following, shown in Figure 17-12.

Figure 17-12 *Configuring Shell Command Authorization Sets*

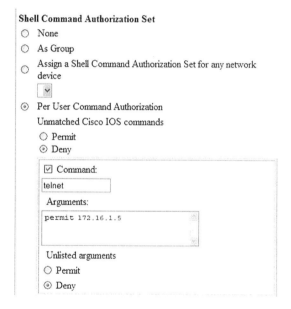

Refer to the network map in Figure 17-13 for the following exercise. The configuration of the PIX Firewall and the Cisco Secure ACS controls access to the host 172.16.1.3.

In the PIX Firewall configuration in Example 17-9, hosts on the internal network are not allowed to make connections to 172.16.1.3 on the DMZ segment except for the PCAnywhere (TCP/5631 and UDP/5632) application. But to allow this connection the Firewall will ask authentication as well as authorization using a Cisco Secure ACS.

Example 17-9 *Configuring AAA Authorization on the PIX Firewall*

```
nameif ethernet0 outside security0
nameif ethernet1 inside security100
nameif ethernet2 dmz1 security50
ip address outside 192.168.0.1 255.255.255.0
ip address inside 10.10.10.254 255.255.255.0
ip address dmz1 172.16.1.254 255.255.255.0
access-list from-inside-to-dmz permit tcp 10.10.10.0 255.255.255.0 host 172.16.1.3 eq 5631
access-list from-inside-to-dmz permit udp 10.10.10.0 255.255.255.0 host 172.16.1.3 eq 5632
access-list from-inside-to-dmz permit tcp 10.10.10.0 255.255.255.0 host 172.16.1.5 eq telnet
access-list from-inside-to-dmz deny ip any host 172.16.1.3
access-list 121 permit tcp any host 172.16.1.3
access-list 121 permit udp any host 172.16.1.3
access-list 121 permit tcp any host 172.16.1.5 eq telnet
access-list 101 permit ip 10.10.10.0 255.255.255.0 host 172.16.1.3
nat (inside) 0 access-list 101
static (inside,dmz1) 10.10.10.1 10.10.10.1 netmask 255.255.255.255 0 0
access-group from-inside-to-dmz in interface inside
aaa-server AuthOutbound protocol tacacs+
aaa-server AuthOutbound (inside) host 10.10.10.4 xxxxxxxx timeout 10
aaa authentication match 121 inside AuthOutbound
aaa authorization match 121 inside AuthOutbound
virtual telnet 172.16.1.5
```

A user on the 10.10.10.1 host would telnet to virtual telnet address at 172.16.1.5, authenticate and afterwards will run his PCAnywhere application with the target host as 172.16.1.3. The Cisco Secure ACS authorizes this user if in its database for this user the Command Authorization configuration of the Cisco Secure ACS is similar to Figure 17-13.

Figure 17-13 *Configuring Shell Commands*

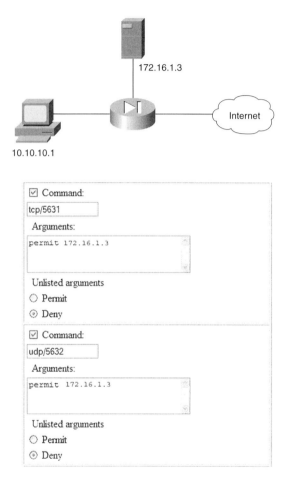

Step 4: Configuring Accounting

You have successfully configured both your Cisco PIX Firewall and your Cisco Secure ACS for authentication and authorization. The final portion is to configure accounting. Accounting is used to track specific traffic passing through the firewall. It also ensures that users are performing functions in keeping with company policies. Log data is commonly stored and can be used to investigate employees who are using their Internet connections for activities not authorized by the employer. The general syntax for the command that accomplishes accounting is as follows:

```
aaa accounting include | exclude acctg-service | if-name local-ip
    local-mask foreign-ip foreign-mask server tag
```

The following items are defined within the **aaa accounting** command:

- **include**—Creates a rule with a specified service.

- **exclude**—Creates an exception to a previously defined rule.

- *acctg-service*—The service that is included or excluded. It is the service that the user is requesting access to via the network. You can configure *acctg-service* as **any, ftp, http, telnet,** or *protocol/port*. When you configure *protocol/port*, the *protocol* is listed as a number:

  — ICMP—1

  — TCP—6

  — UDP—17

- *if-name*—The interface name from which the users should be authenticated and accounting should be performed.

- *local-ip*—The host address or network segment with the highest security level. As with the other address definitions on the PIX Firewall, 0 is used to define "any."

- *local-mask*—The subnet mask that applies to the *local-ip*; 0 is used to define "any."

- *foreign-ip*—Defines the address space with the lowest security level. The use of 0 defines "any."

- *foreign-mask*—The subnet mask that applies to the *foreign-ip*; 0 is used to define "any."

- *server-tag*—The name used for the AAA server group. The *server-tag* is also used in the **aaa-server, aaa authorization,** and **aaa accounting** commands.

Example 17-10 shows how to configure AAA accounting on the PIX Firewall.

Example 17-10 *Configuring AAA Accounting on the PIX Firewall*

```
PIXFirewall(config)# aaa accounting include any inbound 0 0 0 0 TACACS+
PIXFirewall(config)# aaa accounting include any outbound 0 0 0 0 TACACS+
```

As with authentication and authorization, it is possible to configure the PIX Firewall to match an access list, as demonstrated in Example 17-11.

Example 17-11 *Configuring AAA Accounting to Match an ACL*

```
PIXFirewall(config)# access-list PIXTEST permit tcp any host 65.197.254.5 eq 80
PIXFirewall(config)# access-group PIXTEST in interface outside
PIXFirewall(config)# aaa accounting match PIXTEST inbound TACACS+
```

> **NOTE** To remove AAA accounting from the configuration, enter **no aaa accounting**.

Viewing Accounting Information in Cisco Secure

Now that the Cisco PIX Firewall is configured to perform accounting, you need to ensure that the Cisco Secure ACS is properly configured to log the events. Select System Configuration in the navigation panel to open the System Configuration window, shown in Figure 17-14; then, click the Logging link in the Select pane, and check off the log format and the items you want to log (see Figure 17-15). Logs can be saved in a CSV (flat file) or ODBC (database) format.

Figure 17-14 *Cisco Secure ACS System Configuration Window*

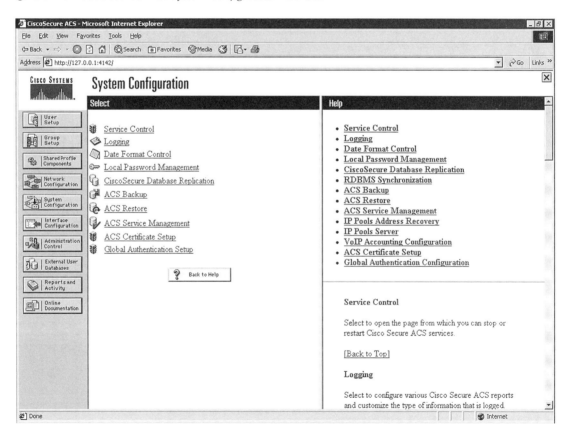

Figure 17-15 *Cisco Secure ACS Logging Targets and Options*

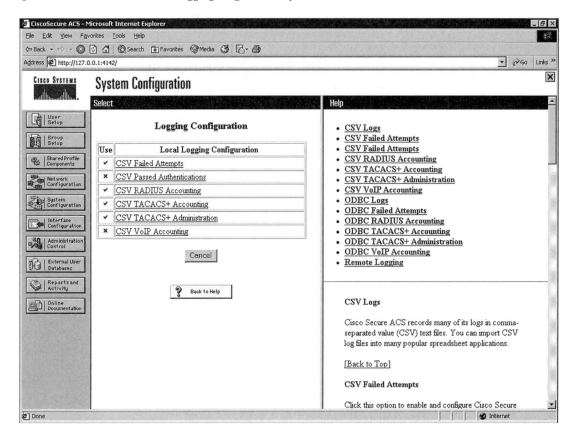

You can view several reports from the Cisco Secure ACS browser interface. Select Reports and Activity from the navigation bar to open the Reports and Activity window, shown in Figure 17-16. Then, choose the report you want by clicking the applicable button in the Reports list. Reports are available for TACACS+ and/or RADIUS only if an AAA client has been configured to use that protocol.

Figure 17-16   *Cisco Secure ACS Reports and Activity Window*

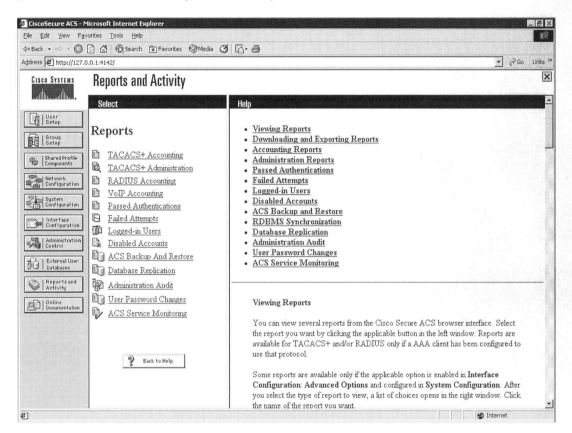

Reports are generated daily and can be viewed or downloaded in comma-separated value (CSV) format. Figure 17-17 lists the titles of the TACACS+ reports that are available. Notice that there are gaps in the dates of available reports. This is because this particular Cisco Secure ACS is not in production, and the system generates logs and, therefore, reports only when it is running.

Figure 17-17   *Available TACACS+ Reports*

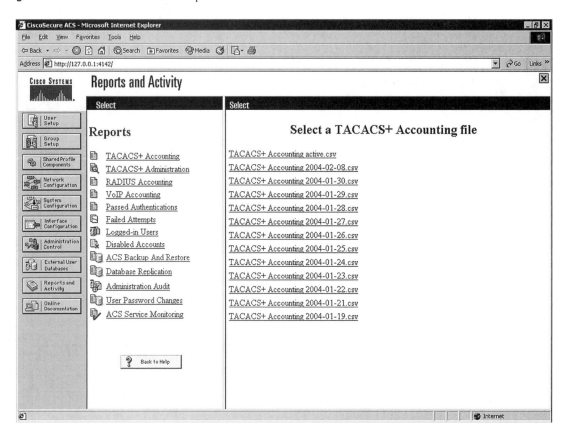

Some reports are available only if the applicable option is enabled in the Interface
Configuration window, Advanced Options pane (see Figure 17-18) and configured in the
System Configuration window. After you select the type of report to view, a list of choices
appears in the right window. Click the name of the report you want.

Figure 17-18 *Interface Configuration Options for Cisco Secure ACS Reports*

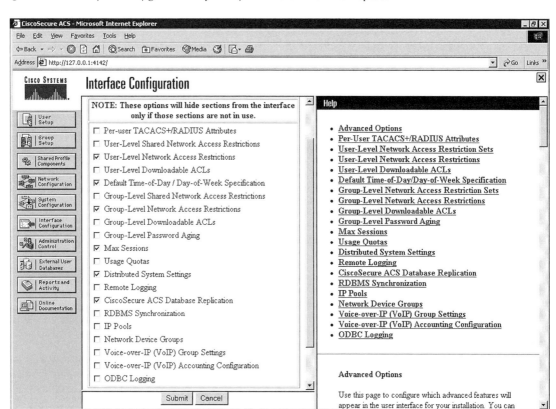

Cisco Secure and Cut-Through Configuration

Cut-through proxy is a feature of the Cisco PIX Firewall that enables it to open connections after authenticating and authorizing a user with the AAA server. This feature was discussed in Chapters 1 and 2. The user initiates a connection to their destination and is prompted for a username and password by the PIX Firewall. The user-provided information is verified by the AAA server, and the connection is allowed by the firewall.

Configuring Downloadable PIX ACLs

Version 3.0 and later of Cisco Secure ACS allows you to create a "downloadable ACL" using the shared profile component. The downloadable ACL configuration is supported only for RADIUS servers. To verify that your configuration is for a RADIUS server, select Network

Configuration from the navigation bar and click AAA Client. Verify that RADIUS (Cisco IOS/PIX) is selected, as shown in Figure 17-19.

Figure 17-19 *RADIUS (Cisco IOS/PIX) Configuration*

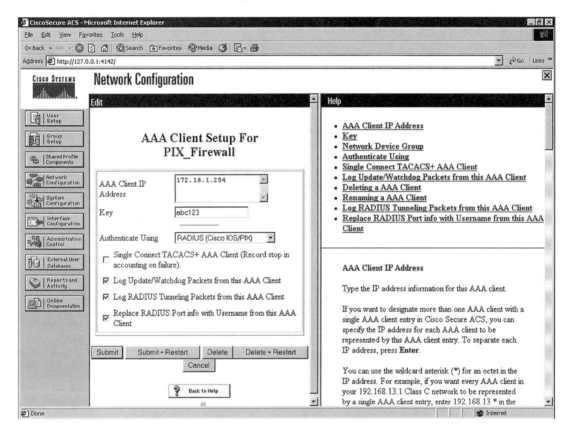

Select Shared Profile Components from the navigation bar, click the link for Downloadable PIX ACL, and select Add.

> **NOTE** If you are not configured for a RADIUS server, the Downloadable PIX ACL link is unavailable.

If the Cisco Secure ACS is configured as a RADIUS server, but you still do not have the Downloadable PIX ACL option available, you must select either User-Level or Group-Level Downloadable ACLs in the Advanced Options menu of the Interface Configuration window, shown in Figure 17-20.

Figure 17-20 *Advanced Options Menu*

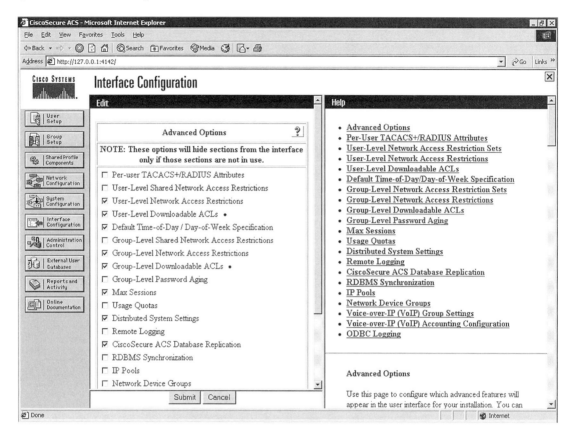

Add the following information in the Downloadable PIX ACLs configuration box, and click Submit:

- **Name**—The access list name.

- **Description**—A description of the access list.

- **ACL Definitions**—A test of the command. This should use the same format as the command used on the PIX Firewall, except for the access list name and the fact that there is no requirement for the keyword "access-list." It also is not necessary to add the access list to an access group. This is done automatically when the ACL is downloaded to the PIX Firewall.

Figure 17-21 shows a downloadable ACL configured to allow outbound access to www.cisco.com.

Figure 17-21 *Creating a Downloadable ACL*

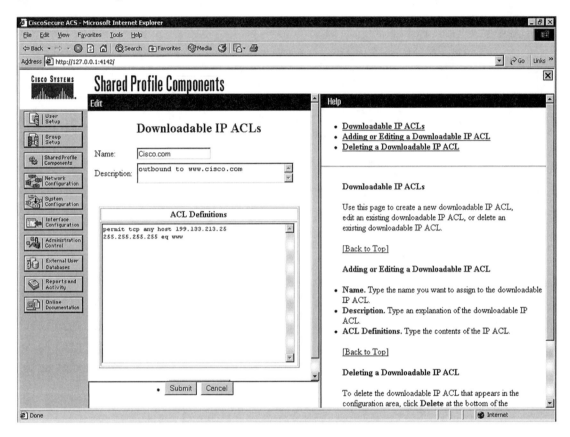

After you configure the downloadable ACL in the Shared Profile Components window, you can add it to either an individual user setup or a group setup. Figure 17-22 shows the Downloadable ACLs box in the Group Setup window. To add the downloadable ACL to the group, simply check the Assign IP ACL box and select the ACL name from the drop-down box.

Figure 17-22 *Selecting a Downloadable ACL*

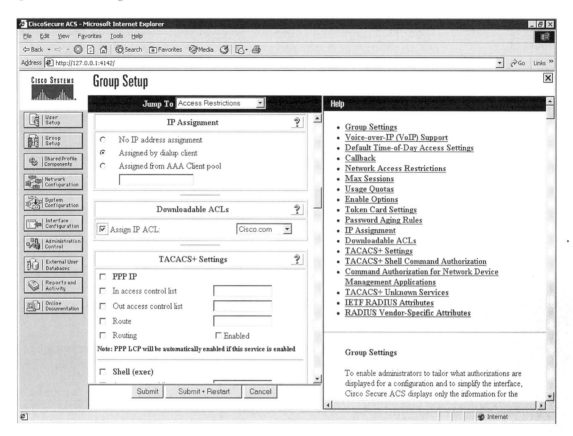

Troubleshooting Your AAA Setup

Troubleshooting your AAA configuration can be a simple function or a difficult process, depending on how complicated the configuration is and how well you documented it. It is always in your best interest to document any configuration and to be as detailed as possible when doing so. It is also recommended that you use best practices such as adding users to groups and applying rules to groups rather than to users, using a *standardized* naming convention, and completing the description fields and comment blocks when creating elements, rules, components, and so on. Neglecting these basic steps can turn a relatively simple issue into an extremely difficult troubleshooting event. It also is a good idea to remember the basic troubleshooting method of "divide and conquer." In other words, do not start checking the PIX Firewall or the Cisco Secure ACS configuration until you have verified connectivity between the two devices.

Checking the PIX Firewall

The most effective command for troubleshooting the PIX Firewall is **show**. The **show** command is run in configuration mode and can be used to show the configuration for all the AAA components on the PIX Firewall. The following is a list of the **show** commands pertaining to the AAA configuration:

- **show aaa-server**—Shows you the different *group-tag*s, which protocol is used for each *group-tag*, and the *ip-address*, *key*, and *timeout* for each AAA server.

- **show aaa**—Provides you with the output of the following commands:

    — **show aaa authentication**—Shows you all AAA authentication rules

    — **show aaa authorization**—Shows you all AAA authorization rules

    — **show aaa accounting**—Shows you all AAA accounting rules

    — **show timeout**—Shows the maximum idle time for a session

    — **show timeout uauth**—Shows the duration in hours, minutes, and seconds before the authentication and authorization cache times out

    — **show auth prompt**—Shows the prompt, accept, and reject text messages when a user attempts to authenticate via a Telnet session

    — **Show uauth**—Shows the number of authenticated users and the number of authentications in progress

Troubleshooting Authentication

If you encounter issues with your AAA authentication, you can use the **debug aaa authentication** command to display the communication between the Cisco PIX Firewall and the AAA server. This command lets you determine the method of authentication and verify successful communication between the PIX Firewall and the AAA server. Example 17-12 shows where a login causes the PIX Firewall to initiate a connection to the AAA server at 17.16.1.2, requesting a login using TACACS+ and generating an eight-digit session ID. The session ID is used to distinguish between multiple concurrent authentication requests.

Example 17-12 debug aaa authentication *Command Output (Continued)*

```
PIX-Firewall# debug aaa authentication
10:15:01: AAA/AUTHEN: create-user user='' ruser='' port='tty19'
  rem-addr='172.16.1.2' authen-type=1 service=1 priv=1
10:15:01: AAA/AUTHEN/START (0): port='tty19' list='' action=LOGIN service=LOGIN
10:15:01: AAA/AUTHEN/START (0): using "default" list
10:15:01: AAA/AUTHEN/START (12345678): Method=TACACS+
10:15:01: TAC+ (12345678): received authen response status = GETUSER
10:15:02: AAA/AUTHEN (12345678): status = GETUSER
10:15:02: AAA/AUTHEN/CONT (12345678): continue-login
```

Example 17-12 debug aaa authentication *Command Output (Continued)*

```
10:15:02: AAA/AUTHEN (12345678): status = GETUSER
10:15:02: AAA/AUTHEN (12345678): Method=TACACS+
10:15:02: TAC+: send AUTHEN/CONT packet
10:15:03: TAC+ (12345678): received authen response status = GETPASS
10:15:03: AAA/AUTHEN (12345678): status = GETPASS
10:15:03: AAA/AUTHEN/CONT (12345678): continue-login
10:15:03: AAA/AUTHEN (12345678): status = GETPASS
10:15:03: AAA/AUTHEN (12345678): Method=TACACS+
10:15:03: TAC+: send AUTHEN/CONT packet
10:15:03: TAC+ (12345678): received authen response status = PASS
10:15:03: AAA/AUTHEN (12345678): status = PASS
```

Troubleshooting Authorization

If you encounter issues with your AAA authorization, you can use the **debug aaa authorization** command to display the communication between the PIX Firewall and the AAA server, as demonstrated in Example 17-13.

Example 17-13 debug aaa authorization *Command Output*

```
PIX-Firewall# debug aaa authorization
10:15:01: AAA/AUTHOR (0): user='jdoe'
10:15:01: AAA/AUTHOR (0): send AV service=shell
10:15:01: AAA/AUTHOR (0): send AV cmd*
10:15:01: AAA/AUTHOR (123456789): Method=TACACS+
10:15:01: AAA/AUTHOR/TAC+ (123456789): user=jdoe
10:15:01: AAA/AUTHOR/TAC+ (123456789): send AV service=shell
10:15:01: AAA/AUTHOR/TAC+ (123456789): send AV cmd*
10:15:01: AAA/AUTHOR (123456789): Post authorization status = FAIL
```

Troubleshooting Accounting

If you encounter issues with your AAA accounting, you can use the **show accounting** command to step through the sessions and, if necessary, print records of actively accounted sessions. The **debug aaa accounting** command is used to display the output of AAA accounting and is independent of the protocol used to transfer records to the log server, as demonstrated in Example 17-14.

Example 17-14 debug aaa accounting *Command Output*

```
PIX-Firewall# debug aaa accounting
10:15:01: AAA/ACCT: EXEC acct start, line 10
10:15:01: AAA/ACCT: Connect start, line 10, glare
10:15:01: AAA/ACCT: Connection acct stop:
task-id=70 service=exec port=10 protocol=telnet address=172.16.1.13 cmd=glare
bytes-in=308 bytes-out=76 paks-in=45 paks-out=54 elapsed-time=14
```

If you believe you have encountered a protocol-specific problem, you can view the individual protocols using the following commands:

- **debug tacacs**—Displays the packet information for communication between the PIX Firewall and the AAA server. Example 17-15 demonstrates typical output from this command.

- **debug radius**—Displays the output of the RADIUS communication. This is more difficult to read, except for the obvious "Access-Accept" or "Access-Reject" message. Example 17-16 demonstrates typical output from this command.

Example 17-15   debug tacacs *Command Output*

```
PIX-Firewall# debug tacacs
10:15:01: TAC+: Opening TCP/IP connection to 172.16.1.2 using source 172.16.1.1
10:15:01: TAC+: Sending TCP packet number 123456789-1 to 172.16.1.2 (AUTHEN/START)
10:15:01: TAC+: Receiving TCP packet number 123456789-2 from 172.16.1.2
10:15:01: TAC+ (123456789): received authen response status = GETUSER
10:15:01: TAC+: send AUTHEN/CONT packet
10:15:02: TAC+: Sending TCP packet number 123456789-3 to 172.16.1.2 (AUTHEN/CONT)
10:15:02: TAC+: Receiving TCP packet number 123456789-4 from 172.16.1.2
10:15:02: TAC+ (123456789): received authen response status = GETPASS
10:15:02: TAC+: send AUTHEN/CONT packet
10:15:03: TAC+: Sending TCP packet number 123456789-5 to 172.16.1.2 (AUTHEN/CONT)
10:15:03: TAC+: Receiving TCP packet number 123456789-6 from 172.16.1.2
10:15:03: TAC+ (123456789): received authen response status = PASS
10:15:03: TAC+: Closing TCP connection to 172.16.1.2
```

Example 17-16   debug radius *Command Output*

```
PIX-Firewall# debug radius
10:15:01: Radius: IPC Send 0.0.0.0:1645, Access-Request, id 0xE len 12
10:15:01:        Attribute 5 5 CDA14568
10:15:01:        Attribute 7 9 B475B47A
10:15:01:        Attribute 6 2 45C4E78A
10:15:01:        Attribute 4 1 14568521
10:15:01: Radius: Received from 172.16.1.2:1645, Access-Accept, id 0xE len 33
10:15:01:        Attribute 2 2 0000000F
```

> **NOTE**   It is important that you not run the **debug** command continuously because these commands can generate a significant amount of output.
>
> The command to terminate the debug is **no debug** *insert your command here.*

Checking the Cisco Secure ACS

After you verify your settings on the Cisco PIX Firewall, you should double-check the settings on the Cisco Secure ACS to ensure that they match the PIX Firewall. You also can use the extensive logging information available in the Cisco Secure ACS Reports and Activity window. You can find a list of troubleshooting information for the Cisco Secure ACS in the Cisco Secure ACS online documentation. Simply enter **Troubleshooting Information for Cisco Secure ACS** in the Search box at Cisco.com to find this documentation.

Foundation Summary

The "Foundation Summary" provides a convenient review of many key concepts in this chapter. If you are already comfortable with the topics in this chapter, this summary can help you recall a few details. If you just read this chapter, this review should help solidify some key facts. If you are doing your final preparation before the exam, this summary provides a convenient way to review the day before the exam.

The Cisco PIX Firewall and the Cisco Secure ACS combine to make an effective AAA solution. The **aaa-server** command configures the PIX Firewall to communicate with the AAA server. This command determines the authentication protocol used between the PIX Firewall and the AAA server, the IP address of the AAA server, and the *group-tag* or the name of the group the AAA server is in.

The PIX Firewall can group up to 14 servers and handle up to 14 server groups. The Cisco Secure ACS is installed on either a Windows NT server or Windows 2000 server. It considers itself an AAA server and the PIX Firewall the AAA client. Command-line entries are put on the PIX Firewall to configure authentication, authorization, and accounting. User accounts, groups, logging, and downloadable PIX ACLs are all configured on the Cisco Secure ACS. Although you can assign authorization to individual users, it is recommended that you assign users to groups and assign authorization rules to the groups.

There are three main steps for troubleshooting AAA issues:

- Verify connectivity between the PIX Firewall and the Cisco Secure ACS.
- Verify the configuration of the PIX Firewall.
- Verify the configuration of the Cisco Secure ACS.

Table 17-2 outlines the commands and syntax necessary to configure the PIX Firewall as a NAS.

Table 17-2 *Commands to Configure the PIX Firewall as a NAS*

Command	Description
aaa authentication include | **exclude** *authen-service if-name local-ip local-mask foreign-ip foreign-mask group-tag*	Implements AAA authentication to include or exclude a specific service that is inbound or outbound in a specific interface for a specific source and destination address assigned to a specific AAA server group as assigned by the group tag.
aaa authentication match *acl-name if-name server-tag*	Matches the requirement for AAA authentication with a specific ACL.

Table 17-2 *Commands to Configure the PIX Firewall as a NAS (Continued)*

Command	Description
show aaa	Displays your AAA configuration.
debug aaa authentication	Displays the authentication communication between the NAS and the AAA server.
aaa authorization include | exclude *author-service if-name local-ip local-mask foreign-ip foreign-mask server-tag*	Implements AAA authorization to include or exclude a specific service that is inbound or outbound in a specific interface for a specific source and destination address assigned to a specific AAA server group as assigned by the group tag.
aaa authorization match *acl-name* inbound | outbound *if-name group-tag*	Matches the requirement for AAA authorization with a specific ACL.
debug aaa authorization	Displays the authorization communication between the NAS and the AAA server.
aaa accounting include | exclude *author-service if-name local-ip local-mask foreign-ip foreign-mask server-tag*	Implements AAA accounting to include or exclude a specific service that is inbound or outbound in a specific interface for a specific source and destination address assigned to a specific AAA server group as assigned by the group tag.
aaa accounting match *acl-name if-name server-tag*	Matches the requirement for AAA accounting with a specific ACL.
show aaa accounting	Steps through individual recorded logs.
debug aaa accounting	Displays the accounting communication between the NAS and the AAA server.

The commands listed in Table 17-3 let you display protocol-specific communication between the NAS (PIX Firewall) and the AAA server.

Table 17-3 *Commands to Display Communication Between the PIX Firewall and the AAA Server*

Command	Description
debug tacacs	Debugs TACACS communications between the PIX Firewall and the AAA server.
debug radius	Debugs RADIUS communications between the PIX Firewall and the AAA server.

Q&A

As mentioned in the Introduction, the questions in this book are more difficult than what you should experience on the exam. The questions are designed to ensure your understanding of the concepts discussed in this chapter and adequately prepare you to complete the exam. You should use the simulated exams on the CD to practice for the exam.

The answers to these questions can be found in Appendix A.

1. Both your Cisco PIX Firewall and your Cisco Secure ACS are configured for TACACS+, but you cannot configure the downloadable PIX ACLs. What is the problem?

2. What is the command to get authorization to work with access lists?

3. What Cisco Secure ACS window is used to configure the PIX Firewall, and what is the firewall considered?

4. How do you put text messages into the logon prompt for a Telnet session?

5. What three messages can you change with the **auth-prompt** command?

6. If your **timeout uauth** is set to 0:58:00, when is the user prompted to reauthenticate after the session times out?

7. What two formats can logs be written to using the Cisco Secure ACS?

8. You have added a new RSA SecurID Token Server to the network. In which two places do you configure the Cisco Secure ACS to use it?

9. What commands are most commonly used to check your AAA configuration on the PIX Firewall?

10. What is the total number of AAA servers to which the PIX Firewall can connect?

11. How do you disable caching of user authentication?

This chapter covers the following subjects:

- Multimedia support

- Attack guards

- Intrusion detection

CHAPTER 18

Attack Guards and Advanced Protocol Handling

The primary function of the Cisco PIX Firewall is to prevent and to protect internal hosts from malicious attacks from the outside network. Some hackers try to gain access to the internal network, but others attack network resources to disrupt network services. This chapter describes some of the features of the Cisco PIX Firewall that are used to mitigate known attacks against network resources. This chapter also discusses how the PIX Firewall handles multimedia application protocols.

How To Best Use This Chapter

The PIX Firewall provides various attack guards that protect your network by actually decoding traffic received for various protocols. Besides identifying attacks against certain protocols, protocol inspection on the signaling traffic can enable the PIX Firewall to dynamically open up the ports necessary for the communicating systems to transfer data. The PIX Firewall also provides some intrusion detection capability along with the ability to dynamically shun intrusive traffic when combined with an Cisco IDS Sensor. Test yourself with the "Do I Know This Already?" quiz and see how familiar you are with the attack guard and multimedia functionality available on PIX Firewalls.

"Do I Know This Already?" Quiz

The purpose of the "Do I Know This Already?" quiz is to help you decide if you really need to read the entire chapter. If you already intend to read the entire chapter, you do not necessarily need to answer these questions now.

The ten-question quiz, derived from the major sections in the "Foundation Topics" portion of the chapter, helps you determine how to spend your limited study time.

Table 18-1 outlines the major topics discussed in this chapter and the "Do I Know This Already?" quiz questions that correspond to those topics.

Table 18-1 *"Do I Know This Already?" Foundation Topics Section-to-Question Mapping*

Foundations Topics Section	Questions Covered in This Section	Score
Multimedia Support	3, 4	
Attack Guards	1, 2, 5 to 7	
Intrusion Detection	8 to 10	

CAUTION The goal of self assessment is to gauge your mastery of the topics in this chapter. If you do not know the answer to a question or are only partially sure of the answer, you should mark this question wrong for purposes of the self assessment. Giving yourself credit for an answer you correctly guess skews your self-assessment results and might provide you with a false sense of security.

1. What does the Flood Defender feature on the PIX Firewall do?

    a. It prevents the PIX Firewall from being flooded with water.

    b. It protects the inside network from being engulfed by rain.

    c. It protects against SYN flood attacks.

    d. It protects against AAA attacks.

2. Which PIX feature mitigates a DoS attack that uses an incomplete IP datagram?

    a. Floodguard

    b. Incomplete Guard

    c. Fragguard

    d. Mail Guard

3. Which of the following multimedia application(s) is(are) supported by PIX Firewall?

    a. CuSeeMe

    b. NetMeeting

    c. Internet Video Phone

    d. All of the above

4. Which is the default port that PIX inspects for H.323 traffic?

    a. 1628

    b. 1722

    c. 1720

    d. 1408

5. Which of the following describes how the Mail Guard works on the PIX Firewall?

    a. It lets all mail in except for mail described by an access list.

    b. It restricts SMTP requests to seven commands.

    c. It revokes mail messages that contain attacks.

    d. It performs virus checks on each mail message.

6. Which of the following statements about DNS Guard is true?

    a. It is disabled by default.

    b. It allows only a single DNS response for outgoing requests.

    c. It monitors the DNS servers for suspicious activities.

    d. It is enabled by default.

7. Which of the following are PIX Firewall attack mitigation features?

    a. DNS Guard

    b. Floodgate Guard

    c. Mail Guard

    d. Webguard

8. Which command enables the PIX Firewall IDS feature?

    a. ids enable

    b. ip audit

    c. ip ids audit

    d. audit ip ids

9. What is the default action of the PIX IDS feature?

    a. Nothing

    b. Drop

    c. Alarm

    d. Reset

10. What does the reset action do in the PIX Firewall IDS configuration?

    a. Warns the source of the offending packet before it drops the packet

    b. Drops the offending packet and closes the connection if it is part of an active connection with a TCP RST

    c. Waits 2000 offending packets, and then permanently bans the connection to the source host

    d. Reports the incident to the syslog server and waits for more offending packets from the same source to arrive

The answers to the "Do I Know This Already?" quiz are found in Appendix A, "Answers to the 'Do I Know This Already?' Quizzes and Q&A Sections." The suggested choices for your next step are as follows:

- **8 or less overall score**—Read the entire chapter. This includes the "Foundation Topics," "Foundation Summary," and "Q&A" sections.

- **9 or 10 overall score**—If you want more review on these topics, skip to the "Foundation Summary" section and then go to the "Q&A" section. Otherwise, move to the next chapter.

Foundation Topics

Multimedia Support on the Cisco PIX Firewall

Chapter 7, "Configuring Access," begins a discussion of some applications that require special handling by the Cisco PIX Firewall. Multimedia applications have special behaviors that require special handling by the PIX inspection feature.

During normal mode of operation, multimedia application protocols open more than one communication channel and several data channels. For example, a client might transmit a request on Transmission Control Protocol (TCP), get responses on User Datagram Protocol (UDP), or use dynamic ports. The **fixup protocol** command is used to help the PIX Firewall identify such protocols so that it can perform inspections.

Here are the multimedia applications supported by the PIX Firewall:

- Microsoft Netshow
- Microsoft NetMeeting
- Intel Internet Video Phone
- VDOnet VDOLive
- RealNetworks RealAudio and RealVideo
- VocalTech
- White Pine Meeting Point
- White Pine CuSeeMe
- Xing StreamWorks
- VXtreme WebTheatre

The PIX Firewall dynamically opens and closes UDP ports for secure multimedia connections. There is no need to open a range of ports, which creates a security risk, or to reconfigure any application clients.

The PIX Firewall supports multimedia with or without Network Address Translation (NAT). Many firewalls that cannot support multimedia with NAT limit multimedia usage to only registered users or require exposure of inside Internet Protocol (IP) addresses to the Internet.

Many popular multimedia applications use Real-Time Streaming Protocol (RTSP) or the H.323 suite protocol standard.

Real-Time Streaming Protocol

RTSP, described in RFC 2326, controls the delivery of real-time data, such as audio and video. It is used for large-scale broadcasts and audio- or video-on-demand streaming. It supports applications such as Cisco IP/TV, RealNetworks RealAudio G2 Player, and Apple QuickTime 4 software.

RTSP applications use port 554 with TCP (and rarely UDP) as a control channel. The TCP control channel is used to negotiate the two UDP data channels that are used to transmit audio/video traffic. RTSP does not typically deliver continuous data streams over the control channel, usually relying on a UDP-based data transport protocol such as standard Real-Time Transport Protocol (RTP) to open separate channels for data and for RTP Control Protocol (RTCP) messages. RTCP carries status and control information, and RTP carries the actual data.

The **fixup protocol** command is used for RTSP connections to let the Cisco PIX Firewall do inspection. The **fixup protocol rtsp** command lets the PIX dynamically create conduits for RTSP UDP channels. For example, the standard RTSP port 554 is enabled by the following command:

```
fixup protocol rtsp 554
```

Application Inspection Support for Voice over IP

The steady growth of Voice over IP (VoIP) technology has also seen the development of new standards. IP phones and devices, unlike their regular phone counterparts, are not fixed to a specific switch device, so they must contain processors that enable them to function and be intelligent on their own, independent from a central switching location. Regular phones are relatively inexpensive because they do not need to be complex; they are fixed to a specific switch at a central switching location. Why is this important to you? Well, you might be running a network that supports VoIP and would want a firewall that supports the different protocols that are involved with it. PIX Firewall Version 6.3 and later support application inspection of the major protocols and applications that provide VoIP services including the following, each of which is discussed in the following sections.

- Computer Telephony Interface Quick Buffer Encoding (CTIQBE)
- H.323
- Media Gateway Control Protocol (MGCP)
- Skinny Client Control Protocol (SCCP)
- Session Initiation Protocol (SIP)

Computer Telephony Interface Quick Buffer Encoding

The Telephony Application Programming Interface (TAPI) and Java Telephony Application Programming Interface (JTAPI) are used by many Cisco VoIP applications. Cisco TAPI Service Provider (TSP) uses CTIQBE to communicate with Cisco CallManager. CTIQBE protocol is disabled by default. The **fixup protocol ctiqbe 2748** command enables CTIQBE protocol inspection that supports NAT, Port Address Translation (PAT), and bidirectional NAT. This enables Cisco IP SoftPhone and other Cisco TAPI/JTAPI applications to work successfully with Cisco CallManager for call setup across the firewall.

There are, however, instances when CTIQBE application inspection has limits or does not support some configuration types. CTIQBE application inspection does not support the following:

■ Stateful failover of CTIQBE calls

■ CTIQBE messages fragmented in multiple TCP packets

■ Configurations that use the **alias** command

The following summarizes special considerations when using CTIQBE application inspection in specific scenarios:

■ If two Cisco IP SoftPhones are registered with different Cisco CallManagers, which are connected to different interfaces of a PIX Firewall, calls between these two phones will fail.

■ When Cisco CallManager is located on the higher-security interface compared to Cisco IP SoftPhones, if NAT or outside NAT is required for the Cisco CallManager IP address, the mapping must be static because Cisco IP SoftPhone requires the Cisco CallManager IP address to be specified explicitly in its Cisco TSP configuration on the PC.

■ When using PAT or outside PAT, if the Cisco CallManager IP address is to be translated, its TCP port 2748 must be statically mapped to the same port of the PAT (interface) address for Cisco IP SoftPhone registrations to succeed. The CTIQBE listening port (TCP 2748) is fixed and is not user-configurable on Cisco CallManager, Cisco IP SoftPhone, or Cisco TSP.

H.323

The H.323 collection of protocols collectively uses up to two TCP connections and four to six UDP connections. Most of the ports, with the exception of one TCP port, are negotiated just for that particular session. Figure 18-1 shows the H.323 protocols in relation to the Open System Interconnection (OSI) reference model.

Figure 18-1 *H.323 Protocols Mapped to the OSI Reference Model*

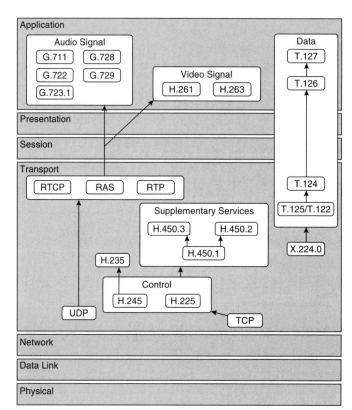

As shown in Figure 18-1:

- H.225 Registration, Admission, and Status (RAS) messages define communications between endpoints and gatekeepers.
- H.225 administers security and authentication.
- H.245 negotiates channel usage.

The content of the streams in H.323 is far more difficult for firewalls to understand than existing protocols because H.323 encodes packets using Abstract Syntax Notation (ASN.1).

The H.323 control channel handles H.225 and H.245, and H.323 RAS. H.323 inspection uses the following ports:

- **1718**—Gatekeeper discovery UDP port
- **1719**—RAS UDP port

■ 1720—TCP control port

> **NOTE** PAT support for H.323 is available in PIX Firewall Version 6.2 software.

fixup protocol h323 Command

The Cisco PIX Firewall inspects port 1720 (default) connections for H.323 traffic. If you need to change port 1720 because you have applications using H.323 on other ports, use the **fixup** command:

```
fixup protocol h323 h225 7430-7450
```

Use the **no** form of this command to disable the inspection of traffic on the indicated port.

An H.323 client might initially establish a TCP connection to an H.323 server using TCP port 1720 to request Q.931 call setup. The H.323 terminal supplies a port number to the client to use for an H.245 TCP connection.

The two major functions of H.323 inspection are as follows:

■ Performs NAT on the embedded IP addresses in the H.225 and H.245 messages. In other words, it translates the H.323 payload to a NAT address. (PIX Firewall uses an ASN.1 decoder to decode the H.323 messages.)

■ Dynamically creates conduits for TCP and UDP channels to allocate the negotiated H.245 and RTP/RTCP connections.

Each UDP connection with a packet going through H.323 inspection is marked as an H.323 connection and times out with the H.323 timeout as configured by the administrator using the **timeout** command. To clear all previous **fixup protocol h323** commands and reset port 1720 as the default, use the **clear fixup protocol h323** command.

Media Gateway Control Protocol

MGCP is a voice protocol that runs in conjunction with Signaling System 7 (SS7), an interoffice signaling protocol for circuit-switched services, and an IP protocol such as H.323 or SIP to bridge circuit-switched and packet networks. MGCP separates the signaling and call control from the media gateway. A media gateway is typically a network element that provides conversion between the audio signals carried on telephone circuits and the data packets carried over the Internet or over other packet networks, such as trunking gateways, residential gateways, and business gateways.

Application inspection for MGCP is disabled by default. To use MGCP, you typically need to configure at least two ports: one on which the gateway receives commands and one for the port on which the call agent receives commands. Normally, a call agent will send commands to port 2427, whereas a gateway will send commands to port 2727.

To enable MGCP application inspection for call agents and gateways using the default ports, enter the following commands:

```
fixup protocol mgcp 2427
fixup protocol mgcp 2727
```

MGCP messages are transmitted over UDP. A response is sent back to the source address (IP address and UDP port number) of the command, but the response may not be sent from the same address to which the command was sent. Multiple MGCP call agents can be supported by the PIX Firewall.

```
mgcp call-agent ip-address group-id
mgcp command-queue limit
mgcp gateway ip-address group-id
```

The **mgcp call-agent** command specifies a group of call agents that can manage one or more gateways. The **mgcp command-queue** command specifies the maximum number of MGCP commands that will be queued waiting for a response. The range of allowed values for the *limit* option is 1 to 4,294,967,295. The default is 200. The **mgcp gateway** command is used to specify which group of call agents are managing a particular gateway.

Example 18-1 limits the MGCP command queue to 320 commands, allows call agents 10.1.1.30 and 10.1.1.35 to control gateway 10.1.2.20, and allows call agents 10.1.1.12 and 10.1.1.14 to control gateway 10.1.2.21.

Example 18-1 *Sample MGCP Configuration*

```
mgcp call-agent 10.1.1.30 101
mgcp call-agent 10.1.1.35 101
mgcp call-agent 10.1.1.12 102
mgcp call-agent 10.1.1.14 102
mgcp command-queue 320
mgcp gateway 10.1.2.20 101
mgcp gateway 10.1.2.21 102
```

Skinny Client Control Protocol

Cisco IP Phones using SCCP can coexist in an H.323 environment. When used with Cisco CallManager, the SCCP client can interoperate with H.323-compliant terminals. Application layer functions in the PIX Firewall recognize SCCP Version 3.3. The functionality of the application layer software ensures that all SCCP signaling and media packets can traverse the firewall by providing NAT of the SCCP signaling packets.

Application inspection for SCCP is enabled by default. You can use the **fixup** command to change the default port assignment for SCCP. The command syntax is as follows:

```
fixup protocol skinny [port[-port]]
```

To change the default port assignments from 2000, use the *port* option. Use the *-port* option to apply SCCP application inspection to a range of port numbers.

Although the PIX Firewall does support PAT and NAT for SCCP, it does have limitations, including the following:

■ PAT will not work with configurations using the **alias** command.

■ Stateful failover of SCCP calls is not supported.

■ Using the **debug skinny** command may delay sending messages, which can have a performance impact in a real-time environment.

■ No support for fragmented SCCP messages is provided.

■ Outside NAT or PAT is not supported.

PIX Firewall does not support NAT or PAT of the file content transferred using Trivial File Transfer Protocol (TFTP), if the address of a Cisco CallManager server is configured for NAT or PAT to a different address or port and outside phones register to it using TFTP. Even though PIX Firewall does support NAT of TFTP messages and opens holes for the TFTP file to pass through the firewall, PIX Firewall cannot translate the Cisco CallManager IP address and port embedded in the Cisco IP Phone's configuration files that are transferred using TFTP during phone registration.

> **NOTE**   Cisco IP Phones need to reregister with the Cisco CallManager to establish calls through the PIX Firewall if the **clear xlate** command is entered. This is because the xlates for the Cisco CallManager are permanently deleted.

Session Initiation Protocol

SIP, RFC 2543, is a signaling protocol for Internet conferencing, telephony, presence, events notification, and instant messaging. SIP was developed in the mid-1990s by the Internet Engineering Task Force (IETF) as a real-time communication protocol for IP voice, and it has expanded into video and instant-messaging applications. SIP works with Session Description Protocol (SDP), RFC 2327, for call signaling. SDP specifies the ports for the media stream. Using SIP, the PIX Firewall can support any SIP VoIP gateways and VoIP proxy servers.

To support SIP calls through the PIX Firewall, signaling messages for the media connection addresses, media ports, and embryonic connections for the media must be inspected, because although the signaling is sent over a well-known destination port (UDP/TCP 5060), the media streams are dynamically allocated. Also, SIP embeds IP addresses in the user data portion of the IP packet. SIP inspection applies NAT for these embedded IP addresses.

Application inspection for SIP is enabled by default. You can use the **fixup** command to change the default TCP port assignment for SIP. The command syntax is as follows:

```
fixup protocol sip <udp> [port[-port]]
```

Attack Guards

Hackers use several methods to cause network service disruption. Denial of service (DoS) is a popular way of causing network disruption. Cisco PIX Firewall has some attack mitigation features to combat against some of the following attacks:

- Fragmentation
- Domain Name System (DNS) attacks
- Simple Mail Transfer Protocol (SMTP)–based attacks
- SYN flooding
- Authentication and authorization attacks

Fragmentation Guard and Virtual Reassembly

Breaking a single IP datagram into two or more smaller IP datagrams is called *IP fragmentation*. DoS attacks overwhelm the host with fragmented IP datagrams. By using the **fragment** command on the PIX Firewall, you can prevent fragmented packets from traversing it. The IP Fragguard feature is enabled by default. To specify the maximum number of packets into which a full IP packet can be fragmented, use the following syntax:

```
fragment chain chain-limit [interface]
```

Setting the chain limit to 1 means that all packets must be whole; that is, unfragmented. The default is 24. The following example shows a configuration that prevents fragmented packets from entering on the outside interface:

```
pixfirewall(config)# fragment chain 1 outside
```

The Fragguard feature enforces the checks recommended by RFC 1858, with two additional security checks protecting against many IP fragment-style attacks such as teardrop:

- The checks ensure that each noninitial IP fragment has an associated valid initial IP fragment.

- In Version 6.2, by default IP fragments of more than 24 elements cannot pass through the PIX; however, this is configurable. The fragment database can process 200 fragmented packets at a time. This value is also configurable but should be set less than the total number of blocks in the 1550 or 16384 pools.

Virtual reassembly is enabled by default. This feature uses syslog to log any fragment overlapping and small fragment offset anomalies. Here is an example of such a message:

```
% PIX-2-106020: Deny IP teardrop fragment
   (size=num, offset=num)from IP-addr to  IP-addr
```

Domain Name System Guard

To understand the DNS attack protection provided by Cisco PIX Firewall, it helps to understand how DNS can be exploited to cause a DoS attack. DNS queries are sent from the attacker to each of the DNS servers. These queries contain the target's spoofed address. The DNS servers respond to the small query with a large response. These responses are routed to the target, causing link congestion and possible denial of Internet connectivity.

The port assignment for DNS cannot be configured on the Cisco PIX Firewall. DNS requires application inspection so that DNS queries will not be subject to generic UDP handling based on activity timeouts. The PIX allows only a single DNS response for outgoing DNS requests. The UDP connections associated with DNS queries and responses are torn down as soon as a reply to a DNS query is received, dropping all other responses and averting a DoS attack. This functionality is called *DNS Guard*. DNS Guard is enabled by default.

DNS inspection performs two tasks:

- It monitors the message exchange to ensure that the ID of the DNS reply matches the ID of the DNS query.
- It translates the DNS A record on behalf of the **alias** command.

Only forward lookups are translated using NAT, so pointer (PTR) records are not touched. DNS zone transfers can also trigger built-in intrusion detection signatures on the PIX Firewall.

> **NOTE** A pointer record is also called a reverse record. A PTR record associates an IP address with a canonical name.

Cisco PIX Firewall Version 6.2 introduces full support for NAT and PAT of DNS messages originating from either inside (more-secure) or outside (less-secure) interfaces. This means that if a client on an inside network requests DNS resolution of an inside address from a DNS server on an outside interface, the DNS A record is translated correctly. This also means that the use of the **alias** command is now unnecessary.

Mail Guard

An SMTP server responds to client requests with numeric reply codes and optional human-readable strings. SMTP application inspection controls and reduces the commands that the user can use, as well as the messages the server returns. SMTP inspection performs three primary tasks:

- It restricts SMTP requests to seven commands: **HELO, MAIL, RCPT, DATA, RSET, NOOP,** and **QUIT.**
- It monitors the SMTP command-response sequence.
- It generates an audit trail–audit record 108002 when an invalid character embedded in the mail address is replaced. For more information, see RFC 821.

By default, the Cisco PIX Firewall inspects port 25 connections for SMTP traffic. SMTP inspection monitors the command-response sequence for the following anomalous signatures:

- Truncated commands.
- Incorrect command termination (those not terminated with <CR><LF>).
- Unallowed characters. The **MAIL** and **RCPT** commands specify the sender and recipient of the mail. Mail addresses are scanned for strange characters. The pipe character (|) is deleted (changed to a blank space), and < and > are allowed only if they are used to define a mail address (> must be preceded by <).
- An unexpected transition by the SMTP server.
- Unknown commands, for which the PIX Firewall changes all the characters in the packet to X. In this case, the server generates an error code to the client. Because of the change in the packet, the TCP checksum has to be recalculated or adjusted.

The **fixup** command is used to change the default port assignment for SMTP. The command syntax is as follows:

```
fixup protocol smtp [port[-port]]
```

The **fixup protocol smtp** command enables the Mail Guard feature. This restricts mail servers to receiving only the seven commands defined in RFC 821 section 4.5.1 (**HELO, MAIL, RCPT, DATA, RSET, NOOP,** and **QUIT**). All other commands are rejected.

The strict implementation of RFC 821 section 4.5.1 sometimes causes problems for mail servers that do not adhere to the standard. For example, Microsoft Exchange Server does not strictly comply with RFC 821 section 4.5.1 and uses extended SMTP commands such as **EHLO**. The Cisco PIX Firewall converts any such commands into **NOOP** commands, which, as specified by the RFC, forces SMTP servers to fall back to using minimal SMTP commands only. This might cause Microsoft Outlook clients and Exchange servers to function unpredictably when their connection passes through the PIX Firewall.

Mail Guard, however, is not the magic bullet for all mail server–related attacks. It protects your mail server only from known attacks.

Flood Defender

The Flood Defender feature of PIX Firewall protects inside systems from a DoS attack that floods an interface with half-open TCP (embryonic) connections, otherwise known as *SYN flooding*. Creating a threshold for the number of embryonic connections or limiting the number of connections to the host mitigates such attacks. When the configured embryonic limit is reached, the PIX Firewall intercepts the SYN bound for the host and responds with a SYN/ACK on the host's behalf.

You enable this feature by setting the *emb-limit* (maximum embryonic connections) option or *max-conn* (maximum connection) option on the **nat** and **static** commands. For example:

```
static (inside,outside) 192.168.10.10 10.10.10.10 netmask 255.255.255.255
   300 500000
```

This example sets the maximum connection to host 10.10.10.10 to 300 and sets the embryonic connection limit to 500,000.

If you set *max-conn* too low, you deny legitimate user access, creating a denial of service for yourself. There is no magic number for the *max-conn* and *emb-limit* arguments because every network has a unique environment. The best number is one that does not negatively affect the network. You can observe the number of connections and embryonic connections to your host, before and after *max-conn* and *emb-limit* implementation, using the **show local-host** *host-ip* command.

The **static** command with the maximum connection or embryonic connection arguments set mitigates inbound DoS. The **nat** command with the same arguments can prevent the users in your network from committing TCP SYN attacks on someone else.

AAA Floodguard

Cisco PIX Firewall has a Floodguard feature that helps it monitor and recover resources tied up in the user authentication (auth) subsystem. As with DNS, the service of authentication is maliciously exploited to create a DoS attack. Authentication attacks are done on the premise that each authentication request has to be processed. Sending an enormous number of authentication requests bogs down the target's finite resources, forcing a shutdown in the worst case.

When the Cisco PIX Firewall is inundated with authentication requests, it displays messages indicating that it is out of resources or out of TCP users. TCP user resources in different states are reclaimed in the following order depending on urgency:

1. Timewait
2. LastAck
3. Finwait
4. Embryonic
5. Idle

The Floodguard is enabled by default. It can be disabled using the **floodguard disable** command.

PIX Firewall Intrusion Detection Feature

Cisco PIX Firewall includes an IP-only intrusion detection feature. It provides visibility at network perimeters or for locations where additional security between network segments is required.

The PIX IDS identifies more than 53 common attacks using signatures to detect patterns of misuse in network traffic. Traffic passing through the PIX Firewall can be identified to be audited, logged, and/or dropped.

After it is configured, the IDS feature watches packets and sessions as they flow through the firewall, scanning each for a match with any of the IDS signatures. When suspicious activity is detected, the PIX Firewall responds immediately and can be configured to do the following:

1. Send an alarm to a syslog server.
2. Drop the packet.
3. Reset the TCP connection.

Cisco PIX Firewall supports both inbound and outbound auditing. Auditing is performed by examining the IP packets as they arrive at an input interface. If a packet triggers a signature and the configured action does not drop the packet, the same packet can trigger other signatures. The IDS feature allows a signature to be acted upon differently depending on the interface on which it was detected. It also allows signatures to be individually disabled if reoccurring false positives are detected.

> **TIP** You can find an excellent explanation of the IDS messages that are generated from IDS events in the section "Messages 400000 to 407002" of the document "System Log Messages" at http://www.cisco.com/univercd/cc/td/doc/product/iaabu/pix/pix-sw/v-63/63syslog/pixemsgs.htm#1138590

Intrusion Detection Configuration

An *audit policy* (audit rule) defines the attributes of all signatures that can be applied to an interface, along with a set of actions. Using an audit policy can limit the traffic that is audited or specify actions to be taken when the signature matches. Each audit policy is identified by a name and can be defined for informational or attack signatures. Each interface can have two policies—one for informational signatures and one for attack signatures. If a policy is defined without actions, the configured default actions take effect. Each policy requires a different name.

The **ip audit** command enables the IDS feature on the Cisco PIX Firewall. The **ip audit** command can be used to create a global audit policy or a per-interface policy.

The global audit policy specifies the default actions to be taken when an attack or informational signature is matched.

In all the **ip audit** commands, the **action** can be any combination of **alarm, drop,** and **reset.** If nothing is configured, the default action is **alarm.** The **alarm** option indicates that when a signature match is detected in a packet, the PIX Firewall reports the event to all configured syslog servers. The **drop** option drops the offending packet. The **reset** option drops the offending packet and closes the connection if it is part of an active connection.

The syntax of the **ip audit attack** command is as follows:

```
ip audit attack [action [alarm] [drop] [reset]]
```

The syntax of the **ip audit info** command is as follows:

```
ip audit info [[action [alarm] [drop] [reset]]
```

Table 18-2 describes the complete command parameters for the **ip audit** command.

Table 18-2 ip audit *Command Parameters*

Command Parameter	Description
attack	Specifies the default actions to be taken for attack signatures
action *actions*	alarm, drop, reset

continues

Table 18-2 ip audit *Command Parameters (Continued)*

Command Parameter	Description
info	Specifies the default actions to be taken for informational signatures
interface	Applies an audit specification or policy (using the **ip audit name** command) to an interface
audit name	Specifies informational signatures, except those disabled or excluded by the **ip audit signature** command, as part of the policy
audit signature	Specifies which messages to display, attaches a global policy to a signature, and disables or excludes a signature from auditing
name *audit-name*	The name assigned by the PIX Firewall admin for the audit policy
clear	Resets name, signature, interface, and attack information to default values
signature-number	IDS signature number

The following example shows the creation and application of policy1 and policy2 on the outside and inside interface:

```
ip audit name policy1 info action alarm
ip audit name policy1 attack action alarm drop reset
ip audit name policy2 attack action alarm drop
ip audit interface outside policy1
ip audit interface inside policy2
```

Table 18-3 describes the **show** commands used to verify the IP audit configuration.

Table 18-3 show *Commands to Verify IP Audit Configuration*

Command	What the Output Displays
show ip audit attack	The default attack actions
show ip audit info	The default informational actions
show ip audit interface	The interface configuration
show ip audit *audit-name* [**name** [**info** | **attack**]]	All audit policies or specific policies referenced by name and possibly type
show ip audit signature [*signature-number*]	Disabled signatures

The Cisco PIX Firewall IDS feature does not cover the entire set of intrusion detection signatures that is available to a Cisco IDS unit.

Dynamic Shunning

The dynamic shunning functionality allows a Cisco PIX Firewall, when combined with a Cisco IDS 3.0 or later sensor that is configured appropriately, to respond dynamically to an attacking host by preventing new connections and disallowing packets from any existing connection. Just like a router, the IDS unit tells the PIX Firewall to stop any new connections and to time out existing connections with the sources of traffic that are determined to be malicious. The **shun** command applies a blocking function to the interface receiving the attack. Packets containing the IP source address of the attacking host are dropped and are logged until the blocking function is removed manually or by the Cisco Secure IDS master unit. The shun feature is disabled by the **no shun** command. The syntax for the **shun** command is as follows:

```
shun src-ip [dst-ip sport dport [protocol]]
```

NOTE   The *protocol* parameter is optional and is either UDP or TCP when used.

In the following example, the offending host (10.10.10.14) makes a connection with the victim (10.25.25.32) using TCP. The connection in the PIX Firewall connection table contains a line similar to the following:

```
TCP out 10.10.10.14:555 in 10.25.25.32:666 idle 0:00:01 bytes 3905
```

Applying the following **shun** command:

```
shun 10.10.10.14 10.25.25.32 555 666 tcp
```

deletes the connection from the PIX Firewall connection table and also prevents packets from 10.10.10.14 from going through the PIX Firewall. The offending host can be inside or outside the PIX Firewall.

The application of the blocking function of the **shun** command does not require the specified host to be in active connection. Because the **shun** command is used to block attacks dynamically, it is not displayed in your PIX configuration. Shun statistics are available by using **show** commands, syslog messages, and PIX Device Manager (PDM) monitoring. The following is a sample output of the **show shun** command applied to the outside interface:

```
Outside=ON, cnt=2, time=(20:14:02)
```

Although the idea of dynamic shunning seems be an innovative way of dealing with offending hosts, it sometimes produces false positives that might cause a denial of service to legitimate users. This feature is available only on PIX Firewall Version 6.0(2) and later.

ip verify reverse-path Command

The **ip verify reverse-path** command is a security feature that does a route lookup based on the source address. Usually, the route lookup is based on the destination address. This is why it is called *reverse path forwarding*. With this command enabled, packets are dropped if no route is found for the packet or the route found does not match the interface on which the packet arrived. This command is disabled by default and provides Unicast Reverse Path Forwarding (Unicast RPF) functionality for the PIX Firewall.

The **ip verify reverse-path** command provides both ingress and egress filtering. Ingress filtering checks inbound packets for IP source address integrity and is limited to addresses for networks in the enforcing entity's local routing table. If the incoming packet does not have a source address represented by a route, it is impossible to know whether the packet has arrived on the best possible path back to its origin. This is often the case when routing entities cannot maintain routes for every network.

Egress filtering verifies that packets destined for hosts outside the managed domain have IP source addresses that can be verified by routes in the enforcing entity's local routing table. If an exiting packet does not arrive on the best return path back to the originator, the packet is dropped, and the activity is logged. Egress filtering prevents internal users from launching attacks using IP source addresses outside the local domain, because most attacks use IP spoofing to hide the identity of the attacking host. Egress filtering makes the task of tracing an attack's origin much easier. When employed, egress filtering enforces which IP source addresses are obtained from a valid pool of network addresses. Addresses are kept local to the enforcing entity and therefore are easily traceable.

Unicast RPF is implemented as follows:

- Internet Control Message Protocol (ICMP) packets have no session, so each packet is checked.
- UDP and TCP have sessions, so the initial packet requires a reverse route lookup. Subsequent packets arriving during the session are checked using an existing state maintained as part of the session. Noninitial packets are checked to ensure that they arrived on the same interface used by the initial packet.

> **NOTE**   Before using this command, add static **route** command statements for every network that can be accessed on the interfaces you want to protect. Enable this command only if routing is fully specified. Otherwise, the Cisco PIX Firewall stops traffic on the interface you specify if routing is not in place.

The following example protects traffic between the inside and outside interfaces and provides **route** command statements for two networks, 10.1.2.0 and 10.1.3.0, that connect to the inside interface by a hub:

```
ip address inside 10.1.1.1 255.255.255.0
route inside 10.1.2.0 255.255.255.0 10.1.1.1 1
route inside 10.1.3.0 255.255.255.0 10.1.1.1 1
ip verify reverse-path interface outside
ip verify reverse-path interface inside
```

The **ip verify reverse-path interface outside** command protects the outside interface from network ingress attacks from the Internet, whereas the **ip verify reverse-path interface inside** command protects the inside interface from network egress attacks from users on the internal network.

The **clear ip verify** command removes **ip verify** commands from the configuration. Unicast RPF is a unidirectional input function that screens inbound packets arriving on an interface. Outbound packets are not screened.

Because of the danger of IP spoofing in the IP protocol, measures need to be taken to reduce this risk when possible. Unicast RPF, or reverse route lookup, prevents such manipulation under certain circumstances.

Foundation Summary

The "Foundation Summary" provides a convenient review of many key concepts in this chapter. If you are already comfortable with the topics in this chapter, this summary can help you recall a few details. If you just read this chapter, this review should help solidify some key facts. If you are doing your final preparation before the exam, this summary provides a convenient way to review the day before the exam.

PIX Firewall Version 6.3 and later support application inspection of the major protocols and applications that provide VoIP services including the following:

- CTIQBE
- H.323
- MGCP
- SCCP
- SIP

Cisco PIX Firewall has built-in features that help it mitigate most known attacks:

- **DNS Guard**—DNS queries and responses are torn down as soon as a reply to a DNS query is received, dropping all other responses and averting a DoS attack.
- **Mail Guard**—The **fixup protocol smtp** command enables the Mail Guard feature, which restricts mail servers to receiving only the seven commands defined in RFC 821 section 4.5.1 (**HELO, MAIL, RCPT, DATA, RSET, NOOP,** and **QUIT**). All other commands are rejected.
- **Flood Defender**—Protects inside systems from DoS attacks that flood interfaces with half-open TCP (embryonic) connections, otherwise known as SYN flooding.
- **AAA Floodguard**—Monitors and recovers resources tied up in the user authentication (auth) subsystem, averting a DoS attack.
- **IP Frag Guard**—Prevents DoS attacks caused by fragmented IP datagrams overwhelming the hosts.

Cisco PIX Firewall also includes an intrusion detection feature with 53 common attack signatures. PIX Firewall supports both inbound and outbound auditing. When an attack signature is detected, the PIX Firewall can send an alarm, drop the packet, or reset the TCP connection.

Q&A

As mentioned in the Introduction, the questions in this book are more difficult than what you should experience on the exam. The questions are designed to ensure your understanding of the concepts discussed in this chapter and adequately prepare you to complete the exam. You should use the simulated exams on the CD to practice for the exam.

The answers to these questions can be found in Appendix A.

1. Which PIX feature mitigates a DoS attack using an incomplete IP datagram?

2. On which port does the PIX Firewall inspect for H.323 traffic by default?

3. How do you enable the PIX Firewall Mail Guard feature?

4. What are some of the PIX limitations on CTIQBE application inspection?

5. What is an embryonic connection?

6. Which actions are available in the PIX IDS configuration?

7. How does DNS Guard on the Cisco PIX Firewall prevent DoS attacks that exploit DNS?

8. How does **ip verify reverse-path** secure the PIX Firewall?

9. How does the Mail Guard feature prevent SMTP-related attacks?

10. How do you enable MGCP application inspection for call agents and gateways using the default ports?

This chapter covers the following subjects:

- FWSM Overview

- Using PDM with FWSM

In addition, this chapter also covers the following supplemental topics:

- Typical FWSM Deployment Scenarios
- Basic FWSM Configuration Tasks
- Basic Troubleshooting Task

CHAPTER 19

Firewall Services Module

The Cisco Firewall Services Module (FWSM) is an integrated module for the Catalyst 6500 Series switch and the Cisco 7600 Series Internet router. By providing firewall functionality on a line card, the operation of the firewall can be tightly integrated into the normal switch operation, thus providing a robust security infrastructure.

How to Best Use This Chapter

Adding firewall functionality to your core switching infrastructure enables you to enhance the overall security of your network dramatically. The FWSM provides this firewall functionality by directly integrating into your Catalyst 6500 switches using a switch module card. Test yourself with the "Do I Know This Already?" quiz and see how familiar you are with the FWSM.

"Do I Know This Already?" Quiz

The purpose of the "Do I Know This Already?" quiz is to help you decide if you really need to read the entire chapter. If you already intend to read the entire chapter, you do not necessarily need to answer these questions now.

The ten-question quiz, derived from the major sections in the "Foundation and Supplemental Topics" portion of the chapter, helps you determine how to spend your limited study time.

Table 19-1 outlines the major topics discussed in this chapter and the "Do I Know This Already?" quiz questions that correspond to those topics.

Table 19-1 *"Do I Know This Already?" Foundation Topics Section-to-Question Mapping*

Supplemental or Foundations Topics Section	Questions Covered in This Section	Score
Cisco Firewall Services Module (FWSM) Overview	1, 9	
Basic Deployment Scenarios	6, 10	
Initializing the FWSM	2, 3, 5	
Using PDM with the FWSM	4	
Troubleshooting the FWSM	7, 8	

CAUTION The goal of self assessment is to gauge your mastery of the topics in this chapter. If you do not know the answer to a question or are only partially sure of the answer, you should mark this question wrong for purposes of the self assessment. Giving yourself credit for an answer you correctly guess skews your self-assessment results and might provide you with a false sense of security.

1. Which of the following is true?

    a. The FWSM supports more interfaces than the Cisco PIX Firewall.

    b. The FWSM supports fewer interfaces than the PIX Firewall.

    c. The FWSM and the PIX Firewall support the same number of interfaces.

    d. None of the above

2. When using Cisco IOS software, the switch passes traffic from which VLANs to your FWSM?

    a. All configured VLANs

    b. All VLANs configured for all firewall vlan-groups

    c. The firewall vlan-group associated with the specific FWSM module

    d. Any VLAN

    e. None of the above

3. What traffic is initially allowed by the FWSM?

   a. All traffic

   b. Traffic from your protected networks

   c. Traffic from the inside interface only

   d. No traffic

   e. None of the above

4. To connect to PDM on the FWSM, you use which protocol?

   a. HTTP

   b. HTTPS

   c. SSH

   d. Telnet

   e. None of the above

5. To cause switch traffic (using Cisco IOS software) to be controlled by the FWSM, what must you do?

   a. Place the VLAN for the traffic in a firewall vlan-group.

   b. Configure the VLAN normally because all VLANs are controlled by the FWSM.

   c. Define the IP network addresses on the switch to be passed to the FWSM.

   d. Define the IP interfaces on the MSFC to be passed to the FWSM.

   e. None of the above

6. What properties identify each firewall interface? (Choose three.)

   a. VLAN

   b. IP Address

   c. Security Level

   d. Switchport

   e. MSFC interface

7. What is the color of the status LED when the FWSM is operating normally?

   a. Red

   b. Orange

   c. Green

   d. Yellow

   e. White

8. Which Cisco IOS switch command enables you to reset the FWSM?

   a. session

   b. reset

   c. nameif

   d. hw-module

   e. None of the above

9. Which of the following is true?

   a. The PIX Firewall supports more concurrent connections than the FWSM.

   b. The PIX Firewall and FWSM support the same number of concurrent connections.

   c. The FWSM supports more concurrent connections than the PIX Firewall.

   d. None of the above

10. Which configuration(s) is valid to regulate the flow of traffic on the Catalyst 6500 switch between the MSFC and the FWSM?

   a. MSFC as the inside router

   b. MSFC as the outside router

   c. MSFC not directly connected to FWSM

   d. Answers a, b, and c

The answers to the "Do I Know This Already?" quiz are found in Appendix A, "Answers to the 'Do I Know This Already?' Quizzes and Q&A Sections." The suggested choices for your next step are as follows:

- **8 or less overall score**—Read the entire chapter. This includes the "Foundation and Supplemental Topics," "Foundation Summary," and "Q&A" sections.

- **9 or 10 overall score**—If you want more review on these topics, skip to the "Foundation Summary" section and then go to the "Q&A" section. Otherwise, move to the next chapter.

Foundation and Supplemental Topics

Cisco Firewall Services Module Overview

The Cisco Firewall Services Module (FWSM) is a high-performance firewall solution, providing 5 gigabits per second (Gbps) of throughput from a single FWSM. Combining multiple modules in a single chassis enables you to scale this throughput to 20 Gbps. Some features of the FWSM include the following:

- Is fully virtual LAN (VLAN) aware
- Supports dynamic routing
- Integrates firewall functionality and switching in a single chassis
- Supports the entire Cisco PIX Firewall Version 6.0 feature set and some Version 6.2 features
- Allows up to 1 million concurrent connections
- Supports 5-Gbps throughout
- Enables multiple FWSMs per chassis
- Supports intrachassis and interchassis stateful failure
- Provides multiple management options

Initially, the FWSM provided several features that were not available with the PIX software. These included features such as Open Shortest Path First (OSPF) functionality and support for VLAN tagging. As of PIX Firewall Version 6.3, many of these features have been incorporated into the PIX software. Table 19-2 outlines the major differences between the FWSM (Version 1.1.2) and the PIX software (Version 6.3).

Table 19-2 *FWSM and PIX Feature Comparison*

Feature	FWSM	PIX 535
Performance	5 Gbps	1.7 Gbps
Interfaces	100	24
Concurrent Connections	1,000,000	500,000

> **NOTE** The PIX software supports both logical and physical interfaces. The maximum number of interfaces supported on the PIX 535 is 24. You can have a maximum of 10 physical interfaces and a maximum of 22 logical interfaces. The total number of interfaces (both physical and logical) cannot exceed 24. For more information on logical interfaces, see Chapter 9, "Routing and the PIX Firewall."

Because the FWSM command set is derived from the PIX 6.0 feature set, many of the configuration tasks that you use to configure the FWSM are similar if not identical to the PIX configuration tasks. Therefore, this chapter focuses on the following aspects of the FWSM:

■ Basic deployment scenarios

■ Initializing the FWSM

■ Using PIX Device Manager (PDM) with the FWSM

■ Troubleshooting the FWSM

Basic Deployment Scenarios

Figure 19-1 shows a basic network configuration in which a central switch is used to connect various VLANs both at Layer 2 and at Layer 3. Protecting the perimeter of the network with a firewall is the first step in securing this network configuration. Securing the flow of traffic between multiple internal VLANs, however, can be a more difficult task.

Figure 19-1 *Basic Switched Network*

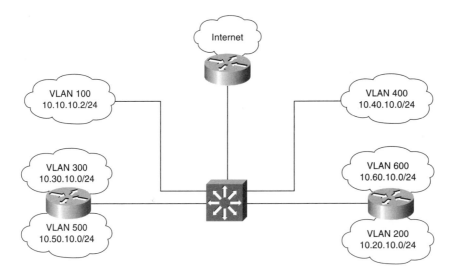

Because the FWSM is tightly integrated with the switch, securing the traffic flowing between multiple VLANs on your network becomes an easier task to manage. When you place a FWSM in your central Catalyst 6500 switch, the configuration has the following characteristics:

- Each firewall interface is a Layer 3 interface that is associated with a VLAN, security level, and Internet Protocol (IP) address.
- Traffic from all nonfirewall VLANs in the switch (those not part of a firewall group) is routed through the Multilayer Switch Feature Card (MSFC) without being examined by the firewall.
- The MSFC may be configured as a connected router on any firewall interface.
- Traffic for all VLANs that are part of a firewall group is protected and controlled by the FWSM, whereas other VLANs are considered to be outside the firewall.

When integrating the FWSM into your network's security configuration, you need to decide on the location of the MSFC. The MSFC enables your switch to forward traffic between multiple VLANs because it performs routing or Layer 3 functionality. You can configure your MSFC in one of the following three configurations. Each is discussed in more detail in the following pages.

- MSFC as inside router
- MSFC as the outside router
- MSFC not directly connected to FWSM

Multilayer Switch Feature Card as the Inside Router

Figure 19-2 shows a FWSM configuration with the MSFC used as a router on the network inside the firewall. VLANs 100, 200, and 700 are configured as firewall VLANs. The MSFC is connected to VLAN 100 (which is a firewall-controlled VLAN). In this configuration, traffic between VLANs 300, 400, 500, and 800 is routed by the MSFC without passing through the FWSM. All other traffic is routed through the FWSM.

NOTE   The MSFC provides multiprotocol routing and multilayer switching for the Catalyst 6000 family of switches.

Figure 19-2 *MSFC Inside FWSM Network*

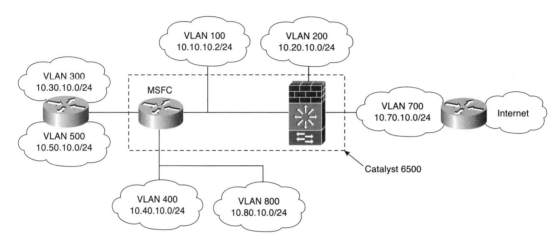

Multilayer Switch Feature Card as the Outside Router

Figure 19-3 shows a FWSM configuration with the MSFC used as a router on the network outside the firewall. All of the VLANs (except VLAN 600 and 700) are controlled by the FWSM. Therefore, only traffic from the Internet to VLAN 600 is handled by the MSFC. All other traffic is subject to the rules on the FWSM.

Figure 19-3 *MSFC Outside FWSM Network*

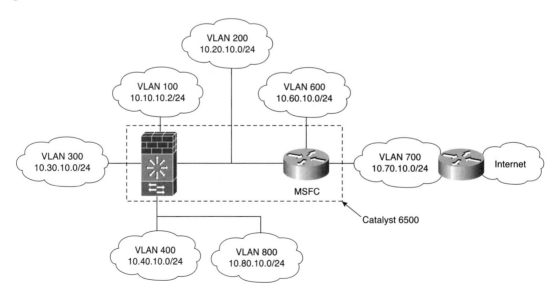

Multilayer Switch Feature Card Not Directly Connected to FWSM

Besides connecting the MSFC to either the inside or outside of the FWSM, you can also set up a configuration in which the MSFC is not directly connected to any of the FWSM interfaces. In this situation, there is no interaction between the MSFC and the FWSM.

Initializing the Firewall Services Module

When you configure a PIX Firewall, you can run the **setup** command and the firewall is ready to go. The FWSM, on the other hand, receives traffic directly from the Catalyst switch's backplane. This increases the initial configuration task required to make the FWSM operational. Initially configuring the FWSM involves the following tasks:

- Switch configuration
- Basic FWSM configuration

Switch Configuration

Before you can use the firewall functionality on your network traffic, you need to perform several configuration tasks on the switch. To configure the switch to operate with your FWSM, you need to perform the following steps:

Step 1   Create VLANs.

Step 2   Define a firewall vlan-group.

Step 3   Associate the firewall vlan-group with a module.

> **NOTE**   The switch configuration steps outlined in the following sections assume that your switch is running Cisco IOS software. If you are using the Catalyst operating system (CatOS), please refer to the documentation for the configuration steps.

Create Virtual LANs

Each interface on the FWSM receives traffic from specific VLAN(s) on your switch. To create VLANs on your switch you use the **vlan** command. The syntax for this command is as follows:

```
vlan vlan-number
```

Next you need to be able to route traffic between VLANs using the MSFC. By default, routers route traffic between the networks to which they are physically connected. With the MSFC, you can create virtual interfaces connected to the various VLANs on your switch. These virtual interfaces enable your switch to control the flow of traffic between the different networks defined by the configured VLANs. To create a virtual interface for a VLAN, use the **interface vlan** command. The syntax for this command is as follows:

```
interface vlan vlan-number
```

Define Firewall vlan-group

At a minimum, you need to specify two VLANs when configuring your FWSM. One of these VLANs represents the network being protected by the FWSM. All traffic for this VLAN will be sent through the FWSM for analysis before being sent to the actual devices on the VLAN. The other VLAN represents the network outside the FWSM.

Normally, the switch passes traffic to the MSFC, and the MSFC routes traffic between the various VLANs configured on the switch. When using the FWSM, however, you want certain traffic to be sent to the FWSM instead of to the MSFC. To accomplish this, you need to define a group of VLANs that will be controlled by the FWSM by using the **firewall vlan-group** command. The syntax for this command is as follows:

```
firewall vlan-group firewall-group vlan-range
```

Table 19-3 describes the parameters associated with the **firewall vlan-group** command.

Table 19-3 firewall vlan-group *Parameters*

Parameter	Description
firewall-group	A number that is used to reference the set of VLANs associated with this firewall VLAN group.
vlan-range	A range of VLANs to be included in the firewall group. Individual VLANs can be separated by commas, and a range of VLANs can be specified by using a dash (for example, 200–250).

After the firewall vlan-group is defined, the switch will then send traffic for these VLANs to the FWSM instead of to the MSFC. This enables the FWSM to enforce security policy rules against the traffic from or to these VLANs.

Associate the vlan-group with the Module

Finally, you need to inform the switch in which switch slot the FWSM is located. You can have multiple FWSMs in a single switch, so this command is used to identify which blade will receive the traffic for a specific firewall vlan-group. This association is defined using the **firewall module** switch command, and its syntax is as follows:

```
firewall module module-number vlan-group firewall-group
```

Table 19-4 describes the parameters associated with the **firewall module** command.

Table 19-4 **firewall module** *Parameters*

Parameter	Description
module-number	The slot in the switch where the FWSM is located
firewall-group	The number of the firewall vlan-group that you want to associate with the specified module (from the **firewall vlan-group** command)

Assume that your FWSM is located in slot 5 on a switch that is running Cisco IOS software. Example 19-1 shows the switch configuration commands necessary to set up a FWSM configuration with the MSFC as the inside router (as shown in Figure 19-2).

Example 19-1 *Configuring the MSFC on the Inside Interface*

```
Switch# configure terminal
Switch(config)# vlan 100
Switch(config-vlan) no shut
Switch(config-vlan) exit
Switch(config)# interface vlan100
Switch(config-if) ip address 10.10.10.1 255.255.255.0
Switch(config-if) no shut
Switch(config-if)# exit
Switch(config)# vlan 200
Switch(config-vlan) no shut
Switch(config-vlan) exit
Switch(config)# interface vlan200
Switch(config-if) ip address 10.20.10.1 255.255.255.0
Switch(config-if) no shut
Switch(config-if)# exit
Switch(config)# vlan 300
Switch(config-vlan) no shut
Switch(config-vlan) exit
Switch(config)# interface vlan300
Switch(config-if) ip address 10.30.10.1 255.255.255.0
Switch(config-if) no shut
Switch(config-if)# exit
Switch(config)# vlan 400
Switch(config-vlan) no shut
Switch(config-vlan) exit
Switch(config)# interface vlan400
Switch(config-if) ip address 10.40.10.1 255.255.255.0
Switch(config-if) no shut
Switch(config-if)# exit
Switch(config)# vlan 700
```

continues

Example 19-1   *Configuring the MSFC on the Inside Interface (Continued)*

```
Switch(config-vlan) no shut
Switch(config-vlan) exit
Switch(config)# interface vlan700
Switch(config-if) ip address 10.70.10.1 255.255.255.0
Switch(config-if) no shut
Switch(config-if)# exit
Switch(config)# vlan 800
Switch(config-vlan) no shut
Switch(config-vlan) exit
Switch(config)# interface vlan800
Switch(config-if) ip address 10.80.10.1 255.255.255.0
Switch(config-if) no shut
Switch(config-if)# exit
Switch(config)# firewall vlan-group 10 100,200,700
Switch(config)# firewall module 5 vlan-group 10
Switch(config)# exit
```

Basic Firewall Services Module Configuration

To initially set up the FWSM, perform the following tasks on it:

■ Run the **setup** command

■ Configure interfaces

■ Define access lists

Because you are initially configuring the FWSM, you need to gain access to the command-line interface (CLI) on the FWSM from the switch CLI. The **session slot** command enables you to access the CLI on your various switch modules. The syntax for this command is as follows:

```
session slot module-number processor processor-id
```

> **NOTE**   When accessing the FWSM, you use a processor ID of 1.

If your FWSM is located in slot 3 on your switch, you would use the following command to connect to the FWSM CLI from the switch CLI:

```
stat-6000#session slot 3 processor 1
The default escape character is Ctrl-^, then x.
You can also type 'exit' at the remote prompt to end the session
Trying 127.0.0.31 ... Open

FWSM passwd:
Welcome to the FWSM firewall
Type help or '?' for a list of available commands.
FWSM>
```

At the passwd prompt, you need to enter the password for Telnet console access on the FWSM.

> **NOTE**   The default password for Telnet console access is *cisco*. For security reasons, you should change the default password using the **passwd** command from the privileged mode on the FWSM.

Running the setup Command

Just like on the PIX Firewall, the **setup** command enables you to configure many of the basic parameters on the FWSM quickly, such as the following:

- Host name
- Domain name
- Enable password

Example 19-2 is a sample of the output and questions provided by the **setup** command:

Example 19-2

```
FWSM(config)# setup
Pre-configure FWSM Firewall now through interactive prompts [yes]?
Enable password [<use current password>]:
Inside IP address [10.10.10.2]:
Inside network mask [255.255.255.0]:
Host name [FWSM]: FWModule
Domain name: cisco.com
IP address of host running FWSM Device Manager: 10.10.10.4
The following configuration will be used:
Enable password: <current password>
Clock (UTC): 06:26:43 Feb 13 2004
Inside IP address: 10.10.10.2
Inside network mask: 255.255.255.0
Host name: FWModule
Domain name: cisco.com
IP address of host running FWSM Device Manager: 10.10.10.4
Use this configuration and write to flash? yes
Building configuration...
Cryptochecksum: dc097768 111d2643 5ec3f1a7 b9775f45
[OK]
```

Configuring the Interfaces

Unlike the PIX Firewall, the FWSM does not have a default inside and outside interface. Initially, you associate two or more VLANs with the FWSM (using the **firewall vlan-group** and **firewall module** switch commands). On the FWSM, however, you must assign each

VLAN to a specific interface name and assign each interface an IP address. To assign a switch VLAN a specific interface name on the FWSM you use the **nameif** command. The syntax for this command is as follows:

```
nameif vlan-number interface-name security-level
```

The parameters for the **nameif** interface commands are shown in Table 19-5.

Table 19-5 nameif *Parameters*

Parameter	Description
vlan-number	The switch VLAN that will be assigned to the interface. You can specify only VLANs that are assigned to the firewall vlan-group for your FWSM module (from the **firewall vlan-group** command).
interface-name	The name of the interface that you want to assign to the specified VLAN.
security-level	The security level of the interface being created. Valid values range from 0 to 100, with 0 being the lowest security level and 100 being the highest.

After creating your FWSM interfaces by assigning an interface name to each interface, you need to specify an IP address for each interface. You use the **ip address** command to configure the FWSMs IP address; its syntax is as follows:

```
ip address interface-name ip-address netmask
```

Table 19-6 shows the parameters for the **ip address** command. Besides the IP address, you need to provide a netmask that identifies the network portion of the IP address.

Table 19-6 ip address *Parameters*

Parameter	Description
interface-name	The name of the interface on which you want to assign an IP address (from the **nameif** command)
ip-address	The IP address for the specified interface
netmask	The netmask for the specified IP address.

NOTE The IP address and netmask for the inside interface are configured when you run the **setup** command.

Configuring the Access Lists

Traffic from the protected network through the PIX Firewall is allowed by default. The FWSM, on the other hand, explicitly defines access lists on all its interfaces. Therefore, even traffic from your protected network is denied unless you create an access list to allow it. To define access lists, you use the following two commands:

- access-list
- access-group

The **access-list** command defines the traffic that you want to allow. Then you use the **access-group** command to assign your access list to a specific interface. Chapter 7, "Configuring Access," explains the commands in more detail.

Using PIX Device Manager with the Firewall Services Module

Just like the PIX Firewall, you can manage the FWSM using the Cisco PDM. Before you can use PDM, however, you need to perform the following tasks:

- Perform initial preparation
- Install the PDM image
- Launch the PDM

Initial Preparation

The initial switch configuration tasks to use PDM include the same configuration tasks required to configure the FWSM initially, such as the following switch configuration:

- Configuring VLANs
- Configuring a firewall vlan-group
- Associating the firewall vlan-group with a module

You also need to perform the initial FWSM configuration tasks, which include the following:

- Running the **setup** command
- Defining interfaces
- Defining access lists

Running the **setup** command enables access to PDM from the host that you specify in response to the following prompt:

```
IP address of host running FWSM Device Manager: 10.10.10.4
```

In addition, you must configure your access lists to enable traffic to reach the PDM web server (HTTP over SSL, or HTTPS) from the PDM client IP address.

> **NOTE** You also can enable Hypertext Transfer Protocol (HTTP) access using the **http server** command and define which systems have HTTP access to the FWSM using the **http** *<local-ip>* command.

Installing the PIX Device Manager Image

The FWSM (Version 1.1) does not come with PDM preinstalled. You need to place the PDM software image on your FWSM. The FWSM Version 1.1 requires PDM Version 2.1. To install the PDM software on your FWSM, you use the **copy tftp** command. The syntax for this command is as follows:

```
copy tftp://server-location/pathname flash:pdm
```

For instance, suppose that the following information matches the PDM image that you want to install on your FWSM:

- Trivial File Transfer Protocol (TFTP) server—10.200.10.10

- PDM image file location—/pdm/pdm-211.bin

The following command will install this image on your FWSM:

```
copy tftp://10.200.10.10/pdm/pdm-211.bin flash:pdm
```

You can verify that PDM is installed on your FWSM by using the **show version** command as shown in the following:

```
FWSM# show version
FWSM Firewall Version 1.1(2)
FWSM Device Manager Version 2.1(1)
Compiled on Tue 25-Mar-03 17:26 by awatiger
FWSM up 7 days 16 hours
Hardware:   WS-SVC-FWM-1, 1024 MB RAM, CPU Pentium III 1000 MHz
Flash  V1.01   SMART ATA FLASH DISK @ 0xc321, 20MB
0: gb-ethernet0: irq 5
1: gb-ethernet1: irq 7
2: ethernet0: irq 11
Licensed Features:
Failover:       Enabled
VPN-DES:        Enabled
VPN-3DES:       Enabled
Maximum Interfaces:    100
Cut-through Proxy:     Enabled
Guards:         Enabled
Websense:       Enabled
Throughput:     Unlimited
ISAKMP peers:   Unlimited
Serial Number: SAD072806ER
Configuration last modified by enable-15 at 06:05:16 Feb 13 2004
FWSM#
```

Launching PIX Device Manager

When accessing PDM to configure your FWSM, you use a secure HTTP connection (HTTPS). The address to which you connect is one of the IP addresses that you configured for one of the interfaces on the FWSM.

> **NOTE**   The browser that you use to connect to PDM must have Java and JavaScript enabled. For complete details on the browser requirements, refer to the "Cisco PIX Device Manager Installation Guide."

Suppose the address of your FWSM is 10.10.10.1. To connect to PDM, you would enter in your browser a Uniform Resource Locator (URL) similar to the following:

```
https://10.10.10.1
```

Troubleshooting the Firewall Services Module

Besides the basic software troubleshooting commands available through the FWSM (similar to PIX debugging commands), you also can debug the operational status of the FWSM from the switch. These basic troubleshooting operations fall into the following categories:

■   Switch commands
■   FWSM status LED

Switch Commands

To troubleshoot the operation of your FWSM, you can use several switch commands. The switch commands to troubleshoot the operation of the FWSM fall into the following categories:

■   Module status
■   Memory test
■   Resetting and rebooting

Module Status

To verify that the Catalyst 6500 switch correctly recognizes the FWSM, you can use the **show module** switch command. The syntax for this command is as follows:

```
show module [module-number¦all]
```

By viewing the output of this command, you can verify that the switch recognizes the correct card type (Firewall Module) for the module number where you have installed the FWSM.

You also can check the FWSM status. Using the **show module** command without any arguments provides information on all of the modules on the switch, as shown in Example 19-3.

Example 19-3 *Viewing Module Status*

```
stat-6000#show module
Mod Ports Card Type                                Model              Serial No.
--- ----- ---------------------------------------- ------------------ ----------
  1     2 Catalyst 6000 supervisor 2 (Active)      WS-X6K-SUP2-2GE    SAL0605HFH7
  2    48 48 port 10/100 mb RJ-45 ethernet         WS-X6248-RJ-45     SAD050504C1
  4    48 48 port 10/100 mb RJ45                    WS-X6348-RJ-45     SAD041606Y5
  5     6 Firewall Module                          WS-SVC-FWM-1       SAD060300N9
  6     6 Firewall Module                          WS-SVC-FWM-1       SAD0707016K
Mod MAC addresses                      Hw     Fw            Sw            Status
--- ---------------------------------- ------ ------------- ------------- --------
  1 0006.d65a.9694 to 0006.d65a.9695   3.5    6.1(3)        7.5(0.6)HUB2 Ok
  2 0001.c96d.64d0 to 0001.c96d.64ff   1.4    5.4(2)        7.5(0.6)HUB2 Ok
  4 00d0.c0cd.86c8 to 00d0.c0cd.86f7   1.1    5.3(1)        7.5(0.6)HUB2 Ok
  5 00e0.b0ff.3438 to 00e0.b0ff.343f   0.201  7.2(1)        2.2(0)6       Ok
  6 0002.7ee4.f610 to 0002.7ee4.f617   1.1    7.2(1)        2.2(0)6       Ok
Mod Sub-Module                Model          Serial           Hw      Status
--- ------------------------- -------------- ---------------- ------- --------
  1 Policy Feature Card 2     WS-F6K-PFC2    SAL06100RH2      3.2     Ok
  1 Cat6k MSFC 2 daughterboard WS-F6K-MSFC2  SAL06090F5F      2.2     Ok
  4 Inline Power Module       WS-F6K-PWR                      1.0     Ok
Mod Online Diag Status
--- ------------------
  1 Pass
  2 Pass
  4 Pass
  5 Pass
  6 Pass
stat-6000#
```

Memory Test

By default, the FWSM performs only a partial memory test when the module boots up. You can change this behavior so that it performs a full memory test. When the FWSM is configured for a full memory test, it takes longer to boot. Table 19-7 shows the time required to perform full memory tests for two different memory sizes.

Table 19-7   *Full Memory Test Times*

Memory Size	Test Time
512 MB	3 minutes
1024 MB (1 GB)	6 minutes

To configure a full memory test when using Cisco IOS software, you use the **hw-module** command with the following syntax:

```
hw-module module module-number mem-test-full
```

NOTE   The **hw-module** command is specific to Cisco IOS and is not available if your switch is running the Catalyst operating system (CatOS) software.

Resetting and Rebooting

If you cannot access the FWSM either through Telnet or the **session** command on the switch, you need to reset the module from the switch. For Cisco IOS software, the **hw-module** switch command resets individual modules. The syntax for this command when resetting a module is as follows:

```
hw-module module module-number reset
```

For instance, to reset the FWSM located in slot 4 you would use the following command on the switch:

```
hw-module module 4 reset
```

NOTE   You also can use the **hw-module** command to access the maintenance partition on the FWSM. To reboot the module into the maintenance partition, you use the following command:

```
hw-module module module-number reset cf:1
```

NOTE   The **hw-module** command is available only in Cisco IOS software. If you are using CatOS, you need to use the **reset** command to reset/reboot the FWSM from the switch command line or access the maintenance partition.

Firewall Services Module Status LED

Each FWSM has a status LED on its front panel that indicates its current operational state. Table 19-8 describes the different states the status LED indicates.

Table 19-8 *Status LED States*

Color	Description
Green	The FWSM is operational and passed all of its diagnostic tests.
Red	A diagnostic test (other than the individual port test) failed.
Orange	The FWSM is in one of the following states: • Module is running boot and self-test diagnostics. • Module is disabled. • Module is shut down.
Off	The module is powered off.

Foundation Summary

The "Foundation Summary" provides a convenient review of many key concepts in this chapter. If you are already comfortable with the topics in this chapter, this summary can help you recall a few details. If you just read this chapter, this review should help solidify some key facts. If you are doing your final preparation before the exam, this summary provides a convenient way to review the day before the exam.

The Cisco Firewall Services Module (FWSM) is a high-performance firewall solution, providing 5 Gbps of throughput from a single FWSM. Combining multiple modules in a single chassis enables you to scale this throughput to 20 Gbps. Some features of the FWSM include the following:

- Is fully VLAN aware

- Supports dynamic routing

- Integrates firewall functionality and switching in a single chassis

- Supports the entire PIX Firewall Version 6.0 feature set and some Version 6.2 features

- Allows up to 1 million concurrent connections

- Supports 5-Gbps throughout

- Enables multiple FWSMs per chassis

- Supports intrachassis and interchassis stateful failure

- Provides multiple management options

Table 19-9 outlines the major differences between the FWSM (Version 1.1.2) and the PIX Firewall software (Version 6.3).

Table 19-9 *FWSM and PIX Feature Comparison*

Feature	FWSM	PIX 535
Performance	5 Gbps	1.7 Gbps
Interfaces	100	24
Concurrent Connections	1,000,000	500,000

Because the FWSM is tightly integrated with the switch, it becomes an easier task to secure the traffic flowing between multiple VLANs on your network. The basic deployment scenarios are as follows:

- MSFC as inside router
- MSFC as the outside router
- MSFC not directly connected to FWSM

Before you can use the firewall functionality on your network traffic, you need to perform the following configuration tasks on your switch.

- Create VLANs
- Define firewall vlan-groups
- Associate vlan-groups with the module

When first setting up the FWSM, you start by configuring the following parameters on the FWSM:

- Host name
- Interfaces
- Access lists

Just like on the PIX Firewall, you can manage the FWSM using the Cisco PDM. Because the FWSM (Version 1.1) does not come with PDM preinstalled, however, you need to place the PDM software image on your FWSM to use PDM.

Besides the basic software troubleshooting commands available through the FWSM, you can also debug the operational status of the FWSM from the switch. These basic troubleshooting operations fall into the following categories:

- Switch commands
- Status LEDs

The switch commands to troubleshoot the operation of the FWSM fall into the following categories:

- Module status
- Memory test
- Resetting and rebooting

Each FWSM has a status LED on its front panel that indicates its current operational state. Table 19-10 lists the different states indicated by the status LED.

Table 19-10 *Status LED States*

Color	Description
Green	The FWSM is operational and passed all of its diagnostic tests.
Red	A diagnostic test (other than the individual port test) failed.
Orange	The FWSM is in one of the following states: • Module is running boot and self-test diagnostics. • Module is disabled. • Module is shut down.
Off	The module is powered off.

Q&A

As mentioned in the Introduction, the questions in this book are more difficult than what you should experience on the exam. The questions are designed to ensure your understanding of the concepts discussed in this chapter and adequately prepare you to complete the exam. You should use the simulated exams on the CD to practice for the exam.

The answers to these questions can be found in Appendix A.

1. What are some of the major features of the FWSM?

2. What are the basic deployment scenarios for the FWSM?

3. What are the three switch configuration steps necessary to set up your FWSM?

4. Which Cisco IOS switch commands define the VLANs to be controlled by the FWSM?

5. Which Cisco IOS switch command shows the status of the FWSM?

6. Which Cisco IOS switch command enables you to reset the FWSM?

7. What does an orange FWSM status LED indicate?

8. What does a red FWSM status LED indicate?

9. Which two FWSM commands define which traffic is allowed through the FWSM?

10. Which FWSM command associates a VLAN and security level to a FWSM interface?

11. Which switch command associates a firewall vlan-group with a specific switch module?

CHAPTER 20

Case Study and Sample Configuration

The DUKEM consulting firm is a medium-size company with 700 employees. It has three offices across the continental United States. Twenty percent of DUKEM's employees are mobile or telecommute. Figure 20-1 shows the current DUKEM network infrastructure.

Figure 20-1 *DUKEM Network Infrastructure*

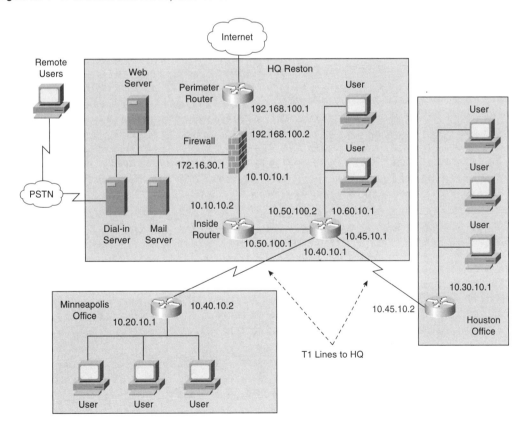

Remote Offices

The branch offices are connected to headquarters (Reston) by T1 connections. All Internet-bound traffic goes out through Reston. Telecommuting and mobile users call an 800 number that connects to a pool of modems at Reston.

Firewall

A server-based application firewall is used at headquarters (HQ). The firewall cannot be configured for Internet Protocol Security (IPSec) or generic routing encapsulation (GRE). The firewall has a history of irregular behavior, which has created network disruptions.

Growth Expectation

DUKEM has grown by 13 percent during each of the past two years and expects to have an average growth rate of 15 percent over the next few years. It also has experienced an increase in the number of employees who telecommute.

DUKEM's CIO has put forth the following requirements:

- A highly available firewall solution
- Secure communication channels between branch offices and HQ, telecommuters and HQ, and possible business partners

An information technology (IT) consulting firm hired by DUKEM has recommended that Cisco PIX Firewall replace the existing firewall system. You have been selected to do the Cisco PIX Firewall configuration for DUKEM.

Figure 20-2 shows the Cisco PIX Firewall solution in the new network design.

Use the information in Figure 20-2 to configure your firewalls by completing the following tasks:

> Task 1—Basic configuration for the Cisco PIX Firewall
> Task 2—Configuring access rules on HQ
> Task 3—Configuring authentication
> Task 4—Configuring logging
> Task 5—Configuring a virtual private network (VPN) between HQ and remote sites
> Task 6—Configuring a Remote Access VPN to HQ
> Task 7—Configuring failover

Good luck!

Figure 20-2   *Proposed Network Design with PIX Firewall*

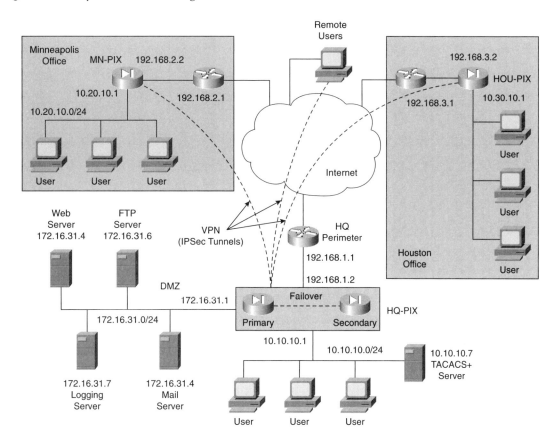

Task 1: Basic Configuration for the Cisco PIX Firewall

Tables 20-1 through 20-5 list the information required for you to configure the Cisco PIX Firewall at the Reston headquarters. Use the information from the tables to configure your Cisco PIX Firewall according to the network diagram shown in Figure 20-2.

Basic Configuration Information for HQ-PIX

Table 20-1 lists the physical interfaces of the Cisco PIX Firewall that is installed in the Reston headquarters. This table includes the interface name, physical interface ID, assigned address, and speed/duplex.

Table 20-1 *PIX Interface Information for HQ*

Interface Name	Hardware ID	Interface IP Address	Interface Speed
Outside	Ethernet0	192.168.1.2	100full
Inside	Ethernet1	10.10.10.1	100full
DMZ	Ethernet2	172.16.31.1	100full
Failover	Ethernet3	1.1.1.1	100full

Table 20-2 shows what routing information needs to be configured on the PIX. Note that the only route required is the default route. No specific routes are defined on the firewall.

Table 20-2 *PIX Routing Information for HQ*

Interface Name	Destination Network IP Address	Network Mask	Gateway (Router) IP Address
Outside	0.0.0.0	0.0.0.0	192.168.1.1

Table 20-3 shows which outside addresses or address ranges are available for the global address pool. Remember that the global addresses are used in conjunction with the **nat** command to assign the addresses to which the PIX is translating (this is not the original source but the translated source).

Table 20-3 *Recording Global IP Information for HQ*

Interface Name	NAT ID Number	Beginning of IP Address Range	End of IP Address Range
Outside	1	192.168.1.12	192.168.1.150
Outside	1	192.168.1.152	
DMZ	1	172.16.31.12	172.16.31.100

Table 20-4 shows which Internet Protocol (IP) addresses or network segments are to be translated (into the global addresses) as they pass through the firewall.

Table 20-4 *NAT IP Information for HQ*

Interface Name	NAT ID Number	Network Address	Network Mask for This Address
Inside	1	10.10.10.0	255.255.255.0
DMZ	1	172.16.31.0	255.255.255.0

Table 20-5 shows static IP address mapping for resources that are accessed from the outside (public) network. The static IP address is the address that is configured on the individual server, and the host IP address is the IP address that the PIX uses when answering for the server.

Table 20-5 *Static IP Address Mapping Information for HQ*

Interface on Which the Host Resides	Interface Name Where the Global Address Resides	Static IP Address	Host IP Address	Description
DMZ	Outside	192.168.1.4	172.16.31.4	Mail server
DMZ	Outside	192.168.1.5	172.16.31.5	Web server
DMZ	Outside	192.168.1.6	172.16.31.6	FTP server

Example 20-1 shows the individual configuration commands for all the items documented in Tables 20-1 through 20-5.

Example 20-1 *Firewall Configuration for the Reston Headquarters*

```
nameif ethernet0 outside security0
nameif ethernet1 inside security100
nameif ethernet2 DMZ security80
nameif ethernet3 failover security90

interface ethernet0 100full
interface ethernet1 100full
interface ethernet2 100full
interface ethernet3 100full

ip address inside 10.10.10.1 255.255.255.0
ip address outside 192.168.1.2 255.255.255.0
ip address DMZ 172.16.31.1 255.255.255.0
ip address failover 1.1.1.1 255.255.255.0
```

continues

Example 20-1 *Firewall Configuration for the Reston Headquarters (Continued)*

```
hostname HQ-PIX
nat (inside) 1 10.10.10.0 255.255.255.0
global (outside) 1 192.168.1.12-192.168.1.150 netmask 255.255.255.0
global (outside) 1 192.168.1.152 netmask 255.255.255.0
global (DMZ) 1 172.16.31.12-172.16.31.100 netmask 255.255.255.0
static (DMZ,outside) 192.168.1.4  172.16.31.4 netmask 255.255.255.255 0 0
static (DMZ,outside) 192.168.1.5  172.16.31.5 netmask 255.255.255.255 0 0
static (DMZ,outside) 192.168.1.6  172.16.31.6 netmask 255.255.255.255 0 0

route outside 0.0.0.0 0.0.0.0 192.168.1.1
```

Basic Configuration Information for MN-PIX

Tables 20-6 through 20-9 provide the information needed to configure the PIX Firewall at the Minneapolis office.

Table 20-6 shows information about the physical interfaces on the PIX Firewall.

Table 20-6 *PIX Interface Information for Minneapolis*

Interface Name	Hardware ID	Interface IP Address	Interface Speed
Outside	Ethernet0	192.168.2.2	100full
Inside	Ethernet1	10.20.10.1	100full

Table 20-7 depicts which routes need to be configured on the PIX Firewall in the Minneapolis office.

Table 20-7 *Routing Information for the Minneapolis PIX*

Interface Name	Destination Network IP Address	Network Mask	Gateway (Router) IP Address
Outside	0.0.0.0	0.0.0.0	192.168.2.1

Table 20-8 lists the global IP addresses or address ranges that are used in conjunction with Network Address Translation (NAT) for translation purposes.

Table 20-8 *Global IP Address Information for the Minneapolis PIX*

Interface Name	NAT ID Number	Beginning of IP Address Range	End of IP Address Range
Outside	1	192.168.2.12	192.168.2.250
Outside	1	192.168.2.252	

Table 20-9 lists which addresses are dynamically translated on the PIX Firewall.

Table 20-9 *NAT IP Address Information for the Minneapolis PIX*

Interface Name	NAT ID Number	Network Address	Network Mask for This Address
Inside	1	10.20.10.0	255.255.255.0

Example 20-2 depicts the individual configuration commands for each of the items listed in Tables 20-6 through 20-9.

Example 20-2 *Firewall Configuration for the Minneapolis Office*

```
nameif ethernet0 outside security0
nameif ethernet1 inside security100

interface ethernet0 100full
interface ethernet1 100full

ip address inside 10.20.10.1 255.255.255.0
ip address outside 192.168.2.2 255.255.255.0

hostname MN-PIX

nat (inside) 1 10.20.10.0 255.255.255.0
global (outside) 1 192.168.2.12-192.168.2.250 netmask 255.255.255.0
global (outside) 1 192.168.2.252 netmask 255.255.255.0


route outside 0.0.0.0 0.0.0.0 192.168.2.1
```

Basic Configuration Information for HOU-PIX

Tables 20-10 through 20-13 provide the information needed to configure the PIX Firewall in the Houston office.

Table 20-10 shows information about the physical interfaces of the Cisco PIX Firewall.

Table 20-10   *Interface Information for the Houston PIX*

Interface Name	Hardware ID	Interface IP Address	Interface Speed
Outside	Ethernet0	192.168.3.2	100full
Inside	Ethernet1	10.30.10.1	100full

Table 20-11 depicts which routes need to be configured on the PIX Firewall in the Houston office.

Table 20-11   *Routing Information for the Houston PIX*

Interface Name	Destination Network IP Address	Network Mask	Gateway (Router) IP Address
Outside	0.0.0.0	0.0.0.0	192.168.3.1

Table 20-12 lists the global IP addresses or address ranges that are used in conjunction with NAT for translation purposes.

Table 20-12   *Global IP Address Information for the Houston PIX*

Interface Name	NAT ID Number	Beginning of IP Address Range	End of IP Address Range
Outside	1	192.168.3.12	192.168.3.250
Outside	1	192.168.3.252	

Table 20-13 lists which addresses are dynamically translated on the PIX Firewall.

Table 20-13   *NAT IP Address Information for the Houston PIX*

Interface Name	NAT ID Number	Network Address	Network Mask for This Address
Inside	1	10.30.10.0	255.255.255.0

Example 20-3 depicts the individual configuration commands for each of the items listed in Tables 20-10 through 20-13.

Example 20-3 *Firewall Configuration for the Houston Office*

```
nameif ethernet0 outside security0
nameif ethernet1 inside security100

interface ethernet0 100full
interface ethernet1 100full



ip address inside 10.30.10.1 255.255.255.0
ip address outside 192.168.3.2 255.255.255.0



hostname HOU-PIX

nat (inside) 1 10.30.10.0 255.255.255.0
global (outside) 1 192.168.3.12-192.168.3.250 netmask 255.255.255.0
global (outside) 1 192.168.3.252 netmask 255.255.255.0



route outside 0.0.0.0 0.0.0.0 192.168.3.1
```

Task 2: Configuring Access Rules on HQ

After configuring the basic PIX Firewall parameters, you must create the access rules for the PIX Firewall at the Reston site (HQ-PIX). The access rules are necessary to enable the remote sites to connect to the Reston location while limiting access from unauthorized locations. The following steps define the access rules needed on HQ-PIX.

Step 1   To allow users on the outside interface access to the mail server on the demilitarized zone (DMZ) interface, enter the following commands:

```
access-list acl-out permit tcp any host 192.168.1.4 eq smtp
access-group acl-out in interface outside
```

The **access-group** command binds the **acl-out** access list command statement group to the outside interface.

Step 2   To allow users on the outside interface to access the web server on the DMZ interface, use the following command:

```
access-list acl-out permit tcp any host 192.168.1.5 eq www
```

Step 3   To allow users on the outside interface to access the File Transfer Protocol (FTP) server on the DMZ interface, use the following command:

```
access-list acl-out permit tcp any host 192.168.1.6 eq ftp
```

Example 20-4 shows the access list configured on the HQ PIX.

Example 20-4 *Access List on the HQ PIX*

```
access-list acl-out permit tcp any host 192.168.1.4 eq smtp
access-list acl-out permit tcp any host 192.168.1.5 eq www
access-list acl-out permit tcp any host 192.168.1.6 eq ftp
access-list acl-out permit udp any host 192.168.1.8 eq 514
access-group acl-out in interface outside
```

Task 3: Configuring Authentication

Incoming FTP connections to HQ-PIX are authenticated using the Terminal Access Controller Access Control System Plus (TACACS+) server located on the internal network. To use a TACACS+ server for authentication, you must first identify the IP address of the TACACS+ server and then indicate which connections will use the TACACS+ server. This configuration requires the following two steps:

Step 1   Configure the TACACS+ server:

```
aaa-server TACACS+ (inside) host 10.10.10.7 tacpass
```

Step 2   Configure authentication, authorization, and accounting (AAA) authentication for FTP access:

```
aaa authentication include ftp inside 0.0.0.0 0.0.0.0 TACACS+
```

Example 20-5 shows the TACACS+ configuration.

Example 20-5 *TACACS+ Configuration*

```
aaa-server TACACS+ (inside) host 10.10.10.7 tacpass
aaa authentication include ftp inside 0.0.0.0 0.0.0.0 TACACS+
```

Task 4: Configuring Logging

To help protect your network configuration it is important to log events that are happening on the network. This log information provides valuable insight into what is happening on the network, especially when the network is being attacked or proved. The following steps outline the commands necessary to enable logging at the three locations.

Step 1   Enable logging on HQ-PIX to the logging server:

```
logging on
logging trap informational
logging host DMZ 172.16.31.7
```

Step 2   Enable logging on HOU-PIX:

```
logging on
logging trap informational
logging host outside 172.16.31.7
```

Step 3   Enable logging on MN-PIX:

```
logging on
logging trap informational
logging host outside 172.16.31.7
```

> **NOTE**   Sending logging information from Houston and Minneapolis to the actual logging server IP address (172.16.31.7) prevents the logging traffic from traversing the Internet in the clear. Sending the logging traffic through the VPN tunnel prevents the logging information from being observed on the Internet, but the real IP address (172.16.31.7) is reachable only when the VPN tunnel is active.

Task 5: Configuring a VPN Between HQ and Remote Sites

The two remote sites communicate with the Reston location (HQ-PIX) using VPN connections that traverse the Internet. To enable these VPNs, you must define the VPN characteristics at the headquarters location, as well as at the remote sites. Configuring the VPN connections between HQ-PIX and the two remote sites (MN-PIX and HOU-PIX) involves the following tasks:

- Configuring the central PIX Firewall, HQ-PIX, for VPN tunneling

- Configuring the Houston PIX Firewall, HOU-PIX, for VPN tunneling

- Configuring the Minneapolis PIX Firewall, MN-PIX, for VPN tunneling

> **NOTE**   The VPN tunnels shown in this example enable the two remote sites (Houston and Minneapolis) to communicate with the main location at Reston. If the two remote sites also must be able to communicate with each other, you would also need to establish a VPN tunnel from HOU-PIX to MN-PIX. This example assumes that the two remote sites need to communicate only with the main location and not with each other.

Configuring the Central PIX Firewall, HQ-PIX, for VPN Tunneling

Both remote sites connect to the Reston location using VPN tunneling. The VPN protects the traffic coming from the remote sites. The following steps define the VPN characteristics on HQ-PIX.

Step 1   Configure an Internet Security Association and Key Management Protocol (ISAKMP) policy:

```
isakmp enable outside
isakmp policy 10 authentication pre-share
isakmp policy 10 encryption des
isakmp policy 10 hash md5
isakmp policy 10 group 1
isakmp policy 10 lifetime 1000
```

Step 2 Configure a preshared key and associate it with the peers (Houston and Minneapolis):

```
isakmp key C2I#ghi address 192.168.3.2
isakmp key B2I#def address 192.168.2.2
```

Step 3 Configure the supported IPSec transforms:

```
crypto ipsec transform-set myset esp-des esp-md5-hmac
```

Step 4 Create an access list:

```
access-list 130 permit ip 10.10.10.0 255.255.255.0 10.30.10.0
  255.255.255.0
access-list 130 permit ip 172.16.31.0 255.255.255.0 10.30.10.0
  255.255.255.0
access-list 120 permit ip 10.10.10.0 255.255.255.0 10.20.10.0
  255.255.255.0
access-list 120 permit ip 172.16.31.0 255.255.255.0 10.20.10.0
  255.255.255.0
```

Step 5 Define a crypto map for both Houston and Minneapolis:

```
crypto map Dukem-Map 20 ipsec-isakmp
crypto map Dukem-Map 20 match address 120
crypto map Dukem-Map 20 set peer 192.168.2.2
crypto map Dukem-Map 20 set transform-set myset

crypto map Dukem-Map 30 ipsec-isakmp
crypto map Dukem-Map 30 match address 130
crypto map Dukem-Map 30 set peer 192.168.3.2
crypto map Dukem-Map 30 set transform-set myset
```

Step 6 Apply the crypto map to the outside interface:

```
crypto map Dukem-Map interface outside
```

Step 7 Specify that IPSec traffic is implicitly trusted (permitted):

```
sysopt connection permit-ipsec
```

Step 8 Configure a NAT 0 policy so that traffic between the offices is excluded from NAT:

```
access-list VPN permit ip 10.10.10.0 255.255.255.0 10.30.10.0
  255.255.255.0
access-list VPN permit ip 172.16.31.0 255.255.255.0 10.30.10.0
  255.255.255.0
access-list VPN permit ip 10.10.10.0 255.255.255.0 10.20.10.0
  255.255.255.0
access-list VPN permit ip 172.16.31.0 255.255.255.0 10.20.10.0
  255.255.255.0
nat (inside) 0 access-list VPN
```

Example 20-6 shows the complete configuration for the HQ-PIX.

Example 20-6 *HQ PIX Firewall Configuration (Continued)*

```
nameif ethernet0 outside security0
nameif ethernet1 inside security100
nameif ethernet2 DMZ security80
nameif ethernet3 failover security90
enable password 8Ry2YjIyt7RRXU24 encrypted
passwd 2KFQnbNIdI.2KPPU encrypted
hostname HQ-PIX
fixup protocol ftp 21
fixup protocol http 80
fixup protocol h323 1720
fixup protocol rsh 514
fixup protocol smtp 25
fixup protocol sqlnet 1521
fixup protocol sip 5060
names
access-list acl-out permit tcp any host 192.168.1.4 eq smtp
access-list acl-out permit tcp any host 192.168.1.5 eq www
access-list acl-out permit tcp any host 192.168.1.6 eq ftp
!--- Traffic to HOU-PIX:
access-list 130 permit ip 10.10.10.0 255.255.255.0 10.30.10.0 255.255.255.0
access-list 130 permit ip 172.16.31.0 255.255.255.0 10.30.10.0 255.255.255.0
!--- Traffic to MN-PIX:
access-list 120 permit ip 10.10.10.0 255.255.255.0 10.20.10.0 255.255.255.0
access-list 120 permit ip 172.16.31.0 255.255.255.0 10.20.10.0 255.255.255.0
!--- Do not Network Address Translate (NAT) traffic to other branches:
access-list VPN permit ip 10.10.10.0 255.255.255.0 10.30.10.0 255.255.255.0
access-list VPN permit ip 10.10.10.0 255.255.255.0 10.20.10.0 255.255.255.0
access-list VPN permit ip 172.16.31.0 255.255.255.0 10.30.10.0 255.255.255.0
access-list VPN permit ip 172.16.31.0 255.255.255.0 10.20.10.0 255.255.255.0
pager lines 24
logging on
no logging timestamp
no logging standby
no logging console
no logging monitor
no logging buffered
logging trap
no logging history
logging facility 20
logging queue 512
logging host DMZ 172.16.31.7
interface ethernet0 100full
interface ethernet1 100full
interface ethernet2 100full
```

continues

Example 20-6 *HQ PIX Firewall Configuration (Continued)*

```
mtu outside 1500
mtu inside 1500
ip address outside 192.168.1.2 255.255.255.0
ip address inside 10.10.10.1 255.255.255.0
ip address DMZ 172.16.31.1 255.255.255.0
ip address failover 1.1.1.1 255.255.255.0

ip audit info action alarm
ip audit attack action alarm
no failover
failover timeout 0:00:00
failover poll 15
failover ip address outside 192.168.1.3
failover ip address inside 10.10.10.2
failover ip address DMZ 172.16.31.2
arp timeout 14400

global (outside) 1 192.168.1.12-192.168.1.150 netmask 255.255.255.0
global (outside) 1 192.168.1.152 netmask 255.255.255.0
nat (inside) 1 10.10.10.0 255.255.255.0
!--- Do not NAT traffic to other PIXes:
nat (inside) 0 access-list VPN

static (DMZ,outside) 192.168.1.4  172.16.31.4 netmask 255.255.255.255 0 0
static (DMZ,outside) 192.168.1.5  172.16.31.5 netmask 255.255.255.255 0 0
static (DMZ,outside) 192.168.1.6  172.16.31.6 netmask 255.255.255.255 0 0
access-group acl-out in interface outside
route outside 0.0.0.0 0.0.0.0 192.168.1.1
timeout xlate 3:00:00
timeout conn 1:00:00 half-closed 0:10:00 udp 0:02:00 rpc 0:10:00
h323 0:05:00 sip 0:30:00 sip-media 0:02:00
timeout uauth 0:05:00 absolute

aaa-server TACACS+ protocol tacacs+
aaa-server RADIUS protocol radius
aaa-server TACACS+ (inside) host 10.10.10.7 tacpass

aaa authentication include ftp inside 0.0.0.0 0.0.0.0 TACACS+
aaa authentication include telnet inside 0.0.0.0 0 0.0.0.0 TACACS+
no snmp-server location

no snmp-server contact
snmp-server community public
snmp-server enable traps
floodguard enable
sysopt connection permit-ipsec
no sysopt route dnat
```

Example 20-6 *HQ PIX Firewall Configuration (Continued)*

```
crypto ipsec transform-set myset esp-des esp-md5-hmac

!--- Traffic to HOU-PIX:
crypto map Dukem-Map  20 ipsec-isakmp
crypto map Dukem-Map  20 match address 120
crypto map Dukem-Map  20 set peer 192.168.3.2
crypto map Dukem-Map 20 set transform-set myset

!--- Traffic to MN-PIX:
crypto map Dukem-Map 30 ipsec-isakmp
crypto map Dukem-Map  30 match address 130
crypto map Dukem-Map  30 set peer 192.168.2.2
crypto map Dukem-Map  30 set transform-set myset
crypto map Dukem-Map  interface outside

isakmp enable outside
isakmp key ******** address 192.168.3.2 netmask 255.255.255.255
isakmp key ******** address 192.168.2.2 netmask 255.255.255.255
isakmp identity address
isakmp policy 10 authentication pre-share
isakmp policy 10 encryption des
isakmp policy 10 hash md5
isakmp policy 10 group 1
isakmp policy 10 lifetime 1000
telnet timeout 5
ssh timeout 5
terminal width 80
Cryptochecksum:fb446986bcad922ec40de6346e9e2729
: end
```

Configuring the Houston PIX Firewall, HOU-PIX, for VPN Tunneling

Similar to configuring the VPN characteristics on HQ-PIX, you also must define the VPN characteristics at each of the remote sites. The following steps outline the commands necessary to define the VPN characteristics on HOU-PIX at the Houston remote site:

Step 1 Configure an ISAKMP policy:

```
isakmp enable outside
isakmp policy 10 authentication pre-share
isakmp policy 10 encryption des
isakmp policy 10 hash md5
isakmp policy 10 group 1
isakmp policy 10 lifetime 1000
```

Step 2 Configure a preshared key and associate it with the peer (HQ-PIX):

```
isakmp key A1!#abc address 192.168.1.2
```

Step 3   Configure the supported IPSec transforms:

```
crypto ipsec transform-set myset esp-des esp-md5-hmac
```

Step 4   Create an access list:

```
access-list 110 permit ip 10.30.10.0 255.255.255.0 10.10.10.0
  255.255.255.0
access-list 110 permit ip 10.30.10.0 255.255.255.0 172.16.31.0
  255.255.255.0
```

Step 5   Define a crypto map for HQ-PIX:

```
crypto map Dukem-Map 20 ipsec-isakmp
crypto map Dukem-Map 20 match address 110
crypto map Dukem-Map 20 set peer 192.168.1.2
crypto map Dukem-Map 20 set transform-set myset
```

Step 6   Apply the crypto map to the outside interface:

```
crypto map Dukem-Map interface outside
```

Step 7   Specify that IPSec traffic is implicitly trusted (permitted):

```
sysopt connection permit-ipsec
```

Step 8   Configure a NAT 0 policy so that traffic between the offices is excluded from NAT:

```
access-list VPN permit ip 10.30.10.0 255.255.255.0 10.10.10.0
  255.255.255.0
access-list VPN permit ip 10.30.10.0 255.255.255.0 172.16.31.0
  255.255.255.0
nat (inside) 0 access-list VPN
```

Example 20-7 shows the Houston PIX configuration.

Example 20-7   *Houston PIX Firewall Configuration (Continued)*

```
nameif ethernet0 outside security0
nameif ethernet1 inside security100
enable password 8Ry2YjIyt7RRXU24 encrypted
passwd 2KFQnbNIdI.2KPPU encrypted
hostname HOU-PIX
fixup protocol ftp 21
fixup protocol http 80
fixup protocol h323 1720
fixup protocol rsh 514
fixup protocol smtp 25
fixup protocol sqlnet 1521
fixup protocol sip 5060
names
!--- Traffic to Reston HQ:
access-list 110 permit ip 10.30.10.0 255.255.255.0 10.10.10.0 255.255.255.0
```

Example 20-7 *Houston PIX Firewall Configuration (Continued)*

```
access-list 110 permit ip 10.30.10.0 255.255.255.0 172.16.31.0 255.255.255.0
!--- Do not NAT traffic to Reston HQ:
access-list VPN permit ip 10.30.10.0 255.255.255.0 10.10.10.0 255.255.255.0
access-list VPN permit ip 10.30.10.0 255.255.255.0 172.16.31.0 255.255.255.0
pager lines 24
logging on
no logging timestamp
no logging standby
no logging console
no logging monitor
no logging buffered
logging trap 6
no logging history
logging facility 20
logging queue 512
logging host 192.168.1.8
interface ethernet0 100full
interface ethernet1 100full
mtu outside 1500
mtu inside 1500
ip address outside 192.168.3.2 255.255.255.0
ip address inside 10.30.10.1 255.255.255.0
ip audit info action alarm
ip audit attack action alarm
no failover
failover timeout 0:00:00
failover poll 15
failover ip address outside 0.0.0.0
failover ip address inside 0.0.0.0
arp timeout 14400

global (outside) 1 192.168.3.12-192.168.3.250 netmask 255.255.255.0
global (outside) 1 192.168.3.252 netmask 255.255.255.0
nat (inside) 1 10.30.10.0 255.255.255.0
!--- Do not NAT traffic to Reston HQ:
nat (inside) 0 access-list VPN
route outside 0.0.0.0 0.0.0.0 192.168.3.1 1

timeout xlate 3:00:00
timeout conn 1:00:00 half-closed 0:10:00 udp 0:02:00 rpc 0:10:00
h323 0:05:00 sip 0:30:00 sip-media 0:02:00
timeout uauth 0:05:00 absolute
aaa-server TACACS+ protocol tacacs+
aaa-server RADIUS protocol radius
no snmp-server location
no snmp-server contact
```

continues

Example 20-7 *Houston PIX Firewall Configuration (Continued)*

```
snmp-server community public
no snmp-server enable traps
floodguard enable
sysopt connection permit-ipsec
no sysopt route dnat
crypto ipsec transform-set myset esp-des esp-md5-hmac
!--- Traffic to Reston HQ:
crypto map Dukem-Map  10 ipsec-isakmp
crypto map Dukem-Map  10 match address 110
crypto map Dukem-Map  10 set peer 192.168.1.2
crypto map Dukem-Map  10 set transform-set myset
crypto map Dukem-Map  interface outside
isakmp enable outside
isakmp key ******** address 192.168.1.2 netmask 255.255.255.255
  no-xauth no-config-mode
isakmp identity address
isakmp policy 10 authentication pre-share
isakmp policy 10 encryption des
isakmp policy 10 hash md5
isakmp policy 10 group 1
isakmp policy 10 lifetime 1000
telnet timeout 5
ssh timeout 5
terminal width 80
Cryptochecksum:b23cc9772a79ea76d711ea747f182a5f
```

Configuring the Minneapolis PIX Firewall, MN-PIX, for VPN Tunneling

Similar to configuring the VPN characteristics on HQ-PIX, you also must define the VPN
characteristics at each of the remote sites. The following steps outline the commands
necessary to define the VPN characteristics on MN-PIX at the Minneapolis remote site:

Step 1   Configure an ISAKMP policy:

```
isakmp enable outside
isakmp policy 10 authentication pre-share
isakmp policy 10 encryption des
isakmp policy 10 hash md5
isakmp policy 10 group 1
isakmp policy 10 lifetime 1000
```

Step 2   Configure a preshared key and associate it with the peer (HQ-PIX):

```
isakmp key A1l#abc address 192.168.1.2
```

Step 3   Configure the supported IPSec transforms:

```
crypto ipsec transform-set myset esp-des esp-md5-hmac
```

Step 4   Create an access list:

```
access-list 110 permit ip 10.20.10.0 255.255.255.0 10.10.10.0
    255.255.255.0
access-list 110 permit ip 10.20.10.0 255.255.255.0 172.16.31.0
    255.255.255.0
```

Step 5   Define a crypto map for HQ-PIX:

```
crypto map Dukem-Map 20 ipsec-isakmp
crypto map Dukem-Map 20 match address 110
crypto map Dukem-Map 20 set peer 192.168.1.2
crypto map Dukem-Map 20 set transform-set myset
```

Step 6   Apply the crypto map to the outside interface:

```
crypto map Dukem-Map interface outside
```

Step 7   Specify that IPSec traffic be implicitly trusted (permitted):

```
sysopt connection permit-ipsec
```

Step 8   Configure a NAT 0 policy so that traffic between the offices is excluded from NAT:

```
access-list VPN permit ip 10.20.10.0 255.255.255.0 10.10.10.0
    255.255.255.0
access-list VPN permit ip 10.20.10.0 255.255.255.0 172.16.31.0
    255.255.255.0
nat (inside) 0 access-list VPN
```

Example 20-8 shows the configuration for the Minneapolis PIX Firewall.

Example 20-8   *Minneapolis PIX Firewall Configuration*

```
nameif ethernet0 outside security0
nameif ethernet1 inside security100
enable password 8Ry2YjIyt7RRXU24 encrypted
passwd 2KFQnbNIdI.2KPPU encrypted
hostname MN-PIX
fixup protocol ftp 21
fixup protocol http 80
fixup protocol h323 1720
fixup protocol rsh 514
fixup protocol smtp 25
fixup protocol sqlnet 1521
fixup protocol sip 5060
names
!--- Traffic to Reston HQ:
access-list 110 permit ip 10.20.10.0 255.255.255.0 10.10.10.0 255.255.255.0
access-list 110 permit ip 10.20.10.0 255.255.255.0 172.16.31.0 255.255.255.0
```

continues

Example 20-8 *Minneapolis PIX Firewall Configuration (Continued)*

```
!--- Do not NAT traffic to Reston HQ:
access-list VPN permit ip 10.20.10.0 255.255.255.0 10.10.10.0 255.255.255.0
access-list VPN permit ip 10.20.10.0 255.255.255.0 172.16.31.0 255.255.255.0
pager lines 24
logging on
no logging timestamp
no logging standby
no logging console
no logging monitor
no logging buffered
logging trap 6
no logging history
logging facility 20
logging queue 512
logging host outside 192.168.1.8
interface ethernet0 100full
interface ethernet1 100full
mtu outside 1500
mtu inside 1500
ip address outside 192.168.2.2 255.255.255.0
ip address inside 10.20.10.1 255.255.255.0
ip audit info action alarm
ip audit attack action alarm
no failover
failover timeout 0:00:00
failover poll 15
failover ip address outside 0.0.0.0
failover ip address inside 0.0.0.0
arp timeout 14400

global (outside) 1 192.168.2.12-192.168.2.250 netmask 255.255.255.0
global (outside) 1 192.168.2.252 netmask 255.255.255.0
nat (inside) 1 10.20.10.0 255.255.255.0
!--- Do not NAT traffic to Reston HQ:
nat (inside) 0 access-list VPN
route outside 0.0.0.0 0.0.0.0 192.168.2.1 1

timeout xlate 3:00:00
timeout conn 1:00:00 half-closed 0:10:00 udp 0:02:00 rpc 0:10:00
h323 0:05:00 sip 0:30:00 sip-media 0:02:00
timeout uauth 0:05:00 absolute
aaa-server TACACS+ protocol tacacs+
aaa-server RADIUS protocol radius
no snmp-server location
no snmp-server contact
snmp-server community public
no snmp-server enable traps
```

Example 20-8 *Minneapolis PIX Firewall Configuration (Continued)*

```
floodguard enable
sysopt connection permit-ipsec
no sysopt route dnat
crypto ipsec transform-set myset esp-des esp-md5-hmac
!--- Traffic to Reston HQ:
crypto map Dukem-Map 10 ipsec-isakmp
crypto map Dukem-Map 10 match address 110
crypto map Dukem-Map 10 set peer 192.168.1.2
crypto map Dukem-Map 10 set transform-set myset
crypto map Dukem-Map interface outside
isakmp enable outside
isakmp key ******** address 192.168.1.2 netmask 255.255.255.255 no-xauth
  no-config-mode
isakmp identity address
isakmp policy 10 authentication pre-share
isakmp policy 10 encryption des
isakmp policy 10 hash md5
isakmp policy 10 group 1
isakmp policy 10 lifetime 1000
telnet timeout 5
ssh timeout 5
terminal width 80
Cryptochecksum:d962d33d245ad89fb7c9b4f0db3c2dc0
```

Verifying and Troubleshooting

After you configure the PIX for VPNs, the next step is to verify the configuration. The **show**, **clear**, and **debug** commands are used to verify and troubleshoot your configuration.

show Commands

- **show crypto ipsec sa**—Displays the current status of the IPSec security associations. This is useful in determining whether traffic is being encrypted.

- **show crypto isakmp sa**—Displays the current state of the Internet Key Exchange (IKE) security associations.

Debug Commands

If you have problems establishing any of the VPN tunnels, use the following commands for troubleshooting:

Step 1   If you are connected to the PIX by the console port, enable debugging on the console using this command:

```
logging console debugging
```

If you are connected to the PIX by Telnet, enable debugging using this command:

```
logging monitor debugging
```

Step 2   To view debug information related to the VPN configuration, use the following commands:

- **debug crypto ipsec**—Used to debug IPSec processing

- **debug crypto isakmp**—Used to debug ISAKMP processing

- **debug crypto engine**—Used to display debug messages about crypto engines, which perform encryption and decryption

Step 3   To clear security associations (SAs), use the following commands in the PIX configuration mode:

- **clear [crypto] ipsec sa**—Deletes the active IPSec SAs. The keyword **crypto** is optional.

- **clear [crypto] isakmp sa**—Deletes the active IKE SAs. The keyword **crypto** is optional.

Task 6: Configuring a Remote Access VPN to HQ

Similar to the remote sites, the remote users must also have a secure mechanism to connect to the Reston location. The remote users, however, do not use fixed VPN tunnels. Instead, the remote users use Easy VPN remote to connect to the headquarters location and dynamically establish a VPN tunnel. The configuration process involves performing the following tasks:

- Create an IP address pool

- Define a group policy for mode configuration push

- Enable IKE dead peer detection (DPD)

Create an IP Address Pool

For instance, suppose that you want to assign the remote clients addresses in the range from 10.20.100.1 through 10.20.100.254. Using a pool name of *vpn-pool*, the command line would be as follows:

```
ip local pool vpn-pool 10.10.10.154-10.10.10.200
```

Define a Group Policy for Mode Configuration Push

When remote VPN clients connect to HQ-PIX, the firewall must push certain configuration information to them. You configure these parameters using the **vpngroup** command.

```
vpngroup remote-users password B#!42Dd
vpngroup remote-users dns-server 10.200.10.35
vpngroup remote-users wins-server 10.100.10.25
vpngroup remote-users default-domain dukem.com
vpngroup remote-users address-pool vpn-pool
vpngroup remote-users idle-time 10
```

> **NOTE** You also need to configure the VPN client software on the remote user PCs. This configuration involves identifying the IP address of HQ-PIX and indicating the VPN group name (remote-users) and group password (B#!42Dd).

Enable IKE Dead Peer Detection

You need to specify the number of seconds between DPD messages and the number of seconds between retries (if a DPD message does not receive a response). The syntax for this command is as follows:

```
isakmp keepalive seconds [retry-seconds]
```

Task 7: Configuring Failover

Failover is configured on the PIX only at the Reston site (HQ-PIX). When configuring failover, you first configure the failover parameters on the primary PIX Firewall (leaving the secondary PIX Firewall powered off). Then you configure the failover parameters on the secondary PIX Firewall. The steps to configure failover are as follows:

Step 1   Make sure that failover is enabled on the primary PIX Firewall using the following command:

```
failover
```

Failover is not enabled by default.

Step 2   Configure **failover ip address** for all interfaces that have an IP address configured on them:

```
failover ip address inside 10.10.10.2
failover ip address outside 192.168.1.3
failover ip address DMZ 172.16.31.2
failover ip address failover 1.1.1.2
```

Step 3   Check the status of your failover configuration:

```
show failover
```

```
Failover On
Cable status: Unknown
Reconnect timeout 0:00:00
Poll frequency 15 seconds
This host: primary - Active
Active time: 225 (sec)
Interface failover (1.1.1.1): Normal (Waiting)
Interface dmz (172.16.31.1):  Normal (Waiting)
Interface outside (192.168.1.2): Normal (Waiting)
Interface inside (10.10.10.1): Normal (Waiting)
Other host: secondary - Standby
Active time: 0 (sec)
Interface failover (1.1.1.2: Unknown (Waiting)
???Authors: Missing ')' bracket. Thanks - Izak
Interface dmz (172.16.31.2): Unknown (Waiting)
Interface outside (192.168.1.3): Unknown (Waiting)
Interface inside (10.10.10.2): Unknown (Waiting)
```

Step 4   Enable stateful failover:

failover link failover

Step 5   Connect the failover cable between the two PIX Firewalls if you have
              not already connected it.

Step 6   Power on the secondary unit.

Step 7   Check the status of your failover configuration:

```
HQ-PIX# show failover
Failover On
Cable status: Normal
Reconnect timeout 0:00:00
Poll frequency 15 seconds
        This host: Primary - Active
                Active time: 123(sec)
                Interface failover (1.1.1.1): Normal
Interface dmz (172.16.31.1): Normal
                Interface outside (192.168.1.2): Normal
                Interface inside (10.10.10.1): Normal
        Other host: Secondary - Standby
                Active time: 0 (sec)
                Interface failover (1.1.1.2):Normal
                Interface dmz (172.16.31.2): Normal
                Interface outside (192.168.1.3): Normal
                Interface inside (10.10.10.2): Normal
```

```
Stateful Failover Logical Update Statistics
        Link : failover
        Stateful Obj    xmit        xerr        rcv         rerr
        General         435     0           0           0
        sys cmd         415     0           0           0
        up time         0           0           0           0
        xlate           27          0           0           0
        tcp conn        203     0           0           0
        udp conn        0           0           0           0
        ARP tbl         0           0           0           0
        RIP Tbl         0           0           0           0

Logical Update Queue Information
                Cur     Max     Total
        Recv Q:     0       0       0
        Xmit Q:     0       1       614
```

What Is Wrong with This Picture?

Now that you have successfully gone through the configuration scenarios in the previous sections, this section focuses on problem solving after or during an implementation of Cisco PIX Firewall. Examples 20-9 through 20-11 show the configuration of three PIX Firewalls for this exercise.

Example 20-9   *Atlanta PIX Firewall Configuration*

```
1.   : Saved
2.   :
3.   PIX Version 6.2(2)
4.   nameif ethernet0 outside security0
5.   nameif ethernet1 inside security100
6.   nameif ethernet2 DMZ security70
7.   enable password ksjfglkasglc encrypted
8.   passwd kjngczftglkacytiur encrypted
9.   hostname Atlanta
10.  domain-name www.BranchVPN.com
11.  fixup protocol ftp 21
12.  fixup protocol http 80
13.  fixup protocol smtp 25
14.  fixup protocol skinny 2000
15.  names
16.  access-list inbound permit icmp any host 192.168.3.10
17.  access-list inbound permit tcp any host 192.168.3.10  eq www
18.  access-list inbound permit tcp any host 192.168.3.10 eq 443
19.  access-list DMZ permit udp 172.16.3.0 255.255.255.0 host 10.10.3.240 eq ntp
20.  access-list VPN permit ip 10.10.3.0 255.255.255.0 10.10.2.0 255.255.255.0
```

continues

Example 20-9 *Atlanta PIX Firewall Configuration (Continued)*

```
21.  access-list VPN permit ip 10.10.3.0 255.255.255.0 10.10.10.0 255.255.255.0
22.  access-list LosAngeles permit ip 10.10.3.0 255.255.255.0 10.10.10.0
     255.255.255.0
23.  access-list Boston permit ip 10.10.3.0 255.255.255.0 10.10.2.0 255.255.255.0
24.  pager lines 24
25.  logging on
26.  logging timestamp
27.  interface ethernet0 auto
28.  interface ethernet1 auto
29.  interface ethernet2 auto
30.  mtu outside 1500
31.  mtu inside 1500
32.  ip address outside 192.168.3.1 255.255.255.0
33.  ip address inside 10.10.3.1 255.255.255.0
34.  ip address DMZ 172.16.3.1 255.255.255.0
35.  arp timeout 14400
36.  global (outside) 1 192.168.3.20-200
37.  nat (inside) 1 0.0.0.0 0.0.0.0 0 0
38.  nat (inside) 0 access-list VPN
39.  static (DMZ,outside) 192.168.3.10 172.16.3.10 netmask 255.255.255.255 0 0
40.  access-group inbound in interface outside
41.  access-group DMZ in interface DMZ
42.  route outside 0.0.0.0 0.0.0.0 192.168.3.254 1
43.  timeout xlate 3:00:00
44.  timeout conn 1:00:00 half-closed 0:10:00 udp 0:02:00
45.  timeout uauth 0:05:00 absolute
46.  aaa-server TACACS+ protocol tacacs+
47.  aaa-server RADIUS protocol radius
48.  no snmp-server location
49.  no snmp-server contact
50.  snmp-server community public
51.  no snmp-server enable traps
52.  floodguard enable
53.  sysopt connection permit-ipsec
54.  crypto ipsec transform-set BranchVPN esp-3des esp-md5-hmac
55.  crypto ipsec transform-set NothingNew esp-3des esp-sha-hmac
56.  crypto map BranchVPN 10 ipsec-isakmp
57.  crypto map BranchVPN 10 match address LosAngeles
58.  crypto map BranchVPN 10 set peer 192.168.1.1
59.  crypto map BranchVPN 10 set transform-set BranchVPN
60.  crypto map BranchVPN 20 ipsec-isakmp
61.  crypto map BranchVPN 20 match address Boston
62.  crypto map BranchVPN 20 set peer 192.168.2.1
63.  crypto map BranchVPN 20 set transform-set BranchVPN
64.  crypto map BranchVPN interface DMZ
65.  isakmp enable outside
66.  isakmp key ******** address 192.168.1.1 netmask 255.255.255.255
```

Example 20-9 *Atlanta PIX Firewall Configuration (Continued)*

```
67.   isakmp key ******** address 192.168.2.1 netmask 255.255.255.255
68.   isakmp identity address
69.   isakmp policy 20 authentication pre-share
70.   isakmp policy 20 encryption 3des
71.   isakmp policy 20 hash md5
72.   isakmp policy 20 group 2
73.   isakmp policy 20 lifetime 86400
74.   terminal width 80
75.   Cryptochecksum:e0c04954fcabd239ae291d58fc618dd5
```

Example 20-10 *Boston PIX Firewall Configuration*

```
1.    : Saved
2.    :
3.    PIX Version 6.2(2)
4.    nameif ethernet0 outside security0
5.    nameif ethernet1 inside security100
6.    nameif ethernet2 DMZ security70
7.    enable password ksjfglkasglc encrypted
8.    passwd kjngczftglkacytiur encrypted
9.    hostname Boston
10.   domain-name www.BranchVPN.com
11.   fixup protocol ftp 21
12.   fixup protocol http 80
13.   fixup protocol smtp 25
14.   fixup protocol skinny 2000
15.   names
16.   access-list inbound permit icmp any host 192.168.2.10
17.   access-list inbound permit tcp any host 192.168.2.10  eq www
18.   access-list inbound permit tcp any host 192.168.2.10 eq 443
      access-list DMZ permit tcp 192.168.1.13 255.255.255.255 192.168.2.11 eq 1521
19.   access-list DMZ permit udp 172.16.2.0 255.255.255.0 host 10.10.2.240 eq ntp
20.   access-list VPN permit ip 10.10.2.0 255.255.255.0 10.10.10.0 255.255.255.0
21.   access-list VPN permit ip 10.10.2.0 255.255.255.0 10.10.3.0 255.255.255.0
22.   access-list LosAngeles permit ip 10.10.2.0 255.255.255.0 10.10.10.0
      255.255.255.0
23.   access-list Atlanta permit ip 10.10.2.0 255.255.255.0 10.10.3.0 255.255.255.0
24.   pager lines 24
25.   logging on
26.   logging timestamp
27.   interface ethernet0 auto
28.   interface ethernet1 auto
29.   interface ethernet2 auto
30.   mtu outside 1500
31.   mtu inside 1500
32.   ip address outside 192.168.2.1 255.255.255.0
```

continues

Example 20-10 *Boston PIX Firewall Configuration (Continued)*

```
33.  ip address inside 10.10.2.1 255.255.255.0
34.  ip address DMZ 172.16.2.1 255.255.255.0
35.  arp timeout 14400
36.  global (outside) 1 192.168.2.20-200
37.  nat (inside) 1 0.0.0.0 0.0.0.0 0 0
38.  nat (inside) 0 access-list VPN
39.  static (DMZ,outside) 192.168.2.10 172.16.2.10 netmask 255.255.255.255 0 0
     static (DMZ,outside) 192.168.2.11 172.16.2.11 netmask 255.255.255.255 0 0
40.  access-group inbound in interface outside
41.  access-group DMZ in interface DMZ
42.  route outside 0.0.0.0 0.0.0.0 192.168.2.254 1
43.  timeout xlate 3:00:00
44.  timeout conn 1:00:00 half-closed 0:10:00 udp 0:02:00
45.  timeout uauth 0:05:00 absolute
46.  aaa-server TACACS+ protocol tacacs+
47.  aaa-server RADIUS protocol radius
48.  no snmp-server location
49.  no snmp-server contact
50.  snmp-server community public
51.  no snmp-server enable traps
52.  floodguard enable
53.  crypto ipsec transform-set BranchVPN esp-3des esp-md5-hmac
54.  crypto ipsec transform-set NothingNew esp-3des esp-sha-hmac
55.  crypto map BranchVPN 10 ipsec-isakmp
56.  crypto map BranchVPN 10 match address LosAngeles
57.  crypto map BranchVPN 10 set peer 192.168.1.1
58.  crypto map BranchVPN 10 set transform-set BranchVPN
59.  crypto map BranchVPN 20 ipsec-isakmp
60.  crypto map BranchVPN 20 match address Atlanta
61.  crypto map BranchVPN 20 set peer 192.168.3.1
62.  crypto map BranchVPN 20 set transform-set BranchVPN
63.  crypto map BranchVPN interface outside
64.  isakmp enable outside
65.  isakmp key ******** address 192.168.1.1 netmask 255.255.255.255
66.  isakmp key ******** address 192.168.3.1 netmask 255.255.255.255
67.  isakmp identity address
68.  isakmp policy 20 authentication pre-share
69.  isakmp policy 20 encryption 3des
70.  isakmp policy 20 hash md5
71.  isakmp policy 20 group 2
72.  isakmp policy 20 lifetime 86400
73.  terminal width 80
74.  Cryptochecksum:e0c04954fcabd239ae291d58fc618dd5
```

Example 20-11 *Los Angeles PIX Firewall Configuration*

```
1.   : Saved
2.   :
3.   PIX Version 6.2(2)
4.   nameif ethernet0 outside security0
5.   nameif ethernet1 inside security100
6.   nameif ethernet2 DMZ security70
7.   enable password HtmvK15kjhtlyfvcl encrypted
8.   passwd Kkjhlkf1568Hke encrypted
9.   hostname LosAngeles
10.  domain-name www.BranchVPN.com
11.  fixup protocol ftp 21
12.  fixup protocol http 80
13.  fixup protocol h323 1720
14.  fixup protocol rsh 514
15.  fixup protocol smtp 25
16.  fixup protocol sqlnet 1521
17.  fixup protocol sip 5060
18.  fixup protocol skinny 2000
19.  names
     access-list inbound permit tcp any host 192.168.1.9 eq ftp
20.  access-list inbound permit icmp any host 192.168.1.10
21.  access-list inbound permit tcp any host 192.168.1.10  eq www
22.  access-list inbound permit tcp any host 192.168.1.10 eq 443
23.  access-list inbound permit tcp any host 192.168.1.11  eq www
24.  access-list inbound permit tcp any host 192.168.1.11 eq 443
25.  access-list inbound permit tcp any host 192.168.1.12  eq www
26.  access-list inbound permit tcp any host 192.168.1.12 eq 443
27.  access-list inbound permit tcp any host 192.168.1.13  eq ftp
28.  access-list Exchange permit tcp any host 192.168.1.14 eq 25
     access-list Exchange permit tcp any host 192.168.1.14 eq 443
     access-list DMZ permit tcp 172.16.1.13 255.255.255.255 10.10.11.221 eq 1521
29.  access-list DMZ permit udp 172.16.1.0 255.255.255.0 host 10.10.10.240 eq ntp
30.  access-list VPN permit ip 10.10.10.0 255.255.255.0 10.10.2.0 255.255.255.0
31.  access-list VPN permit ip 10.10.10.0 255.255.255.0 10.10.3.0 255.255.255.0
32.  access-list Boston permit ip 10.10.10.0 255.255.255.0 10.10.2.0 255.255.255.0
33.  access-list Atlanta permit ip 10.10.10.0 255.255.255.0 10.10.3.0 255.255.255.0
34.  pager lines 24
35.  logging on
36.  logging timestamp
37.  interface ethernet0 auto
38.  interface ethernet1 auto
39.  interface ethernet2 auto
40.  mtu outside 1500
41.  mtu inside 1500
42.  ip address outside 192.168.1.1 255.255.255.0
43.  ip address inside 10.10.10.1 255.255.255.0
```

continues

Example 20-11 *Los Angeles PIX Firewall Configuration (Continued)*

```
44.  ip address DMZ 172.16.1.1 255.255.255.0
45.  failover
46.  failover timeout 0:00:00
47.  failover poll 15
48.  failover ip address outside 192.168.1.2
49.  failover ip address inside 10.10.10.2
50.  failover ip address DMZ 172.16.1.2
51.  arp timeout 14400
52.  global (outside) 1 192.168.1.20-250
53.  nat (inside) 1 0.0.0.0 0.0.0.0 0 0
54.  nat (inside) 0 access-list VPN
55.  static (DMZ,outside) 192.168.1.10 172.16.1.10 netmask 255.255.255.255 0 0
56.  static (DMZ,outside) 192.168.1.11 172.16.1.11 netmask 255.255.255.255 0 0
57.  static (DMZ,outside) 192.168.1.12 172.16.1.12 netmask 255.255.255.255 0 0
58.  static (DMZ,outside) 192.168.1.13 172.16.1.13 netmask 255.255.255.255 0 0
     static (DMZ,outside) 192.168.1.14 172.16.1.14 netmask 255.255.255.255 0 0
59.  access-group inbound in interface outside
     access-group Exchange in interface outside
60.  access-group DMZ in interface DMZ
61.  route outside 0.0.0.0 0.0.0.0 192.168.1.254 1
62.  timeout xlate 3:00:00
63.  timeout conn 1:00:00 half-closed 0:10:00 udp 0:02:00 rpc 0:10:00 h323 0:05:00
     sip 0:30:00 sip-media 0:02:00
64.  timeout uauth 0:05:00 absolute
65.  aaa-server TACACS+ protocol tacacs+
66.  aaa-server RADIUS protocol radius
67.  no snmp-server location
68.  no snmp-server contact
69.  snmp-server community public
70.  no snmp-server enable traps
71.  floodguard enable
72.  sysopt connection permit-ipsec
73.  no sysopt route dnat
74.  crypto ipsec transform-set BranchVPN esp-3des esp-md5-hmac
75.  crypto ipsec transform-set NothingNew esp-3des esp-sha-hmac
76.  crypto map BranchVPN 10 ipsec-isakmp
77.  crypto map BranchVPN 10 match address Boston
78.  crypto map BranchVPN 10 set peer 192.168.2.1
79.  crypto map BranchVPN 10 set transform-set BranchVPN
80.  crypto map BranchVPN 20 ipsec-isakmp
81.  crypto map BranchVPN 20 set peer 192.168.3.1
82.  crypto map BranchVPN 20 set transform-set BranchVPN
83.  crypto map BranchVPN interface outside
84.  isakmp enable outside
85.  isakmp key ******** address 192.168.2.1 netmask 255.255.255.255
86.  isakmp key ******** address 192.168.3.1 netmask 255.255.255.255
87.  isakmp identity address
```

Example 20-11 *Los Angeles PIX Firewall Configuration (Continued)*

```
88.  isakmp policy 20 authentication pre-share
89.  isakmp policy 20 encryption 3des
90.  isakmp policy 20 hash md5
91.  isakmp policy 20 group 2
92.  isakmp policy 20 lifetime 86400
93.  terminal width 80
94.  Cryptochecksum:e0clmj3546549637cbsFds54132d5
```

After you have reviewed the configuration files for the three PIX Firewalls, answer the following questions (the answers appear in Appendix A, "Answers to the 'Do I Know This Already?' Quizzes and Q&A Sections"):

> **NOTE** The questions should be answered in order and the later questions assume that the configuration changes needed to correct previous problems have already been applied. For instance, question 4 assumes that the configuration changes needed to resolve questions 1 though 3 have been applied to the configurations listed in the chapter when considering the answer to question 4.

1. The VPN session is established, but no traffic, or just one-way traffic, is passing between the Boston firewall and Los Angeles firewall. Ellen starts debugging the problem using **debug icmp trace**. She pings the other end of the VPN node and gets the following results:

   ```
   LOCAL-PIX(config)#
   609001: Built local-host inside:10.10.2.21
   106014: Deny inbound icmp src outside:10.10.10.31 dst
   inside:10.10.2.21 (type 8, code 0)106014: Deny inbound icmp src
   outside:10.10.10.31 dst
   inside:10.10.2.21 (type 8, code 0)
   106014: Deny inbound icmp src outside:10.10.10.31 dst
   inside:10.10.2.21 (type 8, code 0)
   106014: Deny inbound icmp src outside:10.10.10.31 dst
   inside:10.10.2.21 (type 8., code 0)
   106014: Deny inbound icmp src outside:10.10.10.31 dst
   inside:10.10.2.21 (type 8, code 0)
   609002: Teardown local-host inside:10.10.2.21duration 0:00:15
   ```

   What do these results indicate and what could be causing this problem? How would you help Ellen resolve this issue?

2. Eric cannot get the VPN tunnel to work from HQ to the Atlanta branch office. He starts a debug and gets the following results:

   ```
   crypto-isakmp-process-block: src 10.10.10.40, dest 10.10.3.34
   VPN Peer: ISAKMP: Added new peer: ip:10.10.10.40 Total VPN Peers:1
   VPN Peer: ISAKMP: Peer ip:10.10.10.40 Ref cnt incremented to:1
     Total VPN Peers:1
   OAK-MM exchange
   ISAKMP (0): processing SA payload. message ID = 0
   ```

```
ISAKMP (0): Checking ISAKMP transform 1 against priority 10 policy
ISAKMP:        encryption DES-CBC
ISAKMP:        hash MD5
ISAKMP:        default group 1
ISAKMP:        auth pre-share
ISAKMP:        life type in seconds
ISAKMP:        life duration (basic) of 2400
ISAKMP (0): atts are acceptable. Next payload is 0
ISAKMP (0): SA is doing pre-shared key authentication using id type ID-IPV4
 -ADDR
return status is IKMP-NO-ERROR
crypto-isakmp-process-block: src 10.10.10.40, dest 10.10.3.34
OAK-MM exchange

ISAKMP (0): processing KE payload. message ID = 0
ISAKMP (0): processing NONCE payload. message ID = 0
ISAKMP (0): processing vendor id payload
ISAKMP (0): processing vendor id payload
ISAKMP (0): remote peer supports dead peer detection
ISAKMP (0): processing vendor id payload
ISAKMP (0): speaking to another IOS box!

return status is IKMP-NO-ERROR
crypto-isakmp-process-block: src 10.10.10.40, dest 10.10.3.34
OAK-MM exchange
ISAKMP (0): processing ID payload. message ID = 0
ISAKMP (0): processing HASH payload. message ID = 0
ISAKMP (0): SA has been authenticated

ISAKMP (0): ID payload
        next-payload : 8
        type         : 1
        protocol     : 17
        port         : 500
        length       : 8
ISAKMP (0): Total payload length: 12
return status is IKMP-NO-ERROR
crypto-isakmp-process-block: src 10.10.10.40, dest 10.10.3.34
ISAKMP (0): processing NOTIFY payload 24578 protocol 1
        spi 0, message ID = 2457631438
ISAKMP (0): processing notify INITIAL-CONTACTIPSEC(key-engine): got a queue
  event...
IPSEC(key-engine-delete-sas): rec'd delete notify from ISAKMP
IPSEC(key-engine-delete-sas): delete all SAs shared with   10.10.10.40

return status is IKMP-NO-ERR-NO-TRANS
crypto-isakmp-process-block: src 10.10.10.40, dest 10.10.3.34
OAK-QM exchange
oakley-process-quick-mode:
OAK-QM-IDLE
ISAKMP (0): processing SA payload. message ID = 133935992
ISAKMP : Checking IPSec proposal 1
ISAKMP: transform 1, ESP-DES
ISAKMP:    attributes in transform:
ISAKMP:       encaps is 1
ISAKMP:       SA life type in seconds
ISAKMP:       SA life duration (basic) of 28800
```

```
ISAKMP:       SA life type in kilobytes
ISAKMP:       SA life duration (VPI) of  0x0 0x46 0x50 0x0
ISAKMP:       authenticator is HMAC-MD5
IPSEC(validate-proposal): invalid local address 10.10.3.34
ISAKMP (0): atts not acceptable. Next payload is 0
ISAKMP (0): SA not acceptable!
ISAKMP (0): sending NOTIFY message 14 protocol 0
return status is IKMP-ERR-NO-RETRANS
crypto-isakmp-process-block: src 10.10.10.40, dest 10.10.3.34
ISAKMP (0:0): phase 2 packet is a duplicate of a previous packet.
```

What could be the cause of this problem?

3. Bruce is having problems establishing a VPN session to the Atlanta office. He gets the following debug results:

```
IPSEC(crypto-map-check): crypto map BranchVPN 20 incomplete. No peer or
    access-list specified. Packet discarded
```

What is causing this problem, and how would you help Bruce successfully establish a VPN tunnel to the Atlanta office?

4. The web administrator in Los Angeles needs to maintain the web servers in the DMZ from the internal network using Terminal Services (Transmission Control Protocol [TCP] port 3389). Is the firewall in Los Angeles configured to allow this access? Explain your answer.

5. The web administrator in Los Angeles also needs to administer the web servers in Boston and Atlanta. Are the three firewalls configured to allow this access? Explain your answer.

6. The Web server 172.16.1.13 needs to access an Oracle database server that sits on a segment connected to the internal network at 10.10.11.221. The web server initiates the connection on TCP port 1521 and retrieves inventory data. Can this connection be completed? Explain your answer.

7. The web server 172.16.1.13 needs to access an Oracle database server on the DMZ in Boston using the address 172.16.2.11. The web server initiates the connection on TCP port 1521 to retrieve financial data. Can this connection be completed? Explain your answer.

8. Is the configuration solution to question 7 a good idea? Explain your answer.

9. The company has installed an FTP server on the DMZ segment in Los Angeles that customers can access to download updates. The FTP server address is 172.16.1.9. Can all external users access this FTP server? Explain your answer.

10. The exchange server is installed on the DMZ segment in Los Angeles using the address 172.16.1.14. The firewall is configured to allow Simple Mail Transfer Protocol (SMTP) access for inbound mail and Secure Sockets Layer (SSL) access for users who want to connect using Outlook Web Access over an HTTP over SSL (HTTPS) connection. Will any users be able to receive their mail with this configuration? Explain your answer.

11. What needs to be done in Los Angeles to allow access to the mail server?

Answers to the "Do I Know This Already?" Quizzes and Q&A Sections

Chapter 1

"Do I Know This Already?" Quiz

1. Which single method is the best way to secure a network?

    a. Allow dialup access only to the Internet

    b. Install a personal firewall on every workstation

    c. Use very complex passwords

    d. Implement strong perimeter security

    e. None of the above

    Answer: e

2. What are the three types of cyber attacks? (Choose three.)

    a. Penetration attack

    b. Access attack

    c. Denial of service attack

    d. Destruction of data attack

    e. Reconnaissance attack

    Answer: b, c, e

3. What type of threat is directed toward a specific target normally for a specific purpose?

    a. Structured threats

    b. Directed threats

    c. Unstructured threats

    d. Political threats

    e. None of the above

    Answer: a

4. What type of threat normally scans networks looking for "targets of opportunity"?

   a. Structured threats

   b. Scanning threats

   c. Unstructured threats

   d. Script kiddies

   e. None of the above

   Answer: c

5. What type of scan looks for all services running on a single host?

   a. Ping sweep

   b. Service scan

   c. Horizontal scan

   d. Vertical scan

   e. All of the above

   Answer: d

6. What type of attack determines the address space assigned to an organization?

   a. Ping sweep

   b. DNS queries

   c. Vertical scan

   d. Horizontal scan

   e. None of the above

   Answer: b

7. What are the steps of the security process?

   a. Secure, test, repair, retest

   b. Test, repair, monitor, evaluate

   c. Lather, rinse, repeat

   d. Evaluate, secure, test

   e. None of the above

   Answer: e

8. What constant action sits between the individual steps of the security process?

    a. Test

    b. Retest

    c. Evaluate

    d. Repair

    e. Improve

    Answer: c

9. True or false: Cisco AVVID uses only Cisco products.

    Answer: False

10. Which of the following is *not* a component of Cisco SAFE?

    a. Perimeter security

    b. Policy implementation

    c. Identity

    d. Security management and monitoring

    e. Application security

    Answer: b

Q&A

1. What is the difference between the network security policy and the network security process?

    Answer: The network security process is an ongoing process that ensures the constant improvement of security in accordance with the security policy.

2. For unstructured threats, what is the normal anatomy of an attack?

    Answer: The attacker first gains information about the network by launching a reconnaissance attack against specific targets and then attempts to exploit vulnerabilities discovered during the reconnaissance.

3. What information can you gain from a ping sweep?

    Answer: Replies from ICMP requests will tell you which addresses on the network are assigned to running systems.

4. What is the single most important component when implementing defense in depth?

    Answer: There is no single most important component. Defense in depth is a combination of products, processes, and architecture used to identify and mitigate attacks.

5. Why could an organization be legally responsible if its systems are compromised during an attack?

    Answer: Organizations are expected to exercise "reasonable care" to secure their networks and resources.

Chapter 2

"Do I Know This Already?" Quiz

1. True or false: Packet filtering can be configured on Cisco routers.

    Answer: True

2. What design feature enables the Cisco PIX Firewall to outperform conventional application firewalls?

    a. The Packet Selectivity Algorithm

    b. Super-packet filtering

    c. A single embedded operating environment

    d. Hot standby proxy processing

    Answer: c

3. True or false: Cut-through proxy technology allows users to do anything they want after authenticating at the firewall.

    Answer: False

4. What steps are required to add an ARP entry to a Cisco PIX Firewall?

    a. Edit the /etc/interfaces/outside/arp.conf file.

    b. You do not need to add an ARP entry on a PIX Firewall.

    c. Add the ARP entry using the GUI.

    d. Use the **set arp** command in interface config mode.

    Answer: b

5. True or false: There is no limit to the number of connections an application proxy firewall can handle.

   Answer: False

6. True or false: The Adaptive Security Algorithm requires a tremendous amount of processing by the firewall. Although the PIX Firewall is not very efficient at processing the ASA, it can handle the task.

   Answer: False

7. True or false: Redundancy allows you to configure two or more PIX Firewalls in a cluster to protect critical systems.

   Answer: False

8. Of the three firewall technologies, which one generates a separate connection on behalf of the requestor and usually operates at the upper layers of the OSI reference model?

   a. Stateful inspection

   b. Packet filtering

   c. High-speed packet filtering

   d. Application proxy

   e. None of the above

   Answer: d

9. Which of the following is *not* one of the three basic firewall technologies?

   a. Stateful inspection

   b. Packet filtering

   c. High-speed packet filtering

   d. Application proxy

   e. None of the above

   Answer: c

10. Which firewall technology is commonly implemented on a router?

    a. Stateful inspection

    b. Packet filtering

    c. High-speed packet filtering

    d. Application proxy

    e. None of the above

Answer: b

Q&A

1. What items does a packet filter look at to determine whether to allow the traffic?

Answer: Source address/port, destination address/port, and protocol.

2. What are the advantages of the Cisco PIX Firewall over competing firewall products?

Answer: The Cisco PIX Firewall has a single embedded operating system, the adaptive security algorithm, cut-through proxy, and redundancy.

3. How many PIX Firewalls can you operate in a high-availability cluster?

Answer: The PIX Firewall can be configured in a failover configuration consisting of two firewalls.

4. What is the ASA, and how does the Cisco PIX Firewall use it?

Answer: The Adaptive Security Algorithm is what the PIX Firewall uses to perform stateful inspection. The ASA not only tracks the session information in the state table but also randomly generates TCP sequence numbers to ensure that a session cannot be hijacked.

5. Why is cut-through proxy more efficient than traditional proxy?

Answer: Cut-through proxy is a feature that the Cisco PIX Firewall uses to authenticate and authorize a user during the initial creation of the session. Cut-through proxy uses the ASA to track session information but does not perform any proxy services. This greatly increases the firewall's performance compared to traditional proxy firewalls.

6. What are the advantages of a real-time embedded system?

Answer: The advantages are improved security, functionality, and performance.

Chapter 3

"Do I Know This Already?" Quiz

1. True or false: You do not need a license for any Cisco PIX Firewall. If you own the appliance, you can do anything you want with it.

   Answer: False

2. How many physical interfaces does the PIX 525 support?

   a. Eight 10/100 interfaces or three Gigabit interfaces

   b. Eight 10/100 interfaces and three Gigabit interfaces

   c. Six 10/100 interfaces or three Gigabit interfaces

   d. Six 10/100 interfaces and three Gigabit interfaces

   e. None of the above

   Answer: a

3. What are the three firewall technologies?

   a. Packet filtering, proxy, connection dropping

   b. Stateful inspection, packet filtering, proxy

   c. Stateful proxy, stateful filtering, packet inspection

   d. Cut-through proxy, ASA, proxy

   Answer: b

4. How are optional component cards installed in the PIX Firewall?

   a. ISA slot

   b. USB port

   c. Serial connection

   d. PCI slot

   e. PCMCIA slot

   Answer: d

5. What is the maximum clear-text throughput of the PIX 535?

   a. 1.0 Gbps

   b. 1.7 Gbps

   c. 100 Mbps

   d. 565 Mbps

Answer: b

6. How many physical interfaces does a PIX 501 have, and how many network segments does it support?

   a. Six interfaces, two network segments

   b. Six interface, six network segments

   c. Five interfaces, four network segments

   d. Two interfaces, two network segments

   e. None of the above

Answer: e

7. What happens to a reply that does not have the correct TCP sequence number?

   a. It generates an alert.

   b. The connection is dropped.

   c. The connection information is added to the state table.

   d. The session object is modified.

   e. None of the above

Answer: b

8. Which of the following is the best way to remove the ASA from a PIX Firewall?

   a. Use the ASA removal tool, downloaded from Cisco.com.

   b. Use the **asa disable** command in the config mode.

   c. Configure all NATs to a single external address.

   d. Configure all NATs to a single internal address.

   e. You cannot remove the ASA from the PIX Firewall.

Answer: e

9. Which of the following four authentication methods is not supported by the PIX Firewall for performing cut-through proxy?

   a. Local Database

   b. TACACS+

   c. RADIUS

   d. Active Directory

   e. All of the above

   Answer: d

10. What encryption algorithms does the PIX Firewall *not* support?

   a. Data Encryption Standard

   b. Triple Data Encryption Standard

   c. Diffie-Hellman

   d. Advanced Encryption Standard 128

   e. Advanced Encryption Standard 256

   f. Answers c, d, and e

   Answer: c

Q&A

1. What is the ASA, and how does the Cisco PIX Firewall use it?

   Answer: The ASA is an algorithm used by the PIX Firewall to provide better security than packet filters and better performance than application proxies.

2. Why does the ASA generate random TCP sequence numbers?

   Answer: The initial TCP sequence numbers for outbound connections are randomly generated by the PIX Firewall to greatly reduce the chances of an inbound TCP session being hijacked.

3. What components of a TCP session does the ASA write to the state table to create a session object?

   Answer:

   — Source IP and port

   — Destination IP and port

   — TCP sequencing information

   — Additional TCP and UDP flags

   — A new random TCP sequence number

4. What can cause a session object to be deleted from the state table?

   Answer: The session is not authorized by the security policy, the session has ended, or the session has timed out.

5. What are the three ways to initiate a cut-through proxy session?

   Answer: Initiate an HTTP, FTP, or Telnet session.

6. What X.509 certificates do SCEP and the PIX Firewall support?

   Answer:

   — Entrust Technologies, Inc.—Entrust/PKI 4.0

   — Microsoft Corp.—Windows 2000 Certificate Server 5.0

   — VeriSign—Onsite 4.5

   — Baltimore Technologies—UniCERT 3.05

7. How many physical interfaces does the PIX 515E support?

   Answer: PIX 515E supports up to six 10/100 interfaces.

8. What is the lowest model number of the PIX Firewall family to support failover?

   Answer: The PIX 515E is the lowest model to support failover.

9. What are three methods of managing a Cisco PIX Firewall?

Answer:

- Command-line interface (CLI)
- PIX Device Manager (PDM)
- CiscoWorks Management Center for Firewalls (PIX MC)

10. List four advantages of the ASA.

Answer:

- It is more secure than packet filtering.
- It has greater performance than application proxy.
- It can guard against session hijacking.
- It is part of the embedded PIX operating system.

Chapter 4

"Do I Know This Already?" Quiz

1. Which command upgrades a PIX Firewall 525 device running a 5.3 OS version to 6.3?

   a. install

   b. setup

   c. copy 6.3

   d. copy tftp flash

   Answer: d

2. Which binary file is required to perform a password recovery procedure on a PIX device running OS Version 6.3?

   a. np63.bin

   b. pix52.bin

   c. bh52.bin

   d. pass52.bin

   Answer: a

3. What circumstance(s) warrant(s) the use of a boothelper disk in the OS upgrade procedure?

    a. A corrupt binary image

    b. A PIX 520 device

    c. A PIX device running a 6.0 or later PIX OS

    d. No circumstance warrants the use of a boothelper disk.

    Answer: b

4. To what is the console password set after a successful password recovery procedure?

    a. password.

    b. cisco.

    c. secret.

    d. It is erased and set to blank.

    Answer: d

5. How many privilege levels are there on the PIX Firewall?

    a. 2

    b. 16

    c. 32

    d. 4

    Answer: b

6. Which of the following is the highest level of privilege to which a user account can be assigned?

    a. 32

    b. 16

    c. 8

    d. 15

    Answer: d

7. Which command changes the SSH password for login?

   a. change ssh password

   b. secret

   c. password

   d. ssh pass

   Answer: c

8. What is the default amount of time a Telnet session can be idle?

   a. 2 minutes

   b. 15 minutes

   c. 5 minutes

   d. 12 minutes

   Answer: c

9. Which of the following pieces of information are sent to an SNMP management station by the PIX Firewall?

   a. Link up and link down

   b. Running configuration

   c. Show command outputs

   d. Authentication failure

   Answer: a, d

10. Which version of SSH does the PIX Firewall support?

   a. 2.1

   b. 2.2

   c. 3.1

   d. 1

   Answer: d

Q&A

1. How many ways can you access the PIX Firewall?

   Answer: You can access the PIX Firewall through Telnet, SSH, PDM, and the console port.

2. What is the command to change the Telnet password?

    Answer: passwd or Password

3. Which command would you use to view the privilege level assigned to the **access-list** command?

    Answer: show privilege command access-list

4. Which version of SSH does PIX Firewall support?

    Answer: The PIX Firewall supports SSH version 1.

5. What is the activation key?

    Answer: The activation key is the license key or number for the PIX Firewall.

6. Give one reason why you would need to change the activation key on your PIX Firewall.

    Answer:

    — **Your Cisco PIX Firewall does not have failover activated.**

    — **Your PIX Firewall does not currently have VPN-DES or VPN-3DES encryption enabled.**

    — **You are upgrading from a connection-based license to a feature-based license.**

7. How many privilege levels are available on the PIX Firewall?

    Answer: 16

8. How do you determine which version of the PIX Firewall operating system is installed?

    Answer: The show version command displays the version information on your PIX Firewall.

9. Which command would you use to create locally a user called mason with a password of Fr33 on the PIX Firewall?

    Answer: username mason password Fr33

10. How do you find out what your activation key is?

    Answer: Use the show activation-key command for versions earlier than 6.2, and use the show version command for Version 6.2 and later.

Chapter 5

"Do I Know This Already?" Quiz

1. By default, how long will an embryonic connection remain open?

   a. 2 minutes

   b. 3600 seconds

   c. 1800 seconds

   d. Unlimited

   e. 30 minutes

   Answer: d

2. You have configured two additional DMZ interfaces on your PIX Firewall. How do you prevent nodes on DMZ1 from accessing nodes on DMZ2 without adding rules to the security policy?

   a. Route all traffic for DMZ2 out the outside interface.

   b. Dynamically NAT all DMZ2 nodes to a multicast address.

   c. Assign a higher security level to DMZ2.

   d. All of the above

   Answer: c

3. Which of the following is not a method of address translation supported by the PIX Firewall?

   a. Network Address Translation

   b. Socket Address Translation

   c. Port Address Translation

   d. Static Address Translation

   Answer: b

4. What happens if you configure two interfaces with the same security level?

   a. Traffic will pass freely between those connected networks.

   b. Traffic will not pass between those interfaces.

   c. Specific ACLs must allow traffic between those interfaces.

   d. The two interfaces will not apply the **nat** or **global** commands.

   Answer: b

5. When should you run the command **clear xlate**?

   a. When updating a conduit on the firewall

   b. When editing the NAT for the inside segment

   c. When adding addresses to the global pool

   d. All of the above

   Answer: d

6. How do you define the **global** addresses used when configuring NAT?

   a. Define a subnet.

   b. Define an address range.

   c. Define individual IP addresses.

   d. You can define only /24 address segments for global addresses.

   e. None of the above

   Answer: b

7. How many external IP addresses are required to configure PAT?

   a. A single address

   b. A /24 subnet

   c. A defined address range

   d. Any of the above

   e. None of the above

   Answer: a

8. What command shows all active TCP connections on the PIX Firewall?

   a. **show conn**

   b. **show xlate**

   c. **show connection status**

   d. **show tcp active**

   e. None of the above

   Answer: a

9. Why is it difficult to penetrate the PIX Firewall over UDP port 53?

   a. The PIX Firewall allows multiple outbound queries but randomizes the UDP sequence numbers.

   b. The PIX Firewall allows queries to go out to multiple DNS servers but drops all but the first response.

   c. The PIX Firewall allows responses only to outbound DNS queries.

   d. All of the above

   Answer: b

10. How many connections can you hide behind a single global address?

    a. 65,536

    b. 255

    c. 17,200

    d. An unlimited number

    e. None of the above

    Answer: e

Q&A

1. What is the difference between TCP and UDP?

   Answer: TCP is a connection-oriented protocol, and UDP is a connectionless protocol.

2. What is the default security for traffic origination on the inside network segment going to the outside network?

   Answer: By default, traffic is permitted from the inside (higher security level) to the outside (lower security level) network as long as the appropriate nat/global/static command has been configured.

3. True or false: You can have multiple translations in a single connection.

   Answer: False. Multiple connections can take place in a single translation.

4. What commands are required to configure NAT on a Cisco PIX Firewall?

   Answer: nat and global are required to configure NAT on a Cisco PIX Firewall.

5. How many nodes can you hide behind a single IP address when configuring PAT?

    Answer: You can hide approximately 64,000 nodes. This is determined by subtracting the 1024 previously assigned ports from the 65,535 available ports. It is also estimated that that number could be significantly lower because there might be multiple connections occurring behind a single translation.

6. What is an embryonic connection?

    Answer: An embryonic connection is a half-open TCP session.

7. What is the best type of translation to use to allow connections to web servers from the Internet?

    Answer: Static translations provide a one-to-one translation from external to internal/ DMZ addresses.

8. How does the Cisco PIX Firewall handle outbound DNS requests?

    Answer: The PIX Firewall allows multiple outbound queries but allows only a single query response. All responses after the first are dropped.

9. True or false: The quickest way to clear the translation table is to reboot the PIX Firewall.

    Answer: False. The command clear xlate is the fastest method of clearing the translation table.

10. True or false: If you configure a static translation for your web server, everyone can connect to it.

    Answer: False. You also need to configure an ACL or conduit allowing the connection.

11. What does the PIX Firewall normally change when allowing a TCP handshake between nodes on different interfaces and performing NAT?

    Answer: The PIX Firewall translates the local address to a global address and randomly generates a new initial TCP sequence number.

12. What does the PIX Firewall normally change when allowing a TCP handshake between nodes on different interfaces and performing PAT?

    Answer: The PIX Firewall changes the local address and source port to a global address and random port, and generates a random initial TCP sequence number.

13. True or false: TCP is a much better protocol than UDP because it does handshakes and randomly generates TCP sequence numbers.

    Answer: False. Each transport protocol has its strengths and weaknesses. UDP is connectionless and has much less overhead than TCP, however TCP is more reliable.

14. What are the two commands (syntax) to perform Network Address Translation of all internal addresses?

    Answer:

    — LabPIX(config)# nat (inside) 1 0.0.0.0 0.0.0.0

    — LabPIX(config)# nat (inside) 1 0 0

15. When would you want to configure NAT and PAT for the same inside segment?

    Answer: You would want to configure NAT and PAT for the same inside segment when you have more internal users than addresses in the global pool. If you use only PAT, you limit all of your local addresses to a single global address.

16. What is RFC 1918?

    Answer: RFC 1918 defines specific address ranges that are not routable across the Internet. These addresses are reserved for private networks.

17. Why is there an *id* field in the **nat** command?

    Answer: The nat command has an *id* field so that the PIX Firewall can map a specific nat statement to a global statement.

Chapter 6

"Do I Know This Already?" Quiz

1. Which command tests connectivity?

    a. ping

    b. nameif

    c. ip address

    d. write terminal

    Answer: a

2. Which command saves the configuration you made on the Cisco PIX Firewall?

   a. write terminal

   b. show start-running config

   c. write memory

   d. save config

   Answer: c

3. Which command assigns security levels to interfaces on the PIX Firewall?

   a. ip address

   b. route

   c. nameif

   d. secureif

   Answer: c

4. Which command flushes the ARP cache of the PIX Firewall?

   a. flush arp cache

   b. no arp cache

   c. clear arp

   d. You cannot flush the ARP cache.

   Answer: c

5. Which of following configures a message when a firewall administrator enters the **enable** command?

   a. banner motd enter the enable password

   b. banner enable enter the enable password

   c. banner exec enter the enable password

   d. banner login enter the enable password

   Answer: c

6. Why would you want authentication enabled between the PIX and the NTP server?

   a. To ensure that the PIX does synchronize with an unauthorized NTP server

   b. To maintain the integrity of the communication

   c. To increase the speed of communication

   d. To reduce latency

   Answer: b

7. How do you access the enable mode?

   a. Enter the **enable** command and the enable password.

   b. Enter the **privilege** command and the privilege password.

   c. Enter the super-secret password.

   d. Enter only the **privilege** command.

   Answer: a

8. How do you view the current configuration on your PIX Firewall?

   a. show running-config

   b. show current

   c. write memory

   d. save config

   Answer: a

9. In a DHCP client configuration, what is the command to release and renew the IP address on the outside interface?

   a. ipconfig release

   a. ip address dhcp outside

   a. outside ip renew

   a. ip address renew outside

   Answer: b

Q&A

1. How do you access privileged mode?

   Answer: Enter the enable command and the enable password to access the privileged mode.

2. What is the function of the **nameif** command?

   Answer: The name if command is used to name a PIX Firewall interface and assign a security level.

3. Which six commands produce a basic working configuration for a Cisco PIX Firewall?

   Answer: The six commands that are used to create a very basic PIX configuration are nameif, interface, ip address, nat, global, and route.

4. Why is the **route** command important?

   Answer: The route command is important because it instructs the PIX Firewall where to send a packet that arrives at its interfaces.

5. What is the command to flush out the Address Resolution Protocol (ARP) cache on a Cisco PIX Firewall?

   Answer: clear arp

6. What is the syntax to configure a message-of-the-day (MOTD) banner that says, "System shall not be available on 18:00 Monday January 19th for 2 hours due to system maintenance"?

   Answer: First, enter the configuration mode on the PIX Firewall. Then enter the following command: banner motd System shall not be available on 18:00 Monday January 19th for 2 hours due to system maintenance.

7. What is the command used to configure PAT on the PIX Firewall?

   Answer: The NAT command, nat (*if-name*) *nat-id local-ip* [netmask], is used to configure PAT on the Cisco PIX Firewall.

8. Which command releases and renews an IP address on the PIX?

   Answer: ip address outside dhcp

9. Give at least one reason why it is beneficial to use NTP on the Cisco PIX Firewall.

    Answer: You can use NTP on the PIX Firewall (1) for certificate revocation lists (CRLs) because it is time stamp sensitive; and (2) because it makes troubleshooting events easier.

10. Why would you want to secure the NTP messages between the Cisco PIX Firewall and the NTP server?

    Answer: To prevent the Cisco PIX Firewall from synchronizing with unauthorized NTP servers.

Chapter 7

"Do I Know This Already?" Quiz

1. Which of the following are constraints when configuring policy NAT?

    a. A global address *can* be used concurrently for NAT and PAT.

    b. An access list must be used *only twice* with the **nat** command.

    c. Access lists for policy NAT *cannot* contain deny statements.

    d. An access list must be used only once with the **nat** command.

    Answer: c, d

2. What is the maximum number of access list entries in one access list that TurboACL supports?

    a. 19

    b. 2000

    c. 16,000

    d. 10

    Answer: c

3. What is the minimum number of access list entries needed in an access list for TurboACL to compile?

    a. 4

    b. 19

    c. 16,000

    d. No minimum is required.

    Answer: b

4. Which of the following is *not* one of four options for object types when you create an object group?

   a. Network

   b. Protocol

   c. Application

   d. Services

   Answer: c

5. Which command lets you create a network object group?

   a. **object-group network** *group-id*

   b. **enable object-group network** *group-id*

   c. **create network object-group**

   d. **network object-group enable**

   Answer: a

6. Which command enables TurboACL globally on the PIX Firewall?

   a. **turboacl global**

   b. **access-list compiled**

   c. **access-list turboacl**

   d. You cannot enable TurboACL globally.

   Answer: b

7. What is the minimum memory requirement for TurboACL to work?

   a. 8 MB

   b. 100 KB

   c. 2.1 MB

   d. 4 MB

   Answer: c

8. How many SMTP commands are made by the PIX application inspection function?

   a. 3

   b. 2

   c. 7

   d. 5

Answer: c

9. What will be the results if you disable FTP fixups?

   a. Nothing

   b. All inbound FTP is disabled.

   c. All outbound FTP is disabled.

   d. FTP traffic will be disabled in both directions.

Answer: b

10. Which of the following is the correct syntax for mapping an internal web server with an IP address of 10.10.10.15 to an outside IP address of 192.168.100.15 for HTTP traffic?

   a. static (inside, outside) 192.168.100.15 80 10.10.10.15 netmask 255.255.255.255 eq www

   b. static (inside, outside) 192.168.100.15 80 10.10.10.15 netmask 255.255.255.255

   c. static (inside, outside) tcp 192.168.100.15 80 10.10.10.15 www netmask 255.255.255.255

   d. static (inside, outside) 192.168.100.15 80 10.10.10.15 netmask 255.255.255.255

Answer: c

Q&A

1. What do static NAT settings do?

Answer: Static NAT creates a one-to-one mapping between a host/network on both the interfaces.

2. What is the difference between regular network address translation and policy-based network translation?

Answer: The Policy NAT feature lets you identify traffic for address translation by specifying the source and destination addresses (or ports) in an access list, whereas regular NAT uses only source addresses/ports.

3. Which command would you use to create the description/remark "Linda's group extranet server access" for access list 112?

   Answer: **access-list 112 remark Linda's group extranet server access**

4. About how many ACEs in one access list does TurboACL support?

   Answer: **16,000**

5. How would you change the default port assignment for FTP?

   Answer: **Use the fixup protocol ftp [*port*] command to change the default port assignment for FTP.**

6. What is the minimum memory required to run TurboACL?

   Answer: **2.1 MB**

7. What is the command to enable TurboACL globally on the PIX Firewall?

   Answer: **access-list compiled**

8. What is the minimum number of ACEs needed for TurboACL to compile?

   Answer: **19**

9. What is the function of object groups?

   Answer: **Object groups are used to group hosts/networks, services, protocols, and icmp-types. Object grouping provides a way to reduce the number of access rules required to describe complex security policies.**

10. What are the four object type options available when you are creating object groups?

    Answer: **network, protocol, service, and icmp-type**

Chapter 8

"Do I Know This Already?" Quiz

1. What is the command for sending syslog messages to the Telnet session?

    a. logging console

    b. logging monitor

    c. telnet logging

    d. send log telnet

    Answer: b

2. Which of the following is the correct command syntax to set the logging level to 5 for syslog message 403503?

    a. logging message 403503 level 5

    b. logging 403503 5

    c. logging message 403503 5

    d. logging 403503 level 5

    Answer: a

3. The PIX Firewall can be configured to send syslog messages to all of the following except which one?

    a. Console

    b. Telnet session

    c. Serial port

    d. Syslog server

    Answer: c

4. Which of the following is *not* an example of a severity level for syslog configuration?

    a. Emergency

    b. Alert

    c. Prepare

    d. Warning

    Answer: c

5. What is syslogd?

    a. A message type that forms the syslog services

    b. A service that runs on UNIX machines

    c. A hardware subcomponent that is required for syslog configuration on the PIX

    d. Cisco application software

    Answer: b

6. Which port does syslogd use by default?

    a. UDP 512

    b. TCP 514

    c. TCP 512

    d. UDP 514

    Answer: d

7. Which of the following logging severity levels are matched up correctly?

    a. Error → 4

    b. Alert → 2

    c. Warning → 4

    d. Notification → 1

    Answer: c

8. Which of the following is the highest-importance logging level?

    a. 9

    b. 7

    c. 0

    d. 3

    Answer: c

9. By using which command could you view the logging setting from the command line?

   a. show log setting

   b. show logging

   c. show syslog

   d. view log

   Answer: b

Q&A

1. What command would you use to view logs that are in memory?

   Answer: show logging buffered

2. On which port does syslogd listen by default?

   Answer: Syslogd listens on UDP port 514 by default.

3. What is the total number of logging facilities available for PIX Firewall syslog configuration?

   Answer: Eight logging facilities are commonly used for syslog—facilities 16 to 23.

4. What is the command for sending syslog messages to Telnet sessions?

   Answer: logging monitor

5. For what is the **logging trap** command used?

   Answer: The logging trap command determines which levels of syslog messages are sent to the syslog server.

6. What is the command used to enable logging on the failover PIX unit?

   Answer: logging standby

7. Why would you use the *timestamp* command parameter?

   Answer: The *timestamp* command parameter specifies timestamp values on the syslog messages sent to the syslog server for later analysis of the logs.

8. What is PFSS?

   Answer: The PIX Firewall Syslog Server (PFSS) is a Windows NT–based syslog server designed for use with the PIX Firewall.

Chapter 9

"Do I Know This Already?" Quiz

1. Which dynamic routing protocol(s) are supported by PIX Firewall Version 6.3?

    a. RIP

    b. OSPF

    c. BGP

    d. EIGRP

    e. Answers a and b

    Answer: e

2. Which command do you use to configure static routes?

    a. interface

    b. mroute

    c. route

    d. static

    e. None of the above

    Answer: c

3. Which command do you use to configure the PIX Firewall to statically receive a multicast session?

    a. **igmp forward**

    b. **igmp static**

    c. **multicast static**

    d. **igmp join-group**

    e. None of the above

    Answer: d

4. What type of Ethernet VLAN tagging does the PIX Firewall support?

   a. ISL

   b. 802.1x

   c. 802.1q

   d. 802.3

   e. None of the above

   Answer: c

5. IP multicasting is a technique that

   a. consumes more network bandwidth by sending IP traffic to multiple hosts on the network.

   b. enables the PIX Firewall to communicate with multiple hosts on the network.

   c. sends traffic to specific Class C IP addresses.

   d. sends traffic to specific Class D IP addresses, thus enabling multiple recipients to receive the same traffic stream.

   e. None of the above

   Answer: d

6. Which of the following is true with respect to PIX Firewall RIP support?

   a. RIP routing updates cannot be propagated by the PIX Firewall.

   b. The PIX Firewall can advertise a default route.

   c. Authentication is supported only for RIP version 2.

   d. Answers a, b, and c

   e. None of the above

   Answer: d

7. Which PIX Firewall command do you use to create logical interfaces?

   a. interface

   b. nameif

   c. logical

   d. static

   e. None of the above

   Answer: a

8. Which PIX command enables you to configure the security level for logical interfaces?

    a. static

    b. interface

    c. nameif

    d. logical

    e. None of the above

    Answer: c

9. Which OSPF subcommand defines which Type 3 LSA traffic to filter?

    a. network

    b. area

    c. router ospf

    d. prefix-list

    e. access-list

    Answer: d

10. The PIX Firewall can propagate which types of routes?

    a. BGP

    b. OSPF

    c. RIP

    d. Static

    e. None of the above

    Answer: b

Q&A

1. What type of Ethernet tagging does the PIX Firewall support?

    Answer: The PIX Firewall supports 802.1Q tagging.

2. Which command do you use to configure logical interfaces?

    Answer: You use the interface command to define one or more logical interfaces on a single physical interface.

3. What three basic configuration parameters do you need to define for each logical interface?

    Answer: For each logical interface, you need to define an interface name, a VLAN id, a security level, and an IP address.

4. What command do you use to define static routes on the PIX Firewall?

    Answer: The route command enables you to define static routes on the PIX Firewall.

5. What is the default route and what values do you use for the IP address and netmask when creating the default route?

    Answer: The default route is a static route that is used when no other route matches the specified destination address. When configuring the default route, you use 0.0.0.0 for both the destination IP address and the network mask.

6. The PIX Firewall provides functionality for which two routing protocols?

    Answer: The PIX Firewall provides functionality for both RIP and OSPF.

7. Can the PIX Firewall propagate RIP routes?

    Answer: The PIX Firewall only passively listens to RIP routing updates. It cannot propagate this information to other devices. It can, however, advertise a default route for one of its interfaces.

8. Which LSAs can the PIX Firewall filter, and why is this important?

    Answer: OSPF routes are advertised to all the interfaces configured for OSPF. This can send information about private networks to public interfaces. Therefore, you can filter Type 3 LSAs to prevent the public interfaces from receiving information on private networks.

9. Which two commands enable you to configure LSA filtering?

    Answer: The prefix-list command defines which advertisements are permitted and which advertisements are not permitted (denied). The area command then applies this prefix list to a specific OSPF area.

10. What are the steps involved in setting up OSPF on your PIX Firewall?

    Answer: To set up OSPF, you must first enable OSPF. Next, you define the PIX Firewall interfaces that will run OSPF. Finally, you define the OSPF areas. Optionally, you may need to configure LSA filtering to protect private addresses.

11. Can the PIX Firewall operate as a fully functional multicast router?

Answer: **The PIX Firewall cannot operate as a fully functional multicast router, but it can operate as a Stub Multicast Router (SMR), in which case it proxies all IGMP requests to the actual multicast router.**

12. If you have clients that cannot send IGMP messages, which command do you use to statically configure the PIX Firewall to receive messages from a multicast group?

Answer: **To statically configure the PIX Firewall to join a multicast group, you use the igmp join-group command that is available as a subcommand to the multicast interface command.**

13. What is the range of addresses for multicast traffic?

Answer: **Multicast traffic uses Class D addresses in the range of 224.0.0.0 through 239.255.255.255.**

14. If the multicast transmission source is protected by the PIX Firewall, which command do you use to configure the PIX Firewall to allow clients to access it?

Answer: **When the multicast traffic is coming from a protected network behind the PIX Firewall, you need to use the mroute command to statically configure routes for the multicast traffic to the next hop.**

15. Which two commands can you use to view the multicast configuration on the PIX Firewall?

Answer: **To view the multicast configuration on the PIX Firewall, you can use the show multicast command to display multicast settings for one or more interfaces. The show igmp command displays information about one or more IGMP groups, and the show mroute command shows the current multicast routes.**

16. Which command enables you to view the routes currently in use on the PIX Firewall?

Answer: **The show route command enables you to view the routes currently being used by the PIX Firewall.**

17. Which command enables you to pass OSPF routing information between multiple OSPF domains or processes?

Answer: **The redistribute ospf command enables you to pass OSPF routes between multiple OSPF processes on your PIX Firewall.**

18. Why would you run multiple OSPF processes on your PIX Firewall?

    Answer: When you are using your PIX Firewall as an ASBR OSPF router using multiple interfaces, you need to use two OSPF processes if you want to perform address filtering.

Chapter 10

"Do I Know This Already?" Quiz

1. Which of the following causes a failover event?

   a. A reboot or power interruption on the active PIX Firewall

   b. Low HTTP traffic on the outside interface

   c. Issuance of the **failover active** command on the standby PIX Firewall

   d. Low memory utilization for several consecutive seconds

   Answer: a

2. What is the command to view failover configuration?

   a. show failover

   b. failover

   c. view failover

   d. show me failover

   Answer: a

3. Which of the following is/are replicated in stateful failover operation?

   a. Configuration

   b. TCP connection table, including timeout information for each connection

   c. Translation (xlate) table

   d. Negotiated H.323 UDP protocols

   e. All of the above

   Answer: e

4. Which of the following is *not* replicated in stateful failover operation?

   a. User authentication (uauth) table

   b. ISAKMP and IPSec SA table

   c. ARP table

   d. Routing information

   e. All of the above

   Answer: e

5. What is the command to force configuration replication to the standby unit?

   a. write standby

   b. copy to secondary

   c. force secondary

   d. force conf

   Answer: a

6. Which of the following is a stateful failover hardware restriction?

   a. The stateful failover configuration is supported only by PIX Firewall 535 models.

   b. Only fiber connections can be used in a stateful failover hardware configuration.

   c. A PIX Firewall with two FDDI cards cannot use stateful failover, because an additional FDDI interface is not supported.

   d. There is no hardware restriction for stateful failover configuration.

   Answer: c

7. What command assigns an IP address to the standby Cisco PIX Firewall?

   a. secondary ip address *ip address*

   b. failover ip address *if-name ip-address*

   c. ip address *ip address* secondary

   d. ip address *ip address* failover

   Answer: b

8. What is the command to configure a LAN-based failover?

   a. conf lan failover

   b. failover ip LAN

   c. failover lan interface *if-name*

   d. lan interface failover

   Answer: c

9. What is an advantage of a LAN-based failover?

   a. It quickly fails over to a peer when a power failure on the active unit takes place.

   b. It does not have the 6-foot-cable distance limitation for failover communication.

   c. It is preconfigured on the PIX Firewall.

   d. All of the above

   Answer: b

10. What is the default failover poll, in seconds?

    a. 10 seconds

    b. 15 seconds

    c. 30 seconds

    d. 25 seconds

    Answer: b

11. Which of the following is true about the serial link cable connection in a PIX Firewall failover configuration?

    a. Serial link cable can transfer data at 100 Mbps.

    b. The two units maintain the heartbeat network over the cable.

    c. Network link status is not communicated over the serial link.

    d. Keepalive packets and configuration replication are communicated over the serial link.

    Answer: b

Q&A

1. What are some things that trigger a failover event?

   Answer: A failover event may be triggered by a loss of power, cable error, memory exhaustion, or an administrator forcing the standby.

2. What command assigns an IP address to the standby PIX Firewall?

   Answer: The failover ip address *if-name ip-address* command assigns an IP address to the standby PIX Firewall.

3. How many PIX Firewall devices can be configured in a failover configuration?

   Answer: Two PIX Firewall devices can be configured in a failover configuration.

4. What are the disadvantages of LAN-based failover?

   Answer: The following are the disadvantages of LAN-based failover:

   — The PIX Firewall takes longer to fail because it cannot immediately detect the loss of power of the standby unit.

   — The switch between the two units can be another point of hardware failure.

   — A separate interface is required for the failover link, which otherwise could have been used for normal traffic.

5. What is some of the information that is updated to the standby unit in a stateful failover configuration?

   Answer: The following is some information that is updated to the standby unit in a stateful failover configuration: TCP connection table; translation table (xlate); negotiated H.323 UDP ports; port allocation table bitmap for PAT; SIP; HTTP sessions; and MGCP UDP media connections.

6. What command forces replication to the standby unit?

   Answer: The write standby command forces replication to the standby unit.

7. What command configures a LAN-based failover?

   Answer: The failover lan interface *interface-name* command configures a LAN-based failover.

8. What is the default failover poll, in seconds?

   Answer: The default failover poll is 15 seconds.

9. Does configuration replication save the running configuration to Flash memory on the standby unit during normal operations?

Answer: No, the running configuration is only stored in memory on the active unit. When a "write memory" command issued on the active unit, configuration replication causes the changes to the current configuration to be saved on the standby unit.

10. How long does it take to detect a failure?

Answer: Network and failover communication errors are detected within two consecutive polling intervals (by default, 15-second intervals).

Chapter 11

"Do I Know This Already?" Quiz

1. Which type of encryption is stronger?

   a. Group 2 Diffie-Hellman

   b. AES-128

   c. 3DES

   d. AES-192

   e. DES

   Answer: d

2. Which service uses UDP port 500?

   a. IPSec

   b. OAKLEY

   c. IKE

   d. None of the above

   Answer: c

3. Which service uses TCP port 50?

   a. IKE

   b. AH

   c. OAKLEY

   d. ESP

   e. None of the above

   Answer: e

4. What is the size of the output for a MD5 hash?

    a. There is no fixed size.

    b. 256 bits

    c. 255 bits

    d. 128 bits

    e. None of the above

    Answer: d

5. What is the most scalable VPN solution?

    a. **Manual-ipsec** with CAs

    b. IKE using OAKLEY

    c. IKE using CAs

    d. CAs using preshared keys

    e. None of the above

    Answer: c

6. What is the function of the access list with regard to VPNs?

    a. It tells the PIX what traffic should be allowed.

    b. It tells the PIX what traffic should be encrypted.

    c. It tells the PIX what traffic should be denied.

    d. None of the above

    Answer: b

7. What is the configuration value for the unlimited ISAKMP phase 1 lifetime?

    a. Unlim

    b. 99999

    c. 86400

    d. 19200

    e. 0

    Answer: e

8. The X509v3 standard applies to which standard or protocol?

    a. Authentication Header format

    b. ESP header format

    c. Digital certificates

    d. Diffie-Hellman negotiation

    e. AES encryption

    Answer: c

9. What are three types of VPNs?

    a. Hardware, software, and concentrator

    b. Manual, dynamic, and very secure

    c. Dialup, cable, and LAN

    d. Access, intranet, and extranet

    e. Internet, extranet, and dialup

    Answer: d

10. What command will allow you to watch the IKE negotiations?

    a. **debug isakmp sa**

    b. **debug crypto isakmp**

    c. **view isakmp neg**

    d. **view crypto isakmp**

    e. **debug isakmp crypto**

    Answer: b

Q&A

1. Why is **manual-ipsec** not recommended by Cisco?

    Answer: The session keys are manually coded and never change.

2. What is the difference between an access VPN and an intranet VPN?

    Answer: Access VPNs require VPN client software on the remote machine and intranet VPNs do not.

3. Which hash algorithm is configured by default for phase 1?

   Answer: **SHA-1**

4. What are the two methods of identifying SA peers?

   Answer: **By IP address or host name**

5. What happens if you have different ISAKMP policies configured on your potential SA peers, and none of them match?

   Answer: **They will not be able to negotiate the connection.**

6. Where do you define your authentication method?

   Answer: **isakmp policy**

7. What is the default lifetime if not defined in **isakmp policy**?

   Answer: **86,400 seconds**

8. Do your transform sets have to match exactly on each peer?

   Answer: **No, the peers will continue to go through the transforms until they find a match. If there is no match, they will be unable to negotiate the connection.**

9. What is the difference between the **isakmp** lifetime and the **crypto map** lifetime?

   Answer: **isakmp lifetime initiates a renegotiation of IKE based on time only; the crypto map lifetime initiates a renegotiation of the IPSec SA based on time or the amount of traffic the passes through the connection (in kilobytes).**

10. What command do you use to delete any active SAs?

    Answer: **clear crypto isakmp sa**

11. What is the command for defining a preshared key?

    Answer: **isakmp key** *string* **address** *peer-address* **netmask** *peer netmask*

12. What is the first thing you should check if you are unable to establish a VPN?

    Answer: **You should verify connectivity prior to attempting to establish the VPN. If you have connectivity but cannot establish the VPN, you should verify that the configuration of the peers matches.**

13. What is the command to apply an access list to a crypto map?

    Answer: crypto map *map-name seq-num* match address *acl-name*

14. What is the difference between ESP and AH?

    Answer: AH does only header authentication; ESP can perform authentication of the header and the data as well as encryption.

Chapter 12

"Do I Know This Already?" Quiz

1. What is the Easy VPN Server functionality known as *Initial Contact*?

   a. Ability to cause the Easy VPN Server to delete any existing connections, thus preventing SA synchronization problems

   b. The first connection between an Easy VPN Client and Easy VPN Server

   c. The initial message sent from the Easy VPN Server to the Easy VPN Client

   d. The initial message sent from the Easy VPN Client to the Easy VPN Server

   e. None of the above

   Answer: a

2. Which of the following platforms does not support the Easy VPN Remote feature functionality?

   a. 800 Series routers

   b. 900 Series routers

   c. 7200 Series routers

   d. 1700 Series routers

   e. None of the above

   Answer: c

3. Which two IKE authentication mechanisms do the Easy VPN Remote Clients support? (Choose two.)

    a. Username/password

    b. Preshared keys

    c. Diffie-Hellman

    d. Digital certificates

    e. XAUTH

    Answer: d

4. How many different operation modes does the Easy VPN Remote feature support?

    a. 1

    b. 4

    c. 2

    d. 3

    e. None of the above

    Answer: c

5. In which Easy VPN Remote mode are the IP addresses of the remote systems visible on the Easy VPN Server network?

    a. Client mode

    b. Network extension mode

    c. Server mode

    d. No Easy VPN Remote modes support this functionality.

    e. All Easy VPN Remote modes

    Answer: b

6. The Cisco VPN Software Client supports which key management techniques?

    a. IKE main mode

    b. IKE aggressive mode

    c. Diffie-Hellman groups 1, 2, 5, and 7

    d. Answers a and b

    e. Answers a, b, and c

    Answer: e

7. What is Secure Unit Authentication (SUA)?

   a. The ability to require the hosts on the remote protected network to be authenticated individually based on the IP address of the inside host

   b. The ability to require one-time passwords, two-factor authentication, and similar authentication schemes before the establishment of a VPN tunnel to the Easy VPN Server

   c. An authentication mechanism between the remote systems and the Easy VPN Remote Client

   d. An authentication mechanism that the Cisco VPN Software Client uses to connect with the Easy VPN Remote feature

   e. None of the above

Answer: b

8. Which authentication mechanisms are supported with PPPoE?

   a. PAP

   b. CHAP

   c. MS-CHAP

   d. Answers a and b

   e. Answers a, b, and c

Answer: e

9. Which command enables the PIX Firewall to pass configuration parameters learned from a DHCP server to its DHCP clients?

   a. dhcpd auto_config

   b. dhcpd option 150

   c. dhcpd address

   d. dhcpd bind

   e. None of the above

Answer: a

10. Which of the following is false with regard to the PIX Firewall?

    a. You can pass configuration parameters learned from the DHCP client to the PIX's DHCP clients.

    b. You can pass configuration parameters learned from the PPPoE client to the PIX's DHCP clients.

    c. You can enable the DHCP client and the DHCP server simultaneously.

    d. You can enable the PPPoE client and the DHCP client on the same interface simultaneously.

    e. All of the statements are true.

    Answer: d

Q&A

1. Which two major components comprise the Easy VPN solution?

    Answer: The Easy VPN comprises Easy VPN Server and Easy VPN Remote feature.

2. Which three types of devices can serve as Easy VPN Servers?

    Answer: You can use PIX Firewalls, Cisco VPN 3000 Series Concentrators, and Cisco IOS® routers as Easy VPN Servers.

3. What is DPD?

    Answer: DPD enables two IPSec peers to determine if the other is still "alive" during the lifetime of the VPN connection.

4. What is Initial Contact?

    Answer: Initial Contact enables the VPN Client to send an initial message that informs the gateway to ignore and delete any existing connections from that client, thus preventing connection problems caused by SA synchronization issues.

5. Which client platforms support the Easy VPN Remote feature?

    Answer: The Easy VPN Remote feature is supported on the Cisco VPN Software Client, Cisco VPN 3002 Hardware Client, Cisco PIX 501 and 506/506E VPN Clients, and Cisco Easy VPN Remote router clients.

6. Which router platforms can be used as Cisco Easy VPN Clients?

    Answer: The 800 Series routers, 900 Series routers, and 1700 Series routers can serve as Cisco Easy VPN Remote clients.

7. What are the six major steps that occur when the Easy VPN Remote client initiates a connection with the Easy VPN Server gateway?

    Answer: When the Easy VPN Remote client initiates a connection with the Easy VPN Server, it goes through the following six steps: (1) VPN Client initiates the IKE phase 1 process; (2) VPN Client negotiates an IKE SA; (3) Easy VPN Server accepts the SA proposal; (4) the Easy VPN Server initiates a username/password challenge; (5) mode configuration process is initiated; and (6) IKE quick mode completes the connection.

8. When initiating the VPN connection, the client can use which two IKE authentication mechanisms?

    Answer: When initiating the VPN connection, the client can use preshared keys and digital certificates for IKE authentication.

9. What is XAUTH?

    Answer: Extended authentication (XAUTH) enables the Easy VPN Server to require username/password authentication (performed by a AAA server) in order to establish the VPN connection.

10. Which two modes of operation does the Easy VPN Remote support?

    Answer: The Easy VPN Remote supports client mode and network extension mode.

11. In which Easy VPN Remote mode are the addresses of the remote system visible on the Easy VPN Server network?

    Answer: When operating in network extension mode, the remote system addresses are visible on the Easy VPN Server network. In client mode, PAT is used on the Easy VPN Remote client so the remote system addresses are not visible.

12. What feature enables the Cisco VPN Software Client to be simple to deploy and manage?

    Answer: The ability to push VPN access policies automatically from the Easy VPN Server to the Cisco VPN Software Client simplifies deployment and management.

13. Which encryption algorithms are supported by the Cisco VPN Software Client?

    Answer: The Cisco VPN Software Client supports DES, 3DES, and AES (128- and 256-bit) encryption algorithms.

14. What is SUA?

Answer: Secure Unit Authentication (SUA) enables the Easy VPN Remote server to require one-time passwords, two-factor authentication, and similar authentication schemes before the establishment of a VPN tunnel to the Easy VPN Server.

15. What is IUA?

Answer: Individual User Authentication (IUA) causes the hosts on the remote protected network to be individually authenticated based on the IP address of the inside host.

16. What is PPPoE?

Answer: Point-to-Point Protocol over Ethernet (PPPoE) provides an authenticated method for assigning IP addresses to client systems over broadband connections by combining PPP and Ethernet.

17. What type of DHCP functionality does the PIX Firewall (Version 5.2 or later) provide?

Answer: Any PIX Firewall (Version 5.2 or later) provides both DHCP server and DHCP client functionality. As a DHCP server, the PIX Firewall provides hosts protected by the firewall with the network parameters necessary for them to access the enterprise or corporate network. As a DHCP client, the PIX Firewall can obtain its own IP address and network mask and, optionally, a default route from the DHCP server.

18. Which command enables you to configure the PIX Firewall to pass configuration parameters learned by using either PPPoE or DHCP to its DHCP clients?

Answer: To enable the PIX Firewall to pass the learned DHCP configuration parameters automatically to its DHCP clients, you use the dhcpd auto_config command.

Chapter 13

"Do I Know This Already?" Quiz

1. How many tabs does PDM have under its Configuration button?

a. Three

b. Five

c. Eight

d. Six

Answer: b

2. How do you connect to PDM?

    a. By accessing the PIX Firewall through Telnet and entering PDM

    b. By entering http://inside_interface_ip in your browser

    c. By entering https://inside_interface_ip in your browser

    d. By entering https://PIX_PDM in your browser

    Answer: c

3. What version of PIX Firewall software is required for PDM 3.0 to run?

    a. 6.1

    b. 5.2

    c. 6.3

    d. 6.0

    Answer: c

4. Which model of the PIX Firewall does PDM support?

    a. 515

    b. 525

    c. 535

    d. All of the above

    Answer: d

5. Where does PDM reside?

    a. On a Windows NT/2000 server

    b. On a Red Hat Linux 7.0 server

    c. On a Solaris server

    d. In the PIX Flash memory

    Answer: d

6. What default security mechanism does PDM employ for browsers to connect to it?

   a. RSA

   b. Biometrics

   c. MD5

   d. SSL

   Answer: d

7. Which of the following is a prerequisite for access rules to be created?

   a. Hosts or networks must be defined before access rule creation.

   b. Dynamic or static translation must be defined before access rule creation.

   c. There are no prerequisites.

   d. Answers a and b

   Answer: d

8. What is a translation exemption rule?

   a. A rule that exempts addresses from being encrypted or translated

   b. A rule that denies access to addresses

   c. A rule that increases security on selected addresses

   d. None of the above

   Answer: a

9. What is the optimum configuration file size to use with PDM?

   a. 100 KB

   b. 1500 KB

   c. 110 MB

   d. 25 KB

   Answer: a

10. Which of the following is required to access PDM?

    a. Cisco Secure access control server

    b. Transport Layer Security (TLS) enabled

    c. JavaScript and Java enabled on the browser

    d. A VPN connection to the PIX Firewall

    Answer: c

Q&A

1. When reading an existing configuration using PDM, what three situations can cause access rules to become null?

Answer: When reading in an existing configuration (using PDM), access rules can become null for 1) a rule for inbound traffic that does not have a static translation, 2) a rule for outbound traffic that is not NATed, and 3) a rule that has no hosts or networks defined for either the source or destination.

2. What is a translation exemption rule?

Answer: A translation exemption rule specifies traffic that is exempt from being translated.

3. What are the three main buttons on the PIX PDM?

Answer: The three main PDM button are Home, Configuration, and Monitoring.

4. How do you access PDM?

Answer: PDM is accessed via a web browser using SSL. (For instance https://interface IP where interface IP represents the IP address of a PIX Firewall interface that has been configured to allow HTTP access using the http *local_ip [mask] [interface]* command.

5. What version of PIX Firewall software is required to run PDM Version 3.0?

Answer: PIX Firewall Version 6.3 or later is required to run PDM 3.0.

6. Which models of Cisco PIX Firewall are supported by PDM?

Answer: PIX 501, 506/506E, 515/515E, 520, 525, and 535 are supported by PDM.

7. What versions of Windows does PDM support?

Answer: Windows XP, Windows 98, and Windows 2000 are supported by PDM.

8. Where does PDM reside?

   Answer: **PDM resides in the PIX Flash memory.**

9. What is the quickest method to configure site-to-site VPN using PDM?

   Answer: **The quickest method to configure site-to-site VPN using PDM is to use the VPN Wizard.**

10. What is the command to install or upgrade PDM on the PIX Firewall?

    Answer: **The copy tftp flash:pdm command is used to install or upgrade PDM on the PIX Firewall.**

Chapter 14

"Do I Know This Already?" Quiz

1. Which of the following are types of building blocks? (Choose two.)

   a. Network objects

   b. Address translation pools

   c. Access rules

   d. Static translation rules

   e. Dynamic translation rules

   Answer: a, b

2. What are the three types of access rules?

   a. Firewall rules

   b. Static translation rules

   c. AAA rules

   d. Dynamic translation rules

   e. Filter rules

   Answer: a, c, e

3. What are the three reports supported by Firewall MC?

    a. Device Report

    b. Activity Report

    c. Configuration Differences report

    d. Device Setting Report

    e. Deployment reports

    Answer: b, c, d

4. When making changes to device configurations in Firewall MC, the changes can apply to which firewalls?

    a. A single firewall

    b. The firewalls in a group

    c. All of the managed firewalls

    d. Firewalls belonging to multiple groups

    e. Answers a, b, and c

    Answer: e

5. Which software manages login access to the Firewall MC?

    a. CiscoWorks

    b. Firewall MC

    c. Windows OS

    d. Auto Update Server

    e. None of the above

    Answer: a

6. Firewall MC groups comprise which items? (Choose two.)

    a. Configuration lists

    b. Devices

    c. Subgroups

    d. Software images

    e. Access lists

    Answer: b, c

7. What are the three steps involved in updating device configurations when workflow is enabled?

   a. Define, deploy, review

   b. Define, test, evaluate

   c. Create, test, review

   d. Define, approve, deploy

   e. None of the above

   Answer: d

8. Which of the following is not an option when importing devices into Firewall MC?

   a. Import configuration file for a device

   b. Import configuration file for multiple devices

   c. Import configuration from PDM

   d. Create firewall device

   e. Import configuration from device

   Answer: c

9. Which of the following is not a configuration tab in AUS?

   a. Devices

   b. Deployment

   c. Images

   d. Assignments

   e. Admin

   Answer: b

10. Which translation rules define a permanent mapping between an internal IP address and a public IP address?

    a. Dynamic translation rules

    b. AAA rules

    c. Web filter rules

    d. Static translation rules

    e. None of the above

    Answer: d

Q&A

1. Which software performs user authentication for Firewall MC and AUS?

    Answer: CiscoWorks Common Services provides the user authentication for both Firewall MC and AUS.

2. Which type of building block enables you to associate multiple protocols with a single name?

    Answer: Service groups enable you to associate multiple protocols with a single name.

3. What types of translation rules can you configure in Firewall MC?

    Answer: Firewall MC enables you to configure static translation rules, dynamic translation rules, and translation exception rules (NAT 0 ACL).

4. What types of access rules does Firewall MC enable you to configure?

    Answer: Through Firewall MC, you can configure firewall rules, AAA rules, and web filter rules.

5. What types of images does AUS support?

    Answer: AUS supports PIX Firewall software images, PDM software images, and PIX configuration files.

6. Which images can you not add directly through the AUS interface?

    Answer: You cannot add PIX configuration files directly through the AUS interface. They must be deployed from Firewall MC.

7. Which type of translation rule defines a permanent mapping between private IP addresses and public IP addresses?

    Answer: Static translation rules define a permanent mapping between private IP addresses and public IP addresses.

8. What is an address translation pool?

    Answer: Address translation pools enable you to associate a name with a group of addresses that will be used to create dynamic address translations for outbound traffic.

9. What is a network object?

    Answer: A network object associates a name with a range of network addresses, which are specified by an IP address and a network mask.

10.   What are three of the device settings that you can configure through Firewall MC?

Answer: Through Firewall MC, you can configure the following device settings: PIX operating system version, interfaces, failover, routing, PIX Firewall administration, logging, servers and services, advanced security, and Firewall MC controls.

11.   What type of building block do you need to define to create a dynamic translation rule?

Answer: To create a dynamic translation rule, you must first define an address translation pool that specifies the addresses to be used for the dynamic translation.

12.   What is workflow?

Answer: Workflow enables you to require approval for configuration changes and deployment operations. This enables you to divide the responsibility of updating firewall configurations between multiple people. Configuration changes become activities, and deploying those activities becomes jobs.

13.   Can AUS be used to manage firewalls that use dynamic addresses assigned by DHCP?

Answer: AUS can manage firewalls with dynamic addresses because the managed firewalls initiate the communication with the AUS server.

14.   What building blocks can you configure with Firewall MC, and how are they used?

Answer: Firewall MC supports the following types of building blocks: network objects, service definitions, service groups, AAA server groups, and address translation pools. Building blocks enable you to optimize your configuration. Basically, you can use the names of the building blocks in place of corresponding data values when configuring device settings or defining rules.

15.   What three reports does Firewall MC support?

Answer: Firewall MC supports Activity Reports, Configuration Differences reports, and Device Setting Reports.

16.   Name the three possible methods from which each device setting in a managed configuration can be derived.

Answer: Each device setting in a managed configuration can either be inherited, mandatory, or overridden.

17. What are the four steps used to import a device into Firewall MC?

   Answer: The four steps used to import a device into Firewall MC are as follows: select the target group, select the import type, define the firewall basic information, and review the device details.

18. What are the steps required to add images to AUS?

   Answer: The steps involved in adding an image to AUS are as follows: download the image file, and add the image to AUS.

Chapter 15

"Do I Know This Already?" Quiz

1. How does the PIX Firewall filter Java applets and ActiveX objects?

   a. By commenting out the <OBJECT> </OBJECT> tags or the <APPLET> </APPLET> tags in the HTML page.

   b. By deleting the <OBJECT CLASSID> </OBJECT> tags or the <APPLET> </APPLET> tags in the HTML page.

   c. It notifies the content-filtering server, which in turn disables the ActiveX objects and Java applets.

   d. The PIX Firewall does not filter ActiveX objects or Java applets.

   Answer: a

2. What is the command to designate or identify the URL-filtering server?

   a. filter url-server

   b. url-server

   c. filtering server

   d. server url

   Answer: b

3. What is the longest URL length supported by Cisco PIX Firewall Version 6.2 with Websense Enterprise URL-filtering software?

   a. 12 KB

   b. 15 KB

   c. 4 KB

   d. 6 KB

   Answer: d

4. What is the command to filter URLs?

   a. **filter url**

   b. **url-filter**

   c. **url-server**

   d. **filter web page**

   Answer: a

5. What happens when the only URL-filtering server is unavailable?

   a. If the **allow** option is set, the PIX Firewall forwards HTTP traffic without filtering.

   b. SMTP traffic is dropped because the URL-filtering server is unavailable.

   c. HTTP requests are queued until the URL-filtering server is available.

   d. The PIX Firewall reverts to the onboard URL-filtering engine to filter HTTP traffic.

   Answer: a

6. What is the default port used by the N2H2 server to communicate with the Cisco PIX Firewall?

   a. TCP/UDP 1272

   b. TCP 5004 only

   c. TCP/UDP 4005

   d. UDP 5004 only

   Answer: c

7. What command identifies N2H2 servers on a Cisco PIX Firewall?

   a. **websense url** filter *server-ip*

   b. **filter url** *server-ip* **vendor n2h2**

   c. **url-server** (*if-name*) **vendor n2h2 host** *local-ip*

   d. All of the above

   Answer: c

8. How many URL servers can be configured on a single Cisco PIX Firewall?

   a. 5

   b. 12

   c. 3

   d. 16

   Answer: d

9. What command disables URL caching on the Cisco PIX Firewall?

   a. **no url-cache**

   b. **caching-url**

   c. **disable url-cache**

   d. None of the above

   Answer: a

10. Which of the following URL-filtering servers supports FTP and HTTPS filtering?

    a. N2H2

    b. Cisco Works

    c. Websense

    d. CSACS

    Answer: c

Q&A

1. With what two URL-filtering servers does the PIX Firewall work?

   Answer: The PIX Firewall works with the Websense Enterprise and N2H2 Sentian servers.

2. What command filters out Java applets from HTML pages?

Answer: The filter java port *local-ip local-mask foreign-ip foreign-mask* command filters out Java applets form HTML pages.

3. Why are Java applets and ActiveX objects considered a threat?

Answer: Java applets and ActiveX objects are considered a threat because they can be used to execute malicious tasks on the network and the local machine.

4. How does the Cisco PIX Firewall filter Java applets and ActiveX objects?

Answer: Java and ActiveX filtering of HTML files is performed by selectively replacing the <APPLET> </APPLET> tags and the <OBJECT CLASSID> </OBJECT CLASSID> tags with comments.

5. What is the command to designate or identify the URL-filtering server?

Answer: The command to designate or identify the URL-filtering server is url-server.

6. Which PIX Firewall version supports the Websense URL-filtering server?

Answer: Cisco PIX Firewall Version 5.3 and later support the Websense URL-filtering server.

7. What is the longest URL filter, in bytes, that is possible with Cisco PIX Firewall Version 6.1 and earlier?

Answer: The longest URL filter that is possible with Cisco PIX Firewall Version 6.1 and earlier is 1159 bytes.

8. What is the longest URL filter that is supported by Cisco PIX Firewall 6.2?

Answer: The longest URL filter supported by Cisco PIX Firewall 6.2 is 6 KB.

9. What is the command to filter URLs?

Answer: The command to filter URLs is filter url.

10. How would you configure the PIX Firewall to buffer the response from a web server if its response is faster than that from the N2H2 or Websense URL-filtering server on the PIX Firewall?

Answer: The url-cache command provides a configuration option to buffer the response from web servers that respond faster than the available URL-filtering servers.

Chapter 16

"Do I Know This Already?" Quiz

1. Which platform does Cisco Secure ACS for Windows Version 3.2 currently support?

    a. Windows XP Professional

    b. Windows 2000 Server

    c. Windows NT Workstation

    d. Windows 2000 Professional

    Answer: b

2. What is a new feature of Cisco Secure ACS for Windows Version 3.2?

    a. A password generator

    b. A password database

    c. Additional configuration steps for your Cisco IOS Network Access Server

    d. New graphics and tables

    Answer: c

3. If you are installing Cisco Secure ACS 3.2 for Windows and do not understand a configuration option, what should you do?

    a. Check the explanation page.

    b. Push F7 for help.

    c. Select the About Cisco Secure ACS drop-down option.

    d. Open a case with Cisco TAC.

    Answer: a

4. Which of the following are *not* connection types for authenticating to a PIX Firewall? (Select all that apply.)

    a. Telnet

    b. SSH

    c. FTP

    d. HTTPS

    Answer: b, d

5. When installing Cisco Secure ACS Version 3.2 for Windows, you have the option to authenticate users against an existing user database. Which database can you check?

   a. A currently configured Cisco Secure ACS

   b. Any RADIUS server on the network

   c. The primary domain controller (PDC)

   d. The Windows user database

   Answer: d

6. What access does cut-through proxy allow a user after they have successfully authenticated?

   a. Access to anything on the network

   b. Access only to web servers

   c. Access based on the user profile (authorization)

   d. Access only to the Cisco Secure ACS

   Answer: c

7. What options are available to authenticate users on a PIX Firewall?

   a. Local user database

   b. Remote RADIUS server

   c. Remote TACACS+ server

   d. All of the above

   e. None of the above

   Answer: d

8. What technologies does the Cisco Secure ACS use to communicate with the NAS? (Choose two.)

   a. TACACS

   b. RADIUS

   c. TACACS+

   d. RADIUS+

   e. Virtual Telnet

   Answer: b, c

9. What does the Cisco Secure ACS consider the PIX Firewall to be (i.e., what is it referred to as, during configuration of the Cisco Secure ACS)?

   a. A perimeter security device

   b. A Network Access Server

   c. Cisco Secure ACS does not work with the PIX Firewall.

   d. None of the above

   Answer: b

Q&A

1. What is the relationship between the Cisco PIX Firewall and the AAA server?

   Answer: The Cisco PIX Firewall acts as the AAA client to the Cisco Secure ACS (AAA Server). Although the PIX Firewall acts as the AAA client, it is referred to as the network access server (NAS) when configuring the Cisco Secure ACS.

2. What three methods are used to authenticate to the Cisco PIX Firewall?

   Answer: HTTP, Telnet, and FTP are the three methods used to authenticate to the Cisco PIX Firewall.

3. How does the Cisco PIX Firewall process cut-through proxy?

   Answer: The user connects to the PIX Firewall using HTTP, FTP, or Telnet, and the PIX Firewall either authenticates to a local database or forwards the authentication request to the AAA server. After the authentication is completed, the PIX Firewall allows whatever connection is authorized by the rulebase for that user.

4. What are the main differences between RADIUS and TACACS+?

   Answer: RADIUS is connectionless and combines the authentication components. TACACS+ is connection-oriented and sends the authentication and authorization separately.

5. What patch level must you have Windows 2000 Professional configured to before you install Cisco Secure ACS?

   Answer: Trick question . . . Cisco Secure ACS must be installed on Windows 2000 Server.

6. Why is it important to authenticate a user before you complete authorization?

   Answer: Permissions can be assigned only after the user account has been authenticated.

7. What are the three layers of authentication?

   Answer: The three layers of authentication are something you know (password), something you have (token), and something you are (biometrics).

8. What is the purpose of the Explain button during the Cisco Secure ACS installation?

   Answer: Clicking the Explain button opens a window that explains the possible configuration options for the window in which the button appears.

9. What do you need to verify before installing Cisco Secure ACS?

   Answer: You need to verify that the systems are up to date, meet the minimum hardware/ browser requirements, and have connectivity with the PIX Firewall (NAS).

10. Why is it important to have Internet Explorer up to date on your Cisco Secure ACS?

    Answer: Cisco Secure ACS is managed via a browser-based web interface and has specific minimum browser requirements.

11. True or false: With authorization configured, cut-through proxy authenticates users and then allows them to connect to anything.

    Answer: False. Cut-through proxy allows users to access only resources to which they have been authorized access.

12. True or false: The Cisco Secure ACS installation on Windows Server is a relatively simple, wizard-based installation.

    Answer: True. The Cisco Secure ACS installation uses an installation wizard.

Chapter 17

"Do I Know This Already?" Quiz

1. What is the best way to authenticate an H.323 connection?

   a. Authenticate to the H.323 server

   b. Telnet to the H.323 server

   c. Virtual Telnet to the PIX Firewall for authentication

   d. Virtual HTTP to the Cisco Secure ACS for authentication

   Answer: c

2. What three services are used to authenticate by default in the PIX Firewall?

    a. FTP, HTTP, HTTPS

    b. FTP, Telnet, SSH

    c. Auth-proxy, Local-auth, console

    d. FTP, HTTPS, Telnet

    e. None of the above

    Answer: e

3. Which options are mandatory in every **aaa authentication** command on the PIX Firewall? (Select all that apply.)

    a. **include/exclude**

    b. **inbound/outbound**

    c. **local-ip/mask**

    d. **group-tag**

    e. **acl-name**

    Answer: a, b, d

4. How do you configure client IP address assignment on the Cisco Secure ACS when using the PIX Firewall as the AAA client?

    a. Edit the AAA-client IP address in the System Configuration window.

    b. Edit the AAA-client information in the Network Configuration window.

    c. Edit the AAA Server information in the Interface Configuration window.

    d. Edit the PIX Firewall information in the Network Configuration window.

    e. None of the above

    Answer: b

5. Why is it a good idea to rename your groups in Cisco Secure ACS?

    a. To get the groups into a hierarchical format

    b. To increase the performance of the Cisco Secure ACS

    c. To simplify administration of users and groups

    d. You cannot rename groups after they have been created.

    e. None of the above

    Answer: c

6. You are trying to create downloadable IP ACLs in Cisco Secure ACS, but the option is not available. What are two possible reasons?

   a. You are running an older version of Cisco Secure ACS that does not support downloadable ACLs.

   b. The PIX Firewall cannot connect to the Cisco Secure ACS.

   c. Your authentication protocol is not RADIUS.

   d. You do not have User-Level or Group-Level Downloadable ACLs selected in the Interface Configuration window, Advanced Options pane.

   Answer: c, d

7. Where do you see the logs on the Cisco Secure ACS?

   a. Interface Configuration window

   b. Reports and Activity window

   c. Network Configuration window

   d. System Configuration window

   Answer: b

8. You are installing Cisco Secure ACS on your new Windows 2000 Professional, but you cannot get it to load correctly. What is most likely the problem?

   a. Cisco Secure ACS requires server software.

   b. Your patch level is not up to date.

   c. You are running a personal firewall or host-based IDS that is blocking the installation.

   d. You do not have administrative privileges on that system.

   e. All of the above

   Answer: a

9. True or false: Cisco Secure ACS comes with its own online documentation.

   Answer: True

10. True or false: The **show aaa** command shows you everything that has to do with your AAA server in its configuration.

    Answer: False

11. What happens to virtual HTTP if you disable **timeout uauth absolute**?

    a. The user cannot authenticate.

    b. The user authenticates and never has to reauthenticate because the connection stays open.

    c. The user can authenticate but cannot connect to the server.

    d. None of the above

    Answer: c

Q&A

1. Both your Cisco PIX Firewall and your Cisco Secure ACS are configured for TACACS+, but you cannot configure the downloadable PIX ACLs. What is the problem?

   Answer: Downloadable ACLs are supported only by RADIUS.

2. What is the command to get authorization to work with access lists?

   Answer: The command to get authorization to work with access lists is aaa authorization match *acl-name if-name server-tag*.

3. What Cisco Secure ACS window is used to configure the PIX Firewall, and what is the firewall considered?

   Answer: The PIX Firewall is configured as an AAA Client in the Network Configuration window.

4. How do you put text messages into the logon prompt for a Telnet session?

   Answer: You use the auth-prompt command put text messages into the logon prompt for a Telnet session.

5. What three messages can you change with the **auth-prompt** command?

   Answer: You can change the prompt, accept, and reject messages with the auth-prompt command.

6. If your **timeout uauth** is set to 0:58:00, when is the user prompted to reauthenticate after the session times out?

   Answer: By default, timeout uauth absolute does not prompt the user to reauthenticate until they start a new connection after the uauth timer has expired.

7. What two formats can logs be written to using the Cisco Secure ACS?

    Answer: Logs are written to either the CSV or ODBC formats.

8. You have added a new RSA SecurID Token Server to the network. In which two places do you configure the Cisco Secure ACS to use it?

    Answer: The RSA SecurID Token Server must be configured as an external user database, and you must select it for password authentication in the User Setup window.

9. What commands are most commonly used to check your AAA configuration on the PIX Firewall?

    Answer: The show aaa or show aaa-server commands are most commonly used to check the AAA configuration on the PIX Firewall.

10. What is the total number of AAA servers to which the PIX Firewall can connect?

    Answer: The total number of AAA servers that the PIX Firewall can connect to is 196 (14 groups, each group containing a maximum of 14 servers).

11. How do you disable caching of user authentication?

    Answer: You use the timeout uauth 0 command to disable caching of user authentication.

Chapter 18

"Do I Know This Already?" Quiz

1. What does the Flood Defender feature on the PIX Firewall do?

    a. It prevents the PIX Firewall from being flooded with water.

    b. It protects the inside network from being engulfed by rain.

    c. It protects against SYN flood attacks.

    d. It protects against AAA attacks.

    Answer: d

2. Which PIX feature mitigates a DoS attack that uses an incomplete IP datagram?

    a. Floodguard

    b. Incomplete Guard

    c. Fragguard

    d. Mail Guard

    Answer: c

3. Which of the following multimedia application(s) is(are) supported by PIX Firewall?

    a. CuSeeMe

    b. NetMeeting

    c. Internet Video Phone

    d. All of the above

    Answer: d

4. Which is the default port that PIX inspects for H.323 traffic?

    a. 1628

    b. 1722

    c. 1720

    d. 1408

    Answer: c

5. Which of the following describes how the Mail Guard works on the PIX Firewall?

    a. It lets all mail in except for mail described by an access list.

    b. It restricts SMTP requests to seven commands.

    c. It revokes mail messages that contain attacks.

    d. It performs virus checks on each mail message.

    Answer: b

6. Which of the following statements about DNS Guard is true?

    a. It is disabled by default.

    b. It allows only a single DNS response for outgoing requests.

    c. It monitors the DNS servers for suspicious activities.

    d. It is enabled by default.

Answer: d

7. Which of the following are PIX Firewall attack mitigation features?

    a. DNS Guard

    b. Floodgate Guard

    c. Mail Guard

    d. Webguard

Answer: c

8. Which command enables the PIX Firewall IDS feature?

    a. ids enable

    b. ip audit

    c. ip ids audit

    d. audit ip ids

Answer: b

9. What is the default action of the PIX IDS feature?

    a. Nothing

    b. Drop

    c. Alarm

    d. Reset

Answer: c

10. What does the reset action do in the PIX Firewall IDS configuration?

   a. Warns the source of the offending packet before it drops the packet

   b. Drops the offending packet and closes the connection if it is part of an active con-nection with a TCP RST

   c. Waits 2000 offending packets, and then permanently bans the connection to the source host

   d. Reports the incident to the syslog server and waits for more offending packets from the same source to arrive

   Answer: b

Q&A

1. Which PIX feature mitigates a DoS attack using an incomplete IP datagram?

   Answer: Fragguard mitigates IP fragmentation attacks that cause denial of service.

2. On which port does the PIX Firewall inspect for H.323 traffic by default?

   Answer: Port 1720

3. How do you enable the PIX Firewall Mail Guard feature?

   Answer: The Mail Guard feature is enabled by default. If it is disabled, it can be enabled by using the fixup protocol smtp command.

4. What are some of the PIX limitations on CTIQBE application inspection?

   Answer: Some of the limitations of the application inspection for CTIQBE include 1) stateful failover of CTIQBE calls is not supported, 2) CTIQBE messages that are fragmented across multiple TCP packets are not supported 3) configurations that use the alias command (which was deprecated after the introduction of outside NAT in PIX Firewall Version 6.2) are not supported.

5. What is an embryonic connection?

   Answer: An embryonic connection is a half-open TCP connection.

6. Which actions are available in the PIX IDS configuration?

   Answer: alarm, drop, reset

7. How does DNS Guard on the Cisco PIX Firewall prevent DoS attacks that exploit DNS?

   Answer: The PIX Firewall allows only a single DNS response for outgoing DNS requests. Any other responses are dropped.

8. How does **ip verify reverse-path** secure the PIX Firewall?

   Answer: It provides a mechanism for checking source IP addresses before receiving or sending packets.

9. How does the Mail Guard feature prevent SMTP-related attacks?

   Answer: Mail Guard allows only a restricted set of SMTP commands, namely, HELO, MAIL, RCPT, DATA, RSET, NOOP, and QUIT.

10. How do you enable MGCP application inspection for call agents and gateways using the default ports?

    Answer: Use the fixup protocol mgcp 2427 and fixup protocol mgcp 2727 commands.

Chapter 19

"Do I Know This Already?" Quiz

1. Which of the following is true?

   a. The FWSM supports more interfaces than the Cisco PIX Firewall.

   b. The FWSM supports fewer interfaces than the PIX Firewall.

   c. The FWSM and the PIX Firewall support the same number of interfaces.

   d. None of the above

   Answer: a

2. When using Cisco IOS software, the switch passes traffic from which VLANs to your FWSM?

   a. All configured VLANs

   b. All VLANs configured for all firewall vlan-groups

   c. The firewall vlan-group associated with the specific FWSM module

   d. Any VLAN

   e. None of the above

   Answer: c

3. What traffic is initially allowed by the FWSM?

    a. All traffic

    b. Traffic from your protected networks

    c. Traffic from the inside interface only

    d. No traffic

    e. None of the above

    Answer: d

4. To connect to PDM on the FWSM, you use which protocol?

    a. HTTP

    b. HTTPS

    c. SSH

    d. Telnet

    e. None of the above

    Answer: b

5. To cause switch traffic (using Cisco IOS software) to be controlled by the FWSM, what must you do?

    a. Place the VLAN for the traffic in a firewall vlan-group.

    b. Configure the VLAN normally because all VLANs are controlled by the FWSM.

    c. Define the IP network addresses on the switch to be passed to the FWSM.

    d. Define the IP interfaces on the MSFC to be passed to the FWSM.

    e. None of the above

    Answer: a

6. What properties identify each firewall interface? (Choose three.)

    a. VLAN

    b. IP Address

    c. Security Level

    d. Switchport

    e. MSFC interface

    Answer: a, b, c

7. What is the color of the status LED when the FWSM is operating normally?

   a. Red

   b. Orange

   c. Green

   d. Yellow

   e. White

Answer: c

8. Which Cisco IOS switch command enables you to reset the FWSM?

   a. session

   b. reset

   c. nameif

   d. hw-module

   e. None of the above

Answer: d

9. Which of the following is true?

   a. The PIX Firewall supports more concurrent connections than the FWSM.

   b. The PIX Firewall and FWSM support the same number of concurrent connections.

   c. The FWSM supports more concurrent connections than the PIX Firewall.

   d. None of the above

Answer: c

10. Which configuration(s) is valid to regulate the flow of traffic on the Catalyst 6500 switch between the MSFC and the FWSM?

   a. MSFC as the inside router

   b. MSFC as the outside router

   c. MSFC not directly connected to FWSM

   d. Answers a, b, and c

Answer: d

Q&A

1. What are some of the major features of the FWSM?

    Answer: Some of the major features of the FWSM include the following: it is fully VLAN aware, supports dynamic routing, integrates firewall functionality and switching in a single chassis, supports the entire PIX Firewall Version 6.0 feature set and some Version 6.2 features, allows up to 1 million concurrent connections, supports 5-Gbps throughout, enables multiple FWSMs per chassis, supports intrachassis and interchassis stateful failure, and provides multiple management options.

2. What are the basic deployment scenarios for the FWSM?

    Answer: The basic deployment scenarios for the FWSM are MSFC as the inside router, MSFC as the outside router, and MSFC not directly connected to FWSM.

3. What are the three switch configuration steps necessary to set up your FWSM?

    Answer: The three switch configuration steps to set up the FWSM are to create VLANs, define firewall vlan-groups, and associate the vlan-groups with specific switch modules.

4. Which Cisco IOS switch commands define the VLANs to be controlled by the FWSM?

    Answer: The firewall vlan-group command defines the VLANs to be controlled by the FWSM.

5. Which Cisco IOS switch command shows the status of the FWSM?

    Answer: The show module switch command displays the status of the FWSM.

6. Which Cisco IOS switch command enables you to reset the FWSM?

    Answer: The hw-module module *module-num* reset switch command resets the FWSM from the switch CLI.

7. What does an orange FWSM status LED indicate?

    Answer: An orange status LED on the FWSM indicates that the FWSM is in one of the following states: module is running boot and self-test diagnostics, module is disabled, or module is shut down.

8. What does a red FWSM status LED indicate?

    Answer: A red status LED on the FWSM indicates that a diagnostic test (other than the individual port test) failed.

9.   Which two FWSM commands define which traffic is allowed through the FWSM?

   Answer: The access-list and access-group commands define which traffic is allowed through the FWSM.

10.   Which FWSM command associates a VLAN and security level to a FWSM interface?

   Answer: The nameif FWSM command associates a VLAN and security level to a specific FWSM interface.

11.   Which switch command associates a firewall vlan-group with a specific switch module?

   Answer: The firewall module command associates a firewall vlan-group with a specific switch module.

Chapter 20

1.   The VPN session is established, but no traffic, or just one-way traffic, is passing between the Boston firewall and Los Angeles firewall. Ellen starts debugging the problem using **debug icmp trace.** She pings the other end of the VPN node and gets the following results:

```
LOCAL-PIX(config)#
609001: Built local-host inside:10.10.2.21
106014: Deny inbound icmp src outside:10.10.10.31 dst
inside:10.10.2.21 (type 8, code 0)106014: Deny inbound icmp src
outside:10.10.10.31 dst
inside:10.10.2.21 (type 8, code 0)
106014: Deny inbound icmp src outside:10.10.10.31 dst
inside:10.10.2.21 (type 8, code 0)
106014: Deny inbound icmp src outside:10.10.10.31 dst
inside:10.10.2.21 (type 8., code 0)
106014: Deny inbound icmp src outside:10.10.10.31 dst
inside:10.10.2.21 (type 8, code 0)
609002: Teardown local-host inside:10.10.2.21duration 0:00:15
```

What do these results indicate and what could be causing this problem? How would you help Ellen resolve this issue?

Answer: The sysopt connection IPSec statement is missing from the configuration on the local PIX (Boston) and needs to be added. By default on the PIX Firewall, any inbound session must be explicitly permitted by a conduit or access list statement. With IPSec-protected traffic, the secondary access list check could be redundant. To ensure that IPSec-authenticated inbound sessions are always permitted, make sure that the configuration contains the following command:

```
sysopt connection permit-ipsec
```

2. Eric cannot get the VPN tunnel to work from HQ to the Atlanta branch office. He starts a debug and gets the following results:

```
crypto-isakmp-process-block: src 10.10.10.40, dest 10.10.3.34
VPN Peer: ISAKMP: Added new peer: ip:10.10.10.40 Total VPN Peers:1
VPN Peer: ISAKMP: Peer ip:10.10.10.40 Ref cnt incremented to:1
  Total VPN Peers:1
OAK-MM exchange
ISAKMP (0): processing SA payload. message ID = 0

ISAKMP (0): Checking ISAKMP transform 1 against priority 10 policy
ISAKMP:      encryption DES-CBC
ISAKMP:      hash MD5
ISAKMP:      default group 1
ISAKMP:      auth pre-share
ISAKMP:      life type in seconds
ISAKMP:      life duration (basic) of 2400
ISAKMP (0): atts are acceptable. Next payload is 0
ISAKMP (0): SA is doing pre-shared key authentication using id type ID-IPV4
 -ADDR
return status is IKMP-NO-ERROR
crypto-isakmp-process-block: src 10.10.10.40, dest 10.10.3.34
OAK-MM exchange

ISAKMP (0): processing KE payload. message ID = 0
ISAKMP (0): processing NONCE payload. message ID = 0
ISAKMP (0): processing vendor id payload
ISAKMP (0): processing vendor id payload
ISAKMP (0): remote peer supports dead peer detection
ISAKMP (0): processing vendor id payload
ISAKMP (0): speaking to another IOS box!

return status is IKMP-NO-ERROR
crypto-isakmp-process-block: src 10.10.10.40, dest 10.10.3.34
OAK-MM exchange
ISAKMP (0): processing ID payload. message ID = 0
ISAKMP (0): processing HASH payload. message ID = 0
ISAKMP (0): SA has been authenticated

ISAKMP (0): ID payload
        next-payload : 8
        type         : 1
        protocol     : 17
        port         : 500
        length       : 8
ISAKMP (0): Total payload length: 12
return status is IKMP-NO-ERROR
crypto-isakmp-process-block: src 10.10.10.40, dest 10.10.3.34
ISAKMP (0): processing NOTIFY payload 24578 protocol 1
        spi 0, message ID = 2457631438
ISAKMP (0): processing notify INITIAL-CONTACTIPSEC(key-engine): got a queue
  event...
IPSEC(key-engine-delete-sas): rec'd delete notify from ISAKMP
IPSEC(key-engine-delete-sas): delete all SAs shared with   10.10.10.40
```

```
return status is IKMP-NO-ERR-NO-TRANS
crypto-isakmp-process-block: src 10.10.10.40, dest 10.10.3.34
OAK-QM exchange
oakley-process-quick-mode:
OAK-QM-IDLE
ISAKMP (0): processing SA payload. message ID = 133935992
ISAKMP : Checking IPSec proposal 1
ISAKMP: transform 1, ESP-DES
ISAKMP:    attributes in transform:
ISAKMP:        encaps is 1
ISAKMP:        SA life type in seconds
ISAKMP:        SA life duration (basic) of 28800
ISAKMP:        SA life type in kilobytes
ISAKMP:        SA life duration (VPI) of  0x0 0x46 0x50 0x0
ISAKMP:        authenticator is HMAC-MD5
IPSEC(validate-proposal): invalid local address 10.10.3.34
ISAKMP (0): atts not acceptable. Next payload is 0
ISAKMP (0): SA not acceptable!
ISAKMP (0): sending NOTIFY message 14 protocol 0
return status is IKMP-ERR-NO-RETRANS
crypto-isakmp-process-block: src 10.10.10.40, dest 10.10.3.34
ISAKMP (0:0): phase 2 packet is a duplicate of a previous packet.
```

What could be the cause of this problem?

Answer: The crypto map has not been applied to the correct interface. This is a common problem. Examining the Atlanta configuration, you notice that the crypto map has been applied to the DMZ instead of the outside interface. To fix the problem apply the crypto map to the outside interface using the following command:

```
crypto map BranchVPN interface outside
```

3. Bruce is having problems establishing a VPN session to the Atlanta office. He gets the following debug results:

```
IPSEC(crypto-map-check): crypto map BranchVPN 20 incomplete. No peer or
    access-list specified. Packet discarded
```

What is causing this problem, and how would you help Bruce successfully establish a VPN tunnel to the Atlanta office?

Answer: The crypto map statements on both peers must match each other. Examining the configuration reveals that the match address statement (for Atlanta) is missing from the HQ-PIX crypto map. The following command needs to be added to the HQ-PIX configuration:

```
crypto map BranchVPN 20 match address Atlanta
```

4. The web administrator in Los Angeles needs to maintain the web servers in the DMZ from the internal network using Terminal Services (Transmission Control Protocol [TCP] port 3389). Is the firewall in Los Angeles configured to allow this access? Explain your answer.

    Answer: Yes. Since the web administrator is coming from the inside interface, which has a security level of 100, and is going to the DMZ interface, which has a security level of 70, the traffic is allowed without a specific access list. Traffic from a higher-security-level interface is automatically allowed to traverse to a lower-security-level interface without a conduit or access list.

5. The web administrator in Los Angeles also needs to administer the web servers in Boston and Atlanta. Are the three firewalls configured to allow this access? Explain your answer.

    Answer: No. Although VPNs are configured between Los Angeles and the other two locations (and the sysopt connection permit IPSec line is in the configuration), the VPNs permit traffic only between each location's internal network segments. To access the web servers, you need to configure a VPN connection from the internal network in Los Angeles to the DMZ segments of Boston and Atlanta.

6. The Web server 172.16.1.13 needs to access an Oracle database server that sits on a segment connected to the internal network at 10.10.11.221. The web server initiates the connection on TCP port 1521 and retrieves inventory data. Can this connection be completed? Explain your answer.

    Answer: No. Although an access list allows traffic between the web server and the database server on port 1521, there is no route to the 10.10.11.X network segment. Therefore, traffic for the 10.10.11.X network is routed to the default route (192.168.1.254) instead of going to the internal web server.

7. The web server 172.16.1.13 needs to access an Oracle database server on the DMZ in Boston using the address 172.16.2.11. The web server initiates the connection on TCP port 1521 to retrieve financial data. Can this connection be completed? Explain your answer.

    Answer: Yes. An access list on the Boston firewall allows the inbound connection, and static IP address translations are configured on both firewalls. An access list is not required for the web server in Los Angeles to initiate outbound connections.

8. Is the configuration solution to question 7 a good idea? Explain your answer.

    Answer: No. With the current configuration, the financial data retrieved from the database would traverse the Internet in the clear (without being encrypted). An attacker could watch this traffic and observe sensitive financial information.

9. The company has installed an FTP server on the DMZ segment in Los Angeles that customers can access to download updates. The FTP server address is 172.16.1.9. Can all external users access this FTP server? Explain your answer.

   Answer: No. The configured inbound access lists allow incoming FTP traffic to hosts 192.168.1.9 and 192.168.1.13. A static translation exists for 172.16.1.13, but there is no static translation for 172.16.1.9.

10. The exchange server is installed on the DMZ segment in Los Angeles using the address 172.16.1.14. The firewall is configured to allow Simple Mail Transfer Protocol (SMTP) access for inbound mail and Secure Sockets Layer (SSL) access for users who want to connect using Outlook Web Access over an HTTP over SSL (HTTPS) connection. Will any users be able to receive their mail with this configuration? Explain your answer.

    Answer: No. It appears that the access list named "Exchange" permits the users to access port 25 (SMTP) because it is applied to the outside interface. Unfortunately, only one access group can be applied to a specific interface for a specific traffic direction. The "inbound" access list has already been applied to the outside interface for incoming traffic.

11. What needs to be done in Los Angeles to allow access to the mail server?

    Answer: By changing the access list statements labeled "Exchange" to "inbound," the statements become part of the existing access group that is already applied to the outside interface.

Index

Numerics

E

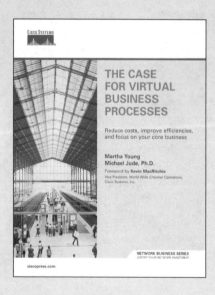

FUNDAMENTALS SERIES
ESSENTIAL EXPLANATIONS AND SOLUTIONS

When you need an authoritative introduction to a key networking topic, **reach for a Cisco Press Fundamentals book**. Learn about network topologies, deployment concepts, protocols, and management techniques and **master essential networking concepts and solutions**.

Look for Fundamentals titles at your favorite bookseller

802.11 Wireless LAN Fundamentals
ISBN: 1-58705-077-3

**Cisco CallManager Fundamentals:
A Cisco AVVID Solution**
ISBN: 1-58705-008-0

Data Center Fundamentals
ISBN: 1-58705-023-4

IP Addressing Fundamentals
ISBN: 1-58705-067-6

IP Routing Fundamentals
ISBN: 1-57870-071-X

Voice over IP Fundamentals
ISBN: 1-57870-168-6

CISCO SYSTEMS

Cisco Press

CISCO CERTIFICATION SELF-STUDY
#1 BEST-SELLING TITLES FROM CCNA® TO CCIE®

Look for Cisco Press Certification Self-Study resources at your favorite bookseller

Learn the test topics with **Self-Study Guides**

CCNA Self-Study:
Interconnecting Cisco Network Devices (ICND)
Second Edition

Cisco authorized self-study book for CCNA® 640-801
and ICND 640-811 foundation learning

Edited by:
Steve McQuerry, CCIE No. 6108

Gain hands-on experience with **Practical Studies** books

CCNA® Practical Studies

Practice for CCNA exam #640-607 with
hands on networking lab scenarios

Gary Heap, CCIE®
Lynn Maynes, CCIE

Prepare for the exam with **Exam Certification Guides**

CCNA® Self-Study
CCNA ICND
Exam Certification Guide

The official self-study test preparation guide
for the Cisco CCNA ICND exam 640-811

Wendell Odom, CCIE® No. 1624

Practice testing skills and build confidence with **Flash Cards and Exam Practice Packs**

CCNA® Self-Study
CCNA Flash Cards
and Exam Practice Pack
Second Edition

More than 1100 flash cards, practice questions,
and quick reference sheets for the CCNA 640-801,
INTRO 640-821, and ICND 640-811 exams

Eric Rivard
Jim Doherty

Visit **www.ciscopress.com/series** to learn more
about the Certification Self-Study product family
and associated series.

Learning is serious business.
Invest wisely.

Cisco Systems

Cisco Press

NETWORKING TECHNOLOGY GUIDES
MASTER THE NETWORK

Turn to Networking Technology Guides whenever you need **in-depth knowledge of complex networking technologies**. Written by leading networking authorities, these guides offer theoretical and practical knowledge for **real-world networking applications and solutions**.

Look for Networking Technology Guides at your favorite bookseller

Cisco Access Control Security:
AAA Administration Services
ISBN: 1-58705-124-9

Cisco CallManager Best Practices:
A Cisco AVVID Solution
ISBN: 1-58705-139-7

Designing Network Security,
Second Edition
ISBN: 1-58705-117-6

Network Security Architectures
ISBN: 1-58705-115-X

Optical Network Design
and Implementation
ISBN: 1-58705-105-2

Top-Down Network Design, Second Edition
ISBN: 1-58705-152-4

Troubleshooting Virtual Private Networks
ISBN: 1-58705-104-4

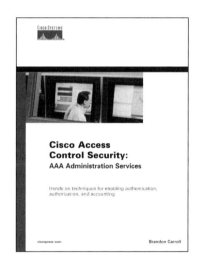

Visit **www.ciscopress.com/series** for details about Networking Technology Guides and a complete list of titles.

Learning is serious business.
Invest wisely.

SEARCH THOUSANDS OF BOOKS FROM LEADING PUBLISHERS

Safari® Bookshelf is a searchable electronic reference library for IT professionals that features more than 2,000 titles from technical publishers, including Cisco Press.

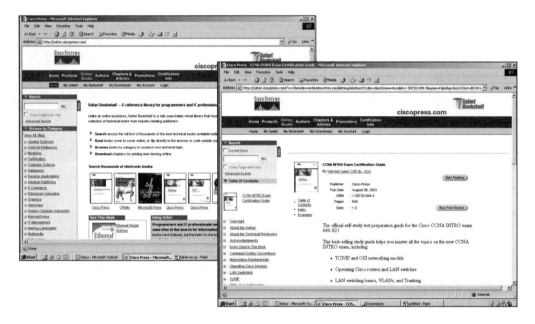

With Safari Bookshelf you can

- **Search** the full text of thousands of technical books, including more than 70 Cisco Press titles from authors such as Wendell Odom, Jeff Doyle, Bill Parkhurst, Sam Halabi, and Karl Solie.

- **Read** the books on My Bookshelf from cover to cover, or just flip to the information you need.

- **Browse** books by category to research any technical topic.

- **Download** chapters for printing and viewing offline.

With a customized library, you'll have access to your books when and where you need them—and all you need is a user name and password.

TRY SAFARI BOOKSHELF FREE FOR 14 DAYS!

You can sign up to get a 10-slot Bookshelf free for the first 14 days. Visit **http://safari.ciscopress.com** to register.